A TRAVEL GUIDE TO
JEWISH EUROPE

A TRAVEL GUIDE TO
JEWISH EUROPE

THIRD EDITION

By Ben G. Frank

PELICAN PUBLISHING COMPANY
Gretna 2001

First edition, April 1992
Second edition, January 1996
Third edition, February 2001

Library of Congress Cataloging-in-Publication Data

Frank, Ben G.
    A travel guide to Jewish Europe / by Ben G. Frank. — 3rd ed.
    p. cm.
    Includes bibliographical references and index.
    ISBN 1-56554-776-4 (pbk. : alk. paper)
    1. Jews—Europe—History. 2. Kosher restaurants—Europe-
-Directories. 3. Synagogues—Europe—Directories. 4. Jews—
Europe–Societies, etc.—Directories. 5. Europe—Guidebooks. I.
Title.

DS135.E8 F7 2000
940'.04924—dc20   00-062323

Maps and cover art by Joseph Honig

*Information in this guidebook is based on authoritative data available at
the time of printing. Prices and hours of operation of businesses are subject
to change without notice. Readers are asked to take this into account when
consulting this guide.*

Printed in Canada

Published by Pelican Publishing Company, Inc.
1000 Burmaster Street, Gretna, Louisiana 70053

To my wife, Riva

Contents

Acknowledgments

It is one thing to write a first travel book; it is another to write a second and then a third one in order to bring the first and second ones up to date and to add new chapters. Patience and skill are not enough. One needs the encouragement, advice, and help of friends, colleagues, and fellow writers, as well as many wonderful individuals and groups. It could not have been done without them.

Of necessity, this travel guide, with its detailed information, could not have been written without the expertise and professionalism of the tourist offices and airlines of France, Great Britain, Germany, Holland, Belgium, Switzerland, Portugal, Spain, Greece, Austria, Ireland and Turkey, as well as those of Italy, Norway, Denmark, Sweden, the Czech Republic, Romania, Bulgaria, Slovakia, Hungary, and Poland.

For this and other editions, I especially want to cite for their cooperation George Hern, former public-relations director of the French Government Tourist Office; Robin Massee, public-relations director of the French Government Tourist Office; and Marion Fourestier, public-relations assistant; Bruce C. Haxthausen, formerly of Air France and now Chelsea Communications; Rosario Mariani, vice president of sales, Alitalia Airlines, North America and Mexico; Allen Stolz, formerly of Air France and now president of World Travel Consultants; Hedy Wuerz, senior associate, Sullivan and Associates; Helga Brenner-Khan, manager of the Public Relations Department of the German National Tourist Office; Ronnie Golz and Olaf Kolbatz, both of Berlin, excellent guides and wonderful historians in their own right; Kevin Kennedy, of

Potsdam, guide and historian; Andrew J. Lazarus, president of A. J. Lazarus Associates; Chris Lazarus, vice president of A. J. Lazarus Associates; Balazs Szucs, director of the Hungarian National Tourist Office, North America; Andrea Szakal, media-relations manager of the Hungarian National Tourist Office; Frederique Raeymaekers, director of the Belgian National Tourist Office; Annette Choynacki, who is in charge of the Trade Department of the Belgian National Tourist Office; Liliane Opsomer, who is in charge of press and public relations at the Belgian National Tourist Office; Dagobert Scher, formerly of Rail Europe; Erika Lieben, manager of public relations at the Swiss National Tourist Office; Vladimir Hulpach of CEDOK, Central Europe travel service; Miroslav Ehl, general manager for North America of Czech Airlines, CSA; Rina Allalouf of Czech Airlines, CSA; Stefan Adamec, Slovakia Travel Service and representative of SATUR; Peter Gomori of Ibusz Hungarian Travel; and Joram Kagan, director of special projects, LOT Polish Airlines.

I would be remiss not to thank the organizations whose patient staffs were always there when I needed them. They are the American Jewish Joint Distribution Committee (JDC), the American Jewish Committee, Chabad Lubavitch, the World Jewish Congress, and the World Union of Progressive Judaism.

For much help in the new chapters on Romania and Bulgaria and the expanded one on Hungary, I must cite two devoted experts on the situation of the Jews in Eastern Europe: Amir Shaviv, assistant executive vice president for special operations of the American Jewish Joint Distribution Committee; and Kim Bayer, former desk director for Central and Eastern Europe of the American Jewish Joint Distribution Committee.

In Romania, Dr. Zvi Feine, country director for Romania for the JDC, was very helpful. My appreciation for all her work and effort toward my writing about Romania goes to Franca Oprescu-Aronovici, a dedicated social worker with the Jewish Community of Bucharest. A hard-working and knowledgeable JDC Jewish Service Corps volunteer, Yosef Hirsh, was of great assistance to me in Bucharest and back in the United States.

In Bulgaria, I want to thank Jorge Diener, the JDC country director for Bulgaria. I truly can say I became enamored with this wonderful Jewish community because of two energetic and devoted Bulgarian Jewish leaders: Robert Djerassi, assistant to the JDC country director for Bulgaria; and Stefan Oscar, JDC community development consultant for Bulgaria. Certainly mention must be made of Hadara Stanton in Bulgaria, a JDC Jewish Service Corps volunteer who worked with small Jewish communities outside of Sofia and who helped me with information on the Jewish community in Plovdiv.

In Hungary, Dr. Israel Sella, director of JDC in Hungary, and Dr. Geza Ilona Seifert, head of JDC visiting missions, deserve my admiration and appreciation for opening up the wide world of Hungarian Jewry to me. Through them, I met the Jews of Budapest. I also was aided in my understanding of the Hungarian Jewish community by discussions with Gilad Eliezer, director of The Jewish Agency for Israel in Budapest, and Joszi Croitoru, an assistant at the Budapest office of The Jewish Agency for Israel. A great deal of the background and history of the Jewish community and of Hungary could not have been transmitted to me without the aid of Nandor Gerei, a wonderful guide and historian who helped me both in Budapest and when I returned to New York. I thank him. Many Jewish community leaders in Europe were very helpful and sent me information, but deep gratitude goes to my friend Leon Masliah, honorary executive director of the Consistoire Central in Paris; and Dr. Leon Zelman, director of The Jewish Welcome Service of Vienna.

For my chapter on Poland, I must thank the following, all of whom helped me chart "unknown waters": Rabbi Haskel Besser, chairman for Poland of the Ronald S. Lauder Foundation; Basia Jakubowska, assistant to Rabbi Besser; Rabbi Michael Schudrich, former director of the Ronald S. Lauder Foundation in Poland and now the rabbi of the Nozyk Synagogue in Warsaw; Yale J. Reisner, director of Research and Archives of the Ronald S. Lauder Foundation in Warsaw; Grazyna S. Pawlak, Ph.D., former executive director of the Jewish Historical Institute of Poland; Henryk Halkowski, historian, writer, guide, and community leader in Cracow; Joachim S. Russek, director of the Jagiellonian University Research Center on Jewish History and Culture in Poland and the

Center for Jewish Culture in Kazimierz, Cracow; Stanislaw Krajewski, Jewish community leader in Warsaw; Dr. Yehuda Nir, author, lecturer, and professor; and Manlio Dell'Ariccia, JDC country director for Poland.

Encouraging me in my task were longtime friends, relatives, and colleagues: Joseph Honig, designer and graphic artist who designed and added maps to this edition as well as past ones; Doris Gold, editor; Françoise Bartlett, editor; Maxwell J. Lillienstein, Esq.; and Deborah Kahn, computer consultant, all of whom believed in my idea from the beginning; my brother and sister-in-law, Dr. Ivan and Malke Frank, who helped me on the chapters on Spain, Portugal, Poland, and Bulgaria. Of course, many kudos to Elizabeth Ackley, that patient, accurate, and proficient computer consultant who word-processed the updated and new chapters of this third edition of *A Travel Guide to Jewish Europe,* and to Ross Golden, computer instructor, who guided me through the world of cyberspace.

Gathering information and historical background was obviously a daunting task, and I am forever grateful to the entire staff of the Chappaqua Library in New York: Director Mark Hasskarl; reference librarians Martha Alcott, Carolyn Jones, Paula Peyraud, Jane Peyraud, Carolyn Reznick, Michele Snyder, and Maryanne Eaton; and staff members Marilyn Coleman, Mary McGrath, Peggy Gaillard, Judy Lauder, and Joan Kuhn.

I also wish to thank my traveling colleagues, relatives, and friends who on their return to home base briefed me with the latest tourist information: Howard Green for photos and information on Germany; Jessica Spitalnic for information on England; Eva and Robert Fischer for my chapter on Italy; Dr. Joshua and Amy Fogelman for their help on England, France, and Germany; Ed Robin for his knowledge of Eastern Europe; Aaron Meyer for his help on Hungary; Vivian and Joseph Goldreich, Sheila and Jerry Rosenkranz, Ronnie and Larry Ackman, Elysia and Stephen Wolnek, Elliott and Ruth Bier, Dr. Gene and Gloria Sosin, Manual and Natalie Charach, Dr. Maurice and Marcia Cohen, and Haya and Sam Urman for their help on the Czech Republic, Hungary, and other countries.

Truly helpful always were friends and professionals Raphael Rothstein, national director of marketing and communications for Israel Bonds; Jerry Goodman, executive director of the National Committee for Labor Israel; Richard Berman, media consultant; Yitzhok Fuchs, CPA and international tax expert; and Ambassador Herbert Donald Gelber.

I can only hope that I am not omitting any names. If I am, I apologize. I am especially indebted to the unnamed helpful residents of many countries who pointed me in the right direction.

I offer praise and appreciation to Dr. Milburn Calhoun, publisher and president of Pelican Publishing Company, and the entire staff at Pelican, who immediately saw the need for this travel book all the way to a third edition. I owe a special debt of gratitude to my editors at Pelican, Nina Kooij and Susan Smits, who helped make this edition the book that it is.

My deepest thanks, of course, go to my family: my late parents, Nathan M. Frank and Sonya Winerman Frank, and my wife's late parents, Rabbi Solomon Spitz and Jeanette Joskowitz Spitz. They inspired my wife, Riva, and me to learn more about and keep alive the traditions of the Jewish people, and this certainly encouraged us to seek out details of our roots and of the Jews of Europe. It is also an amazing reward for a father to have two sons who can aid him in such a momentous book project, now in its third edition. I am deeply indebted to my journalist-writer son, Martin N. Frank, for spending long hours editing the manuscript. I also owe a debt of gratitude to my lawyer son, Monte E. Frank, who represented me in this endeavor. Our children and grandchildren, Martin, Jodi, and Randall Stuart, and Monte, Leah, and Rebecca Naomi, have been a source of strength to me.

Finally, any author knows how at times, especially as deadline approaches, pressure can become burdensome on one's wife—or husband. As for my wife, Riva, her love and devotion, her encouragement and steadfastness, not only kept my resolve moving on track but also reinforced what we both knew: that this was a worthwhile project for not only this generation but also future generations.

Introduction

This is a unique travel guide. It is a practical, anecdotal, and adventurous journey through historic Jewish Europe, including kosher restaurants, cafés, synagogues, and museums, plus cultural and heritage sites.

The reader will visit more than fifty cities, including some of the most fascinating capitals on the European continent: Paris, London, Madrid, and Lisbon. He or she will saunter along the "Italian honeymoon trail" of Venice, Florence, and Rome. The traveler who peruses this guide will inhale the excitement of Central Europe's "Golden Triangle": Prague, Budapest, and Vienna, as well as Sofia and Bucharest.

This book is for the tourist to use as a full resource to search for his or her roots in the rich past that was Polish Jewry, as well as for the Jewish traveler who stands silently in the death camps and recalls loved ones and others who perished in the Holocaust. With this volume, the traveler can join in an activity of the struggling but still amazingly alive Polish Jewish community in Warsaw, Cracow, and Lublin and the small but energetic and friendly Jewish community of Bulgaria. It is all here!

This book chronicles my third sojourn to Jewish Europe. This writer still identifies himself as Benjamin of New York, who, like his twelfth-century namesake, Benjamin of Tudela, travels and chronicles the Jewish world in Europe, Asia, and Africa. Like Benjamin of Tudela, this author records the Jewish population, describes the people, tells their history, comments on their rulers, and defines the Jewish community structure.

Since 1960, the cities of Europe have served as my grazing

grounds, so to speak, though I spent much of that time west of the old "Iron Curtain." Indeed, the first edition of *A Travel Guide to Jewish Europe* did not fully discuss the Jewish sites or institutions of Eastern Europe that after World War II struggled to survive "forty years of Communist darkness."

But in 1989, Communism crumbled. The Cold War ended. New destinations beckoned. The traveler, tourist, and business person refocused and came up with a new mindset that propelled them to push away the past anxiety and fear of visiting a Communist country and to return to nations breathing freedom for the first time in four decades.

This author, too, followed the "yellow brick road" to such "refreshed" cities as Prague, Budapest, Bratislava, Warsaw, Cracow, united Berlin, Bucharest, and Sofia. The result is this third edition of *A Travel Guide to Jewish Europe.*

Prague is in. Budapest is in. Cracow is in. Sofia is in. When I visited these cities, I carried on my tradition of not only seeing places of interest but also visiting with Jews—learning how they live, exchanging ideas—and attending Sabbath services, bar mitzvahs, and social functions.

Now, besides having danced at parties in Marseilles, dined with Rothschilds in Paris, lunched with the Abouaziz family in Cannes, chatted with Israelis in Rome, or met Jews in Granada, I have spent a Sabbath afternoon around a table with the Jews of Prague. We shared food at a *shalosh s'udot* (a gathering for the third meal of the Sabbath). As we studied and talked, the Sabbath drew to a close and we sang *zmiros* (Sabbath songs). Then we recited the evening prayer—all this in the oldest standing synagogue in Europe, the *Altneuschul,* where you can almost feel the spirit of the famous Rabbi Judah Loew ben Bezalel, known as the *Maharal* (the Hebrew acronym for "most venerated teacher and rabbi"), and the *golem,* a robot figure serving the rabbi for his good works.

Near the Ukrainian-Slovakian border, I talked with American Jewish builders and developers who were helping the new nation of Slovakia. I visited the concentration camp at Terezin in the Czech Republic and uttered, "*Zachor*" ("Remember") and "Never again." I listened to hypnotic gypsy music in Budapest, "the Queen of the Danube." I strolled through the streets of Bratislava, where once Yeshiva students walked in the shadow of buildings that housed the greatest Talmudic schools of learning in Europe. I walked the streets of the Warsaw Ghetto, shed tears in Auschwitz, and sang Hebrew songs with young Polish Jews in Kazimierz, the still-preserved old Jewish section of Cracow. I sat with Jewish students in a café in Sofia and talked about life in our respective countries.

Of course, major differences in culture, history, religion, customs, and traditions mark Eastern Europe from Western Europe. Every state sports a different shape today than it did seventy-five years ago. The complexities of Eastern Europe, the suspicions, the mistrust, the hatreds are still there. And Eastern Europe, including Russia, certainly bore the greatest burden of World War II. Whereas France has 700,000 Jews and England has 300,000, the Czech Republic has only 13,000 Jews. And Hungary, the largest Jewish community in Eastern Europe, records about 100,000 Jewish citizens. Poland, once the second-largest Jewish community in the Diaspora, with about 3.5 million Jews, now contains perhaps 8,000. More and more Jews are openly declaring their heritage, and Jewish leaders say there could be thousands more living more discreetly. For sure, Jewish life in Eastern Europe, with all its difficulties, is reviving. Though anti-Semitism exists worldwide, it is amazing how it flourishes in Eastern Europe, where very few Jews live. I still label it "anti-Semitism without Jews." Challenges such as the growth of rightwing, anti-Semitic nationalist movements cause Jewish communities concern but not panic. Jewish leaders in Europe, too, have learned that the price of liberty is eternal vigilance.

In Western Europe, the Jewish community is struggling with assimilation, but in Eastern Europe, the Jewish community is being reborn despite higher rates of mixed marriages. It is seeking to educate, locate, and greet Jews who voluntarily or involuntarily have hidden and may even still hide their Jewishness. Despite difficult economic situations in some countries, Jewish communities are springing up in Central and Eastern Europe and are rapidly strengthening.

Moreover, American Jews want to meet their co-religionists. I have discovered not only that today's American Jews want to travel to Eastern Europe to find their roots, but they want to do it with their parents and grandparents, their sons and daughters. This updated guide to Jewish Europe will help them.

Though this is a travel book, it is more than that. I have attempted to answer some of the questions that will help us learn how the Jewish people, forced to disperse throughout the world almost two thousand years ago, continue to share a sense of identity.

This volume is an attempt to provide some of the information necessary to answer these questions. It contains my experiences and observations as a Jewish journalist who has traveled to Jewish communities in Europe. It explores the customs, mores, and politics of Jews in societies as diverse as Dusseldorf, Madrid, Budapest, Prague, Warsaw, Lublin, Cracow, Istanbul, and Bucharest.

Each chapter contains a description of Jews within a specific society and their institutions, customs, places of interest—even their restaurants. Each chapter explores the relationships among Jews, and between Jews and non-Jews. Also cited are Jews' contributions to the countries of their origin.

Travel stimulates the mind, and the love of travel is inherent in the Jewish consciousness. Jews have been traveling for centuries. Obviously, expulsion has a lot to do with it. Some of the journeys were extremely unpleasant, to say the least: wandering through the desert to the Promised Land, being expelled brutally and oppressively, escaping from the Spanish and Portuguese inquisitions, evading the *pogroms,* fleeing Nazi terror, and running the British naval blockade to reach the shores of Palestine. All this bitter uprooting taught the Jews how to move about, and quickly; how to seek a comfortable and tranquil home; and how to long for the Holy Land and finally regain it as a nation of their own. *A Travel Guide to Jewish Europe* will help you understand the significance of those events as they relate to the present and the future.

On May 14, 1948, when the State of Israel was established, Jews began traveling with increasing frequency. Only this time, they were driven to see the new nation.

On their way to and from Israel, Jews and non-Jews would stop off in other lands. I discovered an interesting phenomenon: People who would rarely visit a synagogue or church in their own town or city not only toured shrines throughout Europe but prayed in the houses of worship of their religion.

Moreover, American Jews who might not even keep Jewish traditional dietary laws would hasten to unearth a kosher restaurant in Paris, London, or Nice, and upon their return to the States would immediately tell their friends of the tasty and spicy pastrami sandwiches they had devoured near the Champs-Elysées, or the dumplings in the kosher restaurant in Prague, or the Hungarian goulash in the kosher establishment near the beautiful Dohany Street Synagogue in Budapest.

I recall observing American businessmen, who, for a whole week, savored the best *Michelin Guide* cuisine until one night they stole away to Goldenberg's kosher-style restaurant in the Jewish section of Paris. They would go there even after terrorists shot up the place. Stopping at Goldenberg's became an "act of faith" for them.

Along with insights into Jewish life, I provide lists of synagogues, kosher restaurants, hotels, and Jewish sites, along with travel descriptions of the wonderful cities I have visited.

It is now a half-century since the end of a war in which evil came close to winning. Jews and humanity in general have yet to recover fully from that conflagration and the Holocaust.

But this book dispels the myth that after World War II, Jewish life ceased to exist on the Continent. Today, Jewish communities are thriving throughout Europe, even growing.

So join me on a third trip in this edition of *A Travel Guide to Jewish Europe.* Jewish and non-Jewish travelers will find more than the basic ingredients of a travel guide in this book. It will also help the businessperson plan his or her journey.

"You cannot tell the players without a scorecard," as they say, and you cannot truly appreciate a site without fully knowing its origin. So let us fly away and visit Prague, now called "the Left Bank of the new century." Or let us take a trip to Budapest, often called "Europe's most seductive capital." Neither city has reason to feel inferior to any other. We can still stop and stroll along the *rue de la Paix* in Paris, or the *Bahnhofstrasse* in Zurich, or Regent Street in London, or Taksim Square in Istanbul.

Yes, let us begin our journey. As the Chinese say, the journey of a 1,000 *li* begins with the first step.

A TRAVEL GUIDE TO
JEWISH EUROPE

France
The Fourth Largest Jewish Community in the World

France is the home of the largest Jewish community in Europe, the third largest in the Diaspora, and the fourth largest in the world.

France is the home of 700,000 Jews, more than 300 Jewish organizations and associations, several hundred synagogues, about 30 day schools, 180 Talmud Torahs (Jewish schools), many kosher butcher shops, as well as B'nai B'rith lodges, a Jewish art museum, and a Jewish library of more than 160,000 volumes.

France today is the home of 300,000 Jews from North Africa, who, in the 1960s, settled in towns and villages where at the time there were no Jews.

France, which has a diverse Jewish population, is one of the few countries outside of Israel where Sephardic Jews now outnumber the Ashkenazic. "Sepharad" is the Hebrew word for Spain. Sephardim are those Jews who trace their origins to Spain or Portugal before the 1492 expulsion, and include Jews from the Mediterranean basin who share a common cultural legacy, as well as those Jews who follow the traditions, customs, rituals, and culture of the Jews of Spain and Portugal.

Ashkenazic Jews are those whose religious rites and customs stem from Germany and Eastern Europe, and whose household language at home was Yiddish.

A Brief History

Jewish history in France probably begins with the Roman period after the conquest of Jerusalem, and certainly by the fourth century, when Jews pitched their tents along the great trade routes. Jews migrated to the French Mediterranean coast in and around Marseilles. Soon they settled in the south of Gaul, near Bordeaux and Avignon.

By the fourth and fifth centuries, Jews lived in Metz, Poitiers, Avignon, Arles, Brittany, Clermont-Ferrand, and Narbonne. By 524, they settled in Valence. A synagogue was founded in Paris in 582. Jews served as merchants, physicians, and sailors. Although restricted by Christianity, they lived comfortably. They fared well under Charlemagne and his successors in the eighth and ninth centuries.

The days of the intellectual glory of French Jewry did not occur until the eleventh and twelfth centuries. This Golden Age of French Jewry was sparked by such luminaries as Rabbenu Gershom, the Light of Exile (960-1030), and Rashi (1040-1105), the great commentator on the Bible who lit up the sky of Jewish religious thought. By the mid-eleventh century, Joseph B. Samuel Bonfils taught in Limoges, and Moses haDarshan in Narbonne.

The first significant act of anti-Semitism in the form of a blood libel charge occurred in 1171 in the Loire town of Blois. Thirty-two Jews were burned at the stake. A similar event had already taken place in Norwich, England, in 1144.

Many times since, the Jews of France and Europe were to suffer from the false charge of murdering Christians and draining their blood for Passover. Thus began a period of expulsions and murder. In 1182, King Philip Augustus expelled the Jews—only to recall them sixteen years later.

In the next century, severe anti-Jewish persecutions erupted. In 1242, at the instigation of the Catholic Church, copies of the Talmud were seized from French Jewish homes, libraries, and synagogues and hurled into town squares, where they were burned.

On July 22, 1306, Philip IV, known as the "Fair," seized Jewish property and banished the Jews from France. More than

100,000 Jews fled. They found refuge in Belgium, Italy, and Spain. Several decades later those Jews who had remained in France would again be victimized. Now they would be charged with poisoning the wells during the Black Plague.

The great creativity of medieval French Jewry soon ended, even though they were readmitted to France in 1315. We know that Jewish communities thrived in Bayonne, Bordeaux, Toulouse, Marseilles, Limoges, Poitiers, Nantes, Angers, Dijon, Le Havre, Rouen, Verdun, Valence, and, of course, in Alsace and Lorraine in such cities as Mulhouse, Colmar, and Strasbourg. While some were purveyors to the Imperial Court, most were engaged in finance.

In 1394, Charles VI expelled the Jews once again. For two hundred years, only a handful of Jews remained on French soil—in Alsace-Lorraine and Avignon, the latter called the "Pope's Jews" because they were protected by the pope. Much has been written about these Jews of Avignon who, with their brothers and sisters of Carpentras, Cavaillon, and L'Isle-sur-la-Sorges, comprised the four communities of the Comtat Venaissin (lands of the pope). Here Jews established centers and historical sites, one of which is the Synagogue in the Round in Avignon. Large concentrations of Jews had settled there in the fifth and sixth centuries.

After 1394, Jews in France did not practice their religion openly. Yet, following the Spanish Inquisition and expulsion in 1492, Marranos (secret Jews) began to arrive in the southwest corner of the country. Called members of the "Portuguese Nation" or "Portuguese merchants," they crossed the border near the Pyrenees. It was safer to be Portuguese than to be known as a Jew. Starting in 1550, under the guise of being "New Christians," these Marranos were granted letters of protection by Henry II, who permitted them to live in France wherever they desired. Other Marranos and Jews settled in Bayonne and Bordeaux and in numerous small cities in this Atlantic-coast corner of France. Some went north to La Rochelle, Nantes, and Rouen.

The 1648 Chmielnicki massacres in the Ukraine caused Jews to flee to France from Poland and Russia and to settle in Alsace-Lorraine. By 1657, there were 96 Jewish families in

Metz. After the Treaty of Westphalia in 1648, Jews were allowed to remain in Lorraine. For the first time since 1394, Jews were legally permitted to live in France.

Later Cardinal Richelieu invited Marranos to settle in French port cities for the purpose of expanding French overseas trade.

By the close of the seventeenth century, Jews were welcome in France because of the policies of Jean-Baptiste Colbert, finance minister to Louis XIV. Colbert believed in mercantilism, that the purpose of the state was to increase its wealth. Colbert figured Jews would bring business skills to France. This they certainly did, including chocolate-making in Bayonne. They enhanced shipping and trading in the port of Bordeaux.

By the beginning of the eighteenth century, Jews began to return to Paris. They were peddlers who sold secondhand clothes and rags. Because of occupational restrictions, Jews were forced to become moneylenders, military purveyors, and petty traders.

Two groups existed side by side in France: Sephardic Jews in Bordeaux, Avignon, and Comtat Venaissin, and Ashkenazim in Alsace-Lorraine and other provinces.

In 1732, Sephardic Jews were formally recognized by royal decrees and permitted to practice Judaism. In 1787, on the eve of the French Revolution, 40,000 Jews lived in France, 20 times more than in the fledgling Jewish community in that new land across the ocean, the United States.

Notable French Jews

By the end of the nineteenth century, the Jewish population increased to 90,000, of which 50,000 lived in Paris, the center of European capitalism. It was then that Jews achieved fame in France, which until World War I was certainly the cultural center of the world. Before World War I, Jewish painters and sculptors helped make the so-called "Paris School" famous: Pissarro, Soutine, Pascin, Modigliani, Chagall, Mane Katz, as well as Benn. (They also used Jewish subjects in their works.)

The names of Jacques Offenbach, Claude Kahn, Darius

Milhaud, Paul Dukas—all of whom are Jews—are well known in French music; and Jews in French literature are legion, both past and contemporary.

France boasts two Jewish Nobel laureates, Henri Bergson in literature and Rene Cassin, winner of the World Peace Prize in 1968. Writers include Marcel Proust, Andre Maurois, Edmond Fleg, Eugene Ionesco, Armand Lurel, Albert Memmi, Clara Malraux, and Joseph Kessel of the Académie Française. Goncourt Prize winners include Roger Ikor, Romain Gary, Andre Schwarz-Bart, and Anna Longfus. Philosophers and writers Bernard-Henri Levy, Alain Finkelkraut, Victor Malka, Roland Goetschel, and novelists Andre Schwarz-Bart and Marek Halter, have achieved world acclaim. The writer Elie Wiesel, who received the Nobel Peace Prize in 1986, is well known in France. He lived there after his release from the Nazi death camps and wrote distinguished literary works in French.

Jews in academic life include Raymond Aron, Robert Aron, George Steiner, Claude Levi-Strauss, Georges Friedman, and Bernhard Blumenkranz.

French Jews have starred in the theater, film, and television: Rachel, Sarah Bernhardt, Jules Dassin, Simone Signoret, Marcel Marceau, Anouk Aimee, Jean-Pierre Aumont, Claude Lelouch, Claude Berri, Regine, and Claude Lanzmann. The latter won a "Cesar," France's equivalent of the Oscar, for his epic *Shoah,* the film on the Holocaust.

Some notable French Jews who excelled in science include: Henri Moissan, Andre Lwoff, Gabriel Lippman, François Jacob (all Nobel Prize winners from France), Henri-Marc Baruk, Bernard Halpern, and Eugene Minkoski.

In industry, Max Hymans and Bernard Attali each served as the director general of Air France. Andre Citroën founded the famous French automobile company.

Finally, Jews played a role in government and politics. Leon Blum, Rene Mayer, and Pierre Mendes-France were prime ministers. Daniel Mayer, Jules Moch, Pierre Masse, Georges Mandel, Jean Pierre-Bloch, Simone Veil, Lionel Stoleru, and former Minister of Justice Robert Badinter, who now serves as president of the Constitutional Council, all achieved prominence in government.

Jack Lang, a minister of culture, is Jewish. Isaac-Adolphe Cremieux was a foreign minister; he gave French citizenship to Algerian Jews. Nearly a hundred years later, his act enabled the Jews of Algeria to leave and resettle in France as full citizens of the Republic.

Jewish Life in France

Apart from a few wealthy capitalists, the great majority of French Jews were middle class—peddlers, merchants, craftsmen, painters, hat makers, tailors, and shoemakers.

By 1914, the Jewish population of France included 20,000 Eastern European Jews. Their brothers and sisters migrated to Paris during the upheaval caused by the Russian Revolution. In 1935, 260,000 Jews lived in France.

Between World War I and World War II, Eastern European Jews continued to flee to France, which had become a land of refuge. By 1939, there were about 300,000 Jews in France, half of whom were not French citizens.

In the late 1930s, as in all of Europe, a wave of anti-Semitism enveloped France. Following Franco's win in Spain, France found itself facing totalitarianism on three of its borders, Spain, Italy and Germany. "The Jews in France believed in the strength of the Third Republic, and the Jews of East Central Europe believed in France. Few imagined that Nazi Germany could become a real threat beyond its own borders," wrote Friedlander in *Nazi Germany and the Jews*. France would surrender in 38 days and its capitulation would result in Vichy's surrender and its subsequent collaboration with the Nazis. Despite the roundups and the terror, more than two-thirds of the estimated 350,000 Jews who were living in France in 1940 were saved. After the war, Jews from Eastern Europe flocked to France, many on their way to the future Jewish state in Palestine. For a decade, the old-time French Jewish community was weak. On the one hand it tried to aid the Jewish displaced persons and on the other it sought to revitalize itself. Only the arrival of the Sephardim from North Africa actually rejuvenated the community, and in France today, Jews are vocal and visible.

The one "burning issue" uniting all French Jews is the survival of the State of Israel and the activism that is needed to ensure that survival. This ideal and goal has been enhanced by the influx of North African Jews.

In the 1970s, activism on behalf of Israel found its expression in *Renouveau Juif,* Jewish Renewal. This group galvanized the community and encouraged Jews to be more vociferous in espousing the cause of Israel and the Jewish people. They felt that, to reach French public opinion, they had to hold rallies and demonstrations against the policy of the French government toward Israel, a policy that from time to time has tilted towards the Arabs.

As we have seen, observers of French foreign policy have noted that since 1967, France and Israel have been on a rocky road regarding their relationship. So when French Prime Minister Lionel Jospin made a visit to Israel in 2000, commentators noted his favorable comments regarding Israel and his criticism of Hezbolah terrorists who were operating in Lebanon. It was a high for French Jews in the often "tepid relations" between France and Israel.

The Jews from Algeria, Morocco, and Tunisia were also more observant than their Ashkenazic co-religionists.

Major publishing houses began printing well-known Jewish authors, Hebrew classics, and contemporary books on French history, theology, Israel, and Jewish tradition.

At the universities, Hebrew studies programs leading to advanced degrees have been established. The purpose of Jewish Renewal was "to create a sense of renewal in the Jewish community, to unify the community through political activism and to integrate French Jews into Jewish life."

Enrollment in Jewish schools today is higher than ever, consisting of 10 percent of school-age children. About 16,000 students are enrolled full-time in France's more than 30 Jewish schools. An equal number attend Sunday School. The new economic prosperity of the Sephardim fuels a revival of religious education. They realize that only Jewish education can save them from rampant assimilation.

Jews around France can tune in to any of 13 radio stations playing Hebrew and Yiddish songs and broadcasting cultural programs and news commentaries. The three Paris stations alone claim a daily audience of 37,000 Jews. *Judeotel,* a video magazine, has introduced programs that consist of Jewish news and culture and is accessible on the Internet.

Jewish publications have more readers than ever. Numerous weeklies are distributed free of charge in Jewish centers and shops. The monthly *L'Arche,* aimed at France's educated middle class, reaches about 10,000 subscribers. Every year, an international festival of Jewish films is held.

Many Jews, including Michel Boujenah, a Jewish actor of Tunisian origin, are involved in the film industry. In June of each year a Yiddish festival takes place.

There has been a continued blossoming of Jewish culture by the French public. Nelly Hansson noted in the 1988 edition of the *American Jewish Yearbook* that "even as many Jews were becoming personally de-Judaized, French society was becoming culturally Judaized."

The French rightist politician LePen and his brand of anti-Semitism probably do not constitute a crisis for French Jews today, though these extremists are always a danger if there is no "eternal vigilance." LePen's appeal seems to be waning in "multicultural" France. Today's Jewish problems consist of assimilation and mixed marriages.

France is changing. With the new united Europe, the French are accepting minorities and are less nationalistic, it is said. Marek Halter was probably right when he declared, "Jews never lived so freely as they do today in France," and they stand by Israel. In 1991, during the Gulf War, when the Jewish State was being bombarded by SCUD missiles, about 1,500 French Jewish men, women, and children, in a show of solidarity, visited Israel. They were the largest solidarity group to arrive from the Diaspora. Also, once every two years, more than 40,000 Jews gather at Le Bourget Airport for a *Yom Ha-Torah,* a day of Torah study.

Jewish Paris

For nearly everyone, there is the Paris of art, culture, and romance; the banks of the River Seine; the galleries, museums, and cathedrals; the Champs-Elysées; the Eiffel Tower; the parks; the superb restaurants, as well as thousands of sidewalk cafés and bistros. To arrive in the "City of Light" for the first time or the tenth time is to be touched by beauty.

It has been said that one half of Paris makes love to the other half. Wherever you go, Paris boasts the best-dressed women, the best food, the best wine. That's at least what the guidebooks say, especially since this wonderful city is known as the "City of Love."

This is the city of Hugo, Dumas, Flaubert and Balzac; Zola, Baudelaire, and other literary dreamers. This is a city mad on pleasure and passionate about food. Movies and especially books by Ernest Hemingway, William Carlos Williams, John Dos Passos, and other American writers who described the city on the Seine for two decades between the world wars helped enhance America's love for this city.

As author William L. Shirer said, Paris is "as near to paradise on this earth as any man could ever get." The writer John Galsworthy said, "Paris pets the senses." Observe the cafés; sail on the river; walk along the boulevard St-Michel; inhale the "Paris of the common man, the Paris born of the French Revolution."

For Jews, there is another Paris. It can be found on the Left Bank and on the Right Bank, on the avenue de Wagram, in the student quarter on the boulevard St-Michel, in the rue Richer and the rue des Rosiers.

Before there was France, even before there were a people called the French, there was Paris. And Jews have lived in Paris since the year 582.

The capital of France is the center of French Jewish activities. Half of the 700,000 French Jews live in and around Paris. You meet them everywhere: on the Champs-Elysées, in the fashionable Sixteenth Arrondissement, in the attractive suburb of Neuilly, in the elite shops of the exquisite rue Faubourg de St-Honoré, in the restaurants on the rue Richer, on the *bateaux mouches* that cruise up and down the Seine, and in the immaculate and superb gardens and parks of this beautiful metropolis. Indeed, Jewish travelers to Paris are increasing 5 to 10 percent each year.

Jewish Paris is alive and full of contrasts. One can see a Chassidic Jew on a bicycle delivering kosher takeout Chinese food.

In the elegant Place des Vosges, one of the most beautiful squares in Europe, just outside the Temple des Vosges at No. 14, I saw a bride and groom leave the synagogue after a Jewish wedding where the shamash was dressed in the *bicorne* (cocked hat of the Napoleonic era), knee-length black coats, and silver chains of office.

JEWISH SITES IN PARIS

Visit the **Pletzel.** This neighborhood is still a visible center of Jewish life in Paris, and is located in the Marais/St. Paul section of the city.

The Pletzel is located on the site of the thirteenth-century ghetto of Paris known as the **Juiverie.** When the Jewish people were permitted to return to the Kingdom of France in 1198, they settled on what is now the rue Ferdinand Duval, then called "street of the Jews." Once it was in the neighborhood of the rich, but after the storming of the Bastille on July 14, 1789, the poor moved in. When those first Jewish immigrants settled in this section in the twelfth century, they called it "little square," or in Yiddish, the "Pletzel."

Today, several thousand Jews, many of them religious, live in the Pletzel. On Friday afternoons, one can observe Chassidim dressed in long black coats with their round *shtreimels* (fur hats), scurrying home to prepare for the Sabbath Queen.

Seen in shop windows in the Pletzel are religious goods, such as *yarmulkes* and *talesim* (skullcaps and prayer shawls); Israeli and Yiddish newspapers; and Israeli food products, including humus and falafel and matzoh for Passover.

As you walk through the maze of those tight alleys and winding streets with walls of quaint old buildings forming odd angles at the narrow streets below, you quickly sense that you are taking a sentimental journey. Depending on the world situation, you can always spot the Jewish synagogue, community center, or museum from several blocks away, simply because there are armed security forces standing in front of these institutions. Fear, however, does not appear to linger in the air in the Pletzel. Residents bustle about this old-world neighborhood, which has always exuded a Jewish atmosphere. Usually when I go to old neighborhoods such as the Pletzel, it is just as if I am meandering along the Lower East Side of New York. As I watch the bearded Orthodox men with long black coats and fur *shtreimels,* all engaged in deep conversation, I romanticize that this is the way it must have been 75 years ago, when the Jews started settling here in large numbers.

To this day in the Pletzel, on the rue des Rosiers, rue des Hospitalieres-St-Gervais, rue des Ecouffes (pawnbrokers), rue Ferdinand Duval, rue Geoffroy l'Asnier, and rue Vieille du Temple, you will find a Jewish atmosphere of small synagogues, shops, apartments, restaurants, delicatessens, and monuments; in short, "the old neighborhood." To start, here are some art and book stores in the Pletzel:

Bibliophane, 26, rue des Rosiers, 75004, Paris. Tel: 48-87-82-20.

Diasporama, 20, rue des Rosiers, 75004, Paris. Tel: 42-78-30-50. FAX: 42-74-38-76. Open Sunday to Friday, 10 A.M.-7:30 P.M., except Friday when it closes before the Sabbath. It stays closed on the Sabbath. Diasporama is a fine Judaica store featuring menorahs, silver and pewter items, kiddush cups and seder plates, original paintings, audio and video tapes, and Limoges plates. Chana and Patrick Hagistare are the proprietors.

Librairie Hebraica-Judaica, 12 rue des Hospitalières St-Gervais, 75004, Paris. Tel: 48-87-32-20.

Librairie du Marais, 7, rue des Rosiers, 75004, Paris. Tel: 48-87-99-97. Books, religious items, tapes.

JEWISH RESTAURANTS IN PARIS

In Paris, one place to meet Jews is in restaurants and cafés. Meeting people in a café is typically French, for the Parisians include the surrounding eating establishments in their definition of home.

Most would agree that Paris is the gastronomic capital of the world. This city loves a carefully prepared meal that is appreciatively savored. According to Parisians, a meal is a very special

A store selling religious goods in the rue des Rosiers, Paris. (Photo courtesy of the French Government Tourist Office)

Jewish bookstore in the Marais, Paris. (Photo by Dr. Joshua Fogelman)

experience, a pleasure of life. The French do not eat; they dine. The traveler seeking **kosher** cuisine does not have to be wary about finding it in Paris, where there may be more kosher facilities than in New York, Chicago, and Los Angeles combined. One can certainly enjoy a wide variety of French, Eastern European, and North African specialties here.

Kosher restaurants are usually open from noon to about 3 and from 6 until 11, except for Friday and Saturday. Some open Saturday night, depending on the season. Addresses and hours change, so it is best to telephone ahead to confirm hours and make reservations. More than 100 kosher restaurants in Paris will certainly meet the traveler's needs. Most kosher restaurants carry the sign of the Beth Din of Paris, certifying "kosher here," but some also have the approval sign of Lubavitch.

Jewish restaurants are institutions where people are ready to extend a warm welcome to the visitor. Ironically one of the best-known Jewish tourist spots in Paris is a Jewish restaurant that is not kosher, but kosher-style. I call it "Chez Goldenberg."

Goldenberg's, 7, rue des Rosiers, 75004, Paris. Tel: 48-87-20-16 or 48-87-70-39. A mainstay eatery in the Marais. It remains open everyday from 8 A.M. to 2 A.M.

Jo Goldenberg likes to say his meals are for the *"kleine or groysse fresser."* Gastronomes will enjoy Goldenberg's pastrami and corned beef, although it is spicier than that in the United States. Also available are pickled fleish, borscht, schmaltz herring, pickled flanken, chopped liver, smoked salmon, herring, matjes herring, and, of course, Eastern European specialties such as zakuski, pojarski, and Hungarian goulash. A lively lunch atmosphere also percolates from the takeout deli counter, table areas in the front, and the red leather sofa-chairs in the back, during the long midday meal. And you never know who is going to drop in from government, business, and the professions during that time. This restaurant is an "in" place to eat and be seen. Famous guests include former President of the Republic François Mitterrand and former Prime Minister Michel Rocard, who dined here often; Abba Eban, Charlie Chaplin, Barbra Streisand, Charles Aznavour, and Simone Veil, who served as president of the European Parliament.

Jo Goldenberg's popular kosher-style restaurant in the Marais, Paris. (Photo by Dr. Joshua Fogelman)

At night, there is singing and dancing, and music fills the air. Call for reservations and plan to arrive at about 9 P.M. That's the best time for the gaiety.

Jo Goldenberg is a delightful man, and an engaging host. He still hops from table to table. He embraces guests. He tastes everything—he munches bread, he samples the strudel, he sips a glass of tea.

One of Jo Goldenberg's hobbies is to collect samovars. He has them lined up on the staircase of his two-story establishment. He is a child of the Marais: he speaks French, Yiddish, Hebrew, and some English. He points proudly to a photo on the second floor of the restaurant, a picture of his father, who opened a deli and restaurant in the 1920s, just down the street from the present Goldenberg's.

Jo circles the bullet holes. That the restaurant functions to this day is a victory over a terrorist attack on the place in 1982.

Kosher Restaurants

Boulangerie Patisserie Murciano, 14-16, rue des Rosiers, 75004, Paris. Tel: 48-87-48-88.

Kosher Pizza, 11, rue de Rosiers, 75004, Paris. Tel: 48-87-17-83. Delicious, strictly kosher pizza.

La Petite Famille, 32, rue des Rosiers, 75004, Paris. Tel: 42-77-00-50.

Le Mazel-Tov, 25, rue des Rosiers, 75004, Paris. Tel: 40-27-87-40.

Micky's Deli, 23 bis, rue des Rosiers, 75004, Paris. Offers glatt kosher meat sandwiches. The small counter and good takeout service make this a nice stop on a sojourn in the Marais.

Pita Burger, 23, rue des Rosiers, 75004, Paris. Tel: 42-77-59-41.

Tutti Frutti, 38, rue des Rosiers, 75004, Paris. Tel: 42-76-04-75. This is a very popular takeout place with a small counter. It is especially known for grilled panini sandwiches of tuna and cheese. It also serves yogurt. English and Hebrew are spoken here. (Tutti Frutti is strictly kosher, "Halav Yisrael.")

Yahalom, 24, rue des Rosiers, 75004, Paris. Tel: 42-77-12-35.

Le Tamy's kosher pizzeria in the Marais, Paris. (Photo by Dr. Joshua Fogelman)

This place is strictly glatt kosher. They offer you falafel, humus, tahini, and eggplant. Full-course meals include Israeli dishes as well as meat dishes. You will find that snacks are also available.

Contini, 42, rue des Rosiers, 75004, Paris. Tel: 48-04-78-22.

Hamman Café, 4, rue des Rosiers, 75003, Paris. Tel: 42-78-04-76.

La Pita, 26, rue des Rosiers, 75004, Paris. Tel: 42-77-93-13.

Chinese Kosher

Le Lotus de Nissan, 39, rue Amelot, 75011, Paris. Tel: 43-55-80-42. For a change of pace, excellent kosher Chinese food awaits the tourist in Paris. This charming kosher Chinese restaurant presents a menu that includes fried wonton, chop suey, spring rolls, duck, and beef. Reservations advised.

Lotus de Nissan has a kosher takeout that will deliver right to your hotel for lunch or dinner. The takeout facility is located at 53, rue Amelot, 75011, Paris. Tel: 43-57-44-05.

Other Kosher Restaurants

Adolphe, 14, rue Richer, 75009, Paris. Tel: 47-70-91-25.

Allo Sarina, 38 rue Curial, 75019, Paris. Tel: 40-35-08-98.

Auberge de Belleville, 110 blvd. De Belleville, 75020, Paris. Tel: 43-15-02-59.

Benittah, 49 quai de Seine, 75019, Paris. Tel: 40-05-99-00.

Berberche Burger, 42, rue Richer, 75009, Paris. Tel: 47-70-81-22.

Brasserie du Belvedere, 109, avenue de Villieres, 75017, Paris.

Cash Food, 63, rue des Vinaigriers, 75010, Paris. Tel: 42-03-95-75.

Centre Communautaire, 5 rue Rochechouard, 75009, Paris. Tel: 45-95-95-92.

Centre Edmond Fleg, 8 bis, rue de l'Eperon, 750006, Paris. Tel: 46-33-43-31.

Chez Chlomi, 159/161 rue de Flanders, 75019, Paris. Tel: 46-07-54-76.

Chez Marco, 34, rue Curial, 75019, Paris. Tel: 40-05-05-99.

Chez René et Gabin, 92, boulevard de Belleville, 75020, Paris. Tel: 43-58-78-14.

Chochana, 54, avenue Secretan, 75019, Paris. Tel: 42-41-01-16.
Cotel Maaravi, 69 avenue Armand-Carel, 75019, Paris. Tel: 42-06-13-00.
Darima, 89 avenue des Ternes, 75017, Paris. Tel: 45-72-50-50.
Dolly's Food, 9, rue Cite Riverain, 75010, Paris. Tel: 48-03-08-40.
Dizengoff Café, 27 rue Riche, 75009, Paris. Tel: 47-70-81-97.
El Guacho, 1 Allee Darius Milhaud, 75019, Paris. Tel: 40-03-02-88.
Eugenie, 103, Jouffroy d'Abbans, 75017, Paris. Tel: 47-64-33-11.
Fradji, 42, rue Poncelet, 75017, Paris. Tel: 47-54-91-40.
Gin Fizz, 157 blvd. Semurier, 75019, Paris. Tel: 42-00-51-28.
Isacharl's, 36, blvd. Barbes, 75018, Paris. Tel: 42-52-68-50.
Juliette, 14, rue Duphot, 75001, Paris. Tel: 42-60-18-05 or 42-60-18-10.
King Solomon, 46. Rue Richer, 75009 Paris. Tel: 42-46-31-22.
La Brasserie des Champs, 64 avenue Marceau, 75008, Paris. Tel: 56-32-31-31.
La Libanaise, 13,rue des Sablons, 75016, Paris. Tel: 45-05-10-35.
Les Jardins du Belvedere, 111, avenue de Villiers, 75017, Paris. Tel: 42-27-16-91. Highly recommended. Excellent food.
Le Manahattan, 231, blvd. Voltaire, 75011, Paris. Tel: 43-56-03-30.
Les Cantiques, 16, rue Beaurepaire, 75010, Paris. Tel: 42-40-64-21.
Lumieres de Belleville, 102, blvd. de Belleville, 75020, Paris. Tel: 47-97-51-83.
Natania, 27, rue Poissonniere, 75002, Paris. Tel: 42-33-58-36.
Nini, 24, rue Saussier-Leroy, 75017, Paris. Tel: 46-22-28-93. Excellent food and highly recommended. Nini is very popular with American Jews. It has been called a "Tunisian-chic restaurant." Served here are steaks, veal, lamb chops, mixed grill, and couscous.
Nini Japonais, 6, rue Fourcroy, 75017, Paris. Tel: 46-22-28-93.
Restaurant Henri, 13/15, Passage du Ponceau, 75002, Paris. Tel: 40-13-91-72.
Restaurant "Les Ailes," 34 rue Richer, 75009, Paris. Tel: 47-70-62-53. Grill and Tunisian specialties. Also high on the list of kosher diners.

Resto Flash, 10, rue Lucien-Sampaix, 75010, Paris. Tel: 45-23-85-00.

Yun Pana, 115, blvd. Voltaire, 75011, Paris. Tel: 43-79-20-48.

Wang's, 159/161 Semurier, 75019, Paris. Tel: 40-03-00-03.

Zazou Burger, 19, rue du Faubourg-Montmartre, 75009, Paris. Tel: 40-22-08-33.

LODGING

Lebron, 4, rue Lamartine, 75009, Paris. Tel: 48-78-75-52. FAX: 49-95-94-64. Besides fine hotel rooms with TVs, this kosher facility maintains a glatt kosher restaurant, dining room, and conference room. One can order meals ahead of time for the Sabbath. The hotel is near numerous synagogues and not far from Temple Victoire, as well as the synagogue on rue Buffault. Chabad House is several doors down, at 8, rue Lamartine. Moreover, the hotel is near fine kosher restaurants in rue Richer and the surrounding area.

The quarter around rue Richer is another Parisian section where one can often meet Jews. Throughout the world, No. 32 rue Richer is known as the Folies Bergeres. This is one of the most dynamic streets of Paris.

Walk along the rue Richer, between rue du Faubourg-Poissonniere and rue Faubourg-Montmartre. Explore the side streets. Lunch or dine in one of the many kosher restaurants and snack bars.

Browse in one of the largest Jewish bookstores, the **Colbo,** at No. 3, rue Richer. Tel: 47-70-21-81.

SYNAGOGUES IN PARIS

The Jewish tourist in France has no difficulty finding a synagogue to visit, whether in Paris or the countryside. Several hundred exist in France. There are more than 50 Jewish houses of worship in Paris alone. And many of the Parisian suburbs contain synagogues. To check times of services, please contact the **Consistoire Central,** 19, rue St-Georges, 75009, Paris. Tel: 49-70-88-00, or the Consistoire de Paris, 17, rue St-Georges, 75009, Paris. Tel: 40-82-26-26.

Temple Victoire, 44, rue de la Victoire, 75009, Paris. Tel: 45-26-95-36. Metro: LePetetier or Notre-Dame-de-Lorette. A must for American visitors. This beautiful, austere building is frequently referred to as the Rothschild Synagogue because members of the renowned family attend services here. Built in 1874 in neo-Romanesque style, it is lavishly decorated with marble and stained glass, and is dominated by opulent candelabras. It is often called the "Cathedral Synagogue."

The synagogue is on a relatively narrow street. Jewish officials had hoped to have the façade on the somewhat more conspicuous rue St-Georges, from which one now enters the community offices, but the empress's confessor, reportedly a converted Jew, did not want the building to be visible on a heavily traversed thoroughfare. So the congregation had to put up with the resulting incorrect orientation of the Holy Ark, writes Carol Herselle Krinsky in *Synagogues in Europe*. The interior is impressive.

Because the Rothschilds pray here, let us reflect on this family of financiers and philanthropists, who have contributed greatly to Jewish causes. The head of the Rothschild family was Mayer Amschel Rothschild of Frankfurt (1744-1812), who had five sons. They were Amschel Mayer (1773-1836), who stayed in Frankfurt; Solomon Mayer (1774-1855), who went to Vienna; Nathan Mayer (1777-1855), to London; Karl Mayer (1788-1855), to Naples; and James Jacob (1792-1868), to Paris.

The French branch of the family was founded when James, the youngest of the sons, settled in Paris in 1812. As an agent of his brother Nathan, James established the firm of Rothschild Freres. Financially, he aided the Bourbon and Orleans families, the kings of France, and Napoleon III. From then on, apart from its banking activities, the Rothschild family was active in the French Jewish community.

James de Rothschild built the Rothschild Hospital, which still stands today in Paris. An early railroad entrepreneur, James helped set up many government railroad lines. The Rothschilds financed the main rail networks in France, including the Chemin de Fer du Nord.

The Rothschild family assumed positions of responsibility in the French Jewish leadership, holding respected posts. Baron Guy de Rothschild was president of Fonds Social Juif Unifié (FSJU). He was succeeded by his son, David Rothschild. The late Baron Alain de Rothschild was president of the Consistoire and headed the Representative Council of Jewish Organizations in France (**CRIF**). Baron Elie de Rothschild was active in the French United Jewish Appeal.

Synagogue services: Friday nights at 6:30, Saturday mornings at 9:30. (Metro: Le Peletier). There is also a Tunisian and an Egyptian congregation on the premises.

Agoudas Hakehilos, 10, rue Pavée, 75004, Paris. Tel: 48-87-21-54. A school is located here. Austere on the outside and beautiful inside, this Orthodox synagogue in the Pletzel was designed in 1913 by Hector Guimard, the famous art nouveau architect of the Metro, who fled to the United States in 1942 and whose wife was Jewish. The building itself is neo-Gothic in feeling. There are two lateral aisles, each having two rows of overhead galleries for the women's section, supported by four massive pillars, plus wooden benches. Orthodox Ashkenazic services are offered every day. Sabbath morning services at 9:20. (Metro: St-Paul).

A second synagogue, located at 23, rue Petion, 75011, Paris, opened in March 1991. Services are held Friday evenings at 6:30 and Saturday mornings at 10. (Metro: Voltaire-Leon Blum).

Ohel Avraham, 31, rue Montevideo, 75016, Paris. Tel: 45-04-66-73.

Oratoire, 223, rue Vercingetorix, 75014, Paris. Tel: 45-45-50-51. (Metro: Daumesnil).

Oratoire, 42, rue des Saules, 75018, Paris. Tel: 46-06-71-39. (Metro: Jules Joffrin).

Oratoire, 120, boulevard de Belleville, 75020, Paris. Tel: 47-97-46-96.

Oratoire, 13, rue Fondary, 75015, Paris. Tel: 45-04-66-73. (Metro: Grenelle).

Synagogue, 15, rue Notre-Dame de Nazareth, 75003, Paris. Tel: 42-78-00-30. (Metro: Republique).

Synagogue, 21 bis, rue des Tournelles, 75004, Paris. Tel: 42-74-32-80. This is a Sephardic synagogue known for its wrought-iron-work interior. It is situated back-to-back with the Ashkenazic synagogue known as **Temple des Vosges,** which fronts on the Place des Vosges, 14, Place des Vosges, 75004, Paris. Tel: 48-87-79-45. A must for the visitor, the Place des Vosges, located in the heart of the Marais, is probably one of the most beautiful squares in all of Paris. Victor Hugo lived at No. 6; the house is now a museum. (Metro: Bastille).

Synagogue (Rabbinical Seminary), 9, rue Vauquelin, 75005, Paris. Tel: 47-07-21-22. FAX: 43-37-75-92. (Metro: Monge).

Synagogue, 28, rue Buffault, 75009, Paris. Tel: 45-26-80-87. (Metro: Cadet).

Synagogue Kahal Yreim, 10, rue Cadet, 75009, Paris. Tel: 42-46-36-47. (Metro: Cadet).

Synagogue Berith Shalom, 18, rue St-Lazare, 75009, Paris. Tel: 48-78-45-32 and 48-78-38-80.

Synagogue Rachi, 6, rue Ambroise-Thomas, 75009, Paris. Tel: 48-24-86-94. This synagogue is named after Rashi, who is considered the leading commentator on the Bible and the Talmud. Born in Troyes in 1040, he learned a great deal about viticulture and husbandry. In Rashi's time, Jews lived in Champagne and other wine districts of northern France. He himself studied in Worms and Mainz. About 1070, he founded a school in Troyes that made French Judaism renowned for its scholarship. But not all was tranquil. During the First Crusade, Rashi had to flee anti-Jewish riots in and around Troyes. Once he established himself in Worms, Germany, he lived and studied there. Rashi died in 1105. His burial place is not known. (Metro: Cadet).

Synagogue, 130, rue du Faubourg-St Martin, 75010, Paris. (Metro: Gare de l'Est).

Synagogue Don Isaac Abravanel, 84-86, rue de la Roquette, 75011, Paris. Tel: 47-00-75-95. (Metro: Bastille).

Synagogue, 14, rue Chasseloup-Laubat, 75015, Paris. Tel: 42-73-36-29. (Metro: Segur).

Synagogue de Montmartre, 12, rue Ste-Isaure, 75018, Paris. Tel: 42-64-48-34. (Metro: Jules Joffrin).

Synagogue de Neuilly, 12, rue Ancelle, Neuilly Sur-Seine. (Metro: Las Sablons). Tel: 46-24-49-15.

Synagogue Or Torah, 15, rue Riquet, 75019, Paris.

The Liberal Synagogue, 22-24, rue Copernic, 75116, Paris.

Tel: 47-04-37-27. On Friday night and Saturday, many American visitors and residents pray at the Union Liberale Israelite de France (The Liberal Synagogue). Services at 6 on Friday evenings and at 10:30 A.M. Saturdays. Holiday services at 10 A.M. On Passover, there is an attempt to have part of the traditional seder in English. An English-speaking secretary is available all week long to aid travelers. (Metro: Victor Hugo. Bus: 22, 82, 30, 52).

Movement Juif Liberal de France, 11, rue Gaston de Cailavet, 75015, Paris. Tel: 44-37-48-48 or 44-37-48-50. Spiritual leaders are Rabbi Daniel Farhi and Pauline Bebe. Services at 6:15 on Friday evenings and 10:30 Saturday mornings. Telephone first for directions. (Metro: Charles Michels).

CJL-Communaute Juive Liberale Ile de France, 6 rue Pierre Ginier, 75018, Paris. Tel: 47-04-37-27. Fax: 47-27-81-07.

Assembly of Masorti Synagogues

Adath Shalom, 8 rue George Bernard Shaw, 75015 Paris. Tel.: 45-67-9796. FAX: 45-56-89-79. E-mail: RUZIEDR@aol.com. Services are held here at 6:30 P.M. Friday nights and Saturday mornings at 10 A.M.

Kehilat Gesher, 10 rue fe Pologne, 78100, St. Germain en Laye. Tel: 39-21-97-19.

OFFICIALS AND ORGANIZATIONS

Chief Rabbi Joseph Sitruk serves as chief rabbi of France. His office is at 19, rue St-Georges, 75009, Paris. Tel: 49-70-88-00. FAX: 42-81-03-66.

Rabbi David Messas is the grand rabbi of Paris. His office is located in Consistoire de Paris, 17, rue St-Georges, 75009, Paris. Tel: 40-82-26-26. FAX: 42-81-92-46.

Note: For American travelers, questions regarding synagogue services, religious matters, and tickets for high holidays should be directed to Consistoire Central, 19, rue St-Georges, 75009, Paris. Tel: 49-70-88-00. FAX: 42-81-03-66. Many officials here also speak English and

Hebrew. One person to contact is Leon Masliah, honorary executive director.

Paris is the center of Jewish activities in France, as all major institutions have their headquarters there.

Conseil Representatif des Institutions Juives de France, (CRIF), 39, rue Broca, 75005, Paris. Tel: 42-17-11-11. FAX: 42-17-11-13. **CRIF,** the representative council of Jewish organizations, was founded in 1944 to protect the rights of Jews in the Republic. Today, more than 35 groups belong to **CRIF,** which speaks and acts on behalf of the organized Jewish community in representations to the government.

Consistoire Central, Union des Communautés Juives de France, 19, rue St-Georges, 75009, Paris. Tel: 49-77-88-00. FAX: 42-81-03-66. The Consistoire is a major force in French Jewish organizational life. The Consistoire Central recently moved its headquarters next door to 19 rue St-Georges. The building contains an assembly hall for lectures and ceremonies and special offices. **Leon Masliah** is honorary executive director. Frederic Attali is director of the Consistoire.

Fond Social Juif Unifie (FSJU), 39 rue Broca, Paris. Tel: 42-17-10-10. FAX: 42-17-10-45. The words on the banner at the entrance of this important institution tell the story of the goals of the revitalized Jewish community of France:

For a strong community
To help Israel.
For your active participation in Jewish life.

These words define the goals of the Fonds Social Juif Unifie, translated as the United Jewish Social Fund, similar to a federation and welfare fund in the United States.

The FSJU coordinates, supervises, and plans major social, educational, and cultural activities and enterprises of the French Jewish community. This building also houses the offices of L'Appel Unifie Juif de France (the French UJA) and the Conseil Representatif des Institutions Juives de France (**CRIF**), which is a council of Jewish organizations.

The "Appel" has introduced American fund-raising techniques in soliciting funds.

Lubavitch is very active and maintains more than 40 Chabad Centers in France, as well as many synagogues. The main **Synagogue and Center** is located at **Beth Loubavitch,** 8, rue Lamartine, 75009, Paris. Tel: 45-26-87-60. Orthodox Shabbat service is at 10:30 A.M. on Saturdays. Call for a list of group activities and services. You will be welcome.

In addition to the above, there are hundreds of distinguished groups, international and local, which are active. A partial list includes the World Jewish Congress, ORT, B'nai B'rith, a number of Sephardic and Zionist groups, the American Jewish Joint Distribution Committee, the Jewish Agency for Israel, the Weizmann Institute, the France-Israel Alliance, and WIZO (Women's International Zionist Organization).

American Jewish Joint Distribution Committee, 5 av. Malignon, 75008, Paris. Tel: 56-59-79-79. FAX: 56-59-79-89.

B'nai B'rith, 9, rue de Chaillot, 75116, Paris. Tel: 42-80-03-30. FAX: 40-70-17-05.

Embassy of Israel, 3, rue Rebelais, 75008 Paris. Tel: 40-76-55-00. FAX: 40-76-55-55.

Federation of Zionist Organizations of France, 17 bis rue de Paradis, 75010, Paris. Tel: 48-24-03-44. FAX: 48-24-04-63.

Femmes Pionnieres, 12 rue de l'Echiquier, 75010, Paris. Tel: 47-70-21-75.

Jewish Agency, 140 blvd. Malesherbes, 75017, Paris. Tel: 47-63-00-68.

K.K.L. (Jewish National Fund), 11, rue du 4 Septembre, 75002, Paris. Tel: 42-86-88-88. FAX: 42-60-18-13.

O.R.T., 44 avenue. Victor Hugo, 75116, Paris. Tel: 45-00-74-22. FAX: 45-01-80-21.

WIZO, 54 rue de Paradis, 75010, Paris. Tel: 48-01-97-70. FAX: 48-01-97-77.

ORT-France—Organisation Reconstruction, Travail Association, 10, Villa d'Eylau, 75116, Paris. Tel: 4500-74-22. ORT, as it is known throughout the world, operates vocational and technical schools.

World Jewish Congress, 78, avenue des Champs-Elysées, 75008, Paris. Tel: 43-59-94-63. FAX: 42-25-45-28.

Youth Organizations

BBYO, 5 bis, rue de Rochechouart, 75009, Paris. Tel: 40-82-91-00. FAX: 40-82-95-75.

Lubavitch Youth, Beth Lubavitch, 8 rue Lamartine, 75009, Paris. Tel: 45-26-87-60.

B'nei Akiva, 28, rue Bichat, 75010, Paris. Tel: 42-40-56-00.

Jewish Community Activity Centers

Centre Bernard Lazare, 10, rue Saint-Claude, 75003, Paris.

Centre Communautaire Maison des Jeunes, 5, rue de Rochechouart, 75009, Paris. Tel: 49-95-95-92. FAX: 42-80-10-66. Located here are many activities, such as sports, lectures, theater programs, and an ulpan to study Hebrew. A kosher cafeteria serves lunch from 12 noon to 2 P.M. and dinner from 6 to 8 P.M. There are services on Friday nights and at 8:45 A.M. on Saturdays.

Centre Edmond Fleg, 8 bis, rue de l'Eperon, 75006, Paris. Tel: 46-33-43-31. This is a university student center, sponsored by the Consistoire de Paris and named after a French Jewish writer. Young visitors should inquire about activities. A cafeteria serves hot kosher lunches.

Centre Israel Jeffroykin, 68, rue de la Flie Maricourt, 75011, Paris. Located near the Bastille. (Metro: Oberkampf).

Centre Rachi, 30, boulevard Port-Royal, 75005, Paris. Tel: 43-31-98-20 or 43-31-75-47. Open from 9 A.M. to 11 P.M. A good spot, especially for university students and adults interested in intellectual activities. Seminars, lectures, and films. A kosher cafeteria and circular coffee bar make it a fine gathering place. Services are at 8 Friday night and 8 Saturday morning in the summer; 4:30 P.M. Friday and 9 A.M. Saturday in the winter.

Centre Rambam, 19-21, rue Galvani, 75017, Paris. Tel: 45-74-52-80 or 45-74-51-81. Located in a growing Jewish neighborhood, this Sephardic center contains a beautiful Moroccan-style synagogue, library, meeting rooms, reception, and catering area. Sabbath services. This is a good site to reflect upon the impact of the arrival in the 1960s of Sephardim to France.

During the thirty years since their departure from North Africa, Sephardic Jews from Morocco have established this Sephardic center in Paris. The center, which was named Rambam, hosts study groups devoted to Spanish Jewish traditions as well as organizes lectures. Rambam is the acronym of Rabbi Moses ben Maimon (1135-1204), or as he is more widely known, Maimonides, one of the most illustrious figures of the post-Talmudic era.

The massive flux in the 1950s and 1960s of Sephardic Jews from North Africa to France was one of the most exciting movements of immigration in contemporary European history. Nearly 300,000 Sephardic Jews came to France in the early 1960s. They revitalized and revolutionized French Jewry to such an extent that some have called the present community the Second French Jewry.

The Sephardim brought activity and momentum, an infusion of new blood. They set up community institutions, synagogues, and Talmud Torahs. They were proud of their Jewishness. Although half settled in and around Paris, many moved into towns such as Avignon, Arles, Aix-en-Provence-towns that had heretofore contained few Jews.

This was one of the few times in Jewish history when the Jewish community changed from Ashkenazic to Sephardic. Not only was their arrival welcome, their integration into Jewish and French society was also very successful. They launched themselves into key positions in French government, education, art, and science.

Maison France-Israel. Located only a few short blocks from the Arc de Triomphe is the Maison France-Israel, at 64, avenue Marceau, 75008, Paris. Tel: 44-43-36-36. FAX: 44-43-35-20. This can be a home away from home for American tourists. First of all, this new institution contains three strictly kosher restaurants as well as meeting rooms. Established and led by former government minister Lionel Stoleru, the officers and staff want visitors to feel at home. In the courtyard stands the superb statue, *La Fontaine de Rachi,* named after the great French Talmudist, Rashi, and dedicated to the enhancement of two cultures: France and Israel. Here in this building are halls named after Chagall and Rothschild. Dedicated by former French President François Mitterrand and former Israeli President Chaim Herzog, the mansion houses the Simon Wiesenthal Center, Friends of the Israel Museum in Jerusalem, L'Alliance France-Israel, the France-Israel Chamber of Commerce, and other organizations. Kosher restaurants include a gastronomic restaurant called Le Table de David, and Le Sabra, which specializes in Israeli food. Several Jewish radio stations, including Radio Shalom, broadcast from this building, Tel: 44-43-36-03.

Rabbinical School of Paris, 9, rue Vauquelin, 75005, Paris. Tel: 47-07-21-22. American students may want to contact this Orthodox, rabbinic seminary for a schedule of activities, classes, and religious services. A synagogue is located here as well.

MUSEUMS

The Jewish artists Soutine, Pascin, Chagall, Pissarro, Modigliani, Mane-Katz, Benn, and Lipchitz worked and created masterpieces in France. Many of their works are exhibited in various Parisian museums.

Centre National d'Art et de Culture Georges Pompidou, better known as Beaubourg, on rue Beaubourg, 75004, Paris. Tel: 42-77-12-33. **The Centre National d'Art et de Culture Georges Pompidou** has been refurbished. Repairs were needed as attendance at this museum far outstrips other popular institutions. In 20 years, Beaubourg has served 160 million visitors and is far more popular than the Versailles Palace and the Louvre Museum. Paintings by Jewish artists, such as Chagall, Soutine, and Modigliani. Hebrew and Yiddish language lessons available on taped cassettes. Numerous books on Jewish history, Judaica, Israel, and Jewish literature. The Pompidou Centre, which is visited by about 25,000 persons daily, is not far from the Pletzel in the Marais section.

Musee d'art et d'historoie du Judaisme, Hotel de Saint-Aignan, 71 rue du Temple, 75003, Paris, Tel: 01-53-0186-60, FAX: 01-42-72-97-47; E-mail:info@mahj.org. A half century in the making; the Jewish Museum has moved from its perch high above Montmartre to the wonderful **Hotel de Saint-Aignan,** 17 rue due Temple. Located near the Pompidou Centre, the Metro stop is Rambuteau, Hotel de Ville. Hours are Monday to Friday: 11A.M. to 6 P.M.; Sunday, 10 A.M. to 6 P.M. **The Museum of Jewish Art and History** is housed in one of Paris' most palatial mansions in the historic Marais quarter, for many years considered the Jewish quarter. The museum traces the historical evolution of Jewish communities from the Middle Ages to the 20th Century through their cultural and artistic heritage. Although the focus is on the history of the Jews in France, Jewish communities in Europe and North Africa are also represented. Here one will see religious items, textiles, manuscripts, and documents depicting Jewish history, including the archives of the Dreyfus Affair. Some of the artists represented here are Chagall, Modigliani, Soutine, Kikoine and other Jewish painters.

Built in 1650, the Hotel de Saint-Aignan first served as the home of Comte d'Avaux, Mazarin's superintendent of finance. The Duc de Saint-Aignan bought the house in 1688. During the Revolution, the mansion became the town hall of Paris's 7th district. After 1842, it housed workshops, with Jewish craftsmen moving in at the end of the century. In 1962, the Hotel de Saint-Aignan was bought by the City of Paris who made it available to the Museum of Jewish Art and History. The mansion's restoration and conversion into a museum were financed by the Ministry of Culture and Communication and the City of Paris.

Exhibitions of photography, graphic arts highlight the presentations of the Museum. Cultural events occur here, too. One can see that no expense was spared in setting up the museum

Library of the Alliance Israelite Universelle, 45, rue la Bruyere, 75009, Paris. Tel: 42-80-35-00 or 47-44-75-84. More than 100,000 books of Judaic interest, including manuscripts. Permission to visit needed.

Musée Carnavalet, 23, rue de Sevigne, 75003, Paris. Tel: 42-72-21-13. Open 10 to 5:40 every day except Monday. The aim of the museum is to illustrate the history of Paris from its origins to the present day. The building and mansion display a number of personal souvenirs and artifacts of Rachel, one of France's most famous Jewish actresses.

The building also houses the Museum of the History of Paris, which covers the sixteenth to the nineteenth centuries. The museum has branched out into a new addition next door, the Hotel le Peletier-St-Farglau, which includes the bedroom of the famous Jewish writer Marcel Proust. Open 10 to 5:40 every day except Monday.

A wonderful exhibit entitled "The French Revolution" enhances this inspiring structure and is well worth seeing. At the time of the French Revolution, about five hundred Jews resided in Paris. Many had bribed the chief of police for permission to settle there. Looking back to the days of the French Revolution, we learn that the Jews of that time were indebted to liberal Count Mirabeau and a liberal Catholic cleric named Abbe Gregoire, who supported Jewish equality. The Declaration of Human Rights was passed in the summer of 1789. The Jewish question did not come up for debate until December 24, 1789. The revolutionary Count Mirabeau simply did not possess the votes. The matter was tabled until the next month. On January 28, 1790, Talleyrand brought in a report by the Committee of the Constitution in favor of "equality."

On that day, however, only the Sephardic Jews, those "who were known in France by the names of the Portuguese, Spanish, and Avignonnais Jews," would henceforth enjoy the rights of active citizens. Twenty months would pass until equal rights were given to the Ashkenazic Jews. On September 27, 1791, after much debate and many delays, the Ashkenazim who lived in Alsace and the surrounding area were emancipated.

Regarding the impact of the French Revolution on the Jews, "for the first time in the modern history of the West, all the Jews within the borders of a European state were united with all its other citizens, as equals before the law," writes Arthur Hertzberg in *The French Enlightenment and the Jews.* A new era in Jewish history was born.

Robespierre himself was one of the first to demand citizenship for the Jews. True, some synagogues were closed during the Revolution because of the anti-religious policy, which the Jacobins directed against the powerful Catholic Church. But the

Jacobins fought against all religious symbols. Although there was anti-Jewish discrimination, neither during the Reign of Terror nor during the Thermidor was a Jew executed solely because he was a Jew.

Soza Szajkowski, author of *Jews and the French Revolution of 1789, 1830, 1848,* says that "the vast majority of Jews did favor the new regime, but because of their diverse economic and regional attachments, Jews were active in all factions of the Revolutionary regime."

A Jewish Jacobin Club sprung up in the "Jewish suburb" of St-Esprit in Bayonne. A synagogue still stands in that very section— at 35, rue Maubec in Bayonne.

The armies of the Revolution and, later, of Napoleon himself carried the banner and, more important, put into practice "Liberty, Equality and Fraternity." For Jews, the cry meant freedom. Napoleon was the liberator of the Jews of Europe.

While on the one hand the French gave Jews human rights, virulent anti-Semitism existed in the philosophical writings of such Frenchmen as Voltaire and Diderot. While the Enlightenment helped the Jews, these French thinkers were widely read and their anti-Semitic writings would in the end harm the Jewish people.

Still, the Republic attracted Jews from all over the world. Because of the country's liberal immigration policy, Jews from Eastern Europe poured into France. In the nineteenth century, this flow would increase. One outcome of the Revolution of course was the Sanhedrin. In 1806, Napoleon convoked a Grand Sanhedrin which codified religious decisions. It met in 1807. Napoleon was determined to provide the Jews of France with a central organization supervised by the State and loyal to the government. He followed the example of the arrangements he had already introduced for other religions.

The emperor possessed an ulterior motive. He wanted Jews assimilated. He felt their emancipation had not produced the anticipated results. Jews, he said, were really a nation within a nation. But because of its group nature, the Sanhedrin was distorted by anti-Semites as an international conspiracy plotting ritual murder.

The Consistoire Central in France was established on July 17,

1808, along with the institution of the chief rabbinate. Following the Revolution of July 1830, the French government proposed that the Jewish religion have equal status with the Catholic Church and Protestantism. One year later it was done.

Musée Cluny, 6, Place Paul-Painleve, 75005, Paris. Tel: 43-25-62-00. Contains furniture, Jewish engagement rings, sculpture, fragments representing kings of Judea. Displayed here are the famous Strauss-Rothschild collections of Jewish ritual objects.

Musée du Louvre, rue de Rivoli, 75001, Paris. Tel: 42-60-39-26. Every day in Paris, thousands of tourists from around the world enter the **Musée du Louvre** by way of an enormous glass pyramid. Standing 70 feet high and constructed from 200 tons of glass and steel, **La Pyramide du Louvre** welcomes more than five million tourists each year. The pyramid was designed by American architect I.M. Pei and is located in the center of the Napoleon Courtyard. On March 30, 2000, the Pyramid celebrated its 10th anniversary. The entrance designed by I. M. Pei and Partners leads from ground level down to the welcoming area. From below ground level, one proceeds to various pavilions, such as the Sully, Danton, or Richelieu Pavilions, or to the museum's cafeteria or bookstore. The Palais du Louvre contains many Jewish archeological items and antiques from Israel, such as a terra-cotta ossuary discovered in a funeral cave in Azor near Tel Aviv. The museum itself contains about six thousand paintings. In 1993, part of the collection was housed in the Richelieu Pavilion in the rue de Rivoli. This pavilion had been used for offices by the French Ministry of Finance. Open Thursday, Friday, Saturday, and Sunday, 9 to 6; Monday and Wednesday, 9 A.M. to 9:40 P.M. (Closed Tuesday). The Pyramid is open every day except Tuesday. (Metro: Palais Royal Musée du Louvre).

Musée d'Orsay, 62, rue de Bellechasse, 75007, Paris. Tel: 45-49-48-14. A former belle époque railroad station was renovated in 1986 to become a modern museum of nineteenth-century art, including the works of two well-known French Jewish artists, Pissarro and Modigliani. Contains impressionist paintings by Manet, Monet, Van Gogh, Degas, Sisley, Renoir, Cezanne, Seurat, Signac, and Gauguin. Open daily from 10 to 6 and until 9:45 on Thursday. Closed Monday.

Bibliothèque Nationale (The National Library), 58, rue de

Richelieu, 75009, Paris. Tel: 47-03-81-26. Magnificent Hebrew manuscripts, Dead Sea Scroll fragments, Bibles, Haggadoth, ketubot. More than 30,000 volumes are in the Hebraic section. A regular exchange with Israel has ensured the acquisition of all books published there since 1953. One must write for permission to see the manuscripts or use the library.

MEMORIAL SITES

Memorial in Le Drancy, avenue Jean-Jaures, Le Drancy. Drancy is a town three miles from Paris, a short express ride on the RER train (suburban express subway). Located here is one of the most befitting memorials to the six million Jews who were murdered by the Nazis and to those Jews deported from France, often with the help of the collaborationist Vichy government. Drancy was the site of an internment camp that supplied the concentration camps with inmates.

More than 12,000 Jews were held in this transit camp before being transferred to their death in the East. Drancy was "the ante-room of Auschwitz," say French Jews.

Established in 1940, it was an unfinished housing project with apartment buildings on three sides of a rectangular court. Jews were quartered in the large, grim buildings that still stand today as part of a municipal housing project. The gathering camp was supervised by Alois Brunner, one of the last major Nazi war criminals still at large and believed to be living in Syria. He is still in the news, as Jewish groups are demanding his extradition from Syria.

The outdoor monument in the form of a statue was dedicated in 1976. It bears a quotation from Lamentations 1:12: "Behold, and see if there be any pain like unto my pain." Just behind the monument is an old railroad boxcar once used in the deportation process. Inside the railroad car is a pictorial exhibit showing the roundups of Jews, their boarding the railroad cars, and their crowded quarters in camps.

The monument is dedicated to the martyrs, victims of the barbaric Nazis. One poster reads, "Never Again a Camp at Drancy. Never Again Auschwitz."

The town of Drancy itself was a stronghold of the Resistance.

The key to the railroad car exhibit must be obtained in advance from the town hall, except on Saturday. However, travelers can visit the railroad boxcar from 2 P.M. to 4 P.M. every Saturday, except when Saturday falls on a bank holiday. On other days, one may be able to obtain the key from the Cultural Department of the Mayor's Office located in the town hall at Place Maurice Thorez, 93700, Le Drancy. Take the RER at Gare du Nord. At Drancy station, take bus number 148, direction Pantin, to the memorial. If it is not Saturday, ask to get off at City Hall to obtain the key to the boxcar. Tip: Arrangements should be made in advance.

If the collapse of France and the ultimate establishment of the Fascist state of Vichy under Pétain and Laval were painful to France, they were far more tragic for Jews. And yet nearly sixty years after the war, France is coming to grips with the collaborationist Vichy regime role in deporting some 76,000 Jews. In 1994, at least one Frenchman, Paul Touvier, who was then 79, was brought to trial for crimes against humanity during the war—the first Frenchman brought to trial for crimes against humanity. He served in a pro-Nazi militia during the German occupation of France. Touvier was a key aide during World War II to Gestapo chief Klaus Barbie, who was tried in 1987 for war crimes and sentenced to life imprisonment. Barbie died in 1991.

Touvier picked at random seven Jewish prisoners and lined them up in front of the cemetery wall at Rillieux-la-Page, outside of Lyon. They were shot by a firing squad. In April 1994, a French court convicted him of the charge of crimes against humanity and he was sentenced to life imprisonment. Writing in *The New York Times,* on April 20, 1994, Alan Riding stated, "The trial assumed special significance because it was the first time a French court had examined any aspect of French persecution of Jews when the country was under German occupation between 1940 and 1944." Touvier died in a prison hospital in July 1996. He was 81.

Another Vichy aide accused of war crimes, Rene Bousquet, had been shot dead by a lone gunman at his home in Paris in 1993, thus precluding a long-promised public trial.

Also accused of complicity in crimes against humanity was Maurice Papon, a former high-ranking French official.

Condemned on April 2, 1998, to 10 years of criminal detention, he had been found guilty on two counts of having helped organize the arrest and the deportation of Jewish men, women and children from Bordeaux where he was a young official of the Vichy regime between 1942 and 1944. Papon rose to be the powerful head of the Paris police, a member of parliament and then finance minister under President Giscard d'Estaing (1978-81). His career was halted when a newspaper alleged he was behind the deportation of more than 1,500 Jews while administering the southwestern province of Gironde whose center was Bordeaux. At liberty pending an appeal, Papon appeared in the news in October, 1999 when it was discovered he had fled to Switzerland. The Swiss returned him to France and he is now serving his sentence.

To this day, the memory of Vichy remains a stain on the nation. All the trials force the French more and more to assign responsibility to Vichy France for its "complicity" with the Nazis in the deportation of Jews from France, a fact that many in France have known but have preferred to remain silent about. As Susan Zuccotti has shown in her book, *The Holocaust, the French, and the Jews,* Vichy was overtly and actively chauvinistic and anti-Semitic.

Some believe that President Charles deGaulle may have inflated the role of the Resistance in liberating France in 1944 in order to expunge the memory of Vichy. In his memoirs, he called Vichy null and void. He argued that "real France" had not capitulated to Germany.

In the Holocaust, about 250,000 Jews, or two thirds of the community, survived, while 76,000 were sent to the death camps. At first, Vichy, which was subservient to Germany, turned over only foreign Jews to the Nazis. Later, when the Germans seized all of France, Jews—French-born or not—were seized. Still, of the approximately 75,000 Jews deported to the concentration camps, only 15,000 were of French descent. The remaining 60,000 were either naturalized or immigrants. If we include all the other Jews who found themselves on French soil when the Armistice was declared, we find that 10 percent of French Jews died. This contrasts with the death of 40 percent of immigrant or recently arrived Jews. France lost about 25 percent of her Jews, including foreigners, in comparison to 55 percent for Belgium and 86 percent for Holland.

French Jews played an outstanding role in the Resistance. Some say that one-quarter of the Resistance was Jewish.

Today, a new organization, the **Association of Conservatoire Camp de Drancy,** reminds men and women everywhere of the camp, which was liberated on August 17, 1944. One of the apartments has been made over into a flat just as it was during the war. For further information on the former camp and the model apartment, contact the **Association du Conservatoire Camp de Drancy,** 15 Cite de la Muette, 93700 Le Drancy. Tel: 48-32-11-21 or 48-95-35-05.

A **synagogue** in Drancy is located at 15, boulevard St. Simon, Drancy. Tel: 48-32-54-82.

Memorial of the Unknown Jewish Martyr, 17, rue Geoffroy l'Asnier, 75004, Paris. Tel: 42-27-44-72. FAX: 48-87-12-50. Metro: Pont-Marie or Saint-Paul. This four-story memorial is one of the most moving Jewish sites in Paris and a tribute to the six million Jews who perished in the Holocaust. The museum displays documents and photographs of Nazi camps and prisons and contains material devoted to the Archives of the Centre Documentation Juive Contemporaine. Before one enters the building, however, one passes through a massive courtyard that actually is the roof of an underground crypt. In the street-level courtyard is a large bronze cylinder shaped in the form of a burial urn. On it are engraved the names of some of the notorious concentration camps and the Warsaw Ghetto. Below the courtyard-two flights down-is a tomb of black marble in the form of a Star of David. An "eternal flame" flickers at its center. Erected in 1956, the memorial building contains archives, books, and a library reading room. Open Monday through Friday, 10 to noon and 2 to 5; open Sunday, 2 to 5.

In 2000, plans were underway to enlarge the museum by building more exhibition space and library facilities. This was made possible by monies from the national government and the City of Paris, in the amount of 50 million French francs.

Regarding the Holocaust, mention also should be made of Varian Fry who went to France as the agent of the American

Emergency Rescue Committee. He rescued not only the two hundred persons he had been sent to save, but nearly two thousand more in France. According to Andy Marina in *A Quiet American: The Secret War of Varian Fry*, Fry smuggled out of France such noted professionals and personalities as Hannah Arendt, Franz Werfel, Heinrich Mann, Walter Gropius, Marc Chagall, Lion Feuchtwanger and Enrico Fermi.

Memorial to the Deported is located in a garden behind Notre Dame on the tip of the Ile de la Cité, not far from the Pletzel. This memorial is dedicated to the 200,000 French men and women of all races and religions who died in the Nazi death camps during World War II.

Vél' d'Hiv, located at 8, boulevard Grennelle, Paris, 15th Arrondissement (Metro: Bir Hakeim). A plaque on this monument commemorates the imprisonment of Jews rounded up by the French police and placed in the Vélodrome d'Hiver Stadium on July 16, 1942. This was a huge indoor sports arena for winter bicycle races, eventually torn down in 1989. When a large-scale manhunt was conducted in Paris on July 16, 1942, about 13,000 Jews, including 4,000 children, were arrested and corralled at the sports facility. "The operation was poetically christened 'Spring Wind' by the French Police, who executed the German orders with almost excessive zeal," writes Annie Cohen-Solal in *Sartre: A Life*. Later they were moved to Drancy, a gathering camp, and sent to Auschwitz. More Jews were rounded up during the summer. The July and August transports included 25,000 French Jews. In the Holocaust, some 75,000 Jews were deported from France to death camps, and only 3,000 of those survived. A square located at the intersection of quai de Grenelle and boulevard de Grenelle, near the former stadium, has been named "Place des Martyrs Juifs du Vélodrome d'Hiver" (Square of Jewish Martyrs of the Winter Velodrome).

The late, former President Francois Mitterrand proposed that bygones be allowed to be bygones regarding France's past. But by this time, Mitterrand had himself been badly compromised by revelations that during World War II, he did a stint with the Vichy regime, before joining the Resistance.

On July 16, 1995, French President Jacques Chirac's admission of national guilt for deporting Jews to Nazi death camps during

Memorial to the Jewish Martyrs rounded up by the French police in July, 1942 and held in the Velodrome D'Hiver, Paris.
(Photo by Dr. Joshua Fogelman)

World War II was received as a "significant historical step," and Jewish leaders throughout the world praised the French President's commentary on Vel d'Hiv. Chirac said in his speech, "Fifty-three years ago..450 French police officers, acting under the authority of their chiefs, complied with the Nazis' demands." He added, "the criminal insanity of the occupier was assisted by the French people, by the French state." Until then, no French leader had acknowledged the state's role in collaborating with the Germans in deporting Jews.

OTHER SITES

Hotel de Castille, 37, rue Cambon. This is the building in which Theodor Herzl, the father of modern Zionism, wrote his famous tract, *The Jewish State.* The spark was the trial of Capt. Alfred Dreyfus. Nearly 100 years after emancipation, the Jews of the Republic and the world were shocked by the Dreyfus Affair. For most of the nineteenth century, anti-Semitism had been a weapon in the hands of the royalists, the clergy, and the military. These forces also opposed successive Republican governments. The battle lines were being drawn. Usually, the conservative anti-Republican forces disliked the Jews.

Incidentally, research shows that the Hotel Castile itself was once part of the Ritz. The Hemingway Bar is directly across from the hotel building which counts107 rooms. Located in the fashion district, the hotel's neighboring streets include the rue de la Paix and the Faubourg St. Honoré. Electrifying to shoppers and costly, too, are the shops on this street. Chanel is next door to the hotel. The legendary **Place Vendome, Louvre** and the **Palais Royal** are nearby as are **Hermes,** 24 rue Faubourg St. Honoré and **Lancel** is at 8 place de l'Opera.

Statue of Capt. Alfred Dreyfus, on the Boulevard Raspail in a small park near the intersection with Notre Dame de Champs. Captain Dreyfus, a Jew, was a member of the general staff of the French Army. The victim of a forgery, he was framed and unjustly court-martialed in a secret trial in 1894. There were many reasons to go after Dreyfus: "he was rich, he was snobbish and he was a Jew."

The charges, the trial, and the resultant riots tore France asunder. They unleashed a wave of anti-Semitism. Every family was affected. The French were split down the middle; you were either for, or against, Dreyfus. A crisis of conscience had penetrated France and the repercussions caused an upheaval in political life that translated into serious consequences for Jewish life. Shock waves rocked Europe. Found guilty of treason, Dreyfus was relegated to Devil's Island, where he spent almost five years. However, some citizens of France rallied to his side. Among them was the writer Emile Zola (1840-1902), who on January 13, 1898, published an open letter to the president of the Republic. It appeared on the front page of the newspaper *L'Aurore* and was entitled, "J'accuse." Proclaiming Dreyfus's innocence, it accused his attackers of libel. Zola is buried in the Pantheon.

Dreyfus was retried by a military court. But again, he was found guilty by army officers who just could not admit the army was guilty of conspiracy. Later, after he had been exonerated and pardoned, Dreyfus was reinstated in the army. On July 28, 1906, he received the Order of the Legion of Honor. In World War I, he served with dignity and honor. He died in the 1930s as a colonel in the French Army. He is buried in the Montparnasse Cemetery, Division 29. As a result of the trumped-up charges against Dreyfus and the new anti-Semitism, Theodor Herzl, then a Viennese journalist in Paris, founded the Zionist movement, which brought about the State of Israel. In the cobblestone military courtyard, as Dreyfus was being marched around the square and drummed out of the army, Herzl heard the captain shout: "I am innocent." Stefan Zweig wrote that the incident "convulsed Herzl's soul." Herzl knew Dreyfus was innocent: "He [Dreyfus] had brought the horrible suspicion of treason on himself merely by being Jewish." Subsequently, Herzl wrote his famous pamphlet, *The Jewish State*, in the Hotel de Castille.

CEMETERIES

Père Lechaise, boulevard de Menilmontant, Paris. (Another entrance is at rue des Rondeaux, and for this, take the Metro to the Gambretta stop). This is Paris's most impressive cemetery and many famous Jews are buried here, including many of the Rothschild family (Division 7). Some of the more noted Jewish persons buried here are the actresses Rachel (Division 7) and Sarah Bernhardt (Division 44), the painter Rosa Bonheur (Division 44), and writers Marcel Proust and Gertrude Stein (Division 85). The cemetery was opened in 1803.

Sephardic Cemetery, 44, rue de Flandres. Many Sephardic Jews who lived in Paris before the Revolution are buried here. Apply at the office of the Consistoire Central of Paris for the key. 17. rue St-Georges, 75009, Paris. Tel: 40-82-26-26.

RECOMMENDED HOTELS

Recommended hotels in Paris include Hotel Intercontinental, 3, rue de Castiglione, 75040, Paris, Tel: 44-77-11-11; and Le Grand Hotel at 2, rue Scribe, Paris, Tel: 40-07-32-32, FAX: 42-66-12-51. Both of these are fine, first-class hotels. The Inter-Continental offers a full range of services and facilities for business and vacation travelers. It has recaptured its past history and it still has old-time charm and comfort. The Grand Hotel has undergone a drastic restoration and renovation. This is a palace-type hotel and it has close proximity to the Opera.

Also recommended are the Le Warwick and Westminster hotels. The Warwick often has kosher catered events. The Warwick is located at 5, rue de Berri, 75008, Paris, just 50 meters from what many call the "most beautiful avenue in the world," the Champs-Elysées. That is important because today there is no hotel on the Champs-Elysées itself. This is a good and unique business person's hotel as it contains conference rooms, telex, FAX machines, and parking with direct access to the lobby. The hotel is a fully air-conditioned, modern deluxe hotel.

Hotel Westminster at 13, rue de la Paix, 75002, Paris. Tel: 42-61-57-46. This one is a favorite, as it is located between the historical Opera and Place Vendome. Surrounded by world famous jewelry shops, the Hotel Westminster offers 102 elegant rooms and suites decorated in classical French style. Antique furniture, marble bathrooms, and crystal chandeliers complete the luxurious interior of the hotel.

The French Countryside

Paris dominates the cultural, business, governmental, and entertainment life of France. But that certain French "sweetness of life" is also found in Angers and Avignon, Biarritz and Bordeaux, St-Tropez and St-Jean-de-Luz, Lyon and Limoges, Strasbourg and St-Malo, Nice and Cannes.

THE LOIRE IS HEARTLAND FRANCE

A good place to start is the fabled valley of Loire, the Garden of France, and its special section, Touraine, which encompasses the famous town of Tours.

Step back into a magnificent past. Visit the amazing chateaux at **Amboise** with its sumptuous setting and wonderful views, **Brissac** with its two round defensive towers on a building standing in a fine park, **Chambord** with its rich Renaissance decoration, **Chaumont-sur-Loire** with its beautiful site on the Loire, and **Chenonceaux** with its gardens and edifice astride the gentle river. It is indeed a horticultural delight.

Follow the majestic river Loire through the heart of France. Travel alongside it from Orleans westward to Angers and Nantes on to the Atlantic Ocean. Jews settled in Touraine at the time of the Romans. They lived along the river and were active in shipping, commerce, and boating.

Centers of Jewish life flourished in the Loire Valley in the towns of Orleans, Tours, Chinon, and Angers. Today a Jewish community thrives again because thousands of Sephardic Jews from North Africa have migrated here to give the area new energy.

Visit a few of these Loire towns.

Angers

Angers is a town to roam around. The counts and dukes of Anjou made it their cultural center. Throughout the ages, it has remained the gateway to the west of France and to Brittany.

Angers is a major hub of commerce, transportation, and culture. Its gastronomy and wine cellars, parks and gardens, proximity to the chateaux at Brissac and Saumur, as well as its galleries, museums, and modern new library, make it a wonderful stop.

This capital of the Maine et Loire boasts a very fine, hospitable Jewish community.

The Jewish traveler will probably have a rewarding experience attending a Friday night service. At the Orthodox synagogue, there is usually a small minyan (quorum of 10 men) on the Sabbath eve. The congregation welcomes you with warm informality; they are extremely friendly.

Synagogue and Community Center, 12, rue Valdemaine, 49100, Angers. Tel: 41-87-48-18 or 41-87-48-10. FAX: 41-37-11-79. Passover seder and holiday celebrations are held.

About 50 Jewish families live in Angers. Mr. Samuel Marciano conducts the services, but on special occasions, a rabbi from Nantes visits the community.

Today, two town streets are named after two notable Jewish personalities: Place Pierre Mendes-France, one of France's prime ministers, and Place Anne Frank (formerly known as de la Juiverie).

Tourist information can be obtained at the **Office of Tourism,** Place Kennedy, B.P. 2397, 49023, Angers. Tel: 41-88-69-93.

Orleans

"Paris is the head of France, Orleans is its heart," they say. Once Orleans was the second most important city in France. On May 8, 1429, Joan of Arc entered the city as its deliverer from the English and persuaded Charles VII to claim his throne.

Jews lived in Orleans before the sixth century. During the Middle Ages, its Jewish community was an important center of Jewish learning. In the fourteenth century, the Jews were expelled, not to return until the beginning of the nineteenth century.

A view of Angers, France. (Photo courtesy of the French Government Tourist Office)

The historical museum, Musee Grevin, in Tours, France. (Photo courtesy of the French Government Tourist Office)

The **Synagogue and Community Center** are located at 14, rue Robert-de-Courtenay, 45000, Orleans. Tel: 38-62-16-62. FAX: 38-77-97-71. The synagogue is the heart of the Jewish community. This house of study, meeting place, and sanctuary is not difficult to find. It is next door to the cathedral, which dates from the Middle Ages. For further information, visitors can call Mr. Cogos, Tel: 38-88-40-13 or Mrs. Klein, Tel: 38-53-16-47.

Tourist information can be obtained at the **Office of Tourism,** boulevard Aristide Briand, 45000, Orleans. Tel: 38-53-05-95.

Tours

This is the home of Rabelais, Descartes, and Balzac—the home of good books, fine food, and distinctive wine.

Tours is probably one of the best starting points from which to see the impressive chateaux of the Loire. It is a convenient place from which to make excursions. Tours possesses one of the oldest Jewish communities in France. The first Jews probably arrived here in 570. Later, in medieval times, a Jewish quarter and synagogue thrived in this market town and provincial capital. Today, about 200 Jewish families live in Tours.

Well worth a visit is the **Musée des Beaux-Arts,** 18, Place François-Secord, 37000, Tours. Tel: 47-05-68-73.

Historial de Touraine, Musée Grevin, Chateau Royal, Quai D'Orleans, 37000, Tours. Tel: 47-61-02-95. Brought to life here is the history of Touraine from the Gallo-Roman period to the mid-twentieth century. In almost lifelike scenes, painters, doctors, writers, and politicians are all on view: in one scene, French Jewish Prime Minister Leon Blum, and in another, Nobel Prize-winner Henri Bergson, the French Jewish philosopher.

Synagogue, 37, rue Parmentier, 37000, Tours. Tel: 47-05-56-95. Services are held at 6:30 Friday evenings in the winter and 7 P.M. during the summer. Saturday morning services are at 9. A study class conducted by the rabbi takes place every Saturday evening at 7. The synagogue was founded in 1908.

For those needing to stock up on or replenish kosher food

for their journey through France, go to the store at 38, rue Parmentier, which sells kosher items. Open five days a week. Call the synagogue first for more information as to exact hours.

A **Jewish Community Center** is located at 6, rue Chalmel, Tours. Tel: 47-05-59-97.

Tourist information can be obtained at the **Office of Tourism,** Place du Marechal Leclerc, 37000, Tours. Tel: 47-05-58-08.

REIMS

All the kings of France were crowned in Reims, now conveniently a less than two-hour drive from Paris. It was in the cathedral in 1429 that Joan of Arc, after a legendary ride, achieved her wish of seeing Charles VII crowned king of France.

Reims proudly possesses one of the most beautiful and unique synagogues in the northeast part of France. Built in 1879, its architecture is imposing indeed. A synagogue functioned here in medieval times. After the expulsion of the Jews from France in the fourteenth century, they did not reside in Reims for about 500 years. In 1820, a small group settled in the city.

Fifty years later, Jews from Alsace-Lorraine began to arrive in Reims, which is famous for its champagne wineries, its historic cathedral, as well as the schoolhouse where Supreme Allied Commander Dwight D. Eisenhower's representatives accepted the German surrender in May 1945.

The Germans made a complete and unconditional surrender to the three Allied powers at 0341, the morning of May 7, 1945. A more formal ratification of the surrender by the German High Command took place in Berlin on May 9; but May 8 is celebrated as V-E Day because the act of the May 7 became effective at 0001 on the 9th of May, Zone B, which in Central European Time, (ZoneA) was 2301, May 8, according to *The Invasion of France and Germany, 1944-1945,* by Samuel Eliot Morison.

Today 150 Jewish families live in Reims.

The **synagogue** at 49, rue Clovis, Reims, also has a community center. Tel: 26-47-68-47.

Tourist information is available at the **Office of Tourism,** 1, rue Jadart, 51100, Reims. Tel: 26-47-68-47.

STRASBOURG

Known as the Jerusalem of France, Strasbourg is an active, highly organized, intellectual Jewish community of about 12,500 persons. Most of the chief rabbis of France have come from this center of Jewry, which has deep roots in the province of Alsace.

The large, beautiful **Synagogue de la Paix** with its community center is located on la rue du Grand-Rabbin-Rene-Hirschler (avenue de la Paix), 67000, Strasbourg. Tel: 88-14-46-50. FAX: 88-24-26-69. Dedicated in 1958, the synagogue features a bronze menorah and a bronze grill which grace the front of the structure. Visitors have included the late President of the Republic Charles de Gaulle, Moshe Dayan, and Golda Meir. This new synagogue replaced the historic Synagogue Consistoriale du Quai Kleber, which was destroyed by the Nazis in the war. The city has yeshivot and Talmud Torahs.

Jews and non-Jews here share many common memories. How would you like to live in a city that has changed hands four times in a little more than 100 years? That is why a war memorial in Strasbourg depicts Alsace as an allegorical mother cradling her lost sons. One of them is French, the other German. Erected in 1936, it shows what an ancient frontier city, this truly is. In 1871, the city became German for almost a generation; then French again in 1918; and then German again in 1940. In 1939, the city had been completely evacuated because a German attack was expected. Many Jews, victims of the Holocaust, would not return. And many of the Jewish survivors settled in the south of France where they are able to hide during the war. Since 1945, the city is French and it truly stands as a European city, for it is the location of the Council of Europe and shares with Brussels, the home of the European Parliament.

As the capital of Alsace, Strasbourg leads the region in

business, culture and intellectual pursuits. But today in the 21st century, the Germans also contribute to the shaping of the city, which, after all is in a strategic location—it sits among a dense system of water and land paths.

Strasbourg is situated in northeastern France, nestled between the Vosges Mountains and the Rhine River. The city borders Germany to the north and east and shares many links to the country across the Rhine River. While French is the official language, many inhabitants speak German as well as the regional dialect Alsatian, a mixture of the two.

A rich gastronomical center, this city boasts many beautiful gardens, parks, buildings and museums, and a famous Cathedral.

Akiba, 9-10, quai Zorn, 67000, Strasbourg. Tel: 88-35-48-58. Seven hundred students are enrolled in this famous day school.

Beth Chabad, 59 faubourg de Pierre, 67000, Stasbourg. Tel: 88-75-66-05.

Union Juive Liberale de Strasbourg, BP 4 67015, Strasbourg Cedex. In 2000, this group, a member of the World Union for Progressive Judaism, did not have its own building for worship.

Lubavitch Youth, 59, faubourg de Pierre, 67000, Strasbourg. Tel: 88-36-46-16

Alsatian Museum, 23, quai St-Nicolas, Strasbourg. This site has a rich collection of Jewish ritual objects in an exhibit entitled "History of the Jews of Alsace-Lorraine."

Worth visiting is Strasbourg's **"La Petite France,"** an ancient quarter of 400-year-old houses.

Kosher Restaurants in Strasbourg

Visitors to Strasbourg can enjoy a kosher meal in the **Restaurant Chalom** in the **Commmunity Center of the Synagogue** at la rue du Grand-Rabbin-Rene-Hirschler, Strasbourg. Tel: 88-36-56-30.

King, 28 rue Sellenick, Strasbourg. Tel: 88-52-17-71.

Massada, 7 rue Baldung Grien, Strasbourg. Tel: 88-35-43-43.

Restaurant Universitaire, 11, rue Sellenick, Strasbourg. Tel: 88-76-74-76.

Struthof Concentration Camp

Struthof Concentration Camp. F 67130 Natzweiller. Located on Route D 130, 50 kilometers west of Strasbourg in Alsace. On this site stands the only concentration camp built by the Nazis in France. They called it the "Konzentrationlager Natzweiller Elsass." Set up on May 12, 1941, its victims were from throughout Europe and included, French, German, Dutch, and Russian prisoners of war. Horrible medical experiments were conducted on 87 Jewish victims, including 30 women, all of whom perished. The camp was liberated by the First French Army and the Sixth American Army Corps on November 23, 1944.

A **Memorial to the Deported** was inaugurated by President Charles de Gaulle on July 23, 1960. The 41.5-meter-high concrete shaft spirals. Designed by architect B. Monnet, it not only symbolizes the flame of the crematorium, but also infinite freedom. The emaciated silhouette sculpted on the memorial by Lucien Fennaux recalls the hunger that precedes death. An inscription honors an "unknown deported prisoner." Another commemorative tablet reads: "Aux heros et martyrs de la Deportation, la France reconnaissante," (To the heroes and martyrs transported, The French Republic is grateful). A visitor to the camp sees barracks, memorial stones, a national cemetery, and the crematorium. The crematorium has been preserved as well as an ash pit located between two huts and down close to the forest where the ashes of the victims were spread. A commemorative tablet with the Star of David memorializes the 87 Jews who were killed in this camp's gas chamber, as well as the six million Jews who were murdered by the Nazis throughout Europe during World War II. A museum has been placed at the entrance of the camp. Located close to the camp is the sand quarry where camp inmates were forced to toil. Three kilometers down the road back towards Struthof, visitors can view the gas chamber where they were put to death. For further information on the Struthof Concentration Camp, contact the Historical Society of the Jews of Alsace and Lorraine, c/o Andre Marc Haarscher, Secretaire, 20 rue Erwin, F 67000 Strasbourg. Tel: 88-22-01-02. FAX: 88-75-67-64. Hours: 9 A.M. to noon and 2 P.M. to 5 P.M. The site is closed from December 25 to February 28. Entrance fee: FF8 (8 French francs) per person or FF5 per person for groups of ten or more. Children under 16 are free. Information: Camp de Concentration du Struthof, F 67130 Natzweiller. Tel: 88-97-04-04 or Tel: 88-76-76-76, ext. 6383, for the Direction Departementale des Anciens Combattants, Service du Struthof. Directions: 56.5 kilometers west of Strasbourg. From Strasbourg, take Highway A 35 followed by N 420 in the direction of Schirmeck/St-Die. In Schirmeck, take direction Rothau, then direction Natzweiller (Route D 130). The camp is located in the mountains on Road D 130, next to the village of Natzweiller. Coming from Paris on Highway A 4, take the Saverne exit. Then take direction Molsheim on Road N 4. In Molsheim, take direction Schirmeck Road N 420, and follow as above.

Tourist information is available at the **Office of Tourism, Place des Congres, avenue Schutzenberger, 67000, Strasbourg.** Tel: 88-35-03-00.

DIJON

Visit Dijon, provincial capital of Bugundy, the home of the legendary dukes. Here are the palaces of the dukes who in 1196 placed the Jews under their protection. Here is a small Arc de Triomphe in a city that is an important rail link in one of Europe's technologically advanced train systems.

About 250 Jewish families live in this charming university town in central France, 200 miles southeast of Paris. This fifteenth-century city of clean, winding pedestrian streets, of quaint shops, cafes, and homes, is also the headquarters of famous Dijon mustard and cassis. No wonder Dijon is often called the gastronomical capital of France, and, of course, boasts rare wines to go with delicious cuisine. Dedicated in

1879, the **synagogue** in Dijon is the focal point of the Jewish community. It is located at 5, rue de la Synagogue 21000, Dijon. Services are held Friday evenings and Saturday mornings. Activities for young people are held in the synagogue on Sundays. For information about kosher food and services, contact synagogue officials at Tel: 80-66-46-47 or Rabbi Simon Siboney, Tel: 80-67-50-98.

Many Jewish tourists visit Dijon for wine tasting and begin week-long vacations on the popular barge waterway program on the Bugundy Canal and Saone River.

Tourist information can be obtained at the **Office of Tourism,** Place Darcy, 21000, Dijon. Tel: 80-43-56-05.

LYON

To inhale the quality of French life outside of Paris, visit Lyon. This 2,000-year-old city on two rivers should be a stop on any tour of France. All roads lead to Lyon, France's second largest metropolitan area. More than 35,000 Jews call Lyon home, a unique location along the banks of the Saone and Rhone Rivers. They live in the Lyon area, including Villeurbanne. They support over 20 synagogues, 15 kosher butcher shops, several kosher restaurants and day schools, and 13 Talmud Torahs.

Happily, Lyon keeps the charm of a great provincial city. This city of bridges is noted for the manufacture of silk. Lyon boasts pleasantly paced living with parks, an extraordinary rose garden, sweeping pedestrian malls, a giant shopping center, plus 24 major museums.

Savor Lyon. It is the financial and cultural hub of the Rhone-Alpes region, the jumping-off point for skiing in the Alps or for visiting vineyards to the north and south of this city. If it is great cuisine you want, this is the place to visit. This city is the gastronomic center of La Belle France. Good food is a fact of life. The area boasts more top chefs honored with little guidebook stars, forks, and tongues than any other part of the country.

You can reach Lyon in just two hours by nearly 20 daily TGV

trains speeding from Paris at 168 miles per hour. After your arrival you can have your pick of 20 museums, including an excellent Fine Arts Museum.

Make sure you take the funicula, or cable car, to the top of a high hill, an exceptional view of the city of bridges and two rivers.

I like Lyon even if, as Ted Morgan notes, it "has always been in the shadow of Paris." It sports the Palace Bellecour, one of the largest public squares in France. It stands as a prosperous trading center and, let us face it, Lyon means serious gastronomy; it is, after all, a city of "haute cuisine," with its superb restaurants.

Many consider Lyon the capital of the French Resistance in World War II. Significantly, Lyon broke into the news headlines in the 1980s as the city that hosted the trial of the Gestapo commander, the late Klaus Barbie, otherwise known as "The Butcher of Lyon." This city not only served as the base for the French Resistance, but as a center of French Jewry. Barbie was stationed in Lyon and was responsible for the sending of area Jews—including the homeless, orphaned children at Izieu—to the gas chambers, as well as the torture and killing of French Resistance leaders, including Jean Moulin. Twice condemned to death in absentia after the war, Barbie lived in Latin America for several decades until he was tracked down by Beate Klarsfeld, who searches for Nazis, in Bolivia in 1972 and brought to France 11 years later. He was convicted in 1987 as the chief enforcer of a Nazi reign of terror. Sentenced to life imprisonment, he died a prisoner in a French hospital in Lyon in the fall of 1991.

Musée Memorial des Enfants d'Izieu (Izieu Childrens Home and Museum) The Village of Izieu. I kept focussing on the staircase of this farmhouse in the village of Izieu, about 60 miles from Lyon. That was the set of steps that one of the young leaders raced up to escape the German seizure of the children of Izieu. He had been walking down the steps, when a young girl, who could have been his sister we are told, yelled to him to go back up because the Germans were there. He ran up the steps; opened a nearby window; jumped to the ground below and fled through a nearby field. He survived, but for the rest of his life he would remember the children of Izieu who were rounded up by the Germans.

The world learned about the children from the trial of Klaus Barbie, otherwise known as "butcher of Lyon." Stationed in Lyon, this Gestapo officer was responsible for the torture and killing of the children. The museum, known as the **Izieu Childrens' Home and Museum,** remains a site that should be visited. While not per se a Holocaust Memorial; it certainly could be. For here in a former modest farm house and in a large building on the premises, the traveler will soon know the story of the 44 children who spent the final year of their lives in this building in the farm area above the Rhone River. It is quiet here. The visitor naturally asks, how could this be the site where one day in April, 1944, the Germans captured the 44 unarmed young children and a half dozen or so adults. It is also a question asked by the thousands of today's French children from the surrounding area and beyond who come here every day. About 20,000 people visit the museum every year and they certainly see the 44 trees planted behind the memorial.

The displays in the museum consist of drawings and letters the children wrote to parents who probably had been sent to Nazi concentration camps. Also exhibited are the photographs of the 44 youngsters who were seized. Audio-visual displays record the fate of the 11,000 French Jewish children who were sent from France to the death camps by Vichy and its German officials, a small fraction of the more than one million Jewish children murdered in Europe.

In the 1970's Serge Klarsfeld, the French historian and Nazi hunter, began a 20 year-campaign to identify these children whose murderers "had wished them to die anonymously. Klarsfeld went on the radio in France, the U.S. and Israel to request family photographs and testimonials. He sifted through French archives. He went to court to force the French police to produce photographs of the victims. And in 1996, he published the results of his labors in *French Children in the Holocaust,* a book that contains photographs and descriptions of more than 2,500 of those children. The Jewish Welfare Organization, OSE, saved children in homes such as that at

Izieu. OSE became an underground organization providing children with false identity papers and housing them with Christian families and organizations. OSE would then smuggle them across the border to Switzerland. The method saved more than 1,000 children.

While OSE sponsored 14 homes in France, they hid more than 1,000 of these children until the organization's American branch obtained visas for them. Under OSE's auspices, 253 children were able to leave France before the Vichy government began blocking emigration in the summer of 1942.

In France today, a reawakening interest has arisen to study and view the horrors of the Nazi era; to sort out the sins of Vichy and to honor the courage of those righteous French citizens. For example, in Le Chambon-Sur-Lignon, local Protestants shielded thousands of Jews from arrest and deportation. An example of another town—and there were many more—which saved Jewish children was Chabannes, an isolated and insulated rural village in the Creuse region of central France. In August, 1942, Vichy had rounded up 10,000 Jews for deportation. But only six of Chabannes 400 Jewish students were deported and just four perished, thanks to various artful dodges, schemes and ploys by a man named Felix Chevrier who ran a chateau that housed a school.

Centre d'Histoire de la Resistance et de la Deportation.Centre of the History of Resistance and Deportation, 14 Ave., Berthelot, Lyon. Dimly lit corridors, films, photographs and biographies of the hundreds of men, women and children who fought the Germans in France are displayed here. Many of these freedom fighters were arrested. Open daily from 9 A.M. to 5:30 P.M. Mention should also be made here of the more-than-above-the-call-of-duty of French Jews who flocked to the Resistance. "Charles DeGaulle was reputed to have been bitter that among the few Frenchmen who joined him during the first days in London many were Jews—not because DeGualle was anti-Semitic, but because he knew and felt that the presence of so many Jews in his small patriotic grouping would make it unrepresentative and unpopular," according to John Lukacs. Jews were among the first and all alone in the Resistance.The proportion of Jewish participation in the war and the Resistance in all its forms is by far the highest, comprising approximately a quarter of the Jewish population capable of action.

Sites in Lyon

Fonds Social Juif Unifié, 145 Gde, rue de la Guillotiere, 69007, Lyon. Tel: 78-72-88-23.

Kosher Restaurants

Le Grillon D'Or, 20, rue Terme, 69001, Lyon. Tel: 78-27-33-09. Ask the owners to tell you about the visit of President Bill Clinton in the mid-1990s. In this fine kosher restaurant which promotes itself as offering "the best *couscous* in France. They also boast a fine selection of wines, including the latest kosher Beaujolais.

Lippmann, 4, rue Tony-Toilet, 69002, Lyon. Tel: 78-42-49-82. Lyonnaise kosher cuisine.

Le Jardin d'Eden, 14 rue Jean Jaures, 69100, Villeurbanne. Tel: 72-33-85-65.

Synagogues in Lyon

American visitors will find a warm welcome at the synagogue-office of the Grand Rabbinat de Lyon and Rabbi Richard Wertenschlag, at the historic **Great Synagogue**, 13 Quai Tilsitt, 69002, Lyon, 78- 37-13-43. FAX: 78-38-26-57. Write in advance to the rabbi for information regarding services and kosher food. This synagogue was built in 1864. Many American Jewish tourists attend services here.

Charre Tzedek, 18, rue St-Mathieu, 69008, Lyon. Tel: 78-00-72-50.

Ecole Juive de Lyon, 40, rue Alexandre Boutin, 69100, Villeurbanne. Tel: 78-83-80-20.

La Fraternité, 4, rue Malherbe, 69100, Villeurbanne. Tel: 78-24-38-91.

Lubavitch Youth, 60, rue Crillon, Lyon. Tel: 78-89-08-32.

Neveh Chalom Synagogue and Talmud Torah, 317, rue Duguesclin, 69007, Lyon. Tel: 78-58-18-74. This is a beautiful new Sephardic synagogue and community center. Many activities are held here. This synagogue also has a mikva.

Oratoire Etz Hayim Yechouron, 60, rue Crillon, 69006, Lyon. Tel: 78-89-08-32.

Beth Chabad Loubavitch of Lyon, 203 rue Francis De Pressense, Lyon-Villeurbanne, 69100, 78-89-08-32.

Tourist information is available at the **Office of Tourism, Place Bellecour,** 69002. Tel: 42-25-75. FAX: 37-02-06.

BORDEAUX

Bordeaux, France's fifth largest metropolitan area, has a special place in Jewish history. Bordeaux is important in Jewish history because many of the Marranos—secret Jews—escaped from Spain and Portugal to this port city.

There are many interesting individuals in the area who know much about the Sephardic Jews of Bordeaux. If you're not in a hurry and would like to learn about a rich Jewish past which dates back to the sixth century, Bordeaux is a prime place to begin. On the eve of the French Revolution, only a few thousand Jews lived in France. Most were Sephardic Jews in Bordeaux and Bayonne.

On January 28, 1790, the leaders of the French Revolution declared that all Jews in France who were known as "Portuguese, Spanish and Avignonnais Jews. shall enjoy the rights of citizens." Twenty months later on September 27, 1791, after debate and delays, all the other Jews of France, including Ashkenazim, were emancipated. France became the first European state to grant its Jewish residents the rights of citizenship.

Today, this active city of about 650,000 boasts eighteenth-century architecture, with an elegant Grand Theater in the very center of town. Outside the city are the celebrated vineyards of Mouton Rothschild, Chateau Lafite, Chateau Margaux, and many others.

More than 15 Jewish organizations meet at the **Jewish Community Center** at 15, Place Charles Gruet, 33000, Bordeaux. Tel: 56-52-62-69. There are active B'nai B'rith and B.B.Y.O. groups in the center.

The **synagogue,** built in 1882 in the Spanish-Portuguese style, is at 8, rue du Grand Rabbin-Joseph-Cohen, 33000, Bordeaux. Tel: 56-91-79-39.

The **Consistoire** is located at 213, rue Ste. Catherine, 33000, Bordeaux. Tel: 56-91-79-39. Further information on services and kosher food can be obtained by calling: Tel: 56-91-79-39, at the synagogue.

Tourist information is available at the **Office of Tourism,** 12, cours 30-Juillet, 33000, Bordeaux. Tel: 56-44-28-41.

THE SOUTHWEST

Three towns, Biarritz, Anglet, and Bayonne, located in the southwest, are known as the "BAB" towns. About 250 Jewish families live in these municipalities. Most of the Jews who came here after the Inquisition and expulsion from Spain and Portugal were Marranos. They were called the "Portuguese Nation," for it was safer to be called Portuguese than Jew. They settled in the BAB town area, which is about 25 miles from the Spanish border. In 1619, there were 2,000 Jewish congregants here. They and their descendants flourished in the area. Today, these "Basque-Country" Jews continue to prosper. Let us go first to Biarritz.

Biarritz

Biarritz is a resort town made famous by the monarchs of Europe, including Napoleon III, who built what is now the luxurious **Hotel du Palais** for his wife, Eugenie. The aristocracy summered in this city of nineteenth-century charm, and it remains an attractive summer place.

Synagogue, at corner of rue de la Russie and rue Pellot, 64200, Biarritz. Services during summer and on holidays only. Kosher food is available through the synagogue in nearby Bayonne. Tel: 59-55-03-95.

Tourist information can be obtained at the **Office of Tourism,** Square d'Ixelles, 64200, Biarritz. Tel: 59-24-20-24.

Bayonne

During the early sixteenth century, the Marranos from Portugal and Spain, who practiced Judaism secretly, were fearful that the long arm of the Inquisition would reach across the border from Spain and snare them in Bayonne, if they revealed their identity. They had settled in Bayonne because it was a thriving port and the commercial capital of Gascony. But when they came here, they were forced to live in the St-Esprit section of the city. Today they still live there, voluntarily of course. The neighborhood of St-Esprit, which supports a synagogue, is called Little Jerusalem.

Synagogue, 35, rue Maubec, 64100, Bayonne. Tel: 59-55-03-95.

Musée Basque de Bayonne, 1, rue Marengo, 64100, Bayonne. Tel: 59-59-08-98. The museum, dedicated to Basque history, draws visitors from all over the world. A room is devoted to Jewish religious objects, mezuzoth, prayer books, lithographs, and candles. It is well worth a visit.

Tourist information can be obtained at the **Office of Tourism,** Place de la Liberté, 64100, Bayonne. Tel: 59-59-31-31.

St-Jean-de-Luz

Because the beach resort of St-Jean-de-Luz has a small Jewish population of less than 100, visiting it will be a delightful experience. The town harbored many Jews who fled from Spain in the sixteenth century. During World War II, Jews escaping the Nazis crossed here into Spain. Today the small Jewish community in this fishing village resort attends services in nearby Bayonne.

Tourist information is available at the Office of Tourism, Place du Marechal Foch, 64500, St-Jean-de-Luz. Tel: 59-26-03-75.

Pau

Gateway to the Basque Country, this nineteenth-century resort, popular with the English, was made famous by Henry IV, a Protestant king of France. Here in southwest France, Pau (pronounced "Po"), with a population of about 150,000, beckons every visitor to begin a sojourn by walking along the attractive boulevard des Pyrenees and marveling at the imposing mountain range.

About 160 Jewish families live in Pau. They support an active synagogue and a kosher butcher shop. The **synagogue** is located at 8, rue Trois-Frères-de-Bernadec, 64000, Pau. Tel: 59-62-37-85. A community center and Talmud Torah are part of the synagogue building, which survived World War II.

Services are held Friday evenings, Saturday mornings, and Saturday evenings.

Tourist information can be obtained at the **Office of Tourism,** Place Royale, 64000, Pau. Tel: 59-27-27-08.

Montpellier

Montpellier is a city rich in architecture, with charming eighteenth-century houses, the famous neoclassical pavilion Chateau d'Eau, and the Musée Fabre, one of the best museums outside of Paris. Rabelais once studied medicine here in the city's fine medical facility, part of one of France's most famous universities. Many Jewish doctors and Talmudists resided in medieval Montpellier and contributed to the medical faculty. Today, Montpellier is considered a resort town with sandy beaches.

The **Musée Fabre,** at 37 boulevard Sarrail, is located in a district which boasts beautiful seventeenth- and eighteenth-century palaces.

Synagogue Ben-Zakai, 7, rue Général-Laffon, 34000, Montpellier. Tel: 67-92-02-07.

Synagogue, 18, rue Ferdinand-Fabre, 34000, Montpellier. Tel: 67-79-09-82.

Jewish Radio Station, 45, rue Proudhon. Montpellier.

Jewish Community Center, 500 boulevard d'Antigone, 34000, Montpellier.

Synagogue Lubavitch, 9 rue des Blampiers, Montpellier. Tel: 67-92-86-93.

Toulouse

Toulouse is called *La Ville Rose,* "the pink city," and rightly so, for the sights, the gourmet restaurants, the architecture, the unhurried pace, the atmosphere of a university city (one-third of the population are students) spell out a cultural and intellectual city.

"If you are in Toulouse, you are safe." That is a saying that was not only heard during World War II, but also during the days of the Spanish Inquisition, especially in the fifteenth and sixteenth centuries.

During World War II, Toulouse was one of the principal centers for resistance to the Nazi invaders. Not only did Jews find refuge in this city steeped in history, but the Organisation Juive de Combat was founded in Toulouse and its leaders would often meet there.

One Jewish historian says Jews have resided in the area ever since the destruction of the second temple. Today, more than 28,000 Jewish residents call Toulouse their home. This is a city that has 30 to 40 active Jewish organizations; 6 kosher butcher shops; 3 day schools, including a technical school sponsored by ORT; and 9 synagogues, with 3 functioning every day.

Only an hour's flight from Paris and located in the Midi Pyrenees in the heart of France's Southwest, this region of open spaces, unique and prestigious, stands as an area where everything is possible. And it is right smack in the middle of the old trade routes between Montpellier and Bordeaux. For those interested in Jewish history, this is the road that makes its way from Beziers to Narbonne, to Carcassonne, to Toulouse, the principal cities of Languedoc, this delightful province bordering on the Mediterranean.

Centre Maimonide, 14, rue du Rempart-St-Etienne, 31000, Toulouse. Tel: 61-23-36-59. Located here is the synagogue called the Old-New Synagogue because many of the Jews of Toulouse came from North Africa and brought from those lands some of the synagogue's fixtures, such as the chandeliers.

The Synagogue and Community Center, are located in the same building at Espace du Judaisme, 2, place Riquet, 31000 Toulouse. **Synagogue:** Tel: 62-76-46-46.Telephone for the Community Center is 62-76-45-73. A restaurant is also located here in this new Center.

Les 12 Tribus, 2, place Riquet, Toulouse. Tel: 62-73-56-56.

Synagogue Adath-Israel, 17, rue Alsace-Lorraine, 31000, Toulouse.

Communaute Juive Liberale-Toulouse, 13 rue du Colonel Driant, 31400, Toulouse.Tel:6152-7369.

Restaurant Le Kotel, 9, rue Clemence Isaure, 31000, Toulouse. Tel: 61-29-03-04. When in Toulouse, visit this excellent, strictly kosher restaurant. Hebrew, English, French, and Yiddish are spoken here. American visitors and business people involved with aerospace frequent this establishment. Served here are some favorite dishes such as gefilte fish, couscous, lamb, steak, chicken, and fish. The ownership is dedicated to keeping kosher ritual alive in this city. Hours are from 12 noon to 3 P.M. during the week and 8 to 11 P.M. Saturday night. The piano bar functions in a "cavelike" atmosphere. Closed on Friday night and the Sabbath.

A kosher restaurant is also located at the University. **Restaurant Universitaire,** 14, rue du Rempart, St.Etienne, Toulouse. Tel: 61-23-36-54.

THE SOUTHEAST

Jewish communities dot the Southeast of France in Provence and the Alps. A comfortable way to reach such centers as Avignon, Nimes, and St-Etienne is the speedy and on-time French National Railways, especially T.G.V., the world's fastest train, which averages 186 miles per hour.

Moving southward, a visitor sees and feels the warmth of Provence with its luminous sun, sleepy Roman towns, and striking antiquities. Its bright blue sky has inspired French artists, including Vincent Van Gogh, Paul Cezanne, and Marc Chagall.

Provence is so named because it was the Province of Rome. Towns that attract the traveler are classic Aix-en-Provence, medieval Avignon, Carpentras, Cavaillon, and the great port of Marranos.

Keep in mind that a mere two hours from Marseilles or Avignon are the celebrated ski slopes of the French Alps at the foot of Mont-Blanc, Europe's highest peak.

Provence was once an important European Jewish center—a place where Jews have lived continually in spite of persecutions and expulsions. The earliest evidence of Jews in Provence dates from the fifth century in Arles and the sixth century in Marseilles. Five centuries later, Jews lived in many towns of Provence.

While Rabbenu Gershom and Rashi were the products of Judaism of northern France during the tenth and eleventh centuries, Provence in the south was undergoing its own renaissance of learning. When Benjamin of Tudela visited Provence in 1160, he found renowned scholars teaching hundreds of students.

Much has been told about the Jews of Avignon, who with their fellow co-religionists of Carpentras, Cavaillon, and L'Isle-sur-la-Sorgue comprise the four communities of the Comtat Venaissin, where Jews established important centers of learning. These towns were the cities of the papal states. Here Jews were given protection by the popes and served as financiers and merchants. They were called the "Pope's Jews," and as will be noted in the chapter on Italy, the thinking of the church leaders often was to protect the Jews as a reminder to those who might reject the Catholic Church that they would also be punished.

Nimes

Historically a major center of Jewish life in this part of France, Nimes is proud of two famous native sons, both French Jewish personalities.

Isaac-Adolphe Cremieux (1796-1880), French lawyer and statesman, was minister of justice in the Government of National Defense in 1870. He issued the Cremieux Decree by which the Jews of Algeria received French citizenship. This decree was very meaningful, as it enabled Jews of Algeria to settle in France as French citizens in the 1960s.

Bernard Lazare (1865-1903), liberal publicist, helped obtain the freedom of Capt. Alfred Dreyfus, who had been unjustly accused of espionage.

This handsome city has some of the most remarkable Roman structures outside of Italy—the **Roman Arena** and Maison Carrée—as well as magnificent gardens, fine museums, and a colorful medieval quarter.

Synagogue, 40, rue Roussy, 30000, Nimes. Tel: 66-29-51-81. Built in 1794, it is still used as a house of worship.

Community Center, 5, rue d'Angouleme, 30000, Nimes. Tel: 66-76-27-64.

Tourist information can be obtained at the **Office of Tourism,** 6, rue Auguste, 30000, Nimes. Tel: 66-67-29-11.

Avignon

Mention Avignon, and artists come to mind, as well as the medieval walls of the city and the children's song, "Sur le pont d'Avignon" ("On the Bridge at Avignon"). After 1309, Avignon became the residence of the popes. Joanna, countess of Provence, sold the city to Pope Clement VI and it belonged to the French states of the Holy See until the French Revolution.

Thus, Jews were able to stay there even when they were excluded from the rest of France.

Discover the city's festive ambiance from the vantage point of a café along the **rue de la République** or on the **Place de L'Horloge.**

Another major site is the **Petit Palais Museum** of medieval painting and sculpture. Savor art and music festivals staged in the municipal theater, or performances of choirs in the Palace.

From the nineteenth century onward, Jewish life almost ceased, until it was revived in the 1960s by Sephardic immigrants. There is a very narrow street called **rue de la Vieille Juiverie,** the old Jewish Quarter. Avignon has a small Jewish community of about 2,500.

The **synagogue** is located at 2, Place Jerusalem, 84000, Avignon. Tel: 90-85-21-24. Services are at 6 Friday night, at 7 in the summer, and on Saturday mornings at 9. This unusual circular synagogue was built in the Roman manner. It was erected on the site of the old Jewish quarter of the thirteenth century.

A **community center** is located at 18, rue Guillaume-Puy, Avignon. Tel: 90-82-64-87.

Information can be obtained at the **Office of Tourism,** 41, cours Jean-Jaures, 84000, Avignon. Tel: 90-82-65-11.

Arles

According to a Jewish legend, one of three rudderless ships bearing Jewish exiles arrived in Arles, 27 miles south of Avignon, after the destruction of the Second Temple in 70 C.E. The first evidence of Jewish life here dates back to the fifth century. Rome made Arles famous. An ancient Roman theater and a vast arena still stand in the city.

Benjamin of Tudela, the famous Jewish traveler, notes in the twelfth century that a Jewish community of 200 existed in Arles.Jews were expelled in 1481. After the French Revolution, some Jews from the Comtat Venaissin settled in Arles, the city to which the famous artist van Gogh brought fame.

The **Musée Arlaten**, located in the Palais de Laval-Castellane at 42, rue de la République, founded by the famous Provençal poet Frederic Mistral, preserves the relics of Old Provence. It contains a collection of Jewish religious and cultural objects. The **Arles Museum** houses the Lunel collection.

Tourist information is available at the **Office of Tourism,** 35, Place de la Republique, 13200, Arles. Tel: 90-96-29-35.

Cavaillon

Association Culturelle des Juif du Pape, Musée Judeo-Comtadin, rue Hebraique, 84300, Cavaillon. Tel: 90-76-00-34. A short drive from Avignon is the wonderful, provincial town of Cavaillon, "known throughout France for the succulence of its melons."

Jewish history can also be inhaled and seen in Cavaillon by a visit to this synagogue and Jewish Museum of the Comtat Venaissin on rue Hebraique, between rue Chabran and rue de la Republique. Built in 1772, this elegant rococo building is a national monument. This museum-synagogue was built above the gateway to the old "carriere," a single street similar to a ghetto area The rue Hebraique still shows slightly modified features of the "carriere."

The museum retraces Jewish history. On exhibit are prayer books, Torah scrolls, candelabras, shofars, and an oven used for baking matzoh. Many of these relics date from the 14th and 15th centuries and were housed in a 15th century house of prayer which was on the same site. A small synagogue remains upstairs above the museum. A velvet chair reserved for the Prophet Elijah is located in a niche on the wall high above the wooden circumcision chair.

The story as to how the synagogue survived the Nazi occupation explains that when the Jewish trappings were removed from the house of prayer, it took the appearance of a tearoom. Scheduled to be open from 10 A.M. to 2 P.M. to noon and from 2 P.M. to 5 P.M. every day except Tuesday. If the museum and synagogue are closed, contact Mr. Mathon at 23, rue Chabran of Maurice Palombo, Magasin Gigo, 36 rue Raspail, Cavaillon. Tel: 90-78-02-46.

About 50 to 75 Jews make Cavaillon their home.

Cavaillon Office of Tourism, 79, rue Saunerie,84300, Cavaillon. Tel: 90-71-32-01.

Carpentras

Synagogue, place de la Synagogue, 84200, Carpentras. Tel: 90-63-39-97. Contact Mme. Jenny Levy. This synagogue opposite the Town Hall is open Monday to Thursday from 10 A.M. to 12 noon and from 3 P.M. to 5 P.M. and Fridays, 10 A.M. to 12 noon, and 3 P.M. to 4 P.M. **Services are not usually held in this synagogue.** Please contact the other **Synagogue and Community Center** in place Maurice Charretier, for information re services. Tel: 90 63 39 97. Call here for information and schedule of events and services.

Synagogue and Community Center, place Maurice Charretier, BP190, 84206, Carpentras. Tel: 90-63-39-97. Once Jews sought temporary asylum within the borders of Carpentras. In this town, which boasts a bustling commercial life, stands a **Synagogue** which may well be the oldest in France. Erected in 1367, it was repaired in 1677, 1730 and 1885. Several more restorations were completed in this century. The synagogue of 1367 contained a men's area and a separate women's section in a cellar. In the two basement levels are a matzoh factory and a ritual bath.

Situated in what was the old "carriere," the restricted area, the synagogue was constructed from 1741 to 1743 by architect Antonine d'Allemand. The synagogue contains two levels, the sanctuary on the first discloses a high, light blue ceiling with gold stars. The bimah is situated in the middle of the prayer hall. There is also a miniature velvet armchair for Elijah the Prophet. It occupies a niche on the wall above the ark. It is said that the chair used to be taken to every house when there was a circumcision, but, obviously, it is too small for anyone to sit in. A mikveh and matzah oven are being restored.

Carpentras has about 100 Jewish families and sponsors special activities, such as holiday celebrations. Henry Kamm wrote in *The New York Times* on September 15, 1991, that "the two synagogues

The historic synagogue at Carpentras. (Photo courtesy of the French Government Tourist Office)

of Carpentras and Cavaillon...are reminders of the squalid, over-crowded ghettos in which Jews were forced to live from the mid-1400s until the French Revolution freed them and scattered their communities."

The synagogue here, too, survived because the curator took out all the Jewish elements and then brought in coffins, thus giving it the appearance of a church. The Germans believed this, it was reported.

Carpentras Office of Tourism, 170, avenue Jean-Jaures, 84200, Carpentras. Tel: 90-63-00-78.

COTE D'AZUR

Mention the names Cannes, Nice, Monte Carlo, Cap Ferat, Antibes, Juan-les-Pins, and St-Tropez and you picture beaches, villages, sun terraces on high-rise apartments, promenades, modern art museums, fireworks, flowers, and Mardi Gras carnivals. Mention the words delightful climate, clear sky, refreshing breezes, deep-blue waters, orange groves, and cassia plantations and you bring up before your eyes the French Riviera. Picasso, Matisse, and Renoir succumbed to this azure coast that now boasts film and folk festivals, as well as a vibrant landscape dotted with red tiled roofs and Mediterranean trees and gardens. It is one of the most beautiful areas in the world. The Riviera lies between the Maritime Alps and the Mediterranean Sea. Swathed in sunshine, a monument to leisure, its inviting hills are an open-air atelier for artists, with all the ripe pleasures of summer and sea.

More than 35,000 Jews live and work in this vacationland from Toulon to Menton, Cannes, Antibes, St-Tropez, Nice, and Juanles-Pins. The area offers tourists an exciting visit in scenic luxury.

Monte Carlo

The Monte Carlo Jewish community has undergone some exciting moments recently. A group of Americans, Canadians, and English, many of them retired, have added vitality to the **Sephardic Synagogue,** which is located at 15, avenue de la Costa, 98000, Monaco. Tel: 93-30-16-46. FAX: 93-50-64-15. A community center is located there, too.

Half of the congregation is English-speaking and Ashkenazic. The Ashkenazim have joined with their Sephardic counterparts in attempting to improve the organization of the congregation.

In fact, one condominium on the boulevard des Moulins is the residence of a number of Anglo-Saxons, as they are called. Some of them are officers in the synagogue and leaders in the community. There are also a kosher butcher shop under the supervision of the Beth Din of Nice, a Talmud Torah, and several Jewish organizations.

Nice

Travel to Nice, the capital of the Riviera and of international tourism. Its festivals and jazz concerts are well known, as are its colorful old districts, casinos, markets, and fine hotels, such as the Negresco, the Hyatt Regency, Sofitel Splendid, the Meridien, and the Plaza. The museums of Nice contain fine collections of impressionist and contemporary art. Outstanding French artists such as Dufy, Matisse, and Picasso worked along this Mediterranean coast.

In Nice, which sits beside the beckoning blue waters of the Mediterranean, about 25,000 Jews support a dozen synagogues, about 20 kosher butcher shops, several Talmud Torahs, a yeshiva, and a headquarters for the Lubavitch movement including a youth hostel. In summer, of course, Nice flaunts its tourism. It is close to other resorts along the shore and is a few minutes' drive from the wonderful scenic mountain Corniche-drives to Monte Carlo.

Jewish tourists who seek information regarding synagogues and kosher food in Nice and the area should contact the office of the **Grand Rabbi,** 1, rue Voltaire. Tel: 93-85-82-06.

Nice likes to say that it remains one of the homes of the Jewish artist Marc Chagall in the form of **The National**

Museum Biblical Message of Marc Chagall, located at avenue Docteur Menard and boulevard Cimiez. Tel: 93-81-75-75. It contains the most important permanent collection ever assembled that is devoted to Chagall, including large paintings, preparatory sketches, gouaches, and engravings. Chagall once said, "Perhaps in this abode, one will come and seek an ideal of fraternity and love such as my colors and my lines have dreamt." He commented on his famous Bible paintings hanging in the museum: "I want to leave them in this house so that people may find here a certain peace, a certain spirituality, a religious atmosphere, a feeling for life." Other media include stained-glass mosaics, lithographs, sculptures, and tapestries.

The **Maeght Foundation**, a major museum of contemporary paintings and sculpture, is set in a pine grove of St-Paul-de-Vence.

Synagogues and points of interest in Nice include:

Office of the Grand Rabbi, 1, rue Voltaire. Tel: 93-85-82-06. Rabbi Marc Bensoussan is Grand Rabbi.

Synagogue, 7, rue Gustave-Deloye, 06000, Nice. Tel: 93-92-11-38. Sephardic service. For those seeking an Ashkenazic service, attend **Synagogue Ezras Achim**, 1, rue Blacas.

Synagogue, 8, rue Marceau, 06000, Nice. Tel: 93-85-34-84.

Oratoire, Nice-Nord, 96, avenue St-Lambert.

Union Libérale Israelite de France, 24, rue de France, 06000, Nice. Tel: 93-82-26-15.

Organizations in Nice include:

Centre Michelet, 22, rue Michelet. Tel: 93-51-89-80. This new Jewish center contains a modern synagogue, library, rnikveh (ritual bath), classrooms, and a hall for weddings and bar mitzvahs.

Fonds Social Juif Unifié, 15, rue d'Angleterre. Tel: 93-87-53-20.

Beth Lubavitch-Chabad, 22, rue Rossini, 06000, Nice. Tel: 93-82-46-86. Sponsored by the Lubavitch movement.

Kosher restaurants in Nice

Le Leviathan, 1 av. G. Clemenceau, Nice. Tel: 93-87-22-64.

Kinereth, 37, bis av. G. Clemenceau, Nice. Tel: 93-87-55-36.

Maxime, 6 bd. De la Pinede, Juan. Tel: 92-93-99-40.

Tourist information can be obtained at the **Office of Tourism,** avenue Thiers, 06000, Nice. Tel: 93-87-07-07.

As noted, Nice is an excellent base from which to take day trips.

Cannes

If you are in Nice or Monte Carlo, certainly travel on to Cannes, the radiant city of the French Riviera with its sandy beaches, blue sky, and the beckoning Mediterranean, casinos, yacht harbors, palm trees, and the renowned **Palm Beach Club,** Cannes, is the largest yachting center of the Riviera.

The luxury hotels of Carlton, Martinez, Grey Albion, and the Majestic dress up the city. But there are hotels for every budget.

Cannes has a major Jewish community of about 10,000. Many are involved in enhancing this city known for its film festivals and attractive boulevard La Croisette, as well as Old Port Quarter.

Synagogue, 20, boulevard d'Alsace, 06400, Cannes. Tel: 93-38-16-54.

Centre Communautaire, 3, rue de Bone. Tel: 93-38-47-18. The community center has a kosher restaurant, but check on hours.

Le Toval, 3 rue Gerard Monod, Cannes.Tel: 93-39-36-25.

Pizza Duck, 7 bis rue Mimont, Cannes. Tel: 92-59-10-82.

Tourist information can be obtained at the **Office of Tourism,** Palais des Festivals et des Congrès, 1, La Croisette, 06400, Cannes. Tel: 93-39-24-53.

St-Tropez

Visit this wonderful resort town, a place of beaches, boutiques, cabarets, cafés, and countless yachts. St-Tropez has provided inspiration for so many artists, including Andre Lhote and Raoul Dufy. For those visiting St-Tropez, there is a **synagogue** at nearby **Frejus-St-Raphael,** in rue du Progrés, 83600, in Frejus-Plage. Tel: 94-52-06-87, 94-53-20-30, or 94-53-14-04.

Tourist information can be obtained at the **Office of Tourism,** Quai Jean-Jaures, 83990, St-Tropez. Tel: 94-97-45-21.

Antibes—Juan-les-Pins

Two towns, joined into one, sport a super night life, good shops, a fine beach, as well as a wonderful first-class, still-established family-style hotel, the **Hotel Juana**, avenue de Gallice, Juan les Pins. Nearby is the famous **Hotel du Cap** and its restaurant, **Eden-Roc,** in Cap d'Antibes. Both of these hotels are not to be missed on a trip to the Riviera. The Eden-Roc restaurant with its view of the bay is one of those never-to-be-forgotten sights.

Visit Antibes to see the famous castle of the Gromaldis, now the **Musée Picasso**. Juan-les-Pins, as the storybooks say, is a very popular international resort. It became famous after World War I, popularized by Jay Gould, the American railroad magnate who lived here.

In Juan-les-Pins, in July and August, there is a **kosher-deli restaurant** at 2, rue Roger Gallet.

Antibes-Juan-les-Pins Synagogue, 30, chemins des Sables Villa "La Monada," 06000, Antibes. Tel: 93-61-59-34. A Torah scroll is considered holy, sacred, venerable. To save a Torah scroll is a great mitzvah. The Antibes-Juan-les-Pins synagogue houses a famous Torah scroll, the story of which follows.

It is good to meet fellow co-religionists and exchange ideas and stories. Here is my experience on the Riviera, an experience that tells you much about the people—and one man in particular whom I interviewed, Leon Allouche—who make up French Jewry along this beautiful coast.

For the first 23 years of his life, Allouche lived in Algeria, that wonderful former North African Jewish community, in the city of Bonne. As a result of the Cremieux Decree of the nineteenth century, Algerian Jews were French citizens. So when war clouds broke over Europe in 1939, Allouche was conscripted into the Army of the Republic of France and shipped off to Europe. When France capitulated to the Nazi onslaught in 1940, Allouche was taken prisoner. He escaped four months later and made his way back across the Mediterranean to Algeria, where he lived briefly until that hero of modern France, Gen. Charles De Gaulle, rallied the nation.

Allouche, like French Jewish men and women throughout the French Empire, immediately joined the ranks of General de Gaulle. Once again Allouche sailed across the Mediterranean.

As the Allied armies fought their way across eastern France, Allouche would stop and ask residents along the way, "Is there a synagogue here? Where is it?"

Nearly all Jewish houses of worship were gutted or completely destroyed. Many towns had no Jews. One day in 1944, in a small town in Alsace, Allouche asked several townspeople if there were a synagogue in the area. A civilian who had been jailed previously led him to a shattered building that was stripped bare and from which the Holy Ark had been ripped right out of the wall.

The Germans had transformed this house of worship into an army barracks and dumped all the religious items they could find into a garbage heap 100 yards away. Allouche then commandeered several German prisoners of war to locate the garbage site, and soon his group found it. There, sticking out of the refuse, were the two poles of a single Torah. The POW crew quickly cleared away the area and found three other Torah scrolls.

Because Allouche and his unit had to move out, he left three Torah scrolls at the liberated synagogue for the future Jewish community and took a small one with him on his journey across Nazi Germany. It protected him, he recalled 43 years later.

Discharged in 1945, Allouche carried the Torah back to his home in Bonne, Algeria. In 1962, when France pulled out of Algeria, the Jews departed with the French who lived in Algeria and were known as *pieds noirs* (black feet). About 100,000 Jews fled this North African country and came to France as part of a modern exodus. More than 10,000 went to Israel.

Allouche took the Torah with him to Antibes-Juan-les-Pins where, like his fellow Algerians, he could resume his life as a French citizen. (He would later become police chief of

Antibes-Juan-les-Pins). This beautiful municipality is described as "one of the flashiest places on the Riviera," such is the quality of nightlife and its beaches. Here rests the Torah now, in a town with a timeless Mediterranean charm.

Other synagogues along the Riviera near Antibes-Juan-les-Pins include:

Cagnes-sur-Mer, 5, Imp. Douce-France, 35.

Draguignan, 15, rue de l'Observance.

Grasse, place de la Buanderie.

Hyeres, Chemin de la Ritorte.

Menton, centre "Altyner," 106, cours du Centenaire.

St-Laurent-du-Var, Villa "Le Petit Clos," 35, avenue des Oliviers.

Marseilles

Is this how Jews live in North Africa? Is this Oran? Fez? Cairo? No, it is Marseilles.

Here are Arab men carrying long spits with roasted lamb. The guttural sounds of Arabic permeate the air as the bearers wail haunting Arabic melodies of the Sahara.

I must have attended several hundred bar mitzvah ceremonies in my life, opulent ones and frugal ones. Held in the summer house of a very successful professional, this one certainly belonged to the former category. Cocktails were served poolside, tables were set out on the veranda, champagne flowed, and food abounded-course after course of exotic Sephardic dishes. There even was the familiar bar mitzvah candle-lighting ceremony similar to the one in the United States, where the boy is joined by various relatives as they light each of the 13 candles to signify the boy's thirteenth birthday. Gathered here were many successful, educated North African Jews who would never go back to the continent across the Mediterranean. They were French. They mixed with French society. They were business persons and professionals: they lived well, dressed well in the latest Paris fashions, and belonged to clubs. Many had fashionable apartments on the affluent Avenue Parades and other upper middle-class thoroughfares.

Marseilles, it is said, is a mix of Catholics, Communists, socialists, free thinkers, Armenians, Corsicans, Africans, Arabs, Jews, and Gypsies. Many are newcomers, including repatriated pieds noirs from Algeria, Tunisia, and Morocco. Marseilles has one of France's largest concentrations of Arab immigrants. Lately the newest group are refugees from Vietnam. The city is an important center of France's extreme right political party, the National Front of Le Pen.

Marseilles remains bustling and cosmopolitan. The famous Canebière Boulevard is always full of sailors and crowds at cafes. The city boasts the **Longchamps Palace,** with its **Fine Arts Museum** and the **Natural History Museum.** Atop a hill, **Notre Dame de la Garde Basilica** offers a breathtaking panorama of Marseilles.

Walk around the old port at night. Visit the restaurants, which offer rich gastronomic rewards. The dining establishments, cafes, and fish houses are filled with tourists who come here for a meal that may include bouillabaisse, turbot, white wine, and Chianti. Just southwest of the port lie the islands of Rattonneau and Pomegues. Between them and the mainland is the isle of Chateau d'If, which was the scene of part of Alexandre Dumas's *Le Comte de Monte-Cristo.*

As an emporium, Marseilles trades with the Levant and the Near and Far East. The smell of the sea is everywhere. Called Europort of the South, City of Conventions, and Gateway to the Riviera, Marseilles has also been called a tough harbor city of smugglers, thieves, prostitutes, and undesirables.

Through this ancient harbor in the late 1940s passed thousands of Jews on their way to their homeland in Palestine. The former president of France, François Mitterrand, helped pave the way for Jewish ships to go to Israel. In the three years following the end of World War II in 1945, the French embarrassed the British in Palestine just as the British were trying to keep the French out of the Middle East. France lost Syria and Lebanon. Perhaps the British should lose Palestine, thought a few in the Quai d'Orsay, the French Foreign Office.

As one walks up and down the busy Canebière Boulevard or strolls around the Old Harbor (the Vieux Port), one cannot help but visualize those post-World War II days, when old, unseaworthy Staten-Island-ferry-type boats, their beams bursting from the overcrowding of humans literally stuffed on board, sailed out secretly at night into the blue Mediterranean to run the gauntlet of the British Navy in order to reach the Jewish homeland. The British and the world called them "illegals," these survivors of the Holocaust. They maintained they were neither displaced nor illegal.

Marseilles had been my stomping ground during the days of the recovery of France after World War II, as well as the days of the nightmare following the Algerian War. Some of my happiest and best travel experiences occurred in this thriving seaport. Algeria, they say, was France's Vietnam. In the late 1950s and early 1960s, Jews fled Algeria because they knew that the country would revert to Moslem rule, and they were not sure Moslems would allow them to live in peace.

During the Algerian War, Jews in France leaned toward the French view. After all, they were French citizens according to the 100-year-old Cremieux Decree. While some Jews fought on the Algerian side, they would never feel comfortable in an Arab society, even though, throughout history, the Arabs treated Jews relatively well compared with Christian Europe.

They were beginning a new life in a new land, and even though they knew the language, they struggled to settle in. But unlike other Jewish immigrants from the North African countries, Algerian Jews were French citizens. This instant citizenship granted them rights to health benefits, to the vote, and to hold political office.

The first stop of the North African Jews who came to Marseilles was the **Place de la Bourse,** a large downtown square, a place that has witnessed revolutions, demonstrations, financial crisis, peaceful gatherings, and celebrations. Now new activity began on the square: the welcoming of refugees, newcomers, people looking for jobs. When fighting in Algeria had ended, the OAS went underground in clandestine headquarters here.

Today, about 70,000 Jews live here, many from Morocco and Tunisia. They sponsor about 20 synagogues, day and vocational schools, and youth centers. Marseilles is now the second largest Jewish community in France and the third largest in Western Europe.

Marseilles is a city of Sephardic Jews with names like Chiche, Dahan, Zana, Solal, Amsellem, and Zemmour. They are committed to Judaism. They are proud and active as they try to keep a community alive, fighting assimilation and anti-Semitism.

Their community organizations are enough to boggle the mind: the Fonds Social Juif Unifié, the social welfare agency; community centers; WIZO; ORT; B'nai B'rith; Zionist groups; sports clubs. Many work under the umbrella organization known as **CRIF,** which makes representations to the government.

A Jewish radio station in Marseilles broadcasts cultural programs to the people of all religions. The radio serves an educational purpose; it brings Judaism into the home.

For the Jewish community in France, whether it be Marseilles, Nice, Lyon, or Paris, where nearly two-thirds of the country's 700,000 Jews live, there is a new page in the annals of history. The French Jewish community can no longer be called a group of newcomers or of an immigrant generation.

Four decades after their arrival, Algerian Jews have entered various professions and have done well economically. Unlike their fellow Sephardic Jews in the United States, Sephardic Jews are in the majority in Marseilles and throughout France.

For information while in Marseilles, contact the following:

Appel Unifié Juif de France, 173, rue Paradis, Marseilles. Tel: 91-37-03-21. Similar to the American United Jewish Appeal, this organization is interested in meeting Americans and exchanging views.

B'nai B'rith, 41, cours d'Estienne-d'Orves, 13001, Marseilles. Tel: 91-33-80-50.

C.A.S.I.M., 61, rue de la Palud, 13006, Marseilles. Tel: 91-54-37-36.

Consistoire Israelite de Marseilles, 117, rue Breteuil, Marseilles. Tel: 91-37-49-64.

Coopération Féminine, 67, rue Breteuil, 13006, Marseilles. Tel: 91-81-79-59.

Fonds Social Juif Unifié (FSJU), 67, rue Breteuil, 13006, Marseilles. Tel: 91-37-40-57.

K.K.L. (Jewish National Fund), 95, cours Pierre-Puget, 13006, Marseilles. Tel: 91-33-83-92.

Beth Chabad, 112, boulevard Bary, 13001, Marseilles. Tel: 91-06-00-61.

WIZO, 2, boulevard Theodore Thurner, 13006, Marseilles. Tel: 91-48-64-26.

Tourist information can be obtained at the **Office of Tourism,** 4, Canebière, 13001, Marseilles. Tel: 91-54-91-11.

For prayer service, American visitors can go to the Temple Breteuil, 117, rue Breteuil, 13006, Marseilles'. Tel: 91-37-49-64. This main synagogue conducts a Sephardic service. The chief rabbi has his office at 119, rue Breteuil, 13006, Marseilles.

An Ashkenazic service is held in the **Synagogue** at 8, impasse Dragon, 13006, Marseilles, just nearby.

Other synagogues include the following:

Chalom Rav, 8, impasse Dragon, 13006, Marseilles.

Chevet Ha'him, 18, rue Beaumont, Marseilles. Tel: 91-50-30-07.

Maguen David, 31, avenue des Olives, 13013, Marseilles (La Rose, a suburban area). Tel: 91-70-05-45.

Or Torah, 14, rue St-Dominique, 13001, Marseilles. Tel: 91-90-64-30.

Ozer Dalim, 8, impasse Dragon, 13006, Marseilles. Tel: 91-53-33-73.

Union Libérale Israelite de France, 24, rue Martigny, 13008, Marseilles. Tel: 91-71-97-46.

There are two community centers in Marseilles:

Centre Communautaire Edmond Fleg, 4, impasse Dragon, 13006, Marseilles. Tel: 91-37-42-01.

Centre Maguen David, 31, avenue des Olives, 13013, Marseilles (La Rose). Tel: 91-70-05-45. This center is located in the outskirts of Marseilles.

Kosher Restaurants

Centre Communautaire Edmond Fleg, 4, impasse Dragon,

13006, Marseilles. Tel: 91-37-42-01 or 91-37-42-63. Sunday through Friday, 11 to 3, lunch only. Call for information.

Le Kikar, 58, rue Liandier, 13008, Marseilles. Tel: 91-80-51-20.

Mister Chan-Hai, 1 place due Lycee, 13001, Marseilles. Tel: 91-92-84-21.

Master King, rue St. Suffren, 13006, Marseilles. Tel: 91-92-84-21.

Natanya, 17 rue du Village, 13006, Marseilles. Tel: 91-42-05-31.

Byblos, 38 bd. Barral, 13008, Marseilles. Tel: 91-22-87-87.

There are also numerous kosher pizzerias, including **Pizzeria Gan Eden,** 225, Paul Claudel, Marseilles. Tel: 91-75-12-72.

AIX-EN-PROVENCE

Just a half-hour from Marseilles—only 20 miles—rests the quiet but stimulating municipality of Aix-en-Provence. This delightful academic town is known as the town of spas and arts, of music and fountains. A scholastic center, it boasts three universities and many institutes and it hosts music and art events.

An American school where students from the United States study French language, history, and culture adds to the cultural impact of Aix as it is fondly called. Stroll along the **Cours Mirabeau,** the most celebrated avenue in France and called one of the "most beautiful main streets in the world." At the head of the avenue is a noted fountain, La Rotonde, a monument to nineteenth-century romanticism. Most travel writers advise that the best time to experience the life and sites of the Cours is early morning or late at night.

In spite of wars, construction, and other threats to the landscape, Aix has managed to hold on to its lively fountains along the middle of its lovely streets. It is this music of culture and scenic beauty that keeps many tourists in rapture.

Enjoy the cool, shady plane trees and the eighteenth-century facades of elegant manor houses. Stop at the cafes and watch the world go by. Paul Cezanne and Emile Zola did when they lived here.

Once the capital of Provence, the city has existed for more than 2,000 years. Jews have a long history in Aix. They have lived here since the fifteenth century. Darius Milhaud, the famous French Jewish composer, was born here. His great grandfather helped establish a synagogue in Aix in 1840.

The Aix Jewish community of 600 families nearly ceased to exist after World War II. However, with the influx of North African Jews in the early 1960s, especially those from Algeria, the Jewish community was renewed.

A modern **synagogue** is located at 3 bis, rue de Jerusalem, 13100, Aix-en-Provence. The street may still be known as rue Montperrin since the new name, rue de Jerusalem, was designated only recently by the mayor of the town. Tel: 42-26-69-39. A community center, with classrooms, a library, and social hall, dates from the early 1970s.

Visitors are welcome to attend services each morning at 6:45. Evening services depend on sunset. On Saturday mornings, services are conducted at 8:30.

Tourist information is available at the **Office of Tourism, Place du Général de Gaulle,** 13100, Aix-en-Provence. Tel: 42-26-02-93.

NORMANDY

For centuries, Jews have lived in the serene and peaceful countryside of Normandy. Because of its scenery, splendid architecture, contrasting landscapes, rich agricultural lands, and historic past, it is one of the most attractive French provinces.

The towns of Normandy have retained their character despite wartime destruction and postwar building. In Normandy, too, are the D-day beaches that are part of American and French history: Utah, Omaha, Gold, Juno, and Sword. Farther east is Arromanches, where the British landed. And from the beautiful seaside town of Honfleur, Samuel de Champlain set sail to Quebec to explore the American Great Lakes.

Normandy is considered the home of the best cheese in the world, apple cider, strong Calvados, and tasty duck. It boasts lush, green fields, farmhouses, and estates. Today the Normans, active, friendly people, welcome tourists of all races and religions, just as they greeted the American GIs with glasses of cider following the D-day invasion.

This is the place that recalls the voice of our former president, then General Dwight D. Eisenhower, who on June 6, 1944, declared, "Peoples of Western Europe, a landing was made today on your beaches."

Rouen

This municipality is one of the most interesting in Normandy; its main street is the River Seine. Devastated in World War II, the city was rebuilt in such a way that one is constantly reminded of its rich history, art, and architecture. It was at Rouen that the peasant girl, Jeanne d'Arc, (Joan of Arc) inspired France to oppose the invading English.

An archeological discovery was made beneath the parking lot of the **Palace of Justice**. Uncovered were the remains of a medieval Jewish building, apparently the only Jewish institution of higher learning in Europe whose walls have survived from either antiquity or the Middle Ages. This would account for the fact that the present Palace of Justice fronts on rue aux Juifs (Street of the Jews). Uncovered in the excavations dedicated that day were graffiti on the walls of the medieval academy. This discovery meant that Rouen was a most important medieval center in France for Jewish studies, overshadowing even Paris.

The Jewish school of learning dated back to about the year 1090. (Some believe the building was a synagogue).

For Prof. Norman Golb of the University of Chicago, a specialist in Hebrew and Judaeo-Arabic studies, this find means that the Jewish presence in northern France was not only economic and commercial, but cultural as well. What makes the story even more exciting is that the location of the structure had been predicted by Golb, who reached his conclusion from a study of medieval manuscripts.

Months before the Romanesque building was discovered,

The Palace of Justice in Rouen. (Photo courtesy of the French Government Tourist Office)

the professor had published his hypothesis about the yeshiva in a book entitled *History and Culture of the Jews of Rouen.* It appeared in Hebrew in the spring of 1976.

He had researched 150 manuscripts which he studied in Jerusalem, the British Museum, the Bibliothèque Nationale in Paris, and libraries in Budapest, Amsterdam, and New York, as well as the Vatican Library.

His selection of the site of the yeshiva on Rouen's rue aux Juifs was based on the fact that references to the building stop with the sixteenth century. This was the point at which the highly ornamented Palais de Justice was built. "I surmised that they had razed the Jewish center to make way for the new construction," Golb told me in an interview.

Equally fascinating is the fact that Golb may have discovered why Rouen was overlooked as a center of Judaism during the Middle Ages. It may have been bypassed because Hebrew references to the city were misread by Latin scholars of the Middle Ages. Until the fourteenth century, Rouen was known as Rodom.

In surviving Hebrew manuscripts, the name *Rodom* is written like *Rhodoz,* a medieval city in southern France. What happened was that scholars, in recopying the manuscripts, often mistook the Hebrew letter *samech* for a final *mem.* Golb said he was fascinated by the possibility that the city they were really talking about and writing about as a "thriving Jewish community" was really Rodom or Rouen.

"I went back to the original manuscripts at the British Museum, and my suspicions were immediately confirmed," he said. Subsequent studies of manuscripts in Paris, Amsterdam, and Jerusalem revealed detailed maps, as well as descriptions of the Jewish quarter and of life in the city.

Today in Rouen, there are about 400 Jewish families engaged in professions and academic life, as well as industry and commerce. The Jews who came to Rouen in the 1960s from Algeria and Tunisia brought a Sephardic presence to the area.

With the archeological discovery, more people will be visiting Rouen. Since that day when the find was made, Rouen and the government of France have spent about $1 million on its restoration. It is a Jewish historic landmark in France not to be missed.

Appointments for group visits of no more than 20 persons

should be made with the **Office of Tourism,** 25, Place de la Cathédrale, BP666, 76008, Rouen. Tel: 35-71-01-44.

Synagogue, 55, rue des Bons-Enfants, 76100, Rouen. Tel. 35-71-01-44.

St-Lô

Rabbi Edmond Beldreb is a circuit rabbi. St-Lô is one of the towns he covers. He drives through scenic Normandy on roads flanked by rows of high hedge forming a leafy canopy.

St-Lô was one of the towns that Gen. George Patton made famous. It was from here in June 1944 that his forces broke out of German encirclement, and the enemy front facing the West collapsed. (Behind the roads traveled on by the rabbi are the D-day beaches).

True, there probably were no Jews here when Patton's Third Army moved out against the Germans. But a few Jewish families have now settled in this historic town.

Like the countryside around it, Normandy contains small Jewish communities tied together by joint activities and by visiting rabbis.

There are a few Jewish families in **Evreux,** about 10 families in **Lisieux,** 15 families in **Cherbourg,** 200 families in **Le Havre**, and 400 families in Rouen. And in **Caen**, almost entirely rebuilt after the war, there are about 100 Jewish families. After World War II, the Jews of Caen built their own **synagogue** at 46, avenue de la Libération. Tel: 31-43-60-54. Caen has a small but active Jewish community. Many arrived here from that cultural center of Jewish life in France, Strasbourg.

Memorial: A Museum for Peace, Esplanade Dwight Eisenhower, Caen, in Normandy. On April 26, 1992, a new and very moving exhibit citing the World War II deportations and acts of genocide was opened. The exhibit includes maps of the camps, items from deportations, a painting by Andre Roth, and a scenographic creation of shadows and vacillating lights dramatizing and highlighting the shameful place that the deportation occupies in the history of World War II. Museum hours: Open daily 9 A.M. to 7 P.M.; from July 11 to August 31, open until

9 P.M. Closed January 1 to 15, March 20, and December 25. Tel: 31-06-06-44.

The Jews of Normandy are a close-knit group. New super-highways and high-speed trains offer them the opportunity to go from Caen to Paris in two hours, from Rouen to Paris in a little more than an hour. But there are also intercity happenings. The Jews of Le Havre and Caen hold joint activities: seminars, lectures, and films.

During summer months, thousands of Jews also come to **Deauville**, which is the world-renowned resort of casinos, polo matches, and horse racing. In the summer, I was told, there is even a minyan in Deauville, whose summer population rises from about 10,000 persons to more than 100,000.

RENNES

Rennes is the capital of Brittany, the French province that is west of Paris and juts out into the Atlantic Ocean. Damaged in World War II and liberated by American GIs, the city boasts a beautiful town hall, with curved facades designed by Jacques Gabriel, as well as two important museums, **Musée de Bretagne** and **Musée des Beaux-Arts**, at 20 Quai Emile Zola. Artists such as Gaugin painted here, and writers such as Chateaubriand wrote here.

Rennes existed in the days of Gaul, the capital city of the Celtic tribe of the Redones. In the ninth century, Rennes became part of Brittany and gained prestige as a grand duchy.

There never have been many Jews in Brittany. Jews lived in nearby Nantes in the fifth century and were found in Brittany at the end of the twelfth century.

By an agreement of February 23, 1222, Pierre Mauclerc, Duke of Brittany, confirmed the jurisdiction of the bishop of Nantes over the Jews living in his area. In 1236, many Jews in Brittany were massacred by Crusaders. The remainder were expelled in April 1240 by Duke Jean le Roux, who declared a moratorium on all debts owed to Jews and ordered them to return all pledges of chattel or real estate. For several centuries, therefore, only converted Jews were found living in Brittany.

From the beginning of the seventeenth century, many Marranos settled in Brittany, mainly in Nantes, a little more than an hour from Rennes.

During the eighteenth century, Jewish traders from Bordeaux, as well as Alsace-Lorraine, began to visit area fairs and markets. But in 1780, Jews were expelled. After the French Revolution, Jews returned to Brittany. In 1808, when Jewish community consistories were established in France, only 300 Jews lived in Rennes. Historically, one reason there may never have been many Jews here is that Brittany, unlike Paris, Strasbourg, Lyon, and Marseilles, is not a "gateway" or port city. The thinking goes: you needed a port city to attract Jews who were tradesmen.

What makes Rennes an interesting place to visit is its ancient ramparts with watchtowers and gates, narrow streets, little squares, and half-timbered houses.

Located in the heart of an agricultural region and surrounded by areas of beautiful beach coastline, Rennes maintains a fine university and an excellent medical center. As a French Army administrative center, the city attracts many civil servants or, as the French call them, "fonctionnaires." The municipality is also the headquarters of the prefect, the official who supervises the whole region of Brittany.

There are usually jobs available here, and that is why many Jews settled in during the wave of the North African Jewish immigration in the 1960s.

What will possibly preserve the Jewish communities in the region is the T.G.V. high-speed train of the French National Railways, which makes the Paris-Rennes run in about two hours instead of three. French Railways schedules 14 trains daily to Nantes and Rennes from Paris. They run at about 186 mph.

The Jews in Brittany feel that their ties to Paris (where one-half of France's 700,000 Jews reside) will obviously be much stronger because the trip is now two hours instead of three. A one-day journey from Paris to attend a lecture on Jewish subjects or a visit to attend a Jewish program will help stimulate this small community.

When you visit Rennes, head towards the **Jewish Community Center,** 32, rue de la Marbaudais, 35000, Rennes. Tel: 99-63-57-

18. The street is located within a large apartment complex. According to the plaque on the building wall, the synagogue is called "Centre Communautaire/Beith Hatikvah." The synagogue is part of a larger apartment-complex community center.

Jews must have lived here before World War II, although people don't know too much about the old community. There is a monument in the synagogue reading, "Mortes en Déportation, 1942-1945." I counted more than 60 names on the memorial plaque, victims of the Holocaust.

Services are Friday at 7:15 P.M. They always have a minyan. One of the large community gatherings occurs on the Day of Remembrance, of the Holocaust. The municipal authorities of Rennes attend. According to Mary Elsy and Jill Norman in *Travels in Brittany,* Brittany contributed more men and women than any other province in France to the Free French Resistance movement. Some of World War II's fiercest fighting took place in Brittany, in such ports as Brest, Lorient, St-Nazare, and St-Malo.

Lecturers, such as writers Marek Halter, Victor Malka, and Rabbi Serat, the former chief rabbi, have visited the center.

On Yom Kippur, several hundred Jews pray in the synagogue's large room.

There are regional activities with Jewish communities in Nantes, Brest, and Lorient. One gets the impression they have many joint gatherings. The community is friendly and welcomes visitors.

Here in Rennes, this city of art and history, the second trial of Capt. Alfred Dreyfus took place at the turn of the century. Here again, Dreyfus was unjustly found guilty. But at his Rennes trial it was clear that this Jewish army officer had been framed and several of the judges wavered. The trial took place in the **red brick schoolhouse** that still stands. Later it was named after Emile Zola, the noted French writer who was instrumental in focusing world attention on the injustice to Dreyfus. It was his famous newspaper article that shouted out in a banner headline style, "I Accuse."

Obviously, Jews don't live in a vacuum. They are part of a city and a people with a rich history, and live in a land that should be explored. Brittany offers sandy seaside beaches, rivers, fishing, natural sites, and wildlife. You can live on a boat. You can play golf or ride a horse. You can camp out or stay in a fine hotel. And of course, you can visit a friendly Jewish community.

FRENCH SYNAGOGUES OUTSIDE OF PARIS

There are synagogues and community centers in more than 120 cities and towns in France. Further questions should be directed to the **Consistoire Central,** 19, rue St-Georges, 75009, Paris. Tel: 49-70-88-00.

Here is a partial listing:

Agen, 52, rue de Montesquieu.
Amiens, 90, rue St-Fuscien.
Annecy, 18, rue de Narvik.
Annemasse, 13, rue de la Paix.
Arcachon, 36, avenue Gambetta.
Bastia, 3, rue du Castagno.
Beauvais, rue Jules-Isaac.
Belfort, 6, rue de l'As-de-Carreau.
Besancon, 2, rue Mayence.
Beziers, 19, Place Pierre-Semard.
Brest, 40, rue de la République.
Chalons-sur-Marne, 21, rue Lochet.
Chalons-sur-Saone, 10, rue Germiny.
Chambery, 44, rue St-Real.
Clermont-Ferrand, 6, rue Blatin.
Colmar, 3, rue de la Cigogne.
Compiegne, 4, rue du Dr. Charles-Nicolle.
Creil, 1, Place de la Synagogue.
Dunkerque, 19, rue Jean-Bart.
Elbauf, 29, rue Grémont.
Epernay, 2, rue Placet.
Epinal, 7, rue Charlet.
Evian, avenue des Grottes.
Grenoble, 11, rue Andre-Maginot.
La Ciotat, 1, square de Verdun.
La Rochelle, 40, cours des Dames.
Le Havre, 40, rue Victor-Hugo.

Le Mans, 416, boulevard Paixhans.
Lille, 5, rue Auguste-Angellier.
Limoges, 25-27, rue Pierre-Leroux.
Luneville, 5, rue Castara.
Macon, 32, rue des Minimes
Melun, corner of rues Branly and Michelet.
Metz, 39, rue du Rabbin-Elie-Bloch.
Montauban, 12, rue Sainte Claire
Mulhouse, 19, rue de la Synagogue.
Nancy, 17, boulevard Joffre.
Nantes, 5, impasse Copernic.
Perigeux, 13, rue Paul-Louis-Courier.
Perpignan, 54, rue Arago.
Poitiers, 1, rue Guynemer.
Roanne, 9, rue Beaulieu.
St-Etienne, 34, rue d'Arcole.
St-Louis, rue du Temple.
Sedan-Charleville, 6, avenue de Verdun.
Sens, 14, rue de la Grande-Juiverie.
Sete, 136 chemin de l'Anglore.
Tarbes, 6, rue du Pradeau, Cite Rothschild.
Toulon, avenue Lazare-Carnot.
Troyes, 5, rue Brunneval.
Valence, 1, Place du Colombier.
Valenciennes, 36, rue de l'Intendance.
Verdun, impasse des Jacobins.
Versailles, 10, rue Albert-Joly.
Vichy, 2 bis, rue du Marechal-Foch.
Vitry-le-François, 29, rue du Mouton.
Vittel, rue Croix-Pierrot.

England, which we shall visit in the next chapter, is now clos-er to France, not only because of the European Union, but because in 1994, the Channel Tunnel linking the two countries and the Continent with the British Isles opened and no doubt the two large Jewish communities will forge new links between French and British Jewry. It takes about 2½ hours to go by train from London to Paris.

Suggested Reading

Adler, Jacques. *The Jews of Paris and the Final Solution.*

ben-Sasson, H. H., ed. *A History of the Jewish People.* Cambridge, Mass.: Harvard University Press, 1969.

Bernstein, Richard. *Fragile Glory: A Portrait of France and the French.* New York: Alfred A. Knopf, 1990.

Courthion, Pierre. *Paris in the Past.* Paris: Editions d'Art Albert Skira, 1957.

Culbertson, Judi, and Tom Randall. *Permanent Parisians: An Illustrated Guide to the Cemeteries of Paris.* Chelsea, Vt.: Chelsea Green Publishing, 1986.

Eban, Abba. Heritage: *Civilization and the Jews.* New York: Summit Books, 1984.

Halter, Marek. *The Book of Abraham.* New York: Henry Holt, 1983.

—. *The Jester and the King.* New York: Little, Brown, 1988.

Hertzberg, Arthur. *The French Enlightenment and the Jews.* New York: Columbia University Press, 1968.

Hyman, Paula. *From Dreyfus to Vichy: The Remaking of French Jewry, 1906-1939.* New York: Columbia University Press, 1979.

Johnson, Paul. *A History of the Jews,* New York: Harper & Row, 1987.

Jones, David Pryce. *Paris in the Third Reich.* New York: Holt, Rinehart and Winston, 1981.

Josephs, Jeremy. *Swastika Over Paris: The Fate of the Jews in France.* New York: Little, Brown, 1989.

Krinsky, Carol Herselle. *Synagogues of Europe: Architecture, History, Meaning.* Cambridge, Mass.: MIT Press, 1985.

Liebling, A. J. *Between Meals: An Appetite for Paris.* New York: Simon & Schuster, 1962.

Marrus, Michael R., and Robert O. Paxton. *Vichy France and the Jews.* New York: Basic Books, 1981.

Morgan, Ted. *An Uncertain Hour: The French, the Germans, the Jews, and the City of Lyon, 1940-1945.* New York: William and Morrow, 1990.

Posner, S. *Adolphe Cremieux: A Biography.* Philadelphia: Jewish Publication Society of America, 1940.

Roth, Cecil. *A History of the Jews: From Earliest Times through the Six Day War.* New York: Schocken Books, 1970.

Schnapper, Dominique. *Jewish Identities in France: An Analysis of Contemporary French Jewry.* Chicago: University of Chicago Press, 1983.

Szajkousky, Soza. *Jews and the French Revolution of 1789, 1830, 1848.* New York: Klav Publishing House, 1969.

Vital, David, *A People Apart, The Jews in Europe, 1789-1939,* Oxford, Oxford University Press, 1999.

Wilson, Derek. *Rothschild, the Wealth and Power of a Dynasty.* New York: Charles Scribner's Sons, 1988.

Zuccotti, Susan. *The Holocaust, the French, and the Jews.* New York: Basic Books, 1993.

England
Cromwell, Disraeli, and the Rothschilds

London casts a spell on the American visitor with its parks, museums, art galleries, and history. England was America's "mother country" and London, its capital. In our day, we recall World War II, when Great Britain stood alone against the Nazi tyranny. Bombed at night, the English still rose in the morning to meet the day. They never surrendered, neither during nor after Dunkirk and the blitz.

"Surrender?" a British sergeant asked his men when he heard of Belgium's 1940 collapse in World War II. "Let them all surrender; we never will!" And in modern times Britain has also stood up as America's ally.

A Brief History

The sites and sounds of London excite an American: the Houses of Parliament, Big Ben, the changing of the guard at Buckingham Palace, the British Museum, Her Majesty's Tower of London, the National Gallery, Hyde Park, the Victoria and Albert Museum, Westminster Abbey, Whitehall, the Strand, Trafalgar Square, Madame Tussaud's Wax Museum, the royal parks, the pubs. Jews came to England with William the Conqueror (1027-87), who, in 1066, invaded England, which then was a Saxon-Scandinavian land. Those first Jews who arrived along with William were from France. Even in those days, one did not give up speaking French easily; in fact, we are told, French continued to be the language of the Jews until they were expelled in 1290.

Jews counted themselves among the few Londoners to own stone houses. They lived in that square mile of central London called "the City," which ironically is located next to the East End. Centuries later it would again become the "old Jewish neighborhood," though by then a poorer area. A street called "Old Jewry" survives to this day in this section of central London; it is one of the area's most famous lanes, and contains much history. Located in EC3, it was once known as "Poor Jewry."

An English travel writer described the Jewish merchants of London long ago as having "the ageless eyes of the Jews." Others would translate "Jew" to mean "moneylender." The first impression of Jews in England was that of a peddler with a pack on his back.

As Jews were to become proprietors, and Christians could not float loans, Jews financed these non-Jews, offering capital with payment of interest. The church condemned moneylending as the "heinous sign of usury." Aaron of the town of Lincoln, a leading Jewish European financier in the twelfth century, became one of the wealthiest persons in England.

While Jewish tax collectors thought they were protected by royalty, they actually were "chattels of the King" and possessed few legal rights. Although the king and his associates were heavily in debt to the Jews, royalty soon discovered ways to renege on their payments by canceling the debts or by killing or expelling the Jews.

Another way to wipe out debts was the fable of ritual murder, followed by blood libel. Jews were supposed to have murdered Christians, then to have used the blood of the victims to make matzoh on Passover.

In 1275, King Edward I prohibited Jews from collecting interest. That measure strangled the Jewish community. Later, on July 18, 1290, Edward I banished the Jews from England. By November 1, 1290, All Saints Day, most of the 16,000 Jewish refugees had made their way across the English Channel to France, Flanders, and Germany. Their descendants would not return for 400 years.

After four centuries, what finally would move England to readmit its Jews? British pounds and shillings would play a major role in bringing Jews back onto English soil. The return of Jews to England has its origin in Amsterdam. Working together would be the Puritan dictator Oliver Cromwell and a Dutch Jew named Manasseh Ben Israel (1604-57). As Winston Churchill wrote, "It was left to a Calvinist dictator [Cromwell] to remove the ban which a Catholic king had imposed."

Until 1616, a small colony of secret Jews, mostly Marranos who came to England about 1500, managed to keep Judaism alive. Toleration of the Jewish return to Britain was due in part to the fact that the English read the Old Testament. With Manasseh Ben Israel's pleading and Cromwell's "unwritten permission," Jews began arriving in England in 1656.

During the Revolution of 1688, William of Orange captured the throne of England and sparked the influx of additional Jews to England. The restored Stuarts protected the Jews, who could now earn a living among their Christian neighbors. But it would take 200 more years for them to obtain political rights.

The newcomers were Sephardim from Spain and Portugal. They had names like Pereira, de Castro, d'Oliveira, de Veifa, Mendes da Costa, Gimes, Nunes, Henriques, Alvares, and Lousades.

By the end of the seventeenth century, about 20,000 Jews lived in Great Britain. The majority settled in London. Besides the Bevis Marks Synagogue, three Ashkenazic synagogues were organized. Jews of this era made their living as peddlers and small traders, opticians, physicians, and teachers.

Indirect parliamentary recognition came in 1698. Later, with the Jew Bill of 1753, foreign-born Jews were permitted to acquire privileges enjoyed by native children. Still, despite commercial success, Jews were not permitted to hold political office; nor could they serve in Parliament, vote in municipal elections, or attend the universities. Finally, in 1826, Jews were at least able to become naturalized.

As in many countries, the Jews of England were expected to govern themselves. The Board of Deputies was established in 1760 as the representative house of British Jewry. To this day, it maintains de facto government recognition.

After the Napoleonic Wars, Jewish families, like the Goldsmiths and Rothschilds, played an important role in English finance and society.

By 1830, 30,000 Jews lived in England, two-thirds of them in London. But English Jews looked across the channel and saw that their French co-religionists were already emancipated. They wanted similar rights. By 1840, the last of the so-called disabilities for Jews in England had disappeared, with the exception of the right to sit in Parliament. At that time, the swearing-in ceremony for members of Parliament was taken "on the oath of the true faith, of a Christian," an oath a Jew obviously could not take.

In 1858, Lionel Nathan Rothschild became the first Jew to be admitted to the House of Commons. He was not forced to "take the oath of a Christian." Since then, one or more Jews have served in every Parliament.

In 1860, the Orthodox "United Synagogue" came under the jurisdiction of a chief rabbi. This group consisted of the vast majority of synagogues. Reform and Sephardic groups established their own units.

In the 1880s, Jews began to move from Eastern Europe to the west. A vast wave of immigrants from the east arrived in England. In 1880, 60,000 Jews lived in Great Britain. By 1905, there would be 150,000 Jews.

To Jews, London and the British Isles will always mean a land of temporary refuge. For many on the way to the United States in the nineteenth century, it was a stopping-off place. The first Jewish mayor of New York City, Abraham Beame, was born in England and came to New York City as a young child.

The new Jewish immigrants were Yiddish-speaking proletariat and middle-class Orthodox. They were tailors, boot and shoe manufacturers, and furniture suppliers. As immigrants, they set up their own life-style in the poor neighborhoods of British cities.

By the start of World War I, 300,000 Jews lived in Britain. About 50,000 Jews fought with the Allies during the war and suffered 10,000 casualties. Approximately 1,500 Jews were decorated. Six persons were awarded the Victoria Cross, Britain's highest order.

During World War II, about 90,000 Jews fled from Hitlerism to the British Isles, of which 75,000 came from Germany and Austria, Czechoslovakia, Poland, and Italy. Friction between Britain's Jews and His Majesty's government would increase over the country's League of Nations mandate in Palestine, especially since Britain tightened Jewish immigration to the future Jewish State.

In 1944, with the assassination of Lord Moyne and the 1947 hanging of two British Army sergeants, tension rose in England, which had pursued a pro-Arab policy, to say the least.

Ernest Bevin, the post-World War II British foreign secretary, followed a Palestine policy that "virtually abrogated" the Balfour Declaration. The latter called for a Jewish national home in Palestine. He imposed severe restrictions on Jewish immigration. Nothing moved Bevin, not even the thousands of Jewish survivors still held in displaced persons (D.P.) camps. His anti-Semitism blinded him.

Although they felt betrayed, English Jews rallied and, on May 14, 1948, they too celebrated the establishment of the State of Israel. After World War II, Jews moved to the suburbs, mainly to the northwest to Wembley, Harrow, Stanmore, Edgware, Finchley, Palmers Green, Ilford, Golders Green, and Stamford Hill. Today, Jews are less than one percent of the British population. About three-quarters of Great Britain"s estimated 300,000 Jews live in and around cosmopolitan London, which has 6.6 million people. One suburb, Golders Green, stands out as a comfortable middle-class residential area of northern London. There—and in Stamford Hill—you will find a Jewish neighborhood with Jewish stores and synagogues. While probably not as high as in the United States, the frequency of intermarriage in England is about one out of three. Intermarriage and assimilation are becoming common in Jewish society here, for England, since World War II, has become freer and less stratified.

Notable English Jews

The *Jewish Chronicle,* the first permanent Anglo-Jewish

newspaper, was established in 1841. Located at 25 Furnival St., London EC4, it has the honor of being the oldest Jewish newspaper in the world in continuous publication. On its pages often appeared notices and reports on outstanding Jewish personalities who contributed much to Great Britain and British Jewry.

Many times, of course, mention was made of Sir Moses Montefiore (1784-1885), a famous son of British Jewry. He was probably the outstanding figure in the Jewish community and the most celebrated Jew in England; he lived until the age of 101. Sir David Salomons became the first Jewish mayor of London in 1855; he was also the first Jewish sheriff in 1835, and the first Jewish alderman in 1847. Sir George Jessel was the first Jew to become a member of the government and was appointed solicitor in 1871.

Benjamin Disraeli (1804-81) was born a Jew, and he became one of the United Kingdom's greatest prime ministers.

Herbert Samuel, later viscount, became a British cabinet minister in 1909. He also was named as the first High Commissioner for Palestine in the 1920s. Solomon Schechter, rabbinic scholar and founder of Conservative Judaism, later took the post of president of the Jewish Theological Seminary in the United States, where he served from 1902 until his death in 1915. Sassoon Siegfried was a famous Jewish poet and author of *Memoirs of an Infantry Officer.*

Sites in London

Sites which are a must on a trip to London include **Shakespeare's Globe Theater,** the reconstructed playground of England's greatest bard; the restoration of **Windsor Castle,** after the devastating fire of 1992; the **Tate Gallery of Modern Art, on Bankside, 25 Sumner St.,** now linked to the City of London and St. Paul's Cathedral on the Thames' north bank by the new Millennium Bridge. "To be in London these days is to be endlessly entertained by art, by the museums that show it, the multiplying galleries that sell it and the masses who have become weirdly fascinated by it," writes Michael Kimmelman in *The New York Times,* June 6, 2000. Even the venerable British Museum on Great Russell St., which we have noted earlier, has created London's first covered public square, the Great Court. Visit, too, the Royal Opera House in Covent Garden, at 45 Floral Street. Finally, the new Millennium Dome on Drawdock Road, a vast white edifice and the world's largest dome which looks like an upturned dinner plate. The building in which you can take a wondrous journey from one end of existence, that is, the Big Bang to the present, opened on January 1, 2000.

Jewish London

THE EAST END

The first Jewish word that a Jewish traveler hears in the London of Disraeli, Rothschild, Adler, Schechter, and Balfour deals with Jewish food. The word is *heimisch,* "homey, informal, comfortable."

"Heimisch [homemade] mushroom barley soup," says a man between spiels in the weekly Sunday market in Petticoat Lane. During the week, it is known as Wentworth Street. "Go over to Bloom's and have a bowl," he urges.

London's East End—with its flavor of New York's Lower East Side—deserves a stroll. This neighborhood has changed. Once it boasted many clubs, theaters, shelters, yeshivas, and schools. Today, there are few Jews, and fewer institutions, but the neighborhood is still exciting and vibrant, and it is good to begin a visit to London here in White Chapel and at such streets as Whitechapel High Street, Osborne Street, Brick Lane, Fournier Street, and Greatorex Street.

"The Asians are here now," says Mr. Meyers, the peddler in

Petticoat Lane. "The newcomers want to succeed, so they go where the Jews began," he points out as he looks around at fellow hawkers who sell—from their stalls—leather bags, coats, umbrellas, jeans, mirrors, sweaters, and orange juice squeezers.

Or, put another way, "they're speaking Hindustani where *mamaloshen* [Yiddish] used to be spoken," according to Member of Parliament Grenville Janner.

The East End can be reached by taking the Underground. Take the "tube" to Liverpool Street, Bethnal Green, Aldgate, Aldgate East, or Shoreditch. Several bus lines also serve the area—6, 8, 15, or 25 from Oxford Circus or the 6 or 15 from Charing Cross.

By the way, the area houses several streets and buildings of interest to Jewish travelers, including the home of Abe Saperstein, who founded the Harlem Globetrotters in the United States; the Jewish Working Men's Club on Alie Street, where in 1896, Theodor Herzl launched the Zionist movement.

TOURS

A tour in the East End, the location of the original Jewish settlement, and elsewhere in London, is conducted by **Londinium,** 6 W. Heath Ave., London, NW11 7QL. Tel: 020-8458-2288 or FAX: 020-8455-6612. Valerie Sussman and Sally Pitel conduct the Jewish tour by means of a private car. The tours can be tailor-made to the traveler"s interests. Website: www.Londiniumtours.com.

One way to see the East End is to stroll along with Mr. or Mrs. Joseph, who conduct **walking tours** of the "Jewish East End." They point out all the nostalgic and historic sights of interest. The **Josephs** now take only groups around the area. Make sure you call ahead. Tel: 020-8504-9159.

Historic Tours, 3 Florence Rd., South Croydon, CR2 0PQ. Tel: 020-8668-4019. FAX: same as telephone. This is a historical walking tour tracing Jewish history in England from the time of William the Conqueror to World War II. The tour is conducted on Sundays and Tuesdays at 11 A.M. from Aldgate Underground Station. Please call for details.

JEWISH SITES IN LONDON

The J.F.S. Comprehensive School, 175 Camden Rd. This is a wonderful sight to see regarding Jewish life in Britain. I visited this excellent school and marveled at the sight of 1,500 Jewish boys and girls, ages 11 to 18, reciting the *mincha* (afternoon) service in the school's synagogue. The youths were dressed with blue-knit yarmulkes; blue blazers, grey slacks, and school ties for the boys; and blue blouses and grey skirts for the girls, the much-seen school clothes of British youth. The school is Orthodox and its subjects include Hebrew, Bible, laws, and Talmud, along with math, chemistry, history, tradition, and athletic events in fine facilities.

The Office of N. M. Rothschild & Sons is located at New Court, St. Swithins, in the heart of London. The headquarters of this remarkable Jewish family was responsible for many loans aiding the British government, including funds for the defeat of Napoleon, the relief of the Irish famine, the Crimean War, and, of course, the purchase of the shares of the Suez Canal owned by the khedive of Egypt. After the battle of Waterloo, the Rothschilds became bankers to the Holy Alliance of Christian Monarchs of Russia, Austria, Prussia, and Britain.

The Rothschild family moved to various European capitals to direct financial matters. James made Paris his base; Solomon moved to Vienna; Carl went to Naples; Mayer Amschel remained in Frankfurt. The main center of operations emerged at New Court, London, where the English branch was directed by Nathan Mayer Rothschild (1777-1836). He was the son of founder of the Rothschild dynasty, Mayer Amschel. The son, too, was a financial genius, a creative business person. Nathan Mayer Rothschild, "N.M.," as he was called, had been the first Rothschild to leave Frankfurt. He came to England, entered the textile importing business, and was an agent for his father. He became a British citizen in 1806 and married Hannah Cohen, whose sister married Moses Montefiore. The latter's brother married Nathan's sister, Henriette, and this liaison connected N.M. to the Salomons, Goldsmiths, and other prominent families. He helped establish the Jews"

Free School. He was in the government loan business, especially since London was the financial center of the world. He transformed the Rothschilds into "the world's leading business house."

It took ten years of effort, but finally the son of "N.M." was the first Jew to sit in Parliament. You see, time after time, Lionel Nathan Rothschild had been elected by the City of London as its parliamentary representative. But the British Parliament refused to admit him to the House of Commons because, as a Jew, he refused to take the oath of office, which contained the words "on the true faith of a Christian." Ten years later, the House of Commons ended that oath. Even more time elapsed before a Jew could take his seat in the House of Lords. In 1885, Lionel's son, Nathaniel ("Natty") Mayer Rothschild, became the first "professing" Jew to be raised to the peerage of a Lord and became a member of that august body. He was head of the British Jewish Community and president of the United Synagogue.

KOSHER RESTAURANTS IN LONDON

Kosher Establishments under the Kashrut Division of the London Beth Din

Six-13, 19 Wigmore St., London, W1H 9LA. Tel: 020-7629-6133. What do you get when you add six and 13 together? You get 613. There are 613 *mitzvot,* Jewish rules for living. And if you add 6 plus 13, well, that equals 19, the street number for the restaurant. And that is what we have: A new up-scale kosher restaurant, which opened in July in 2000, in the West End of London. Not only is it kosher, under the supervision of the Kashrut Division of the London Beth Din, but it is reported to be London's first *kosher fusion* restaurant. The current interpretation of kosher-fusion food is a "fusion of flavors incorporating traditional and modern ideas, and the cuisine of different cultures from all over the world." The establishment is loosely based on New York's **Le Marais.** The interior contains a plush setting and fashionable French Art Deco theme. Six-13 offers modern international dishes made entirely from kosher ingredients, dairy and gluten free, combined with "Jewish classics," such as salt beef and chicken soup. Open Sunday to Thursday, 11:00 A.M. to 3:30 P.M. and 7:30 P.M. to 11 P.M.; Fridays from 11:30 A.M. to 2 P.M. (winter) and 4 P.M. (summer). Saturdays, 7:30 P.M. to 11 P.M. (winter only).

Café on the Green, 122 Golders Green Rd., London NW11 8HB. Tel: 020-8209-0232. FAX: 020-7266-2393. Catering specialists, Kenny and Susan Arfin, owners of this successful dairy restaurant in Golders Green, are also involved in the Six-13 restaurant in the West End. The attractive Mediterranean interior gives off a friendly and relaxed atmosphere. A variety of pastas and pizzas are highlights, as are fresh fish dishes that are prepared daily. This air-conditioned restaurant also offers *al fresco* dining, a favorite, the restaurant says, with American and European visitors.

The restaurant, licensed by the London Beth Din, notes that all of its dairy products are *chalov Yisrael.*

Open Sunday through Thursday, 10 A.M. to 11 P.M. Fridays, 10 A.M. to 2 P.M. in winter and 4 P.M. in summer. On Saturdays, **Café on the Green** is open from 7:30 P.M. to 12 A.M. only in winter.

Bloom's, 130 Golders Green Rd., London NW11. Tel: 020-8455-1338. Fax: 020-8455-3033. Everyone knew the former Bloom's in Whitechapel High St., where it was in business for many years before moving to its present location.

Catskills, 1-4 Belmont Court, Finchley Rd., Temple Fortune, London NW11. Tel: 020-7388-0801. Fax: 020-8209-1050.

Kadimah Hotel, 146 Clapton Common, London E5. Tel: 020-8800-5960. FAX: 020-8800-6237.

Kaifeng, 51 Church Rd., London, NW4. Tel: 020-8203-7888. FAX: 020-8203-8263.

Marcus's, 5 Hallswelle Parade, Finchley Rd., London, NW11. Tel: 020-8458-4670.

New Ambassador Hotel, Meyrick Rd. East Cliff, Bournemouth. Tel: 01202-555453.

Sally's, 148a Golders Green Rd., London NW 11. Tel: 020-8455-0004.

Sally's Exclusive, 146-150 Golders Green Rd., London NW11. Tel: 020-8455-2121.

Tasti Pizza, 23 Amhurst Parade, Amhurst Park, London N16. Tel: 020-8802-0018. Also, 252 Golders Green Rd., London N11. Tel: 020-8209-00023.

Kosher Take-Away Delis under the supervision of the Kashrut Division of the London Beth Din

Brownsteins Delicatessen, 24A Woodford Ave., Gants Hill, Essex 1G2 6XG. Tel: 020-8550-3900.

B'te A'von Fine Meals by Oberlander, 1A Cecil Rd., London NW9. Tel: 020-8200-7766. Fax: 020-8200-8253.

Great Food (Steve's Deli), 5 Canons Corner, Stanmore Middlesex. Tel: 020-8958-9446. Fax: 020-8905-4700.

Kosher King, 223 Golders Green Rd., London, NW11. Tel: 020-8455-1429.

Munch Box, 41 Greville St., London, EC1. Tel: 020-7242-5487. Fax: 020-7831-3860.

Hillel Restaurant, 1/2 Endsleigh St., London WC1 H 0DS. Tel: 020-7387-4644 or 020-7380-0111. A fine place that caters to university students in a marvelous college atmosphere in the area around Euston Station. Open Monday to Thursday, noon to 2:30 P.M. and 5:30 to 9 P.M., and on Friday, lunch only, from noon to 2. On Friday night, Shabbat meals are available. Advance booking, as the British say. Tel: 071-388-0801.

Kosher Establishments under Kedasssia Kosher Authority

Amor, (meat), 8 Russell Parade, Golders Green Road, London NW 11. Tel: 020-8458-4221. This restaurant also has take-away.

Milk'n'Honey, (dairy), 124 Golders Green Road, London NW 11. Tel: 020-8455-0664.

Orli Café (dairy), 96 Brent St., London NW4. Tel: 020-8203-7555.

Taboon, (dairy), Russell Parade, Golders Green Road, London NW11. Tel: 020-8455-7451.

Tasti Pizza (dairy), 23 Amhurst Parade, Amhurst Park, London N16. Tel: 020-8209-0023 and 020-8802-0018.

Uncle Shloime's (meat), 204 Stamford Hill, London N16. Tel: 020-8802-9355. This establishment also offers take-away.

Kosher Establishments under the
Federation of Synagogues

Aviv Restaurant, 87 High St., Edgware. Tel: 020-8952-2484.

Cassit, 313 Hale Lane, Edgware, Middlesex. Tel: 020-8958-4955.

Kinneret, 313 Hale Lane, Edgware. Tel: 020-8958-4955.

Macabi, King of Falafel, 59 Wentworth St., London E1. Tel: 020-7247-6660.

Sami's, 157 Brent St., London NW4. Tel: 020-8203-8088.

The White House, 10 Bell Lane, Hendon N.W. 4. Tel: 020-8203-2427.

SYNAGOGUES

Many British Jews, like their co-religionists in the United States, do not want to forget their heritage; hence their many synagogues.

Bevis Marks Synagogue, St. Mary Axe, London EC3. In the East End, this is the oldest Jewish synagogue in England. If you have only one day in London to see Jewish sites, you should make sure to visit this landmark. Services are held on Mondays, Thursdays, and Saturday mornings.

Built in 1701, Bevis Marks is modeled after the Portuguese synagogue in Amsterdam, Holland. It is now a national monument worthy of preservation and located in St. Mary Axe (pronounced "Simmery Axe'). Here is a symbol of the resettlement of the Jews in England in 1656, after having been expelled for 400 years.

Dutch Jews brought the central chandelier from Amsterdam in the late 1600s. On the lectern in front of the Holy Ark are ten great brass candlesticks symbolizing the Ten Commandments. The twelve columns supporting the gallery

Bevis Marks Synagogue, London. (Photo courtesy of the British Tourist Office)

The Holy Ark of the Bevis Marks Synagogue, London. (Photo courtesy of the British Tourist Office)

in the three sides signify the twelve tribes of Israel. Worshippers can sit on the old, highly polished oak benches from the very first synagogue of the resettlement, which was then in Creechurch Lane, a short distance from the present site. The gates are often locked, so visitors wishing to see the Bevis Marks Synagogue should phone ahead. Telephone 624-1274 to check opening hours. Be sure to ask for directions and which entrance to use. The vestry office is at 4 Heneage Lane and the gates are on Houndstitch Street.

Interestingly, according to Carol Herselle Krinsky in *Synagogues of Europe: Architecture, History, Meaning,* Bevis Marks Synagogue was built in a lane because Jews were not allowed to erect a synagogue on Bevis Marks *Street.* Joseph Avis, a Quaker, built the synagogue. When the building costs came to less than the estimate, he returned the difference. Finally, Queen Anne herself is said to have donated a wooden beam for the Bevis Marks Synagogue.

An **Ashkenazic** synagogue that stood in Duke's Place just next door to Bevis Marks was London's chief Ashkenazic place of worship. Called the Duke's Place Shul, it was considered the country's best-known synagogue, and a popular choice for marriages, until it was destroyed in September 1941. The Rothschilds attended services here. A plaque is affixed to International House, which replaced the Duke's Place Shul.

Marble Arch Synagogue, 32 Great Cumberland Pl., West End, London Wl. This synagogue is located in a beautifully designed area by a charming semicircular terrace of houses. Located near many hotels, it is difficult to tell that the building is a house of worship. This Orthodox synagogue took the place of the Great Synagogue on Duke's Place, which was destroyed by German bombers in 1941.

Sephardic Synagogue, Lauderdale Road, Maida Vale, London W9. This famous Spanish-Portuguese synagogue was established in the nineteenth century in a residential section near Paddington Station. A huge dome in the Arabesque style summons Jewish worshippers to prayer. During the service, rabbis and some congregants wear the traditional top hats.

Sephardic Synagogue, 8 St. James Gardens, London W11. Tel: 603-7961. Many of the congregation"s members are from Greece and Turkey.

Central Synagogue, Great Portland Street, London W1. Tel: 020-7580-1355. Here is another synagogue that was destroyed in the blitz of World War II. Today, a modern Orthodox building stands in its place.

Spanish and Portuguese Jews Congregation, 2 Ashworth Rd., London W9 1JY. Tel: 020-7289-2573. This is also the headquarters of the Sephardic community and here the synagogue authorities showed me the registration of circumcision of Benjamin Disraeli, the great British prime minister who shortly before his bar mitzvah was converted by his father to the Church of England (see Statue of Disraeli in "Other Sites" section).

In Stamford Hill, many small Chassidic synagogues dot the area. Here are congregations whose members were born in Morocco, Iran, and India.

Synagogues of the United Synagogue (Orthodox)

The United Synagogue maintains its executive offices at Adler House, 735 High Road, Finchley, London, N12 OUS. Tel: 020-8343-8989. Fax: 020-8343-6262. It is the largest synagogue movement in the United Kingdom. The Chief Rabbinate and its Beth Din administer the religious life of large sections of provincial Jewry. One can also contact that office for more information on synagogue services. Tel: 020-8343-6301. Fax: 020-8343-6310. The Kashrut Division is also housed here. Tel: 020-8343-6250. FAX: 020-8343-6254/6. E-Mail: grossman@kosher.org.uk. The new United Synagogue website gives up-to-date information on kashrut, the calendar, community development, education the Chief Rabbi and a wide range of other news and views, including help lines and useful synagogue location information: www.unitedsynagogue.org.uk.

Chelsea, Smith Terrace, Smith Street, London, SW3. Tel: 020-7747-3931

Dollis Hill, Parkside, Dollis Hill Lane, London NW2.Tel: 020-8958-6777

Edgware, Edgware Way, Edgware, Middlesex. Tel :020-8958-7508

Finchley, Kinloss Gardens, London N33DU.Tel: 020-8346-8551

Golders Green, 41 Dunstan Rd., London NW11 8AE. Tel: 020-8455-2460

Hendon, Raleigh Close, Hendon.Tel: 020-8202-6924.

Ilford, 24 Beehive Lane, Ilford, Essex. Tel: 020-8554-5969

New, Egerton Rd., Stamford Hill, N16. Tel: 020-8800-6003.

New West End, St. Petersburgh Pl., London W2 4JT. Tel: 020-7229-2631

St. John's Wood, 37-41 Grove End Rd., London NW8 9WA. One of Britain's largest synagogues. Tel: 020-7286-6333

South London, 45, Leigham Court Road, London, SW16. Tel: 020-8677-0234

Chabad Houses in London

Lubavitch Foundation, United Kingdom Headquarters, Merkos Menachem, 107-115 Stamford Hill, London, N16 5RP. Tel: 44-20-8800-0022. FAX: 44-20-8809-7324.

Beis Chana, Jewish Womens Centre, 19 Northfield Road, London, N16 5RL. Tel: 44-20-8809-6508.

Chabad on Baker Street, 32 Baker Street, London, W1M 1DG. Tel: 44-20-7486-7077.

Heichal Menachem-Lubavitch, 237 Golders Green Road, London, NW11 9ES.

Chabad House-Southgate, 33 Osidge Lane, London N14 5JL. Tel: 44-20-8361-3044.

Chabad House South London, 42 St. Georges Road, London SW19 4ED. Tel: 44-20-8944-1581. FAX: 44-20-8944-7563.

Lubavitch of Edgware, 230 Hale Lane, Edgware, Middx HA8 9P7. Tel: 44-20-8905-4141. FAX: 44-20-8958-1169.

Chabad Lubavitch Ilford Centre, 372 Cranbrook Road, Ilford, Essex 1G2 6HW. Tel: 44-20-8554-1624. FAX: 44-20-8518-2126

Synagogues of the Beth Din (Orthodox)

Finchley Central, Redbourne Ave., London N3.

Stamford Hill, Beth Hamidrash, 26 Lampard GR., London N16.

Yavneh, 25 Ainsworth Rd., London E9.

Yeshurun, Fernhurst Gardens, Edgware, Middlesex.

Independent, Liberal, Progressive, and Reform Synagogues

Liberal is equivalent to the American Reform Movement of

Judaism and British Reform is similar to the American Conservative Movement of Judaism.

Barkingside Progressive Synagogue (Union of Liberal and Progressive Synagogues), 129 Perrymans Farm Rd., Barkingside, Ilford, Essex. Tel: 020-8554-9682. Friday service, 8 P.M. Saturday, 11 A.M.

Belsize Square Synagogue (Ind), 51 Belsize Square, Hampstead, London NW3. Tel: 020-7794-3949.Friday service, 6:30 P.M. Saturday, 11 A.M.

Ealing Liberal Synagogue,(ULPS) Lynton Avenue, Drayton Green, West Ealing, London. Tel/Fax: 020-8997-0528.

Edgware and District Reform Synagogue (Reform Synagogues of Great Britain), 118 Stonegrove, Edgware, Middlesex HA8 8AB. Friday service, 8 P.M. Saturday, 11 A.M. Tel: 020-8958-9782

Finchley Progressive Synagogue (ULPS), Hutton Grove, Finchley, London N12. Tel: 020-8146-4063.

Finchley Reform Synagogue (RSGB), Fallow Court Ave., Finchley, London N12 OBE. Tel: 020-8446-3244.

Hendon Reform Synagogue (RSGB) Danescroft Ave. Hendon, London, NW4, 2NA.

Kol Chai-Hatch End Jewish Community, (RSGB), 434 Uxbridge Road, Hatch End, Middx,

Liberal Jewish Synagogue (ULPS), 28 St. John's Wood Rd., London NW8. Tel: 020-7286-3591. Friday service, 8 P.M. Saturday, 11 A.M. Located near Regents Park, this is the chief Liberal Synagogue and probably has the largest seating capacity of any British synagogue. Similar to American Reform.

Middlesex New Synagogue, (RSGB) 39 Beesborough Rd., Harrow, Middlesex. Tel: 020-8864-0133. Tel/FAX: 020-8864-0133.

Mill Hill Reform Synagogue(RSGB), 366-A Stag Lane, Henry Harris Centre, Kingsbury, London NW9. Tel: 020-7959-8317.

North London Progressive Synagogue (ULPS), 100 Amhurst Park, Stamford Hill, London N16. Tel: 020-8800-8931. Friday service, 8:15 P.M. Saturday, 11 A.M.

North Western Reform Synagogue (RSGB), Alyth Gardens, Golders Green, London NW11 7EN. Tel: 020-8455-

6763. Friday service, 6:30 P.M. Saturday, 10:30 A.M.

Northwood and Pinner Liberal Synagogue, (ULPS) Oakland Gate, Green Lane, Northwood, Middlesex. Tel: 01923-822592.

Radlett & Bushey Reform Synagogue, (RSGB), 118 Watling St. Radlett, Herts. Tel/Fax: 01923-856110.

Shir Hayim, Hampstead Reform Jewish Community, (RSGB) Hashomer House, 37A Broadhurst Gardens, London, NW63BN. Tel: 020-7794-8488.

South London Liberal Synagogue (ULPS), Prentis Road, Streatham, London SW16. Tel: 020-8769-4787. Friday service, 8:15 P.M. Saturday, 11 A.M.

Southgate Progressive Synagogue (ULPS), 75 Chase Rd., London N14. Tel: 020-8886-0971. Friday service, 8:15 P.M. Saturday, 11 A.M.

West Central Liberal Synagogue (ULPS), 109-13 Whitfield St., London W1P 5RP. Tel: 020-7636-7627. Saturday service, 3 P.M.

West London Synagogue of British Jews (RSGB), Upper Berkeley St., London W1N 6AT. Tel: 020-7723-4404. Friday service, 6 P.M. Saturday, 11 A.M. Located near Hyde Park, this Reform synagogue for Ashkenazim and Sephardim is a fine example of Victorian architecture, and was founded by affluent West End London Jews. It celebrated its 150th anniversary in 1990. Having changed little, it remains one of the prime movers behind the Foundation of the Reform Synagogues of Great Britain, similar to the American Conservative Movement of Judaism. The Foundation consists of 30 other congregations in various parts of the country. The synagogue says its Holy Ark is famous for its open grillwork, which enables one to see the scrolls throughout the service. (Most synagogues cover their arks with a curtain). In the main entrance hall to the synagogue, known as the Goldsmid Hall, there are Memorial Tablets dedicated to the memory of congregants who fell in the world wars.

Westminster Synagogue (Ind), Kent House, Rutland Gardens, London SW7 1BX. Tel: 020-7584-3953. Friday service, 6:30 P.M.; Saturday, 11 P.M. Housed here in the Czech Memorial Scrolls are 1,564 Torahs from the Jewish Museum in Prague, Czech Republic, in the Czech Memorial Scrolls Center, which is open to visitors on Tuesdays and Thursdays from 10 to 4 and at other times by appointment. Please let the center know you are planning a visit. Tel: 071-584-3953/3741.

Wimbledon & District Synagogue, (RSGB) 1 Wueensmere Rd., Wimbledon Park Side, London, SW195QD.Tel: 020-8946-4836.

Assembly of Masorti Synagogues
Conservative Synagogues in England

Edgware Synagogue, Baker Path, Edgware, Middlesex, HA8 7YA. Tel: 020-8905-4096.

New Essex Congregation, Roding Valley Hall, Station Way Buckhurst Hill, Essex. Tel: 020-8506-6873.

New London Synagogue, 33 Abbey Road, St. John's Wood, London, NW8 0AT. Tel: 020-7328-1026.

New North London Synagogue, The Manor House, 80 East End Road, London. Tel: 020-8346-8560.

New Whetstone Synagogue, Henriques House, 120 Oakleigh Road North, Whetstone, N20. Tel: 020-8445-2671.

Hendon Masorti Minyan, Bell Lane, JMI School, Hendon NW4. Tel: 020-8202-9058.

Headquarters of Synagogue Governing Bodies

Adath Yisroel, 40 Queen Elizabeth's Walk, No. 16, London N16 OHH. Tel: 020-7802-6226/7.

Chief Rabbinate Headquarters, Adler House, 735 High Road, Finchley, London, N12 OUS. Tel: 020-8343-6301. Fax::020-8343-6310 Adler House, the office of the chief rabbinate and the London Beth Din. The building is named after Dr. Herman Adler, chief rabbi of the Empire and son of Dr. Nathan Marcus Adler. British Chief Rabbi Dr. Nathan Marcus Adler (1803-90) established Jews' College in 1855 and the Jewish Board of Guardians in 1859. In 1866, he helped create the United Synagogue.

Rabbi Jonathan Sacks is chief rabbi of Great Britain.

Some say that out of the 300,000 British Jews, the Orthodox number about 100,000, the Progressive Liberal (i.e., Reform and Conservative) about 60,000, and the rest—about 50 percent—are unaffiliated.

Edgware Adath Yisroel, 261 Hale Lane, Edgware, Middlesex. This is a Union of Orthodox Hebrew Congregations synagogue.

Federation of Synagogues, 65 Watford Way, Hendon, London. Tel: 020-8202-2263. FAX: 020-8203-0610. The second largest synagogue body in England is the Federation of Synagogues, boasting a membership of 17,000 in some 50 branches. As an Orthodox group, it set up independent courts of Jewish justice, as did the Union of Orthodox Hebrew Congregations and the Reform and Liberal movements of Judaism.

Lubavitch Foundation, Lubavitch House, 107-15 Stamford Hill, London N16. Tel: 020-8800-0022. This is the group's regional headquarters.

Reform Synagogues of Great Britain, The Sternberg Center for Judaism., The Manor House, 80 East End Rd., Finchley, London N3 2SY. Tel: 020-8349-5640. FAX: 020-8343-0901. Similar to American Conservative Movement of Judaism.

Spanish and Portuguese Synagogue, 2 Ashworth Rd., London W9 1JY. Tel: 289-2573. Located here is the Sephardic Kashrut Authority.

Union of Liberal and Progressive Synagogues, 109 Whitfield St., London W1P 5RP. Tel: 020-7580-1663. This is also the headquarters of the World Union for Progressive Judaism (European Board). Tel: 020-7637-7442.

United Synagogue, 735 High Road, Finchley, London, N12 0US. Tel: 020-8343-8989. FAX: 020-8343-6262.

Assembly of Masorti Synagogues, Conservative Synagogues in England, 1097 Finchley Road, London, NW 11 0PU. Tel: 020-8201-8772. FAX: 020-8201-8917.

ORGANIZATIONS

Agudas Israel, Golders Green Road, London NW11. Tel: 020-8458-8424.

Association for Jewish Youth, 50 Lindley St., London E1 3AX. Tel: 020-7790-6407. Information on youth groups can be obtained here.

B'nai B'rith Hillel House, 1/2 Endsleigh St., London WC1. Tel: 020-7387-4644 or 020-7380-0111.

Institute of Jewish Affairs, 11 Hertford St., London W1Y 7DX. Tel: 020-7491-3517.

Jewish Agency, Balfour House, 741 High Rd., London N12 OB9. Tel: 01-446-1477.

Jewish Historical Society of England, 33 Seymour Pl. London W1H 5AP.

Maccabi World Union, North Ends Road, London NW11 7GY Tel: 020-7458-9488/9.

WIZO, 107 Gloucester Pl., London W1. Tel: 020-7486-2691.

World Jewish Congress, 11 Hertford St., London W1Y 7DX. Tel: 020-8491-3517.

MUSEUMS AND LIBRARIES

British Museum, Great Russell Street, Bloomsbury, London WC1. Tel: 020-7636-1555. The Hebrew Library here contains about 50,000 volumes and 3,000 manuscripts including material from ancient Palestine. At times, letters from Benjamin Disraeli are shown. Also permanent exhibits contain archeological finds from the Middle East as well as a philatelic collection of early twentieth-century stamps, including pre-Israel Independence Palestine stamps. The British Museum contains the Balfour Declaration. On November 2, 1917, Foreign Secretary Arthur James Balfour wrote a letter to Lord Rothschild declaring, "His Majesty's Government view with favor the establishment in Palestine of a national home for the Jewish people."

Lord Balfour was interested in Zionism, perhaps as a result of a meeting with Dr. Chaim Weizmann in Manchester. Weizmann had persuaded the British government and influenced Lord Arthur Balfour to favor the establishment of a Jewish state in Palestine. A distinguished scholar and scientist, Weizmann studied chemistry in Germany and Switzerland and as a British subject, he admired England and English ways.

A leading British chemist, he had served as director of the laboratories of the British Admiralty and was instrumental in the "perfection of the most subtle and complex method of obtaining alcohol from wood, at a time when this material, absolutely vital for the production of explosives, was becoming impossible to obtain in sufficient quantities, because of the submarine campaign of the abnormal conditions of war"! After the Balfour Declaration, he became the leader of the World Zionist Movement and is considered a great Jewish statesman. He was named the first president of the State of Israel.

The **Jewish Museum**, Raymond Burton House, 129-131, Albert Street, Camden, London, NW17NB. Tel: 020-7284-1997. FAX: 020-7267-9008.This museum is open from Sunday through Thursday, 10 A.M. to 4 P.M. A wonderful exhibit of British Jewry covers the history of the Jews on this island from 1066 until the expulsion by King Edward I. Also shown is an exhibit of British Jewish history from the days of Oliver Cromwell. Artifacts are displayed. Portraits of Jewish leaders are shown.

Browsing through the framed documents, you might ask museum officials to show you etchings of Levi Salomons, father of Sir David Salomons, the first Jewish lord mayor of London, who was elected to his post in 1855. This and other pieces are representative of British artifacts.

Ask to see an etching or painting of Manasseh Ben Israel. He led the fight for readmission to England. Born to Marrano parents in Madeira in 1604, he was baptized Manoel Dias Soeiro. His family moved to Amsterdam. Upon their arrival, they announced they were Jews. After studying with Rabbi Isaac Uziel, Manasseh was ordained a rabbi. He taught, wrote essays, and edited books, many of them for Christian audiences. He even corresponded with English religious leaders and intellectuals. Much of his motivation was mystical. You see, Manasseh had met a Jew named Antonio (Aaron) de Montezinos, who had told him that he had discovered Jews in America. Manasseh theorized that since Jews were now living in America, they were residents of every country on earth except one, that one of course being England. To make the dispersion cycle complete, and help the Messianic movement reach fulfillment, the Jews needed to reside in Britain. Then the Messiah would come and the Jews would return to their homeland—Palestine. During the conference to decide whether to admit Jews, Manasseh made a logical case for Jewish admission. He argued that wherever Jews live, they develop new branches of economy and trade flourishes. The meeting ended in a so-called compromise, with no official declaration, but it meant Jews were allowed to enter. However, Manasseh, who had fought so hard, took it as a personal defeat. He felt the compromise was a sham. He called for a formal recall of the Jewish people to England. When this did not happen, he returned to Amsterdam, where he died a broken man. He was buried in the cemetery at Ouderkerk, close to the Amstel River, not far from his father, Joseph Ben Israel, and near his teacher, Rabbi Isaac Uziel.

The **Sternberg Centre for Judaism: The Manor House,** 80 East End Rd., Finchley, London N3 2SY. Tel: 020-8349-4731 or FAX: 8349-1143. Also known as The Manor House, this active institution is located on a seven-and-a-half-acre site in North London. Various organizations can be found here, including: **The Manor House Society,** which provides Jewish cultural and intellectual events and publishes a quarterly magazine, Manna; **The Leo Baeck College,** a rabbinical seminary for Britain's Progressive (Reform and Liberal) movements; **Progressive Jewish Students** and **SATMAH,** for college and university students; **The Centre for Jewish Education;** the **Akiva Primary School;** a synagogue; a biblical garden; and a number of other communal organizations.

Located here is part of the former **Jewish Museum,** which was housed in Woburn House. Exhibitions here tend not to go back further than the 19th century when dealing with Jewish History in England. The exhibits here deal with the social history of British Jewry.

To illustrate current Jewish life, history, and religion, there are many visual aids and filmstrips for the numerous Jewish and non-Jewish religious classes that visit the museum.

The Ben Uri Art Society exhibits works by Jewish artists and has also moved to the Sreinberg Center.

The Manor House Bookstore is open Monday through

Thursday, 10 to 4; Sunday, 10 to 2. This well-stocked bookstore has a wide range of books of Jewish interest, educational materials, and Jewish artifacts.

The **Freud Museum**, 20 Maresfield Gardens, Hampstead, London. Tel: 01-435-2002. This museum houses mementos of both Sigmund Freud, founder of psychoanalysis, and his daughter, Anna Freud, a leading authority on child psychoanalysis. In 1938, Sigmund Freud fled the Nazis in Vienna and settled in this house as a refugee. He brought with him his household furnishings, his books, and a collection of about 1,800 classical Egyptian and Oriental antiques. During his last days in 1939, he often asked that his bed be brought downstairs so he could enjoy the garden view. Anna Freud died in 1982. The museum is open Wednesday through Sunday, from noon until 5 P.M.

Institute of Contemporary History and the Weiner Library, 4 Devonshire St., London W1. Tel: 020-7636-7247. This library probably contains more than 50,000 books and periodicals and hundreds of thousands of newspaper clippings on Nazism and the Holocaust.

Jews' College, Albert Road, Hendon, London NW4 2SJ. Founded in 1855, coursework at this college leads to graduate degrees as well as rabbinical ordination. Includes a magnificent library of more than 80,000 volumes.

Leo Baeck College, Sternberg Centre for Judaism, The Manor House, 80 East End Rd., London N3 2SY. Tel: 020-8349-4525.

Library of the Spanish and Portuguese Synagogue, Lauderdale Road, London W9.

Mocatta Library and Museum, University College, Gower Street, London WC1. Sponsored by the Jewish Historical Society, it contains a wonderful Hebraica and Judaica section in the Guild Hall Library. Abraham Mocatta was a leader of the Bevis Marks Synagogue. The family originally came from Spain and the Mediterranean area. The Mocattas were among the first Jews in England, as well as founders of the Bevis Marks congregation. West London Synagogue. They were active on the Jewish Board of Deputies.

Museum of the Jewish East End, Sternberg Centre for Judaism, The Manor House, 80 East End Rd., London N3 2SY.

OTHER SITES

Selfridge's Department Store, 400 Oxford St., London W1, maintains a Jewish book section, as well as a scrumptious kosher food department.

The Statue of Benjamin Disraeli in Westminster Abbey. One of the most popular tourist sites in England is Westminster Abbey, which is the burial site, as well as house of statues, of Great Britain's greatest heroes, scholars, and politicians. In the Statesmen's Corner of the Abbey, next to former Prime ministers Peel and Gladstone, stands a statue of Benjamin Disraeli (1804-81). The guides usually tell you that Benjamin Disraeli was born a Jew, but he was converted by his father.

He was born at **No 22. Theobalds Rd.** There is also a statue of Benjamin Disraeli facing Parliament. He died at 19 Curzon St., London W1, in 1881. A plaque was erected on the building. Disraeli was a statesman, one of the greatest prime ministers of the United Kingdom, and a prolific writer and novelist. Among his books were *Vivian Grey, Alroy, Sybil,* and *Coningsby*. There are Jewish themes in many of his books. In the novel *Tancred,* Disraeli spoke out in favor of national independence of the Jews.

Just before his bar mitzvah, he was baptized by his writer-historian father, Isaac D'Israeli, after the latter had a quarrel with the Sephardic synagogue. The congregation had asked Isaac to serve on the board of trustees and Isaac refused. In those days, if you turned down your position, you had to pay a fine. Isaac refused again and left the congregation.

Even though Benjamin Disraeli was one of the most brilliant diplomats, and even though he was a regular church communicant, he never hid his Jewish origin and sympathies. As Disraeli liked to tell it, the family actually came from Italy, not Spain. "He believed that the Jews, by their virtue and their glorious past, were entitled to special esteem, and he devoted his tremendous audacity and imagination to securing it for them," writes Paul Johnson. Many say that, in Parliament, he spoke as if he were a Jew. He did much to improve the general social and political position of the Jews. As a young man, he had visited the Near East and Jerusalem.

Disraeli boasted of the "superiority of the Jewish race" as a storehouse of energy and vision. He believed Jews were the "aristocrats of mankind." He is quoted as saying, "The most inspiring singers, most graceful dancers and most delicate musicians are the sons and daughters of Israel." He once told Montefiore, "You and I belong to a race that can do everything but fail."

He was a great friend of the Rothschilds. With the financial help of the Rothschilds, he acquired the Egyptian khedive's shares in the Suez Canal to make sure England controlled the vital route to India. This action brought England right smack into the Middle East, next door to Palestine, which the British, under General Allenby, conquered in 1917 during World War I.

Perhaps Disraeli had indeed studied the map. Some historians say that in his bringing England into Egypt and closer to Palestine, perhaps he actually had in mind eventually to plant Britain in Palestine and thus be able to establish a Jewish state. Farfetched? Did not General Allenby invade Palestine from Egypt a half-century later?

His other great diplomatic victory was at the 1878 Congress of Berlin, when he prevented war in Eastern Europe.

Benjamin Disraeli presided at No. 10 Downing Street, the office of the Prime Minister, when it was the seat of the greatest empire the world had ever seen.

He got along splendidly with Queen Victoria, who laid a wreath upon his tomb. The marble tablet placed in the chancel of Hughenden Church after his death says, "To the Dear and Honored Memory of Benjamin, Earl of Beaconsfield. This memorial is placed by His Grateful Sovereign and Friend, Victoria, R.I. Kings love him that speaketh right."

The Statue of Cromwell. In Parliament Square stands the statue of Oliver Cromwell, the "Lord Protector" of England. He had a great deal to do with the Jewish return to England in 1656 after a 400-year absence. Indeed the Standard Jewish Encyclopaedia states that Manasseh Ben Israel's mission to England to petition for the readmission of Jews was probably undertaken at Cromwell's suggestion. Manasseh realized that Cromwell, a Puritan, viewed the Jews favorably and supported their readmission. To Cromwell it made good business sense. Cromwell had hoped to extend Britain's influence and its wealth, and to make England "number one" in Europe. He knew that Jews, as well as Marranos (secret Jews), had enriched other nations, including Holland, whose ships were out-trading the English. He hoped the Jews would do the same for England.

In December 1656, Cromwell convened the Whitehall Conference to consider the matter of the Jews. He himself presided over the opening session. He liked Manasseh Ben Israel, whose speech before the council was one of the most eloquent in Jewish history. It was called "Esperanca de Israel" ("The Hope of Israel"). But Cromwell later dissolved the conference when he realized the council's decision would be a resounding "no" to allowing Jewish immigration. Since he had the power, he could have rammed an admission bill through the meeting. Instead, he connived to allow the Jews to enter the country and stay, giving up attempts to permit their immigration on a formal basis—in short, a compromise.

Soon Jews were permitted to hold services in rented rooms. Later, they would be allowed to build their first synagogue in Creechurch Lane. In the spring of 1656, Cromwell received and granted a petition from the Marranos to establish a cemetery outside of London. Under Cromwell, Marranos obtained seats on the London Stock Exchange. From these trader families, the Jewish community created a network of other families who were prominent in banking, finance, and commerce.

The Statue of Winston Churchill. Near Parliament stands the statue of Winston Churchill. During World War II, Churchill was the voice of the free world. He uplifted men and women all over the globe. He was a leader. As you look at his statue, you cannot but admire this great man who rallied the people all over the world against Nazism. His patriotism, it is said, "was rooted in the very soil of the history of England."

Churchill was an ardent Zionist. His influence established the Jewish Brigade of Palestine in World War II. Churchill once wrote to Franklin D. Roosevelt, "I am strongly wedded to the Zionist policy, of which I was one of the authors." He was a bitter opponent of England's White Paper, which, in 1939, severely limited Jewish immigration and closed off Palestine as a refuge. But, as William Manchester notes, he was "unrepresentative of England's upper class, for even England was not free of anti-Semitism."

John Lukacs writes in his book, *The Duel,* that in 1938, when

Churchill was in such debt that he was about to sell his beloved country house, Chartwell, Sir Henry Strakosch, a London financier of Jewish ancestry, "paid off his debts." Jewish groups would often cite Churchill for his "courageous defense of freedom and denunciation of Nazism." But even with Churchill's sympathy, it was always an uphill battle to establish the Zionist dream of a Jewish homeland. European Jews who were trapped during the war could not emigrate because most countries refused to admit Jews. And several ships, such as the Patria, were sunk because the English refused permission to dock in Palestine. Even after World War II, when Churchill was out of power, the British Labor Party resisted the establishment of a Jewish nation. It appeared that nothing could sway them, not even the death of the six million Jews.

Yet in the face of world opinion in favor of a Jewish state, the British finally relented. After the U. N. Partition Plan of November 1947, they left Palestine forever in 1948, bitter to the end. Almost six decades later, many Israelis say the British treated them not as colonial subjects but as human beings. Aspects of the Israeli parliament, judiciary, and bureaucracy are all patterned after the British, under whom the Jews developed self-government.

Wingate and Chindit Memorial. Victoria Embankment, outside the Ministry of Defence, London. This monument stands in honor of Maj. Gen. Orde Wingate and his Chindit forces of the Burma campaign during World War II. Wingate, friend of the Jews, some say "hero" of the Jews, helped train the Palmach, the "shock troops," of Haganah, the self-defense army of Israel during the British Mandate in Palestine.

Brighton and Hove

Perhaps it is the Royal Pavilion, which houses a museum and art gallery; or the Dome area, which is used for concerts and conferences; or the Lanes and those famous antique shops that attract thousands. Maybe it is the boardwalk, the beaches, and the piers, but whatever the specific attraction, tourists are lured to this wonderful seaside resort on the English Channel, 51 miles south of London.

Many Jews commute from here to London each day, vacation here in the summer, and are active in the community, which has about 12,000 Jews, including a large number of retirees originally from London.

In the middle of the eighteenth century, the town became famous as a resort and wealthy Jews settled here, including the Goldsmids and Sassoons. But the bulk of Jews probably did not settle here until about 1800.

SYNAGOGUES IN BRIGHTON AND HOVE

Synagogue, 66 Middle St., Brighton. Tel: 27785. Brighton is also famous for this synagogue. It is a lovely, small synagogue consecrated in 1875, well known for its interior design.

Brighton & Hove Liberal Jewish Synagogue, 6 Landsdowne Rd., Hove. Tel: 737-223.

Orthodox Synagogue, Holland Road, Hove. Tel: 732-035.

Reform Synagogue, 65 Palmeira Ave., Hove. Tel: 735-343.

Synagogue, 29 New Church Rd., West Hove.

Chabad House, 15 The Upper Drive, Hove, East Sussex BN3 6GR. Tel: 1273-321-919. FAX: 1273-821-518.

LODGING

The Hideaway Helmdon, 1 Furse Hill, Hove BN3 1PA. Tel: 772-038. This is a kosher boardinghouse in Hove.

Manchester

Manchester is often considered the prototypical city of the Industrial Revolution, and the first Jewish settlers arrived here from Liverpool in the eighteenth century. Nathan Mayer Rothschild's first residence in England was in Manchester, from where he exported cotton goods from 1798 to 1805. The large Jewish immigration came here between 1881 and 1914, generally tailors and capmakers. Lord Marks, founder of Marks and Spencer and one of the greatest leaders of the

Zionist movement in Britain, was born in Manchester. In addition to the Manchester Jews who came to the city from Russia and Poland, a large number came here from the Middle East and established the important Sephardic congregations of South Manchester. From 1904 to 1917, Manchester was the home of Dr. Chaim Weizmann, the great Zionist leader and first president of Israel. Here he conducted his early scientific experiments and met the future leaders of the Zionist movement.

There are many synagogues in Manchester, the second largest Jewish community in Great Britain, with a Jewish population of about 35,000.

The Manchester Jewish Museum is located on the premises of the former Spanish and Portuguese Synagogue at 190 Cheetham Hill Rd., Manchester M88LW. Tel: 061-834-9879. The building, completed in 1874, is listed as being of historical importance. The ground floor of the structure has not been altered in any significant way, and is no longer used for worship services. A traveler can visit this remarkable synagogue. The former ladies' gallery now houses the permanent exhibition in which the history of Manchester's Jewish community, now more than 200 years old, is vividly brought to life. Homes, schools, and workshops of long ago have been recreated in detail to portray the lives of ordinary people. The museum opened in 1984. It is open Monday through Thursday, 10:30 A.M. to 4 P.M., and Sunday, 10:30 A.M. to 5 P.M.

The first Jewish school was founded in 1842.

An interesting site is the library in St. Peters Square, which has an excellent Jewish collection.

Fulda's Hotel is a kosher hotel located at 84 Bury Old Rd. in Sulford. Tel: 740-4551.

Lubavitch House Manchester, 62 Singleton Road, Salford, Manchester M7 4LU. Tel: 161-740-9514.

Lubavitch of South Manchester, 2a Old Market Place, Altrincham, Cheshire WA14 4NP. Tel: 161-929-9999, 161-929-9020. FAX: 161-929-7707.

Cheetham Hebrew Congregation, 453-455 Cheetham Hill Road, Manchester, M8 9PA, Tel: 740-7788.

Manchester Reform Synagogue, Jackson Row, Albert Square, Manchester M2 5NH. Tel: 834-0514 FAX: 834-0415.

Manchester Jewish Museum. (Photo by Dr. Gene Sosin)

A special notice of the Manchester Beth Din as shown in the Manchester Jewish Museum. (Photo by Dr. Gene Sosin)

A plaque commemorating Dr. Chaim Weizmann, the first President of Israel, who resided in Manchester from 1904 to 1917. (Photo by Dr. Gene Sosin)

Oxford

There is an old British expression that everyone journeys to Oxford sooner or later. Oxford is a city of all seasons, a city of learning and scholarship, and above all, a city built upon books, "books being read, books being written, books being published." This "sweet city with her dream spires" supports a labyrinth of libraries and dozens of bookstores.

The **Oxford Center for Post-Graduate Hebrew Studies**, 45 Giles St., Oxford OX1 3LP. Mix together a former British country estate, one of the world's greatest universities, nine cottages for Israeli and American Jewish writers, and a college junior-year-abroad program in Jewish studies, and you have an advanced research institute of Judaic studies. The university is Oxford, in the town of Oxford, 56 miles by road from London. The Jewish institute, located just four miles outside the City of Oxford, is the Oxford Center for Post-Graduate Hebrew Studies.

Yarnton Manor, a seventeenth-century manor house that once belonged to the Spencer family from whom Diana, Princess of Wales, was descended, is used for lectures, symposia, seminars, and conferences. At the manor are the Kressel Library and Archives. The library contains 35,000 volumes; the archives contain approximately one-half-million newspaper clippings.

Oxford still remains one of the great centers of England. Historically, Jews came down here from London to sell hats, frocks, and shoes. And now, too, Jewish scholars and students of Judaism are coming to Oxford University, to the Oxford Center for Post-Graduate Hebrew Studies.

These scholars have produced more than 350 academic and literary items, including 80 books, as a result of their stay. Such famous works of Hebrew literature as A. B. Yehoshua's *The Lover* and T. Carmi's *The Penguin Book of Hebrew Verse* were written, in whole or in part, at the center. Other writers who have worked here include Benyamin Tammuz, the Israeli novelist, who wrote *Minotaur* in the Apple Loft, one of the Yarnton Manor's estate cottages. In its English translation, *Minotaur* was chosen by the late Graham Greene as one of the three best novels of 1981.

Dr. David Patterson, founder and president of the center, Cowley Lecturer in Post-Biblical Hebrew, and fellow of St. Cross College in Oxford University, stresses that, during World War II, about 750 institutions of Jewish learning in Europe were lost forever. He recalls that when he started the center, he received the warm support of such leading scholars as Sir Isaiah Berlin and Professor David Daube, the former Regius Professor of Civil Law at Oxford University.

In an interview, Dr. Patterson told me that he knew that Oxford was exceptionally well qualified to serve the needs of an international center for Jewish learning. After all, the chair in Hebrew was established by Henry VIII, and Hebrew has been taught there in an unbroken tradition for more than 450 years since then.

Bodleian Library. Thousands of Hebrew books, handwritten Bibles, priceless Judaica, and manuscripts are located in the Bodleian Library, one of the outstanding libraries in the world. One estimate quotes that more than 30,000 Hebrew volumes are housed here.

Synagogue and Jewish Center, 21 Richmond Rd., Oxford OX1 2JL. Tel: 08-655-3042.

L'Chaim Society Center, 121 St. Aldate's, Carfax, Oxford. This is the Jewish student union, which sponsors speakers and other events.

Chabad House, 75 Crowley Road, Oxford OX4 1HR. Tel: 44-1865-200-158.

B. H. Blackwell, Ltd., 48-51 Broad St., Oxford OX1 3BQ. This impressive and large bookshop contains a Judaica section.

York

Clifford's Tower of York Castle. A tragic episode occurred in York on the Sabbath before Passover, March 16, 1190, the day preceding Palm Sunday. It took place at Clifford's Tower, located just across from the museum. The tragedy was described thusly: At Easter, villagers launched a whispering campaign that Jews were killing Christian children so they could use their blood for Passover rites. Frightened, the Jews of York, headed by Rabbi Yom Tov of Joigny, fled to the castle.

Rather than surrender, they decided to kill each other. Given a so-called safe conduct, a few survivors left the castle. "Kill the Jews," yelled the villagers. After butchering the survivors, they quickly burned the financial debt notes owed to the Jewish moneylenders. York Jewry never recovered from the killings. Today, only about 45 Jews live in York. For an admission fee, one can climb to the top. Open March 15 to October 15, Monday through Friday, 9:30 A.M. to 6:30 P.M. Sundays, 2-4:00 P.M. in summer.

Suggested Reading

Bermant, Chaim. *The Cousinhood.* New York: Macmillan, 1971.

Blake, Robert. *Disraeli.* London: Methuen, 1969.

—. *Disraeli's Grand Tour: Benjamin Disraeli and the Holy Land, 1830-31.* New York: Oxford University Press, 1982.

Corbett, W. *Jews and the Jews of England.* Gordon, 1976.

Hyamson, Albert M. *A History of the Jews in England.* Chatto and Windus, 1908.

Litvinoff, Barnet. *The Burning Bush: Anti-Semitism and World History.* New York: Dutton, 1988.

Morris, James. *Oxford.* New York: Harcourt, Brace & World, 1965.

Morton, H. V. *In Search of London.* New York: Dodd, Mead, 1951.

Wasserstein, Bernard. *Britain and the Jews of Europe, 1939-1945.* New York: Oxford University Press, 1979.

Weintraub, Stanley. *Disraeli: A Biography.* New York: Truman Talley Blochs/Dutton, 1993.

Ireland
Dublin Has Had Jewish Mayors

They call it "Bloomsday" and it remains the major literary festival of Ireland. It celebrates the birthday of Leopold Bloom, the son of a Hungarian Jew and the hero in *Ulysses*, James Joyce's novel that depicts certain elements of Jewish life in Dublin at the beginning of the 20th century. Joyce stands as Dublin's most famous writer and Dublin remains the center of the Jewish community of Ireland.

The Jews of Ireland, most of whom live in Dublin, conduct a meaningful Jewish life with many activities. This Jewish community supports Orthodox synagogues, a large variety of religious, charitable, Zionist, and educational institutions, a religious school, and a museum. Relations between the Jewish community and the Catholic and Protestant populations are good.

A Brief History

The Irish love to link Ireland with biblical tradition, as well as to the ancient Jews. "Legends that the Irish are the Ten Lost Tribes of Israel can prove very convincing when delivered in the midst of a peat bog and when shown the genuine Jacob's ladder to heaven in a secret cave near the Lakes of Killarney," writes Asher Benson, Dublin correspondent for the London *Jewish Chronicle*.

The earliest known reference to Jews in Ireland is in A.D. 613

when St. Columbanus penned an epistle to the pope of Rome, and smugly reported, "None of us has been a heretic, none of us a Jew." In the year 1079, five Jews came over the sea with gifts and were refused entry. Jews were forbidden to land in Ireland in the fifteenth and sixteenth centuries, although Marranos probably resided there.

After an absence of several hundred years, a number of Jewish families of Spanish and Portuguese descent and two or three of Polish or German origin settled in Dublin around 1660.

But Jews did not flock to Ireland in large numbers until after Cromwell permitted them to return to England in 1656. Marranos from London were the first Irish Jewish settlers. In the middle of the seventeenth century, more Marranos settled in the city. Thus, by the first quarter of the eighteenth century, Dublin was the only city in Ireland that had an organized Jewish community. And they came, according to Louis Hyman, because Dublin was the second city of the British Empire and the city was an excellent trading post, with a high society rivaling the heyday of Paris. Eighteenth-century Dublin was a vital, innovative capital.

In 1717, a Jewish cemetery was set up and a synagogue was founded in 1746.

Throughout the eighteenth century, the Irish tried often to convert the Jews of Dublin. According to one testimonial, "the people of this Kingdom constantly rejoice when they see a Jew convert."

About 200 Jews lived in Dublin in 1750. But the failure of the Irish banks in 1727 and the famine of 1748 would hurt the city, including the Jews. Many Jews fled the severe famine, leaving only a few Jewish families in Dublin in the early nineteenth century. In 1816, the Irish Naturalization Act of 1783, from which the Jews had been excluded, was repealed: Jews could now be naturalized in Ireland. Dublin grew again in 1822 with the arrival of Polish and German Jews, most of whom had lived in England, writes Hyman. "In their struggle for political emancipation, the Jews of England found many a champion in Ireland," he adds.

But in the winter of 1845-46, Ireland again was stricken by a potato famine, which left a giant graveyard. One million persons fled to America. The relief measures taken by an unprepared government were almost useless, but there was outside aid in which British and American Jews were prominent. An Irish famine-loan of 8 million British pounds was negotiated by Baron Lionel Rothschild of London, who waived all commission.

After 1882, the Russian Jews arrived and firmly established the Jewish community. They settled in Cork, Limerick, Londonderry, and Waterford. In 1881, there were 472 Jews. By 1901, that figure rose to 3,769.

While the Jewish community maintained neutrality during Ireland's fight for independence, Dublin Jews sheltered many Irish revolutionaries and individual Jews took a leading part in the rebellion, Robert Briscoe among them. Briscoe later became lord mayor of Dublin.

In 1918, the office of the chief rabbi of Eire was established and Rabbi Isaac Herzog (1889-1959) was appointed. He later served as the first Ashkenazi chief rabbi of Israel. Rabbi Herzog was recognized as one of the great rabbinical scholars of his time. He was rabbi in Belfast from 1916 to 1919 and in Dublin until 1936, receiving the title of chief rabbi of the Irish Free State after 1921. He was a friend of Eamon deValera, the Irish leader and prime minister. His son, Chaim, was president of Israel from May 1983 to May 1993.

Belfast-born Chaim Herzog also served Israel as a former intelligence officer, military commentator, military attaché to Washington, and Israel's ambassador to the United Nations.

When Ireland became independent in 1921, the Jews set up their own community council. The 1937 Constitution of the Republic recognized Judaism as a minority faith and guaranteed Jews complete freedom from discrimination.

Israel's independence occurred on May 14, 1948. But, Ireland waited until February 12, 1949, to accord de facto recognition of Israel. In 1995 Ireland finally established diplomatic relations with Israel.

Jewish Dublin

Jews live in Dublin because it is a business center, vacation destination, and port city. It is a city of writers, revolutionaries, and talkers—a city of memories possessing a tragic and yet glorious history.

About 1,200 Jews live in Ireland, most of them in Dublin. A half dozen Jewish families reside in Cork. Once, during World War II, more than 15,000 Jews lived in the country, most of them in Dublin. When there was a large Jewish community, Jews lived in the South Circular Road section. That area was called the Jewish "Little Jerusalem." In 1961, there were 3,255 Jews in Ireland. That number declined to 2,633 in 1971, mostly because of a fall in the birthrate and emigration to Israel. Contemporary demographics indicate the population is shrinking.

SITES IN DUBLIN

Birthplace of Leopold Bloom, 52 Upper Clanbrassil St., Dublin 8. This building is supposedly the birthplace of James Joyce's famous character in Ulysses.

Bloomfield House, Bloomfield Avenue, Dublin 8. This was formerly the Jewish Day School.

Clonyn Castle, Delvin, County Westmeath. More than 100 Jewish orphaned children from concentration camps had a temporary home here until 1948.

The Irish Jewish Museum, 3 and 4 Walworth Rd., Dublin 8. Tel: 453-1797. The museum is near Circular Road. Phone ahead to make sure the museum is open.

Do not be shocked, dear reader, when you enter the **Jewish Museum** at 4 Walworth, near Circular Road, Dublin. Two photographs stare at you: the Lubavitch Rebbe and James Joyce. The Museum contains photos, articles, and documents. The Irish Jewish Museum officially was opened on June 20, 1985, by the then-president of Israel, Chaim Herzog. The building is located in the former Walworth Road Synagogue, which has been completely restored.

In planning the layout of the museum in the existing premises, a division was made between the secular and religious. The secular exhibition has been mounted downstairs in the reception hall of the former synagogue. The displays trace the history of the Jews in Ireland beginning with their arrival, their various commercial and professional activities, the development of their institutions, and their integration to their present position and status.

Upstairs, at the rear of the synagogue in the Harold Smerling Gallery, there is a display of ritual and religious items.

Some of the exhibition topics are James Joyce and the Jewish characters and references in his novels; Jews in Irish provincial cities; anti-Semitism; the Holocaust; Irish Jews and families in public life, in the professions, and in business; the Jewish wedding; women in Judaism; and ritual objects.

Most people, when they think about Irish Jews, do not consider their artistic achievements. Perhaps the most unique aspect of a visit to this museum is to discover that Irish Jewry, which never numbered more than 6,000 persons, and now numbers about 1,200, produced talented painters. Works by Harry Kernoff, David Eichenstein, Estella Solomons, Gerald Davis, and others, are on display. A cabinet of books written by Irish Jews is a highlight of the exhibit.

The museum abounds in material regarding families and personalities. The lives of the chief rabbis are also portrayed. A favorite exhibit is "Irish Jews in Public Life." One such personality, of course, is Robert Briscoe (1894-1969), the first Jewish member of the Irish Parliament and the first Jewish lord mayor of Dublin. He fought for Irish independence in the IRA from 1917 to 1924. One of the few Jews in the IRA, he was a member of Eamon de Valera's party from 1927 to 1965. He supported Revisionist Zionism. Briscoe wrote a book, *For the Life of Me*, which was published in 1958, the year he was elected mayor of Dublin. "All the time I was growing up," he states, "I was being steeped in the dark, stormy, racked, light, short history of my country of Eire."

Through the Easter uprising, the terror, the Black and Tans, the controversial treaty with England, and the civil war, Briscoe—who claimed he was the only Jew in the IRA—fought for Irish independence. Some say he taught Vladimir Ze'ev Jabotinsky, Revisionist Zionist leader, guerrilla tactics he learned while fighting the British. He had listened to

Jabotinsky address groups in Ireland. In his book, he tells how he pioneered and helped raise money for the famous "coffin ships" that smuggled thousands of Jews into Palestine. He said he regarded Zionism as a magnificent inspiration.

His son, Benjamin Briscoe, was Dublin's lord mayor from 1988 to 1989. He was then elected to Parliament from his father's constituency.

The Jewish Old Aged Home, Denmark Hill, Leinster Road West, Rathmines, Dublin 6. Tel: 497-6258. This home was founded in 1950. Services are held here; times vary according to season and needs of senior citizens.

Memorial to the Six Million Jews, in the synagogue grounds between 32 and 34 Rathfarnham Rd., Dublin 6. This monument remembers those Jews who perished in the Holocaust.

Office of the Chief Rabbi and Community Centre, Herzog House, 1 Zion Rd., Dublin 6. Tel: 492-3751.

Rabbi Herzog's Home, 33 Bloomfield Ave., Dublin 8. The first chief rabbi of Ireland resided here.

Stratford College and Dublin Talmud Torah, 1 Zion Rd., Dublin 6. Tel: 967351. This college incorporates kindergarten, primary school, and college secondary school.

SYNAGOGUES IN DUBLIN

The Dublin Hebrew Congregation, 36 Adelaide Rd., Dublin 2. Tel: 761734 or 766745. Dedicated in 1892. In a nearby structure, one finds the office of the chief rabbi of Ireland, the community center, a Talmud Torah and day school, as well as the headquarters of various Jewish organizations and Zionist groups. Services are Fridays at 8:30 P.M. in summer and at sunset in other seasons; every Saturday morning from 9:15 to 11:15.

Dublin Jewish Progressive Congregation, 7 Leicester Ave., Dublin 6. Tel: 490-7605. Services are held Fridays at 8:15 P.M. and first Saturdays in every month at 10:30 A.M.

Machzikei Hadass, rear of 77 Terenure Rd. North, Dublin 6. Tel: 490-8413. Services are held every Saturday at 9:30 A.M. Times for all other services vary according to season.

Terenure Hebrew Congregation, between 32 and 34

Rathfarnham Rd., Dublin 6. Tel: 908037, 905969, or 908544. Services are Fridays at 8:30 P.M. in summer and at sunset in other seasons; every Saturday morning from 9:15 to 11:15.

It is said that Ireland, once visited, is never forgotten. The traveler certainly will find this to be so.

Suggested Reading

Briscoe, Robert, with Alden Hatch. *For the Life of Me*. Boston: Little, Brown, 1958.
Hyman, Louis. *The Jews of Ireland, from Earliest Times to the Year 1910*. Shannon, Ireland: Irish University Press, 1972.

Italy
Jews Sell Cameos
in St. Peter's Square

"All Italians look like Jews and all Jews look like Italians," said the Italian writer, Luigi Barzini.

When I stroll through St. Peter's Square in Rome, I watch Italian men selling religious cameos. At least they look Italian. I soon realize that if these salesmen thought you were Jewish, they might greet you in Yiddish with, "Hello, landsman." Considering that Jews have lived in Europe for hundreds of years, it is not strange to hear Yiddish on the Continent. However, it is uncommon to hear a Yiddish greeting from Jews in Italy who, by and large, are of Sephardic origin, or indigenous Italians who do not know Yiddish.

Anyway, what were Jews doing selling religious cameos in St. Peter's Square in the first place?

Believe it or not, the concession is said to be held by Jews, who know that most American Jewish tourists are Ashkenazim. Like all good business persons, those Italian Jews also get attention by shouting out a Yiddish word in the Vatican, of all places. Incidentally, you will probably meet these Jewish salespersons at the Colosseum and the Pantheon, too.

A Brief History

Welcome to Italy, where beauty reigns supreme and where

Jews have lived longer than in any other country in Europe. Italy was one of the first European countries to which Jews migrated from the Holy Land; today it is home to between 30,000 and 40,000 Jews. Ambassadors of Judah Maccabee set foot on Italian soil in 140 B.C. seeking alliances, and indeed found a warm welcome.

Italy, the only nation in Western Europe in which Jewish settlement has been continuous from the second century, is considered the oldest Jewish community in the Western world. Few towns or regions in Italy stand without a trace of Jewish presence: catacombs from first-century cemeteries, medieval and baroque synagogues, Jewish quarters and ghettos. Italy's museums and churches contain countless Jewish relics, and history's first Hebrew printing press was started here.

IN A.D. 70, thousands of Jews were massacred in Palestine. Thousands more were deported to Rome. At one time, 1,500 Jews arrived in Rome in chains. Roman Jewish slaves worked on the Colosseum, one of the monumental symbols of the Eternal City, until they could buy their freedom. They would continue suffering at the hands of Tiberius, Claudius, and Nero.

When Rome fell and Christianity was accepted as the official religion, Jews were persecuted. The Church wanted the Jewish people preserved, however, as "witnesses of ancient truths." Jews were seen as the enemies of Jesus, responsible for his death and were therefore looked upon as second-class citizens, excluded from public offices and from various professions.

While Jews were persecuted by the Byzantines, these conditions ceased when Pope Gregory I (590-604) began his reign. He protected them and provided safety for Jews in Rome and other cities. After this, it becomes evident that Jewish history in Italy is linked with the papacy. Some popes safeguarded Jews. They even hired Jewish financiers and doctors. On the other hand, many popes were bitterly anti-Semitic.

By the end of the eleventh century, Jews lived in northern Italy in such towns as Verona, Pavia, and Lucca. Talmudic academies existed in Rome. Hostility of the popes erupted in the twelfth century and culminated in the Fourth Lataran Council in 1215, which along with other discriminatory regulations forced Jews to wear a distinguishing badge on their clothes.

In the thirteenth century and the beginning of the fourteenth, Jews were allowed to become moneylenders as the Church prohibited Christians from lending money for interest. After the Catholic monarchs of Spain expelled the Jewish people from Spanish soil in 1492, many Jews, as well as Marranos, found their way to Italy. But the Spaniards invaded the south late in the fifteenth century and forced the Jews to leave Sicily and the Italian south. In 1555, Pope Paul IV issued his infamous *Cum nimis absurdum,* banishing Jews to the ghetto. The document also prohibited them from engaging in any business except the sale of rags and other items.

During the Counter-Reformation, an Inquisition was instituted. Jews were burned at the stake. Many fled to the north or out of Italy to North Africa, Greece, Turkey, and the Levant. Throughout the years, even as late as the eighteenth century, Jews, forced to listen to sermons, were often baptized against their will.

When Napoleon overran Italy in 1796, the Catholic Church's political rule was taken away. Implementing the ideals of the Revolution, the French army freed the Jews. For the first time, Jews became Italian citizens. On July 9, 1798, the yellow badge that Jews had been forced to wear was abolished by an edict of the French general St. Cyr.

With Napoleon's abandonment of Italy and his downfall at Waterloo came reaction. Pope Pius VII returned to Rome in 1814 and re-introduced the Holy Inquisition. Jews would have continued to suffer, except for the Risorgimento movement for freedom that started in the Piedmont region in 1820-21 and culminated in the 1848-49 revolution in Milan, Rome, and Venice, the latter under the leadership of Daniele Manin, a Jew. In 1848-49, the walls of the ghetto of Rome came down. They had stood longer than any other in Western Europe. Yet again a wave of repression occurred. Finally, in 1861, when the united Italian kingdom was established, Jews received equal rights.

Cecil Roth points out in *The History of the Jews of Italy* that after 1861, there was no country in either hemisphere where Jewish conditions "were or could be better," at least until the late 1930s. The 1938 racial laws against Jews restricted Jewish life and devastated the Jewish community.

As Germany's ally, Italy invaded France in 1940. Still, the Jews in Italian-occupied southern France, as well as in Italy itself, were reasonably safe. However, when Italy surrendered to the Allies on September 8, 1943, Jews immediately faced danger from the Germans, who rushed troops into central and northern Italy. At this time Mussolini's puppet regime cooperated with the Nazis. The Gestapo also quickly moved against the Jewish community. On September 24, 1943, they blackmailed the Jewish community, demanding 50 kilos of gold within 36 hours, otherwise 200 Jews would be murdered. Four days later, they got their money. Pope Pius XII offered to provide as much as needed, but enough had been collected by the Jewish community. Nothing was taken from the Vatican. Contributions also came from non-Jews.

On October 16, 1943, "Black Saturday," the Germans surrounded the Jewish quarter and arrested more than 1,000 Jews, who were then shipped to Auschwitz, where all but 16 died. "Until that mass roundup the Jews of Rome believed themselves immune to crimes they heard were being committed by the Nazis against the Jews of other countries," writes Robert Katz.

The number of Italian Jews murdered in the Holocaust is estimated at 7,750 out of a total Jewish population of about 30,000 at the beginning of the German occupation, an 85 percent survival rate, second to Denmark.

According to Susan Zuccotti, in her book *The Italians and the Holocaust,* the Holocaust began relatively late in Italy, in September 1943, when the Germans swooped south. Therefore, the danger period was shorter. The Italian Jews were one-tenth of one percent of the population. Financial resources as well as hard cash helped Jews survive. Physical appearances also mattered, for assimilated Jews could pass as non-Jews. Ordinary Italians, moreover, tried to help the Jews during the German occupation. Italy ranks with Denmark as one of the nations that rescued Jews during the dark years. After the war, Italy was the main "highway for Jewish refugees en route to Palestine," although some went to America. In 1945, the post-Holocaust era of Italian Jewry began with lives that had been disrupted. "Those who remained began a slow and painful reconstruction," wrote Emily Braun in *Gardens and Ghettos*. But they were soon to be joined by Jews from Hungary and North Africa, especially Egypt, who lived in more than 200 Italian cities and towns.

By the 1990s the Jewish population was estimated at about 30,000, including about 2,000 Israeli students, out of a total Italian population of 62 million persons.

A high rate of assimilation and declining enrollment in Jewish schools, as well as an aging population, plagues present-day Italian Jewry. According to the Institute of Jewish Affairs in London, 56 percent of Italian Jews have a diploma or university degree; 34 percent are engaged in trade or business; 13 percent are professionals; 5 percent are workers; and 4 percent are teachers.

In the 1980s there were some anti-Semitic incidents, a number of which were sparked by the war in Lebanon, but Chief Rabbi Elio Toaff spoke out and relations between Christians and Jews in Italy are still good. In 1965, the Second Vatican Council repudiated the notion that the Jews collectively were responsible for the death of Jesus and subsequently affirmed the enduring importance of Judaism. And late in 1993, the Vatican and Israel established diplomatic relations. Yet, with the elections of a Rightist Bloc in Italy's Parliament, Jewish concerns were raised, especially since a number of Rightists have been accused of anti-Semitism. Chances are that Jews will be in Rome for many centuries to come.

Notable Italian Jews

Within one or two generations, the Jews moved from crafts and small commerce to industry, the army, and government. Here are some examples. Luigi Luzzatti (1841-1927) was minister of Finance and prime-minister of Italy in 1910. Camillo Olivetti founded the famous typewriter company and Ernesto Nathan served as mayor of Rome in 1907.

The Italian cultural scene included such contributors as Primo Levi (1919-1987), renowned novelist and writer of books on the Holocaust. A chemist, a member of the antifascist resistance, and a survivor of Auschwitz, Levi died in Turin in April 1987—an apparent suicide. Carlo Levi (1902-1975) was a painter, doctor of medicine, political leader, and author of *Christ Stopped at Eboli*. Natalia Ginzburg (1917-1991) was a novelist and playwright. She was a leader of the Italian Resistance and her husband was a victim of the Nazis. Giorgio Bassani (1916-2000), author of *The Garden of the Finzi-Continis*, wrote many stories dealing with the Holocaust. Novelist Alberto Moravia (1907-1991), born Alberto Pincherle, was one of Italy's outstanding writers; he was estranged from Judaism. Amedeo Modigliani (1884-1920), the painter, was born in Leghorn and studied art in Florence and Venice. At 21 he went to Paris; his brother, Victor Emmanuel, was an active Socialist leader who fought Mussolini. Roberto Melli (1885-1958) was a sculptor forced into hiding during war; painter Mario Cavaglieri (1887-1969) was born in the Jewish quarter of Rovigo and lived in Padua. Tullia Zevi is a noted Jewish leader of the Jewish community. She has been mentioned among twelve women who could become future presidential candidates of Italy. Carlo Di Benedetti, former head of Olivetti, is now chief of the company that runs Italy's Autostrade Dottore. Rabbi Dr.Elio Toaff, (b. 1915) was born in Leghorn. He was rabbi of Ancona and Venice before being called to Rome to succeed David Prato as chief rabbi of that community in 1951.

Jewish Rome

In Rome, you will find that several streets contain Jewish-owned stores. One survey has reported that 70 percent of Rome's clothing shops are operated by Jews. The young people of Rome often go straight from school into their parents' businesses. However, Italy has in recent decades become a "heavily industrialized nation via American-style capitalism," and more and more young Jews are moving into industrial and technological professions.

JEWISH SITES IN ROME

The Ghetto of Rome. To find the ghetto in Rome, take buses 44, 56, 60, or 75 to Ponte Garibaldi near the Great Synagogue (see "Synagogues in Rome" section). Walk to the synagogue and then proceed to the area behind the temple.

Another way to reach the ghetto is to circle the Pantheon, going across the Via Botteghe Oscure and past the Caetani Palace, until you reach the winding, narrow cobbled streets and alleyways. Small piazzas are the hallmark of the ghetto, which is on the left bank of the Tiber. The ghetto once was bounded by the Campo di Fiore, the Piazza di S. Croce, and the Piazza Guidea, ancient streets that still exist today.

A small group of Roman Jews still lives in the old ghetto adjacent to the main synagogue.

Before the ghetto was erected in 1555, and even as far back as the days of imperial Rome, Jews lived in the Trastevere section on the right bank of the Tiber. There may have been about 15 synagogues in that sector. **A medieval house of worship** can still be seen on Vicolo dell'Atleta, No. 13-14. It is located in a narrow alley behind the Cinema Esperia. That synagogue was founded by Rabbi Nathan ben Yehiel in the beginning of the twelfth century. He was the author of Arukh, the famous dictionary of the Talmud and the Midrash.

No Italian ghetto was said to be as severe, in regards to living conditions, as the one in Rome. Wrote Jewish historian Cecil Roth, "The ghetto was situated in the fetid, low lying quarter on the left bank of the Tiber, frequently inundated by the overflowing of the river and heavily visited at the time of plagues."

The civic rules specified that Jews could have only one synagogue; they got around that stricture by maintaining five synagogues with different rites under a single roof. Needless to say, their whole life revolved around the ghetto. Today it seems to be the "in" place to live. But if you really want to see what a ghetto street looked like, head for the **Via della Reginella**. Gloomy and oppressive to this day, it is witness to the "misery that once dwelled here." This area of the Tiber at one time contained between 5,000 and 10,000 persons in one-third of a square mile. Another description says the enclosure was seven acres with 130 houses.

Today, Jews still live in the main street of the quarter, the Via del Portico d'Ottavia. The portico (gate), now in ruins, was built twelve years after the first Jews came to Rome from Palestine. Later this gate and others would be the only entrance and exit of the Jewish ghetto. On this street, you can see old buildings with stores, excellent restaurants that serve Jewish dishes *alla Romana,* kosher butcher shops, and bakeries.

Marmertine Prison. This memorial near the Roman Forum contains the tablet of Gen. Simon Bar Giora, defender of the Jews against the Romans in Jerusalem (70 C.E.). Titus captured him and dragged him before the populace in Rome; he died in this prison.

A **monument** memorializing the massacres at the Ardeatine Caves is located just off the Porto San Paolo, a few yards from the main synagogue. This is an impressive memorial to the 335 persons, including 100 Jews, murdered by the Germans on March 23, 1944. The incident took place in the Ardeatine Caves just beyond the ancient walls of Rome. These lives were ended in retaliation for the killing of Nazis in the Via Rasella by Italian partisans. Thirty-three Germans were killed in that street near Rome's famous boulevard, the Via Veneto. Ten for one was the Gestapo retribution. The 335 hostages were rounded up, taken to the Ardeatine Caves beyond the catacombs, and murdered by the S.S. The Germans tried to conceal the site, but it was soon discovered.

In 1998, former Nazi SS Captain Erich Priebke 85, was sentenced to life in prison. Priebke was found guilty of helping carry out the massacre of 335 civilians in German-occupied Rome in 1944. On March 7, 1998, the court also handed down a life sentence to former SS Maj. Karl Hass, also 85, for helping to carry out the 1944 massacre.

While the monument is here, the dead are buried nearby in **The Mausoleo delle Fosse Ardeatine Fine,** a mausoleum situated just off the Via Appia Antica between the Via Ardeatine and the Via delle Sette Chiese, a short distance from the catacombs of San Sebastian. Three huge figures are shown tied together. Dedicated in 1957, the mausoleum is in a courtyard. The caves are cut into the Ardeatine Hill. The Jewish graves are inscribed with a Star of David.

JEWISH RESTAURANTS IN ROME

Before dining in Rome, do check to see if the eating establishment is kosher and has rabbinic supervision. Below are some recommended spots.

Zi Fenizia Pizza Restaurant, 64 Maria Del Planto, Rome, Tel: 39-06-689-69-76.

Kosher Products store (Makolot) via Maria Corbino, 17, Rome. Tel: 39-06-558-43-63

Private Glatt Kosher Meals, by Mrs. Labi. Tel: 39-06-442-30332.

Restaurant, via del Portico d'Ottavia, Rome.

Da Lisa, Via Ugo Foscolo, 16, Rome (not far from the main railroad station). This restaurant is listed as kosher.

The Jewish Orphanage, Instituto Pitigliani, Via Arco de Tolomei 1. Tel: 39-06-580-05-39. Open for kosher lunch every day. It is important to telephone first to make a reservation.

Tavola Calda, Via Livorno, 8, Rome. Tel: 442-92025. Take the B Metro from the Central Station and get off at the Piazza Bologne. Listed as kosher, but check.

LODGING

Pensione Carmel, Via Gioffredo Mameli 11, Rome. Tel: 580-9921. Many Orthodox Jews stop at this hotel, as it is near the synagogue. Call for reservations. No meals are served here.

SYNAGOGUES IN ROME

The Great Temple (Tempio Maggiore), Lungotevere Cenci 9, on the banks of the Tiber. Tel: 687-5051. Built in 1901, the synagogue, which follows the Italian rite of worship, is Orthodox. There are daily services. A mikveh is located in this synagogue, which is situated between the Via Catalana and Lungotevere Cenci.

The synagogue itself was built on the ruins of the ancient Jewish quarter. Imposing in its Assyro-Babylonian style of architecture, it is set behind wrought-iron gates on the northern side of the Tiber River.

The Great Temple of Rome.

The synagogue interior possesses an Oriental motif. The visitor can see rows of varicolored glass in the top of the dome, stately marble columns and pillars that rise to form wide arcades, windows embellished with cornices, and walls richly painted with stylized floral motifs. Biblical inscriptions adorn the walls. In the synagogue, the Holy Ark comes from the destroyed Sicilian synagogue and bears the date 1586. The six Assyrian columns that surround it are admired for their volutes and elaborate gilded friezes. There are several annexes, such as the Spanish temple, where the Holy Ark was once part of the city's old synagogue.

Memorial tablets of Jews who fell in battle during World War I and of Jews who were deported in World War II grace the walls. A third memorial recalls the Jews who, along with many Christians, were slaughtered by the Nazis in the Ardeatine Caves.

Sephardic services are held in a separate hall of the synagogue as the main service is in the "Italian rite."

The Jewish Museum is located in the same building as the Great Temple. It is open from Monday to Tuesday, 9:30 A.M. to 2 P.M. and 3 to 5 P.M.; Friday, 9:30 A.M. to 1:30 P.M.; Sunday, 9:30 A.M. to 12:30 P.M. Sunday morning is a good time to visit. While tours are conducted, you may have to wait for an Italian-language tour to finish—that is, if you know only English.

The museum is proud of its exhibits dealing with "Two Thousand Years of Jewish History," as well as pages from the Talmud that refer to Italian Jewry. Rare prayer books, reprints of statements of the popes, maps and drawings of the Ghetto of Rome, Torah pointers, rimmonim (Torah ornaments), Hanukkah menorahs, Torah crowns, and candelabra round out the collection.

A guide gives a 20-minute tour of the museum and temple, in English or Italian, in which he describes the manuscripts and Jewish ceremonial objects. The collection includes Torah finials made by Roman goldsmiths in the eighteenth century, when Jews were not allowed to touch gold.

Official German records listing the names of some of the approximately 2,000 Jews who were deported from Rome during the Holocaust can be found here.

The history of the synagogue recalls that in October 1982, Palestinian terrorists attacked the building. A two-year-old child was killed and 37 were wounded. The Italian Jewish community was shocked that this terrorist murder could occur in Italy. At the time, the Jews accused the government of "flirting" with Arab terror groups.

One significant event was the visit of Pope John Paul II to the synagogue in April 1986. It was the first recorded pontifical visit to a Jewish house of worship in Rome in 800 years. Moreover, in 1994, the Vatican highlighted the Roman Catholic church's commitment to the fight against renewed anti-Semitism. Pope John Paul II joined with Holocaust survivors at a concert in the Vatican commemorating the Holocaust. The concert marked the first time in the 50 years since the end of World War II that the Vatican had officially commemorated the Holocaust. Among the guests was Chief Rabbi Elio Toaff.

Synagogue Sephardic, via Garfagnana 4, Rome, Tel: 39-06-442-35640

Synagogue, Via Balbo 33, Rome. Tel: 475-9881. There are two separate synagogues here. The Ashkenazic service is downstairs in this building, where there is a daily minyan. On the main floor, Italian rite services are conducted, but only on Shabbat. This synagogue is near the Piazza Popullo.

Synagogue for Young Adults, Tempio dei Giovianni isola, Tiberino.

ORGANIZATIONS

The Cultural Center, Via Arco Deitalomei, Rome. This center for the Jewish community of Rome is open from 9 A.M. to 1 P.M., but not on Saturdays.

The office of the Grand Rabbi is located here at the Synagogue at Via Catalana 1, Rome. Tel: 687-5051. Nearby at Lungotevere Sanzio 14 and 12 are several schools, including a nursery, seminary, as well as the Italian Rabbinical College. Also at Lungotevere Sanzio 14 are the offices of Hashomer Hatzair and B'nai B'rith. Tel: 581-8346.

The **Israeli Embassy,** Via Michele Mercati 12. Tel: 322-1541/2/3/4.

The **Jewish Agency,** Keren Hayesod, and the Zionist Federation, Corso Vittorio Emanuele 173. Tel: 65-15-14.

The **Jewish National Fund Office,** Via Gramsci 42-A.

Lubavitch, "Beth Chabad of Rome," Via Pancirole 7, Rome 00162. Tel: 39-6-8632-4176. Contact; Rabbi Yitzhak Hazan.

The **Union of Italian Jewish Communities,** Lungotevere Sanzio 9, Rome 00153. Tel: 580-3667. FAX: 589-9569.

MUSEUMS

See the "Synagogues in Rome" section above for a description of the **Jewish Museum.**

The **Borghese Gallery** displays the *David* of Bernini, and *David and Goliath*h by Caravaggio.

The **Doria Pamphili-Gallery** exhibits the *Sacrifice of Isaac,* created by Van Dyck.

OTHER SITES

The **Arch of Titus**. This arch was erected in 81 C.E. by Emperor Domitian (81-91) to celebrate Titus's victory in 70 C.E. in Palestine. A triumphal arch, it symbolically recalls the destruction of the Temple in Jerusalem and shows the Jewish spoils swallowed up by the victors. For centuries, Jews did not walk under the arch. After all, it had been erected to praise Titus for destroying Jerusalem and the Temple. Titus, the son of Vespecian, deported thousands of Jews to Rome and its western provinces, including Sardinia. On one display on the arch, Jewish prisoners are portrayed carrying the booty of the seven-branched menorah, the candelabrum that was taken from the Temple in Jerusalem, as well as the Holy Ark and silver trumpets, the golden shewbread table—all part of the Temple rituals. According to H. V. Morton, "these are the only contemporary sculpted representatives of these objects in existence, and their ultimate fate is even now a mystery."

The prohibition of walking under the arch ended in World War II, when the Jewish Brigade from Palestine, a unit of the British Army, walked under the arch to signify the liberation of the Jewish people. Another report says the ban was broken when the United Nations declared a Jewish state in 1947 and again when Israel was declared a state on May 14, 1948.

On a visit in 1988, I saw scrawled in chalk the words, *"Am Yisrael Chai,"* "the Jewish people live." Today Jews are alive throughout the world. There is silence in the Roman Forum!

Piazza Navona. After you visit the Roman Forum, the Seven Hills, the monuments, the amphitheaters, the Colosseum, the Campo di Fiori, the Spanish Steps, the Trevi Fountain, and the Pantheon, walk around the horseshoe-shaped Piazza Navona, where artists and craftsmen display their wares. But did you know that from the fifteenth to seventeenth centuries, it was a carnival sport and comic spectacle to beat and chase half-naked Jews around this square? Yes, the same Piazza Navona used for bullfights, tournaments, jugglers, tightrope walkers, and other entertainment was the scene of a degrading clownish show. Under Paul II in the fifteenth century, public sport was made of the Jews by forcing some to eat a heavy meal and then run in carnival races. As late as 1667, a guide to Rome noted that during the races "the asses ran first, then the Jews marched with only a band around the loins, then the buffaloes, then the Barbary horses." Clement IX modified the custom the following year: "The victims were allowed to pay a heavy fine to avoid racing," writes E. R. Chamberlain in *Rome: The Great Cities.*

But it was the papacy again, especially during the years of the Holocaust, that aroused a great deal of controversy. Pope Pius XII was silent during the years of mass murder. The Vatican argues that he said nothing in order to prevent even greater slaughter. Others claimed he did so to protect the Catholic Church in Germany. The pope did not want to encourage communism by attacking the Nazis, says this argument. Robert Katz maintains in *Death in Rome* that the pope "interpreted the fall of Fascism as a victory for Communism." In *The Catholic Church and Nazi Germany,* Guenther Lewry writes, "Finally, one is inclined to conclude that the Pope and his advisors—influenced by the long tradition of moderate anti-Semitism so widely accepted in Vatican circles—did not view the plight of the Jews with a real sense of urgency and moral outrage." According to Rolf Hochhuth in *The Deputy,* Pope Pius failed to protest the roundup of Roman Jews for deportation to Auschwitz.

"For years, Jewish and Catholic leaders alike have warned that the beatification of Pius XII could harm reconciliation efforts begun during Vatican II" and cemented by the Pope John Paul II, wrote Alissa Stanley in *The New York Times,* November 3, 1999.

Moreover, evidence has since come to light that the Vatican aided and abetted the escape of "scores if not hundreds of S.S. and other Nazi genocidists...and it did nothing to bar their flight from justice," according to Charles R. Alien, in the magazine *Reform Judaism* (1983).

Pope John Paul has on several occasions apologized for some Catholics' failure to protect Jews during the Holocaust and repeated that regret in a sweeping apology for the historic sins of his church. In Israel at Yad Vashem, in March, 2000, the Pope expressed sadness at "hatred, acts of persecution and displays of anti-Semitism directed against the Jews by Christians at any time and in any place." While the Pope stopped short of an outright apology on behalf of the Roman Catholic Church for what some Jews consider the Vatican's silence, inaction and complicity in the Holocaust, he said in Yad Vashem: "In this place of solemn remembrance, I fervently pray that our sorrow for the tragedy which the Jewish people suffered in the 20th century will lead to a new relationship between Christians and Jews."

Israel Prime Minister Ehud Barak called the Pope's visit and declarations, a "noble act" of reaching out to the Jewish people: "You have done more than anyone else to bring about the historic change in the attitude of the churches toward the Jewish people, initiated by the good Pope John XXII, and to dress the gaping wounds that festered over many bitter centuries."

Rabbi James A. Rudin, the American Jewish Committee's former national inter-religious affairs director, has noted "the extraordinary positive advances in Catholic-Jewish relations," during the last decade of the 20th Century. In the last analysis,

since he became Pope in 1978, John Paul is widely credited
with advancing the Catholic Church towards reconciliation
with the Jews.

San Pietro in Vitcoli (Church of St. Peter in Chains). Here
is the famous Moses of Michelangelo, sculpted in the early sixteenth century. This Moses has horns because of an error in
the translation of the Book of Exodus, where the Hebrew word
keren was translated as horn, instead of *ray of light.*

The Vatican. In the Sistine Chapel of the Vatican are wall
frescoes about the life of Moses in the Old Testament done by
Pinturicchio, Botticelli, and Signorelli, as well as the work of
Michelangelo, the creator of the magnificent ceiling with its
nine biblical scenes.

Ostia Antica. This town is the beach community close to the
Italian capital, one hour from Rome. A Jewish community
once thrived here in this ancient port of Rome as evidenced in
the ruins of an ancient synagogue discovered here in 1961 by
workmen building the Fiumicino Airport.

Among the fragments of columns and pillars uncovered are
the outlines of a prayer room, a study hall, an oven for unleav-
ened bread, and a mikveh (ritual bath). The synagogue
proper, a large hall divided into three aisles with marble
columns, has also been exposed. One of these sections may
have been for women. The wall at the back is slightly curved.
In the oldest hall, the seats were of stone, set against the walls.

In another building, the tabernacle for the Holy Ark rises
behind the pulpit on the left side along its entire length, a few
steps leading to it. Carved into the tabernacle are Jewish symbols that can also be found in other synagogues of that period:
a seven-branched menorah, a shofar, a lulav, and an etrog. The
floor is covered with mosaic. In recent years, many Russian
Jews found a temporary home in the town of Ostia, thus bringing Jews back to an ancient site. As Barbara G. Harrison wrote,
"In Italy, history is never stale."

Milan

What a city! If ever there was a diverse city, indeed Milan is it.

There are 37 ethnic origins alone just among the 6,000 to 7,000 Milanese Jews. Milan contains synagogues, kosher butcher shops, a day school, and several Talmud Torahs (Jewish schools). The Jewish community here boasts diverse Jewish elements, including many Ashkenazim, who in the last century found their way to Milan as they moved down from northern Europe. They first concentrated in the wholesale and export business. Whereas the slower-paced southern Italian looks out to the calm Mediterranean, Jews in Milan scan both north and south in this commercial atmosphere.

One often hears men and women speaking Arabic, especially in the Galleria Vittorio Emanuele II, the galleria that inspired numerous North American imitations. The Arab-speakers may be Jews, for there one can often meet Jewish persons who emigrated from Libya and still speak Arabic. In 1948 and again in 1967, several thousand Libyan Jews came to Italy, although the majority went to Israel. They picked this land because they spoke Italian, for until the middle of World War II, Italy controlled Libya. Like Roman Jews, the Libyan Jews in Milan are by and large shopkeepers and traders. Their connections and linguistic knowledge help them develop trade between Italy and the Arab lands. Incidentally, the Galleria located near the Cathedral and La Scala Opera House is one of the world's first shopping centers, replete with outdoor cafés and famous shops. Located here is the notable establishment Biffi.

Part of the reason Jews settle in Milan is the cultural life of this metropolis. Many Milanese say their city begins in the Piazza della Scala, the location of La Scala Opera House. Since its inauguration more than two centuries ago, the legendary opera house, the home of Verdi and Puccini, has remained the pride of this Lombard capital.

Milan, the gateway to Italy, calls itself the money-maker of this republic, the industrial, commercial, and artisan capital of this nation. It is the most "city-like city in Italy," wrote the Sicilian author Giovanni Vergo a century ago.

Once called "muscular Milan," the city has been described as a city of go-getters and materialistic business persons. About 2 million people live in this bustling urban area located 300 miles northwest of Rome.

The Milanese claim their fashion industry ranks with Paris as a trendsetter. Visit Via Monte Napoleone, the main shopping street, and see for yourself.

Because Milan is so close to the borders of Austria, Switzerland, and France, and because its two airports reach out to the rest of Europe, it always has focused its sights on its European neighbors. Many Jewish business persons fly in for the annual trade fair, one of the most important in the world.

"What do you do in Milan?" I asked a stranger. "You eat!" he exclaimed. Eating is synonymous with Milan, which is famous for its delicious cuisine.

And if you can spot Jewish salesmen in the Vatican, what would you expect to see in various Milanese neighborhoods, such as in the Via Spadari where one finds mouth-watering delicacies? Once a kosher butcher shop was located right next door to the Ambrosiana Museum, which is situated at Piazza Pio XI Square. Ironically, the museum contains Judaica and Hebrew books and manuscripts.

In Italy, the northern and the southern parts of the country vie for attention. This is often mirrored in the Jewish community, too. "Milan makes the money, Rome spends it," said one Jewish citizen of Milan.

Jews—professionals and business people—live and work in this trading center that boasts international fairs, a silk market, nearly 1,000 banks, more than 30,000 firms, and more than 26,000 manufacturers. Italian Jewry lives on because what it loses through assimilation and mixed marriages, it picks up in the immigration of new groups. In the 1980s, for instance, Russian Jews settled in Milan in addition to about 1,000 Iranian Jews. The latter maintain their own synagogue and club for young people. They are excellent business persons and are skilled in the diamond and carpet trades.

As a result of the immigration following the 1956 and 1967 Arab-Israel wars, many Egyptian Jews have settled here, too. The visitor observes streets such as Piazza Tel Aviv and Via Sally Mayer, the latter named for a noted industrialist and philanthropist.

A **synagogue** is located at Via Sally Mayer 4/6, Milan.

JEWISH RESTAURANTS IN MILAN

Eshel Israel, Via Benvenuto Cellini 2, Milan. Tel: 02-545-5076.

Senior Citizens Home, Via Leone XIII No. 1, Milan. This senior citizen home has a kosher facility.

King Solomon, Via Washington 9, Milan.

Pizza Carmel, San Giminyano, 10, Milan, Tel: 02-416-368.

Cedika, Via Della Braida, Milan. Tel: 02-551-88248. This is a kosher products store.

Jewish residents of Milan hold kosher banquets, bar mitzvahs and weddings in, as well as at **Hotel Quark,** Via Lampedusa. Many Jewish business persons gather at the **Hotel Executive,** Viale Sturzo, Milan.

SYNAGOGUES AND DAY SCHOOLS IN MILAN

Beth Shelomo Synagogue, Via Ugo Foscolo 3, Milan. Tel: 02-864-6118. Services are held Friday night, Saturday and Sunday. Check with the congregation regarding other days for prayer.

The Central Synagogue, Via Guastalla 19, Milan. Tel: 02-551-2029. A Sephardic (Persian) synagogue and a mikveh are located here. An Italian rite service is held usually on Monday and Thursdays as well as Saturday mornings. Sephardic service is held every day, but do call ahead to check time of prayers. This house of worship was erected after World War II. The original was destroyed in an Allied bombing raid in 1943. The Holy Ark in the chapel originated in the ancient synagogue of Persia.

Lebanese Synagogue, Via Dei Gracchi, Milan.

Ohel Yaakov Synagogue, Via Benvenuto Cellini 2, Milan. This synagogue follows the Ashkenazi rite.

Synagogue, Via Sally Mayer 4/6.Milan.

Senior Citizens Home, Via Leone XIII No. 1, Milan. A small synagogue is located here. This is a dignified, two-story building and was built in the late 19th Century on the site of ancient buildings in which Jews had lived since 1516 when Europe's first ghetto was created.

Persian Synagogue, Via Monteculuolo, Milan.

Synagogue, Via Eupili 8, Milan. Services are held on Sabbath and festivals. The B'nai B'rith organization also has its office here.

Beth Chabad, Via Arza, Milan. Tel: 02-483-75026. This is a small Beth Chabad synagogue. Call ahead for prayer times.

ORGANIZATIONS

Jewish Community Center, Jewish National Fund and Sally Mayer Hebrew School, Via Sally Mayer 4/6, Milan. At the Documentation Center, I saw young Jews studying the Holocaust period, as well as the history of pre-twentieth century Itlalian Jewish life.

WIZO, Piazza della republica 6, Milan.

Beth Chabad, Via F. Bronzetti 18, 20129, Milan. Tel: 02-70-1000-80. Services are held every day, except in the summer. Check with Chabad as to times.

Zionist Federation, Via DeAmicis 14, Milan.

Venice

The tourist guide usually begins his or her talk to the largely American-Jewish audience thus: "The Jews arrived in Venice in the tenth century. They came from the Levant, Corfu, Greece, and Turkey. In the sixteenth century, the Venetians gave the Jews an area to live and work. They gave that designated plot the Venetian name, the word 'ghetto.' The Jews had to wear a colorful cap so that they could be recognized as Jews. The five synagogues that exist in the ghetto today are the German, the Canton, the Italian, the Levantine, and the Spanish synagogues..." There is so much history in that introductory talk.

Visitors immediately realize that something memorable occurred in this city that was once called "la Serenissima," "the most serene one." For today, millions of people every year pour into this "dream city of lagoons," probably the most beautiful city in the world.

This magical city is often called the loveliest city in the

world. It floods regularly, its painting rots, its canals are green, but its citizens love it and enjoy the outdoor pleasures it offers.

We must also remember that at one moment in the world's history, fifteenth-century Venice was rich and influential, the leader of the West. But just at the time when Venice was booming, a "new India" was discovered to challenge the Venetians. We call that land "America." Trade patterns changed and the city's power faded.

Considered the most important Jewish community of northern Italy, Venice involved Jews in "banking, pawnbroking and second-hand dealing."

The Republic tolerated Jews because Jews were useful. They helped "ring the Venetian cash register." Indeed writer Jan Morris believes that Venice could not have gone on to great heights without Jews. They served as bankers, pawnbrokers, suppliers, outfitters to diplomatic missions, agents, and scholars.

The Jews were usually safe under Venetian rule. But no Jew, not even a local resident, could stay in Venice without a permit, which cost a large sum of money. And it had to be renewed every five years. Jews were often segregated; in the thirteenth century, they were forced to dwell on the island of Spinalunga. We know it as the "Guidecca."

Before 1336, Jews could reside and work only in Mestre, a town just outside of Venice. Only that year did they receive permission to live in the "Lagoon City."

As a kabbalistic mystic center, learning and Hebrew printing thrived here.

Among the most distinguished of the new arrivals from Iberia after the expulsions and inquisitions was Don Isaac Abravanel. He belonged to Spanish diplomatic corps before he settled in Venice. We shall meet him later in the chapters on Spain and Portugal.

THE VENICE GHETTO

This is the city that gave the world the "ghetto." The Italians invented and set up the ghetto. A tourist spot today, it once contained several thousand Jews who were literally locked up at night.

The word *ghetto* comes from the Italian word *gettare*—to cast in metal. When the ghetto was established, it consisted of iron foundries, or *geto novo,* which means *new foundry* in the Venetian dialect.

Interestingly, some think the word *ghetto* comes from the Hebrew word *get* for divorce. These prison neighborhoods served as a way to separate Jews from Christians.

Generally, it is not easy to find Jewish sites in a European city, but not so in Venice. Everyone knows the location of the ghetto. Just ask! Say the word "ghetto." As we have seen, it is after all a Venetian word.

Located near the Venice railroad station, the ghetto can be reached by taking the vaporetti (motor bus-boats) via the Grand Canal. Get off at San Marcuolo landing. Walk away from the canal. Then walk toward Rio Terra San Leonardo. Follow the yellow signs. These signs are in Italian and Hebrew, and say *synagogue.* They will direct you to the ghetto, a lively area composed of Renaissance buildings, medieval houses and columns, and even some wonderful glassmaking shops. Another way to reach the ghetto is via Lake No. 1 Vaporetto, which passes under the Rialto Bridge. Walk a short distance to Calle Rabbia (Rabbi Street), turn right, and there you are.

While Rome's ghetto was crowded and unhealthy, Venice's remained larger. The ghetto district was located on an island cut off from Cannaregio by wide canals. It was also separated from its surroundings by a wall, gates, and drawbridges. Later in 1541, the "geto vecchio" ("the old foundry") was added to house more Jews. By 1663, the ghetto was so crowded that it was allowed to occupy the neighboring "Ghetto Nuovissimo," the site of the last remaining foundry in the district. In the fifteenth and sixteenth centuries, 5,000 people resided there. As street peddlers, rag pickers, dealers in secondhand merchandise, and pawnbrokers, they transformed the ghetto into a thriving beehive.

As a home for refugees, a medieval ghetto provided a certain amount of security. One felt safe from attack; sometimes its walls kept out the mob. On the other hand, when bigots wanted Jews killed, they knew where to find them. Established on April 10, 1516, the second day of Passover, the Venice

Ghetto, as an institution, quickly spread throughout various cities of Italy. Unfortunately, it became accepted practice.

As you stand in the large square of the ghetto, remember that this was the meeting place of the community, and also the site of the well where water was obtained and gossip exchanged. A number of outstanding persons were born or lived in the Venetian ghetto. David Reuveni was one. He appeared in Italy in 1524. He asserted that his brother Joseph ruled over the tribes of Gad and Reuben and half the tribe of Manasseh. He claimed to have traveled in disguise as a Moslem through Ethiopia, Egypt, and the Land of Israel. Reuveni said he came to Europe to obtain the military assistance of the Christian powers for the liberation of the Holy Land from the Turks. His "project" failed and he died in a Spanish prison.

When crowding became a problem, Jews always built upwards. Tall houses resembling skyscrapers were erected. Within the ghetto, there were several autonomous congregations. People worshipped in their own synagogues, according to their own rites, and as we shall see there were at least five different synagogues. The synagogue was the center of Jewish communal life in the ghetto.

When Napoleon's armies broke down the gates of the Venetian ghetto in 1797, it contained little more than a few old huts. The walls were torn down on July 10, 1797, the eve of the fast of the 17th of Tammuz. Emancipation came in 1866.

Although the Jews of Italy were guaranteed full civil equality by King Victor Emmanuel II in 1866, a large group of Jews voluntarily lived in the Venice ghetto until the days of Mussolini.

During World War II, more than 200 Jews, one-fourth of all Venetian Jews, were deported to concentration camps in Germany. They never returned. Today, a **monument** to the Holocaust, consisting of seven bronze tablets, stands on the western side of the Ghetto Nuovo, with the following message:

Men, women, children,
Masses for the gas chambers,
Advancing toward horror,
Beneath the whip of the executioners.
Your sad Holocaust is
Engraved in history.

And nothing shall purge
Your death from our memories
For our memories are your only grave.
The City of Venice remembers the Venetian Jews
who were deported to the Nazi concentration camps
on December 6, 1943 and August 7, 1944.

Jews still live in the ghetto. But today, most of the 650 to 700 Jews of Venice reside outside that neighborhood.

Jewish Rest Home, Ghetto Nuovo 2874. Tel: 71-60-02. It is possible for tourists to obtain kosher meals here, but do book early. Many stop here for meals, especially on the Sabbath. It is located in the ghetto's main square, the Campo Ghetto Nuovo.

The Jewish Community Center (Comunita Ebraica) and Rabbi's Study, Via Cannaregio 1188-A, Ghetto Vecchio. Tel: 71-50-12.

The Jewish community of Venice today is quite different from those of the past. While the religious observances and ceremonies are Orthodox, the community is not. Still, during the year, the congregation gathers together. People are not as busy in the winter as in the summer.

Jews and non-Jews are proud to live in Venice. It is said that people come here because it is unique. As long as Venice will be Venice, Jews will live and visit here.

Beth Chabad, Cannaregio 2884, Venice, 30121. Tel: 39-41-716-214.

Five Synagogues in the Venice Ghetto

Five synagogues rise within the ancient boundaries of the Venice ghetto. The five are the German, Italian, and Canton, situated in the Campo Ghetto Nuovo; the Levantine and Spanish, located in the Campello delle Scole.

They were erected by various Jewish groups that emigrated to Venice from other nations or other parts of Italy. (Sometimes, not all the synagogues are open to the public because of repairs). Space in the ghetto was limited, so many of the prayer halls are located within a single room. In the synagogues, crystal chandeliers are in sharp contrast with the wooden benches of the worshippers. The *aron ha-kodesh* (Holy Ark) is usually at one end, the bimah at another.

In the summer in Venice, tourists may take one of the three synagogue tours in the morning at 10:30, 11:15, and noon; or three tours in the afternoon at 3:30, 4:15, and 5. The tours are offered from March 16 to November 15.

German Synagogue. The German synagogue, located in the Campo Ghetto Nuovo, is the popular one. This Ashkenazic house of worship is known as the Scola Tedesca Grande and is the oldest. Highlighting this temple are five interesting windows, three of which are walled up. The arches are in white stone. There is a beautiful gilded Holy Ark and a bimah. The women's gallery is an oval balcony. The synagogue was restored between 1890 and 1910.

The **Jewish Museum**, known as Museo della Comunita Ebraica, is located on the floor below the German synagogue, Scola Tedesca Grande, built in 1528 in the Campo Ghetto Nuovo. It features a collection of Jewish ritual silver articles and pieces of woven and embroidered materials, as well as a *hummash*—a Pentateuch—used by Maimonides.

The Italian Synagogue. The Italian Synagogue, Scola Italiana, was built in 1575. It is located in the Ghetto Nuovo. Crystal chandeliers are common here, and there are simple wooden benches. At one end stands the *aron ha-kodesh* (Holy Ark) dating from the early 1800s, a gift of Beniamino di Consiglio. This building is not in use, but is now being restored by the Italian Committee for Venice and the Committee for Jewish History of Venice.

The Canton Synagogue. Constructed in 1531, this synagogue is named after a German Ashkenazi banking family and is built into the corner of the piazza. Hebrew writing (names of donors) on the steps leading to the Holy Ark is an interesting sight. The synagogue is closed because of restoration being financed by the Venice Committee of St. Louis, Missouri.

The Levantine Synagogue. Located in the Campello delle Scole, this synagogue is used in the winter because it is heated. Founded in 1538, it is situated across the square from the Spanish synagogue. A plaque commemorates the visit of Sir Moses Montefiore, British Jewish philanthropist and leader, in

1875. Above the entrance to this synagogue is written: "Happy are they that dwell in thy House. They will ever praise thee" (Ps. 84:5).

Long benches fill the sanctuary. The men's pews have wooden stage cases inscribed with the names of members. Woodcarvings decorate the ceiling, walls are covered alternately with wooded frames and damask panels, and four Corinthian columns surround the Holy Ark. The doors are inscribed with the Ten Commandments; the bimah features numerous carvings and wood sculptures. Surrounded by two wide curving stairways, the pulpit is framed by two decorated twisted columns resembling marble. This imitates Solomon's Temple. The women's gallery is above the long entrance side.

Spanish Synagogue. The Spanish synagogue (built in 1555 and restored in 1840), located in the Campello delle Scole, is called the Scola Spagnola. This Spanish-Portuguese synagogue was designed in classical baroque. Summer services are held here. The main sanctuary is an elongated space. The Holy Ark is in a classical-baroque style and is situated along the eastern wall; the bimah stands along the western wall. The bimah is composed of four Corinthian columns, two of them actually half-columns set against the west wall. The seating runs parallel along the north and the south walls. An oval gallery for women is an outstanding feature of the structure. The women used to sit upstairs, but now they are on the main level.

The building contains memorial plaques for Jews deported from Venice in World War II.

Florence

It is not difficult to find the Jewish community of Florence. Head for Via Luigi Carlo Farini 4, not far from San Marco Square, near St. Ambrose Church and off of Via dei Pilastri. Located in a large single compound, the Florence **synagogue** is one of the most beautiful in Europe. On the grounds of this large house of worship stand a Jewish day school, the offices of the Jewish community, as well as the headquarters of the B'nai B'rith and other organizations.

Italy often is pictured as a museum. Thousands of tourists visit Michelangelo's *David* in the Academy of Arts Museum in Florence in the province of Tuscany. The city stands as the great collector of Brunelleschi, Donatello, and Michelangelo. In one year alone, 1505, Michelangelo, Leonardo da Vinci, Machiavelli, and Raphael were working at the same time and within a few blocks of each other. The city contains more fine art per square mile than any other in Italy; be sure to visit the Uffizi Gallery, the Pitti Palace, the Accademia della Belle Arti, the Bargello, the Duomo, the Baptistery, and the Medici Chapels. Florence is also advertised as a shopping center where Ferragamo and Gucci have their headquarters.

If at one time on your trip you sit in Florence's town center in Florence in an outdoor cafe, you just might be at leisure in what once was the area of the ghetto.

We know that during the Renaissance, the Jews of Florence did not live in a ghetto. That enclosure would come later. The Jewish community of Florence was established in 1437, when some Jewish financiers were invited to open loan banks. During the time of Lorenzo de Medici (1449-92), Jewish intellectual life corresponded to the rich achievements of Florentine culture. The Medici in Florence were well disposed toward the Jews.

The heyday of the Florentine Jewish community was between the years 1437 and 1494, the most resplendent period in the history of Florence "or perhaps in any city in the world since recorded history began." Jewish literature, Jewish poetry, and Jewish learning flourished in fifteenth- and sixteenth-century Florence, even though the community did not number more than 100 families.

On October 3, 1570, Grand Duke Cosimo I, a Medici duke called "the Great," banished the Jews to a ghetto because they allegedly broke the law. He feared the Jews would fraternize with Christians, so he forced them to wear a yellow badge. The ghetto restricted Jewish culture in the city known as the "Athens of Italy" and the cradle of the Italian Renaissance.

In 1799, Napoleon and his army freed the Jews. But a year after the French emperor withdrew, a period of repression set in. In 1859, when Tuscany became part of the Kingdom of

Italy, the Jews were recognized as citizens of the new kingdom. Free at last!

There are about 1,000 Jews in Florence and the surrounding towns. About half that number live in the city itself. And they are active in such organizations as B'nai B'rith, Anti-Defamation League, WIZO, Maccabi and the Italian-Friendship Society. The community still maintains a kindergarten, a Talmud Torah through Bar Mitzvah age, which is located next to the synagogue.

JEWISH SITES IN FLORENCE

Beth Haknesset Firenze (The Synagogue of Florence), Via Farini 4. Tel: 245-252. One of the most beautiful synagogues in Europe, this structure is more than 100 years old. Whether seen from an airplane, from another tall structure in Florence, or from the popular tourist vista of Michelangelo Square, this landmark of Judaism in Italy stands out under the city's azure sky. Possessing a distinctive Moorish architectural style of three separate seaweed-green cupola domes and huge arched windows, this house of worship remains a tribute to Italian Jewry. What makes the synagogue so attractive are the elements that make the sculpture and art of Florence so meaningful, that artistic magnet that has drawn thousands of visitors to it each year.

The synagogue in Florence has a Moorish flavor and is the third largest dome in the city. It is said that it was the first edifice in the city to be built with reinforced concrete. This enormous building is impressive, indeed.

Designated a historical museum, the synagogue attracts Jews and non-Jews. Florence remains one of the few cities in Europe where guides point out the local synagogue. It is not that in other cities tour leaders fail to mention Jewish houses of worship because of prejudice; it is because synagogues in Europe are generally not conspicuous. But the synagogue in Florence is considered a beautiful temple and a tourist site.

Unlike other synagogues, this one possesses its own compound and is not located on a congested street; nor is it hidden behind high walls. Standing tall and proud, surrounded by a

Beth Haknesset Firenze, the Synagogue of Florence.

garden of flowers and palm trees, it can be seen from distant hills. The synagogue, built in 1882, symbolizes the emancipation of the Jews of Italy and freedom from the ghetto. The Jewish community also wanted to contribute to the architecture of Florence. They wanted a building that would show their pride.

What style should they choose for the religious building? In the early nineteenth century, many of the synagogues built in Europe were in the Gothic style. Florentine Jewry felt that Gothic was too much associated with Christianity. Instead, the Jewish community adopted the Moorish style, with a central cupola. Eastern influence is also shown by its polychromatic decoration. They wanted to portray an association with the Golden Age of Spain, although Carol Herselle Krinsky, in *Synagogues of Europe,* says many of its features are found in Ashkenazic synagogues.

The construction is pure Moorish style, completely covered with frescoes on the inside and rich Venetian mosaics in the Ehal (area of the Holy Ark) and on the vaulted ceilings. The doors on the Holy Ark are gilded. The bulk of the funds for the temple came from a David Levi, president of the Council of the Jewish University between 1860 and 1870. In his will, dated March 15, 1868, he requested that his assets be utilized for the building of a monumental temple worthy of Florence. At Levi's death on February 16, 1870, it was disclosed that he had left 1,492,255 lire. In 1874, the first stones came from Jerusalem and were laid on October 24, 1882, the date the building opened.

This Sephardic synagogue contains 1,000 pews in a beautiful chandeliered hall. As in many Orthodox synagogues, the women sit upstairs in a balcony. On Saturdays, because of a scarcity of worshippers, prayers are conducted in a special section on the right-hand side of the sanctuary. On holidays, however, it is packed.

The temple has survived wars, barbarism, floods, destruction, and plagues. During World War II the synagogue was dynamited by the Germans; sections were severely damaged. One can still see the bayonet marks inflicted by the "Nazi Fascists," as the guides refer to them, on the doors of the Holy Ark. The Germans used the temple as a garage where they repaired trucks.

On November 6, 1943, the first group of Jews was deported from the synagogue to the extermination camps. It was from the temple, too, that the Nazis arrested the beloved Rabbi Natan Cassuto and others. The rabbi was the son of Umberto Cassuto, who had abandoned his own career as a physician and had assumed the post of rabbi of the community. Ironically, together with a group of Italian Catholic priests, the rabbi forged documents that permitted Jews to escape to Switzerland or sail to Allied lines. His secret cell was caught in 1943, and its members, rabbis and priests, were sent to Auschwitz. On June 6, 1944, 16 old Jews were taken from the Home for the Aged and sent to Germany. The synagogue was occupied, bombed, and heavily damaged. After the war, Jews held services in a theater until the sanctuary was repaired.

A total of 243 Jews were deported from Florence, of whom only 13 returned. Eight more Jews were shot and 4 out of 22 who had taken part in the underground struggle fell.

During World War II, the prayer books and scrolls were hidden in Catholic churches and even in banks. But it was Alfiero Borghini, the *shamash* (beadle) who had been a member of the Italian partisans, who told me that they had also been hidden in a garden in a small town nearby. The shamash later joined the Jewish Brigade, the unit from Palestine that fought its way through Italy in World War II.

The destructive flood of November 4, 1966, was another recent traumatic experience for the synagogue and Florentine Jews. The muddy waters of the Arno River inundated the beautiful structure, causing great damage to the sacred objects and the library. More than 90 Sifrei Torahs (Torah scrolls) were lost. Fifteen thousand Jewish books were destroyed.

The building raises funds from the donations of people who take the synagogue tour. In the synagogue, the eternal theme of Judaism greets each visitor: "Bless he that cometh, bless he that goeth."

A **Jewish school** is also located here. The two-story building was named after the chief rabbi of Florence, Natan Cassuto, who was murdered by the Nazis. About 35 children attend this school.

Another attraction of Florence's synagogue is its **Jewish**

Museum, a sight certainly worth seeing. It is on the second floor of the synagogue and opened in 1987. Religious articles, such as rimmonim and kiddush cups; prayer shawls; and a pictorial display are all here to be absorbed. There are other ritual objects, including silver ornaments and embroidered vestments.

The museum was founded by the Friends of the Jewish Museum of Florence, a nonprofit association whose aim is to contribute to the maintenance of the exhibition and to the enrichment of the historic and artistic collection.

Kosher vegetarian restaurant is located next door to the main synagogue on Via Farini, Florence. This establishment is open only on weekdays until 2 P.M.

Chabad House, Via Dei Banchi, Florence, No, 6. Tel: (50123) 055-212-474. Kosher food is available here. Services every day. **Chabad Hospitality Center,** Via Dei Pilastri, 9R, Florence.

Naples

"See Naples and die," is an Italian proverb. Well you certainly won't die from taking in the beauty of this metropolis.

Naples is home to famous tenor, Luciano Pavarotti, who often sings in the magnificent opera house Teatro San Carlo, and who frequently rides on a Vespa motor bike while singing the folk songs of this busy harbor and the arias made famous by him and native son, Enrico Caruso. This is also the home of the famous actress Sophia Loren.

Naples of course has had a bum rap. Like all port cities, it has its dangers. While walking the streets one doesn't carry large sums of cash and leaves valuables in the hotel. While it remains one of the most chaotic cities in the world regarding traffic, it does have a street life of its own, as part of one of the most beautiful blue bays in the world alongside the superb vacation lands of the Sorrento Peninsula.

Always in the background is the lofty Vesuvius, often considered to be the "emblem" of Naples. Every tourist realizes this, of course, when he or she visits Pompei, which was destroyed on August 24, A.D. 79. Its latest eruption was in 1944.

Naples is famous for its art galleries, its catacombs and of course, the National Archaeological Museum considered to possess one of the richest collections of Greco-Roman antiques in the world.

Near Naples, which has a population of about 3 million and which is the third largest city in Italy, rests the beautiful Amalfi coast, with such hill-perched villages as Positano, Ravello and of course the island of Capri.

Indicative of the survival of small Jewish communities in Europe is the Naples synagogue, with only 154 members.

Synagogue, via Cappella Vecchia 31, Naples. Tel: 081-764-3480. Services are held only on Saturday morning. There is a small Talmud Torah. The office is open Monday, Wednesday and Friday from 10 A.M. to 12 noon. All the holidays are celebrated. Call for time of services.

The synagogue, by the way, is located in the building once occupied by Lady Hamilton, who is thought to have been the mistress of Lord Nelson. The congregation also is just off the Piazza dei Marteri (Martyrs Square), which is surrounded by famous designer shops.

In an interview, Mrs. Gabriella Cohen, secretary of the congregation told this writer that on so many occasions, the congregation decided to close, only to rescind the measure. Most religious Jews move away from the city because there is no kosher food available, no kosher restaurant, nor services during the week.

During World War II, the community was spared because Allied forces landed on the southern beaches of Italy on September 9, 1943, about 30 miles from Naples. The American and British forces quickly raced up the coast towards Naples. On October 31, the day before they arrived in the city, however, a clerk who later was honored by Israel and the Jewish people as "a righteous Gentile," stalled the Germans and Italian fascists who had come to his office for the list of Jewish residents. "Come back tomorrow," the clerk is reported to have said, and they left. The next day, Allied troops arrived in the city and the Jewish community was saved.

Suggested Reading

Chamberlain, E. R., and the editors of Time-Life Books. *Rome: The Great Cities.* Amsterdam: Time-Life Books, 1976.

Cornwell, John, *Hitler's Pope, The Secret History of Pius XII,* New York, Viking, 1999.

Harrison, Barbara G. *Italian Days.* New York: Weidenfeld, 1989.

Hochhuth, Rolf. *The Deputy.* New York: Grove Press, 1964.

Hughes, H. Stuart. *Prisoners of Hope: The Silver Age of Italian Jews, 1924-1974.* Cambridge, Mass.: Harvard University Press, 1983.

Kahler, Erich. *The Jews Among the Nations.* New York: Frederick Ungar, 1967.

Katz, Robert. *Black Sabbath.* New York: Macmillan, 1969.

Lewry, Guenther. *The Catholic Church and Nazi Germany.* New York: McGraw-Hill, 1964.

Mann, Vivian B., ed. *Gardens and Ghettos: The Art of Jewish Life in Italy.* Los Angeles: University of California Press, 1989.

Michaelis, Meir. *Mussolini and the Jews: German-Italian Relations and the Jewish Question in Italy 1922-1945.* Oxford University Press, 1978.

Morton, H. V. *A Traveler in Southern Italy.* New York: Dodd, Mead, 1964.

Roth, Cecil. *The History of the Jews of Italy.* Philadelphia: Jewish Publication Society of America, 1946.

Segre, Dan Vittorio. *Memoirs of a Fortunate Jew.* Bethesda, Md.: Adler and Adler, 1987.

Vogelstein, Herman. *Rome.* Philadelphia: Jewish Publication Society of America, 1940.

Zuccotti, Susan. *The Italians and the Holocaust: Persecution, Rescue and, Survival.* New York: Basic Books, 1988.

Spain
Columbus, a Jew?

"O Spain, one-half of thy face is fiesta and the other, misery." So wrote novelist Perez Galdos of his nineteenth-century homeland. Spain is the home of Cervantes, El Greco, flamenco and castanets, the bullring, and the conquistadors.

The enchanting cities of Castile and Andalusia are found here, as well as the Alhambra of Granada and its surrounding gardens that recall the Arabian Nights. The Moors and the Jews, the Christians and the Inquisition make up Spain's history. Hemingway and the Civil War, Franco and the Lincoln Brigade—there is no question that many world-famous events and figures are linked to this country.

But for the Jewish traveller who arrives in Spain, the nation has a special meaning—*history*. Coming here is like coming home, except that no longer is it a "Jewish neighborhood." Synagogues have become churches. Vanished are the Hebrew academies and the libraries. We visit Spain to recount our glorious past, when one-third of the population of Iberia once contained Jewish blood.

A Brief History

The Jewish people still recall their "Golden Age" in Spain. To this day, Jewish history does not record a similar success story anywhere else in Europe, as Jews have rarely lived as "harmoniously or creatively" as in Spain.

For in Spain, moreover, the people of culture were Jewish. They contributed to the developing societies of both Moslem and Christian Spain. Jews who had been in Spain since the destruction of the First Temple lived peacefully with the Arabs on the Iberian peninsula ever since that wintry night in 711 when Tarik Ibn Ziyad ferried an army across the Strait of Gibraltar and freed the Jews from the barbarous Visigoths.

The Moslems went on to cultivate science, medicine, philosophy, and poetry. The Spanish Jewish communities produced doctors, mathematicians, philosophers, court advisors, diplomats, and military leaders.

Nearly 1,000 years ago, there were cities in Spain where most of the inhabitants were Jewish. Spain contained the largest Jewish community in Europe.

In the Middle Ages, several hundred thousand Jews, one-half of world's Jewry, lived in Spain. To this day, we call these Jews "Sephardim," after "Sepharad," the Hebrew word for Spain. Some of the greatest Hebrew scholars in Jewish history, who devoted themselves to studying both the written and the oral law of Judaism, were from Spain, including Maimonides (1135-1204), known as the *Rambam,* which stands for Rabbi Moses ben Maimon. These scholars fostered the study of all branches of Jewish literature. They spoke Arabic and established schools and libraries. They wrote the finest Hebrew poetry ever created. The Zohar, the main work of Jewish mysticism, is said to have been written by Moses Ben Shem Tov de Leon (1240-1305) of Guadalajara. He is thought to have been born in Avila. And the works of the Hebrew poets Yehudah HaLevi, Solomon Ibn Gabirol, and Moses Ibn Ezra move us to this day.

But as often happens, history took a turn for the worse for the Jews. By the 1300s, they became vulnerable, no longer needed. In 1391, terrible anti-Jewish riots occurred throughout the country. About 20,000 Jews simply gave up the fight and converted. These "New Christians" were called "Conversos," but many of them only pretended to be Christians; secretly they practiced Judaism. We know them also as "Marranos," the Spanish word for "swine," or "criptojudios," "false Jews." They were never trusted by the Spaniards.

Soon one of the most horrible words in the lexicon of the

Jewish people was created—the Inquisition. Spain had to be pure Catholic.

Between "4,000 and 8,000 secret Jews and suspects were burnt alive" in the 15 years of Tomas de Torquemada's reign. During the three centuries of its terror in Iberia, nearly 350,000 people were indicted and about 30,000 "Judaizers" were burned at the stake. Another 15,000 were burned in effigy and several hundred thousand were "penanced" because it was thought they were Jews. The burning of New Christians was to be a lesson to the converted: don't dare revert to Judaism.

Tragically, the Inquisition taught many in the world to focus on "pure blood" and "pure race." If you possessed a certificate of *limpieza de sangre* or "certificate of pure blood," you could rise to the top. The others dropped out. In the end, Spain suffered because it excluded too many bright, intellectual persons. It "surrendered itself to the chimera of racial purity", notes Barnet Litvinoff. It never regained the glory it had achieved before it expelled its Jews, who went on to settle in Africa, Turkey, Italy, Portugal, and France. Dr. M. Kayserling maintains, moreover, that the Inquisition and the expulsion had one purpose: to grab the property of secret Jews for the state treasury, even if they had to do it under the guise of religion.

Thus, in 1492, the year Columbus set sail for America, several hundred thousand Jews were expelled, not to return until 1859. The numbers of Jews expelled vary; I have seen estimates from 100,000 to a half-million and upwards. For 400 years, if a Jew was found in Spain, he could be punished by death.

Jews began to trickle into Seville after the Constitution of 1869 decreed liberty for religious faiths. By 1877, there were 406 Jews in Spain. Refugees fleeing from Czarist Russian pogroms reached Madrid in the 1880s. By 1910, a Jewish community had been set up. One of its founders, Ignazio Bauer, was the first Jew elected to the Spanish parliament.

During World War I, many Sephardic Jews of Spanish ancestry moved from Salonika, Greece, and Istanbul, Turkey, to Barcelona and Madrid. Zionist leader Max Nordau, who was an Austrian citizen, was forced to leave France during World War I, and he, too, moved to Spain.

After World War I, Jewish communities existed in Seville,

Madrid, and Barcelona. In 1924, Prime Minister Primo de Rivera declared that those who were descendants of the Sephardic exiles of 1492 would be recognized as Spanish citizens.

In 1927, Spain offered citizenship to all Sephardic Jews. Under the new Constitution of 1931, Jews enjoyed "full legal equality." This legislation and the Constitution was later nullified by Franco.

About 4,000 Jews resided in Spain when the Spanish Civil War broke out in 1936. "An inner psychic wound" was the way Barbara Probst Solomon described the conflagration. Figures vary, but some say, nearly one million lives were lost in the struggle. Terror reigned; there were excesses on both sides. The overwhelming majority of Jews were on the side of the Republic—10 percent of the 40,000 foreign volunteers who fought for the Republic were Jewish. But Franco and his Fascist generals were victorious. At the start of the Second World War, Spain was closely tied to Nazi Germany but was nonbelligerent. As the war progressed, she quickly became neutral; obviously the Axis powers were losing.

By 1940, Jews were trying to return to Spain and Portugal as Hitler engulfed the Continent. Large numbers of refugees from Nazi-occupied France fled across the Pyrenees into Spain. Although most were interned by the Spanish, they were not deported.

Stanley G. Payne, in his book, *The Franco Regime, 1936-1975,* writes: "Altogether, during the first part of the war, some 30,000 Jews had received safe passage through Spain, and there is no indication of any Jew who reached Spanish soil being turned back to German authorities. Approximately 7,500 more may have passed through between 1942 and 1944, and during the latter phases of the S.S. roundup in Hungary and the Balkans, Spanish consular officials managed to provide protection (through citizenship status) to more than 3,200 additional Jews, many of them Sephardic."

But Spain never exhausted its capabilities in saving Jews during the Holocaust. At times it allowed Jews to cross the border from France to safety. In the second half of the war, it saved more than 10,000 Jews, according to Haim Avni in *Spain, the Jews and Franco.*

Post-World War II Jews moved cautiously as Franco continued to tighten his grip over Spain.

A number of people claim Franco had direct Jewish ancestry that could be traced back to the Inquisition. Perhaps! But many people in Spain, it is said, have "Jewish blood."

After World War II, Spain followed the lead of the Vatican, which failed to recognize Israel as a state in 1948. In 1950, Israel voted against Spain in the U.N. when the world body revoked a resolution condemning Spanish actions during the war. This hardened Franco's position not to recognize Israel.

After the death of Franco in 1975, a new life began for all Spaniards, including Jews. Today dynamic, vibrant Spain, with 40 million citizens, has molded itself into a democracy. Spain, a member of the European community, is often called Europe's "moveable feast," with its famous dress designers, rock stars, and chic café people.

A decline in religious observance has marked post-Franco Spain. Although the 1492 expulsion edict has never been officially annulled (it is still "on the books"), the Constitution of 1978, which guaranteed non-Catholics "the right of religious freedom and religious equality," abrogated it de facto. On February 21, 1990, the government signed an accord that officially placed Jewish and Protestant faiths on par with Roman Catholicism. In 1992, King Juan Carlos I signed a royal decree officially canceling the 1492 Edict of Expulsion of the Jews.

After a long and arduous diplomatic effort, Spain and Israel established diplomatic relations in 1986, and, in the same year, Spain became a member of the European Union.

Yes, there are Jews in Spain today. Indeed, a renascence of Jewish life has occurred. A few schools and synagogues serve about 14,000 Jews, who are devoted to leading a full Jewish life. They are building a community.

Andalusia

Fly to Andalusia in the south of Spain. The Moslems called it "Al-Andalus," their appellation for the conquered lands of Iberia. For millions, the image of Spain is Andalusia.

In the days of Moslem Spain, the heart of Andalusia was represented by three great cities: Seville, Cordoba, Granada. They are Moorish cities, and even today Moorish traditions remain strong. But they were also Jewish cities with literary salons, Talmudic schools, and synagogues. Visit Andalusia and your eyes will view luscious landscapes, singing birds in olive groves, and fertile valleys.

SEVILLE

Let us begin our journey with Seville, the capital of Andalusia—city of romance, poetry, and art; Spain's fourth largest urban area, and the largest city in southern Spain.

Seville, with its approximately one and a half-million persons, is the mythical home of Don Juan, Carmen, and Figaro; the Alcazar, the fourteenth-century palace for Christian kings built like the Alhambra; the Columbus Archives of the Indies, a museum: the *Torre del Oro,* Tower of Gold, and the huge, imposing Seville Cathedral; and the spiritual home of flamenco, bullfights, and Gypsies.

Today there are 15 Jewish families in Seville.

A **synagogue** is located at Bustos Tavera 8, 41003, Seville. Tel: 34-95-427-5517. In the summer services are at 8:30 P.M. on Friday evenings.

What is remarkable is that there is a synagogue at all in Seville and that there are Jews here: 70 at the latest count.

Some 600 years ago, there were 23 synagogues (all destroyed), thousands of Jews, and a Jewish quarter whose remnants we can see today. This Jewish section is called **Barrio de Santa Cruz,** a tourist attraction in this city that Columbus helped to make famous.

Tragedy, of course, came to Seville, in the form of riots, pogroms, conversion of synagogues into churches, and the Inquisition.

Today, in this Santa Cruz section of Seville, you can stroll through the narrow lanes of whitewashed homes and realize that the "Sephardim" (Spanish Jews) lived a full, comfortable life and that members of the Jewish community were even advisors to the vizier.

Passageway in the Barrio de Santa Cruz, the old Jewish quarter in Seville. (Photo courtesy of the Tourist Office of Spain)

The Santa Cruz quarter contains the remains of the old Jewish quarter, which may have run as far as the Alcazar. There is indeed a new hotel called **Las Casas de la Juderia** (The Houses of the Jewish Quarter), made up of individual apartments and located in the midst of the labyrinth of the old Jewish quarter. Located near the Plaza Santa Maria la Blanca, near the Murillo Gardens, the address is 7 Callejon de DOS Hermands. Tel: 441-5150. FAX: 442-2170.

One legend that came out of that time concerns a street in the Barrio de Santa Cruz called **Calle Susona,** street of Susona. Once it was named Calle de la Muerte, street of death.

Visit it; it has an interesting tale. Don Diego Suson, a Marrano whose ancestors originally had converted to Catholicism in 1391, organized a group of Marranos who were trying to halt the Inquisition. Don Diego's daughter, who was called "Beautiful Susanna," may have betrayed a secret meeting of the Marrano group to her Christian lover, who in turn reported it to the authorities. Don Diego and his associates were burned to death as "false Jews." Shocked beyond grief, Susanna placed herself in a convent. But when she was about to die, she repented. She asked that her corpse, and later her skull, be hung in front of the house she had betrayed. The street was known as Calle de la Muerte for many years.

Within a decade, Jews were expelled from Spain. Romantic Seville became a tragic port of embarkation for Jewish refugees from western Andalusia, most of whom left for North Africa.

Today, interestingly, most of the Jews in Spain (and in Seville) are also from North Africa, from cities across the Mediterranean Sea, some of whose exotic names are Ceuta and Melilla, the latter still governed by Spain. These Moroccan Jews, besides having a synagogue, hold a Passover Seder in Seville, celebrate Jewish holidays as best they can, teach their children Hebrew, and bury their dead in a Jewish cemetery. They face the same problems as Jews all over the world: assimilation, intermarriage, and a desire for Jewish education and knowledge.

But they are not that isolated at the end of the twentieth century. The Jews of Seville belong to a National Federation of Spanish Jewish Communities; they visit Jewish communities in nearby Malaga. It is only an hour's flight on Iberia, airline of Spain, to Madrid where there are about 4,000 Jews. And, of course, there is Israel, which most of them have visited.

Sites in Seville

In the **Seville Cathedral,** Jews of Seville presented a symbolic key to Fernando III when he conquered the city from the Moors in 1248. The key is still located in the cathedral treasury, engraved in Hebrew: "The King of Kings will open, the King of the Lord shall enter." The silver tomb of Fernando III rests in the cathedral, with an epitaph written in Latin, Arabic, and Hebrew.

When the Moslems ruled here the cathedral was the city's main mosque. Today, it stands as one of Christendom's most spectacular houses of worship; only the squares of Rome's St. Peter's and London's St. Paul's are larger.

Interesting to both Jews and non-Jews is **Columbus Archives of the Indies** at 3 Avenida Queipo de Llano, which contains the account books of Luis de Santangel, a descendant of a Marrano family. A supporter of Columbus, he has been called the "Disraeli of Spain." He held the posts of chancellor of the Royal Household and controller general of finance in Aragon. He made a private loan of 17,000 ducats to Columbus, "money out of his own pocket," writes Dr. M. Kayserling. Without Santangel's enthusiastic support, "the first voyage of Christopher Columbus would never have taken place," says Cecil Roth. Incidentally, Columbus's first letter telling of his trip was written to Santangel, who with "his kinsman Gabriel Sanchez were the most zealous patrons of Columbus," according to Dr. Kayserling. Other Marranos may have pitched in to help Columbus, but Abraham Seneor, the crown rabbi of Castile, a go-between in the royal marriage of Ferdinand and Isabella, also supported Columbus, as did Don Isaac Abravanel, formerly of Lisbon, now the Jewish spokesperson in Spain, says Litvinoff. Seneor himself would eventually convert. Santangel, though a devout Catholic and counsel to the king and queen, also tried to alleviate the situation of the Jews.

The 1992 world's fair in Seville celebrated the 500th anniversary of Columbus's discovery of America. Columbus returned often to Seville; they like him here.

Was Columbus descended from a Jewish, or ex-Jewish, family? Was he a Marrano, a secret Jew? We simply do not know. Evidence exists on both sides. He could have been a converted Jew and/or Marrano. The famous writer Blasco Ibanes was convinced that Columbus was indeed a Marrano—i.e., ostensibly a Christian, but actually of Jewish descent. Other Spanish authors have said he was of Iberian Jewish stock.

Why did Columbus begin the account of his famous voyage with a reference to the expulsion of the Jews from Spain, scholars ask. Others say the expulsion of Jews and Columbus's voyage are a coincidence: "In the same month in which their majesties issued the edict that all Jews should be driven out of their kingdom and its territories, in the same month they gave me the order to undertake with sufficient men my expedition of discovery to the Indies."

Finally, other scholars note Columbus was mysterious about his religion. He seemed to have something to conceal. He had a strange affinity for Jewish and Marrano society. He deliberately postponed the day of his sailing until August 3, 1492. Why did he wait one day? Perhaps it was that the previous day, August 2, was the "unpropitious fast day of the Ninth of Av known as *Tisha B'Av,*" which commemorates the destruction of the Second Temple. As Cecil Roth notes in *Responsibilities and Events in Jewish History,*" One who does work on the Ninth of Ab, the rabbis say, will never see a blessing therefrom."

Professor Roth maintains Columbus had an obsession with Jewish matters. He points to the theory that the Colombo family were Spanish Jews who settled in Genoa and who, "following the traditions of their race, had remained faithful to the language of their country of origin." "He indubitably had a curious mystical Jewish obsession and was always referring in his notes to the facts of ancient Jewish history," writes Professor Roth.

Also, letters that Columbus wrote to his son, Diego, have been preserved. In the corners were written the Hebrew letters *Bet Heh,* for "B'ezrat Ha Shem" (with the help of God). According to the *Encyclopedia Judaica,* Columbus "boasted cryptically about his connection with King David."

Columbus may have studied Jewish literature firsthand. But Professor Yosef Yerushalmi is quoted as saying: "There is not a shred of convincing evidence that he was either a Jew, a Marrano, or a proto-Semite, although many *Conversos* helped fund his ventures. After all, it was a business." In part, the voyage can be considered a Jewish enterprise because exploration was a business, and Jews were involved in efforts to find new lands. Those who overwhelmingly supported Columbus were "men of Jewish extraction," such as Luis de Santangel, Gabriel Sanchez, and Alfonso de la Caballeria.

Luis de Torres, a Marrano, was Columbus's interpreter on his historic journey. A linguist, he spoke Hebrew. Luis de Torres may have been baptized just before Columbus set sail. "He was the first European on these expeditions to step upon American soil," says Erich Kahler in *The Jews Among the Nations*. Dr. Kayserling also notes that Luis de Torres was the first European who discovered the use of tobacco and "was the first person of Jewish stock who settled in Cuba." There may have been other Jews among Columbus's crew.

We know that, in his journeys, the explorer used the nautical instruments perfected by Joseph Vecinho, who was Jewish.

Navigation was traditionally a Jewish trade.

Abraham Zacuto compiled the navigational almanac. Zacuto, who had ties to the University of Salamanca, went to Portugal at the time of the expulsion and apparently died in Damascus. One of his major contributions was the invention of the copper astrolabe.

The key mapmakers were all Jews. The most famous, of course, were Abraham and Yehuda Cresques, who established a school of cartography in Palma de Mallorca.

Jewish sites of those days still stand, like the **Plaza de Santa Cruz,** the **Arco de laJuderia,** and the streets with Jewish names: **Calle de Cal** (Kahal)—street of the congregation; **Calle de Cal Major**—street of the large congregation; **JuderiaVieja,** the Old Jewish Quarter; **Calle de dos Tintes**—street of the dyers.

In 1492, there were three events that changed the world. The Moslems were defeated in their last battle with Christianity at Granada and Spain was reunited under the Catholic kings. Then

Jews, who were seen as the "traitor burrowing from within," were expelled and would not return for 400 years. And on August 3, 1492, Columbus sailed for America, a day or two after the last Jews left the soil of Spain and one day after *Tisha B'av*, the Jewish holiday that laments the destruction of the Temple.

With 1492 being so important, it is no wonder that the International Jewish Committee Sepharad '92 was formed to commemorate the 500th anniversary of the expulsion of the Jews from Spain, and celebrate the rebirth and subsequent growth of the Sephardic heritage and its place in Jewish history. And so as one walks through Seville, one thinks of Columbus, the Jews, and the Inquisition. But the sounds and sights are of the present. This is a city to tour and absorb. The Moors and the Jews loved Seville. A proverb says, "If one were to ask for bird's milk in Seville, one would be able to get it."

As I walked through the open areas of the middle of the city, I recalled that 500 years ago, 700 *Conversos* were burned at the stake and more than 5,000 were reconciled with the Catholic Church, all within seven years. Even in 1484, Tomas de Torquemada, a converted Jew himself, chaired a convention of the Inquisition in this city to define the procedures of the torture process used to obtain so-called truth. A Spanish Jew once told me, "They tried to kick us out, but we're still here; we were stronger than they were."

CORDOBA

It is good to visit Cordoba after Seville. About 100 miles separate the two cities. To those Jewish travelers interested in Jewish history and culture, Cordoba evokes memories of a brilliant Jewish intellectual center in the Golden Age of Spain. Today one can visit one of the three existing Jewish synagogues of ancient Spain; gaze at the statue of Maimonides in Tiberias Square; or walk in the narrow alleys of the famous Juderia (Jewish Quarter) near the cathedral and the alcazar, where tourists and students sit in the Plaza de Juda Levi and sip coffee or a soft drink.

Cordoba, where once lived Averroes, the Arab philosopher

who was a contemporary of Maimonides, is a Moorish city with narrow winding streets, gardens, olive and orange groves, and a population of one and a quarter million. The capital of the caliph, it contained 200,000 buildings, 3,000 mosques, 27 free schools, and a university that attracted scholars from throughout the world. In the Middle Ages, Cordoba, a scientific center, possessed a vibrant economy that made it the largest city in the world, and the wealthiest and most civilized city in Western Europe. Stanley G. Payne, professor of history, says: "In size, services, culture and economy, the city was without a peer in Western Europe and was rivaled in the East only by Constantinople."

Famous for its libraries and bookshops, Cordoba was the high-water mark of the Arab civilization in Europe. It once contained a library of 400,000 catalogued volumes.

The past and its rich cultural and religious mix can be seen in La Mezquita (mosque) building, which shares the same foundation as the cathedral. The combined structure—not far from the Jewish Quarter—boasts a Moslem forest of pillars and white Moorish arches with a domed ceiling, a testimonial to the days when Cordoba was the capital of Islamic Spain. But after the Christian conquest ended in 1492, 60 columns were torn out of the mosque to make room for the cathedral in the mosque's center.

Today, once again, Jews live in Cordoba, which the poet Antonio Machado y Ruiz called "Roman, Moorish and silent." To be sure, there are only a few Jews here in this Andalusian city of about 750,000, the birthplace of the genius scholar, Maimonides. Once, too, it was the temporary home of Yehudah HaLevi, one of the great Hebrew poets. It was the home of Hasdai ibn Shaprut (915-70), physician, diplomat, and advisor to the caliph, who established the first Talmudic school here. This city contained a galaxy of Hebrew scholars, philosophers, and poets who attended the court of Abd-al Rahman III (912-61).

When I was in Cordoba, I talked with an American Jew, Mrs. E. Fereres, who with her husband, Elias, had been living in Cordoba for five years. As she tells it, the Spaniards often confuse the Jews with the Moors. Doesn't Maimonides wear a turban? One thing she did say was that there is a heightened interest in Jews among Spaniards, especially in the Sephardic past. She cited a group of Catholics who organized themselves into a group called Beit Sephardim.

There are a number of people who speak Hebrew here. A Greek Jew, Eli Nachmias, who lives here part of the year, has been instrumental in helping to restore one of the synagogues. Jewish history courses are taught at the Faculty of Philosophy and Letters, a fine college here. In 1985, the 850th anniversary of the birth of Maimonides brought much attention to the Jewish past in Spain, and there were symposia held, bringing about increased Jewish consciousness.

The Jewish Quarter in Cordoba

When you enter the Moorish gateway known as the **Puerta de Almodovar** (it was once called "Bab-al-Yahud"), you are in the **Juderia,** which is located between the Plaza de las Tendillas and the River Guadalquivir. Turn right down the **Calle de los Judios** in the Jewish Quarter. You have to imagine that Cordoba was once the "New York City of Europe," that along these narrow passageways of flower-laced streets and white-washed abodes, of gardens and orange groves, a population of one and one-quarter million thrived and lived in this capital of the caliph. The Jews flourished in Cordoba. Under the Moors, the Talmudic school of Cordoba was famous throughout Europe. Jews served in high positions as ambassadors and advisors. Many of the caliphs hired Jewish physicians.

The Statue of Maimonides, erected in 1964, is located near the synagogue on Calle de los Judios. Actually, it is just down the street from the synagogue in a square named **Plaza Tiberias** to perpetuate the ties between his Spanish birthplace and Tiberias, the city in Israel where he is buried.

Maimonides was one of the greatest Jewish thinkers and scholars of all time, author of the *Guide of the Perplexed,* and a doctor who lived from 1135 to 1204. Barnet Litvinoff says Maimonides "stands as the most significant Jewish intellect and teacher from the time of the Prophets until Spinoza."

Statue of Maimonides. (Photo by M. Serels)

Born Maimonides, this remarkable figure in post-biblical Jewish history fled from his native Cordoba because of persecution from the Almohad sect, whose military forces rampaged Andalusia in 1146. He mastered medicine and, through tireless study, absorbed many other fields of knowledge, such as mathematics and astronomy. By 1185, he was already a leading physician at Saladin's court in Egypt and knew Richard Coeur de Lion. In 1180, he compiled the *Mishneh Torah,* "Repetition of the Law." His 13 articles of belief would be incorporated in the creeds of Judaism, and his *Guide of the Perplexed* scrutinized the revelation at Sinai through the lens of reason. It is not hard to imagine Maimonides walking through the old Jewish Quarter in Cordoba.

The courtyard is small and the statue of Maimonides, sitting in the middle, dominates the area of plain, whitewashed walls. The sage sits on a marble bench atop an attractive cube. He is wearing the robes and twisted turban of the desert. In his lap, he holds a book, his right thumb marking the spot. His face, his posture, and his robes are those of a philosopher and, as you look at the statue, you understand why his admirers said, "From Moses to Moses there was no one like Moses."

Just up the street from the statue of Maimonides is the small, "cubicle-in-shape" **synagogue** built in 1315. On the east wall of the small Moorish-designed building is a vacant niche that once held the Ark of the Law. On the south wall can be seen intricately designed Scripture and prayers in Hebrew. In his book, *Travels in Jewry,* Israel Cohen writes that one of the verses in Hebrew says: "A little sanctuary and a house of testimony which was built by Isaac Mehab, son of the wealthy Ephraim, erected in the year 75 [1315] as a temporary structure. Arise, O Lord and hasten to rebuild Jerusalem." Upstairs, in the upper part of the south wall, you can clearly make out a women's gallery. The building later served as a church, the Church of Saint Crispin.

The spirit of Maimonides is everywhere. Right in the Juderia, not far from the statue of Maimonides, you will find a square called **Plazuela de Maimonides.** This may have been the site where Maimonides lived when he resided in Cordoba.

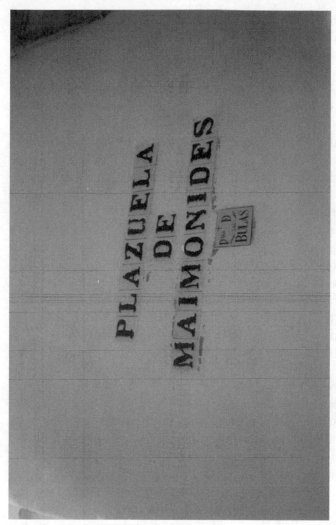

Plazuela de Maimonides in Cordoba. (Photo by Malke Frank)

Visualize silversmiths, silk embroiderers, and leather-goods makers who sold their products. Extending from this street is **Calle Rambam Maimonides.**

Walk to 5 Calle de los Judios, along the street that was the main street of the medieval ghetto. This is **Casa Maimonides,** the actual spot (if not the house itself) where the great Maimonides was born.

In 1935, the Spanish government sponsored an 800th birthday celebration of Maimonides. Jews came from all over the world. For the first time in 443 years, a Jewish prayer service was held in Cordoba. In the synagogue courtyard, the municipality of Cordoba erected this plaque: "On the occasion of the eight-hundredth anniversary of the birth of Rabbi Moses ben Maimon, the Spanish government, in the name of the entire nation, expresses its recognition of that immortal Jewish spirit. Cordoba, his birth place, honors his memory."

During the Moslem period, the Jewish Quarter was located near the alcazar (fortress) in the northwest section of the city. It continued in existence after the Christian reconquest.

Walk down **Juda Levi Street,** named for the Jewish poet who was born in Tudela in 1075, but who lived for a number of years in Cordoba.

The proprietor of the cafe in the **Plaza de Juda Levi** spoke to me about the poet, philosopher, and physician for whom this historical square is named. Born in Tudela (1085-1140), he traveled south to the literary salons of Andalusia and passed through Cordoba on his way, with the intention of going on to Granada. In Cordoba, HaLevi participated in a poetry writing contest and won the competition for imitating a complicated poem by Moses Ibn Ezra, who invited HaLevi to his home. HaLevi lived in many communities in Spain. When he lived in Toledo, he practiced medicine.

"His was the sweetest and most poignant of all the nightingale voices of that time," writes Chaim Raphael. He gave the Jewish people the electrifying "Ode to Zion"; "Songs of Exile"; and "Poems of Zion," or as we know them, "Zionides." "He was the most beloved poet in post-Biblical Hebrew literature," says Raphael. He dreamed of reaching the Land of Israel and freeing himself of the enslavement of Exile. One of his most famous lines is "My heart is in East, and I in the uttermost West." Finally,

Plaza de Juda Levi in Cordoba. (Photo by Malke Frank)

he did leave Toledo. According to legend, HaLevi reached Jerusalem, which was occupied by Crusaders. He bowed down and kissed its stones. As he recited the opening words of one of his elegies, "Zion, wilt thou not ask if peace be with the captive," an Arab horseman pierced his heart with a lance.

But the more likely story is that he died six months after reaching Egypt and was buried there. His "Ode to Zion" expresses Israel's yearning for its homeland. He said the ideal existence for the Jew was attainable only in his own homeland. A Spanish writer, Filipe Torroba Bernaldo de Quiros, says that he united "Sefardite nostalgia of Spain with Palestinian Zionism."

The café owner, too, decries the decision 500 years ago of the Jewish expulsion. "Spain today is not racist," she says. "It is not possible to have one people; we have to have many peoples."

Today, the Spanish people are still remarkably hospitable. There is a feeling in Spain that the country has moved forward once again toward democracy. It is in the air, on TV, in the press.

Of course, despite progress, Spain possesses many of the same problems prevalent in the world today: drugs, crime, and the decline of moral values. Spain, however, has passed through a peaceful transition from repressive dictatorship to parliamentary government.

GRANADA

Once it was called "Gharnata' al-Yahud," "Granada of the Jews." It was also known as "Villa de Judios," the description of the city by the first great poet of Hebrew Spain, Samuel haNagid (Ibn Nagrela). This poet, "the Prince," was also a philosopher-soldier, who lived in Granada.

"Whoever has not seen the splendor of the Jews of Granada, their fortune and their glory, has never seen true glory for they were great with wisdom and piety."

The best place to find Granada's Jews is the **University of Granada,** at the Cartuja Campus. Chances are that, at the university, you will first run into dynamic Dr. Maria Jose Cano, a Catholic who teaches in the Department of Semitic Studies. Dr.

Cano, who studied at the Jewish Theological Seminary in New York and who attended the Hebrew University and Tel Aviv University, speaks and reads Hebrew and has written scholarly papers on the poetry of Solomon Ibn Gabirol and Maimonides.

Here is her story. When she was a young girl, at Easter time the children of her village would travel to a nearby village and make papier-mâché targets depicting Jews. They would then throw stones at them.

Her father told her this was wrong, so she never participated in this hatred. Her father explained to her that Jews are people like all people—not the devil as depicted by the children. She believed her father was an upright, honest man and what he said must have been true. So she pursued her interest in this people, the Jews, because her father had shown kindness toward them. She went to Israel and studied Hebrew in a kibbutz ulpan as well as at the Hebrew University in Jerusalem.

"Interest in Jewish studies and Israel is rising in Spain," she said in an interview in her office at the university, "especially with the finalization of diplomatic relations between Spain and Israel in early 1986." For example, the town in which she grew up commissioned her to write a paper on Jewish life in that village as it was centuries ago. Dr. Cano hopes her students will also engage in research into the Sephardic past.

I met a number of Spanish students who were eager to visit Israel. They talked about Israel and the Jewish people.

One problem in the Department of Semitic Studies is a lack of books on Jewish history and Israel. Persons willing to contribute books in English, Spanish, and Hebrew can mail them to Dr. Maria Jose Cano at the University of Granada, Department of Semitic Studies, Faculty of Philosophy and Letters, Cartuja Campus, Granada, Spain. Being interested in Judaism, she is a good source on Jews who live in Granada.

On a trip to Spain a number of years ago, I met a Jewish family in Granada, Dr. and Mrs. Shaul Belilty Cohen, who are from Spanish-ruled Melilla in North Africa. Dr. Cohen is a urologist. He enjoys Granada and does not hide the fact that he is Jewish—all his friends and colleagues know it. He often travels to Malaga, an hour and a half away, where there is a Jewish community. The Cohens light candles and say kiddush on Friday nights. He has visited Israel several times and has relatives there, as well as in Morocco.

He grew up as a member of Hashomer Hatzair in Morocco and attended the University of Granada. He has two children. While he has a good life in Granada, he worries about raising his children Jewish. He tries to help Dr. Cano expand the Department of Semitic Studies at the university.

People like Dr. Cano and Dr. Cohen, by their work and by their presence, try to tell the story of the past and still keep Judaism alive.

The Alhambra Palace and the Jews

The Alhambra, the palace of paradise, is also of historic significance to Jews. It is the "apex of Moorish design extravagance." All routes led to the Alhambra Palace, which is one of the most beautiful monuments in all Spain. The royal palace—which is a fortress—was constructed on a 35-acre plateau atop a last spur of the Sierra Nevada to express the spirit of the civilization that was Moslem Spain.

It is said that the best time to view Granada is when the colors of the sky are lilac, rose, gray, blue, hazel, aquamarine, red, and dusty-gold. Surrounding the Alhambra are flowering gardens, courtyards, and splashing fountains. The scene brings to mind an idea of what life must have been like under the Arabs. Nightingales sing in the Alhambra Gardens, a wonderful legacy of the Moors, who "designed their gardens not only in the visual sense, but also aimed to catch a visitor's ear, arouse his tastebuds and coax him into touching all that summoned him."

Looking up at the Alhambra, one recalls that the Ibn Nagrela family may have had something to do with building part of the structure. Joseph Ibn Nagrela was the son of the famous Samuel Ibn Nagrela, "The Nagid" (933-1055). Samuel, the vizier of Granada, achieved the highest position as a Jew in medieval Moslem Spain. Joseph, who succeeded his father, built a huge palace. It is believed that this was later destroyed, and the present Alhambra built on that site.

Joseph came to an untimely end as a result of a palace intrigue. He was assassinated on December 30, 1066, and a day after his murder, a Moslem mob stormed through the Jewish Quarter of Granada in what was one of the few recorded pogroms of Moslems against Spanish Jews.

The Moors who conquered Spain in the eighth century believed that the fertile plain of Granada would be heaven, as told in the Koran. They built a grand city here and created the impressive fountains of the Alhambra, whose walls owe their redness to bricks made from ferrous mud. The "Red Fort" is still one of the most admired monuments in Spain.

The guides who take you around the Alhambra cite Jewish influence in the "ruddy hue" of the palace. Some say the famous "Lion Fountain," "Court of the Lions," was a gift of the Jews of Granada. Others say the 12 lions are patterned after 12 oxen of King Solomon's Temple, which Joseph Ibn Nagrela had copied for his palace.

The Alhambra is history. Perhaps that is why two million persons visit here each year. The Alhambra, a symbol of Moorish surrender to the "Catholic kings," still stands as the last bastion of Islam in Spain. It fell on January 2, 1492. But this Moorish architectural gem contains within its silent walls much of Jewish history in Spain.

Let us go first to the **Hall of the Ambassadors.** Under its 60 feet high domed ceiling, the Catholic kings, on March 31, 1492, signed the document expelling the Jews. The huge square room contains nice large windows from which one can look down to the city of Granada.

In the very same room, Ferdinand and Isabella signed an agreement allowing Columbus to sail west to America.

Here in this hall, Don Isaac Abravanel (1437-1508), Jewish philosopher, statesman, and supporter of Columbus, and Abraham Seneor of Segovia tried to change the minds of their Catholic rulers about the expulsion of the Jews in 1492 by offering a large bribe. They almost succeeded, but as Litvinoff writes: "Tomas de Torquemada, Confessor to the Queen, Inquisitor General of the Inquisition and converted Jew, is said to have taunted Abraham Seneor, a confidant of Isabella, who then converted." Torquemada stopped any wavering on the part of the "Catholic kings," and the Jews were forced out.

After the expulsion decree, incidentally, Don Isaac Abravanel

left Spain on May 31, 1492, first to Italy, then to Corfu, and finally
to Venice in 1503, where he wrote mystical works and biblical
commentaries. He died in 1508 at the age of 71 and was buried
in Padua. The expulsion edict was promulgated at the end of
April, and the Jewish exodus began in May and continued until
August 2, 1492. More than 100,000 Jews went to Portugal, just
across the border. They were seeking a haven. Instead, they ran
right smack into danger once again. In Portugal, they would
soon be forced into baptism and sold into slavery.

Jewish Madrid

It is only about an hour's flight from Granada to Madrid, a
city of bullfights and "machismo." Hemingway called it "the
most Spanish of all cities, the best place to live in, the finest
people."

Madrid symbolizes the New Spain—busy and active, now
moving at a fast pace to make up for lost time. The energy is
addictive.

Greater Madrid boasts five million Madrileños, who traverse
wide boulevards and bask in the sun at dramatic fountains and
statues of heroes. Here Cervantes wrote *Don Quixote*, Lope de
Vega wrote plays and El Greco painted.

Madrid, which became the capital in 1561, lies almost in the
center of the Iberian peninsula, the highest capital city in
Europe. Situated in the Meseta, this somewhat isolated city
rests on an undulating plateau of sand and clay. Because it suffered severe damage in the Civil War, which ended half a century ago, many of its buildings and homes were rebuilt. Rarely
seen is a piece of physical damage of the two-and-a-half-year
civil war that ended on March 28, 1939, when Franco's troops
entered the capital.

SITES IN MADRID

In 1977, a new day school, including a Jewish college,

Collegio Estrella Toledano, was established on Paseo de la Cobendas in the suburb of Moraleja. It was dedicated by leading dignitaries, including Sephardic Chief Rabbi OvadiaYosef. The school offers classes in Hebrew and Jewish history.

Arias Montano, Institute of Jewish Studies, 4 Calle del Duque de Medinaclli, in front of the Palace Hotel and American Embassy. Located in the heart of Madrid, this library contains more than 16,000 volumes, manuscripts, and publications about Sephardic Jewish history. It was opened in 1940, during World War II, at a time when Franco was an admirer of Hitler.

University City offers courses in Hebrew and Sephardic studies.

Sefarad Handicrafts: This Jewish religious article and handicraft store has three outlets in Madrid. They are: **Sefarad I,** Gran Via, 54, 28013, Madrid. Tel: (91) 547-61-42 or (91) 547-25-77, FAX: (91) 547-61-42. Open 10 A.M. to 2 P.M. and 4 P.M. to 10 P.M. **Sefarad II,** Gran Via, 43 bis, (esq Silva) 28013 Madrid. Tel: (91) 547-07-22 or (91) 547-74-59. FAX: (91) 547-61-42. Open 10 A.M. to 8 P.M. **Sefarad III,** Paseo del Prado, 12, 28014, Madrid. Tel: (91) 429-21-19. FAX: (91) 429-11-09.

Walk down the **Calle de la Fe,** the "street of the faith." Some say it was once called "Calle de la Synagogue." On this street, Jews once owned stores and real estate. In the riots of 1391, many Jews were massacred here. Others were converted on the spot. A synagogue destroyed during those disturbances stood next to the San Lorenzo Church. Other streets in the old Jewish quarter, called the **Juderia,** are **Calle de Bailen, Plaza de Oriente,** and **Plaza de Lavapies.**

BETH YAAKOV SYNAGOGUE

Beth Yaakov Synagogue and Jewish Community Center, 3 Calle Balmas, Madrid. Tel: 445-9843. Located near the Plaza Sorolla. Sephardim from Europe and North Africa began settling in Spain after World War II, but it was not until the public dedication of a new synagogue in Madrid on September 17, 1968, that recognition and a new era began for the Jews in

Spain. It was 476 years after the Jews were expelled from Spain. Today, laws in Spain grant Jews the legal right to observe their religion. Present at the historic ceremony were the archbishop of Madrid and representatives of the Foreign and Justice ministries. Baruch Garzon Serfaty had the honor of being the first rabbi of the new synagogue. In the year 2000, the rabbi of the JCC is Rabbi Moshe Bendahan.

Actually, the nucleus for this congregation was established after World War II. Later, when many Ashkenazi Jews arrived in Spain, they began to meet in a room at **Calle del Cardinal Cisneros.**

This building on Calle Balmas serves as religious and cultural center and contains a library, a kosher catering facility, a youth lounge, and another small synagogue. Downstairs there is even a letter from President George Washington of the United States of America. Arrangements for kosher meals can be made here, but write and order in advance. There is a kosher kitchen that even dispatches wine and matzah to other Jewish communities at Passover.

Kosher food is limited in Spain. Travelers are advised to bring their own kosher food. Some of the following outlets sell kosher products:

Elias Susana Butchery, Calle Viriato, 35, Madrid.

El Corte Ingles Shipping Mall. Only the "Castellana" branch, at Metro Station, Nuevos Ministerios, in the supermarket section. Look for the sign, "Productos Kosher."

The synagogue, which is Orthodox, contains a separate women's gallery, as well as a meeting hall for youth groups.

The community center section of the building also includes a rabbinical office and a Talmud Torah of about 200 children and a Sunday school of 40 also function. Youth activities include summer camps and a growing Maccabi sport movement.

Friday night services at the synagogue are usually at 7:30 P.M., 8:30 in summer; on Saturday morning they are held at 9:30 A.M. Services are daily and on holidays, but do call to check on times.

When I first went to Spain in 1964, I searched and searched for the synagogue. I had difficulty finding it, for in those days, a Jewish house of worship could not display exterior signs.

I remember I walked up a long flight of steps in an apartment building to reach the nearly hidden synagogue. The synagogue is now not difficult to find. You might easily spot it from a distance because of security. When I visited the congregation, for example, a police car was parked in front of the building.

The Sunday morning I attended services, a small minyan of Moroccan Jews had gathered. As we talked about life in the Spanish capital, cake was served. At the synagogue, I also talked to a Lubavitcher Chassid, Rabbi Yitzchak Goldstein. A teacher, he is the brother of a Lubavitch rabbi at the University of Michigan, Rabbi Aaron Goldstein.

The cornerstone of the new synagogue building reads: "This house of prayer is the first ever to be built in Madrid. May it be a symbol and a memorial for the Jewish communities that existed in this land until 1492 and a portent for the revival of Judaism in Spain."

ORGANIZATIONS

Amistad Judea Christiana. The new climate in the Catholic world of Vatican Council II made possible the organization of the Amistad Society, which eliminates textbook passages of material offensive to the Jewish people and religion. Many Jews in Madrid praise this group.

Chabad Center, There is no Chabad building, but using the following coordinates, the traveler can certainly be in touch with Chabad Lubavitch of Spain, Rabbi Yitzchak Goldstein, Tel/FAX: 34-91-445-9629. E-Mail chabad@wanadoo.es. Mikva is located at Beth Yaakov, Calle Balmes, 3, Madrid. To use the mikva, please call 24 hours in advance: 34-91-591-3131 or 592-8218.

MUSEUMS

Museo Sefardito de Madrid, 18 Calle Zorilla, one block from the American Express office. This museum has an interesting display of Jewish historical documents, art replicas, and other objects related to the history of the Jews in Spain.

National Archaeological Museum, 13 Calle de Serrano. This museum contains castings of Hebrew inscriptions from medieval buildings.

The Prado, Paseo del Prado, Madrid is the home of one of the world's outstanding art museums, the Prado, also called the National Museum of Painting and Sculpture. In 1994, it celebrated its 175th birthday and interestingly, one and a half million persons visited it in 1993. Hemingway wrote that if the city "had nothing else than the Prado, it would be worth spending a month in Madrid every spring, if you have money to spend for a month in any European capital." There are about 2,000 paintings by Spanish and foreign masters, including more than 30 works by El Greco, 100 by Francisco Goya, and 50 by Diego Velazquez.

Of special Jewish interest in the Museo del Prado are Titian's famed *Moses Saved from the Waters* and Murillo's painting of *Rebecca and Eliezer,* as well as two works depicting an auto-da-fé of the Inquisition.

Barcelona

Barcelona makes noise and money.

Even in the twelfth century, that world traveler, Benjamin of Tudela, mentioned the prosperity and beauty of Barcelona, according to Dr. Kayserling.

Before Franco came to power, Barcelona was one of the most creative cities in the world. It still is. Since the Olympics in 1992—a turning point for the city—tourism has become a fast-growing industry. One of the city's biggest tourist attractions is the Sagrada Familia church.

Miguel de Cervantes of Barcelona once wrote, "Barcelona was the fatherland of all valiant men." A beautiful city, it is conveniently situated, and it once welcomed Columbus home from a long journey to the Americas.

Even at midnight, there is a difference between Madrid and Barcelona. Hardworking and energetic, Barcelonians walk fast as if going somewhere in a hurry. Madrid is slower.

Synagogue of Vilajuiga (Jews' Village) near Barcelona.
(Photo by Ruth Serels)

The second city in size and 2,000 years old, Barcelona, with its four and a half-million citizens, stands as the great metropolis of the northeast coast. Some say it would make a better capital than Madrid. As one of the oldest and largest Mediterranean seaports and as the capital of Catalunya, historic Barcelona flaunts itself as an international city and looks across the Mediterranean to Alexandria, Genoa, Pisa, and Venice. Visit the **Ramblas** (long avenue) with its stalls and outdoor cafés; "it's always gay and lively." It was especially so in 1992 when the city was the site of the summer Olympics and with the commemoration of the 500th anniversary of the discovery of America and the expulsion of the Jews.

Once a center of Talmudic learning, Barcelona is known for the great disputation between Rabbi Moses ben Nachman, known as Nachmanides, and members of the Dominican and Franciscan orders. (We shall meet Nachmanides in Gerona, where he was born).

In 1391, Spain's Jewish community was almost destroyed. Barcelona's Jewry never recovered—by 1396 not a single Jew lived in the city. Since Barcelona was a harbor, many of the Jews who were expelled left from this harbor for safer lands. This was the port, too, where Columbus briefed the "Catholic kings" after his first voyage to America.

At the beginning of the twentieth century, a few Jewish peddlers from Morocco and Turkey settled in Barcelona.

The Jewish community was legalized in 1902. After Salonika was taken from the Turks by the Greeks in 1912, more Jews arrived. The Spanish government encouraged settlement of Spanish Jews on its territory, and another wave of Jewish immigration moved in from the Balkans after World War I.

More than 100 Jews lived in Barcelona in 1918. By 1932, the number rose to about 3,000, mostly of Sephardic origin. German Jews, fleeing Hitler, began arriving in 1933, and they brought the figure to more than 5,000 Jews, mostly Ashkenazim. During the Spanish Civil War of 1936-39, however, many of Barcelona's Jews left for France and Palestine. Some of the city's German Jews emigrated after the defeat of the Republic in 1939. But ironically many, if they had not been able to get to America or England, quickly came back, for Barcelona became a center for refugees. After World War II, the government granted permission to open a synagogue in Barcelona.

In 1965, together with leaders of the Madrid Jewish community, Barcelona's Jewish community officers were received by Franco in the first meeting since 1492 between a Spanish head of state and Jewish leaders.

Today, there are about 5,000 Jews in Barcelona.

JEWISH SITES IN BARCELONA

Mountain of the Jews. Much of the Jewish history of Barcelona evolves around two hills called Tibidabo and Montjuich. The latter is on the southern side of the city. Vast amounts of land lie between these two mountains. In Catalan, "Montjuich" means "Mountain of the Jews," where obviously Jews once owned much land. Here again, we meet the old Jewish neighborhood.

In the eleventh and twelfth centuries, Jews helped establish Barcelona's commercial greatness. A Jewish cemetery about 1,000 years old is kept up with a special section still set aside for Jewish graves. Located on Montjuich is the outstanding **Museum of Art,** with its excellent collection of Romanesque art.

Synagogue Maimonides and Community Center, 24 Avenir 08021, Barcelona. Tel: 200-6148 or 200-8513. FAX is also 200-6148. Near the President Hotel, it was established in 1954. From that date one can realize that it was the first synagogue to be built in Spain in almost 500 years. The first floor is the Sephardic prayer hall; the second floor is Ashkenazic, which holds services on Rosh Hashanah and Yom Kippur. The Sephardim hold services every day and there is a *minyan* every day in this synagogue at 7:30 A.M. and evenings at 8:15 P.M. Friday night services are held at 8 P.M. and Saturday mornings at 9 A.M.

The building maintains recreational rooms and classrooms, and many activities are offered.

In the entrance lobby of the five-story edifice, just beyond the outside iron gates, is a tablet in Hebrew and Spanish dedicating the building to Maimonides. For kosher food, call or write the center office. There is also a store at Avenir 29 that sells kosher products, including kosher meat. It is usually open from 10 A.M. to 1 P.M. and 3 P.M. to 7:30 P.M. Friday, 10:00 A.M. to 1 P.M. Closed Saturdays. Check on times when it is open by calling **Chabad,** Tel: 34-93-200-85-13 or 34-93-439-99-34. For kosher meals, please call ahead of time. Kosher products can be obtained at the **Corte ingles** on Calle Diagonal. This store has a section of kosher products.

Chabad of Barcelona, Calle Avenir, 24, 08021 Barcelona. Tel: office, 34-93-200-85-13; home: 34-93-439-99-34. E: Mail: chabad-liber@ctv.es. Contact **Chabad** for kosher meals. Contact Rabbi David Libersohn for information. For the mikveh, contact Mrs. Libersohn at 34-93-439-9934.

Reform Temple, Communitat Hebrea Atid de Catalunya, Calle Castaner 27, 08034. Barcelona. Tel/fax: 34-934-172-704. Rabbi Ruben Sternschein heads a newly formed Reform congregation of about 200 newcomers, many from South America. The congregation is known as **ATID,** or future.

Calle del Call. From the end of the eleventh century, the Jews of Barcelona lived in a special quarter in the heart of the old city, near the main gate and not far from the harbor. The main street of the quarter is still called "Calle del Call" or "Carrer del Call," "the quarter of the kahal." In the Catalan language, *call* is the equivalent of the Hebrew kahal, community. A part of the old ghetto wall is built into a Gothic house at **No. 5 Calle del Call.**

The University of Barcelona offers courses in Judaism.

Vegetarian restaurant, 41 Calle Canuda, Barcelona.

Gerona

If ever there was a place where the footsteps of Jews still seem to echo in the streets, it is Gerona. This Spanish municipality lies in the province of Catalonia in the northeast corner of Spain between the Pyrenees and the Mediterranean Sea. Just 30 miles from the French border and 60 miles from Barcelona, Gerona is called "the mother of Israel," a name given to but a few sites in the world known to be spiritual resting places for "the wandering Jew." Little known is the fact that this city was one of the most important Jewish communities in the area, and that once it was the first center of Kabbala (mysticism) in Spain. Some people consider the well-preserved and old Jewish Quarter here to be the most representative in Europe after that of Prague.

The Call or Jewish Quarter of Girona

An interesting area to visit is the **Call** itself, the Jewish district in Gerona, which probably had its origins back in the ninth century. Renovated in the early 1980s, it may, without doubt, be one of the most interesting visits in Jewish Spain. There were about 300 Jews in the area, also known in Arabic as "Aljama" (or Alsima).

The steep, narrow streets surrounding the broad avenue, **Carrer de la Forca,** were home to the Jewish community of Girona in medieval times. The life of the "Aljama," was concentrated around the synagogue which, over time, was housed in different locations

Today visitors can go to the **Centre Bonastruc ca Porta,** a complex of buildings in an enclosure that preserves the essence of the former Jewish presence. The complex contains the **Institut d'Estudis Nahmanides** (Nahmanides Institute of Jewish Studies), which includes a book and gift shop, an attractive library rooms for lectures and special programs, and a **Jewish Museum** which opened in July, 2000. Tradition has it that the center, which is covered with the mystery of history, is built on or near the site of a former synagogue.

The Patronat Municipal Call de Girona sponsors a series of lectures on Jewish topics, which are also designed to reflect the various cultures existing in feudal Catalonia, as well as today. Experts on culture, philosophy, art, and literature share their knowledge at monthly sessions held at the Institute, mostly in Spanish or Catalan.

Another site to visit is **The Monastery of St. Pere de Galligants** built between the 11th and 12th centuries. This was a Benedictine monastery and now houses the Archeological Museum. It contains a large collection of prehistoric objects as well as those from the Greek and Roman periods. Its unique collection of Hebrew tombstones, inscribed in Hebrew, will be moved to the **Jewish Museum**.

Further information can be obtained at the **Centre Bonastruc ca Porta,** Bonastruc ca Porta, Girona. Tel/fax: 34-972-216-761, or e-Mail: secretaria@redjuderias.org.

Perhaps Gerona's best-known citizen is Rabbi Moses ben Nachman (Nachmanides) who was born here and often called the "Rabbi of Gerona." He has been described as the outstanding personality in Jewry during the thirteenth century. Nachmanides' halachic works rank among the masterpieces of rabbinic literature and many of them have become classics. We also know Nachmanides as a philosopher, Kabbalist, biblical exegete, poet, and physician. As we have seen, there is a street named after him, Bonastruc da Porta, his name in the Catalan language.

Nachmanides was chief rabbi of Catalonia. He is famous for the disputation in Barcelona in July 1263, when at the request of King James I, he debated several Dominicans, including the convert Pablo Christiani. Permitted to speak as he wished, Nachmanides (also known as the Ramban) took full advantage of the opportunity and spoke frankly, for which the king rewarded him. The distinguished historian Yitzhak Baer says of him, "His personality was the product of diverse influences: the Spanish cultural background, French talmudist, German pietism, the mysticism of the Kabbala and an acquaintance with Christian theological writings." He wanted Jewish thought to embrace mystical ideas.

After the Barcelona Disputation, Nachmanides codified his views at the request of the local bishop. Still the Dominicans attempted to put him on trial. Even with the king's help in obtaining his release, Nachmanides barely succeeded in escaping from Spain to Israel.

Toledo

Experts say that if you have only one day to visit Spain, spend it in touring Toledo, once the ancient capital of Spain. Like Florence in Italy, the city is preserved as a museum.

Historic Toledo boasts that it is the most fascinating, aristocratic metropolis in all Spain and among the most interesting cities of Europe. It still stands today just as the great Spanish artist El Greco painted it centuries ago. Indeed, this city of a half-million persons houses his masterpieces, as well as those of artists Goya and Velazquez. Toledo, 40 miles from Madrid, rests on a mountain. A deep-etched gorge caused by the winding Tagus River surrounds it on three sides.

In the Civil War of 1936, the streets of Toledo actually "ran red with blood." The alcazar, which housed an infantry academy, was held by the Fascists. For 72 days, Franco's forces withstood wave after wave of fierce attacks from the Republic's troops and survived.

As the seat of the Spanish primate, Toledo records Catholic history. Its main cathedral, a Gothic masterpiece with paintings by El Greco, stands at the top of the hills of the city. Joseph L. Andrew, Jr., observed in *The Jewish Advocate* of February 23, 1989: "It is apparent even from the city's geography that the Jews had a less lofty status than the Catholics, as you must descend from the summit of Toledo's hills with their cathedrals down to the Jewish Quarter, near the bottom, through narrow lanes, past weathered golden-hued limestone buildings."

Toledo is one of the few towns in Spain where remnants of Jewish edifices have been preserved. Jews came to Toledo in the fourth and fifth centuries. By the seventh century, Toledo possessed a large Jewish population that helped the Moors capture the city from the Visigoths. By the eleventh century, 40,000 Jews resided in Toledo; one-third of the city was Jewish and they lived in peace with the Moors and Christians. The name Toledo comes from "Toledoth," the city of "generations." Legend has it that Toledo was founded 4,000 years ago by a direct descendant of Noah. Others say that the first Jewish exiles to Toledo were members of the tribe of Benjamin.

What we do know for certain, however, is that, because of its

outstanding Jewish scholarship and community structure during the Middle Ages, Toledo became known as the "second
Jerusalem." Perched on a hill and surrounded by walls, it still
resembles Jerusalem. Some say it was the "most important
Jewish city in Spain."

As a center of Spanish Jewry, Toledo, with its schools and
libraries, attracted poets, translators, and writers. Yehudah
HaLevi, the great Hebrew poet, resided here. Surely not all
Jews in Toledo were scholars. They served as tailors, felt makers, masons, butchers, farmers, and craftsmen. The Jewish
Quarter in Toledo, a spacious area, functioned virtually as a
city in itself. For about 600 years, Jews lived in peace. In the
twelfth century, there were 12,000 Jews there. But in 1391,
mobs attacked and nearly slaughtered the entire Jewish com-
munity of Toledo. In a moment of weakness, many wealthy
Jews sought to save their lives by converting; they became New
Christians. Expulsion followed. Today, the Cathedral of
Toledo, completed in 1477, contains, on an interior wall, a
plaque memorializing the Expulsion of the Jews in 1492.
Despite its sad history, Toledo has been named the "World
Sephardic Capital."

Recent reports indicate there are nine Jewish families in
Toledo, but they are not organized. When I visited Toledo, I
found a **restaurant** that is run by a Moroccan Jew. This eating
spot was not kosher, but it had a Jewish-Israeli atmosphere.
Many Israelis came here. The owner said he conducts a
Passover Seder for 140 friends and their families every year.
The establishment is near the El Transito Synagogue (see
below). He told me he knew a man who lights candles every
Friday night and does not eat pork. The man did not know
the religious significance of what he did, but he said he was
told to do it by a grandparent. Shadows of the Marranos, the
secret Jews, over and over again are perceptible in modern
democratic Spain.

SYNAGOGUES IN TOLEDO

Once Toledo housed numerous synagogues. Today, there

are only two. But these two are famous and a "must" on a tour
of Jewish sites in Toledo. They are located in the eastern side
of what was once the Jewish Quarter. Indeed, Santa Maria la
Blanca and El Transito are considered two great architectural
treasures of medieval European Jewry.

Santa Maria la Blanca, with its inspired Almohad art, was
founded in 1203—the oldest Jewish monument in Toledo.
Like all medieval synagogues, it is unimpressive on the outside.
But the inside is a forest of 32 pillars supporting a long vista of
horseshoe-shaped arches, surrounded by limestone block
walls. The octagonal columns are richly decorated with designs
of a Moorish-Jewish motif. There are arched galleries and you
can see signs of a separate women's upper gallery. In the fifteenth century, it was converted into a church by Vicente
Ferrer, who stirred up many riots against Jews and was responsible for many conversions. The church later became a military
barracks, a warehouse, and even a dance hall. Now it is a
national museum.

El Transito Synagogue got its name from a church that the
building housed after the Inquisition. Samuel Levi Abulafia
built the structure in about 1360. He was a finance minister
and advisor to Pedro the Cruel, king of Castille, who ruled
from 1350 to 1369. He not only managed Pedro's finances but,
as a diplomat, defended his interests. His reward was the king's
permission to build a new synagogue despite clergy and city
opposition. Barnet Litvinoff writes that Abulafia "maintained a
style in Toledo almost as regal as the masters." He wanted the
building to be a private synagogue for his own house, which
still stands and supposedly from which there was an entrance
to the synagogue. The artist El Greco lived in this house, which
some say is the Casa El Greco (House of El Greco), now known
as the **El Greco Museum**.

To build the synagogue, Abulafia, it is said, imported cedars
from Lebanon, as did Solomon when he built the Temple in
Jerusalem. The graceful Moorish arches, the artistic designs,
and the quotations from the Torah that line the entire length
of the synagogue walls at ceiling level, bring the entire Golden
Age back to life. The building boasts alabaster columns, a wall
with stone tracery, and 54 elegant windows.

The building of El Transito Synagogue contains the **Sephardic Museum and Library** and is located on the **Calle de Samuel Levi,** an old ghetto lane named after Samuel Levi Abulafia. The museum contains Sephardic relics, documents, other pieces of Judaica, reproductions, and manuscripts. Abulafia hid his wealth here in the house. He had a long tunnel dug out connecting his home in Toledo with the Tagus River so that, in case of a popular uprising, he and other Jews could escape. It did not help him. Pedro the Cruel tortured and executed him.

El Transito served successively as a church, a monastery, a hospital, a military storehouse, and army barracks. But in 1877, it was designated a national monument. The building cannot be restored to its original state because no one knows what it looked like.

In 1964, the El Transito Synagogue became a museum for the history of the Jews in Spain. A synagogue service celebrating the opening of the museum holds the distinction of being one of the first public Jewish meetings in Spain since Jews were expelled.

Marbella

Synagogue, Beth El, 21 Calle Jazmines, Urbanizacion El Real, Km. 184.Tel: 95-277-4074. This synagogue has an Ashkenazic prayer service and a Sephardic one.

Suggested Reading

Ashtor, Eliyahu. *The Jews of Moslem Spain.* Philadelphia: Jewish Publication Society of America, 1973.
Avni, Haim. *Spain, the Jews and Franco.* Philadelphia: Jewish Publication Society of America, 1982.
Baer, Yitzhak. *A History of the Jews in Christian Spain.* Philadelphia: Jewish Publication Society of America, 1966.
Cohen, Israel. *Travels in Jewry.* New York: Dutton, 1953.

Kayserling, Dr. M. *Christopher Columbus and the Participation of the Jews in the Spanish and Portuguese Discoveries.* New York: Hermon, 1968.

Lipschitz, Rabbi Chaim U. *Franco, Spain, the Jews and the Holocaust.* New York: Ktav, 1984.

Litvinoff, Barnet. *Fourteen Ninety Two: The Decline of Medievalism and the Rise of the Modern Age.* New York: Charles Scribner's Sons, 1991.

Morris, Jan. *Spain.* Oxford University Press, 1979.

Morton, H. V. *A Stranger in Spain.* New York: Dodd, Mead, 1955.

Netanyahu, Benzion. *The Marranos of Spain.* Millwood, N.Y: Kraus Reprint Company, 1973.

Payne, Stanley G. *The Franco Regime, 1936-1975.* Madison: University of Wisconsin Press, 1989.

—. *A History of Spain and Portugal.* Madison: University of Wisconsin Press, 1973.

Pritchett, V. S. *Marching Spain.* London: Ernest Benn, 1928.

Raphael, Chaim. *The Road from Babylon: The Story of Sephardic and. Oriental Jews.* New York: Harper & Row, 1985.

Roth, Cecil. *A History of the Marranos.* New York: Hermon Press, 1974.

—. *The Spanish Inquisition.* New York: Norton, 1964.

Wiesenthal, Simon. *Sails of Hope: The Secret Mission of Christopher Columbus.* New York: Macmillan, 1973.

Yahil, Leni. *The Holocaust: The Fate of European Jewry, 1932-1945.* New York: Oxford University Press, 1990.

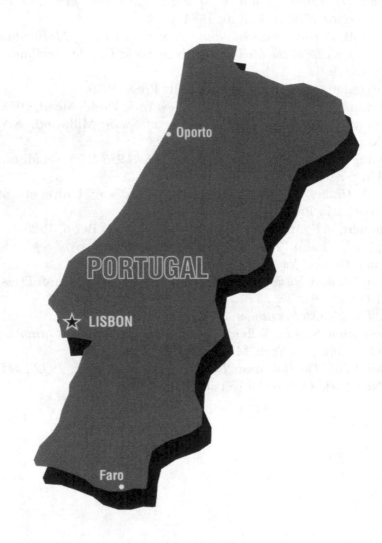

Portugal
Saying the Mourner's Prayer
in Rossio Square

Think of Portugal and you think of the sea, explorers and navigators, and weather-beaten faces of fishermen hauling in the day's catch.

"With its shoreline facing the Atlantic Ocean to the west and to the south, the Portuguese had a long tradition of seafaring as fisherman and traders," says Miriam Estensen in her book *Discovery: The Quest for the Great South Land.* Its location soon determined its vocation to the sea and let us remember that two-thirds of the earth is converged by water.

Think of Portugal and you consider driving up to Estoril, the fashionable resort, and Cascais, "the town of fishermen and kings." You see yourself sitting in the coffeehouses, drinking smooth port wine and strong coffee, and listening to moody *fados,* those melancholy songs of the Portuguese fishermen.

Think of Portugal and you think of Lisbon, the city that attracts many tourists. "By day Lisbon has a naïve theatrical quality that enchants and captivates, but by night it is a fairy-tale city, descending over lighted terraces to the sea, like a woman in festive garments going down to meet her dark lover," wrote Eric Maria Remarque, in his novel, *The Night in Lisbon.*

Some people label Portugal an anachronism. Long ago, Prince Henry the Navigator, Vasco da Gama, Magellan, and Cabral, who sailed uncharted waters, led Portugal into its golden age as a great power. Few European countries reached such seafaring heights. But then it crumbled and lost its colony, Brazil, and later was ruled by a dictatorship. Finally in our own day, a peaceful revolution, "the Revolution of Flowers" of 1974, would install a democracy.

Portugal is one of the smallest countries in Europe. Containing 35,516 square miles, or one-sixth of the Iberian peninsula, it is located on the far western edge of the peninsula. Because Iberia was isolated from Europe for centuries, people said Europe began and ended at the Pyrenees. No longer! A free, democratic atmosphere envelops the country today, bringing tourists to Portugal.

Let us also remember that Portugal is a member of the European Union since 1986 and has enjoyed a steady economic growth.

For Jewish travelers, the Jewish connection lies just beneath the surface, more in knowledge of the past than in the sites themselves. Most of the cities and towns contained an area that was assigned to the Jews and known as "Juderia." Today, many of them can be found. For starters, ask if there is a "street of the Jews."

A Brief History

Some sources say the Jews migrated to Portugal after the destruction of Jerusalem by Nebuchadnezzar, settling there before the establishment of the first Portuguese kingdom. By the year 900, with the Moslems in control, Jews worked as winegrowers. In the reign of Sancho I in the twelfth century, Don Solomon Jachia, a Jew, was a field marshal commanding the Portuguese Army.

For a long time Portugal befriended Jews. Before the sixteenth century, most of the rulers of Portugal considered the Jews a valuable resource, especially their financial and commercial talents. Christian noblemen often married daughters of wealthy Jews.

Until 1497, no profession or occupation was barred to Portuguese Jews. They were active in government, philosophy, botany, finance, medicine, and astronomy. They improved Portuguese typography so that it could compete with Italy and

Germany. A Hebrew printing press was set up in Lisbon at the end of the fifteenth century. Vasco da Gama, who discovered the sea route to India, was advised by Jewish scholars and financed by Jewish businessmen. He also followed maps and instruments made by Jewish manufacturers. Jewish physicians were on board his ships. Jews possessed a great reputation in the sciences. Portuguese Jewish doctors rivaled their co-religionists in Spain.

During the thirteenth to fifteenth centuries, Portugal's rulers even allowed a synagogue to develop in Lisbon. By the end of the fifteenth century, Portugal's 200,000 Jews made up one-fifth of the population. Included were many of the several hundred thousand Jewish refugees who had been expelled from Spain in 1492. The reception, while not warm, was tolerant. Jews were forced to pay a poll tax of eight cruzados per adult and agree not to remain longer than eight months.

Romance, intrigue, and expulsion now entered the history of the Portuguese Jewish community in the person of Emanuel I, the Fortunate (1495-1521). He was an unfortunate monarch for the Jews. Ambitious, he soon initiated Machiavellian scenarios. Assuming power in 1495, he hoped to rule all of Iberia. He would do this simply by marrying the Spanish princess Isabella, the daughter of Ferdinand and Isabella. But as a condition for marriage, the Spanish king and queen demanded that Emanuel expel the Jews from Portugal. He had to "purify" his kingdom, and then, as Barnet Litvinoff writes, he could "Christianize Portugal."

Emanuel reluctantly banished the Jews and Moslems in December 1496, a month after the royal marriage, but soon changed his edict—because he needed their revenues. He tried to persuade them to convert to Christianity. He then went so far as to strike at the parents through the children. "Be baptized or die," he decreed. On March 19, 1497, all Jewish children between the ages of 4 and 14 were forcibly baptized in one single day in an attempt to keep the parents in Portugal. On another occasion, shortly thereafter, when 20,000 parents were forced to gather in Lisbon, only seven or eight badly beaten persons escaped the forced baptism. But like their Spanish brothers and sisters, these Jews would become Marranos and flee the country. By 1499, however, Marranos were denied emigration and had to revert to subterfuge to leave.

For several decades, Jews in Portugal managed to ward off the Inquisition. However a papal brief on May 23, 1536, ordered Portugal to establish a Holy Office of the Inquisition to be patterned after the Spanish model. An auto-da-fé was held in Lisbon on September 20, 1544. Sebastion Jose de Carvalho e Mello halted the Inquisition in 1821. History knows him as Marqués de Pombal. During the three centuries of the Inquisition, more than 40,000 persons were indicted, of whom 30,000 were sentenced at autos-da-fé in Portugal. About 1,200 persons were actually burned at the stake.

Sir George Young suggests that had the Jews been left alone, Lisbon might have become the commercial capital of Europe, a position the country was firmly headed toward a hundred years before London.

The Portuguese Jews who left Iberia between 1540 and 1800 would establish communities or join their Sephardic brothers and sisters in such cities as Venice, Hamburg, Amsterdam, London, and Bordeaux in Europe; Recife in Brazil; Surinam in South America; Curaçao, Jamaica, Barbados, Nevis, and St. Thomas in the West Indies; and New York City and Newport, Rhode Island in the New World. Some of them became international Jewish personalities. One son of a Portuguese Marrano whom we know as Baruch Spinoza, the seventeenth century philosopher, later would be excommunicated by his own people in Holland.

Trade caused the return of Jews to Portugal after 400 years. It is said that an admiral invited two Jews from Gibraltar to come to Portugal to create a commercial outlet. The two merchants, Isaac Aboab and Moses Levi, accepted the offer. Thus began the return of the Jews to Portugal.

By 1820, the city of Faro had a small Jewish community. Jews began to arrive as merchants when foreigners were allowed freedom of worship under the Charter of 1826. In 1868, the Jews were recognized as a colony. At the turn of the century, Eastern European Jews found in Portugal a haven from persecution.

Official recognition permitting religious services was granted to Jews in 1892. A synagogue was erected in 1902. The new Portuguese republic, established by the revolution of

1910, finally gave the Jewish community official status in 1912.

During the Holocaust, neutral Portugal adopted a liberal immigration policy, with about 45,000 Jewish refugees entering the country. Later, Portugal would at times withhold asylum because of its concern that the country would be overrun with refugees, and sailings across the Atlantic were limited. Still, it granted consular protection to Jews in occupied countries. Indeed, Portugal, with other neutral countries in 1944, managed to save many Hungarian Jews.

Ironically, even as late as the Holocaust, some Christians or descendants of Marranos would help Jews. One such person was Aristedes de Sausa Mendes do Amaral e Abranches, a Portuguese consul in Marseilles. He issued 10,000 visas to stranded Jews in defiance of his own government. He did the same thing in Bordeaux. (With a Portuguese visa you could travel through Spain). Ousted from the diplomatic corps, where he worked around the clock to save Jews, he was never reinstated, according to Rabbi Chaim U. Lipschitz, but was helped by a Jewish organization. He died in 1954, forgotten and impoverished. In 1961, Israel and Yad Vashem planted 20 trees in the Martyrs Forest in his memory, and in 1967, posthumously awarded him a medal in deep appreciation and gratitude.

The story of Portuguese Jewry makes it seem like a miracle that this Jewish community is still alive. After World War II, 12,000 Jews resided in Portugal, which has a population of slightly more than 10 million.

This is one Jewish community that is really shrinking in numbers. According to the author's sources there are about 300 Jews in Lisbon. There also are several hundred Jews in nearby Estoril. Still, there are activities held by the community. And relations with the Government are said to be friendly.

Lisbon is the capital, chief port, and largest metropolis of the country. Strategically, it is "the most splendidly situated capital in Europe," says V. S. Pritchett in *At Home and Abroad: Travel Essays*. Lisbon—called the quintessence of Portugal—is home to nearly two million Portuguese. This city, whose sea aroma wafts from the Atlantic Ocean, may pale next to expansive Paris or London. Yet, there is much for the tourist to see and do, including the Sao Carlos Opera House, Castle of Sao

George, Tower of Belem, the Museum of Ancient Art, the city's many public squares, statues of national heroes, tree-lined avenues and small parks, and the 25th of April Bridge, one of the longest suspension bridges in the world.

Notable Portuguese Jews

While the Jewish schools of Portugal may not have produced a Maimonides, they could boast of their Abravanels, as well as many others whose names resound among great literati.

Other Jews contributed much to Portugal. Abraham Zacuto, innovator of navigational instruments such as the first astrolabe in copper and astronomical tables, also emigrated from Spain to Portugal at the time of the expulsion and went on to become royal astronomer to advise Vasco da Gama on his voyage to India. In 1497, when King Emanuel forced the Jews to convert, Zacuto left Portugal and went to Spain. Cresques headed the Academy of Navigation founded by Prince Henry the Navigator. Pedro Teixeira explored South American territories in the early seventeenth century. Joseph Vechino was a court physician and advisor to Joao II. The nation's first printing press was set up by Samuel Porteira. And of course Jewish scholar Judah Abravanel served as royal treasurer of Joao I.

Jewish Lisbon

ROSSIO SQUARE

Imagine landing in the middle of Lisbon's main square and reciting "kaddish," the Hebrew prayer for the dead. That is what a group of Jews would do if they stood in the Plaza Rossio (Rossio Square) in this busy capital of Portugal. Here in the center of the city, not far from the Royal Palace in 1506, between 2,000 and 4,000 New Christians, known as Marranos, were butchered.

In the Plaza Rossio stood the Palace of Estaos, which housed the Inquisition. The building was destroyed by the earthquake of 1755, and the National Theatre of Dona Maria was constructed in its place. During the Inquisition, Jews were forcibly baptized at the Church of Sao Domingo, which is located in the adjacent square. Rossio Square is a good spot to stand and reflect on the world of the Marranos, a world in which no one could trust anyone.

A vast difference existed between Spain and Portugal in terms of the Inquisition. Portuguese Jews had 20 to 30 years longer to adjust to Christianity and practice Judaism secretly before the Inquisition came on the Portuguese scene. This meant that crypto-Judaism in Portugal contained deep roots and enabled these New Christians to revert to their former Jewish faith whenever they managed to escape to free lands.

But Elias H. Lindo writes in *History of the Jews of Spain and Portugal* that the Inquisition of Portugal exercised the same cruelty as that of Spain towards the New Christians. Those who were discovered or suspected of practicing Jewish rites, and under torture confessed their Judaism, suffered death and expired in the flames of the autos-da-fé.

The Inquisition concentrated on rooting out all traces of Judaism. Basically it succeeded. In fact, many of the victims of the Inquisition were not guilty. There are those historians who claim that the purpose of the Inquisition was really to enrich church coffers. But it never completely crushed the Marrano movement, which is important to understand.

The visitor on a trip to Portugal keeps hearing and seeing the word *Marrano*. The term *Marrano* is derived from a Spanish word meaning swine; it was an ugly, contemptuous word. Jews prefer to use the Hebrew word *anussim*, meaning those whose change of religion was forced upon them, but "who lived according to the precepts and laws of their ancestral faith," writes Dr. M. Kayserling.

In Portugal and Spain, they were also called New Christians, or "Conversos." The church was suspicious of the Conversos. They suspected that these newcomers had not given up their the Sabbath and holidays, assembled in subterranean or other secret synagogues, and practiced Jewish rites in their homes." The true-born Christians, the old Christians, "who were free from any taint of Moorish or Jewish blood," frequently participated in riots against the New Christians.

These secret Portuguese Jews, some believe, are considered the first modern Jews of the Diaspora. They set the stage for the center of world trade, moving from southern to northern Europe. The Marranos were always looking for a home where they could openly proclaim their religion. Many of them, joined by their Spanish and Portuguese brothers and sisters, settled in the West Indies, but especially in Brazil. They also tried to get to Holland, which had turned Protestant and welcomed persons of all religions. Remember, Marranos were valued because European businessmen perceived them as having connections with relatives and friends throughout the world. These Jewish merchants and entrepreneurs knew Spanish and Portuguese. They had helped make Lisbon the commercial center of the continent. They maintained contact with Jews who had settled in North Africa after the 1492 expulsion from Spain. They controlled more than a quarter of the stock of the Dutch East India Company. But even though they were respected traders outside of Portugal, many were still afraid to say openly that they were Jews. So they called themselves Portuguese. Thus, "Portuguese" became synonymous with "Jewish." Others, as soon as they felt secure, openly professed Judaism. To understand the story of the Marranos is to understand Portuguese Jewish history.

KOSHER FOOD IN LISBON

Kosher meals can be obtained by calling **Mrs. R. Assor,** rua Rodrigo de Fonseca, 38, Lisbon. Tel: (21) 386-03-96.

SYNAGOGUES AND ORGANIZATIONS IN LISBON

Shaare Tikvah Synagogue, rua Alexandre Herculano, 59,

Lisbon. Tel: (21) 385-8604. Isaac Assor, the son of the late Rabbi Assor leads the congregation in Sabbath services held on Friday evenings and Saturday mornings. A *kiddush* is held on Saturday. The cornerstone bears the Hebrew name, *Kehilla Kedusha Shaare Tikvah*, in Portuguese, *Portas da Esperanca* (Gates of Hope). On the Holy Ark, it says in Hebrew, "Know before whom thou standest."

The building contains 20-foot wooden gates and high concrete walls that enclose the synagogue. A beautiful courtyard extends behind the building. There are several candelabra, common to Sephardic houses of prayer, in the sanctuary. Services are Friday night at 8 P.M. and Saturday morning at 9. The service is Sephardic ritual.

In the year 2002, this famous synagogue will celebrate its 100th anniversary. Plans were underway to repair and remodel various sections, including the beautiful rugs in the building. The second floor of this house of worship serves as a museum and includes memorabilia of the community.

Within walking distance from hotels, the building features a blend of Eastern and North African styles inside. In 1948, the congregation rebuilt sections of the building. The then chief rabbi of France, Jacob Kaplan, attended this public dedication ceremony that symbolized the rebirth of the Portuguese Jewish community. "After an interval of 500 years, the inhabitants of Lisbon looked on with curiosity and admiration at the procession of the sacred Jewish scrolls, which their forefathers had outlawed, despoiled and put to flames," wrote one reporter. In 1949, a second balcony and additional seats were added to the synagogue. As you walk into the synagogue, on the left-hand side you will see a memorial room to victims of the Holocaust. Refugees from Nazi-occupied France knew that neutral Portugal was their best hope of fleeing the Germans in World War II.

Ashkenazic Synagogue, rua Elias Garcia, 110, Lisbon. This synagogue, which is more on the order of a shtibel (small house of prayer), is rarely open. Yet, from time to time, there are services and holiday celebrations here.

Belmonte, Guarda, Covilha

Visit the towns of Belmonte, Guarda, and Covilha. Marranos live here as well as in **Monsanto** and **Castelode Vide.** Samuel Schwartz, the Polish Jewish mining engineer, discovered these villages in 1919.

Belmonte is a farming and wine area in the northern province of Beira Alta. In 1988, Michael Fink reported a community center of two cramped rooms: "On the walls are a tiny Israeli flag, a roster of the members of the community and a generic synagogue dedication in Hebrew." Recent reports indicated that there are 200 Marranos in Belmonte, with a rabbi from Israel to lead them.

Schwartz said that Marranos in Belmonte "were completely ignorant of the existence of other Jews with different religious rites." The old Marrano women who acted as "keepers of the faith" did not recognize Schwartz's Hebrew prayers and rejected him. Obviously, these Marranos lived outwardly as Christians—they attended Catholic Church services and joined in Catholic sacraments—but kept alive secretly some form of Jewish rites. Observers say their distrust of outsiders made them wary even of fellow Jews. (They seemed to believe that they were the only remaining pure Jews).

More and more, conversos or crypto-Jews, are formally converting to Judaism, such as in Belmonte. Even today, Belmonte's Jews find it hard to be open about their religion. They still attend Mass with their Catholic neighbors at the village church where, for so many generations, they have been baptized, married, and buried under marble tombstones, writes Paul Ames of the Associated Press in *The Jewish Week* of June 22, 1990. According to Colette Avital, Israel's former ambassador to Portugal, "They've lived on the outside like Christians. On the inside, in their houses, they were not Christians, they were Jews, and they have transmitted this from father to son."

Descendants of the original Marranos who still live in and around Belmonte are uncircumcised and baptized, but otherwise practice Judaism in secret, lighting their Sabbath lamps in the cellar. They do not eat pork; they marry amongst themselves and are known by their neighbors as Judeos—Jews. They are not officially recognized by world Jewry. Although they were discovered in 1919, attention was not drawn to them until the neighboring town of **Guarda** was "twinned" with the Israeli town of Safed in 1982.

According to *Time* magazine of April 11, 1977: "The Marranos shun all Saturday work: a telltale sign of their identity. But paradoxically, most of the men have not been circumcised because that could disclose their secret."

Here is another description in *The Jerusalem Post* of these descendants of Jews who fled from the Inquisition: "They get together for Yom Kippur eve services; they observe the Purim eve Taanit Esther fast, but not the Purim celebration. They observe baking their own matzot, according to a generations-old recipe, reciting certain traditional blessings at various stages of the process; they have a short seder meal that includes bitter herbs, but they do not read the haggada."

When Marrano communities were discovered, Jewish organizations began to raise money to bring them back into the fold. But success has been limited. The Marranos have been difficult to reach.

Anthropologists have found the Marrano communities living in semi-isolation and cut off from most of the developments in the world and from their own religion. The estimate of the number of these Marranos has been revised downward. They seemed to be disappearing. Decades and even centuries of intermarriage were noted in the poor health of community members. Most were poor and earned their livelihoods as wandering tradesmen. Those who had managed to achieve upward mobility had achieved it through marriage outside the group and subsequent departure from Jewish tradition.

Faro

Faro is the capital of the Algarve and even possesses a medieval wall and a large number of monuments, museums, and Roman ruins. About 300 Jews live in the Algarve area in the extreme south of Portugal. Traces of the Moorish presence are also still seen in the area's unique architecture, terraces, chimneys and whitewashed houses.

Faro was a famous center of Hebrew printing in the fifteenth century. The first printed book in Portugal, a Hebrew edition of the Pentateuch, was published here in 1487 by Samuel Porteira.

Today in Faro, the Jewish traveler will find a medieval **Jewish cemetery** dating from about the fourteenth century. A new cemetery was started in 1820.

Oporto

There are a handful of Jews in Oporto, a city known for its contrasting baroque architecture and modern commercial center.

Kahal Kodosh Mekor Haim Synagogue (Kadoorie Synagogue), rua Guerra Junqueiro 340. Tel: 602-20. This was the first synagogue built by and for native Portuguese Jews in more than 400 years. The cornerstone for the synagogue was set on June 30, 1929, and the dedication ceremony took place on January 16, 1938. It was opened under the initiative of Capt. Burros Bastos, Portuguese hero of Marrano descent. The synagogue received funds from the famous Kadoorie family of Baghdad. For more than 20 years, Bastos led this synagogue. He hoped to bring the Marranos back to Judaism. While the synagogue is still in the building, this house of worship is not often used.

Suggested Reading

Bradford, Sarah. *Portugal.* New York: Walker, 1973.
Estensen, Miriam, *Discovery, The Quest for the Great South Land,* New York, St. Martin's Press, 1998.
Mocatta, Frederic David. *The Jews of Spain and Portugal, and the Inquisition.* New York: Cooper Square, 1973.

Kahal Kodosh Mekor Haim Synagogue, Oporto. (Photo by Ed Robin)

Austria
Where Jews Have Memories

"Something out of the dim past... when Vienna was a free city, where Herzl lived and worked and created the Zionist movement, where the *Neue Freie Presse* was one of the great liberal newspapers in the world; where Freud developed his ideas; where Yiddish writers... could be found..." This passage by Joseph Leftwich comes to mind as the car leaves the city of Vienna and heads toward the green forest around the capital. The tourist guide-driver turns on the cassette tape and the music of Strauss's "Tales from the Vienna Woods" bursts forth. You can visualize the majestic, uniformed men and the gowned ladies waltzing in the grand ballroom. All you need is a piece of *sacher torte mit schlag,* cake with whipped cream. But that comes later when you are back in Vienna and after you visit Stadtpark, that pleasant place where the statues of Strauss and Beethoven lure you back to the city's heyday where Haydn, Mozart, Brahms, and Schubert also composed.

Walk to the Ringstrasse, one of the most beautiful streets to be found anywhere. On this main boulevard are situated the university, the town hall, the Parliament buildings, the National Library, the Museum for Natural History and the History of Art, the State Opera House, the famous hotels, and stately offices.

In Vienna you practically inhale nostalgia. Where else can you still buy picture postcards of Emperor Franz Joseph or books on the Hapsburg Empire of 100 years ago?

251

But like other Jewish communities in Europe, 50 years after the fall of the Nazis, Vienna for some may no longer be a popular place for Jewish settlement. Some feel the Holocaust actually began in this capital. Here lived the art student Hitler, who became insane with the idea that he had to murder Jews; and this city, say some commentators, is "the cradle of modern political anti-Semitism." Says author Judith Miller, Austria also has become synonymous with the country of Kurt Waldheim, the former United Nations Secretary General [and former] President of Austria, who lied about his past for 40 years, who told Austrians that he had only done his duty in yielding so willingly to the Third Reich. Waldheim, who did not run for a second term in 1992, was shunned by virtually every Western European leader after it was disclosed that he had covered up his service in a German Army unit that was accused of atrocities in the Balkans in World War II. His 1986 political campaign was marked by anti-Semitic overtones that obviously affected the small Austrian Jewish community. Throughout Waldheim's presidency, Austrian-Israeli relations remained strained and were reinstated only after Waldheim left office.

In 1993, Austrian Chancellor Franz Vranitzky was the first head of the Austrian government to visit Israel.

But it would not be long until divisiveness again raised its ugly head in Austria in the form of Jorg Haider's far-right Freedom Party joining the cabinet in the Austrian government.

Once again it was Austria who dominated the headlines in early 2000 and reminded men of good will everywhere of that country's role in support of fascism, the Nazis, and the murder of Jews.

Once again, it was xenophobia and racism out of Austria.

Once again, Austria was seen as the pariah of Europe, raising "echos," said a *Washington Post* editorial of Februrary 3, 2000, "of the 1930s that are a good deal too clear for comfort: repugnant is one word that comes to mind."

Once again, as Rabbi A. James Rudin, formerly of the American Jewish Committee, put it, the inclusion of Jorg Haider's party in the government "set off alarm bells around the world."

The European Union decided to freeze relations with Austria because of the inclusion of the rightist Freedom Party in its government. That party won 27 percent of the vote for Parliament in the parliamentary elections in the fall of 1999.

The overwhelming majority of Austrians protested the new government. Thousands of Austrians held numerous rallies to protest Haider and his party and the inclusion of that group in the government. In one such demonstration a quarter of a million people marched. Leon Zelman, head of the Jewish Welcome Service which aids Jewish visitors to Austria, called on Jewish groups not to abandon the overwhelming majority of Austrians who oppose Haider but to help them in their fight. "Europe is reacting the way it must react. But at the same time, I will be happy to find an understanding world for the thousands and thousands of young people who go out on the street to protest this new government, " he said in an interview with Ruth Gruber of the Jewish Telegraphic Agency.

But Joanna Nittenberg, the editor of the Vienna Jewish monthly, *Neue Welt,* warns against overstating the case. "The FPO in government is our worst dream," she said. "But Haider is not Hitler. Haider is a populist, he wants power, he wants to be chancellor. But comparing him to Hitler minimizes Hitler. If we exaggerate too much, we can lose credibility," she said, according to Ruth Gruber of the *Jewish Telegraphic Agency.*

Haider is notorious for his anti-immigration policies and his remarks showing sympathy to the Third Reich. When it appeared the Freedom Party might become part of the Austrian ruling coalition, Haider apologized for his remarks, but the suspicion remains his real views have not changed, according to Rabbi Rudin. He has been widely condemned for his remarks seen by many as attempts to play down the crimes of the Nazis who ruled in Austria from 1938 to 1945. He has since resigned as leader of the party, but said he may seek to become chancellor in the future.

The French, the Belgians, the Germans, and the Israelis condemned the action. Israel's ambassador left Vienna immediately, as did the U.S., Germany, Spain, and Belgium. Denmark froze their political relations with Austria because of Haider's rise in power. The unprecedented sanctions imposed by Austria's 14 European Union partners and the U.S. were directed far beyond Austria's borders at a rising tide of xenophobia and extreme-right parties that has spread across both Eastern and Western Europe. However, in the fall of 2000, EU diplomatic sanctions were lifted.

Actually, the late Chancellor Kreisky, who was Jewish, was among the first to make the Freedom Party respectable. His Austrian socialist government joined with the Freedom Party between 1983 and 1986, when it was not led by Haider. That party then was headed by a former member of the Waffen SS, according to author Wistrich.

Within the last few years, Austria for the first time has acknowledged that Austrians were responsible for crimes against Jews. The country has passed legislation setting up a National Fund that provides token sums to Austrian Jews who suffered as a result of Nazi rule. The Austrians also have passed a law establishing ways to return Jewish artworks seized during war to the proper owners or their heirs. The government has called on banks and insurance companies to settle claims put forward by Jewish organizations that deal with the restitution of money.

Today about 90 percent of the Austrian Jewish community lives in this capital of 1.6 million, although small Jewish communities exist in Salzburg, Linz, Graz, and Innsbruck.

Nine-tenths of what the world celebrated as Viennese in the nineteenth century was "promoted, nourished and created by Viennese Jewry," wrote novelist Stefan Zweig (1881-1942). Zweig was to take his own life in Brazil because he could not stand the horrible crimes being committed against the Jewish people.

A Brief History

Jews probably arrived in Austria with the Roman legions. By the tenth century, they are mentioned as "paying tolls on merchandise." An early Jewish tombstone dating from 1130 was found near St. Stephan (Carinthia) and is the earliest evidence that exists of a permanent Jewish settlement is 1194.

A synagogue was built in Vienna in 1204. By the thirteenth century, Austria had become a center of Jewish learning, and a ghetto would grow around the Judenplatz square. The ghetto is gone but the square still exists today near the main synagogue.

At the end of the thirteenth century and during the fourteenth century, Vienna was recognized as the leading community of German Jewry. In 1421, the Jews were expelled from most of Austria, including Vienna. In the fifteenth and sixteenth centuries, only a small number of Jews remained in Vienna; they were restricted to ghettos.

Community life was revived at the beginning of the seventeenth century, especially in the Leopoldstadt section, named after Leopold I. At one time, about 500 Jewish families occupied 136 houses.

During the Turkish War of 1683, the Imperial Armies were financed by court Jews Samuel Oppenheimer and Samson Wertheimer. The latter was called the "Jewish Emperor." They helped stop the Turks at the gates of Vienna. Wertheimer's home in Eisenstadt, capital of the State of Burgenland, 60 miles south of Vienna, where many Jews once resided, became the site of the Austrian **Jewish Museum** in 1982.

By 1753, about 500 Jews lived in Vienna, many in the provinces. The ruler of Austria was Maria Theresa (1740-80), who hated the Jews—unless they converted to Christianity, that is. Maria Theresa once wrote of Jews: I know no worse plague than this nation, therefore, as far as possible they are to be kept away from here and their numbers kept down." But the financial motive was so strong during her reign that she was forced to cultivate wealthy members of the Jewish community. Her son Emperor Joseph II, known as the "lover of mankind," brought about Jewish emancipation. In 1782, this enlightened monarch issued his *Toleranzpatent*, which guaranteed Jews certain rights, such as allowing them to attend general schools and to engage in agriculture and handicrafts.

The Revolution of 1848 altered the course of Jewish and Hapsburg history when the ghetto walls came down. Modern Austrian Jewish history begins with this period. Jews had been very active in the Revolution, including Adolf Fischer, who was chief of the new police force, and Ignaz Kuranda, the first Jewish parliament member.

Only 197 Jewish families lived in Vienna in 1848. The very

next year, thousands arrived from Czech lands, as well as from Galicia. The Austria-Hungary Constitution of 1867 extended basic civil and religious rights to all in the Hapsburg Empire, including Jews.

In the early 1900s, Vienna had the largest Jewish population in Western Europe, 175,318 by 1910 with only Warsaw and Budapest having greater numbers of Jews. Every tenth Viennese was Jewish. Sixty percent of Vienna's physicians were Jews, reminiscent of fifteenth-century Spain. Vienna was said to be a "land-locked version of New York City. "Jewish travel from Eastern Europe to Western Europe went via Vienna, still a transfer point.

World War I began the process that led to the destruction of European Jewry. During that war, thousands of Jews died for Austria.

It was Serbia's refusal to allow Austro-Hungarian police onto its soil in 1914 to investigate the murder of the Habsburg crown prince that precipitated World War I. About 10 million persons died in that war, which swept away the great empires of Central and Eastern Europe. As John Keegan points out in his book, *The First World War,* remaining was " a legacy of political rancor and racial hatred so intense that no explanation of the causes of the Second World War can stand without reference to those roots."

After 1918, the powerful Hapsburg monarchy shrank and Austria became the state no one wanted. The Jews became the scapegoat for its defeat. No matter what they did, even reminding the Austrians of the part they played in the country's development, "they could do nothing to counter the violent hatred against the Jews ingrained in wide sectors of the Austrian population."

Still, Jews there considered themselves Austrians, first. Even in 1933, few could foresee that the disaster that would soon crush German Jewry would be repeated in Austria five years later. "The Jews underestimated the danger of persecution by Hitler," says Nazi-hunter Simon Wiesenthal.

Jewish life was doomed by the German annexation of Austria, the Anschluss, in March 1938. But as Stephen Brook says in *Vanished Empire,* "The idea that staunch little Austria was brutally invaded by the Nazi hordes in 1938 is a fiction, for the ground had been prepared ever since 1934 for closer ties with Germany." The vast majority of Austrians not only welcomed Hitler, but unleashed "a violent explosion of race hatred the like of which even the Jews of Germany, who had already endured five years of Nazi rule, had not experienced," wrote George Clare. Fortunately, about 120,000 frightened Viennese Jews would escape Austria between 1938 and 1941.

World War II soon erupted and engulfed the world. Ironically, the Allies, hoping Austria would resist Nazi occupation, made the mistake of calling Austria "the first victim of the Nazis." It left the Austrians believing they were innocent.

During that war, one-third of Austria's Jewish population, about 60,000 to 65,000 out of approximately 180,000, was killed.

"My Fuehrer, I report to you that Vienna has been cleared of all Jews." Baldur von Schirach, Vienna's Nazi gauleiter, sent that message to Hitler. In 1945, 29 Jewish children remained in Vienna and only a few hundred adults. After the Holocaust, between 250 to 500 persons, the remnants of Vienna's original 180,000 Jews, survived. But it was not the end.

First impressions are crucial, but often misleading. One can easily leave Vienna with the feeling that the Jewish community today is dying. But a community that publishes several Jewish newspapers and maintains about a dozen synagogues, a community center, a day school that includes primary and secondary education, Talmud Torahs, kosher facilities, and a modern senior citizens home is not dormant. And since the Waldheim affair, the Jewish community has become more active. Thousands of Jews joined with a quarter of a million Austrians in 1993, in the same square where a crowd of similar size cheered Adolf Hitler more than 55 years ago. In the infamous Heldenplatz—the same spot where Hitler addressed the Viennese masses after Nazi Germany annexed Austria in the 1938 Anschluss—crowds gathered in 1993 to hear speakers with a different message, such as Rabbi Paul Chaim Eisenberg, Austria's chief rabbi.

The present Jewish population is composed of those who returned from Western countries where they had fled from Hitler or those who emigrated from former Iron Curtain cities, including 3,000 to 4,000 Soviet Jews, Polish and Romanian Jews, as well as Iranian Jews. Today, about 12,000 Jews live in Austria, of whom only 6,300 are registered with the community. Of all the Austrian Jews today, it is estimated that only about 2,000 of them are from the pre-1938 generation. A large percentage of the community consists of Jews who arrived here during the Hungarian Revolution in 1956. Above all, as Georg Haber, managing director of the new Jewish Museum put it in an interview, "it is a very heterogenous community as far as its origins and today's culture of the people are concerned." This community also participates in the growth of Austria, and a significant event regarding Austria took place in the summer of 1994 when that nation was admitted to the European Union. The Austrians later approved the admission.

Between 1945 and 1952, 400,000 Jews from Eastern Europe passed through Vienna en route to Israel. And between 1968 and 1988, more than 270,000 Soviet and Iranian Jews used Austria as a gateway to freedom.

The Viennese Jewish population is elderly: more than half the population is over 60 years old. More members of Austria's Jewish community are over 85 than are under 5 years of age. The senior citizens are single, or if married, without extended families.

On the whole, however, Austrian Jews live a nice life. Despite all the difficulties of combatting the anti-Semitism that arose as a result of the Waldheim case and the threats of the Haider affair, Jews will probably remain here. They are active in community events, according to Rabbi Paul Chaim Eisenberg. However, he noted that there is a generation missing because of the Holocaust. He refers, of course, to those Jews who would have been born between 1938 and 1945 and who now would be in their fifties, had they lived.

Notable Austrian Jews

Some prominent Jews of Austrian culture include Gustav Mahler, composer; Arnold Schoenberg, initiator and creator of the Vienna School of Music; Solomon Suizer in religious music; and Sir Rudolf Bing, general manager of the New York City Metropolitan Opera. In drama, there are the well-known Max Reinhardt, founder of the Salzburg Festival; and Berthold Viertel and Billy Wilder, producers.

Jewish Nobel Prize winners of Austrian origin were Alfred Hermann Fried, Nobel Prize for Peace, 1911; Karl Landsteiner, 1930, and Otto Loewi, 1936, Nobel Prize for Medicine; Robert Barany, Nobel Prize for Physiology, 1914; and Elias Canetti, Nobel Prize for Literature, 1981. Isidor Isaac Rabi won a Nobel Prize for Physics (1944).

Jewish contributions to psychiatry included Sigmund Freud; his daughter, Anna Freud; Alfred Adler; William Reich; and Theodor Reik.

Austrian Jews prominent in journalism and literature were Hugo Bettauer, Martin Buber, Hans Habe, Franz Kafka, Franz Werfel, Stefan Zweig, Arthur Schnitzler, and Hugo von Hofmann. Arthur Koestler, although born in Hungary, was educated at the university in Vienna.

JEWISH SITES IN VIENNA

Community Headquarters, Seitenstettengasse 4, 1010 Vienna 1. Tel: 531-040, FAX: 53104-108. The Jewish Community of Vienna, the only representative body of Viennese Jewry "recognized by the authorities," naturally comprises all religious and political organizations. The 24 members of its governing board are elected to a four-year term by the members of the community. A newspaper called *Die Gemeinde* is published once a month. In the foyer of the headquarters is an exhibit of Jewish religious items.

Leopoldstadt, now the Second District, is indeed an interesting neighborhood. The area holds 1,500 of Vienna's approximately 12,000 Jews. In 1937, one-third of Vienna's Jews, about 60,000, lived in Leopoldstadt, where they were one-half of the district's total population. For Jews, Leopoldstadt meant home, even if it was a ghetto. Even as far back as the seventeenth century, it was known as the Metropolis of Learning. Especially famous were the district's doctors.

Rossauer Cemetery, Seegasse 9, 1090 Vienna. Recently, this First Vienna Jewish cemetery, the oldest Jewish cemetery in the city, was completely renovated and rededicated. The cemetery was restored with funding by the City of Vienna along with the local Jewish community. About a third of the destroyed tombs and headstones have been restored. The oldest tombstone is dated 1582, with the last funeral taking place there in 1783. Later the cemetery became a historical monument.

Buried here is Samuel Oppenheimer, along with other famous eighteenth-century Jewish financiers. Open Sunday through Thursday, 7 A.M. to 5 P.M.; Friday, 7 A.M. to 3 P.M.

The Vienna Central Cemetery, Simmering Hauptstrasse, Vienna XI. Tel: 76-62-52. Graves of famous rabbis, authors, and artists can be found here. Gate 4 is an entrance to the Jewish section; Gate 1 is for an older section. At the Simmering Hauptstrasse entrance, the hours are Sunday through Thursday, 8 A.M. to 5 P.M. and Friday, 8 A.M. to 3 P.M. At the Zentralfriedhof entrance of Gate 1, contact Mr. Pagler, who is coordinator of the restoration of the old part of the cemetery; Tel: 877-1371.

KOSHER DINING IN VIENNA

Alef-Alef kosher restaurant, Seitenstettengasse 2, 1010, Vienna 1. Tel: 535-25-30. This restaurant next to the synagogue entrance on the Judengasse (the old ghetto) is strictly kosher and under Orthodox kosher supervision. It opened in early 2001.

Kosher Bakery, Hollandstrasse 7, (1020 Wien) Vienna 2. Tel. 214-5617.

Kosher Shop, Tempelgasse 8, 1020 Vienna 2. Tel: 24-83-94. This store sells kosher food.

Kosher Supermarket and Kosher Bakery, Hollandstrasse 10, 1020 Vienna 2. Tel: 216-96-75. Also located here is a Jewish bookstore.

SYNAGOGUES IN VIENNA

Stadttempel, Seitenstettengasse 4, 1010 Vienna 1. For a guided tour, telephone the Jewish Community Center, Tel: 531-04-105 or 531-04-16. The chief rabbi is Rabbi Paul Chaim Eisenberg. The synagogue serves as a rallying point for the community, which has maintained and centralized facilities that consist of a community center, and Alef-Alef restaurant often frequented by Jewish travelers to Vienna. There are two buildings that compose the complex: The synagogue and the offices of the Jewish community are located at 4 Seitenstettengasse and the community center hall and the restaurant, Alef-Alef, are situated at 2 Seitenstettengasse.

The Stadttempel, located in one of the oldest sections of the city, opens Monday through Friday at 7 A.M., Sunday at 8 A.M., and Sabbath morning, Saturday, at 9 P.M. Daily services are held in the afternoon for mincha and in the evening for maariv. The pale blue and gold sanctuary is a fitting tribute to a once very large congregation.

Although badly damaged by the Nazis during Kristallnacht in 1938, the synagogue remained the only house of worship not destroyed by the Germans. (The Nazis leveled 22 synagogues and 40 small prayer houses).

This synagogue, the oldest existing Jewish house of prayer in Vienna, was founded on April 9, 1826. The builder was Josef Kornhausel. The structure is also noted as the burial place of the founder of modern political Zionism, Theodor Herzl (1860-1904), who died in Vienna on July 3, 1904. After World War II, Herzl's remains were taken to Jerusalem for final burial. Thousands of Viennese lined the streets. Thus, it is difficult to walk through the streets around the Judenplatz and not think of Herzl, that "black-bearded prophet of the Jewish people who led them back to Zion restored." Vienna was the headquarters of the Zionist movement under Herzl. His book *The Jewish State* called for a sovereign Jewish nation for those who wished to go there.

Herzl, born in Budapest, was a student of law in Vienna from 1878 to 1883. He wrote journals for the Vienna newspaper *Neue*

Freie Presse and became the Paris correspondent for the paper in 1891. *Neue FreiePresse* was comparable to *The Times* in England or *Le Temps* in France. Writers such as Anatole France, Ibsen, Zola, and Shaw were associated with this journal.

Herzl had earlier experienced a tide of economic anti-Semitism in 1891 and in 1894. He was appalled to see France in an alliance with Russia when pogroms were killing Ukrainian Jews. Witnessing the degradation of Capt. Alfred Dreyfus framed by the French military, Herzl was moved by the need to create a Jewish state. He became the hero of the Jewish world, especially to the East European masses, although the term "Zionism" had been coined in May 1890 by a Vienna-born journalist, Nathan Birnbaum (1864-1937).

Agudas Yeshurun, Riemergasse 9, 1010 Vienna 1. Orthodox.

Bet Hamidrash Torah Etz Chayim, the former Schiffschul, Grosse Schiffgasse 8, Vienna 2. Orthodox.

Mizrachi Synagogue, Judenplatz 8, 1020 Vienna 1. Tel: 535-4153. Open for prayer Monday through Friday, 7 A.M.; Sunday, 8 A.M.; Sabbath, 9:30 A.M. The sanctuary and banquet hall are on the second floor. Here also are the headquarters of the Zionist religious youth, Bnei Akiva. Call for information on activities and lessons.

Nearby is **Judenplatz** or Jews Square, where there are plaques recalling the site of an older synagogue, hospital, and place where Jews lived in medieval times.

Ohel Moshe, Lilienbrunngasse 19, 1020 Vienna 2. Tel: 26-88-64. Orthodox. Shomre Haddas, Glasergasse 17, 1090 Vienna. Orthodox.

Synagogue Agudas Israel, Grunangergasse 1,1010 Vienna 1. Tel: 512-83-31. This synagogue opens Monday through Friday at 7 A.M., Sunday at 8 A.M., and Sabbath at 8 A.M.

Synagogue Agudas Israel, Tempelgasse 3, 1020 Vienna 2. Tel: 214-92-62.

Synagogue Machzeke Haddas, Desider Friedmann-Platz 22, Vienna 1. Tel: 512-52-62. Services are held Monday through Friday at 6:30, 7:30, and 8 A.M. in summer; 7, 7:30, and 8 A.M. in winter; Sunday at 7 and 8 A.M.; and on Sabbath at 8:30 A.M. Call to confirm hours.

Or Chadasch, Rosentalgasse 5-7/4/3, A-1140, Vienna.

Tel/FAX: 967-1229. This is a Reform congregation and member of the World Union for Progressive Judaism.

A recommended hotel in the Second District, but a 10-15 minute walk to the main synagogue, is **Hotel Stefanie,** Taborstrasse 12, 1020 Vienna, Tel: 21-150-0. FAX: 21-150-160.

ORGANIZATIONS

Jewish Welcome Service, Stephansplatz 10, 1010 Vienna 1. Tel: 533-88-91. Fax 533-40-98. Dr. Leon Zelman, director, and his staff will be glad to help you contact the Jewish community. This Jewish Welcome Service, a branch of the Austrian Tourist Office, is located at one of the busiest subway stops in Stephansplatz, in the shadow of the 700-year-old St. Stephan's Cathedral, a landmark that is to Vienna, this very Catholic city, what Notre Dame is to Paris. No matter where you are in Vienna, you can see the cornice of St. Stephan's. When he can find the time, Dr. Zelman stands in front of his office in the square where the station is located and watches hundreds of subway passengers emerge from the underground on an escalator, out into the square where they cannot help seeing the sign: "Jewish Welcome Service—Israel Tourist Information."

Dr. Zelman, a leader of the Vienna Jewish community and a Holocaust survivor, is proud of that sign. It is almost as if it is a reminder to Europe, and to the world, that a Jewish community is very much alive in the capital of Austria and under the shadow of St. Stephan's. Dr. Zelman says no one dreamed that a Jewish community would ever again exist in the land of the Anschluss. Jewish leaders saw no future for the Jews in Austria. Young people emigrated to other lands. But Dr. Zelman is convinced that the Austrian Jewish community will continue as a vital and viable entity. His theory about the Jews of Vienna may be extended to other Jewish communities in Europe. He disagrees with those Jews who say that after World War II, Jews should have abandoned Europe completely, leaving for good. "Many of us who stayed sometimes feel that we have done so because we didn't want to give Hitler his victory." The task, as

Dr. Zelman sees it, remains to keep the light of Judaism shining in Vienna.

B'nai B'rith, Taubstummengasse 17, 1040 Vienna 4. Tel: 504-18-52.

Hashomer Hatzair, Desider-Friedmann Platz, 1b, Vienna 1. Tel: 53-74-99.

The Jewish Old Age Home, Bauernfeldgasse 4, Vienna. Tel: 368-16-55.

Jewish Students Organization, Wahringerstrasse 1020 24, 1090 Vienna 9. Tel: 317-54-99.

Jewish Youth Home, Krummbachgasse 8, 1020 Vienna 2.

Lubavitch Organization, Rabbiner-Schneerson-Platz, 1, 1020 Vienna. Tel: 334-18-18.

WIZO, Desider-Friedmann Platz, 1010 Vienna 1.

Zionist Federation, Poale Zion and the Revisionist Zionists, Seitenstettengasse 2, 1010 Vienna 1.

Zvi Perez-Chajes School, Casteliezgasse 35, 1020 Vienna 2. Tel: 216-40-47. Housed in the refurbished building of the old Chajes Gymnasium and located a few steps from the Leopoldstadt section. Opened in 1984. It contains a preschool, a kindergarten, an elementary school, and a high school.

MUSEUMS

Jewish Documentation Center, Salztorgasse 6, 1010 Vienna 1. Tel: 533-91-31. This primary source of information on Nazism is under the direction of Simon Wiesenthal. Obtain an appointment before visiting; permission needed. This building is a stone's throw from the Gestapo headquarters.

Nearly sixty years after World War II, there must be many who are afraid of the man whose office and small staff are located in the building at Salztorgasse 6. Simon Wiesenthal has spent more than half his life tracking down evidence against living Nazis. As founder and head of the Jewish Documentation Center, Wiesenthal has acted as the nemesis of the Nazis. He has guided more than 1,000 cases to trial and has been named the head of the Association of Jewish Victims of the Nazi Regime.

Melodramatic but true: no Nazi war criminal can rest in peace with Wiesenthal stalking him. His most famous conquest was Adolf Eichmann. Through the collaborative efforts of Wiesenthal and Israeli agents, Adolf Eichmann was located in Buenos Aires, Argentina, in 1959, where he was living under the alias of Ricardo Klement. Captured and brought to Israel for trial, Eichmann was found guilty of mass murder and executed on May 31,1961.

Wiesenthal grew up in a small town in Galicia at the easternmost extremity of the Austro-Hungarian Empire. His mother perished in the Holocaust. Most of his wife's relatives did not survive the concentration camps. A total of 89 members of both families perished. He ended up in the Mauthausen concentration camp located near Vienna. Weighing less than 100 pounds and lying helplessly in a barrack where the stench was so strong that even hard-boiled S.S. guards would not enter, Wiesenthal was barely alive when Mauthausen was liberated by an American armored unit on May 4, 1945.

His main point hits home: the trials of ex-Nazis remain an educational experience for the world. Wiesenthal was often at loggerheads with the late Bruno Kreisky, a Jew, who was prime minister of Austria from 1970 to 1983. Kreisky was described as "born a Jew, but he became a hater of Israel and a front-line activist against the Jewish state," according to Edmund Schechter in his *Viennese Vignettes: Personal Recollections.* Obviously, Kreisky's relations with Israel were tense because of his policy of talking with the PLO. In view of the famous "handshake" in Washington, D.C., in 1993 between Prime Minister Yitzhak Rabin of Israel and Yasir Arafat of the PLO, some say they admire "Kreisky's foresight." History will tell.

In 1993, Wiesenthal, who was 85 years old that year, became embroiled in charges that he discovered and concealed evidence of alleged World War II crimes committed by Kurt Waldheim. But Wiesenthal wrote that the accusations being made against him "have no basis in fact." He denied the author's allegations.

Meanwhile, even into 1994, Wiesenthal was often invited to speak to schools and university audiences in Austria, where he is regarded as a leading representative of survivors of the Holocaust and he rarely refuses. Indeed, all of the city's high school students were offered a free screening of the movie *Schindler's List,* and then the students were given the chance to question Holocaust survivors. The first witness was Weisenthal, according to a report by the Austrian Information Services.

Sigmund Freud Museum, 19 Berggasse, 1090 Vienna 9. Tel: 319-15-96. The apartment building at 19 Berggasse where Dr. Sigmund Freud lived and worked for 47 years looks like any multi-unit building in this section of North Vienna, except it was the home of the man whom author Peter Gay calls the "Columbus of the mind." The Sigmund Freud Museum is open Monday, Wednesday, Friday, 9 A.M. to 12:30 %p.m.; Tuesday, 3 to 6 P.M.; Saturday, 10 A.M. to 1 P.M. Closed Thursdays, Sundays, and public holidays. Guided tours by prior arrangement. The house and the study on Berggasse (*berg* means mountain) have been restored and the consulting rooms converted into a museum. The site is sponsored by the Sigmund Freud Society and the Vienna Municipality.

The staircase to the 14 rooms where Freud lived from 1891 to 1938 has not been changed. The rooms contain memorabilia, some 420 items on display in four museum rooms. There are 60 items from Freud's own archaeological collection. Much of the museum is devoted to the history of psychoanalysis.

On a visit to Freud's apartment you see his rooms, his desk, his collection of Greek, Roman, and Egyptian antiques, pieces of sculpture, his books, and his Oriental rugs. The traveler will see Freud's waking cane, his hiking flask, his hat, a suitcase, as well as his comprehensive library. Near his study, note that Freud's youngest daughter Anna set up her office dedicated to the psychoanalysis of children in the mid-1920s. The displays in this memorial room, accessible to the public from late 1991 on, show original documents from Anna Freud's psychoanalytic work with children.

Sigmund Freud, the founder of psychoanalysis and the best-known Austrian throughout the world after Johann Strauss, was born to Jewish parents on May 6, 1856, in Freiberg, a small town in Moravia, now the Czech Republic. He attended school in Vienna and entered the university as a medical student where, it is said, he encountered anti-Semitism. Because of his Jewishness, he was sometimes excluded from the academic community of Vienna, the center of world medicine. However, he found a haven in Ernest Brueck's psychological laboratories. The rest is history.

Freud was not a practicing Jew. He wrote that he did not understand Hebrew. Some would accuse him of being estranged from Judaism. But author Amos Elon asserted in the *New York Review of Books* that "Freud was attached to the Jewish world with ties he knew to be indestructible," and is even said to have contemplated briefly, in 1922, settling in Palestine. He remained a steadfast member of the Jewish community and of the Vienna B'nai B'rith lodge, which author George E. Berkley says he had helped found. Freud once wrote: "My parents were Jews, and I remained a Jew myself."

Sigmund Freud Park and Memorial, located in front of Vienna's Votive Church, only steps from the Medical School of the University of Vienna and from Bergasse. Freud lectured at the university. The park was dedicated in 1985. In the park, which adjoins the University on one side, Vienna's Mayor and Governor, Dr. Helmut Zilk, unveiled a memorial to Freud. It is a simple stone facing the university and bearing the Greek letters, psi alpha, and the inscription, "The voice of reason is soft." Freud himself had used the Greek letter combination psi alpha as the logogram of psychoanalysis and it has become worldwide scientific shorthand.

Jewish Museum of the City of Vienna, Dorotheergasse 11, Vienna. It was a cold, partially snowy day on Sunday, November 21, 1994, and yet they stood in the cold waiting to enter, this the first day of the new Jewish Museum. Even more significant was the fact that this inauguration brought out huge crowds, which made it necessary for long lines to go around the building. It was an opening day in which "The Jewish Museum introduces itself." Admission was free and a special post office was established for stamp collectors.

Vienna Jewry and the city have made a serious commitment to this museum, which is open to the public Sunday to Friday, 10 A.M. to 6 P.M., except on Thursday, when it's open until 9 P.M.

The Jewish Museum of Hohenems, Austria, which is housed in the historical Villa Heimann-Rosenthal built in 1864. One room is dedicated to the music of Hohenems-born Solomon Sulzer (1804-90), who composed religious music. (Photo by Monica Wollner of New York, great granddaughter of Malwina Rosenthal, whose family owned the Villa.)

In addition to general museum work such as exhibitions and collections, the Jewish Museum says it intends to become a place of meeting and contact where Jews and non-Jews can exchange ideas at lectures and presentations, symposia and seminars, film shows and musical events.

The museum also is proud of a lecture hall/cafeteria called "Cafe Teitelbaum," and a bookstore offering a selection of books and magazines on Jewish history and culture.

A highlight of the museum is the Berger collection, which with its approximate 10,000 items includes religious and ritual objects, medals, paintings, prints, and archive material. The exhibit covers the entire spectrum of Ashkenazi art. A collection on the Jewish community of Vienna contains material from the old Jewish Museum, which was closed in 1938 by the Nazis. Another important collection is that of Martin Schlass, which was donated to the Jewish Museum in 1993. This collection contains 5,000 items of anti-Semitic objects such as figurines, household utensils, manuscripts, prints, and postcards.

The first Jewish Museum was opened in 1897 and lasted until the Nazi era. Where were all the objects now housed in the new museum? After the war, all the Jewish objects found in different parts of Austria and Vienna itself were handed over to the Jewish community for keeping.

A municipal Jewish museum was located in the Vienna Jewish community center-synagogue until the museum opened in Dorotheergasse. The new museum building was originally a palace that dates back to the sixteenth century when it was separated from the adjacent Dorotheestift convent. After frequent changes of ownership over the centuries, it finally became in this century an art gallery and in the last decades, it has housed the art department of Vienna's biggest auction house. In 1993, the auction agency put the palace at the disposal of the Jewish Museum of the City of Vienna.

The museum has made it clear that the Jewish Museum "will always have to be aware of the fact that the Nationalist Socialist policy of persecution and annihilation has created a traumatic counterpoint in the history of Jews and non-Jewish Austrians." It added, "the memory of the Holocaust will therefore permeate all activities undertaken by the Museum; at the same time, the

Museum also represents a new beginning, by employing the methods available to a museum of cultural history to reconstruct and preserve the past."

Georg Haber is the managing director of the new museum. The director is Professor Julius H. Schoeps from Germany, who is professor of history at the newly created University of Potsdam and also director of the Moses-Mendelssohn Center for European Jewish Studies.

If the first day was any example, the exhibits on display were superbly presented. Travelers to Vienna would do well to visit this wonderful museum.

MEMORIAL SITES

Gestapo Victims Monument. The monument in Morzinplatz honors hundreds who were murdered here, including many Jews. The Gestapo headquarters were located in the Hotel Metropole. Although Austrians accounted for only 8 percent of the population of the Third Reich, about one-third of all people working for the S.S. extermination machinery were Austrian. Almost half of the six million Jewish victims of the Hitler regime were killed by Austrians.

The Mauthausen Concentration Camp, A-4310, Mauthausen-Marbach 38. Tel: 07-238-2269. The Mauthausen memorial site consists of watchtowers, barbed wire, and a gas chamber. Mauthausen is located 17 miles from Linz and 80 miles west of Vienna. About 200,000 persons perished here, and one-third were Jews. Methods of execution included pushing inmates from one of the 186 steps that they had to climb while carrying rocks from the quarry or ordering them to run to the barbed wire and then shooting them as escapees. The University of Stuttgart concluded its report on Mauthausen with, "deliberate extermination played a more significant role in this camp than in other concentration camps."

According to James E. Young, author of *The Texture of Memory: Holocaust Memorials and Meaning in Europe, Israel, and America,* "Mauthausen has been transformed from a hellish scar on the landscape to a clean, beautifully maintained state memorial."

There are 20 national monuments here, and the Jewish

memorial monument is one of them. It consists of a menorah and a stylized Hebrew lettering spelling out *zachor* "remember."

Young points out that the former Soviet Union's monument to victims of fascism at Mauthausen, "seems inspired partly by Nathan Rapoport's Warsaw Ghetto Monument."

The visitor can see all the buildings of the former concentration camp and its museum with 133 pictures and exhibits. A guide is available or you can obtain a tape as well as a film. Additional exhibits show the fate of Austrians in the concentration camps of Dachau, Buchenwald, Sachsenhausen, Ravensbruch, Auschwitz, and Theresienstadt. Every May 4, ceremonies are held to honor the camp's liberation by the Americans.

Sculpture Monument. A sculptured figure of a Jew forced to scrub political slogans off the street, a common scene during the 1938 Anschluss, when Nazi Germany marched into welcoming Austria, can be viewed. This stone ensemble is located on a square behind the Opera and the Sacher Hotel. Alfred Hrdlicka is the sculptor. The sculptural ensemble by Mr. Hrdlicka, one of Austria's most prominent sculptors, was meant to guide the viewer through Austria's suffering under Hitler, through its participation in the German crime, and finally its liberation from the Nazi hell.

Holocaust Memorial, Judenplatz, Vienna. This memorial, on the site of the burning of a medieval synagogue, resembles an inside-outside library. It honors the memory of about 65,000 Austrian Jews killed by the Nazis. The sculpture is about 12 feet high, 24 feet wide, and 33 feet long. The double doors on the front do not open and the names of the Nazi death camps are inscribed around the base. A museum to display newly excavated remains of the burned synagogue as well as the renovation of the Orthodox Jewish Center in the square—known as Mizrachi House—were also to begin in 2001.

Suggested Reading

Bassett, Richard. *A Guide to Central Europe.* New York: Viking, 1987.

Berkley, George E. *Vienna and Its Jews: The Tragedy of Success 1880-1980s.* Lanham, Md.: Madison Books, 1988.

Fraenkel, Joseph, ed. *The Jews of Vienna, Essays on the Life, History and Destruction.* London: Valentine Mitchell, 1967.

Herzstein, Robert Edwin. Waldheim: *The Missing Years.* New York: William Morrow, 1988.

Hofmann, Paul. *The Viennese: Splendor, Twilight, and Exile.* New York: Doubleday, 1988.

Lengyel, Emil. *The Danube.* New York: Random House, 1939.

Magris, Claridio. *Danube: A Journey Through the Landscape, History and Culture of Central Europe.* Farrar, Straus and Giroux.

Miller, Judith. *One, by One, by One: Facing the Holocaust.* New York: Simon &: Schuster, 1990.

Schechter, Edmund. *Viennese Vignettes: Personal Recollections.* New York: Vantage Press, 1983.

Wiesenthal, Simon. *Justice Not Vengeance.* New York: Grove Weidenthal, 1989.

Young, James E. *The Texture of Memory: Holocaust Memorials and Meaning in Europe, Israel, and America.* New Haven: Yale University Press, 1993.

Switzerland
Home of the First World Zionist Congress

Welcome to Switzerland, one of Europe's most popular tourist destinations. An Israeli I once met said that the most beautiful place in the world is Switzerland, the country of the Alps, of civilized behavior, famed for cheese, chocolate, clocks, and watches. Many Jewish travelers favor Switzerland because for 700 years it has remained without conflict and seems calm and content. Golda Meir, the former prime minister of Israel, once said that Jews were the most nervous people in the world. So there is Switzerland, a place to soothe their nerves.

This "heart of Europe" covers 15,941 square miles or about one-third the area of France Switzerland's population of 7,275,467 includes about 20,000 Jews, or 0.3 percent of the population, who live mostly in the big cities. Five large cities dominate Switzerland: Zurich has 357,000 citizens; Basel, 178,000; Geneva, 170,000; Bern, the capital, 130,000; and Lausanne, 118,000. Sixty-five percent of the people speak Swiss German; 18 percent speak French; 12 percent speak Italian; and 1 percent speak Romansch.

A traveler to Switzerland will see that its people are both orderly and literary. Zurich, Basel, Bern, Lausanne, and Geneva have more bookstores than other big cities in the world. Two of the world's greatest educators, Jean Jacques Rousseau and Henrich J. Pestalozzi, hail from this land-locked state. Well-known Swiss painters include Alberto Giacometti and Paul Klee.

Switzerland is an independent nation, supporting an economy based on international trade and banking. The Swiss banker is known the world over. It is said that "the responsibility of the Swiss is to prosper."

In World War II, while Europe destroyed itself, neutral Switzerland was untouched. Only the Swiss resisted involvement in two world wars. With a freely convertible currency, Switzerland served as an international finance and communication center. After New York and London, Swiss Banks are rated third in the world. But the Swiss banking industry became tarnished when the World Jewish Congress led an investigation into banks that had accepted Nazi-looted gold. At stake were millions of dollars of gold from Jews who had perished in the Holocaust, as well as Swiss accounts that belonged, but were no longer accessible, to Holocaust survivors after World War II.

After several years of investigation and prodding by several groups including the U.S. government, New York state officials, and the World Jewish Congress, Swiss banks in 1998 agreed to a settlement of $1.25 billion with respect to most of Holocaust-related financial claims against Switzerland and Swiss industry. Specifically, this agreement will cover the bank accounts that Holocaust victims placed in Swiss banks for safekeeping and were unable to recover after the war, according to the World Jewish Congress.

A Brief History

The Swiss date their origin from 1291. Men from Uri, Unterwalden, and Schwyz gathered to form the nucleus of the Swiss Confederation. To this day, a Swiss's First loyalty is to his or her canton, of which there are 23. In 1315 the Hapsburg invaders were defeated; the cantons were united to form a confederation.

During the sixteenth century, Switzerland was considered the headquarters of the Protestant Reformation.

In 1798, the French occupied Switzerland. The Confederation

set up a formal constitution that established the Helvetian Republic. The Congress of Vienna recognized Switzerland's "perpetual neutrality," a condition that has endured to this day. A new confederation was established in 1848, with Bern as its capital. The Swiss have the peculiar distinction of being the only country in the Western Hemisphere to delay the right of women to vote until the 1970s. (Before the modern era, some cantons allowed the vote, while others did not).

A Jewish presence in Switzerland appears in the thirteenth century. Jews first settled in Basel in 1213, in Lucerne in 1252, followed by Bern in 1262, and finally in Zurich in 1273. A French expulsion edict in 1306 caused French Jews to move here, only to experience the Black Plague (1348). For allegedly having poisoned the wells, a common medieval anti-Semitic accusation. Jews were tortured.

In 1622, Jews were expelled again. Later, only a handful of Jewish physicians was allowed to remain in some towns, with a few in the canton of Baden.

Until the French Revlution, Jews lived mainly in the canton of Aargau in northern Switzerland. Two Jewish villages, **Endingen and Lengnau,** actually became the cradle of today's Swiss Jewry. If you have a half-day's time in Switzerland, you should definitely visit the two villages and their synagogues, not quite an hour's drive from Zurich. Endingen, by the way, is the only village in Switzerland that has a synagogue and no church, although there are practically no Jews living there anymore. The **Jewish cemetery** located between the two villages, its oldest section romantically secluded in a small forest, is "one of the most touching in Europe," says Willy Guggenheim of the Zurich Jewish community.

But in the 1850s, the United States, England, Holland, and especially France pressed Switzerland to end its discrimination against Jews. Again under French pressure, the Federal Constitution of 1866 was revised to allow Jews to live anywhere in Switzerland. The cantons followed suit and finally, in 1879, Endingen at last granted emancipation to Jews.

Today Zurich is home to about 8,000 Jews;

Geneva, 4,321; Basel, 2,577; and Lausanne, more than 1,000. The "Schweizerische Israelitische Gemeindebund" (SIG),

A silver Torah ornament from Endingen. (Photo courtesy of the Swiss National Tourist Office)

"Union of Swiss Jewish Communities," is the umbrella organ-
ization of Swiss Jewry and has 22 member communities.
The majority of Swiss Jews are Ashkenazic but since 1945,
Sephardic Jews from the Mediterranean area have arrived.
"The community is largely middle class, its members increas-
ingly employed in the specialized professions, large corpora-
tions and the civil service," according to the Institute of Jewish
Affairs' book. *The Jewish Communities of the World.*

Notable Swiss

Switzerland has been known to be a refuge to many expatriates and to the persecuted. Here are the tombs of Rainer Maria
Rilke, Thomas Mann, James Joyce, Robrt Musil, George Kaiser,
and E. Weicher. Goethe, Byron, Franz Liszt, Johannes Brahms,
Stefan Zweig, Eric Maria Remarque, Albert Einstein, Thomas
Mann, and Paul Klee all found peace and a chance to carry on
their work in Switzerland after they had been forced to flee
their own native countries. Ernest Bloch lived in Switzerland,
as did Wolfgang Pauli, physicist, and Tadeus Reichstein, the
medical researcher who won Nobel Prizes in Physiology and
Medicine in 1950.

The President of Switzerland at the beginning of the new
millennium was Ruth Dreifuss. She became the first Jewish
head of state in the nation.

Basel

Basel Stadt Casino, 14 Steinenberg. In the story of Zionism
and the State of Israel, Basel looms large. The Basel Program—
"to create a publicly recognized secured home for the Jewish
people"—was adopted here. Theodor Herzl would later write
in his diary: "In Basel I found the Jewish state. If I said this out
loud today, I would be answered with universal laughter.
Perhaps in 5 years, certainly in 50, everyone will know it."

The First World Zionist Congress began on August 29, 1897.

A view of the Basel Town Hall. (Photo courtesy of the Swiss National
Tourist Office)

Frankfurt Jewry had refused its city as the site of the Congress, so it was held in the Basel Stadt Casino, which in 1938 was replaced by a new concert hall on Steinenberg Street. Today a plaque commemorates the Congress. The English Jewish writer Israel Zangwill referred to the First World Zionist Congress when he wrote: "By the rivers of Babylon we sat down and wept as we remembered Zion. By the rivers of Basel, we resolved to weep no more."

In this city of museums on the Rhine River, Herzl was elected president of the World Zionist Organization. The year 1997 was the 100th anniversary of the first Zionist Congress and a celebration was held.

Centuries ago, Jews were not allowed to live in Basel. They had to live outside the city walls. Indeed, still standing is a city gate where Jews were required to pay a special fee. Ironically, Basel became a center for Hebrew printing.

People enjoy living in Basel, the second largest Swiss city. It is an academic as well as chemical/pharmaceutical center. An aura of scholarship, history, humanism, publishing, and love of the arts permeates the place. The city likes to be known as the "cultural heart" of Switzerland.

Three Kings Hotel (Hotel Drei Könige/am Rhein), 8 Blumenrain, is only a hotel, but it is a symbol for Jews. Every American tourist is familiar with the claim, "George Washington slept here." Well, Theodor Herzl, the founder of modern Zionism, did sleep here during the First World Zionist Congress in 1897 and several times afterward. Mounted on many a wall throughout the world is the famous photo of him standing on the balcony of his room in the Three Kings Hotel overlooking the Rhine and its bridges in the background.

Another fine hotel is **Hotel Euler Basel,** 14 Centralbahnplatz, 4002, Basel.

The **Hotel Basel Hilton,** Tel: 271-66-22, offers special weekends, including "Herzl Weekend" packages.

The **synagogue,** known as the Israelitische Gemeinde Basel, is located at 24 Leimenstrasse. Daily services are held. A Hebrew school and a day school are housed here.

The Jewish Community Center adjoins the synagogue and houses a kosher restaurant known as Topas (Tel: 271-87-00 or 22-87-01). According to Swiss law, ritual slaughtering of animals is forbidden and kosher meats are imported from France.

As for most Jewish residents in Europe, assimilation remains a major problem. New leadership is hard to find and often one leader serves for many years in many roles.

Still, Basel Jewry is active: B'nai B'rith, a local World Zionist Organization, a UJA group, and Bnei Akiva are the main groups. The community sponsors kosher meals on wheels for its senior citizens.

The **Jewish Museum**, 8 Kornhausgasse. Tel: 25-95-14. This museum is the only Jewish museum in Switzerland and is certainly worth visiting. It reflects the Jewish population of more than 2,000 in Basel and exhibits the history of Swiss Jews, who now number approximately 20,000. Although a small museum, it exhibits some exceptionally rare and remarkable items, such as tiny tefillin and rare books of Esther (the story of Purim), as well as havdalah candles, a Polish-Jewish Hanukkah menorah and other Judaic items, and memorabilia from the First World Zionist Congress of 1897. Open from 10 A.M. to noon and from 2 to 5 P.M., Monday, Wednesday, and Sunday.

The Basel Tourist Board is located at Blumerain 2, CH-4001, Basel, Switzerland.

Lugano

The whole world seems to come to Lugano, a summer resort whose city population is about 30,000. They call it the "Rio de Janeiro of the Old World," because of its subtropical vegetation and the peaks of San Salvatore.

Located on Lake Lugano on the southern edge of the Alps, this town has a distinctive Mediterranean character. It "dances in sunshine and is fringed with palms and mimosa trees," making it one of Switzerland's most popular summer holiday resorts. Most of the tourists walk along the calm, cool lakeside promenade. Others visit the sector known as Castagnola. The Villa Favorita, perched at the town's border, contains one of the finest private art galleries in Europe. Day trips on the lake round out the visitor's trip to this garden city.

About 800 Jews live here; many are black-coated, black-kneesocked, bearded Chassidim who are seen in the city streets. The community boasts Orthodox families, many of them Chassidim, a Talmud Torah (afternoon school), a day school, and a synagogue. About 50 Orthodox families live and work in Lugano.

Hotel Dan, Via Fontana. Tel: 54-10-61. This kosher hotel is an institution in this small Jewish community. Hotel owner Moshe Gefen hails from Keltze, Poland. Mr. Gefen, who settled here after the war, speaks Italian, French, German, Hebrew, Yiddish, Polish, and, of course, a little English. His hotel is efficient, clean, and *heimisch*. The glatt kosher food is tasty and well cooked. Mr. Gefen has owned the hotel for more than 25 years, remarkable for a precarious business such as a kosher hotel. He prides himself on doing much of the cooking.

Many Jewish business persons, he said, stay in the kosher facility, which holds religious services during the morning and evening and draws worshippers from throughout the city. Many stay in the hotel during the merchandise fairs held in Milan, Italy, about an hour's drive south. Although politically Swiss from 1512, Lugano remains Italian in ambiance and culture.

Many Jewish retirees reside in apartments and in the hotel during the year, some of them receiving reparations from Germany. The air and the lifestyle help people relax. The hotel is open all year, but sometimes closes "in deep winter," as Mr. Gefen puts it.

Using Lugano as an example, Jews in Switzerland today appear to be comfortable, with complete equality and religious freedom. They feel at home.

A **synagogue** is located at 11 Via Maderno. Tel: 23-61-34. The **Conservative synagogue** of the Associazione Ebraica de Canton Ticino is situated at Via E. Bosia 15-17 in the Lugano Paridiso district.

Geneva

Old-fashioned elegance is one way to describe the setting of Geneva, often called "the city of God" or "the city of Calvin." A "geographic crossroads" and "peace hub of the world," it takes international crises in its stride, although it is the seat of many peace and disarmament conferences and administrative headquarters of the International Committee of the Red Cross and 150 other global organizations.

Here is Geneva, Switzerland's most cosmopolitan city, where the art and jewelry dealings are endless; where one out of three residents is a foreigner. On the banks of a beautiful lake, the sights are attractive, including a new Red Cross Museum and the Opera at the Grand Theatre. Here stands the Palais des Nations, with architecture similar to Versailles. Here sat the League of Nations from 1936 to 1939. And here is the European headquarters of the United Nations.

When Philip Augustus expelled the Jews from French soil in 1182, many businessmen and doctors resettled in Geneva. They were not welcomed with open arms, for, if you were Jewish and passing through the city, you had to pay a poll tax.

Officially recognized in 1853, the Geneva Jewish community founded a synagogue in 1859.

The World Jewish Congress was set up in Geneva in 1936. In August 1939, the last Zionist Congress before World War II took place here. During that war, Geneva served as an important center for information regarding the fate of Jews in Nazi-occupied Europe.

After the war, Eastern European Jews arrived in Geneva. Later came Jews from North Africa and the Middle East. In 1945, the Jewish population was 2,245, by 1968, 2,700. Now it has passed the 4,000 mark.

KOSHER RESTAURANTS IN GENEVA

Restaurant Jardin, 10 rue St.-Leger, Geneva. Tel: 317-89-10.

Open 12 A.M. to 2 P.M., Monday through Thursday. Only lunch is served.

SYNAGOGUES IN GENEVA

The Liberal Synagogue (Bet Gil), Quai du Seujet. Tel: 732-32-45. Services on Friday evening at 6:30 and Saturday morning at 10:30. Beautiful sanctuary. There are Talmud Torah classes, activities, conferences, community dinners, and a sisterhood. Many people here speak English. Established in 1984, the congregation has about 400 family members of Reform or Conservative movement backgrounds. Services are in French and Hebrew; some are in English. During the community seder, prayers are in English. Rabbi François A. Garai, originally from France, speaks excellent English. A friendly atmosphere invites visitors.

The Great Synagogue, Place de la Synagogue. A memorial plaque stands in front of the courtyard at this 100-year-old synagogue honoring the six million Jews who died in the Holocaust.

This would be a good place for the Jewish traveler to consider the Holocaust and the Swiss role in that event.

There are many sides of the debate as to how much Switzerland could or could not have done during the Holocaust. What is true is that by 1942, the situation of the Jews in Europe became extremely dangerous. Yet to understand the problem, we must go back to 1938. On July 6 of that year, in nearby Evian, which is located on the French side of Lake Geneva, an international conference was called to solve the refugee problem. Nobody "lifted a finger." There was only silence. Some even reduced the refugee quota. No one wanted Jews. Switzerland maintained it could only be a transit country for fugitives from Germany. "This was by no means a glorious chapter in Swiss history," says Dr. Guggenheim.

Wartime Swiss officials refused entry to thousands of Jewish refugees, even after "it was known that they faced almost certain death in Nazi Germany," wrote Elizabeth Olson in *The New*

York Times of December 11, 1999. Citing an announcement of a group of independent international historians who had issued a 350-page report, she noted that Swiss authorities were aware that Jews were being annihilated by the Third Reich. By its sending thousands of Jews to their death, Switzerland helped the Nazi effort. Yes, Switzerland saved 21,000 Jews, but it abandoned more than 25,000 and in 1942 closed the border because it was afraid Germany would invade.

The historians said there was no evidence that accepting many more asylum seekers would have put neutral Switzerland in danger of "invasion by the Axis or caused insurmountable economic difficulties." They rejected an argument advanced in Switzerland's defense after earlier disclosures of the country's treatment of Jews trying to escape the Holocaust.

Switzerland did not reverse its policy of keeping out Jews until July 1944, when it declared that persecution for being Jewish was a valid ground for granting asylum.

Remember, too, that it was a Swiss—the head of the police administration in the Ministry of Justice—who concluded that J' for 'Juden' inscribed in German, in passports held by Jews, would help Hitler control the flight of Jews from Germany." Four years later in August 1942, Switzerland closed its borders. Leni Yahil says Switzerland "took the position that the right of asylum is the sole prerogative of the State—not that of the refugee." A Swiss official compared Switzerland to a lifeboat, with thousands of drowning people clamoring to get into that only available lifeboat with very limited space and provisions. In August 1942, at about the time of the sealing of the borders, he said that the lifeboat was full.

From 1939 to 1945, a total of 295,381 fugitives received asylum in Switzerland, some for only a short time. But about 25,000 Jews were refused admission. Many did not even hazard an attempt to get across the freedom line. During the war years, about 21,000 Jewish refugees were saved and taken care of in Switzerland, according to Dr. Guggenheim.

Nearly 1,700 Jews from Hungary were brought to Switzerland via Bergen Belsen, 1,200 Jews from Theresienstadt were rescued, as well as the 400 children who came from the Buchenwald concentration camp. After the war, many left for other lands.

The Machsike Hadass Synagogue, 2, Place des Eaux Vives. Tel :735-22-98. Call ahead for times of services as they may change, depending of course, on the season.
Hekhal Haness, 54 ter, route de Malagnou. Tel: 736-96-32. Sephardic.
Bet Chabad, 42 rue due Lac, 1207 Geneva. Tel: 736-36-82. FAX: 736-38-26. E-mail:%uHabad@Lub.com. Every day, morning and evening services are held, as well as Shabbat services, and activities for children.

ORGANIZATIONS

Travelers should know that the **U.S. Consulate** is located on rue de Temple.
Many Jewish organizations maintain offices in Geneva:
American Jewish Joint Distribution Committee and HIAS (Hebrew Immigrant Aid Society), 75, rue de Lyon, 1211, Geneva. Tel: 345-93-50. HIAS is the international migration agency of the organized American Jewish community.
The Jewish Community Center, 10, rue St-Leger. Tel: 317-89-00. This building is the center of the Jewish community. There are lectures, Talmud Torah classes, a fine library that also has books in English, and a kosher snack bar that is open Monday to Thursday for lunch.
ORT, 1, rue de Varembe. Tel: 734-14-34.
World Jewish Congress, 1, rue de Varembe. Tel: 734-13-25.

HOTELS

Hotel Churchill, 15 rue du Simplon, 1207 Geneva. Tel: 700-88-88. FAX: 700-88-78. A few minutes to Bet Chabad and 10 minute walk to other synagogues.
Hotel Diplomate, 46 rue de la Terrossiere. 1207 Geneva.
One recommended **hotel** is **Le Warwick,** 14 rue de Lausanne, CH-1201, Geneva. Tel: 731-62-50. FAX: 738-99-35.

This 169-room hotel is located in the city's new commercial center across from the main Cornavin railway station with a six-minute direct airport connection. It is a short stroll to the lakefront, the pedestrian mall, and the old city.

Israel Mission, 9 chemin Bon Vent, 1206 Geneva/Cointrin. Tel: 798-05-00.

Zurich

"Athens on the Limat River" is how Zurich is described. This is Switzerland's largest city and the commercial and financial capital. It is a Swiss "New York City," known for its efficiency and exactness. This second city of psychoanalysis stands as a prime gateway to Europe.

Even if it is a communications and industrial center, Zurich is still one of Europe's most beautiful cities because of the hills surrounding it, the fresh air blowing down from the mountains, and the red geraniums, roses, and begonias that decorate this urban area.

Zurich is a city for strollers, especially on the luxurious and prosperous Bahnhofstrasse, where one might just by chance meet one of the city's 6,000 Jews.

Jews first arrived in Zurich in 1273 and were mainly money-lenders. But eventually came bad times and bad memories, among them the Black Death of 1348 when Jews were burned at the stake, as well as the expulsion from Switzerland in 1634. After the French Revlution in 1789, a few Jews returned to Zurich. The Swiss waited until 1866 to grant civil and legal equality, and only then did a new Jewish community arise. Swiss Jewry, and especially Zurich's Jews, are very well organized into the 22-member SIG, the umbrella organization of Swiss Jewry.

A must for the first-time or even second-trip visitor is the city's attractive section across the river, "the East Bank." This area is fast becoming a preserved area of guildhalls and medieval houses. These charming Old World structures are still among the most precious landmarks in the old town.

The Zurich skyline. (Photo courtesy of the Swiss National Tourist Office)

SITES IN ZURICH

Marc Chagall, France's famed Jewish artist, is also well known in Zurich. His five stained-glass windows are located in the chancel of the **Fraumunster Church.** There is the Prophets Window, Jacob Window, Christ Window, Zion Window, and Law Window.

The Jewish ghetto here was once called the **Judengasse.** You would never know it now; there isn't very much left. We do know, however, that one small street now called **Froschaugasse** was located in the ghetto. Book and antique stores give the street a peaceful shopping appearance. Nearby is the building where Nikolai Lenin lived from February 1916 to April 1917. The sign on the building calls him "the Father of the Russian Revolution."

SYNAGOGUES IN ZURICH

The main address of the Zurich community is the **Cultural and Community Center** at 33 Lavaterstrasse, 8027, Zurich. Tel: 201-1659. The building contains an extensive library and meeting halls. A synagogue is located here, too, as well as a kosher "cafe-restaurant," called **Schalom.** Tel: 201-14-76. The library is open Monday, 10 A.M. to noon, and 3 to 6 P.M. Closed Tuesday. On Wednesday, 12 noon to 5 P.M.; Thursday, 10 A.M. to noon. Closed Friday. Sunday, 10 A.M. until noon. It is closed the last Sunday of the month.

Placed just off the fashionable Bahnhofstrasse and its designer stores is the oldest **synagogue** in Zurich, at 10 Lowenstrasse, 8001, Zurich. Built in 1883 in a Moorish style, it has two magnificent cupolas and an exterior of brown and whitish stone. While the rabbi is Orthodox and the service is Orthodox, many non-Orthodox Jews attend services here, I was told. Around the corner at Nuschelerstrasse 36, Zurich, is the entrance to the **prayer hall of the synagogue.** Tel: 211-68-80.

Beth Chabad Lubavitch, Rudigerstrasse 10, 8038, Zurich. Tel: 289-7050.

Chabad Esra, Witillikerstrasse, Zurich. Tel: 386-8403.

A traditional **German Orthodox Congregation** stands at 37 Freigutstrasse, 8002, Zurich. Tel: 201-67-46.

Or Chadasch, a Liberal or Progressive synagogue, is at 13 Fortunagasse, 8001, Zurich. Tel: 221-11-52 or 221-11-53.

The Orthodox community here is the third largest in Europe after London and Antwerp.

KOSHER RESTAURANTS

Fein & Shine, Schonpalstrasse 14, Zurich. Tel: 241-3040.

Ascot, Bonifege Neufeld Birmensdorfstrasse, Zurich.

Suggested Reading

Hasler, Alfred A. *The Lifeboat Is Full: Switzerland and the Refugees, 1933-1945.* New York: Funk and Wagnalls, 1969.

Martin, Lawrence and Sylvia. *Switzerland: An Uncommon Guide.* New York: McGraw-Hill, 1965.

Schwarz, Urs. *The Eye of the Hurricane: Switzerland in World War Two.* Boulder, Colo.: Westview Press, 1980.

Sorell, Walter. *The Swiss: A Cultural Panorama of Switzerland.* New York: Bobbs, Merrill, 1972.

Belgium
Diamonds, Rubies, and the Most Luxurious Ghetto in the World

Belgium does not have to boast it is the heart of Europe. Everyone knows it is. With its capital city, Brussels, designated as headquarters of both the European Union and NATO, this small country has achieved that goal.

Belgians not only speak English, they openly solicit and welcome English-speaking travelers. They have turned their beautiful canal and seashore cities and towns into tourist attractions. Explore Bruges, Ostend and Ghent and you will marvel at Belgian skills in welcoming visitors. Certainly Belgian cooking is giving the French a run for their money. We even found what probably is the best kosher restaurant in Europe in Antwerp at Hoffy's, which we shall discuss when we visit that city, which contains a vibrant, Orthodox Jewish community.

You can spend a week in this urbane country and enjoy every minute of it, including shopping for lace and tapestry and savoring world-renown, delicious Belgian chocolate.

Sandwiched between Germany and France, bordering, too, on the Netherlands and Luxemburg, and facing Britain across a narrow strip of the North Sea, this kingdom has seen wave after wave of invading armies. When you talk to these citizens about their role among nations, some bitterness creeps into the conversation. As they say, the whole world marched onto this tiny land to fight on Belgian battlefields: Waterloo, where Napoleon ended his military career; Flanders Fields in World War I, where a generation of English and French lads were

wiped out halting the invading Germans; at Bastogne in World War II, where American troops withstood a last-gasp attack by the German Army.

So let us begin our journey to Brussels, Ghent, Bruges, Antwerp and Mechelen. After all, "if it is Tuesday, it must be Belgium."

Here along the North Sea lies Belgium, a rich nation of 12,000 square miles—the size of the state of Maryland—with outstanding cultural and artistic complexes blanketing the country.

As nations go, Belgium is a youngster, becoming an independent entity only in 1830. Its nineteenth-century creators hewed out an "artificial state" that had been ruled previously by Rome, Burgundy, Spain, Austria, France, and the Netherlands. It was also to be overrun by Nazi Germany in the twentieth century.

With its 10 million citizens, Belgium also holds the distinction of being the second most densely populated nation in Europe—after its neighbor, the Netherlands, that is. Belgium is flat—trisected by the Scheldt and Meuse rivers with the hills and forests of the Ardennes in the south.

A Brief History

The area came to be known as Belgium because it was settled by Belgic tribes of Celtic origin who were known as Belgica. Much of Jewish settlement in Europe began with the Roman conquests; Jews followed the path of those Roman legions in Belgium in the years 53 to 57 C.E. A group of Jews may have reached the country just after the destruction of the Second Temple in the year 70 C.E. Even with limited evidence, we know that Jews lived in Belgium from the ninth through the thirteenth centuries.

As in most countries of Europe, Belgian Jews were sometimes tolerated and at other times persecuted, depending on who ruled. Jews who were expelled from England in 1290 and from France in 1306 settled in Belgium and Holland. But in 1309, crusaders rampaged the area. Then came the Black Death of 1348, with its scapegoat, the Jews, who were charged with poisoning the wells and the Christians massacred nearly the entire Jewish community of Belgium. In 1380, Jews were accused of desecrating Christian religious symbols. They were dragged from their homes and burned at the stake.

Belgium remained Catholic; Holland had become Protestant. The Belgians never welcomed the Jews as warmly as did the Dutch. And so, the Jews did not come in any significant number until the sixteenth century. Attracting them to Belgium and Holland were the commercial cities of Zeeland and Flanders. The latter needed skilled newcomers for the lively markets of Antwerp and Bruges.

Enter the Marranos, the "secret Jews" who arrived in the Belgian cities in the early sixteenth century. Antwerp's star was rising and the Marranos were sharp businessmen. Because Antwerp needed them, the city fathers gave these Iberians or "New Christians" safe-conduct passes. The Marranos accepted the offer, settled down, and introduced the flourishing silk trade in 1526.

Marranos could not go directly from Spain or Portugal to southern lands in the Mediterranean, so some would pass through Antwerp en route to, of all places, "hospitable" Turkey. An underground railroad from Spain and Portugal via Antwerp to Holland and Turkey was set up. For example, Joao Miguez, a famous Jewish personality of the day who became the future Duke of Naxos and known as Joseph Nasi, came to Antwerp to reach Turkey. He maintained many important commercial contacts. Antwerp also became the first stop on the long odyssey of the Marranos over the Alps into Italy or the Balkans. The clergy, enforcing the Inquisition, watched every move of these New Christians, many of whom secretly practiced Judaism and sought religious freedom.

Later, with the establishment of a free Jewish community in Amsterdam, the main tide of Marrano settlement from Iberia moved from Antwerp toward Amsterdam, which then became the metropolis of the Marrano Diaspora. Still, because Belgium displayed a high quality of life, it would continue to attract Jews.

But waves of unrest surfaced in the seventeenth and eighteenth centuries. Holland and Belgium were split when the northern provinces under Maurice of Nassau won their independence from Spain in 1609. That division continues to this day.

Belgians have learned that they must get along with each other in order to survive. The country exists as a bicultural, bilingual state. People here speak both Flemish and French and some German.

One group, the Flemings, speak Flemish (a dialect of Dutch). They outnumber the other group, the Walloons, by about two million. The Flemings live in Flanders, along the North Sea and on the northern plains, in an area rich in agriculture. The Walloons live in Wallonia, which is in the southern plains and in the hills of the Ardennes. Bordering on France and Luxembourg, they speak French.

When Belgium, which had been governed by Spain since 1519, was turned over to Austria in 1713 according to the Treaty of Utrecht, the Jewish community began to live in relative freedom and attracted Eastern European Jews.

In 1794, the French invaded the Netherlands, which then included Belgium, and immediately introduced religious equality for the 800 Jews. In 1808, Napoleon established the Consistoire Central Israelite, which to this very day stands as the representative body of Belgian Jewry.

After Napoleon was defeated in the Battle of Waterloo, the great powers, meeting at the Congress of Vienna in 1815, did not feel France should rule Belgium. The British pushed for a single state for both the Dutch and Belgians. Nobody bothered to ask the people of Holland and Belgium what they thought about a unified state. The union lasted 15 years.

In 1830, Belgium began its revolt against Dutch rule and soon won its independence. In the new state, religion received official recognition and Jewish religious freedom was written into the constitution guaranteed by the Concert of Europe.

Throughout the nineteenth century, the Jewish population in Belgium increased. By 1900, Antwerp contained 8,000 to 10,000 Jews, including many who would soon be on their way to the United States. Others were attracted to the city by the diamond industry. Jewish life, however, was interrupted by World War I, as Belgian neutrality was scrapped by the invading Germans.

Between World Wars I and II, the Jewish population in Belgium continued to grow, reaching about 100,000, a quarter of them refugees from Nazi Germany. After the Nazis' rise to power in 1933, Antwerp counted 55,000 Jews and Brussels, 30,000. When the Germans unleashed their blitzkrieg strike on the Western front on May 10, 1940, many Belgian Jews fled to France. But they were not safe there, as France, too, was conquered and large numbers of Jews would later be rounded up and returned to Belgium, which itself capitulated to the Germans in May 1940.

By August 1942, the Nazis began transporting Belgian Jews to Auschwitz. Within a year, about one-third of the Jews in Belgium were murdered. By war's end, about 40,000 of the 85,000 Jews who had lived in Belgium perished. After the war, thousands of Jewish refugees from Eastern Europe, many of whom awaited permission to enter the United States and Israel, poured into the country. By the 1960s, both immigration and emigration decreased. The community stabilized.

Today, the majority of Belgian Jews are middle class and are active in the fur, textile, and diamond industries. Total Jewish population is approximately 40,000. About 20,000 Jews live in Brussels, 15,000 in Antwerp. Small Jewish communities exist in Charleroi, Ostend. Ghent, Liege, Mons, Arlon, Knokke and Namur.

Jewish Brussels

The city welcomes, shelters, and entertains diplomats. No wonder this ancient metropolis employs thousands of civil servants and "ex-pats," many of them American. Flocking to the cobble stone Grand Place, tourists gape at this lovely square; they focus on the superb architecture of these Old World buildings, and they enjoy its fine cafés, restaurants, and nearby shops.

The city of 135,000 stands as the nation's fifth largest city. But if you count the suburbs, it becomes the country's largest metropolitan area. People have been moving to the outlying suburbs, such as Waterloo.

Brussells is shaped like a heart. The oldest section, called the lower city, is in the center. This area includes the Grand

Place, which is surrounded by elaborately decorated buildings built in the 1600s to house merchant and craft guilds. The Brussels town hall actually dates from the 1400s.

Jews probably arrived here in the mid-thirteenth century. The Black Death nearly wiped out the entire Jewish community in 1348. Further unrest and exclusion kept the Jewish population at a low level.

From time to time, Marranos found their way here, and in 1713 the Treaty of Utrecht brought Austrian rule and the return of some Jews. In 1757, the Jewish community of Brussels consisted of 21 men, 19 women, and 26 children, many of whom had moved here from Holland. But with the French annexation of Belgium in 1794, Jews again began flocking to Brussels in large numbers. Over the next 150 years Jews came from Holland, Germany, and Eastern Europe. By 1939 10,000 Jews lived in Brussels.

JEWISH SITES IN BRUSSELS

These "Little Belgians" as the French call them, have welcomed and absorbed Jews into their country. When Belgium became independent in 1830, Jews became equal citizens.

Of the approximate 40,000 Jews in Belgium today, about 20,000 reside in Brussels; 15,000 in Antwerp; and about 5,000 in Ostend, Charleroi, Liege and Ghent.

Travelers need to recognize that two separate Jewish communities existing in the same country could not be as different as Brussels and Antwerp.

Let us visit the Brussels Jewish community first.

"It's not easy to be Jewish in Brussels," says Rabbi David Mayer of the Liberal Synagogue. He cringes at what he claims is a 70 percent intermarriage rate which may be on the high side. Even the optimists, however, say the figure hovers around 50 percent. With that rate, Jews will disappear, opines Rabbi Mayer. Jews are so spread out over the city and young couples are moving out to the suburbs so fast that it is difficult to find Jews in Brussels, he explains.

The Grand Palace, Brussels. (Photo by Ben G. Frank)

The president of the Consistoire, says that many parents send their children to Israel to finish high school

Chassidim may be "catalysts for Jewish life," but in Brussels, 80 percent of the Jews here are not Orthodox. In fact, there is only one kosher butcher in Brussels and one Jewish bookstore. Still, Jewish education is stressed in both the Orthodox and non-Orthodox communities. As in other European communities, Jewish leaders feel strongly that Judaism will survive.

Consistoire Central Israelite de Belgique, (C.C. I.B.) rue Joseph Dupont, 1000 Brussels. Tel: 02-512-21-90. FAX: 02-512-35-78. Since Belgium became a nation in the 19th Century, the C.C.I.B. acts as the representative of the Belgian Jewish community to the Belgian government.

Communaute Israelite de Brussels, rue Joseph Dupont 2, 1000 Brussels. Tel: 02-512-43-34. FAX: 02-512-92-37. This group respresents the Jewish community of Brussels.

Communaute Israelite Orthodoxe de Brusells, 67 a rue de la Clinique, 1070 Brussels.Tel: 02-521-12-89.

Communaute Israelite Sephardite de Brussels, 47 rue du Pavillon, 1020 Brussels. Tel: 02-215-05-25.

SYNAGOGUES, SCHOOLS, AND ORGANIZATIONS

The Great Synagogue, 32 rue de la Regence, 1000, Brussels. Tel: 02-512-4334. This is a magnificent synagogue on a magnificent, stately boulevard, a boulevard that contains important Protestant and Catholic churches. Built in 1878, it was not damaged during the Holocaust. The building was described by a Belgian writer in the 19th century as " one of the most successfully carried out buildings of modern Brussels." Today, the chief rabbi maintains his office here. There is a minyan every day: Services on weekday mornings are held at 8 o'clock and in the evening depending, of course, on sunset. Friday night services are held around 6 P.M. or 7 P.M. and on Saturday mornings, prayers begin at 9:30 A.M. Call the synagogue for exact times.

The architect for this synagogue, which was constructed between 1875-1878, was Desire DeKeyser. On the façade, there are ornamental features, such as a rose window. A feature of this house of worship is the three-storeyed gabled central section

The Great Synagogue, Brussels. (Photo by Ben G. Frank)

flanked by slightly recessed four-storeyed towers which conceal low-glass-covered passages running along the north and south sides of the building, according to Carol Herselle Krinsky, author of *Synagogues of Europe: Architecture, History, Meaning.*

Nearly a million francs was spent on building the synagogue and the community administration building which is next door and whose entrance is on **rue Joseph Dupont.** Use this entrance for weekday services as well as services on some Saturday mornings.

Oratoire, rue Joseph Dupont, 2, 1000 Brussels. Next door to the Great Synagogue. Often used for weekday prayers.

Synagogue Adath Israel, 126 rue Rogier, 1030 Brussels. Tel: 02-241-1664.

Synagogue Or HaHaym, 77 rue Pierre Decoster, 1190 Brussels. Tel: 02-344-2342.

Congregation Sepharadite de Brussels. Place Constantin, Meunier 14, 1180 Brussels. Tel: 02-345-2394.

Communaute Israelite de Waterloo, av Belle Vue, 140, 1410 Waterloo. Tel: 02-354-68-33.

Synagogue Chaare Tsion, 303 Chaussie d'Alsemberg, 1190 Brussels.

Liberal Synagogue, av. de Kersbeek, 96, Brussels. Tel: 02-332-25-28. This congregation, about a 20-minute taxi ride from the Grand Place, has about 400 members. Services are at 8 P.M. on Friday nights and 10:30 A.M. on Saturday mornings. Many Americans attend services here. This synagogue has an active program for Jews who live in the suburbs.

Musee Juif de Belgique, av. de Stalingrad, 1000 Brussels. The Jewish Museum is open Monday to Friday, from 12 noon to 5 P.M.; Sunday, from 10 A.M. to 1 P.M. In 2002, a new Jewish museum will open in the **rue des Minimes, Brussels.**

B'nai B'rith, 68, avenue Duepetiaux. Tel: 02-537-39-17.

Fédération Nadonale des Anciens Combattants et Résistants Juifs Armés de Belgique, 148, Chaussée d'Ixelles.

Jewish Community Center, Centre Communautaire Laïc Juif, 52, rue Hotel des Monnaies. Brussels. **The Federation of Jewish Youth** is also here. Tel: 02-532-82-16.

FAX de Jerusalem, semi-monthly review of the Zionist organization of Belgium, 66-68, avenue Duepetiaux, Brussels.

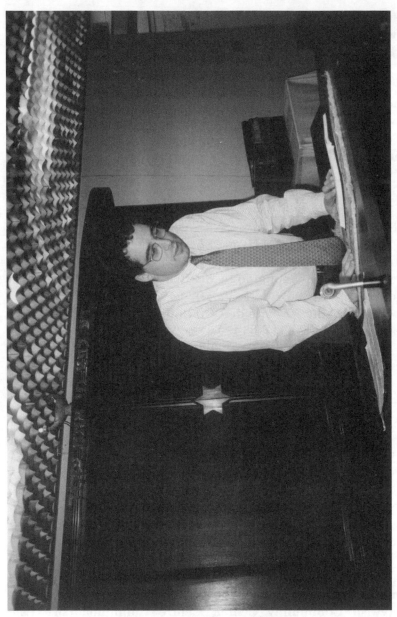

Rabbi David Mayer in the sanctuary of the Liberal Synagogue of Brussels. (Photo by Ben G. Frank)

At 68, avenue Duepetiaux is **The Zionist Federation** (Tel:02-538-56-29) and the **Comité de Coordination des Organizations Juives de Belgique** (Tel: 02-537-16-91). **The Union of Deportees Organization and the World Jewish Congress (Belgian Section)** are also here. **Union of Progressive Judaism,** 61, rue de la Victoire, 1060 Brussels. Tel: 02-537-82-45.

Athenee Maimonide, 67 Bd. Poincare, 1070, Brussels. Tel: 523-63-36. This school has a full primary and secondary program. About 400 children attend. It also maintains a kosher lunch program available to tourists, but telephone ahead.

Beth Aviv, 123, avenue Miliere. Brussels. Tel: 02-347-37-19. A primary and secondary school of about 560.

Ecole Ganenou, 3, rue du Melkriek, 1180 Brussels. Tel: 02-376-11-76. A primary and secondary school of about 560.

Institut d'Etudes du Judaisme—Institut Martin Buber, 17, avenue Franklin Roosevelt, Brussels. Tel: 02-650-33-48. FAX: 02-650-33-47. This is part of the Free University of Brussels. Conducting studies in Judaism at the university level, it is also known as Institut Universitaire d'etudes du Judaisme Martin Buber. **The Centre National des Hautes Etudes Juives (the National Center of Higher Jewish Studies)** is also located here. Tel: 02-648-81-58, ext., 3348.

Cercle Ben Gourion and Radio Judaica, Chee de Vleurgot, 89, 1050 Brussels. Tel: 648-18-59. Many activities for students are held here.

Jewish Student Union, Avenue A. Depoge, 3, 1000 Brussels. Tel: 649-08-08.

Jewish Old Age Home, "Heureux-Sejour," 31-35 rue de la Glacier, 1060, Brussels. Tel: 02-537-76-66.

Beth Chabad, 87 av. Du Roi, 1060, Brussels. Tel: 02-537-11-58.

Guide: Louis Berkowicz, Rerum Novarumlaan 9, 1700 Dilbeek, 02-511-92-67. 02-466-29-12. Louis Berkowicz who speaks excellent English is available for city tours on foot or by car. He also conducts tours to Jewish sites.

Tourist Information Services, Hotel de Ville, Grand Place, B-1000, Brussels. Tel: 02-513-89-40; 02-548-04-48. FAX: 02-514-45-38.

An impressive **National Monument to the Jewish Martyrs** of Belgium is at rue Emile Carpentier and rue de Goujons in the district of Anderlecht. The square is called Square of the

Jewish Martyrs, and 23,838 names are inscribed on the wall. A small museum is also located here. Office: U.D.J.B. 68 Av. Duepetiaux. Tel: 02-538-98-66.

KOSHER DINING IN BRUSSELS

Chez Gilles, 21, rue de la Clinique, 1070 Brussels. Tel: 02-522-1828.

Ghent

"Welcome to Flanders," the guides will tell you.

They do not have to add, "enjoy your stay in Flanders," because you will. Not only is Ghent one of the most beautiful historic cities in Flanders, it was its capital. Today it is less than an hour from Bruges, Antwerp, Brussels and the airport. I found it a quiet city with high-quality events.

Americans will realize that here in the early 19th century, peace talks were underway at Ghent, with the aim of ending the War of 1812 between the U.S. and Great Britain. The final treaty did exactly that and was signed on December 24, 1814. Among those representing the U.S. were Henry Clay, John Quincy Adams and Albert Gallatin. I recalled that when I entered college I was shocked to learn that the U.S. actually lost the war itself, but won a victory at the peace table at Ghent. Here I was in the city where the Treaty of Ghent in reality settled none of the disputes that caused the war, but merely restored the situation that existed previously, without the British boarding our ships.

The waterways right in the center of the town are quite attractive and add to the peace of the municipality. At one time Ghent had 76 bridges. This city once was a power in Europe and you can still see the spirit of enterprise in the facades of the guild houses.

The flower markets, the fruit markets, the vegetable markets add to the atmosphere of a city that is in effect part museum.

Jewish Ghent

There is no synagogue in Ghent. Nor is there a kosher butcher shop or a single kosher restaurant. But there is a Jewish community and there are Jews in Ghent—perhaps 100 live and work in the area. Non-Jews will lead you to one of the town's leading citizens who is Jewish: if you stop a native of Ghent on the street and ask if there's a synagogue in Ghent, chances are he or she will send you to Blochs Bakery, J Veldstraat 60, Ghent. Tel: 09-225-70-85. This concern has had a presence in this town for many, many years. It is a fine establishment and the minute you enter you know you are in a Jewish establishment. There, facing you on the shelves of this bakery and tea room (non-kosher), are several Jewish National Fund boxes.

Ghent is an historic Jewish community. It was founded at the end of the 19th century, and grew between World Wars I and II. Many Eastern Europeans study at the university here.

Jewish leaders of the community, Jacques Bloch and Mrs. Elan Sperling (137 Vaskenslaan 900, Ghent; Tel: 09-333-3297) told me that there are activities sponsored by the community, such as Chanukah and Purim parties, a community Passover seder, lectures, and weekly Hebrew and Bible studies.

The synagogue is not the center of Jewish life here and the Jewish community is not religious. Judaism here is "not linked to religion."

A very important site in Ghent is the **Holocaust Memorial, Coupure rechts and Linden lei**. This Holocaust memorial is in the shape of a dreidel and is located at the confluence of a major canal. But it is not easy to locate. Often tourists are told about it when they are walking in the area or come upon it by accident. More than half of the Jewish population of Belgium survived the war, according to Holocaust historian Yehuda Bauer. He explains that the Christian population and the activities of various Jewish underground groups helped save Jews. Unlike the Dutch, the Belgians did not follow the orders of the Germans or of the Jewish leaders to register and report for assignments in work camps elsewhere, which, as we know, turned out to be located in the killing fields of Poland.

The Holocaust Memorial in Ghent. (Photo by Ben G. Frank)

Another memorial to the Holocaust is located on a wall of the city's university building. There is a memorial plaque citing the deportation of Jewish students during World War II.

Ghent Jewish Community. M. Bloch, Blochs Bakery, J Veldstraat 60, Ghent. Tel: 09-225-70-85.

INFORMATION

Hotel Gravensteeen, Jan Breydelstraat 35, 9000 Ghent. Tel: 09-225-11-50. FAX 09-225-18-50.

Ghent Tourist Office, Presikherenlei 2, B-9000, Ghent. Tel: 09-225-36-41. FAX: 09-225-62-88.

Bruges

As long as I can remember: mention Belgium, and travelers answer, "Bruges."

And they are right. This sophisticated, small, pretty city will not let you down.

As far as we can tell, there are no Jews living in Bruges. We were told Jews work there, but they are commuters, driving in from Antwerp or Ghent or other nearby cities.

Bruges long ago figured out exactly how to attract tourists and went about doing it. The city sports canals, excellent eateries, from fine, gourmet restaurants to moderate establishments, and historic structures that invite exploration. The shops and stores here are geared for tourists, especially for keen shoppers. Even in the rain, even in late fall, even in early winter, the town is packed with visitors. True, you can jump onto a little yellow mini van for a city tour. Or you can see Bruges by boat or bike or horse-drawn cab. All this is fine as long as some place along the line, as they say, you get out of a car and become a pedestrian. You see, Bruges is a walking town and the traveler will just love the shops, the museums, the banks of the Lake of Love and the picturesque canals. Walking is the best way to discover Bruges. The city is rather small. You can easily walk across it in a half-hour.

A familiar sight in Bruges. (Photo by Ben G. Frank)

Don't forget to visit the City Hall, the Old Country House, the Fish Market and the city's many museums.

Bruges was once a world-famous trading center and a cradle of Flemish art. It started as a Gallo-Roman settlement in the Second and Third centuries. From the 11th Century, Bruges became an international commercial center, thanks to its direct access to the sea. Around 1350, Bruges had about 45,000, twice the amount it counts today. In the 15th Century, Flanders became part of the Burgundian state. But at the end of the 15th Century, the Burgundians left Bruges and the city's "Golden Age" ended. First, the city lost its outlet to the sea because of the silting up of the coastal area. Then, Antwerp pulled ahead of Bruges and took over the wool trade. It took several hundred years, but Bruges finally regained its position as an art and tourist city. Europe still thinks that it is a fine place to visit. In 2002, Bruges bears the title of "Cultural Capital of Europe."

Travel is much faster today in Europe. For example, you can take high-speed trains in direct runs between Brussels and Charles de Gaulle Airport in Paris. The trains are called Thalys (a made-up name, pronounced TAL-iss). They are capable of speeds up to 186 miles an hour. This journey takes about 1 hour 25 minutes to travel between the Paris airport and Brussels. But now let's hop a train to that inviting port city of Antwerp.

Antwerp

A proverb says: "Antwerp owes the Scheldt to God and everything else to the Scheldt River." The latter made Antwerp the business and commercial capital of Northern Europe and the second largest city of Belgium.

Antwerp is Antwerp and here they speak Flemish, which is basically Dutch. Only Flemish has less gutteral sounds than the Dutch they speak in Holland. (In Brussels, they speak both French and Flemish). Antwerp with its 463,000 citizens is Belgium's largest metropolis. It thrives as a lively commercial center and a very active harbor. Busy as it is during the week, on Sundays, the city's populace goes outdoors and strolls on the promenade along the Schelde River or sits in the cafes in Old City. The natives, joined by the tourists, love to devour mussels and *frites* (french fries).

In the age-old tradition of one of its major occupations, that is, diamonds of course, Antwerp's art also dazzles, for this city is also Rubens, Van Dyck, Jordaens, Bruegel and Plantin. The city owes much of its cosmopolitan atmosphere to its art, its diamond business and its shipping center.

Antwerp is proud of its many museums: the Plantin Moretus and the Fine Arts Museum are the best known.

The old **Plantin Moretus Museum** in the Vrijdagmarkt has examples of Jewish printing, as well as the Polyglot Bible. This was the home of the great sixteenth-century printer Moretus and of his descendants. In 34 years, he published about 1,500 different works, a phenomenal achievement. Included were editions of classical authors, Hebrew Bibles, and liturgical pieces. The pressroom, foundry, proofreaders' room, and bookshop are still in their original state. The Plantin Moretus Museum also contains an exceptional collection of manuscripts, books, wood blocks, copperplates, and tapestries, as well as paintings by Rubens and others. It is well worth a visit.

The Jewish traveler to Antwerp, a world port and a mecca for art lovers, has no problem whatsoever in finding Jews. Head for the streets called **Pelikaanstraat** or **Hovenierstraat**. You'll find synagogues, bookstores, restaurants, kosher bakeries, and, of course, diamond marts. The area just looks Jewish.

"This is the most luxurious ghetto in the world," said one Jew who lived on **Belgielei Street,** where many Jews reside. He quickly added, "It's a free-will ghetto, of course." No doubt the Jews of Antwerp are very tightly knit. They live together and work together. After all, about 90 percent of the Antwerp Jewish population of 13,000 is involved in the diamond industry.

Antwerp always has been a "Jewish" city. As one Jewish leader put it, "The non-Jews of Antwerp are so used to living with Jews, they don't see them as Jews." Non-Jews know that their Jewish friends like to live alone and are not too involved in the political and social life of the city.

Most of the Jews of Antwerp are of Polish origin and Orthodox. They admit they just don't mingle.

One must remember that the letters forming the name Antwerp spell "diamonds" and "Orthodox Judaism."

And the diamond industry is built on everyone knowing everyone else; reputation and trust are paramount. This breeds a certain amount of introversion, to say the least. They live in a "diamond world." More Chassidim live here than in any other city in Europe, five or six different sects, such as Belz, Gur, Lubavitch, Satmar, Chortkov, and Vizhnitz. In fact, some say the Lubavitch are not that active in Antwerp, because at least 75 percent of the community is Orthodox. "It is another life and another world, a religious world," a Jew in Antwerp told me.

Ninety percent of the Jewish children of Antwerp go to Jewish day schools, which include yeshivot of such sects as Belz, Satmar, and Vizhnitz.

Others point out that, unlike other cities in Europe, intermarriage is not high here because obviously people are religious. "If you are in the diamond business, you don't want people to think of you as one married outside the religion," said one merchant.

A Dutch-language weekly is published in Antwerp, as are various Yiddish publications. The Anti-Defamation League in Antwerp publishes a monthly called *In de Naam Van de Vrijheid (In the Name of Freedom)*.

American Jews, religious or nonreligious, who want to inhale the "shtetl" life of Europe before World War II, can still find a shining example in Antwerp. The signs and the institutions are here.

Shabbat (Sabbath) morning here resembles a scene out of B'nei Brak, Israel, or Williamsburg, Brooklyn, USA: Chassidic fathers and sons walking to synagogue or to a shtibel. No business is conducted in the Antwerp Diamond District on Saturdays. The Diamond Exchange employs a large number of the chassidim; you can easily believe you are walking on the street of diamond exchanges on West 47th St. in Manhattan.

Orthodox Judaism is very well organized in Antwerp. Two large Orthodox groups in Antwerp, Shomre Hadass and

Machsike Hadass, are active in the city. No problem of obtaining a minyan here. No problem of children attending Jewish studies, albeit a strictly religious one, here. No problem of intermarriage here. No problem of finding kosher food here. There are other problems, of course: Unemployment and Jews disagreeing with each other. Undoubtedly, as one diamond worker once told me, a number follow religious observances so as not be excluded. Still, Antwerp has been described as "a Jewish ghetto." For example, the travel department of the American Jewish Congress takes their sightseers into the area as if they were viewing religious life on the old Lower East Side in New York City.

JEWISH CENTERS AND SCHOOLS

The Romi Goldmuntz Center, Nerviersstraat 12-D14. Tel: 03-239-39-11. Built in 1968, this beautiful, modern structure maintains a library, meeting rooms, a catering hall, sports facilities, and a kosher snack bar.

Tachkemoni School, Lange Leemstraat 313. Tel: 03-239-04-67. This Jewish day school with about 780 pupils is Zionist oriented.

Yesodei Hatora Beth Jacob, Lange Van Ruusbroeck Straat. This day school has about 1,100 pupils. Some say about 90 percent of the Jewish children in Antwerp attend this school or the Tachkemoni one. The Jewish day schools of Antwerp are unique in Europe, and the Jewish Board of Education maintains good relations with the government's Bureau of Education.

KOSHER RESTAURANTS IN ANTWERP

Nearly a dozen kosher restaurants and delis exist in Antwerp. Here are a few.

Hoffy's, Lange Kievitstraat 52, 2018 Antwerp. Tel: 03-234-35-35. FAX: 03-226-02-82. They are three Orthodox brothers. And they are called Yumi, Yankele and Moishe. But can they cook?

The three brothers of Hoffy's kosher restaurant in Antwerp. (Photo by Ben G. Frank)

It is this author's opinion, that this by far is one of the best strictly kosher restaurants in all of Europe. The restaurant which is open from 11 a.m. to about 10 P.M. at night, serves up stuffed cabbage, schnitzel, chicken, roast. Fish is also served with zucchini, carrots, potatoes etc. One great feature of this superb establishment is that you can go up to the counter and pick what you like; a little bit of this, a little bit of that. Obviously closed on the Sabbath and all holidays.

Moszkowitz, Lange Kievitstraat, 47, Antwerp. Tel: 03-232-03-49. FAX: 03-226-04-71. This is a fine take-out facility.

Blue Lagoon, Appelmanstraat 18. Antwerp. Tel: 03-226-01-14. This is a kosher Chinese restaurant.

Drezsdner, Simonsstraat 10, Antwerp. Tel: 03-231-60-42.

Gelkop, Van Leriusstraat 28. Tel: 03-233-07-53, Antwerp.

Sam's, Diamond Exchange, Pelikaanstraat 78. Antwerp. Tel: 03-233-0753. This is a kosher restaurant; however, you need a member to bring you in.

A **snack bar** is located at the **Romi Goldmuntz Center,** Nerviersstraat 12, Antwerp.

SYNAGOGUES

There are more than 20 synagogues here in Antwerp, plus many "shtieblach" (small prayer halls).

Americans usually pray at the **Romi Goldmuntz Synagogue,** not located at the community center, but at Van den Nestlei 1.

Beth Jacob Synagogue, Jacob Jacobstraat 22, Antwerp. Tel: 03-231-40-39.

Beth Hamidrash Hagadol Synagogue, Oostenstraat, 43, Antwerp. Tel: 03-230-92-46.

Beth Lubavitch, Brialmontlei 48, Antwerp. Tel: 03-218-41-96.

Communaute Israelite du Rite Portugais d'Anvers, Hoveniersstraat 32, 2018 Antwerp. Tel: 03-232-53-39.

"Hollandse" Synagogue, Bouwmeesterstraat 7. Moriah Synagogue, Terliststraat 35. Antwerp. Tel: 03-232-01-87.

Sephardic synagogue, Hovenierstraat 31, Antwerp. Tel: 03-232-5339.

ORGANIZATIONS

There are many Jewish cultural, political, and youth organizations in Antwerp.

Communaute Israelite Shomre Hadass d'Anvers, Terliststraat 35, 2018 Antwerp. Tel: 03-232-01-87.

Communaute Orthodoxe Machsike Hadass d'Anvers, Jacob Jacobstraat 22, 2018, Antwerp. Tel: 03-233-55-67. This is the headquarters of this Orthodox community.

Agudath Israel, Lamorinierestraat 67, Antwerp. Tel: 03-230-85-13.

Keren Hayesod, Schupstraat 1, Antwerp. Tel: 03-232-97-74/232-05-28.

Macabi Sportclub, Pelikaansstraat 92, Bloc D., Antwerp. Tel: 03-239-56-73.

WIZO, Gretrystraat 53, Antwerp. Tel: 03-239-05-71.

B'nai B'rith, Nervierstraat, 14, Antwerp. Tel: 03/230-17-79.

Fédération Sioniste, Schupstraat 1. Antwerp.Tel: 232-97-74.

Jewish National Fund, Hovenierstraat 12.Antwerp. Tel: 03-231-26-28.

Mechelen

Jewish Museum of Deportation and Resistance, Goswin De Stassartstr 15, 2800 Mechelen. Tel: 015-29-06-60. FAX: 015-29-08-76. This museum tells in part the story of the Holocaust in Belgium. Located in the Dossin Barracks which were used in World War II as an assembly point; this facility served as a holding pen for Jews and gypsies prior to deporting them to the concentration camps, This is one of the few Holocaust museums located in a place which was an "ante-room" in the extermination process of Jews.

From these barracks, 25,124 persons including 5,430 children, were dispatched, mostly to Auschwitz. The first convoys left the Dossin Barracks on August 4, 1942. Between that date and July 31, 1944, the Nazis organized twenty-five more convoys. Nearly half of the Jewish population of Belgium was murdered during the Holocaust. Belgian Jews indicate that while every country had its collaborators, Belgium was one of the countries that tried to save its Jewish citizens.

The museum was opened on May 7, 1995 by the King of Belgium.

First, the visitor to the museum will learn about the early history of the Jews of Belgium. Step by step, the museum will show the methods the Germans employed in transforming the Jewish community into a pariah and then moved to destroy every last vestige of Belgian Jewry. But in Belgium, there was resistance, armed struggle, overt or clandestine action. Shown in the museum is "Belgium under the German Occupation of 1940-1942." One can also see drawings made by detainees in the Dossin Barracks.

Open Sundays to Thursdays from 10 A.M. to 5 P.M., Fridays from 10 A.M. to 1 P.M.

The museum is closed on Friday afternoons and Saturdays and on the Jewish holidays of Rosh Hashanah and Yom Kippur as well as on the holidays of Christmas Day and New Year's Day. Also closed during the annual summer holidays in the second and third week of August.

Suggested Reading

Krinsky, Carol Herselle, *Synagogues of Europe: Architecture, History, Meaning,* Cambridge, Mass.: MIT Press, 1985.

Lerman, Anthony, ed. *The Jewish Communities of the World: A Contemporary Guide.* London: Macmillan, 1989.

Pilkington, Roger. *Small Boat through Belgium.* London: 1957.

Holland
The European Jewish Grandees and Anne Frank

Amsterdam conjures up water, canals, and an active port. Sit and watch the barges ply the canals. Stare at gleaming diamonds in polishing factories. Stroll on streets strewn with leaves as the cool sea breeze bites your face. Then follow the path of nearly 200 canals that were created by the dredging of infected marshes.

Visit the city's museums; Van Gogh and Rembrandt are just two Dutch masters to see. Inhale the spirit that covers the home of the young Anne Frank, whose name will live forever.

A Brief History

This is Amsterdam, the Netherlands, a place that has always welcomed political and religious refugees. For centuries, Jews have carried on a love affair with Holland, a relationship that began in the twelfth century. Called "Little Jerusalem" and "Mokum, the place," Holland has never persecuted Jews.

In this country of harbors, the first large-scale immigration of Jews came here via the sea from Spain and Portugal in 1580. The newcomers were Marranos, secret Jews, who had escaped to Holland and were no longer forced to hide their religion. They could also apply their financial acumen to careers in banking, importing, and exporting in the city that was founded

HOLLAND

Amsterdam

☆ THE HAGUE
● Rotterdam

about 700 years ago and which, by the second half of the fifteenth century, was the "emporium of Europe," a commercial capital, a melting pot. This was the place to be, especially for Jews who thrive in a pluralistic society.

These grandees, the aristocracy of Dutch Jews, came here for economic opportunities, religious freedom, and culture. Their names still resound through Jewish history: Spinoza, Cardozo, Pereira, de Castro, Da Costa, Lopes Mendes, Suasso, Teixerira de Mattos. They worked as silk manufacturers, sugar refiners, printers, book dealers, tobacco merchants, brokers, and doctors.

Legend has it that Uri Ha Levi, a rabbi from Emden, came to Amsterdam about 1600 and met his fellow Jews at a tower that still stands, the **Montel-baanstoren Church.** The first Jewish neighborhood was said to have begun here.

Amsterdam would later become the "metropolis of the Marrano Diaspora." With freedom to worship and unrestricted economic choice, most became entrepreneurs. They became involved in the Dutch West and East Indies companies and, as a result, they became plantation owners and merchants in Brazil, Dutch Guiana, Curaçao, and the Dutch East Indies.

Yet, they did not live by bread alone. As heirs of Spanish, Portuguese, and Moorish culture, Dutch Jewry, made up mostly of Sephardim, would become one of the most important "cultural conveyors" of Jewish life in Europe.

In 1601, the Amsterdam Municipal Council approved a law that Jews could live anywhere in the city they desired. Jews held religious services in a home in 1607 and, the very next year, a congregation was established. In 1610, Jews were already living in the Hague, Rotterdam, Haarlem, Amersfoort, and Alaamaar. Two years later, a synagogue was built in Amsterdam.

In 1616, authorities officially sanctioned the community as members of the Hebrew nation, and Rabbi Isaac Uziel writes that the Jews "live peacefully in Amsterdam." A basic law was passed in 1619 declaring that each city in the provinces could adopt its own local policy toward the Jews.

In 1627, the first Hebrew book was printed. Fifty years later came a Spanish-language paper and Yiddish biweekly, the *Kurant,* according to Jules B. Farber in his *Amsterdam, City of the Seventies.*

In some localities, Jews were singled out, excluded from many trades, guilds, and professions. But compared with Jews in Catholic countries, here was "exceptional liberty," granted by liberal-minded Protestants.

And one man who was on particularly good terms with the Christian community was Manasseh Ben Israel (1604-57), alias Manoel Dias Soeiro, a Marrano, born in Madeira. He was one of the most illustrious rabbis of his age and of world Jewry. His parents brought him to Amsterdam in 1605. At age 18 he became rabbi at a synagogue no longer in existence in Waterlooplein. He acquired fame for his knowledge of Hebrew and the classical languages, enabling him to build contacts with many Christian theologians in Holland and abroad, with whom he discussed religious and philosophical matters. His Hebrew printing press in Amsterdam printed more than 70 books.

In 1650, he wrote *Hope of Israel.* In this volume, he discussed a report dealing with the so-called discovery in South America by Aaron Levi Montezinos of the Lost Ten Tribes. He worked day and night to obtain permission for Jews to live once more in England, an event which he maintained had Messianic implications because it would complete the dispersion of the Jews to *Kezeh ha Arez.* (the end of the earth; *Kezeh ha Arez* is the medieval Hebrew term for *Angle Terre* or England). He believed that the Jews would not be redeemed until they were scattered over the four corners of the earth.

His trips to England and his appeals in 1655 to Oliver Cromwell had effect, although Manasseh Ben Israel felt he had failed because neither Cromwell nor the conference had made it official. Even though he had induced Cromwell to admit the Jews to England, he returned to Holland a broken man, and died in 1657.

The year 1648 was a milestone: the Treaty of Westphalia brought an end to 80 years of fighting between the Spaniards and the Dutch. Holland (the United Provinces) was now free, meaning less restrictions on Jews. In 1657, Holland officially recognized the Jews as subjects of the country. Related to independence was the fact that Amsterdam had topped Antwerp as the chief port in northwest Europe and captured the Belgian city's lucrative trade. Jews immediately moved north to their new Dutch home. The Treaty of Westphalia also closed the navigation of the Scheldt River and almost reduced Antwerp to a dormant city, a condition that would last for two centuries. Jews soon realized that Holland was "where the action was."

With their trading contacts in Spain, Portugal, and the Ottoman Empire, Jews also became very useful. They played an important part in Holland's economic growth. They were involved in the East Indies and West Indies companies. Obtaining control of 25 percent of the shares of the East India Company, they brought in capital and established new enterprises.

By 1672, there were 7,500 Jews in Amsterdam, out of a total population of 200,000. In those days, the Jewish quarter resembled a small Lisbon and Madrid. Spanish and Portuguese was spoken on the streets. The city became a center throughout the Jewish world, the mother community of London, New York, and West Indian Jewry. Many of the 10,000 Jews in Amsterdam, at the close of the seventeenth century, served as academicians, teachers, and rabbis in this city of Jewish printing and learning.

By 1780, the Ashkenazim had by far overtaken the Sephardim, so that only 10 percent of Holland's Jews were Sephardim. (By the early twentieth century, it would be only 6 percent Sephardim).

By the middle of the eighteenth century, Amsterdam possessed the largest Jewish community in Europe, and the French Revolution would dramatically alter Jewish life in Holland. In 1795, the French conquered the Netherlands and its 23,400 Jewish residents. On September 2, 1796, the Batavian National Assembly gave Jews full civil rights. Louis Napoleon, Napoleon's brother, ruled the country until 1815.

Holland became the first country in Europe to elect Jews to its parliament. Here was a precedent, for Holland would become one of the few European nations where Jews would hold many government posts.

Rulers and governments might come and go, but for the Jews of Holland, "unqualified religious equality was the rule until the

Nazis entered in 1940." Like other countries in Europe in the nineteenth century, however, assimilation and discrimination would eat away at the vitality of the Jewish community.

Still, many Jews embraced Zionism and the Eighth Zionist Congress was held at the Hague in 1907. By 1940, 1,500 Dutch Jews had settled in Palestine.

In 1933, many German Jews crossed the border into Holland to escape the Nazis. Few realized that seven years later Hitler would follow them there.

Of all the countries in Western Europe, Dutch Jews in Holland suffered proportionately the most in the Holocaust. Holland, after all, was close to Germany, and the Jews were concentrated in the large cities. From the day the Nazis swallowed up the Netherlands in 1940, until the very end of the war five years later, Jews were hunted down and deported to death camps.

At the beginning of World War II, 156,000 Jews lived in Holland. About 107,000 would perish in the Holocaust. "The Dutch Jewish death rate was the highest in Western Europe. In the East, only Poland had a higher kill ratio," writes Judith Miller, in *One, by One, by One*. By 1943, "about the only way a Jew was seen now, was floating down in a canal," wrote Miep Gies in her *Anne Frank Remembered*. Interestingly, "the percentage of Jews deported from France did not exceed 24 percent in contrast to Holland, whence 76 percent were deported," writes Leni Yahil. In Belgium, the percentage was 40 percent in Denmark it was two percent.

Perhaps because of their naiveté and slavishness to rules, many Dutch Jews obeyed deportation call-ups. Feeling very at home in Holland, they may have been lulled into a false sense of security when the Nazi threat hovered. Some, according to Judith Miller, felt the Dutch Jewish councils "let themselves be used for the liquidation of Dutch Jewry." "They collaborated with the Germans by compiling registers of deportees and in many other ways, all of which facilitated the final murder of the Jews," said a Dutch Commission finding, reported by Ms. Miller in her book.

What has happened of late is that the Dutch, too, are being forced to confront their past. More than 80 percent of the Dutch Jewish population had been murdered. This constitutes the highest percentage in Western Europe. Elise Friedman in the May-June 2000 issue of the *B'nai B'rith International Jewish Monthly* explores the question of how the Dutch can account for the orderly disappearance of more than 100,000 Jews in 1943 and 1944.

When we visit the Anne Frank House, we might want to pause and think about Ms. Friedman's argument that for non-Jewish Holland, Anne Frank "embodies the myth of the heroic nation-in-resistance." What is forgotten is the fact that Anne Frank was betrayed, as were thousands of other Jews in the country. There are 800,000 visitors annually at the Anne Frank House, but only 19,000 visit the former theater where the Germans processed most Dutch Jews for deportation, the Hollandse Schouwburg Museum.

"Onderduikers" or "divers" was the name given to those hidden underground. They lived in cellars or secret rooms. Often, Jews who became fugitives or resistance fighters were supported by clandestine organizations. Only 25,000 Jews went into hiding and of those, only 8,000 of them survived the war, according to writer Elise Friedman.

After the war, between 20,000 and 30,000 Jews returned to their former homes. About 30,000 Jews live in Holland today, and two-thirds of them reside in Amsterdam.

The Netherlands survived the war. Most of the Jews did not. Anne Frank, the Jewish proletariat, the rabbis, the Jewish doctors and lawyers, and the diamond cutters did not. But as Jules B. Farber wrote, "Unlike the Dutch, who tallied their war dead, the Jews counted those who were alive."

JEWISH SITES IN AMSTERDAM

The Anne Frank House, 263 Prinsengracht, 1016 GV Amsterdam. Tel: 626-45-33. Open daily 9 to 5 and Sundays 10 to 5, except major Jewish holidays. Trams 13 and 17, buses GVB 21 and 33, or a five-minute walk from Dam Square will take you here. This site is near Westermarkt.

Now an international center against discrimination, this is the four-story house where teenager Anne Frank (1929-45) hid

Inside the Anne Frank House. (Photo by Doris B. Gold.)

from the Nazis and kept a diary. A million Jewish children died in the Holocaust. She became their voice and their symbol. The secret annex, consisting of two upper floors and an attic, is the building behind the structure on 263 Prinsengracht. The building would turn out to be a good hiding place, for Mr. Otto Frank sold herbs and spices and the inventory had to be stored in the dark. It looked natural, therefore, when the windows at the back of the building were blacked out and painted over.

Miep Gies would risk her life and bring food to the Frank family and the others. Her husband Jan, helped hide the Frank family. He died in 1993 at the age of 87.

The entrance to the hiding place was hidden behind a hinged bookcase. The top of the door was hidden by a map. When you pass through, make sure you watch the brief video tape in the first room, after you pay admission.

The first room you see is the room of the Frank family; Mr. and Mrs. Frank and their eldest daughter, Margot, slept here. On the wall, you spy a newspaper map of Normandy. Otto Frank marked the Allied armies' advances with colored pins. Next to the map, you see the pencil marks where the Franks and the Van Daans measured the height of their teenage children.

Anne's room comes next. She shared the room with Mr. Albert Dussel, the dentist. Recently, a collection of letters and photographs belonging to Mr. Dussel were found and are now displayed in the Anne Frank House. Anne cut movie star pictures out of magazines and pasted them on the walls. They can still be seen. As you walk through to the narrow top floor of the house, you think, "What was it like to live in secret?" Privacy was impossible. Emotions had to be contained. Silence was an absolute necessity, even at night and on weekends. Caution was paramount. Garbage had to be burned in the stove.

Visit the next room, the Van Daan family room. The washroom and toilet were next to Anne's room. The facilities could be used only when people were not working downstairs.

A steep stairway leads from the washroom to the room of Mr. and Mrs. Van Daan, which also served as the hideaway's kitchen and living room. There were a kitchen stove and sink. In the evening, all the windows had to be blacked out.

Peter Van Daan's room is preserved, too. Peter's room can be entered by mounting the stairs leading to the attic. The room contained the only window that could be opened safely. A small supply of food was stored here.

Downstairs, you see a photo exhibit on Anne Frank and her diary and the Holocaust. Her dairy has been translated into more than 40 different languages. On the other side of the room, you find panels on current events that show modern examples of prejudice, discrimination, and repression.

The end of the story came on August 4, 1944, when the police raided the secret annex and destroyed and plundered the apartments. Simon Wiesenthal claims a Dutchman gave them away; he was never found. All eight persons were arrested and sent to concentration camps.

Anne's father, Otto, was the only survivor. In March 1945, two months before the liberation of Holland, Anne died in the concentration camp at Bergen Belsen.

According to Mr. Frank, the SS man who discovered them flung some papers on the floor. Anne's diary was among those papers. "Had he taken the diary with him, no one would have known anything about my daughter." Among the pile of old books, newspapers, and magazines left lying on the floor, Miep Gies and Elli Vossen later found Anne's diary.

After the war, Otto returned to the annex and was given the diary. The world now knows it as *Anne Frank: The Diary of a Young Girl.*

Antiquariaat Spinoza, 26 Den Texstraat, 1017 2B Amsterdam. Tel: 624-23-73. Bookstore.

Bibliotheca Rosenthaliana, 421 Singel, 1012, WP Amsterdam. Tel: 525-23-66. Known as the Rosenthal Collection of the Amsterdam University Library, it contains 500,000 volumes, including the 5,000 volumes of the Rosenthal Collection of Jewish Literature, one of Europe's greatest collections of Hebraica and Judaica. This library is particularly interesting to those who wish to research some aspect of Jewish history and culture.

Hebrew Day School, Buintenveldet.

Huis de Pinto, 69 St. Antoniebreestraat. Established by Isaac de Pinto, a Portuguese Jew from Marrano ancestry who bought the house in 1651, this house is now used as a public library. This is a wonderful street to walk through, as it has a Jewish past. **Waterlooplein** is the old Jewish neighborhood area also known as "Vlooyenburg." Years ago, poor Jews resided around Waterlooplein, which is in the heart of this old section known as "Jodenbuurt" ("Jews' quarter"). By the end of the nineteenth century, the Jodenbuurt had become a slum. It was destroyed between 1941 and 1943. One of its hundreds of famous residents was Baruch Spinoza (1632-77), who lived at 41 Waterlooplein. At No. 33-39 was the synagogue, now demolished, that banned Spinoza.

Who was Baruch Spinoza? He was a Bible scholar and philosopher. Born here in the Waterlooplein area, he was a descendant of Portuguese Marranos. His questioning of ideas angered the leaders of the Jewish community when he criticized aspects of the Bible and refused to consider it as ultimate truth. In 1656, the Jewish community expelled him for his "heretical views." He left for the Hague, where he died in 1677.

The Waterlooplein Flea Market, now held around the Town Hall and Muziek Theater complex, was once the daily market in the Jewish quarter from 1886. Originally, Jews were barred from owning shops, and so they bought and sold on the street. Actually, the old Waterlooplein Flea Market replaced the old market that used to stand on St. Antoniebreestraat and Jodenbreestraat.

KOSHER RESTAURANTS IN AMSTERDAM

Jerusalem of Gold, Jodenbreestraat 148, Amsterdam. Tel: 020-625-09-03. This kosher restaurant is located near the metro station Waterlooplein, which is close to the Jewish Historical Museum and the Portuguese Synagogue. Serves Israeli-style food.

Sal Meijer, Scheldestraat 45, Amsterdam. Tel: 020-673-13-13. This kosher sandwich shop is located near the RAI exhibit and the Convention Center. It is open Sunday through Thursday, from 9:30 A.M. to 7:30 P.M. On Fridays, from 9:30 A.M. until 2 P.M.

NasjViel, De Lairessenstraat 13, 1071 NR Amsterdam. Tel: 020-676-76-22. This establishment caters to young people and students and is located near the Concert Hall, the Van Gogh Museum and the Rijksmuseum.

Carmel, Amstelveenseweg 224, Amsterdam. Tel: 020-675-76-36. An Israeli-style restaurant that is open from Sunday through Thursday, from 2 P.M. until 11 P.M.

Mouwes, Kastelenstraat 251, Amsterdam-Buitenveldert. Tel: 020-661-01-80. A kosher sandwich shop that is open Monday through Thursday, from 9 A.M. until 5 P.M. Fridays, from 9 A.M. until 2 P.M. and Sundays, from 10 A.M. until 5 P.M.

Theeboom, Bolestein 45, Amsterdam-Buitenveldert. Tel: 020-642-70-03. This is a dairy sandwich shop located in a bakery. Open from Sunday through Friday, from 9 A.M. until 5 P.M. Closed on Tuesdays.

The Dutch Chief Rabbinate, Van der Boechorststraat 26, (POB 7967, 1008 AD Amsterdam. Tel: 020-644-3868. Fax: 020-646-46-35. This organization can help with a list of kosher products and other kashrut related matters.

SYNAGOGUES IN AMSTERDAM

The Portuguese Synagogue, 3 Mr. L. E. Visserplein, 1011 RD Amsterdam. Tel: 624-5351. It was just as I pictured it. Still I had to use my imagination to envision the existing huge square building in front of me without the present crisscross of highways and cars, but with several handsome synagogues and thousands of worshippers. This area, this inspirational center of Dutch Jewry, is famous and recognized as the largest historical monument to Jewish Holland.

Like many former Jewish communities in Europe, very few Jews now live in this neighborhood, which includes the street called Jodenbreestraat, the heart of the Jewish neighborhood. They perished in the Holocaust or have moved to other neighborhoods in Amsterdam.

Walk along the heavily trafficked road called Mr. L. E. Visserplein. (Mr. Visser, 1871-1942, was a Dutch Jewish burgher who aided Jews at the beginning of the Holocaust). Here you can see the historic Portuguese Synagogue, the most important building of the old Jewish Quarter. Indeed, it was the first

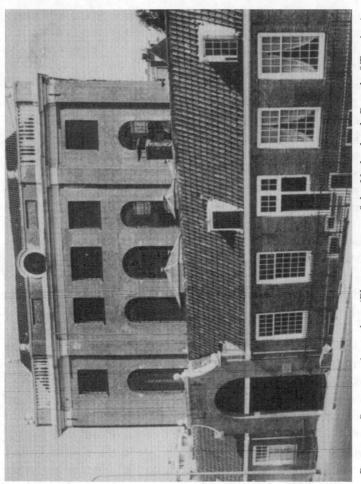

Portuguese Synagogue, Amsterdam. (Photo courtesy of the Netherlands Board of Tourism)

synagogue in Western Europe to be recognized as such and was the model for synagogues in many countries. At one time, it was the largest Jewish house of worship in the world. It is said to be modeled after King Solomon's Temple in Jerusalem, especially the courtyard around the synagogue.

These Sephardic Jews had waited more than 200 years to pray together openly. They wanted the finest synagogue possible and they achieved it. The synagogue was dedicated with such pomp and circumstance that a contemporary witness observed that the people might have been forgiven for thinking they were rededicating the Temple in their homeland.

When it was consecrated in 1675, the mayor and alderman of Amsterdam attended the festivities, which went on for eight days, just as long as the consecration of the Temple in the days of the Maccabees.

The synagogue is always open for services on Saturday mornings at 8:45. It is within walking distance of the major hotels like Krasna Polski, Holiday Inn, the RodeLeeuw, and others. On Sunday mornings at 8:30, and on some Friday nights, services are held, but it is better to telephone ahead to see when services are being conducted, as there are security precautions.

Across the main entrance is a Hebrew text: "For I shall enter your house through your abundant kindness." This is part of the text said upon entering a synagogue.

Enter the hall and you are struck by its size and its spiritual atmosphere. The synagogue itself is one huge room. Twelve stone Ionic columns support the women's galleries and symbolize the 12 Tribes of Israel. Low-hanging brass chandeliers hold 1,000 to 1,500 candles, all of which still have to be lit for services. Seventy-two bow-shaped windows adorn the walls and the light easily shines upon a magnificent ark.

Designed by Elias Bourman in 1675, this house of worship took four years to build and cost 186,000 guilders, an enormous sum in the seventeenth century.

The congregation today consists of 500 to 600 members, but attracts some 25,000 visitors a year. It houses unique works of art, many from the sixteenth and seventeenth centuries, and exquisite antique silver.

In 1993, a major restoration was completed and the building regained much of its original beauty.

Officials still wear traditional dark garb with tall hats. When evening services, bar mitzvahs, and high holiday services are held in the main synagogue, the candles are lit. In the winter, a small attached synagogue is used for prayer when the main hall itself is too cold, as the latter is not heated.

The **Ets Haim Library**, at the Portuguese Synagogue, is open Sundays from 9 A.M. to 1 P.M. Check visiting hours by telephoning 622-6188. This is the library of the Jewish community, one of the major Jewish libraries in the world. It began in 1616 as the library of the Portuguese-Jewish Seminary, an institute that trained rabbis. Its collection contains many remarkable Jewish books, manuscripts, and drawings. There are also copies of famous editions of Hebrew books, such as the books produced by Rabbi Manasseh Ben Israel, one of Dutch Jewry's earliest leaders.

Today, the active synagogues and Jewish center are in the south of the city. Here is a list.

Ashkenazic Synagogues:

Synagogue, 238 Gerard Doustraat is in Jacob Obrechtplein, Amsterdam.

Synagogue, 61 Lekstraat, Rivierenbuurt-Zuider Amstel.

Synagogue, 26 Gerrit Vd. Veenstraat, Zuid.

Synagogue, 105 Linnaeusstraat.

Liberal Synagogue, 8 Jacob Soetendorpstraat, 1079 RM Amsterdam. Tel: 642-35-62. Services are at 8 on Friday evenings and at 10 A.M. on Saturdays. Phone for correct prayer times. This is also the headquarters of the Union of Liberal Jewish Congregations in the Netherlands.

Synagogue, 26 Van der Boechorststraatm, Buitenveldert.

Synagogue, 10 Straat van Messina, Amstelveen.

ORGANIZATIONS

B'nai Akiva, 665 Amstelveenseweg, 1081 JD Amsterdam. Tel: 646-38-72. FAX: 642-58-72.

Beth Chabad, -Lubavitch Holland, De Vlaschaard, 59, 1183KM, Amstelveen-Amsterdam. Tel: 31-20-641-1402.

The Organization of Jewish Communities in the Netherlands, (N.I.K.) Van der Boechorststraat 26, Amsterdam, POB 7967, 1008 AD, Amsterdam. Tel: 020-644-99-68. Tel: 020-644-99-68. Fax: 020-644-26-06. E-mail: info@nik.nl. This is the headquarters of the Dutch Jewish community. Also located here are the Ashkenazic community offices. **N.I.H.S., Jewish Community of Amsterdam,** 26 Van der Bolchorststraat, 1081 BT, Amsterdam. Tel: 646-00-46. Call for information on services.

Mensa Student Youth Groups, 13 de Lairessestraat, 1071 NR Amsterdam. Tel: 676-7622. Kosher facility, but call first for reservation.

Habonim-Dror Zionist Youth, 5 Landskroon, Amsterdam. Tel: 644-14-06.

IJAR Nederland, Student and Youth Movement, 13 de Lairessestraat, Amsterdam. Tel: 676-82-26.

MUSEUMS

The Boas Building, Uilenburgerstraat. This is part diamond museum and part showcase, where diamond cutting is observed by visitors who can view exquisite diamonds and jewelry. Most of the original workers were Jews. In the eighteenth century, observant Jews turned Amsterdam into a fine international diamond center. Many still consider it a "city of diamonds." They became involved in diamond finds in Brazil in 1844.

World War II was the darkest period for these men and women. In 1985, the fortieth anniversary of Holland's liberation from Nazi occupation was observed. Ceremonies were conducted at Westerbork, the deportation site from which more than 100,000 Dutch Jews were sent to the death camps by the Nazis in World War II, including more than 2,000 diamond workers.

Today, only about a third of Holland's diamond workers are Jews.

The Jewish Historical Museum (Joods Historisch Museum), 2-4 Jonas Daniel Meijerplein St., 1011 RH Amsterdam. Tel: 6269-945. Admission can be secured by a $10 museum card,

Inside the New Synagogue of the Jewish Historical Museum. (Photo by Jeroen Nooter, courtesy of the Jewish Historical Museum)

The interior of the Great Synagogue, in the Jewish Historical Museum. (Photo by Jeroen Nooter, courtesy of the Jewish Historical Museum)

Jewish Historical Museum. (Photo by Jeroen Nooter, courtesy of the Jewish Historical Museum)

which grants entrance to all of Holland's museums. For tour guides for the museum or the area Jewish sites, contact Educational Department, Jewish Historical Museum, P.O. Box 16737, 1001, R.E., Amsterdam. Tel: 31-20-626-9945.

Here we see that several synagogues have been restored to their pre-1828 state, and are connected by modern steel bridges and a glass-covered courtyard. The entrance is on the side street, Nieuwe Amstelstraat, once also a heavily populated Jewish street. Queen Beatrix attended the opening ceremony on May 3, 1987, as did Austrian Chancellor Franz Vranitzky and Nazi-hunter Simon Wiesenthal. It is hard to believe that this, an area now crisscrossed by highways, was, during the eighteenth century, the heart of the Jewish community and the site of four Ashkenazic synagogues that adjoined one another and faced the great Portuguese Synagogue. All that hustle and bustle over the centuries, particularly on Friday nights and the holidays, must have generated warmth and inspiration.

The new museum is a complex of Ashkenazic synagogues connected by passageways and is now said to be the largest center of Jewish culture in Europe. The street is named after Mr. Jonas Meijerplein, a jurist. He was the first Jew in the Netherlands to be admitted to the bar. He reconciled the differences between conflicting Jewish congregations during the rule of the French king Louis Napoleon.

Standing in the square facing the Jewish Historical Museum, we are reminded, according to Hebrew scholar Naftali Herz Weisel, that it all began in 1671, when the Jewish community borrowed the equivalent of $8,000 from the City of Amsterdam to build the large and luxurious Grote Shul (Great Synagogue). Facing the museum, this is the synagogue on the right. Adjacent to the shul were a mikveh and study rooms. But the community soon outgrew the large synagogue. In 1686, on an adjacent plot, the community built the Obbene Shul (the Upstairs Synagogue) so named because of the kosher butcher hall constructed under it. It is now a kosher coffee shop and bookstore. In 1700, the Dritt Shul (Third Synagogue) was established. This synagogue is now used as administrative offices for the museum. Finally, in 1730, the expensive Neie Shul (New Synagogue), which could seat close to 1,000, was constructed. (This is the synagogue on the left). These four synagogues functioned separately.

The Jewish Historical Museum has a remarkable history of its own. It was founded in 1932 on a floor of the Historical Museum of the City of Amsterdam, which was in the Waag (Weighing) House, built in 1488. When the Nazis invaded Holland in May 1940, the Waag was closed. In 1943, all the Jewish Historical Museum materials were hauled off to Germany. After the war, however, the majority of the artifacts were recovered. They were not damaged because the Germans wanted to furnish a future Nazi museum for remnants of the "extinguished race."

The museum was reborn in 1955, once again on a floor of the Waag. In 1974, the City Council designated the city-owned synagogue complex, deserted and dilapidated since the war, as the future home of the museum. In the last year of the war, after the Germans had looted the synagogue buildings, the Dutch people, cold and starving, scavenged for any speck of wood and literally ripped up planks from the buildings. After the war, the Amsterdam city government granted restoration permits. The $14 million project began with the synagogues being integrated into what we know today as the Jewish Historical Museum.

The Ashkenazic Synagogue complex, now a museum, remains a memorial not only of the past, but also a monument to the future. The information in the Jewish Historical Museum buildings is divided into three headings: Jewish identity, elements, and aspects; Jewish religion and culture, illustrated through the Jewish festivals and daily life; and then history of the Jews in the Netherlands. Included in the collection are Torah scrolls and a selection of seventeenth-century Hebrew books printed in Amsterdam. The most beautiful objects in the collection of the Jewish Historical Museum date from the seventeenth and eighteenth centuries. Glass showcases display ritual silver objects. One item that brings interest to all is a silver candelabrum with three oranges. It was a gift from the monarch of Holland. In 1688, Prince William III of Orange obtained a loan of two million Dutch gold pieces without interest from a Jewish merchant, Francisco Lopez deSuasso. William and Mary thus proceeded to England to be joint rulers.

Seen throughout the museum will be exhibitions and photos

showing the "gash" in the history of Amsterdam and the Netherlands caused by the Holocaust. And yet, the museum shows that Jewish life has not died but has been rebuilt and is remembered.

The **Museum Route** for the Jewish Historical Museum begins in the renovated eighteenth-century **New Synagogue**. This synagogue was probably designed by city architect G. F. Maybaum. The most impressive part of this building is its glass-domed roof, beautifully decorated both on the inside and outside. The inventory, as well as the richly ornamented ark dating from 1750, was lost in World War II. In the New Synagogue, the visitor is introduced to the theme of Jewish identity. A Holocaust display is located here.

The new section inside the synagogue, the Gallery is used for temporary exhibitions. From here you can reach both the Hans Jaffe room and the extensive "mediatheque" or resource center. The well-stocked mediatheque with its 5,000 books, 4,500 photographs and slides, hundreds of video and sound tapes, and 3,000 documents is open to the public on weekdays from 1 to 5.

The **Great Synagogue** is the oldest public synagogue in Western Europe. The plan and elevation resemble the Protestant churches of city architect Daniel Stalpaert. When this synagogue was restored, the original shades of blue and green were used. A striking feature is the marble ark dating from 1671, placed against the eastern wall. Also noteworthy are the galleries for both men and women, which have been restored to their original state. And during restoration work, the original ritual bath, or mikveh, was found and can now be seen.

The objects of the Great Synagogue emphasize Jewish rituals and prayer: Portuguese silver, a prayer book that Manasseh Ben Israel printed in 1654, a magnificent silk and satin curtain that hung in front of the ark during circumcisions. The oldest item is a large thirteenth-century holiday prayer book. In the **galleries** of the Great Synagogue, attention is focused on the social history of the Jews in the Netherlands. The main theme deals with the concept of "tzedakah," the Hebrew word meaning "generosity and righteousness." This gallery has been linked via a bridge to the gallery in the New Synagogue, which is used for temporary exhibitions.

Rembrandt House Museum ("Het Rembrandthuis"), 4-6 Jodenbreestraat, 1011 NK Amsterdam. Tel: 6249-486. This house stands across the street from the home of Manasseh Ben Israel, who lived there from 1639 to 1657. That latter structure is gone today. But this charming Rembrandt museum is located in the house of Rembrandt's family and it contains about 250 of his etchings and paintings. The house is open daily from 10 to 5, Sundays and holidays from 1 to 4. Directions: From the Central Station, ride to the Nieuwmarkt subway stop or take Tram No. 9 to Waterlooplein.

As a friend of the Jews, Rembrandt van Rijn (1606-69) is deeply involved in Dutch Jewish history.

Rembrandt had a special sympathy for the Jews as "biblical heirs and the patient victims of persecution," according to art historian H.W. Janson. A friend of Ephraim Bueno and Manasseh Ben Israel, Rembrandt, who lived in a Jewish neighborhood, painted Bueno and Ben Israel's portraits. He rarely painted everyday scenes without biblical allusions and the influence of the Jewish neighborhood clearly can be seen in his work. He was often asked by Jews to do their paintings and he loved their biblical faces. He could even mix Ashkenazirn with Sephardim. Rembrandt also studied Jewish law and lore. Biblical prints include *Nebuchadnezzar's Dream and The Triumph of Mordecai.* There is also a sketch, *Jews in the Synagogue.* Scholars have estimated that almost one-fifth of the artist's male subjects were Jewish.

Some say Jozef Israels, Dutch Jewish painter, saved the house from being torn down.

Resistance Museum, 63 Lekstraat, 1079 EM Amsterdam. Tel: 644-97-9'7. Tram 4, 25. Housed as part of a synagogue, this museum is open Tuesday to Friday, 10 to 5; Saturday, Sunday, and holidays, 1 to 5. Closed Mondays.

The Rijksmuseum, Stadhouderskade. There are many paintings of Jewish interest here, including a number by Rembrandt, most famous of which is *The Jewish Bride* (room 221) and *Jeremiah's Lamentations* (room 220). Also in room 221 is A Portuguese Synagogue by Emmanuel de Witte. *Jewish Wedding* by Jozef Israels is on view in room 148. A highlight in this museum of course is Rembrandt's *Night Watch.*

Rembrandt House Museum.

MEMORIAL SITES

The Dutch Playhouse, 24 Plantage Middenlaan. Once a building of joy, then a place of pain and humiliation, today this is a monument. The Nazis took this 1892 structure, a former Dutch theater, at the time called the Jewish Theater, and used it as a detention center before they shipped the Jews off to a concentration camp. Today, only the facade of the playhouse and part of the jagged stone walls are left. The site has been made into a memorial garden. A Ner Tamid (eternal flame) burns in the foyer, and a mourning chamber is filled with paintings from Israel. A plaque commemorates "our Jewish compatriots who were deported between 1940 and 1945 and did not return." The children taken to the theater were often housed in the kindergarten across the street. Many escaped and a plaque on the school building commemorates the fact. The theater is open Monday to Saturday, 10 to 4; Sundays and holidays, 11 to 4.

The Dockworker Statue ("De Dokwerker"), Jonas Daniel Meijerplein Square. This statue, that of a strong, hefty dockworker, stands between the Portuguese Synagogue and the Jewish Historical Museum. Each year on February 25, Dutch Christians and Jews come out and commemorate the bravery of the Dutch people. In 1941, these dockworkers stood up for the rights of their fellow Jewish citizens. Their bravery began when, on February 22, the Nazis rounded up about 400 young Jews for deportation. The Amsterdam dockworkers staged a protest strike that was brutally put down by the Germans. This is perhaps the only time that the population of a city rose against the Third Reich. The statue was designed by Mari Andriessen, who wrote about Amsterdam's collective protest: "Not in Moscow, not in Warsaw, but in Amsterdam, and that is what Amsterdam should always be remembered by."

Gratitude Monument Memorial, Weeperstraat. Established to commemorate those who helped the Jews during World War II, this monument was designed by the sculptor Johan G. Wertheim and erected in 1947 by the Jews of Amsterdam.

The Hague

Kosher food can be obtained at **Jacobs,** 220 Haverkamp the Hague. Tel: 070-347-49-80. Open Sunday through Friday, 10 A.M. to 5 P.M.

Synagogue and Community Center, II Gornelis Houtmanstraat, 2593 RD the Hague. Tel: 070-347-3201. The Hague's Jewish community headquarters is situated here.

Synagogue, 44 Harstenhoekweg, 2587 SL the Hague (Scheveningen).

Rotterdam

Synagogue and Community Center, 4 A. B. N. Davidsplein, 3039 KA Rotterdam. Tel: 4669765. This is the headquarters of the Jewish community in Rotterdam.

For information on **Chabad,** contact Rabbi Jehoeda Vorst, Tel: 10-466-0481 or 10-265-5530. E-Mail: rabbi.vorst@zonnet.nl.

Suggested Reading

Barnouw, Adrian J. *Pageant of Netherlands History.* New York: Longmans, Green, 1952.

Bloom, Herbert 1. *The Economic Activities of the Jews of Amsterdam in the 17th and 18th Centuries.* New York: Kennikat Press, 1969.

Farber, Jules B. *Amsterdam, City of the Seventies.* De Haan/ Bussum, 1975.

Frank, Anne. *Anne Frank: The Diary of a Young Girl.* Garden City, N.Y.: Doubleday, 1952.

Gans, Mozes Heiman. *Memorbook: Pictorial History of Dutch Jewry from the Renaissance to 1940.* Bosch & Keuning, D.V., Baarn, Netherlands, 1977.

Gies, Miep, with Alison L. Gold. *Anne Frank Remembered: The Story of the Woman Who Helped to Hide the Frank Family.* New York: Simon & Schuster, 1987.

Hillesum, Etty. *An Interrupted Life: The Diaries of Etty Hillesum 1941-1943*. Translated by Arnold Pomerans. New York: Pantheon, 1984.

Koning, Hans, et al. *Amsterdam*. Amsterdam: Time-Life Books, 1977.

Presser, Jacob. *Ashes in the Wind: The Destruction of Dutch Jewry*. New York: Dutton, 1969.

Roth, Cecil. *A Life of Menasseh Ben Israel: Rabbi, Printer and Diplomat*. New York: Arno Press, 1975. Originally published by The Jewish Publication Society of America, 1934.

Germany
Jews Do Live There

The German Jewish community is the fastest growing Jewish community in Europe and perhaps in the world.

Today, there are about 80,000 to 100,000 Jews in Germany. By 2006, the figure should reach 120,000 Jews. For Europe, 100,000 Jews is a very large community.

Ronnie Golz, a teacher, lecturer and tour guide, active in the Berlin Jewish community and part of the young leadership generation here, estimates that at any given time there are about 160,000 to 200,000 Jews in Germany. He includes visiting students, the diplomatic corps and Jews who reside here but do not wish to join the community.

While the second and third post-Holocaust generation German Jews have come of age already, much of the Jewish population increase was fueled by Jews from the former Soviet Union. These Russian Jews are giving the German Jewish community a feeling of stability, a sense of permanence and most important—numbers. The doubling of the Jewish community in Berlin, was the result of Russian Jews who arrived here at the rate of about 6,000 a year and who basically came for economic reasons so they could take advantage of Germany's excellent economy and welfare system. They also wanted to escape vestiges of anti-Semitism in the former USSR.

The arrival of Russian and Ukrainian Jews is not without problems for the German Jewish community. Everyone agrees that many of the newcomers know little about Judaism. Few speak German. Dependent on welfare, many find it difficult to obtain employment. In all fairness to these new immigrants, however, German state agencies are often very hard on newcomers, who want to work but must meet stringent licensing examinations. Most of the Jews from the former Soviet Union have settled either in Frankfurt or Berlin.

The German Jewish leadership works at integrating these Russian Jews into various communities throughout the country. No easy task! To train rabbis, to provide Jewish schools, to set up new institutions remains a challenging undertaking, especially in the eastern part of the country, which is burdened with a high rate of unemployment. Paul Spiegel, the new president of the Central Council of Jews in Germany, has said his top priority would be the integration of the 50,000 Jewish émigrés from the former Soviet Union who have come here during the past decade.

There is a Jewish presence in Germany and you see it in the streets and in the media. On German state radio, you can hear the music of the prayer *kol nidre*. In Berlin, you can see young Jewish lawyers, many of them wearing *yarmulkes* arriving at the German foreign ministry to settle reparations claims. You can see Jewish books in the stores. You can feel an interest and eagerness of German youth to learn about Judaism. And you see memorials and monuments to the Holocaust.

Jewish life moves at a fast pace in congregations, day schools, organizations, clubs, WIZO balls, and Jewish community centers. Until the recent millennium, most of the community leaders were older Holocaust survivors, such as the late Ignatz Bubis, who in the words of *The Jewish Week*, of August 20, 1999, "helped create an environment where Jewish life in the country could grow dramatically and flourish as it has, particularly in the last decade."

Ronnie Golz maintains that a somewhat younger German leadership has come into its maturity. The board governing the Jewish community in Berlin, which was elected in the year 2000, contains no members who were born before the war. The Central Council's new president, Paul Spiegel, is seen as a bridge from the older Holocaust survivor community to the native-born German Jews.

The younger generation grew up with the shadow of the Holocaust around them. The new millennium has produced a change in the attitude of those Jews who do call Germany their home. By and large, they no longer feel guilty about residing in this land that murdered six million Jews. Not all Jews are comfortable in the new Germany. There is still anti-Semitism. Many are weary of the increases in xenophobia in recent years, or in the rise of new skinhead groups. They are concerned about the effect of extreme right-wing and anti-Semitic utterances on the Internet. And in June 2000, a Hitler apologist, Ernst Nolte, won a German honor. Though shocked, men and women of good will everywhere were pleased at the storm of protest that did break out when Nolte received the Konrad Adenauer Prize.

The reader might ask how can 80,000 to 100,000 Jews in more than 65 communities live in the country of their murderers. At World War II's end, there were fewer than 100 Jews under the age of 20 in Germany.

Why did Jews return to Munich, Berlin, and Frankfurt after the war? How could they? Many returned to collect German reparations, and stayed. Despite war destruction, Germany became an economic haven even by the mid-1950s. Many Jews also fled the then Communist-ruled East Germany. Some married German spouses and settled in West Germany, where mixed marriages made up a high percentage of the Jewish community.

Many of the parents of Jewish children born in postwar Germany did not tell their offspring of their suffering in the Holocaust. After the war, these children grew up in a Germany where, at least for a few decades, no one dared to express anti-Semitic thoughts.

For the Jewish visitor flying over Germany, it is hard to forget that one's fellow Jews were gassed and burned by Germans. Upon seeing factory smokestacks, the Jewish traveler may "see" the smoke rising from the ovens in the concentration camps. Even if you try to avoid going to a camp, the subconscious visions and symbols may haunt you.

As hard as it for Jews and non-Jews, there obviously is a Germany before 1933 and after 1945, as Fritz Stern points out. We should never play down the achievements of German Jewry and the extent to which they were woven into the fabric of German society, he adds. One-quarter of all the Nobel Prizes won by Germans in the first third of this century were won by German Jews says Otto Friedrich.

A Brief History

It all began when the Romans came to Germany. The Jews tagged along with the centurions as they settled the towns along the Rhine. Jewish traders moved by raft and cart, up and down villages of the Rhine, Rhone, and Danube rivers. By 321, they had settled in Cologne.

In the following centuries, Jewish settlements could be found in Mayence, Metz, Worms, Trier, Speyer, Regensburg, and Wurtzburger.

By the ninth century, the words "merchant" and "Jew" had become synonymous, and later "moneylender" would be added to the vocabulary.

Regarded as a group with initiative and business skills, Jews were given guarantees of rights in various places. For five centuries, the Franks—German pagans who had crossed the Rhine—ruled the Jews but left them alone.

The year 1096 heralded in the First Crusade's murderous wrath against Jews. Jewish communities that lived along the Rhine, however, chose a martyr's death. Rather than allow their children to be baptized, Jewish mothers cut their throats. Jews call that *kiddush hashem* ("the sanctification of the name," loyalty to God).

Disaster and riots plagued Jews in the thirteenth and fourteenth centuries. The Black Plague (1348-50) nearly wiped out one-half of the population of Europe. Jews were accused of having poisoned the wells. By now, Germany was nearly "judenrein," "cleansed of Jews." Still, they would return again and again; they were needed for their financial acumen.

The law forbade usury by Christians so, although excluded from the guilds, Jews served as bankers. "The pecuniary motive explains the continuity of Jewish history in Germany," writes H. G. Adler in *The Jews in Germany*. Emperor Frederick II declared in 1296 that the Jews of Germany were "servants of our treasury."

Not until the seventeenth century, after the disastrous Thirty Years' War, were Jews slowly invited back to help rebuild the devastated north. "Germany could live neither with its Jews, nor without them," according to Marvin Lowenthal.

The institution of "Court Jews," or privileged Jews, began in Germany. They were called "shtadlan" (go-betweens) and were the official representatives of the community, so chosen because they were wealthy and influential. Often they put their financial skill to work for the prince and helped prevent anti-Jewish measures. One such leader was Joseph Oppenheimer (1698-1738), known as "Jew Suess." Another was Samuel Oppenheimer (1635-1703), who financed Vienna's military operations against the Turks who had besieged Vienna.

Later the spirit of the French Revolution would move to Germany. In 1812, Wilhelm von Humboldt and Karl August von Hardenberg liberated the Jews of Prussia. Napoleon created the Confederation of the Rhine. But Jewish rights were soon lost when the Holy Alliance defeated the French emperor.

The first Reform Temple was established in Hamburg in 1818. Abraham Geiger (1810-74) was spiritual father and one of the leaders of the Reform Movement. On the other hand, under the leadership of Rabbi Samson Raphael Hirsch (1808-88), a new Orthodoxy was launched in Germany.

Banking became a Jewish enterprise, with family branches all over Europe. The Mendelssohn family banking house developed the banking firm of Bleichroeder. The House of Rothschild, the Warburg family, including Max, S. G., Paul, and Felix Warburg, the Guggenheims, the Lewisohns, the Kuhns, and the Loebs contributed much to German economic growth.

The Revolution of 1848 helped emancipate the Jews in Central Europe.

After the German victory over Austria in 1866 and the establishment of the North German Confederation, the Reichstag passed a resolution banning religious discrimination. The Constitution of the North German Federation in 1869 ensured full equality, so much so that many cases of assimilation and conversion soon arose. Only Eastern European Jewish immigration into Germany maintained the population level. But then came the anti-Semites.

From 1871-1914, German Jews comprised about 1 percent of the German population, hovering between the 500,000 and 600,000 figure.

More than 100,000 of the 550,000 German Jews fought in World War I, and 80,000 of them were in the front lines. At least 12,000 died in the war. About 35,000 were decorated, with more than 2,000 promoted to officers, and 23,000 received German awards for bravery.

But by the 1930s, "millions of Germans began to believe that Adolf Hitler somehow had the skill and intelligence to solve all the nation's problems," writes Otto Friedrich in his book, *Before the Deluge: A Portrait of Berlin in the 1920's.* As we look back in history, we note the police could have deported him; they did not. Later the democratic world powers could have stopped him; they did not. Many Jews thought Nazism would blow over. People do not just pick up and leave their homes, family businesses, or jobs. They did not foresee the catastrophe of Hitler.Of approximately 500,000 German Jews, about 330,000 would flee between 1933 and 1939. Most of them reached the United States, the United Kingdom, France, and Palestine; the rest would perish.

After the war, the Zionist movement actually opposed Jews returning to Germany, which it called "accursed land." Jews generally do not return to places of tragedy. About 15,000 Jews resettled in Germany. And of these 15,000, only 8,000 would remain; the rest would emigrate to the United States and Israel. By 1986, close to 30,000 German Jews were registered and gave money to the Jewish community.

A law exists in Germany that makes it illegal to spread lies about the Nazi war crimes, lies and crimes that insult the memory of the Jewish dead. Anti-Semitic racism is punishable by law. Millions of Germans under 21 still have never known, seen, or spoken to a Jew.

Jewry here is made up of five groups: those who survived the Holocaust; those who returned after World War II from other countries such as England, Palestine, and China in which they had found refuge; those displaced persons or camp survivors who took temporary refuge in Germany after the war; those emigrants and refugees who were attracted to Germany by its economic prosperity or who fled from persecution; and finally the Soviet Jews of the decades from 1980s to 2000.

Jews in Germany appear to be economically well off. Most do not feel overt anti-Semitism, but they realize that the neo-Nazi extremism has threatened the stability of Central Europe and that means Germany, too. In Germany, it seems the former terrorists have come in from the cold. The unification has brought difficulties to Germans in the West and Germans in the East in comprehending each other. Jews in the 1990s felt the "hostility and discontent," as well as incidents against Jewish institutions, synagogues and Holocaust monuments. Xenophobia, including anti-Semitic and anti-immigrant slurs or attacks are on the rise especially in the eastern part of Germany.

The Jews in Germany praise what they call Christian Jewish societies, which are very active and sponsor various projects. One program invites those who were born or lived in Germany before the war to come and visit their former homes. Some municipalities pay the airfare. Others give the visitors spending money, tickets, and a tour.

Many visitors come from Israel. Indeed, most German Jews have visited Israel; the ties between German Jews and Israel are strong. For example, the Jewish State helps Dusseldorf Jewry by providing and training teachers, principals, and even rabbis.

Jews raise funds for Israel's institutions. German Jewry was proud to state that, after Holland, they came in second in collecting monies for Israel.

On September 10, 1952, the reparations agreement was signed by the representatives of West Germany and Israel. Reparations came to about $8 billion or 25 billion German marks to Israel direct, while 15 billion marks were paid to individuals.

Germany has paid more than $50 billion in reparations to victims of Hitler since World War II. In the first half of 2000, negotiators had hammered out details of a compensation for Nazi-era slave workers and other victims. The agreement focussed on how a $5 billion fund was to be distributed. In principal, an agreement was reached whereby forced and slave laborers of the Nazis will be able to receive a one-time payment from the fund established by German industry and government. Details were still being finalized by mid-2000, but there was hope that payments would begin by the end of that year, according to the World Jewish Congress.

The two nations established diplomatic relations in 1965. Not only is Germany Israel's second trading partner, but many go so far to say that it has positioned itself as the champion of Israel within the European Union. Several decades ago, Germany, it is said, made the decision to back Israel because it felt it had a special obligation to the Jewish state. In 1999, Israel Prime Minister Ehud Barak on a trip to Germany made it clear that the purpose of his trip was to cement his new government's relationship with what he sees as Israel's key ally in the European Union. A rockier relationship has marked French-Israel ties.

In 21st century international affairs, you can not leave Germany out of the larger world picture. Because of its financial strength, it stands as the most powerful economic force in Europe. As the world's third largest economy, Germany, with its 82 million people, is now even becoming more immersed in Central and Eastern Europe. Berlin, we should remember, is only about 50 miles from the Polish border, giving it significant market potential and political influence in the east. Germany accounts for about a third of the gross domestic product of Euroland (that is the 11 nations now sharing the eurodollar). For the first time since Germany became a member of NATO in 1955, a German officer in 1999 took command of an Allied Alliance Kosovo mission outside his homeland, "a strong sign of acceptance of a country slowly shedding its image of an instigator of two world wars," wrote the *Associated Press* in the *International Herald Tribune* of October 8, 1999.

But for many generations, Germany will remain in the spotlight. The world will watch here because even now there are ultraconservatives among the conservatives who deny the existence of gas chambers and the Nazis' extermination of millions of Europeans, including six million Jews. German Jews have called upon their government to take stricter measures against neo-Nazi groups. But in the final analysis, it all depends on whether Germany continues to defend its democratic rights against terrorism and dictatorship.

"For no people can step out of its own history and disown it. It is a legacy which cannot be denied," said former Israeli President Chaim Herzog.

Anson Rabinbach and Jack D. Zipes maintain that ever since the establishment of the Federal Republic in 1949, the policy of the Germans toward Jews has generally been supportive. The obvious reason for this support was to make clear to the world that Germany wanted to overcome its anti-Semitic past. Still the authors say "de-Nazification" was hollow and ritualistic. War criminals were not actively prosecuted in West Germany until after the Eichmann trial of 1960-61.

In a 1988 speech, former German President Richard von Wiezsacher said: "The German nation cannot make others responsible for what it and its neighbors endured under national socialism...Auschwitz remains unique. It was perpetrated by Germans in the name of Germany. This truth is immutable and will not be forgotten."

Yet a generation of Germans who were not even born when the Berlin Wall went up finds it hard to shoulder responsibility for the Germany of fifty years ago Some of them feel that successive governments have done enough penance for the Holocaust. But former Chancellor Kohl pledged on reunification that Germany would fight anti-Semitism and would work to keep alive the memory of the Holocaust. Overall, "anything to do with the Holocaust continues to be treated as an issue of the almost national importance," said the *Economist*.

In the year 2000, much talk went the rounds of intellectuals, writers, politicians and students that Germans want to emerge from history's long shadow. Even Jewish leaders point out that the interest of young Germans to learn about Judaism and the Holocaust has never been as great as it is today. "What did you do during the war, Daddy?" is very close to the question young Germans ask of their fathers and grandfathers: "Where were you when all this happened?" They look incredulous when the grandparents tell them they voted for Hitler, although one said, she did not think that they should have killed the Jews, "just ship them off to Jerusalem." One even admitted she liked Hitler; he got rid of the garbage in the streets and he stopped unemployment.

This grandmother lost her husband on the Russian front. Another said the years 1933 to 1940 were the "best years of her life."

In the Knesset in February 2000, Johannes Rau, German President said, "I ask forgiveness for what Germans have done—for myself and my generation, for the sake of our children and our children's children."

Notable German Jews

German Jews "identified with Germany as their homeland," according to Leni Yahil, and contributed much to their country's political, social, and cultural life. Here are some outstanding German Jews.

Ferdinand Lassalle, an adherent of Marx, founded the German labor movement. German shipping magnate Albert Ballin directed the Hamburg American line, and was a close friend and advisor to Kaiser William II. Kurt Eisner was a Jewish socialist who headed a People's Republic in Bavaria at the beginning of November 1918; he was assassinated in 1919. Nobel Prize laureate Albert Einstein (1879-1955), known as one of the world's greatest physicists, discovered the theory of relativity. David Ben-Gurion, first prime minister of Israel, invited Einstein to become president of the Jewish State.

Germany also boasts a great list of Jewish writers: Ernest Toller, Jakob Wasserman, Arnold Zweig, Alfred Doblin, Kurt Tucholsky, and Walter Benjamin. German Jewish musicians include Felix Mendelssohn, Jacques Offenbach, Otto Klemperer, Bruno Walter, Fritz Kreisler, Paul Hindmith, Kurt Weill, and many others.

Jewish Berlin

"Have a nice day in our capital," says the flight attendant as the plane swoops down onto the runway at Tegel Airport in Berlin. Even the locals are unaccustomed to hear such a greeting. Only in 1999 has Berlin assumed the mantle as the capital of a united Germany, today very powerful and very rich.

And in so doing, Berlin is on its way to becoming a great city of Europe.

For Jewish travelers to this city, there are three Berlins. The Berlin of the past before 1933 when, despite anti-Semitism, Jews were involved in the artistic and cosmopolitan energy of this capital; the Berlin of Hitler, the dark grotestque capital of the dictator and the brutal murder of Jews; and finally the post-war Berlin, the Berlin that existed for 45 years in a Communist East German sea but finally became the German capital.

There was an active Jewish life here before 1933 and there is Jewish life in this metropolis in the 21st century. We must remember that Jews—who had no access to the politics of the country—financed artistic and cultural programs. They hosted salons, started new publications, and backed galleries. Jews, including Jewish artists and thinkers, supported the German counter-culture concept of *Bildung* which was a broad pursuit of humanistic education and inclusion of all human beings regardless of race or religion—all part of the Berlin scene in the 1920s.

For Germany, Berlin is 50 percent New York and 50 percent San Francisco, says Ronnie Golz. Others have said that Berlin is always on a journey and yet never arrives anywhere. East and West Berlin were reunited in 1990, bringing together two halves of a city that had functioned separately for thirty years. Even today, one can notice the differences. The West section of the city around the Ku-Dam features noise and traffic, clubs and halls, and movement, which inspired and still inspires urbanites, foreign and domestic. Yes, the western section of Berlin is busy as ever, with its 8,000 bars and restaurants and all-night clubs. Berlin is still Berlin and today's Berlin especially in the western part reminds one of the 1920's exciting city.

In the East, the quiet atmosphere and revival makes one realize that beneath the surface East Berlin is drab no longer. True, you can still see a few gray, shabby buildings, but the area is quickly changing and becoming the trendy, art and in-section of the city. Walk around the Gendarmenmarkt, the most handsome, elegant-looking square in Berlin and you can sense an exciting and business revival here. Standing in the center of the Gendarmenmarkt square is Schinkel's Schauspielhaus a concert hall, as well as several area churches and cafes. New hotels such as the grand and very modern Four Seasons Hotel catch the traveler's eye. The area was the heart of Berlin before its twentieth century convulsion. This is the still the historic part of Berlin. Just a few blocks away is the Unter den Linden, the grand imperial avenue which is sure to be the heart of the new, unified city. Already, there is much shopping in the area on the Friedrichstrasse which includes Galeries Lafayette and Planet Hollywood.

Top, excellent hotels: Four Seasons, Hilton, Weston, are located in this area. In the 21st Century Potsdammer Platz section, every important corporation is making a construction statement. Skyscrapers, shopping malls, restaurants and concert halls are reaching up to the heavens. In the Mitte district near the Reichstag, on the Hackesche Hofe, stands an Art Nouveau residential complex that also houses cafés, restaurants, galleries and theaters.

Once again the city is being reinvented. Berlin is getting a facelift. Construction cranes dominate the skyline. Splendid art galleries, nightclubs, and a lingering historical presence have made the city attractive to foreigners. This is a city that received a fast break and kick off into the 21st century. The city is again assuming its role as capital of Germany.

In the last decade, the unification of East and West Germany has affected everyone, even the cantor in the drab surroundings of his synagogue at Rykerstrasse 53, in the eastern section of Berlin. He does not always get a minyan on Saturday mornings, but he tells tour after tour of East Germans that their former government, while it did not exactly suppress religion, was not very enthusiastic about it.

But, as noted, the problem of mass immigration into the country already has caused escalation of neo-Nazi violence. This development has set off an alarm in Germany's Jewish community.

Still, Jews will probably settle down here again for a number of reasons. Berlin is the major city between Moscow and Paris, a bridge between East and West. (Lenin said, "He who has Berlin, has Germany, and he who has Germany, has Europe"). Berlin has joined Paris, Brussels, and Rome as being "where the action is." Jews will come to this creative center, mostly for

business, economic, and professional opportunities. How they
will live and how they will withstand the pressure of memory
cannot be foretold. Russian Jews say that they had it so bad in
the former Soviet Union, that the past here does not affect
their functioning in society. Of all the cities in Germany, Berlin
and its landmarks remind you of the Nazis. It is "an open air
museum of the nation's history": Hitler's bunker-grave in the
form of a mound of dirt; the Reichstag; Unter den Linden and
the Brandenburg Gate under which the jackbooted Nazi hooli-
gan army marched singing "Death to the Jews" and "Tomorrow
the World."

Jews who do come here say this city is attractive, scintillating,
and creative. Outwardly, it throbs: the opera, the state library,
the university, and the Kurfürstendamm, that exciting main
boulevard that declares, "Berlin could not be Berlin without
me, the Ku-damm."

Berlin, which once rivaled Paris and London culturally,
inspired the Jews in the nineteenth and early twentieth century, as Paris influenced the world, according to Barnet
Litvinoff. Henry Adams once described the city as a "poor,
keen-witted provincial town, simple, dirty, uncivilized," and
Mark Twain named it "German Chicago." This "European New
York" of about 4 million people evolved over the years along an
east-west axis centered by the Brandenburg Gate, that gigantic
neo-Grecian portal supported by 12 Doric columns, 65 feet
high, and surmounted by a sculpture of four horses drawing
the chariot of the Goddess of Victory.

Jews, who never numbered more than 5 percent in Berlin,
arrived there in the thirteenth century. A cemetery was established in 1543. In 1671, Elector Friedrich Wilhelm admitted 50
Jewish families from Vienna and the community grew. The first
synagogue was built in 1714.

Moses Mendelssohn (1729-86), philosopher, settled in
Berlin in 1743. With access to the king, his home also became
a center for intellectuals of the Enlightenment (Haskalah).
The son of a poor Torah scribe, Mendelssohn was born in
Dessau. This eighteenth-century scholar and philosopher
helped launch the renascence of Jewish culture. Mendelssohn
was a friend of the famous German Christian writer, Gotthold
Ephraim Lessing, who immortalized him in the play, Nathan

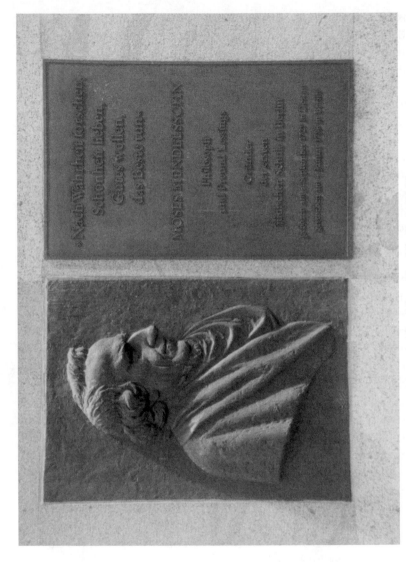

A memorial to Moses Mendelssohn in Berlin.

the Wise. Mendelssohn said that Jews should abandon Yiddish, purify Hebrew, and learn German. In 1768, he published his translation of the Pentateuch for his co-religionists. His followers were called "maskilim" (the Enlightened). They urged Jews "to broaden their minds by studying the culture of those among whom they lived."

The homes of Henriette Herz, Rahel Varnhagen, and Dorothea Schlegel also became centers of the Jewish elite of Berlin.

After the Franco-Prussian War of 1870, Berlin replaced Vienna as the center of the German-speaking world. Jews flocked to Berlin. By the 1930s there were about 150,000 to 180,000 Jews in a city that, before the war, maintained several hundred synagogues and now has seven or eight. About one-third would be murdered in the extermination camps, and the rest would flee. Hitler took power in 1933. Four months later, a boycott of Jewish stores in Germany began; the rest is history. In 1945, Berlin was obliterated by Allied bombing and shelling, with 2.6 billion cubic feet of rubble. Now rebuilt, the city covers more than 550 square miles, is bigger than Chicago, five times the size of the District of Columbia, 15 times the size of Bermuda, and about as large as the five boroughs of New York City. Berlin has about 4 million inhabitants and is thought to be one of the least dense great cities of the world.

Berlin is sure to be Germany's leading city and the gateway to expanding markets in Eastern Europe. And Berlin, considered to be located at the most important crossroads in Central Europe, is vying with Prague as Central Europe's most cosmopolitan city. This point emphasizes the fact that with reunification, Germany has moved from being an Atlantic state to a Central European state and that will be extremely significant in the twenty-first century.

SITES IN BERLIN

Berlin Wall. A 1.3-mile stretch of the Berlin Wall remains. It boasts graffiti and paintings, like an outdoor gallery, with huge, bizarre drawings. By the way, on one of those paintings, there is half a six-pointed Jewish star next to a cracked glass, symbolizing *Kristallnacht.*

Jewish cemetery, Herbert Baumstrasse 45, Berlin-Weissensee, in the northeast suburbs of former East Berlin. Tel: 365-3330. These graves evoke the days of the mid-nineteenth century when Berlin's flourishing and gifted Jewish community played an influential role in the cultural life of the city. Baum incidentally was a German Jewish resistance fighter executed by the Nazis in 1943.

The Jewish Center, Fasanenstrasse 79/80, 1000 Berlin 12. Tel: 884-2030. This is the headquarters of the Berlin Jewish community and is located not far from the Kurfurstendamm, near the Kempinski, Bristol, and Steigenberger hotels.

Jewish Community Center, Fasanenstrasse 79/80, 1000 Berlin 12. Tel: 884-2030. The future of the German Jewish community lies with the young people. A visitor to the Jewish Center can not but notice in a corner of the lobby a computer center alongside a coffee café bar. Here young people can gather information on Jewish subjects and socialize at the same time. This attractive, well-designed Jewish community center was built in 1959 on the Fasanenstrasse site of the Great Synagogue, which seated about 1,700 persons and was completely destroyed on Kristallnacht in 1938. As you face the building, you will see, incorporated right into the facade around the front door, the old portal that once stood above the former main synagogue entrance. The new building was also constructed with a column from the old synagogue, thus showing the crack in human relations on the one hand but also hope for the future.

The center is the focal point of many activities in Berlin, as the community center sponsors lectures, concerts, and dances. A synagogue in the building is used for major holidays such as Rosh Hashanah and Yom Kippur.

In the lobby are photos taken on *Kristallnacht,* which still sears the minds of German Jews. On November 7, 1938, Herschel Grynszpan, age 17, an exile from Germany who was living in Paris, shot Ernst vom Rath, the third secretary of the

German Embassy in Paris. He said he had avenged his parents, who had been among those dumped on the Polish border, a common Nazi tactic and practice. The Germans knew that the Poles would refuse entry to Jews. When vom Rath died, the Gestapo organized a bloodbath designed as a "spontaneous reaction of the people." The date was November 9/10, 1938. *Kristallnacht*, this "Night of Crystal," derives its name from the shattering of glass, as the Nazis literally went berserk when they broke the stained-glass windows of synagogues throughout Germany. The broken glass littered the streets on the morning of the ninth. Edmond Engelman called it "the glitter of the night's flying glass." About 90 Jews were killed during *Kristallnacht*, and about 7,500 Jewish shops were destroyed. Around 25,000 Jews were thrown into concentration camps. Approximately 200 synagogues were destroyed, shops and offices were looted, and plate-glass windows were smashed. Yet it was the Jews who were fined one billion Reichsmarks.

The center also contains a library and kosher restaurant:

Library. Tel: 884-2035. Nine to 10,000 volumes in all languages, which may be circulated. Most of the 2,000 visitors each year are non-Jewish. Arcady Fried is head librarian and speaks English. He welcomes visitors and the library is open to the public. Open Monday to Thursday, 11 A.M. to 8 P.M. and Friday, 11 A.M. to 3 P.M.

Kosher restaurant, second floor. Open every day from 11:30 A.M. to 3:30 P.M. and 6:30 to 11 P.M., on Shabbat from 11:30 A.M. to 2:30 P.M., a buffet on Tuesdays. Those who would like to eat in the restaurant on the Sabbath can order and pay for their meals beforehand.

Reichstag. Seared permanently in this author's mind are two famous photos, the raising of the American flag at Iwo Jima in World War II as well as the photo taken in May 1945, of Russian soldiers hosting their country's flag on the top of a burning Reichstag in Berlin. Perhaps others, including the architects and planners of the new Reichstag, also probably remembered that Second World War photo. Germans who are confronting their history should be reminded of the defeat of Nazism by the Allies and the taking of Berlin by one of the major partners in the battle against the Axis powers. How else do you explain the reconstructed interior of the Reichstag where carved into the walls are pieces of Soviet soldiers graffiti. "Surely no other people would allow itself to be so grossly denigrated in its own Parliament. But then the modern Federal Republic probably places a greater value on a continuous and unabashed confrontation with the past than any other state," wrote Roger Cohen in The Sophisticated Traveler supplement of *The New York Times,* November 21, 1999.

The Reichstag is situated at a critical spot in the city. Beauty and ugliness once enveloped the area. On the one hand always refreshing was the green relaxing Tiergarten. On the other hand for 30 years the infamous Berlin Wall, stood nearby across from the Tiergarten. Much of the building is open to the public.

In 1999, the Reichstag became the seat of the German Parliament when the government moved from Bonn. On the western façade of the Riechstag is an old inscription, "Dem Deutschen Volke, "To the German People,"

Sitting on the top of this noted structure is a glass dome. Inside, a circle of historic pictures lie below the dome. Much of the Reichstag is open to the public. Its new glass dome and winding ramp were designed by the British architect, Sir Norman Foster. You can walk up the Guggenheim Museum-style ramp to the top of the dome for a magnificent view of the Tiergarten.

Walther Rathenau House, Koenigsalle 65. Now a private building containing offices, this was formerly the villa of the noted Jewish industrialist, philanthropist, and statesman. Born in Berlin in 1867, Rathenau managed A.E.G., the electric light complex that was founded by his father. While foreign minister, he negotiated the Rapallo Treaty with the U.S.S.R. in April 1922, which eliminated the political isolation of Germany. He was assassinated by Fascist sympathizers.

Haus der Wannsee Konferenz, The House of the Wannsee Conference, Memorial and Educational Site, Am Grossen Wannsee 56-58, D-D14109 Berlin, in Wannsee section of Berlin. Tel: (030) 80-50-01-0; FAX: (030) 80-50-01-27. (Take the S-Bahn

The bus stop sign for the Villa of the Wannsee Conference, Berlin.
(Photo by Ben G. Frank)

The photos of the SS officers and high ranking civil servants who planned the details of the murder of six million Jews when they met at the Wannsee Conference Villa in Berlin. (Photo by Ben G. Frank)

subway and when you reach Wannsee station, take the 114 bus to the Center). The Hours are Monday to Friday: 10 A.M. to 6 P.M.; Saturday and Sunday, 2 P.M. to 6 P.M. The Reference Library, the videotape collection, audiovisual archives are shown Monday to Friday, 10 A.M. to 6 P.M. (No charge).

The garden is still there. The villa which overlooks the lake is still there. The lake is still there. The bushes are still there. The little cement cherubs are still there. The boats and the yachts and the various yacht club signs are slightly different than they were in 1942, but they are still here. The boats, though newer, are here. You would never in your life guess that this attractive villa which blends into the neighborhood so nicely and that this recreational center for the Gestapo, was the site where on January 20, 1942, Reinhard Heydrich, head of the NS Reich Security Main Office (Reichssicherheitshauptamt) chaired a meeting of 14 high ranking civil servants and SS-officers to organize and implement the "Final Solution." Actually, in a main hall, a long table around which Nazi officials sat and in effect began the execution of the Jewish people in Europe can still be seen. At this table, they took notes on how to conduct the murder of Six Million Jews; then got up and took a break for lunch or walked along the shore.

Called the "Wannsee Conference" because it was held in the Wannsee district of Berlin, these bureaucrats and police offices of the Third Reich made the extermination of Jews of Europe official German state policy. The word, "conference" is a misnomer. It really was a meeting for the killing of European Jewry which already had started during the early stages of the German invasion of the Soviet Union in 1941. John Cornwell notes that a month after the Germans invaded Russia, Heydrich was ordered to make all the necessary preparations for a "complete solution of the Jewish question in the German sphere of influence."

The decision to murder the Jews of Europe had already been made. The significance of the 90-minute meeting at Wannsee was not that a final plan was formulated there, but that decision-making authority was transferred from governmental ministries to the SS hierarchy, assuring the ministries cooperation in a "Final Solution."

A draft had been prepared by Adolf Eichmann. It said that

"in the course of the Final Solution, the Jews should be brought under appropriate direction in a suitable manner to the east for labor utilization." Heydrich had expected that his concept of annihilation of the Jews "would meet with misgivings and objections from the ministerial departments," according to a Villa publication." But he encountered only general agreement and readiness to help in its execution. The discussions dealt solely with details.

For example, among the resolutions adopted at the Wannsee Conference was that the Germans were willing to deport to the German east, the Jews of Romania, Slovakia, Croatia, Bulgaria, and Hungary.

Fifty years later, on January 20, 1992, which marked the 50th anniversary of the conference, a memorial and educational center was opened at the Villa.

The permanent exhibition, called "The Wannsee Conference and the Genocide of the European Jews," is certainly worth while seeing. The documents the conference, the events leading up to it as well as the consequences are all spelled out. Officials at Wannsee say it "provides basic information on the entire process of the segregation, persecution and genocide of European Jews."

The history of Nazism, the racism, the round-ups of Jews in Germany and then Europe, nation by nation, the story of Jewish resistance, the story of the concentration camps, the story of the murder, the shootings, the hangings, the gasing, the killing, it's all here and displayed very graphically and effectively. Guides lead each group and give talks in German before each set of pictures.

About 80,000 persons visit the Villa each year. The exhibit is certainly worth viewing. But you need to obtain an English-language program as there are just major headlines in English over each exhibit. Narrative information is supplied only in written German, not English.

Besides the permanent exhibits, there are always major displays of topics related to the Holocaust. For example, the story of the "Lodz Ghetto, 1940-44," was told in a display.

In the main hall where the Germans planned the roundup and murder of Jews, are the photos of the 15 officials. Easily recognized is Adolf Eichmann whom the Israelis captured in

Buenos Aires in 1962 and who was tried, convicted and hanged for genocide.

The Villa was built in 1914 by the industrialist Ernst Marlier. He told it to Friedrich Minoux who was general director of the Stinnes Trust. In 1940, the site was acquired by SS. After the war, it was occupied by the Soviets and then the Americans. From 1952 to 1988, it was a school vacation home for the school district. The Historian Joseph Wulf drew attention to the role of the Wannsee Conference. In 1965, Wulf proposed establishing an "International Documentation Center for Researching National Socialism and its Consequences" at this site.

The World Jewish Congress supported the idea. In 1986, the Berlin Senate announced that it would establish a Holocaust Memorial at this historical site. On the 50th anniversary of the Conference, the building was opened to the public.

American visitors may have seen some of the photos from previous exhibitions. But put together it is a remarkable visit and well worth the one half-hour subway ride and short bus or taxi trip to the site.

There is a guest book. This author signed it, "Never again."

SYNAGOGUES IN BERLIN

Synagogue, Joachimstalerstrasse 13, Berlin. This Orthodox synagogue, originally built as a Masonic lodge in 1902 and converted into a synagogue after World War II, is the popular house of worship. Also located here are offices of Jewish organizations such as the Jewish Agency, the Jewish National Fund, the Keren Hayesod, and offices to help Russian Jews. Services are at 6 Friday evening and 9:30 Saturday morning. The synagogue holds many activities, including a Passover seder. Out-of-town visitors are welcomed at services. In the synagogue you often see Russian Jews coming for help and aid. They are welcomed.

Synagogue, Pestalozzistrasse 14, Berlin. This is a famous synagogue. An organ is used during services. Open only at prayer times.

Synagogue, Frankelufer 10-12, Berlin.

Synagogue, Dernburgstrasse 26, Berlin.

Synagogue, Rykerstrasse 53, Berlin. This red brick Moorish structure, built in 1903, is located in former East Berlin. Services may not take place according to schedule, for this congregation is not always able to obtain a minyan (quorum of 10 men needed for a service), even on a Saturday morning. By the way, the reason the building was not destroyed during *Kristallnacht* was that the Germans were afraid the apartment buildings next door would catch fire if they torched the synagogue. According to Paul Goldberger in *The New York Times Magazine* on February 5, 1995, during the Nazi era, the Rykerstrasse synagogue "was only a couple of miles from the headquarters of the Gestapo."

Renovations began on the Talmud Torah in the **Rykestrasse Synagogue,** which will house the new school for Jewish educators founded by the Ronald S. Lauder Foundation.

Adass   Israel,   Tucholskystrasse,   Berlin.   E-mail: AdassJisroelBerlin@WEB.DE. Among its many activities, the synagogue sponsors a Passover Seder. To attend the seder call 281-31-35, or FAX: 281-31-22. Services here only on weekends: On Friday nights the start of services depend on sunset, though they usually start at 4 P.M. in the winter. Shabbat morning services usually begin at 9 A.M.

JEWISH ORGANIZATIONS

Leo-Baeck House, Tucholskystrasse 9, Berlin. Once Leo Baeck, Martin Buber taught here. Solomon Schechter and Abraham Joshua Heschel, went to school here. The building, which formerly housed the University of Jewish Sciences, was shut down by the Nazis in 1942. In this house are : **Headquarters of the Jewish Community in Germany (Zentralrat Der Juden un Deutschland),** Tucholskystrasse 9, Berlin. In 1999, the group moved its office from Frankfurt to Berlin, capital of Germany once again. This organization is in charge of religious, communal and financial matters for German Jews. The move to Berlin occurred at the same time that the Reichstag reopened in April, 1999. The then president of Germany, Roman Herzog said the new Jewish office "opens a new chapter in the postwar history of German Jewry."

Also located in the Leo-Baeck House is **Allgemeine Juedische Wochenzeitung,** Germany's main Jewish newspaper,and the **European Jewish Congress.** Another symbolic moved occurred in 1999 when for the first time, the European Jewish Congress opened an office in Germany and placed it at the Leo-Baeck House. **Jewish Teachers School** also calls this building its home.

Chabad House. Ballenstedter St., 16 A, 10709 Berlin. Tel: 30-891-2531.

Liberal Synagogue. A prayer room has been established in the New Synagogue in Oranienburger st. The prayers are described as "The Egalitarian Service"—the language is "not so male oriented," explained one member. The prayer group is really the start of the Reform movement which ironically was founded here in Berlin. Services are held at 7 P.M. Friday night and 9:30 A.M. Saturday morning. The E-mail address of the Gabai: is schenavsky.kohn@T-online. A member of the World Union for Progressive Judaism, this congregation is growing. Services are also held on holidays. During the festivals, about 200 persons attend.

The American Jewish Committee, Berlin office, Leipziger Platz 15, Mosse Palais, 10117, Berlin. Tel: (030) 22-65-94-0. FAX: (030) 22 65 94-14. E-mail: bergerd@ajc.org; Web page: www.ajc.org. Located here in the heart of Berlin, is the Lawrence & Lee Ramer Center for German-Jewish Relations. The American Jewish Committee published a list of 257 active German companies that appear to have used forced labor and have not agreed to pay compensation. The AJC wants to reach out to German youths to educate them as to the history of Jews in Germany and to prevent the rise of extremist groups in the country. The director is Deirdre Berger.

RESTAURANTS

Café Oren, (Restaurant) Oranienburger str, 28, 10117, Berlin. Tel: 030-884-20-339. Located next door to the New Synagogue and the Community Center. This restaurant which is not kosher but kosher style, is open from 12 noon to 1 A.M. Monday through Thursdays. On Friday, it is open from 12 noon to 2 A.M. the following morning. On Saturdays the establishment welcomes guests from 10 A.M. to 2 A.M. the following morning. Sunday hours are from 10 A.M. to 1 A.M. the following morning. Many Israeli dishes are served here.

Rimon Berlin Café-Bar Restaurant, Oranienburger st., 26, 10117, Berlin. Tel: 030-283-840-32. This is an Israeli restaurant located in the trendy Mitte district. It is not kosher; it is kosher style. Open every day, including weekends. A klezmer band is often on hand. Brunch is served on Sundays.

Beth Café, Tucholskystrasse 40, 10117, Berlin. This establishment is strictly kosher and is known as the café-restaurant of the Adass Israel Congregation. Only dairy, no meat is served here. The café is open Sunday to Thursday, from 12 noon to 8 P.M. and Fridays, from 11 A.M. to 3 P.M. Closed on Saturday. On the first Sunday of each month, the restaurant features a klezmer band.

Kolbo, August str. 77/78, 10117 Berlin. Here at this small store, you can buy kosher provisions, including meat as well as some Judaica objects and books for Jewish holidays. Childrens' books and tapes are stocked. The store is open from 11 A.M. until 6 P.M. Monday through Thursday, Fridays, 10 A.M. until 3 P.M.; 10 A.M. to 5 P.M. during the winter and 11 A.M. until 6 P.M. in summer. On Sundays, this concern is open from 11 A.M. until 6 P.M.

MUSEUMS

Niklas Frank, son of Hans Frank, the governor general of Poland, responsible for the killing of three million Jews, has said, "There isn't a day when I don't think about my father and everything that the Germans did. The world will never forget this. Wherever I go abroad, and say that I am German, people think 'Auschwitz,'" he wrote. "And I think that absolutely just," he added, according to *Newsweek*, January 24, 2000.

Writer Andrew Nagorski wrote that he feels the Germans are confronting their country's past. "No other country has examined its dark side as fully as Germany has."

"There's a growing fascination with Judaism and Jewish history," wrote Nagorski.

Harvard Professor Daniel Jonah Goldhagen's book, *Hitler's*

The strictly-kosher Beth Café in Berlin. (Photo by Ben G. Frank)

Willing Executioners, advances the argument that the Holocaust was not perpetrated simply by Adolf Hitler, or by the SS, or by the Nazis—but by the German nation as a whole, with dozens of social elements working together to exterminate an entire people. The *Jewish Exponent* of Philadelphia, points out that "the unique evil perpetrated by Germany was the self-degradation of Europe's most civilized people into the abomination of genocide." That is why every Jewish public building in itself is a memorial to the Holocaust. An example is the new Jewish Museum, which we shall soon visit. Architecturally it towers over all of Berlin and it is only four stories high.

Jewish Museum, Lindenstrasse, 9-14, D-10969, Berlin. Tel: 30-25-99-33; FAX: 49-30-25-99-34-09. Your hotel's concierge will probably warn you: "But there is nothing in the Museum; it is empty." And he or she is correct. Until 2001, you will take a tour of an empty building.

The exhibits are not yet designed or installed. But don't let that stop you. In a little over one year, 145,000 persons also have taken a tour through this most remarkable museum building designed by Daniel Libeskind. They all came to tour the structure even before any exhibits were installed.

Even if you are there when there are no exhibits, it will be one of the most remarkable buildings you will ever encounter. It is a must on your visit to Jewish Berlin. Officials here are quick to say that this is not a Holocaust Memorial; it is a Jewish history museum that is going to show the creative role that Jews played in Germany before 1933. Still, as you walk through this new elongated, sharply angled and folded building, the Holocaust probably will always be on your mind—no matter what officials or the printed program says.

Officials here see this museum as the largest Jewish Museum in Europe and stress that it will depict the history of not only Berlin Jews, but of German Jews as a whole. But, again, it is more than that. As Robert Leiter noted in an article in the *Jewish Exponent* of Philadelphia, "one of the great glories of the architectural rebirth of the unified city of Berlin is its new Jewish Museum." He is correct.

This museum and the Reichstag probably stand as the only pieces of 21st century "avantgardistic architecture."

The Museum is actually composed of two buildings: the former City of Berlin Museum structure and the new Libeskind designed edifice. For just after you enter the new museum from the old City of Berlin Museum building, the floors you walk on in the new building are uneven. You might even feel a little dizzy. At certain points, you will be disoriented. You will stand in space voids. You will enter a dark angular tower, an oppressive space that obviously stands as a symbol of the Holocaust. The outer walls of the building are covered in zinc, pierced by slashes of window that could be lightning or a shattered Star of David.

Anthony Lewis writing in *The New York Times* on October 19, 1999 said that he found the tower "more powerful than museum images of the reality."

You will walk along three museum streets, or axis, that express "historic continuity, emigration and exile and Holocaust and extermination," said one guide. And always light and darkness and black and white, and hope and fear are with you.

All tours are guided.

Three quarters of the visitors here are German, one quarter are Swiss, Dutch and American. In the guest book are quotes in Japanese, Chinese, French, Hebrew, English. They range from "with great admiration," to "I think my grandparents would sigh with relief and grief if they could visit this place. I will lend them my eyes," wrote a woman from the Netherlands. The Jewish Museum Berlin has "lent us its eyes."

The exhibits are scheduled to begin in 2001 and part of the building may be closed, so it is best to check and see if the museum is open.

New Synagogue Berlin, Centrum Judaicum Foundation, Oranienburger Str. 28/30, Mitte District, Berlin. For tours in English: Tel: 030-880-28-316. They stare at you. The men in the photo, the dignified German Jewish men, bedecked in fedoras, black hats, bowlers and suits. They are wearing their overcoats. Either the heat was off or it was very cold that day. A rabbi stands to one side. But more than anything, this huge blown up photo shows us the faces of the men in 1935. Not smiling; not panic either. Their hands were folded in front of them. Already Jews were suffering indignities. This was the

*New Synagogue Berlin, Centrum Judaicum Foundation, on Oranienburger Str.
28/30 in the Mitte District, Berlin. This museum is located in the former
Oranienburger Strasse synagogue.* (Photo by Ben G. Frank)

Great Synagogue on Oranienburger strasse, designed by Eduard Knoblauch who patterned this house of worship after the Alhambra in Spain. Its Moorish style dome was covered with gilded buttresses and was more than 50 meters high.

When you enter the synagogue and view the exhibit in the remaining part of the structure, you will be standing in the remaining one-third of the original synagogue building. Damage from Kristallnacht, damage from the War, damage from the Allied bombing, damage from the post-war construction blasting after the war, left only about one-third standing. The synagogue was set ablaze in 1938 during Kristallnacht. When the Nazi gangs torched the building the police immediately arrived on the scene. They forced the arsonists to leave and even alerted the fire department. The last service of the congregation was held on September 14, 1939. Even though this temple is no longer used for services, thousands come to see and inhale this former center of Jewish life in the capital.

The synagogue also boasts that it once hired the first and only female rabbi in Germany. Her name was Regina Jonas, 1902-1944. Although she did teach, she was never allowed to preach from the pulpit of the New Synagogue. On November 6, 1942, she was deported to Terezin. On October 12, 1944, she was sent to Auschwitz where she perished.

This was once the heart of Jewish life in Berlin. It is intended to be used as a museum and research center. According to Carol Herselle Krinsky, writing in *Synagogues of Europe: Architecture, History, Meaning,* it was the largest synagogue in the world when completed in 1866. "The fact that the Jews could build a synagogue that was as visually impressive as a church, located in central Berlin and on a street rather than a lane, marked a significant victory," she says, adding, "the synagogue, representing the achievements of modern technology and civilization, remained as a skeletal presence besides the Jewish community office building in the former East Berlin." The reworked facade was completed in 1991, the 125th anniversary of the original dedication. The synagogue's exotic dome, topped by a gilded Star of David, was restored. Over the main entrance of the structure is an inscription in Hebrew, "Open ye the gates, that the righteous nation which keepeth the truth may enter in" (Isaiah 26:2).

The hours for viewing the exhibition are Sunday through Thursday, from 10 A.M. to 6 P.M.; Friday, 10 A.M., to 2 P.M.

As we have seen, this edifice now houses an exhibit about the synagogue and Jewish life in Berlin. But it is also home to administrative offices and institutions of the Jewish community.

Library of the New Center is located on the second floor and is open on Mondays from 10 to 12 noon and 1 to 6:30 P.M.; and on Thursdays, from 10 A.M. to 12 noon and 1 P.M. to 4 P.M.

Checkpoint Charlie, The Museum and the former Checkpoint, Friedrichstrasse 44, 10969 Berlin. If you are a traveler to Berlin as this writer was on several occasions, you will enjoy a sign at Checkpoint Charlie that says in part, "Wanderer! Stay and reflect. At this place, the "Western World," ended and the power of the Moscow Kremlin started, from here to Vladivostok. For 40 years, the world experienced the "cold war" and no two words better describe the memory of those four decades in Berlin than "Checkpoint Charley." The sentry point that separated East and West Berlin is today a noteworthy museum. It shows how the famous Berlin Wall went up in August 1961, and came down in late 1989 and early 1990.

Holocaust Memorial, Behrens strasse, corner Friedrich-Ebertstrasse, Berlin, behind the Aldon Hotel and across from the Tiergarten Park, Berlin. In the year 2000, it was an 4.9 acre empty dirt plot with a wire fence near the Brandenburg Gate in the center of the city. Once the Berlin Wall cast its shadow here between East and West. The emptiness of the lot is conspicuous, especially when considering all the nearly completed buildings being erected around it. The huge construction-project signs declare that "on this site, following a resolution of the German Parliament, the Foundation is building a Memorial to the Murdered Jews of Europe which was designed by Peter Eisenman, architect."

About 2,600 stone pillars will be placed in the empty field creating the impression of a huge graveyard and a "documentation center."

The dedication for the memorial was held was held in January 2000 and was attended by German Chancellor Gerhard

"Checkpoint Charlie," a relic of the Cold War, when Berlin was a divided city. (Photo by Ben G. Frank)

The site of the Holocaust Memorial in Berlin, near the Brandenburg Gate and the Reichstag. (Photo by Ben G. Frank)

Schroder, President Johannes Rau, Nobel Laureate Elie Wiesel and other dignitaries. The ceremony finally ended a debate over what type of memorial should be implanted there.

Speaking at the opening in the huge field which is a stone's throw from the final suicide bunker of Hitler, Elie Wiesel pointed out that: "No nation, no ideology, no system has ever inflicted brutality, suffering and humiliation, on any people, as yours has on mine, in such a short period."

There is indeed much symbolism in the site which will cost an estimated $26 million with construction scheduled to begin in the summer of 2001. Across the street from the middle of the block on Ebertstrasse, there is an entrance to Tiergarten park. At one entrance stands a remarkable statue of Germany's greatest poet, Goethe, whose gaze manages to spy a corner of the memorial, underscoring what many have asked before: How could a nation that produced Goethe and Schiller and hundreds of other great cultured, civilized human beings, commit the genocide of a nation, simply because, as in this case, they were Jews?

It took the government 10 years to reach a decision regarding the form of the memorial. Indeed Berlin Mayor Eberhard Diepgen had fought bitterly against the Holocaust Memorial.

But the Germans have made it clear that they are not building this monument solely for the Jewish people. "We are building it for ourselves. It will help us confront a chapter of our history, "Wolfgang Thierse, the Speaker of the Parliament, told the *New York Times* on June 26, 1999.

MEMORIAL SITES

German Resistance Memorial Center, Stauffenbergstrasse 13. Also known as the Bendeerblock. The victims were those generals who rose against Hitler on July 20, 1944. At the wall in the courtyard, a number of generals were shot. A memorial is located at the spot. On the second floor of the former Army High Command building is a museum devoted to the entire range of the German resistance, including the White Rose movement. The White Rose movement was founded by two

Munich students, a brother and sister, who were arrested and executed. Each of the 26 rooms has an exhibit dedicated to a different aspect of the Third Reich and its opponents. Also on display is a section devoted to resistance by Jews.

A Rosa Luxemburg plaque stands alongside the Landwehr Canal in Berlin, not far from the zoo garden area. Gartenufer/ Katharina-Heinroth-Ufer, Berlin. The memorial to Rosa Luxemburg is behind the Hotel Intercontinental. You can see the sign displaying the letters, "ROSA LUXEMBURG" from the boat on the canal.

There is also a square and a street in former East Berlin named after Rosa Luxemburg, who was born on March 5, 1871, in Russian Poland and who emigrated to Germany in 1888. Imprisoned during World War I, she and Karl Liebknecht formed the Spartacus Union.

In October 1918, two German battleships mutinied and hundreds of thousands of Berliners, joining the sailors, poured into the streets calling for a revolution. Liebknecht, who led radical left-wing Spartacus Union, which became the Communist party at the end of 1918, prepared to proclaim a Soviet Republic, with Rosa as a co-founder. Near civil war atmosphere existed; some called it the German Revolution of 1918. But the Free Corps Army crushed the workers and the army picked up Luxemburg and Liebknecht.

The case against them was shaky. Both had moderated their stand and neither seemed to be murderous Bolshevik types, it is said. "Red Rosa," who had taken part in the 1905 Russian uprising, had urged an end to violence. But the army, while moving them to a prison, shot them and dumped their bodies into the Landwehr Canal. A stamp was issued by the East German government in 1955 that depicted Luxemburg as "leader of the German Workers Movement."

"Some of the older men and women in the Communist Party in East Berlin were Jewish. Their ties to the Party and its orthodoxies had to do with the 1930s and with an anti-Nazi movement that found a home and a raison d'être in the Communist underground," writes Jane Kaplan. Until the Communist regime fell over the winter-spring of 1989-90, the East Germans never apologized for the Holocaust. On April 12,

1990, the East German Parliament admitted "joint responsibility on behalf of the people for the humiliation, expulsion and murder of Jewish women, men and children. We feel sad and ashamed and acknowledge the burden of German history. We ask the Jews of the world to forgive us. We ask the people of Israel to forgive us for the hypocrisy and hostility of official East German policies toward Israel and for the persecution and degradation of Jewish citizens also after 1945 in our country."

HOTELS

Four Seasons Hotel Berlin, Charlottenstrasse, 49, 10117, Berlin. Tel: (30) 20-33-8. FAX: (30) 20-33-61-66. Germany's first Four Seasons Hotel rises above the famed Gendarmenmarkt Square in the extremely historical Friedrichstadt district. The Gendarmenmarkt has been described as one of Europe's most beautiful squares. What is splendid about the area which is quiet and serene compared to the busy Ku-dam in the west section of Berlin is the special neoclassical theater built by Karl Friedrich Schinkel and the late baroque French and German cathedrals with their dominant towers. These structures form a trio of buildings, which represent probably the best in Berlin architecture. Here one can explore the heart of the new Berlin. This five-star hotel maintains 24-hour business service, 24-hour concierge services, two fully-equipped business centers, and a restaurant with an open fireplace. The hotel's eight floors feature 204 guest rooms, including 42 suites, all air-conditioned. This is an excellent hotel situated in a fine location.

Art'Hotel Berlin, Mitte, Wallstrasse 70-73, d-1079 Berlin, Tel: 030-240-62-0; FAX: 030-240-62-222. E-mail: berlin@artotel.de. This artsy four-star-109 room- hotel with modern furniture and layout is in the Nikolaiviertel neighborhood. It combines the traditional with the modern, an exemplary piece of architecture, an attractive ensemble. On one side, a modern building; on another and attached to it is the Ermerlerhaus Mansion which radiates the flair of centuries past. Modern paintings—from George B to Andy Warhol—

adorn this four star hotel, usually occupied by musicians, businesspersons, tourists.

Hollywood Media Hotel, Kurfurstendamm, 202, 10719, Berlin. Tel: 030/889-10-0; FAX: 030-889-10-280. E-mail: info@hollywood-media-hotel.de. You will feel as if you are walking into a Hollywood theater, but it is just a film hotel in town. Life- size Oscar statues welcome the guests to the four star hotel. Film equipment and old cameras are used as decoration. "I wanted to bring across a sense of film and television everywhere," said Artur Brauner. He told interviewers that he picked up this idea in Los Angeles where he met all the stars of Hollywood. All 164 rooms and suites have been dedicated to international and German filmstars. Don't worry if you forget the number of your room, you can tell the clerk that you are in the Marilyn Monroe or Humphrey Bogart room.

FAMOUS CEMETERIES

Jewish cemetery. Schonhauser Allee in Prenzlauer Berg, 10435 Berlin. Tel: 030-965-33-30. Many of the gravestones still lie smashed or overturned by the Nazis or Allied bombs. The remaining stones remind one of the remarkable success of German Jewry in the late 19th century and early 20th century.

Jewish cemetery in Charlottenburg, Heer str am Scholzplatz, 14055 Berlin. Tel: 030-304-32-34.

Weissenssee Cemetery, Herbert-Baum st., 45, 13088 Berlin. Tel: 030-965-33-30. Considered as Europe's largest Jewish cemetery, it contains 115,000 graves. This cemetery open for visitations from Sunday through Thursday, from 8 A.M. until 4 P.M. in the winter and until 5 P.M. in the spring and summer, Fridays until 2 P.M.

GUIDES

An excellent guide for Jewish Berlin is **Olaf Kolbatz,** Friedrichstr, 213-214, 10969 Berlin. Tel: (030) 251-69-44 or (030) 252-99-640. FAX: (030) 252-99-641. He can conduct tours to general sites as well. Olaf speaks English and Hebrew. Some of the sites that he can take the visitor to are: Brandenburg Gate, Palace Charlottenburg, Kurfurstendamm, Reichstag, Checkpoint Charley and Unter den Linden with the historical buildings. Also, University (Humboldt), Opera House, Alexanderplatz, Olympic Stadium, and the remains of the Berlin Wall.

Ronnie Golz, 39 Suarez st., 14057, Berlin. Tel: 49-(0)-30-321-76-86. FAX: 49-(0)-30-325-76-52. Mobile: 49-(0)- 177-321-76-86. E-mail: rgolz@t-online.de. Could you expect a guide in Berlin to speak with an English-accent? Meet Ronnie Golz, guide, lecturer, teacher, and active in the Berlin Jewish community. He conducts two coach tours, *Jewish Sites in Berlin in the Past, Present and Future,* and *Art and Memory of the Holocaust in Berlin.* The first tour takes the traveler to synagogues, community buildings and includes a visit to the Jewish cemetery in Berlin-Weissensee as well as Holocaust memorials. The second tour visits Holocaust memorials, including Wannsee Villa, and if requested, Sachsenhausen Concentration Camp. He also has topical walks, such as *The Jewish Quarter in Old and Present Day Berlin,* including a visit to the Centrum Judaicum Museum.

Sachsenhausen Concentration Camp

Sachsenhausen Memorial and Museum, Strasse der Nationen 22, Oranienburg. Tel: 033-010-3715. More than 200,000 political prisoners were interned at Sachsenhausen Concentration Camp. Half of them died from starvation. There was one gas chamber at the camp, which was built in 1943. At times there were more than 6,000 Jewish prisoners. The camp was a training ground for the Nazi SS. In 1942, Himmler ordered the Jews to be deported to Auschwitz. The story did not end in 1945 when Germany surrendered. From 1945 to 1950, the Russians converted this camp into a political prison for about 60,000 Nazi functionaries and opponents of the Communist regime. Under the Soviets, about 12,000 prisoners died here at Sachsenhausen known as the "Camp of Silence." Relatives and friends of prisoners were not allowed to talk about the camp. Two barracks, numbers 38 and 39, remain at the site. A museum nearby can also be visited. In 1992, the late Israeli prime minister, Yitzhak Rabin visited the camp. Immediately afterwards, an arson attack on the two Jewish barracks occurred. In 1998, about 265,000 persons visited the camp.

The museum can be visited from April 1-September 30, 8:30 A.M. to 6 P.M. daily; October 1 to March 31, from 8:30 A.M. to 4:30 P.M. Exhibitions are not shown on Mondays.

Potsdam

A half hour by express train from Berlin brings you to the peaceful town of Potsdam—no longer located in the former Communist state of East Germany but in a united Germany.

For the traveler, for the student, for the history buff, a visit to this thriving tourist site of Potsdam, this "summer-time" capital of Berlin, is a nice reprieve from the hectic schedule of Berlin. The tour guides like to call this city "Berlin's Versailles."

Every summer, this municipality flew the flag of the summer home of the Hohenzollerns and other German royalty. Frederick the Great (1712-1786) had his castles built in this mecca of the German military. Indeed, the bones of Frederick the Great, which the Nazis had evacuated to West Germany to keep them out of the hands of the Russians at the end of World War II, were brought back to Potsdam in 1991. With Chancellor Helmut Kohl standing by, they were ceremoniously reinterred next to the emperor's greyhounds in the park of Sanssouci Palace. The creations of Frederick the Great define the character of the city. As a patron of culture and art, he created the world-renowned *Sanssouci Palace* as well as Sanssouci Park.

At present there is no permanent synagogue in Potsdam, but you can tell there are Jews here. There are only about 350 Jews and they are mostly Russian Jews and you see them in the streets of this prestigious town. There were 400 Jews living here before the war. Russian Jews are coming to Germany and are settling in smaller German cities.

One of the monuments declared "historic" by UNESCO is the New Gardens with the Cecilienhof Palace and its memorial to the Potsdam Conference held in 1945. The hall in which the

The Conference table used at the Potsdam Conference, attended by the U.S., Britain, and USSR. (Photo by Ben G. Frank)

Former Jewish Synagogue, Platz der Einheit, Potsdam. (Photo by Ben G. Frank)

conference was attended by President Harry S. Truman, British Prime Minister Winston S. Churchill and Soviet Premier Joseph Stalin can be seen with its original furnishings. Interestingly, Churchill was replaced at the final meetings of the conference because the results of the British election were announced and Clement Attlee was victorious and arrived at Potsdam as the new prime minister. The Potsdam Conference ran from July 17 to August 2, 1945 and was the longest of the Allied war time conferences. The French were excluded. The Conference dealt not only with Germany with whom hostilities had ceased, but with the continued war with Japan. Regarding Germany, three practical issues faced the conference, according to Gerhard L. Weinberg in his book, *A World At Arms: A Global History of World War II.* "One was the establishment of a government machinery, the second was that of borders, and the third reparations."

Synagogue, Helena Lange Strasse 14, Potsdam. Because there are so few Jews here, a prayer service is held only on Friday evenings and Saturday mornings. Time for evening services, of course, depends on sundown. Shabbat morning services are held at 9:30 A.M. The community eventually may move from this location, a former school.

Former Jewish Synagogue, Platz der Einheit, Potsdam. Directly in back of and across the street from the Victims of Fascism Monument was the site of the Jewish synagogue. A plaque informs the visitor that: "On this spot stood the synagogue of Potsdam. On the night of November 9, 1938, it was plundered and destroyed by fascists."

The first synagogue in the city was built in 1748 on Ebraer strasse or "Hebrews Street." In 1934, the Nazis tore down that street sign and put up a new one with an "aryan" name." But in 1992, the old Jewish name was restored. In 1768, the congregation had moved from the Ebraer strasse location to a new synagogue on the Nauner Plantage, later called Wilheimsplatz. Today that square is known as Platz der Einheit, or "Unity Square." The original synagogue building had to be torn down because of the swampy ground conditions which enveloped the area. So a new synagogue was constructed between 1901 to

The Jewish Cemetery at Potsdam. (Photo by Ben G. Frank)

1903. After Kristallnacht, the Nazis used one undamaged room of the synagogue as a radio broadcast center.

Culture House, Berlinerstrasse 148. Potsdam. Community cultural events are held in one large room in this building. The other room is **Chabad House.** Persons can contact **Rabbi Nahum Pressman** at 0331-270-50-90.

Juedisch Gemeinde Potsdam, Am Lehnitzsee 8, 14476 NeuFahrland. Tel: 33-208-68060, FAX: 33-208-52297. The headquarters of the Jewish community in Potsdam is located here. Here the officers of the community plan activities.

The Jewish Cemetery This Jewish burial ground was once called Judenberg, or Jewish Mountain. In the 19th century it was named Finksburg or Pentacostal Mountain. Opened in 1743, the burial spot was closed by the Nazis in 1943 and never reopened until the fall of the Berlin Wall in 1989. In 1992, it was once again used as a Jewish cemetery. Today, the cemetery is open from 10 A.M. to 1 P.M. only on Sundays. A sign tells visitors, one must wear a *yarmulke* or hat.

Monument Against Fascism, Platz der Einheit, Potsdam. This wall monument still stands. A relic of the Communist days, the following words were inscribed on it: "Our sacrifice, our struggle against fascism and war. Remind the living of their responsibility." A ceremony is held here every January to mark the liberation of the Auschwitz concentration camp. Politically, the town is still controlled by the Socialists who, many claim, are former Communists.

Moses Mendelssohn Center, Am Neuen Markt 8, 14467 Potsdam. Tel: 03-31-280-94-0. FAX: 03-31-280-94-50 An attractive, remodeled building on a quiet street is the headquarters of this important research institute for European Jewish studies. Prof. Dr. Julius H. Schoeps is managing director. The Moses Mendelssohn Center was founded in 1992 on the fiftieth anniversary of the Wannsee Confrence which was discussed in this book in the section on Berlin. The Center was named in honor of the philosopher, Moses Mendelssohn (1729-1786). As an interdisciplinary research unit in history, philosophy, religion and social sciences, it is associated with the University of Potsdam as an active participant in the university's Jewish Studies Program.

The Center emphasizes that special attention is given to the historical relationship between Jews and their non-Jewish environment. A rabbinical seminary is about to open in this institution.

Einstein's Tower, Telegraphenberg, Potsdam. Tel: (0331-288-23-33. Built by Erich Mendelssohn in 1923, the Einstein Tower has been declared a technical monument, a major example of expressionist architecture. The structure was used by Einstein for experiments so he could provide practical evidence of his theory of relativity. It still serves as a sun observatory. Every architectural student in the world is familiar with this building. The "Albert Einstein Science Park" which includes the Potsdam Institute for Climatic Effects. Research, the Potsdam Astrophysical Institute, the Potsdam GeoResearch Centre and the Alfred Wegener Institute for Polar and Marine Research, is open to visitors on the weekend. The tower is about a 20-minute walk from the Potsdam train station. A tour of the tower can be arranged by calling (0331) 288-23-33.

The Einstein House, Waldstrasse 7, Caputh. Einstein himself spent the summer months between 1929 and 1933 in nearby Caputh, about five miles southwest of Potsdam. This "Einstein House" is also known as the lakeside cottage where he vacationed. The Potsdam suburb of Babelsberg is the home of one of Europe's oldest feature film production facilities.

Recommended Guide. Kevin Kennedy. Kevin Kennedy speaks perfect English and German. His knowledge of history is superb. His services can be requested from **Potsdam Information,** Friedrich-Ebert st., 5, 14467, Potsdam. Tel: (0331) 27-55-823. FAX: (0331) 27558-99. His E-mail: Alterfritz@aol.com. Persons can also contact Kevin Kennedy, Gamstr. 17, 14482, Potsdam. Tel: (0331) 740-82-18.

Dusseldorf

Dusseldorf includes an "old town" section: tourist pubs, boutiques, art galleries, an area where one can hear languages from all over the world.

The "desk of heavy industry," Dusseldorf is home to many large corporate headquarters. The region is a very highly industrialized part of Germany, which now has one of the highest standards of living in the world.

Jews have gone back to this urban, vibrant, cosmopolitan, and charming Rhine River city. There are about 2,000 Jews in Dusseldorf out of a total population of 600,000. This metropolis contains the fourth largest Jewish community in Germany, following Berlin, Frankfurt, and Munich.

What strikes one immediately about the community is that 90 percent of the Jewish population is not made up of German Jews, but mainly of Jews who emigrated from Eastern Europe. In recent years, too, a number of Israelis and Russian Jews also took up residence in Dusseldorf.

Jews are attracted to Dusseldorf because it is an artistic and cultural center. It is known as the Paris of Germany because of its fashion industry and famous boulevard of designer shops called the Koenigsallee, which is the heart and showplace of the city. The chic avenue is called the "Ko." Dusseldorf has been described as a "brash town flush with new money and the financial center for the industrial Ruhr."

Here are a few places to visit in Dusseldorf.

Heine Statue, in a small park at Schwanmarkt (a square and park) on Haroldstrasse. Heinrich Heine (1797-1856), the famous Jewish writer and poet who lived in both Germany and France, once wrote that his birthplace, Dusseldorf, "is very beautiful. When you are far away from it, you think of it and you get a strange feeling that says, 'I was born there and I feel as if I would have to go back there immediately.'" Heine was one of Dusseldorfs distinguished citizens.

Heinrich Heine Institute, Bilkerstrasse 14. Original manuscripts of "The Lorelei" and "The Rabbi of Bachrach" are housed in this museum. A great poet, Heine accepted baptism, the "entree card into European culture." Still, he wrote, "I make no bones about my Jewishness to which I have not returned because I never left it." Heine was born in Dusseldorf. In 1831, he emigrated to Paris, where he died in 1856.

In "The Lorelei," he wrote, "When I think of Germany in the night, I am robbed of my sleep.." Heine also said, "What we now call the hatred of the proletariat against the rich was formerly called Jew hatred." Except for the French Jewish writer Marcel

Proust, there was no Jew who could hold a candle to Heine. He feared grave developments in the near future: "Germany is still a little child—but the sun is its nurse. The sun does not suckle it with soothing milk, it suckles it with wild flames." Perhaps he knew that violence would continue forever in Germany, as in the summer of 2000, when a bomb wounded nine immigrants, six of them Jews.

Synagogue, Zietenstrasse 50. Tel: 480-312 or 480-313. Before the war, there was only one synagogue in Dusseldorf, which then had a population of about 5,000 Jews. The synagogue, then located on Kasernenstrasse, was destroyed in 1938 and it is now the site of the *Handelsblatt,* the *Wall Street Journal* of Germany. A stone monument recalls the synagogue.

The synagogue in Dusseldorf calls itself Liberal, meaning it closely resembles the Conservative Movement of Judaism in the United States. Friday evening services are at 6 in the winter, Shabbat morning services are at 9:15, and morning services during the week are at 7:30. There is no kosher restaurant in Dusseldorf, but a kosher kitchen exists at the synagogue's community center and arrangements can be made for kosher meals.

Dusseldorf Memorial Center, Muhlenstrasse, 29, Dusseldorf. Open Tuesday through Sunday. Exhibits and memorials focus on how the Nazi era affected the city. Opened in 1987, it shows the visitor how the Germans themselves remember. There is a memorial book of 2,213 names, the names of Dusseldorf Jews who were deported. Exhibits are in German.

Frankfurt

Located at the center of Western Europe is Frankfurt-am-Main, the financial capital of Germany. Just gaze at the modern all-glass high-rise offices and you can see why Germany is the economic: colossus that it is. Although Frankfurt has only 627,000 people, this Rhine-Main industrial area takes in nearly 400 banking concerns. But then, Frankfurt always has been a center of trade and commerce. Just stand on one of the bridges over the Main River and you can see why trade flourished here. Frankfurt is also the home of Goethe. His home, **Goethehaus**, is open to the public at Grosser Hirschgraben 23. He lived in this house—now a wonderful museum—from his birth until the age of 26.

Some of the famous Jewish native sons of Frankfurt include, of course, the Rothschilds, as well as the artist Moritz Oppenheim, Erik Erikson, Nahum Goidmann, and Daniel Cohn-Bendit. Martin Buber was a professor at Frankfurt University during the Weimar Republic years. Buber, who later emigrated to Israel, sought to resurrect the heritage of Chassidism for the modern Jew and offered his mystical view of the Jewish people. Leopold Sonnemann was the Jewish founder of one of Germany's most prestigious newspapers, *Die Frankfurter Zeitung*.

The book fairs of Frankfurt were always attended by Jewish printers and booksellers. Jewish book people from the United States and Israel still come to the Frankfurt Book Fair, which attracts nearly 250,000 persons. In fact, Sohar, the kosher restaurant here in Frankfurt, is usually the scene of a dinner of Jewish book dealers sponsored by the city's Jewish community.

Jews probably already traded in this flourishing city in the twelfth century. We know that a massacre occurred in 1241. But to Jews, Frankfurt meant the Rothschilds and the ghetto.

JEWISH SITES IN FRANKFURT

The Ghetto. In 1462, the Jews of Frankfurt were transferred to a specially constructed street, known as the Judengasse. It was a ghetto that was enclosed within walls and gates. The Jews possessed their own quarters, but the area could not be enlarged.

The Rothschilds once lived in the ghetto. In the 1560s, Isaac Elchanan, the first Rothschild, obtained a house here that displayed a red sign on the board of a shield, "rot schild" meaning "red sign." While those descendants might have moved, the name Rothschild stuck. On February 23, 1743, Mayer Amschel

Rothschild was born. He later established a relationship with William of Hanau, who loved coin collecting. Mayer Amschel would offer him coins and William in return offered a patronage that eventually blossomed into the Rothschild financial empire.

By 1750, there were 3,000 men, women, and children in the Frankfurt ghetto—all crammed into 200 houses. The building regulations made it impossible to see into the houses of Christians. The side windows of the Jews were walled in and pasted over. The Jews were restricted to the Judengasse, afterwards known as the Bornestrasse; the street still exists. The Jews were locked in after sunset on weekdays and as early as 4 o'clock on Sundays. On certain holidays and festive public occasions, they were forced to remain indoors during the day and were let out only in the evening.

The Bornestrasse is near the Zeil, a pedestrian mall. To get to the Judengasse (Bornestrasse) from the Zeil, head south on Fahrgasse and make a quick left to Ander Staufenmauer. You'll pass through the arch of what was the city wall in the twelfth century and became the ghetto wall in the fifteenth century.

In 1796, the French Revolutionary Army liberated the Jews of Frankfurt, and in 1798, the prohibition on leaving the ghetto on Sundays and holidays was abolished.

Frankfurt became a center of Reform Judaism. In 1845, a conference of rabbis sympathizing with the Reform movement was held there. A leading member was theologian Abraham Geiger, an early German Reform rabbi, first in Frankfurt and then Berlin. Emancipation of the Jews of Frankfurt came in 1864.

Before the Nazis came to power, Frankfurt had a higher percentage of Jewish citizens than any other German city, including Berlin; and Jewish patronage was responsible for the establishment of many of the city's internationally known institutions, including its university and its paper, *Die Frankfurter Zeitung.*

The Bornestrasse Synagogue occupied the same site as the ghetto synagogue until it was destroyed on *Kristallnacht.* A plaque on the building that now houses a city statistical office identifies the site.

The configuration of the street was changed by the Allied bombings of World War II—it now comes to a dead end at a parking lot. Just past the synagogue plaque, the street now curves in the opposite direction from the old Judengasse. The Rothschild home probably stood in a place that is now one block over, near the Canon Copier store on Kurt Schumacherstrasse.

The Frankfurt Municipal Library contains the largest collection of Judaica in Germany, about 25,000 volumes and 325 manuscripts.

The Jewish Community Center in Frankfurt (Judische Gemeinde Frankfurt), Westendstrasse 43, 6000 Frankfurt-am-Main. Tel: 740-7215. The first time the visitor sees this massive structure, he should go to the other side of the building on Savignystrasse 66. On this impressive side, one sees a menorah set high above the entrance. But to the left is a single, blank tablet of law with cracks to symbolize the break between the Germans and the Jewish people. There are about 5,000 Jews in Frankfurt and most make this their center of activity. They sponsor a day school that goes up to the seventh grade, Lectures, movies, senior citizen clubs, and talks by Israeli leaders all add to the program mix offered by this facility. It also contains a gym.

Sohar Kosher Restaurant is located in the Jewish Community Center. Tel: 75-2341. The proprietors are Israelis. The Sohar serves kosher and Israeli-style dishes, Shabbat meals can be ordered in advance.

Jewish Museum, Untermainkai 14-15, 6000 Frankfurt. Tel: 212-8805 or 212-5000. Open Tuesday to Sunday, 10 A.M. to 5 P.M.; Wednesday until 8 P.M. Closed Monday. Significantly, the museum was opened on November 9, 1988, in the former Rothschild Palais on the occasion of the fiftieth anniversary of *Kristallnacht.* The Jewish Museum is the largest of its kind in the German-speaking world. It features a history of Jews in Germany from the Middle Ages to the present with the Jewish community as the main example. The building was the home of Baron Carl von Rothschild and housed a vast library now in the Municipal and University Library. In the words of Georg Heuberger, the director, "the aim of the Jewish Museum is to provide the knowledge relating to the history, culture and religion of the Jewish people necessary for a dialogue between Jews and non Jews." The museum, one of the finest in Europe, includes exhibits on Jewish life, rituals, festivals and holidays, a 1731 Haggadah, and portraits of Gotthold Ephraim Lessing and Moses Mendelssohn.

A videotape shows the history of the Jews of Frankfurt.

The exhibit on the Holocaust is outstanding. A memorial wall bears the names of 11,000 Jews of Frankfurt who lost their lives. It is quite moving!

The museum contains a wooden scale model of the Frankfurt ghetto. The model of both sides of the Judengasse (street) shows Jewish life in the Middle Ages, and was made from plans drawn in 1711. There is an exhibition on the architecture of the synagogue, as well as on Jewish holidays and religious items. Other exhibits are about achievements in the area of civil rights, the development and social structure of the Jewish community, integration (a superb exhibit), assimilation, and anti-Semitism. There is a well-documented section on the Nazi era. Many non-Jews visit this building; it is in effect a learning center.

Museum Judengasse, Karl-Schumacher-Strasse, 10, at Battonnstrasse, 60311 Frankfurt. Tel: (069) 297-7419. This museum located in the old Jewish quarter covers 300 years of Frankfurt's Jewish history. Highlights of this new building are a computerized infobank and other audiovisual instruments. The museum is open from 10 A.M. until 5 P.M. every day, except Mondays. On Wednesdays, the building is open until 8 P.M.

Book-café is a very popular institution in the Jewish Museum in Frankfurt. Hanna Solomon manages this bookstore where one can find German-Jewish and Israeli newspapers and magazines on the racks.

In a room whose theme is the struggle for the Jewish State, Americans will be pleased to see the American flag flown high in a photo exhibit of the liberation of the concentration camp at Dachau. A poster in the display says, "Freedom can only be with the realization of a Jewish National Home in Palestine."

An electronic encyclopedia on Jewish subjects and a bookshop and cafeteria are included in this impressive building.

The Jewish Museum is not the only museum on what is called the Museum Row, Museum Mile, or Museum Embankment. In recent years, Frankfurt, which in 1994 celebrated its 1,200-year anniversary, embarked on much museum construction and it now also is considered a city of art. It has established a Museum Embankment containing a number of museums on Schaumainkai, the tree-lined avenue along the left bank of the Main River. The Jewish Museum is always mentioned as part of this museum complex, although technically, it is located across the river, on Untermainkai, 14-15. Included in the museums that are in the area are the Museum of Applied Arts, Museum of the City of Frankfurt, German Film Museum, German Architecture Museum, Stadel Art Institute, Liebreghaus, an extensive collection of sculpture, and the Jewish Museum. It is also not far from the excellent Franidurter Hof hotel, Bethmannstrasse 33.

Rothschild Park. The affluent Jews of Frankfurt lived in the westend and this is still the home of many Jews, and their cultural and religious center. The park once housed the mansion of the Goldschmidt-Rothschild family and was located behind the Opernplatz.

Senior Citizen Center, Bornheimer Landwehr 79b. Tel: 43-96-02. The Atereth-Zvi Synagogue is also located here.

SYNAGOGUES IN FRANKFURT

Synagogue Baumweg, Baumweg 5-7.

Synagogue, Roderbergweg 29.

Synagogue, Henry and Emma Budge-Stiftung, Wilhelm-shoherstrasse 279. Tel: 47-87-10.

Westend Synagogue, Freiherr-vom-Stein-strasse. This is the only Frankfurt synagogue to have survived Kristallnacht. The grey stone building features vaulting stone arches on four sides under a massive cupola, with Star of David stained-glass windows in blue and white. Although a Liberal Synagogue before the war, it is now Orthodox, as are all the Frankfurt synagogues.

Munich

About 4,000 Jews now live in the Bavarian capital. One thing is certain: they want, and work for, an active Jewish community. And they don't like to be asked, "How can Jews live in Germany?" To them, and to the more than 80,000 Jews in Germany, this is their home. Most of the young people are professionals and of the middle class. Only one-third of Munich's Jews are native-born; Israelis and Polish and Russian Jews make up the rest. Many of the Russian Jews who emigrated from the former U.S.S.R. did not go on to Israel.

Following Berlin and Hamburg, Munich is Germany's third largest industrial city. This warmhearted metropolis is famous for its art collections, its theater, the largest museum of science and technology in the world, and the largest university. Over a million people reside here in Germany's "secret capital." It is said that 60 percent of all Germans would like to live in this area. Surrounded by green valleys and dark green forests, the Muncheners are not poor in nature or wealth; on the contrary, they are probably the richest in all of Germany.

This city of Old-World elegance is a center of art and culture. Alongside its art galleries and museums are open-air beer gardens and the Hofbrauhaus. The Oktoberfest was once described as a Teutonic drunk scene. Fine buildings of every period, grand boulevards and squares, and the Marienplatz all highlight this city. Theodor Herzl, father of modern Zionism, wanted Munich as the seat of the First World Zionist Congress. But the local Jewish community protested because its German patriotism might be questioned. And that is how Basel, Switzerland, came to be the site of the Congress.

In the Schwabing district, the center of European intellectual life, lived Brecht, Mann, Klee, Kandinsky, Trotsky, and Spengler. Munich was the site of the Red Commune in 1919, as well as the birthplace and center of the Nazi movement. In 1923, it was the scene of Hitler's Beer Hall Putsch. In spite of this failed attempt to overthrow the government, Hitler made Munich the headquarters of the Nazi party. In the spring of 1913, Hitler had arrived in this city as a "young artist and German nationalist," according to Stephen Kinzer in *The New York Times*, January 4, 1994. Then, and after World War I, Munich was the scene of great political upheaval. To this day, the area around Munich—the capital of the state of Bavaria—

remains one of Germany's most conservative regions.

Munich also has become synonymous with appeasement. In 1938, British Prime Minister Neville Chamberlain signed the Munich Pact with Hitler at the then Fuhrer Ban (headquarters). "Peace in our time," it was called, but it was clear, outright appeasement, the sellout of Czechoslovakia, and the tragic forerunner of Hitlerian victories.

JEWISH SITES IN MUNICH

Judisches Museum Munchen, Maximilianstrasse 36, Munich. This new museum was dedicated in 1989. Open from Thursdays and Fridays, 2 to 6 P.M.; and Saturdays, 10 A.M. to 2 P.M. Check on hours.

Literatur Hundlung, Furstenstrasse 17, Munich. The owner of this Jewish bookstore in is Rachel Salamander. She once told Jewish Week reporter Toby Axelrod that she had "the biggest collection of Yiddish music and lyrics in Europe." Here are found books on the Middle East, Israel, children's books, and Yiddish records. She is also considered an "unofficial Jewish cultural director" and arranges films, lectures, exhibitions, and readings in Munich.

Youth & Cultural Center of the Jewish Community in Munich, Prinzregentenstr, 91/ Ruckgebaude (back yard), D-81677, Munich. Tel: 0049-89-47-67. FAX: 0049-89-47-054-17. Recreation. Education. Adult Education. These are just some of the highlights of this youth and cultural center. Programs include lectures, speeches, discussions and exhibitions, as well as Hebrew language courses, dance workshops. The community center reaches about 6,000 Jews in Munich. Many non-Jews attend lectures here.

SYNAGOGUES IN MUNICH

Main synagogue, Jewish Community Center, Reichenbachstrasse 27. Tel: 201-4960. Located here is a synagogue, mikveh, restaurant, and various Jewish community organization offices, such as WIZO and United Israel Appeal. The synagogue occupies the site of the old synagogue. Call for information on prayer times, kosher food, and community activities.

Lubavitch Beth Chabad, Ishamingerstrasse 62, 8000 Munich.

Synagogue, Georgenstrasse 71, Schwabing, near the university.

Synagogue, Possarstrasse 15, in Mittersendling.

Synagogue, Schulstrasse 30, in Neuhavsen.

Liberale Judische Gemeinde Munchen Beth Shalom, Munich, Hermann-Hummel str, 18, Grafelfing, 82166, Munich. Tel: 8980-9373. FAX: 8980-9374.

DACHAU

Dachau, nestled in the rolling hills of Munich, is the site of the infamous Nazi death camp and is the fourth most visited site in Germany, with one million visitors in a year, and not all foreigners or school groups.

There are complaints that the Germans have prettied up the camp. But as Thane Rosenbaum notes in a book review of *The Last Survivor,* by Timothy W. Ryback, "no amount of natural scenic beauty can camouflage the death museum that brings a million tourists a year to Dachau."

Dachau boasted the first concentration camp, the first crematory oven, the first gas chambers, the first medical experiments.Robert St. John described Dachau as "an ugly little word." Dachau was opened on March 21, 1933, in what had been a World War I munitions factory. Between 1933 and 1941, the camp was finished and actually had a reputation among inmates as "relatively luxurious," according to James E. Young in his book, *The Texture of Memory: Holocaust Memorials and Meaning in Europe, Israel, and America.* He writes that while several thousand Soviet Army officers were executed here, and Jews were killed at Buchenwald, "the only extermination centers on German territory were Mauthausen and Hartheim Castle in Austria, with their operational gas chambers." But as

The entrance to the concentration camp at Dachau. (Photo by Scott Michaels)

Memorial candles at the concentration camp at Dachau. (Photo by Scott Michaels)

Dachau. (Photo by Scott Michaels)

the war ended and the Soviet troops moved in from the East, "the Germans evacuated masses of starved, diseased ravaged Jews from the death camps in Poland to Germany," according to Young. Dachau became a death camp. "It was inundated with open cattle cars of dead and dying prisoners." Today, there are memorials in Dachau—the sculpture by Nandor Glid of a 45-feet long, black bronze grid of human forms enmeshed in barbed wile, is well-known throughout the world. There is also a Jewish monument of a stone vault. A path descends downward to the vault and on both sides of the path is a barbed iron gate with Stars of David on either side. Inside, one gets the feeling of being in the pit of a furnace looking up through the chimney—it "mirrors the shape of crematorium ovens."

Officials say that Americans are among the most numerous of the foreign visitors to Dachau. Many of the visitors wear yarmulkes. There are German youth from the schools, as well as students arriving on tour buses from Italy. There are English men and women on holiday. They all come to Dachau. An excellent historical museum that traces the brutal rise of Nazism and tells what went on here in the first death camp occupies the premises. Some of the camp's original structures still stand, and two of the barracks have been reconstructed.

What goes on in the visitors' minds? While they say Dachau is not as gruesome in its preservation as, say, Auschwitz, they get the message. Perhaps they hope that the world will be better, that there were righteous Christians even in Germany who saved Jews.

Several miles away from the camp in the town of Dachau itself, I met Johann Waltenberger, principal in the Josef Effner High School, whose student body numbers 1,500. It seems that Waltenberger, who is not Jewish, was moved by the television film *Holocaust*. He immediately set out on his own to bring two peoples, Germans and Israelis, together "to remember the past."

Waltenberger is a religious man. He always has been interested in the Bible and in the Holy Land. He has visited Israel several times and is fond of it. He talks like a Zionist. A number of years ago, with some help from the Jewish community of Munich, he wrote a long letter to a number of Israeli schools and asked them if they would be interested in an exchange program of students and teachers.

The Israelis answered back politely, in effect, "Thank you, but no thank you." Waltenberger said the Israelis wrote that he should teach the Holocaust in his class and drop the matter.

Waltenberger says he understood their reaction but was not deterred. On his next trip to Israel, he visited several of the Israeli educators and personally talked to them about the program.

He was persistent. He says he had to try. After a year of negotiations, six Israeli teachers were scheduled to come to Dachau for a week to exchange ideas, discussions, and methods regarding teaching the Holocaust.

In Waltenberger's school, of course, the Holocaust is taught. His pupils visit the camp, which contains a museum, a sample barracks, several memorials, as well as a synagogue and two churches.

"Emotions," Waltenberger says, "are not enough; dialogue is important. We must do these things." He set up the whole program himself. All of this could be brushed aside as infinitesimal compared to the thousands upon thousands who perished at Dachau. But there are those in the American Jewish community and the German Jewish community who believe that Jews should never cease to remind the world about the Holocaust. As emotionally trying as a visit to Dachau becomes, homage should continue to be paid to the six million Jews on the soil where they died. The world must remember!

Worms

A number of Jewish scholars lived in Worms.

Jewish cemetery. Located just beyond the southwest corner of the city wall is this Jewish cemetery, one of the oldest in Europe. Comprised of 2,000 tombstones, it was probably founded in 1076. Many great scholars are buried in Worms. A section of the cemetery designated as the "Valley of the Rabbis" has directional signs in Hebrew to guide visitors. The municipality tends to the grounds.

Rashi Haus. This is a Jewish museum as well as the city archives and is located next to the synagogue. It was opened in 1982 on the site of a yeshiva where once stood a hospital and an old age home. And just to remind us where we are, there was once on this very site an assembly of Jews, half of which were dispatched to the concentration camp.

Rashi Synagogue. This is one of the most significant Jewish historical sites in Germany. Built first in 1034 and destroyed several times thereafter, it is one of the oldest Jewish houses of worship in Europe. The mikveh (1186) and the Rashi Chapel (1624) were destroyed by the Nazis in 1938, but they have been reconstructed. Although Rashi lived here for only five years, his disciples still come to inhale the atmosphere in which he lived and thrived. The Rashi Chapel has a chair that may have been used by the venerable scholar. A large room to the left of the bimah was a separate women's synagogue built in the thirteenth century. The wall between the two buildings was removed in the nineteenth century and the room now stands empty, except for a memorial marker for the 500 Worms Jews who died in the Holocaust.

Synagogueplatz. This is the square just off the Judengasse that runs parallel to the remnants of the city's north wall.

Suggested Reading

Adler, H. G. *The Jews in Germany: From the Enlightenment to National Socialism.* Notre Dame, Ind.: University of Notre Dame Press, 1969.

Berenbaum, Michael. *The World Must Know: The History of the Holocaust As Told in the United States Holocaust Museum.* Boston: Little, Brown, 1993.

Bolitho, Hector, ed. *Twelve Jews.* Freeport, N.Y.: Books for Libraries Press, 1934.

Cornwell, John, *"Hitler's Pope, The Secret History of Pius XII,* Viking, New York, 1999.

Fest, Joachim C. *Hitler.* New York: Vintage, 1973.

Friedrich, Otto. *Before the Deluge: A Portrait of Berlin in the 1920's.* New York: Harper & Row, 1972.

German National Tourist Office. *"Germany for the Jewish Traveler."* New York.

Herz, Emil. *Before the Fury: Jews and Germany Before Hitler.* Philosophical Library, 1966.

Katcher, Leo. *Post-Mortem: The Jews of Germany Today.* New York: Delacorte, 1968.

Kempe, Frederick, *Father/Land: A Personal Search for the New Germany,* New York, G. P. Putnam's Sons, 1999.

Kramer, Jane. *Europeans.* New York: Farrar, Straus & Giroux, 1988.

Krinsky, Carol Herselle. *Synagogues of Europe: Architecture, History, Meaning.* Cambridge, Mass.: MIT Press, 1985.

Lowenthal, Marvin. *The Jews of Germany: A Story of Sixteen Centuries.* New York: Longmans, Green, 1936.

Meltzer, Milton. *Never to Forget: The Jews of the Holocaust.* New York: Harper & Row, 1976.

Nelson, Walter Henry. *The Berliners, Their Saga and Their City.* New York: David McKay, 1966.

Rabinbach, Anson, and Jack D. Zipes, eds. *Germans and Jews Since the Holocaust: The Changing Situation in West Germany.* New York: Holmes &; Meier, 1986.

Rothschild, Joseph, *East Central Europe between the Two World Wars, Seattle and London,* University of Washington Press, 1974.

Roy, James Charles, *The Vanished Kingdom: Travels Through the History of Prussia,* Boulder, Colorado, Westview Press, 1999.

Ryan, Cornelius. *The Last Battle.* New York: Simon & Schuster, 1966.

Schalk, Adolph. *The Germans.* Englewood Cliffs, N.J.: Prentice Hall, 1971.

Serotta Edward *Jews Germany Memory, A Contemporary Portrait,* Berkubm Nicolai. (Central Europe Center, for Research and Documentation., 1996.

Shirer, William L. *The Rise and Fall of the Third Reich.* New York: Fawcett Crest, 1959.

Shlaes, Amity. *Germany, the Empire Within.* New York: Farrar, Straus & Giroux, 1991.

Sichrovsky, Peter. *Strangers in Their Own Land: Young Jews in Germany and Austria Today.* New York: Basic Books, 1986.

Smyser, W.R., *From Yalta to Berlin: The Cold War Struggle Over Germany,* New York, St. Martin's, 2000.

Weinberg, Gerhard, *A World At Arms: A Global History of World War II,* New York, Cambridge University Press, 1994.

Young, James E. *The Texture of Memory: Holocaust Memorials and Meaning in Europe, Israel, and America.* New Haven and London: Yale University Press, 1993.

Zweig, Stefan. *The World of Yesterday: An Autobiography.* New York: Viking, 1943.

Greece
Grandeur at
the Jewish Museum

Nikos Stavroulakis, founder and former director of Athens' Jewish Museum, sits back and reflectively says, "You know, there always have been Greek-Jewish tensions since the days of the Maccabees. The Greeks have always felt and maintained a strong identity about themselves."

Nikos is right. There was a clash 2,000 years ago between Jewish and Greek culture. Often, Greek merchants envied their Jewish rivals and sought to restrict their progress. Today tension is not felt in the ancient city of Athens, whose majestic Acropolis looks down on you. Jews still live here. They go to the synagogue and they visit the community center. They come and go as they please to Israel. And above all, they keep Judaism alive.

The Jewish traveler can experience Greek Judaism in Athens. He or she will find Athens to be friendly, warm, and quiet—almost like a little peaceful village—despite the rush-hour traffic around Constitution Square and the congestion in the city. The past permeates the air as tourists descend by the millions on this capital.

Athens prides itself on being located at the crossroads of Europe, the Middle East, and Africa. About four million people live in the Athens area, out of a total population of nearly 10 million. This city contains an old Jewish community that originated probably in the first century, before the common era. It is small, but united. About 10 to 15 bar mitzvahs and 17 weddings occur each year. Of course, the death knell of the

Salonika

GREECE

ATHENS

Jewish community in days to come could be the low birthrate. Unfortunately, there are more funerals than births.

This is a wonderful Jewish community: appealing, warm, welcoming. Greek Jewry has a high rate of intermarriage due to the isolation of young Jews in small communities. But because there is no civil marriage in Greece, the intermarriage rate is probably less than in other countries..

In the first century B.C., when the apostle Paul traveled through Greece, active Jewish communities existed in Corinth, Thessaloniki (the ancient name of Salonika), and Patras, as well as on the islands of Rhodes, Somos, and Delos. The original Greek Jews were called Romaniots. Influenced by Greek culture and language, their family names were Greek and their synagogues were known by their Greek names.

Under the Christian rulers of the Byzantine Empire, Jewish rights became limited when Jews were expected to convert to Christianity. Crusaders on their way to the Holy Land would kill Jews living in Greece.

As Christianity spread, substantial legal and economic restrictions were placed on Jews, but they continued to exist. They developed their own variant of Jewish rituals and customs, which came to be known as the Romaniot rite.

Benjamin of Tudela found large numbers of Jews in Greece in 1170 when he toured Jewish communities. He found them in Corfu, Patras, Thebes, Salonika, and other cities, including the Greek islands. They worked in dyeing, weaving, and the making of silk garments. Jews were well off, he reported.

The Turkish conquest in the fifteenth century (Athens was conquered in 1456) ushered in a "Golden Age" for Greek Jewry when the Sephardic migration from Spain and Turkey overwhelmed and absorbed the older Byzantine Jewish communities. The newcomers revived the Sephardic way of life, including the Ladino language.

When Jews were expelled from Iberia, many Spanish and Portuguese Jews settled in Salonika, so much so that by 1553, 20,000 Jews lived there.

The sultan, Bayazid II, had welcomed tens of thousands of Iberian Jews to Istanbul in Turkey and to Salonika, now in Greece but then ruled by the Ottoman Turks, who were to remain in Greece until 1822.

In the sixteenth century, prominent rabbis lived in Salonika. One was Sh'lomo Alqabetz, who wrote the stirring, romantic Shabbat Hebrew song, "L'cha Dodi."

In the seventeenth century "Jewish" Salonika radiated power as the center of rabbinic and Kabbalistic studies and the seat of leading halachic authorities.

Meanwhile, between 1453 and 1821, Greece as a nation-state vanished from history. And it was in 1821-22 that Jews obtained equal and legal rights, even though many Jews lost their lives for backing the Turks.

By 1920 Greek Jews were organized into 24 religious communities with stable institutions and numerous activities. Salonika itself boasted 40 synagogues, which were named after once-famous Jewish communities in Spain. Two newspapers were published in Ladino. After population exchanges between Greece and Turkey in 1923, and the arrival of 100,000 Greeks from Anatolia, the Jewish communities declined somewhat. In 1940, there were 77,000 Jews in Greece. At war's end, only about 10,000 to 15,000 Jews survived the Holocaust. Between 1945 and 1955, 3,500 Greek Jews, mostly Sephardim, settled in Israel, and about 1,200 journeyed to the United States. After the war, Greece promulgated a law that makes racism and anti-Semitism criminal acts. Still, it was one of the few European countries to vote against the 1947 U.N. Partition Plan creating a Jewish state.

Greeks themselves, it appears, are "not indisposed" to the Jews, wrote Arnold Sherman in the *Jerusalem Post*, April 6, 1990, though anti-Israel propaganda at times appears in the press and on television. There are monuments and memorials dedicated to the Jewish victims of Nazism throughout the country that were paid for by municipal or private, non-Jewish funds. Sherman said while Andreas Papandreou inveighed against Israel, more Greek business persons made deals with Israel than ever before. Prime Minister Constantine Mitsotakis changed the policy finally, it appears, with full diplomatic relations between Greece and Israel, in 1990.

If tensions could be kept at bay with the former Yugoslavia, Turkey, and the Republic of Macedonia, Greece could move toward a bright future.

JEWISH SITES IN ATHENS

Beth Shalom Synagogue, 5 Odos Melidoni, Athens. Tel: 325-2773. An attractive white building, with ample seating.

Jewish Community Center, Vissarionos Street and Sina Street. Athens. Activities abound at the Jewish youth and community center: lectures, a seder, Purim, holiday celebrations, Israel Independence Day, Tu B'Shvat. Tel: 36-37-092.

Jewish Community Headquarters and Center, 8 Odos Melidoni, Athens. Tel: 325-2823. Almost the whole Jewish community turns out for high holiday services. Jews in Athens are merchants and industrialists in the textile, garment, and jewelry industries. The members here can tell the traveler about organizations such as WIZO; the Zionist Federation, which organizes summer trips to Israel for teenagers and young adults; and the Pan-Hellenic Jewish Youth movement. A most successful project is the Athens Youth Club. Also at 8 Odos Melidoni is the **Romaniot Synagogue,** which is open primarily on high holidays.

Jewish Youth Square. This area commemorates Jewish youth who perished in the Holocaust. Pafous Square in the Patissia area.

The **Jewish Museum**, 39 Nikis st., Athens. Tel: 322-5882. FAX: 323-1577. E-mail: jmg@otenet.gr and Website: www.jewishmuseum.gr. Open Monday through Friday, 9 A.M. until 2:30 P.M., Saturday and Sunday, 10 A.M. until 2 P.M. Perhaps the history of Greek Jewry haunted the community. Perhaps it plagued the artist, educator, historian and former founder-director, Nikos Stavroulakis so much that he almost single-handedly created one of the finest Jewish museums in Europe. If you are nearby, it is worth a special visit to Greece to see this wonderful museum. The current curator is Zanet Batinou. Nikos created the old museum on Amalias Street. But the new facility on Nikis Street was created through the efforts of curator Zanet Batinou and Sam Benroubi, president of the Board of Directors. The design used here is based on a concept of Nikos: spaces rise spiraling around a central void.

The Jewish Museum is located smack in the heart of Athens, convenient to the city's major hotels. It is a good

Synagogue of Corfu. (Photo by Timothy DeVinney, courtesy of the Jewish Museum of Greece)

The Romaniot Synagogue of Athens. (Photo by Timothy DeVinney, courtesy of the Jewish Museum of Greece)

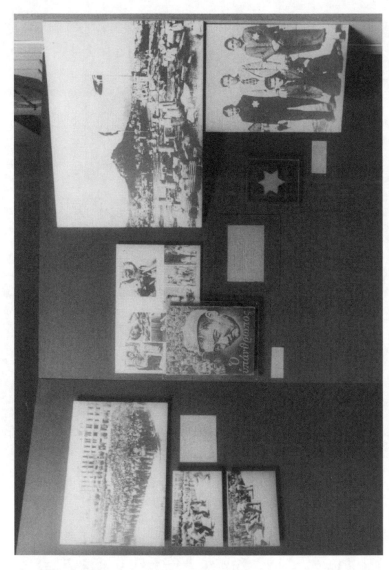

The Holocaust Exhibit in the Jewish Museum of Greece. (Photo by Timothy DeVinney, copyright © Jewish Museum of Greece. All rights reserved.)

place to begin a visit to the Jewish community of Greece. With much to see and study, it is not unusual to spend a good half-day here. Nikos began his museum project by collecting "war leftovers." He obtained 15 cloth bags from the Bulgarian government. The sacks contained 2,800 items that had been confiscated from Greek Jews during the war. Included were watches, rings, and amulets. You can now look at them in this museum: silver from Rhodes, furniture from the Patras Synagogue, and gravestones from Hania in Crete.

He saved and collected and recorded, and today we benefit from his work. Ancient Hebrew books have been preserved.

The Holocaust is remembered and portrayed in the museum. Nearly all of Greek Jewry perished in it, about 80 percent, one of the highest in the Holocaust, according to historian Leni Yahil. The Nazis killed more Jews in Greece proportionately than in any other country except Poland. During the war, almost all of the synagogues had been destroyed or severely damaged.

A U.S. Embassy report once singled out the Greeks as one of the few European peoples who not only helped its Jews, but sheltered them at the risk of being killed if they were discovered.

The Jewish Museum houses the culture of Greek Jewry that was part of the birth and rebirth of Greece. Fittingly, when you walk out of the renovated historic building that now houses the museum, head for nearby busy and noisy Amalias Ave. There you will observe the ancient monument *Pillars of Zeus* across the street.

Those interested in helping or finding out more information about the museum can contact American Friends of the Greek Jewish Museum, P.O. Box 2010, New York, NY 10185. Or, write to the museum directly in Athens.

ORGANIZATIONS

B'nai B'rith, 15 Paparigopoulou, Athens.

The Central Board of Jewish Communities in Greece, 36 Voulis St., Athens. Tel: 324-4315-8. FAX: 331-3852. E-mail: hhkis@hellasnet.gr. The umbrella organization for all Greek

Jewry. Athens, thus, is the home to the Central Board of Jewish Communities in Greece—the governing body of the 6,000-member Greek Jewish community. The council is composed of representatives of the Jewish communities in Athens and other areas of Greece. More than two-thirds of Greek Jewry reside in Athens. **Jewish National Fund,** 2 Nikis St., Athens.

Thessaloniki (Salonika)

An Oriental air hovers over Salonika, Greece's second city, located on the Aegean Sea. It is a gateway to the Balkans, and right on the road between Athens and Istanbul. Thessaloniki is named for the sister of Alexander the Great. It is a short drive from Pella where excavations have revealed Alexander's capital city of Macedonia and from Veria, another city where Jews flourished. Alexander's brother-in-law, Kassandros, who built Thessaloniki, apparently asked the king of Egypt to send him Jewish artisans. This is supposed to have marked the start of the Jewish community of Thessaloniki (Salonika). By the end of the fifteenth century, Salonika became a melting pot for European Jewish communities. Each brought their own exotic sounding names to the city. Calabria, Majorca, and Lisbon were among its thirty separate Jewish communities. Eventually, all the groups embraced Ladino. Also settling here was a large group of Marranos from Portugal.

In the sixteenth and seventeenth centuries, the city of Salonika, then part of Turkey, became a great center of Sephardic Jewry. "Salonika in 17th century terms was as Jewish a city as is New York in the 21st century," says Barnet Litvinoff. This Greek metropolis was known throughout the world for its famous rabbinical scholars and seminaries, Hebrew printing presses, and Jewish libraries. Actually, until the mid-twentieth century, Salonika was "a Jewish city." Shabbetai Zevi, the false messiah born in Smyrna, tried to make Salonika his base of operations. But in 1657, he was expelled from the city.

By the end of the nineteenth century, 80,000 of Salonika's 120,000 citizens were Jews who spoke Ladino. In 1900, 90,000 Jews made up more than half of the city's population. The community supported hospitals, orphanages, schools, daily newspapers, and rabbinical seminaries where Hebrew, Ladino, and French were spoken. Despite hardships, it remained a center of Jewish learning and culture.

In 1912, Greece conquered Turkish-held Salonika and proceeded to Hellenize the city by settling Greeks within it. According to Israel Cohen, a fire in 1917 leveled the Jewish quarter, destroying 20,000 homes, 30 synagogues, 8 schools, and residential and commercial buildings. Nearly two thousand years of history went up in smoke.

While many people emigrated to the then Palestine, the most interesting group who picked themselves up and went to the Land of Israel seems to have been Greek fishermen, relates Cohen. As far as we know, they were the only organized body of Jewish fishermen in the world, descendants of the exiles from medieval Spain. They continued their family occupation and established their own synagogue. For centuries they had been the only fishermen in Salonika. But their monopoly was brought to an end with the Greeks taking over. Some 16 families were transported with all their boats and fishing tackle to a stretch between Atlit and Acre in Palestine.

There are no words to describe the brutal death of Salonika Jewry during World War II. We know 56,000 Jews lived there before the Nazis invaded, with about 85 percent being deported to the death camps, according to Israel Cohen.

Simon Wiesenthal estimates that it took 11 or 12 days to transfer these wonderful, stoic, hardworking Jews from Salonika to Auschwitz, where about 60,000 out of 77,000 Greek Jews were murdered. Of that group, 46,000 were from Salonika.

About 13,000 Jews fought for the Greek army when Germany and Italy attacked.

Today, approximately 1,200 Jews live in Thessaloniki (Salonika), out of a total population of about 6,000 in Greece.

Jewish Thessaloniki (Salonika)

Monastirioton Synagogue, 35 Sygrou st., Thessaloniki. Tel: 031-524-968.

Yad Lezikaron Synagogue, Vassileos Irakleiou st. 26, Thessaloniki. Tel: (031) 223-231.

The Center for Historical Studies, Vassileos Irakleiou st., 26, Thessaloniki. Tel: (031) 223-231.

"Simon Marks" Museum of the History of the Jews of Thessaloniki, Vassileous Irakleiou st., Thessaloniki. Tel: (031) 273-767.

The Jewish Community of Thessaloniki, Tsimiski st., 24,Thessaloniki. Tel: (031) 275-701. FAX: (031) 229-063. E-mail: jct1@compulink.gr. This center is open Monday through Friday, from 9 A.M. to 3 P.M.

Museum of Jewish Presence in Thessaloniki, Agiou Mina st. 13, Thessaloniki. Tel: (031) 250-406 and 250-407. This museum is open from Sunday through Friday, from 9 A.M. to 5 P.M.

Jewish Primary School, "Talmud Torah Hagadot," Fleming st. 7, Thessaloniki. Tel: (031) 830-347 and 837-177.

Cemetery and Memorial to Holocaust Victims. Located in the suburb of Stavroupolis, opposite the "AGNO" Factory. Tel: (031) 655-855.

Square of the Jewish Martyrs. Located between Papanastasiou st. and Priamou st. Thessaloniki. This is a new monument for the Holocaust victims of Thessaloniki. It was created by the late Nandor Glid.

Sources, Guides, and Tours

Website: www.yvelia.com. This is the site where Greek and Jewish culture meet.

Website: www.yvelia.com/kolhakehila. Also, E-mail: kolhake-hila@yvelia.com. Kol haKEHILA is a newsletter and Website on the Jewish heritage of Greece. This site contains information, articles, photographs and genealogy on the Jews of Greece and the Jewish monuments of Greece. The site was created and is operated by Elias Messinas, a Greek-Israeli architect who has studied, surveyed and is involved in the restoration and preservation of the synagogues of Greece.

Jewish Heritage Tours to Greece. The above Website and newsletter indicates tours to Greece in the spring and summer. The cities and towns visited during the tour combine the diverse Jewish cultures of Greek Sephardim and Romaniots (Ioannina and Thessaloniki). The group also visits historic sites of Greek antiquity (Delphi) and the Middle Ages (Meteora). The group will see synagogues and monasteries, ancient temples and theaters, mountains and cities, Jewish quarters (Veroia), as well as ancient mystical sites. Tours include tasting exquisite Greek cuisine and pastries. Sing and dance to the rhythms of Greek music and meet local Greeks and Jews. The KEHILA Jewish Heritage Tours to Greece are organized and guided by experts in the field of Greek Jewish history and architecture and experts in Greek tourism. Accommodations include first and second class hotels and travel by air-conditioned luxury coaches. For more details: www.yvelia.com/greece-tour; E-mail: kolhakehila@yvelia.com. FAX: 972 (2) 563-6690.

Suggested Reading

Brinn, Herb. *Ich Bin Ein Jude*. Middle Village, N.Y.: Jonathan David, 1983.

Cohen, Israel. *Contemporary Jewry*. London: Methuen, 1950.

—. *The Journal of a Jewish Traveler*. New York: Dodd, Mead, 1925.

Elazar, Daniel J., and Harriet P. Friedenreich. *The Balkan Jewish Communities: Yugoslavia, Bulgaria, Greece, and Turkey*. Lanham, N.Y: University Press of America, 1984.

Keeley, Edmund, *Inventing Paradise: The Greek Journey, 1937-1947*, Farrar, Straus and Giroux, New York, 1999.

Messinas, Elias, *"The Synagogues of Salonika and Veroia,"* Athens, Gavielides Editions, 1997.

Patai, Raphael. *The Vanished Worlds of Jewry*. New York: Macmillan.

Turkey
Jewish History from
Constantinople to Istanbul

Turkey awaits you. This gateway to both Europe and Asia is one of the hottest travel destinations, especially for Americans and Israelis. But that alone of course is not the main reason for visiting Turkey.

Turkey, about the size of Texas, shares a border with seven countries that circle this nation of about 65 million. Massive movement of millions of people from country areas to the city has jumped Istanbul's population from about 500,000 in 1920 to about 10 million in 1993. Istanbul, the largest metropolis in the nation, is followed by Ankara, the capital, and Izmir, the third largest city, has seen the outlying villages merge into sprawling suburbs housing hundreds of thousands of residents.

A Brief History

Benjamin of Tudela, who visited Jewish communities in the mid-twelfth century, said of Istanbul (called Constantinople until 1930): "It is a bustling city, with business coming to her from all foreign lands on land and on sea. There is no other city like her except Baghdad. There are the Church of Sophia, and the Pope of the Greeks... and as many churches as there are days in the year, and in them, incalculable wealth... more than in all the churches of the rest of the world [together].

And there is a Hippodrome where the king organizes great games on the birthday of Jesus of Nazareth, and in that place are drawn pictures of all kinds of men in the world before the king and queen with all types of sorcery."

That was eight centuries ago and once upon a time, Istanbul was one of the most important Jewish centers of the world, replete with Jewish schools and scholars. It was even called the Jewish "mother city." Although Jews lived here in Byzantine times, it was not until the Ottoman conquest in 1453 that Muhammad II welcomed Jews. He wanted them to develop business and trade and help Turkey's growth.

Granted asylum after they fled Spain, the Jews who came to Turkey were treated extremely well, especially under Suleiman the Magnificent. They called him "King Solomon," not only because of his name, but also because of his wisdom and legislative programs. During his rule, the Jews of the Ottoman Empire made great cultural and economic strides. Jewish intellectual life rose to new heights. They devoted themselves to secular science, physics, astronomy, math, and medicine.

By the sixteenth century, Istanbul, with 40,000 Jews, had the largest Jewish population in the world. The Jews became a protected minority, although sometimes subject to discriminatory legislation that included dress, taxes, and housing. During this time, the Turkish Jewish community was the home of some wonderful personalities, such as Gracia Nasi and Joseph Nasi.

Gracia Nasi (1510-69) was a Portuguese Marrano who openly returned to Judaism. As a stateswoman and patron, she helped Marranos flee Portugal. In 1537, after her husband's death, she left Portugal and went to Istanbul, where she was joined by Joseph Nasi. Nasi, a Portuguese Marrano, married her only child, Reyna.

When Nasi arrived in Istanbul in 1543, she brought with her large amounts of capital. In addition to her banking and economic activities, she founded yeshivot (religious schools) and synagogues and continued her efforts on behalf of persecuted Marranos and Jews.

Meanwhile Joseph Nasi (1524-79), who became one of the most influential figures in the Ottoman Empire, had been named duke of the island of Naxos and surrounding isles.

Gracia Nasi had obtained a grant to set up a yeshiva in the ruined city of Tiberias, Israel. In 1561, Joseph Nasi extended the grant and began the rebuilding of the ruined walls of Tiberias. This whole enterprise turned out to be one of the practical attempts to establish a Jewish political center in Palestine between the fourth and nineteenth centuries.

In Turkey, too, Joseph Karo (1488-1575) wrote the "Shulhan Arukh," the code of Jewish law. Indeed, Turkey became a great center for the study of Kabbala and was the birthplace of a number of prophetic and messianic movements. Here grew the legend of Shabbetai Zevi. Actually, we cannot visit Turkish Jewry without recalling Shabbetai Zevi, the Kabbalistic mystic who attracted thousands to his following. (See Achrida Synagogue below.)

The visitor to Turkey will also learn about the Karaites and the Dönmeh.

During the eighteenth and nineteenth centuries, Jews began moving westward from Turkey as world trade was shifting from the Mediterranean to the Atlantic coast of Europe. Seeking greater opportunity, Jews now would relocate to Holland, England, and the states along the Danube River.

At the turn of the twentieth century, about 100,000 Jews lived in Turkey. Before World War I, Theodor Herzl approached Constantinople leaders, but could not persuade them to grant a national home to the Jewish people in Palestine. During the reign of the Sultan Abdul Hamid II (1876-1909) the attitude of the Sublime Porte toward Jews was positive. Jews were involved in the economic and political life of the empire. In 1908, the Young Turks overthrew the sultan and Jews actively participated in the Young Turk movement. During World War I, in which the Turks sided with the Germans, the Jews of Istanbul prospered greatly. But after the war, Jews suffered anti-Semitism in former Turkish lands taken over by the Greeks.

Between the wars, Turkey was not fundamentally hostile to Jews; it was anti-foreign and anti-traditional. In 1927, about 82,000 Jews lived in Turkey—46,000 in Istanbul, over 16,000 in Izmir, 5,700 in Edirne, and the rest in 14 other communities. During World War II, however, Turkey was neutral. Many refugees from Nazism found their way here and continued on to

Palestine. After the 1948 Israel Declaration of Independence, Jews began to leave Turkey. Nehemiah Robinson wrote that between 1948 and 1956, about 43,000 Jews emigrated from Turkey. Approximately 22,000 Jews reside in Turkey.

Today, Israel and Turkey have a strong military alliance, an alliance which brings to it the power of the U.S. This group of three is often called the "Phantom Alliance," as William Safire aptly labeled it in his column in *The New York Times*. That alliance has affected the strategic map of the volatile Near and Middle East. For now, at least, Turkey, too, sees its adversaries as Syria, Iraq and Iran.

The volume of civilian trade between Israel and Turkey has reached an annual level of $800 million, double the amount in 1996, wrote Jeremy L. Hirsh in the *Jewish Exponent* of Philadelphia, April 22, 1999.Tourism between the two countries reportedly accounts for an additional $400 million per year in commercial exchange.

Turkish and Israeli pilots now reportedly train in each other's airspace. The Gulf War, the struggle with Greece over Cyprus, the war in Yugoslavia, makes Turkey a major player in the region. During the crisis in Kosovo, Turkey, as NATO's only Muslim member, became a strong American ally. Turkey plays a critical role in protecting American security interests in the region. Linked to the Balkans by 500 years of Ottoman rule, Turkey's planes were involved in air strikes against Yugoslavia.

While the country is more prosperous and complex than ever as author Robert D. Kaplan notes, Turkish governments remain somewhat unstable and the army is always in the background. At century's end, it is hoped that this nation's over-active political scene might be stabilized. Already, according to Kaplan, Turks are "less paranoid and certainly less xenophobic, less vocal, less blaming, perhaps more fatalistic." Still, the government seems to take a hard line against the Kurdish movement which they say threatens national unity and Turkey continues to oppose compromise with Greece over Cyprus, another thorn in the eastern Mediterranean. The Turkish Republic's human rights record also has been criticized.

The country, after all, is a relatively poor Moslem nation of 65 million. Still, the European Union has offered to accept

Turkey as a future member. But Turkey will have to execute some democratic reforms to assure their full integration into the democratic west. One positive aspect of Turkey's situation has changed somewhat at the turn of the millennium and that is that tensions between Greece and Turkey have subsided.

Undoubtedly some anti-Semitism exists. An added encumbrance for Jewish organizations is that they have to go it alone. Turkish law forbids Turkish citizens to have any formal links or even contact with foreign countries or international organizations. This policy applies to all groups.

Many Jews live in suburbs, such as Beyoglu, Sisli, Ortakoy, Kuzguncuk, Kadikoy, Sirkeci, Galata, Tunel, Taksim, Nisantas, Macka, and others. There are large summer communities on three of the islands off of the Bosporus in the Sea of Marmara. The largest communities are located in Buyukada and Heybeli Ada.

JEWISH SITES IN ISTANBUL

This entrepot, this strategic city, this often mysterious, bustling, metropolis enveloped by mighty dome-covered mosques, this city whose thin needle-like minarets puncture the sky, this gray yet golden confluence of great waters—this Bosphorus, this Golden Horn, this Sea of Marmara, it's all here in Istanbul, the city that attracts thousands who arrive here by land, sea and air. I had heard that tourism from Israel to Turkey was at an all-time high. I also knew that the Turks were great salespersons and that Israelis love to shop. But what really convinced me that travel from Israel to Turkey must be setting records occurred when the Turkish street hawkers, with leather jackets slung over outstretched arms, greeted the tour buses picking up passengers at various Istanbul hotels.

"Esrim dollar," ($20). would bark these very mobile merchants in Hebrew.

Hebrew on the streets of Istanbul?

Actually this should not shock Jewish travelers. This is not the first time that Jews and Israelis came to this "land-and-water city" in large numbers as newcomers and tourists.

Five hundred years ago, the Sultan of the then Ottoman Empire opened this country's borders to Jews fleeing the wrath of the Spanish King and Queen Ferdinand and Isabella who in 1492 expelled their Jewish citizens. Not only did Sultan Beyazid welcome Jews to Constantinople, but he had a chosen barb for the Spanish royal family.

"You call Fernando of Spain a wise king—he who has impoverished his country and enriched ours," exclaimed the Sultan who granted Jews immediate asylum to his kingdom.

Although Jews had lived here in Byzantine times, it had not been until the Ottoman conquest in 1453 that Jews were welcome. The Ottomans wanted these Sephardic Jews from Spain and other lands to help the economy especially in perfecting the use of gunpowder.

This city by the Bosphorus remains one of the world's few cities that have a romantic appeal. With the charm of the East reflecting the smells and sights of Istanbul before you, the past projects immediately to the forefront of your thoughts.

Tourists soon realize that from any point of view: history, culture, recreation, lodging, shopping, entertainment, food, this land awakens your senses. Yes, even if it is a few days, you can manage to see the principal attractions, the Hagia Sophia Museum, the Suleymaniye Mosque which is the largest and most grandiose in the city. Then there is the Blue Mosque, the Hippodrome and the Topkapi Palace, (yes, the diamond is still there!). Drive to the Egyptian or spice market and the Covered Bazaar with its 4,000 shops nestled on 50 acres. Both here and in the Egyptian Bazaar you can purchase spices, dried fruits, tea, and of course baklava and taffee. And in the Grand Bazaar, you will find Turkish specialties, rugs, leather and suede goods, golden jewelry with precious stones as well as traditionally shaped pieces in silver. Add pottery and ceramics and the shopping is complete. Restaurants and food shops serve up mouth-watering kebab and shwama. And if its belly dancing you want, you've come to the right country.

Walk slowly around Taksim Square and peek into the stalls selling bazaar type items, including jewelry, books, posters, postcards. I recalled the words of that great French writer, Pierre Loti who once described the then Constantinople:

"The only town in the world, where I have really taken part in the life of the people, the life of this Oriental people noisy, full of color, picturesque but needy and poor, a life busy with a thousand little trades, a thousand chaffererings..."

The so-called "murmur of Constantinople" can be heard in Istiklal Caddesi, the pedestrian street with just an old trolley clinging its bell and moving up and down the street with the flow of the crowd, men, women, children and their pets. Restaurants, fast food spots, shops, art galleries, are at hand.

Of course, don't forget to visit the Dolmabache Palace on the Bosphorus which the travel books tell you is the "richest palace in the world." Your guide should ask you to stand in the magnificent hall of the Dolmabache Palace. Here in this grandeur, the Sultan welcomed visitors to the Sublime Porte as it was called. You will compare it with the Hall of Mirrors in Versailles. Each person decides which is more impressive, the Dolmabache Palace grand room or the mirrored grand hall at Versailles?

I took several boat rides along the Bosphorus, a major strategic waterway. I sailed past the luxury summer homes. The deep Bosphorus links the Black Sea with its dark Russian storms to the Sea of Marmara, to the Dardenelles and then out to the Aegean and the Mediterranean. So much conflict, so much tension, the spot where the roaring Russian bear from the north who has been land locked, shuffles back and forth always trying to break out of her imprisonment. This is the same Russian bear that has always sought a passage through the Dardenelles for her navy. Did not Churchill once describe Russia as "a giant with his nostrils pinched by the narrow exits from the Baltic and the Black Sea."

This bottleneck has certainly been a trouble spot and caused many disputes and even a reason to go to war. "Although the status of the Turkish Straits has been regulated since 1936 by the Montreux Convention, the question of free passage is still topical," says author Nicole Pope.

Throughout World War II, Turkey played a such a masterly game of hide-and-seek that they called "active neutrality, the Germans on one side, the Allies on the other. The Turks in World War II suspected that the Russians had designs not only on Turkey and the Straits but on the Balkans, too, according to Pope.

Now the area is peaceful. Or is it? At the outbreak of the war in Kosova, Russia sent a reconnaissance freighter through the straits, but of course, had to obtain permission from the Turks who granted it.

With all this history surrounding the area, I was interested in having lunch in a café or fish restaurant, overlooking the only sea passage out of the Black Sea where I could watch a fascinating flotilla of freighters, fishing boats, oil tankers, barges, cruise liners—some coming from Russia to the thriving Mediterranean ports of Athens, Haifa, Cairo, Naples, Barcelona, Marseilles and beyond: some going to the former Soviet Union to the famous and attractive port of Odessa. It was indeed a pleasant, and now, peaceful, relaxing sight.

And now let us visit specific Jewish sites and those associated with Jewish History.

Headquarters of Chief Rabbi David Asseo, Yemenici Sokak 23, Beyoglu District. Tel: 144-0472 or 144-5327. This is the headquarters of the Turkish Jewish community and tourists and visitors would do well to stop off here for information on the Jewish community. His staff is friendly and will help tourists.

As you walk to the office, you are apt to recall that as recently as World War II, Turkey contained one of the most creative and distinguished Sephardic communities in the Diaspora. This may be Turkey, but 500 years after their arrival from Iberia, Jews still speak Spanish here. Once Arabic, Armenian, Greek, French, Italian, and yes, even Ladino, was spoken here. Ladino, an archaic form of Spanish, absorbed a considerable vocabulary from the local language, primarily Turkish and Greek, as well as a Hebraic and Talmudic component. This Judeo-Spanish was commonly used in Turkey and some of the Balkan countries ruled by Turkey, according to Bernard Lewis. Under the Ottomans Jews did not normally speak Turkish-only Ladino, which remains the language of the older generation. Ladino still is spoken and read here, as witnessed by the Jewish weekly, *Salom.* That newspaper contains seven pages in Turkish and one in Ladino and is helping keep alive the language of the Sephardim that younger Jews here are increasingly unable to speak. Young people now speak Turkish as their first language. Today, Jews are trying to keep Ladino alive here in Turkey.

Here at the chief rabbi's headquarters, I met the Jewish poet and artist Joseph Habib Gerez, a leader of the Jewish community. He writes in Turkish and describes the glories of Istanbul. He is a man who has traveled the world yet still loves his city, which commands a central position in maritime communications between the Black Sea and the Mediterranean and where you see Russian freighters and cruise ships sailing down the Bosporus. His paintings reflect Jewish life in Istanbul.

The suburb of Galata. Even today, Jews live in Pera and Galata, which is on the heights above the Golden Horn. In Byzantine days, it was a colony of European merchants. The hills north of Galata were favorite places for foreign envoys. The Europeans called that area Pera, from a Greek word meaning "beyond" or "across," i.e., across the Golden Horn from Old Istanbul or beyond the Galata Tower. Many Jews moved to these popular new neighborhoods; at the end of the nineteenth century, half of Istanbul Jewry was living in the Galata and Pera sections. However, the Jews in each quarter maintained their own communal institutions, rabbinical courts, schools, budgets, and councils. According to Hilary Sumner-Boyd and John Freely, the area in front of the Galata Bridge was once a Jewish quarter inhabited by Karaites, a sect that denies Talmudic rabbinical tradition. The Karaites broke off from the main body of Orthodox Jewry in the eighth century.

The Topkapi Palace. The Palace of the Sultans "is the most extensive and fascinating monument of Ottoman civil architecture in existence," according to Sumner-Boyd and Freely. Many Jewish women occupied the palace harem. When you tour the palace and see the harem, remember Esther Kyra. She was a Jewish broker, only she did not deal in stocks and bonds. Her exchange was the royal harem. She had free access to it, where she sold jewels, cosmetics, and rich fabrics and generally made herself indispensable to the ladies. She won the favor of Sultan Murad III's mother, Nur Banu, and of his preferred concubine, the Venetian, Safya Baffo, both of whom had enormous influence. Through them, Esther, in turn, exercised considerable influence in imperial appointments and became involved in political affairs. Her power and wealth spawned jealousy and she was murdered. In 1593, her fortune was confiscated.

The Jewish women in the palace bribed the eunuchs who kept the doors, ruled over the women, and bought and sold for them. The Jewish women became rich. Bernard Lewis tells us that when Sultan Murad III learned that Sephardi girls were wearing choice garments and ornaments with precious stones, he issued a decree to exterminate all Jews throughout all the provinces of his empire. Through the influence of the sultan's mother, the decree was revoked, but an order was given that Jews must wear, in place of the yellow turban, a strange tall hat, pointed above and wide below, like those of the Spaniards.

SYNAGOGUES IN ISTANBUL

There are about 15 synagogues, a Jewish school, a hospital, and a home for the elderly here in Istanbul.

Achrida Synagogue, Kurtci Cesmi Sokak 15, Balat section. In 1992, in honor of the 500th anniversary of the Iberian Jews' arrival here, the Achrida Synagogue was restored. Many festivities, concerts, the opening of a new Jewish Museum, and major ceremonies highlighted the 1992 celebration of 500 years of Jewish history in Turkey. Built in 1412, it existed when the city was in Byzantine hands. Shabbetai Zevi preached here. Born in Smyrna, July 1626, his birthday occurred on the Ninth of Av, the day in which the First and Second Temples had been destroyed. At age 18, he was honored by the rabbis of his town.

According to Barnet Litvinoff, he was the son of a merchant who traded with England. While bathing in the waters of the Aegean Sea, the idea dawned on him that he was the Messiah, the one appointed by God to save the Jews and lead them back to the Holy Land. Late in 1648, during the synagogue service, he stood at the Holy Ark and pronounced the full name of God, an act that only the priest had the right to perform. He proclaimed himself as the Messiah.

Shabbetai Zevi met Raphael Joseph Chelebi in Cairo, who was known as the "prince of the Jews of Egypt and head of that country's treasury." In Gaza, Nathan Benjamin Levi helped Shabbetai, who sojourned for a while in the Holy Land and attracted followers. In 1665, he returned to an ecstatic reception in Smyrna. There he prophesied the impending defeat and abdication of the sultan. The Jews would usurp his empire, said Shabbetai Zevi, reestablishing the Lord's rule in Jerusalem. He, Shabbetai Zevi, would be the king of kings. The Sultan naturally had to get rid of Shabbetai Zevi—either convert him to Islam or put him to death. To save his skin, Shabbetai converted to Islam. So, he was appointed as chamberlain in the royal palace and received a salary. Later he was banished to a small town in Albania, where he died in 1676. His conversion was a severe blow to world Jewry—a betrayal, demoralizing a great part of the Sephardic world.

Ashkenazi Synagogue, Yuksek Kaldirim 37.

Italian Synagogue, Okcu Musa Caddesi 29.

Neve Shalom Synagogue, Buyuk Hendek Caddesi 67. On September 12, 1986, more than 20 people were killed in a terrorist attack on the Neve Shalom Synagogue. The incident shattered the peaceful existence of 500 years, but life goes on. Today, one or two policemen stand guard and a strong security check, including television cameras, is maintained in a bulletproof glass enclosure just inside the door. You can still see the clock that on that Sabbath Saturday stopped at 9:17 A.M., the time the terrorists attacked the house of prayer. Near the bimah, you can see the patched-up bullet holes.

The synagogue also serves as a community center.

Neve Shalom, probably the most modern synagogue in Istanbul, is close to the Pera Palas Hotel, the last of the old-school grand hotels on the Galata Hill, the section of Galata where the Jews live. Located very near the American Consulate, this hotel sports "Old World charm."

The Sisli Synagogue, Efe St. 4, Osmanbey. Tel: 140-6599. Near the Galata Tower. This was the quarter overlooking the Golden Horn where the Jews lived. Sisli Synagogue is close to the Hilton Hotel.

Tour Guide: Ms. Nur Tugberk is an excellent and official

tour guide. Her address is Mazharpasa Sk., 17/9 Engin Apt. 80700, Serencebey /Besiktas, Istanbul. Tel: 0-212-259-91-93. Cel: 0-532-417-29-41.

Suggested Reading

Freid, Jacob. *Jews in the Modern World.* New York: Twayne, 1962.

Lewis, Bernard. *The Emergence of Modern Turkey.* London: Oxford University Press, 1961.

—. *Istanbul and the Civilization of the Ottoman Empire.* Norman, Okia.: University of Oklahoma Press, 1972.

—. *Semites and Anti-Semites.* New York: Norton, 1986.

Loti, Pierre *"Constantinople"*, New York, Frederick A. Stokes, Co., Publishers, 1928.

Mann, Vivian B. *A Tale of Two Cities: Jewish Life in Frankfurt and Istanbul,* 1750-1870. New York: The Jewish Museum, 1982.

Malcomson, Scott L. *Borderlands-Nation and Empire,* Boston-London, Faber and Faber, 1994.

Pope, Nicole *"Turkey Unveiled: A History of Modern Turkey."* New York: The Overlook Press, 1998.

Settle, Mary Lee. *Turkish Reflections.* New York: Prentice-Hall, 1991.

Simon, Joseph. *The Itinerary of Benjamin of Tudela, Travels in the Middle Ages.* Malibu, Calif.: Pangloss Press.

Sumner-Boyd, Hilary, and John Freely. *Strolling Through Istanbul: A Guide to the City.* Istanbul: Redhouse, 1972.

Scandinavia
Something for Everyone

"Scandinavia!" exclaimed a Jewish travel agent. "Why, there are only four Jews there."

Not true; probably more than 25,000 is the accurate figure. It may be small in numbers, but Scandinavian Jewry is alive and well and a visit to four capitals—Helsinki, Stockholm, Copenhagen, and Oslo—will show how that old, dire prediction that Jews will disappear here through intermarriage and assimilation still remains somewhat premature. True, extremely high intermarriage ratios exist; some have put it at 80 percent in Denmark, for example. But having said that, there are valiant efforts being made to stem the tide.

Approximately 20,000 Jews reside in Sweden, about 8,000 in Denmark, 1,000 in Norway, and about 1,300 in Finland. Truly, these numbers are miniscule. In fact, as it was once aptly put, there are more Jews in Minnesota than in all of Scandinavia.

And Jews settled in New York City (1654) before their co-religionists moved into Scandinavia.

For the founders of the Scandinavian Jewish community, these vast northern lands, where anti-Semitism rarely rears its ugly head, were not their first choice. They needed a place of refuge. And one of the places they came to was Denmark and its "fun city," Copenhagen, where, as the travel brochures declare, "there is something for everybody." Copenhagen, which has a population of nearly 500,000 in the city proper and 1.7 million in the metro area, features Tivoli, the enchanting park

next to City Hall in the center of town. Festivities during the season last until the end of September.

Jewish Copenhagen

On my "city tour" in Copenhagen, our very vocal guide made his passengers memorize the years of the reign of Christian IV, who did so much for Copenhagen in the way of institutions, fortifications, and palaces. The years 1588 to 1648 were welded into our minds. In fact, we often were instructed to bellow out the dates in hearty unison.

The guide, however, never mentioned that in 1622, Christian IV invited Portuguese Jews from Amsterdam, probably Marranos, to settle in Gluckstadt. Although now in Schleswig-Holstein in North Germany, it was once an area ruled by Denmark.

Most tourists do not, of course, come to Denmark to learn about Christian IV. They come to see the environment immortalized by the Hans Christian Anderson stories and recounted by the late actor-comedian Danny Kaye; to gaze at the Little Mermaid—and she is indeed little—sitting in the harbor; and to inhale and experience Tivoli, the granddaddy of all amusement parks and one of the tourist wonders of Europe.

Denmark is a good land for Jews. Following King Christian IV was King Frederick III (1657-59), who allowed Sephardic Jews to settle in Denmark. Israel David, a goldsmith, and his partner, Meir Goldschmidt, settled in Copenhagen in 1684. Seven merchants and craftsmen followed. They, too, were Marranos, who had obtained permission to leave their country. At first, they all prayed behind closed doors. But soon, not only would the government decree punishment for anyone who harassed those of another religious faith, it also voided its ban on Jewish employment of Christian servants. By 1766, the first synagogue in Copenhagen was erected.

Nearly 2,000 Jews—merchants, craftsmen, and entrepreneurs—lived in Copenhagen in 1782.

In 1834, more than 4,000 Jews inhabited the country. Chief Rabbi Dr. Abraham Alexander Wolff (1801-91) served as rabbi for 62 years and kept the community united. In 1837, Jews were allowed to hold municipal office. Jews achieved full emancipation when Denmark abolished the absolute monarchy in 1849 and adopted a constitution.

Jews administered their own affairs with little or no anti-Semitism holding them back from assimilation into the country's economic and intellectual life. Prominent Jews have included Mendel Levin Nathanson, father of Danish journalism; Georg Brandes, literary critic and historian; Gen. C. I. De Meza, commander of the Danish Army; the late Victor Borge, who often came home to his native Tivoli in Copenhagen to entertain; and Niels Bohr (1885-1962), a Danish physicist and Nobel laureate who also escaped the Nazis by going to Sweden in a fishing boat in 1943. His mother was from a prominent Jewish banking family.

Following the Kishinev pogrom in 1905, several thousand Jews entered Denmark. By the end of World War I, 96.7 percent of the Danish Jewish community lived in Copenhagen. In the 1930s, many Jewish refugees from Germany poured into Denmark, and then went on to Palestine and the United States. The Jews believed that King Christian X would stand by them. As events would prove, they were correct. They remembered that in 1933, Christian X attended services in Copenhagen's synagogue. This was the year when Hitler took over Germany. Denmark and its ruler, however, were one in protecting their Jewish citizens. A "bone" in his throat, was the way Hitler described Jewish freedom in Denmark. Adolf Eichmann himself, the SS officer who put into operation the execution of Europe's Jews, admitted that in Denmark he could not do as he wished. Not only did the Danes resist the ill treatment of Jews; they saved their Jews (as we shall soon see) in one of the most remarkable rescue operations in history, certainly in recent Jewish history.

After the war, between 1966 and 1967, about 2,500 Polish Jews arrived in Denmark. Poland had unleashed another of one of its waves of anti-Semitism; this time aimed at Jewish members of its Communist party. Not all Polish Jews wanted to go to Israel; Denmark was among the few nations to welcome them. On the other hand, in the last two decades alone, 700 to 800 Danish Jews (close to 10 percent) have emigrated to Israel.

Many Jews visiting Copenhagen head for Israelsplads (Israel Square), where they find a large memorial stone from Israel. A ceremony took place here in 1968. During the event, the name of "Gronttorvet" (the Vegetable Market Place) was changed to "Israel Square." And at the same time, the Beth Hakerem Park in Jerusalem was renamed "Kikar Daniah" (Denmark Square). On weekends, Israel Square turns into a flea market.

In October 1943, the Danish people and the resistance movement defied Nazi occupation of their country to rescue their fellow citizens. During a period of 10 nights, almost all of the Danish Jews were carried across the body of water known as Oresund Strait, in fishing boats and other small craft, to safe Sweden. Israel and Jews all over the world will never forget the rescue. If we were editing the Bible in the 1990s, the saving of the Jews from the Nazis in October 1943 would be told in the Scriptures, similar to the Book of Esther. In the latter biblical event, a wicked Haman wanted to kill the Jews, but the Jewish people were spared. Thus, too, were the Jews of Denmark saved. "This modern-day legend will be commemorated for generations to come," writes Aage Bertelsen in his book, *October, 1943*.

Some headline the events of October 1943 a "Jewish Dunkirk." The Danes rescued virtually the entire Jewish community from the Germans and brought it safely to Sweden. The Nazis had planned to deport the Jews on the night of the Jewish New Year, October 1-2, 1943. But at a religious service on September 29, the acting chief rabbi of Denmark, Dr. Marcus Melchior, rushed into the Great Synagogue on Krystalgade street in Copenhagen and warned his congregants to hide. But where could they find shelter? Where could they flee? Where could they find friends? But they managed: they hid in small groups until their turn came to board the small fishing boats to nearby Sweden.

The Danish police had set up a sea escape route and turned a blind eye to the boats leaving the shore. Some Germans even accepted bribes and allowed trucks of refugees to pass, but it has been conjectured that they did this because they knew if they stopped the vehicles, they might incur the wrath of the Danes. About 7900 Jews escaped, including 686 non-Jews who were married to Jews. About 30 were lost at sea or committed suicide.

On the day of the action, the Germans managed to capture 284 Jews and in the next few weeks, 190 Jews were arrested while trying to escape. Thus, 474 were picked up, of which 101 were non-Danish refugees. Fifty-one of the deported persons died in the concentration camp Terezin (Theresienstadt), in the Czech Republic, while the rest returned safely home in 1945.

A shipping expert in the German Embassy tipped off the Jewish community. He was George Ferdinand Duckwitz (1904-73), according to the book *The Rescue of the Danish Jews*. After the war, he served as West Germany's ambassador to Denmark (1955 to 1958).

But not only did the Danes physically help the Jews escape, they never forgot their Jewish brothers and sisters who were arrested by the Nazis and imprisoned in Theresienstadt. Between October 1943 and April 1945, the Danes pressured the Germans to release all those deported and to allow food parcels to get through. These Danes prevented Denmark's Jews from being transferred from Theresienstadt to the death camp at Auschwitz, and those food packages probably saved the Jews from starvation.

Historian Leni Yahil offers five reasons for the success of the sea evacuation: First, the number of Jews was small. Second, Sweden was nearby. Third, conditions in Denmark were different than in other countries in Nazi-occupied Europe. Fourth, the Germans were reeling after their defeats at El Alamein and Stalingrad. The final reason is "the special character and moral stature of the Danish people and their love of democracy and freedom."

Rabbi Bent Melchior also told me in an interview that the organized church in Denmark was very active in helping to save Jews. To the Danes, he asserted, the treatment of its Jewish citizens was "every citizen's business," not just that of a few leaders or "good souls."

During "Little Dunkirk," Acting Chief Rabbi Marcus Melchior was rescued. Today, his two sons, Rabbi Bent and Arne, are prominent.

Rabbi Bent Melchior is former chief rabbi of Denmark. He is the eighth generation of his family in Denmark, the Melchiors having lived there, it is said, for 300 years. A number of streets in Copenhagen are named after this illustrious family. Rabbi Melchior, who fought in Israel's War of Independence, once told an interviewer, "We have a mission in Denmark. We were saved by the Danes and must continue the community." In 1983, Rabbi Bent Melchior received Denmark's Order of Knighthood.

Arne Melchior holds a high position in the Jewish community of Denmark and in the government. Having served as a cabinet member and a member of Parliament, he also was in the Haganah in Israel's War of Independence. He is a cantor and has flown to Oslo to lead holiday services. Now his nephew, Michael, son of brother Bent, is a member of the Israeli cabinet, Minister of the Diaspora. Another of Rabbi Marcus Melchior's grandsons, Rabbi Uri Schwartz, served in Finland and now is in Israel. Rabbi Bent Lexner is chief rabbi of Denmark.

Religiously, Danish Jews belong to the "Mosaic Community," which is governed by a 20-member board of delegates selected every two years.

JEWISH SITES IN COPENHAGEN

Caroline Skoline, 18 Bomhusvej. Tel: 29-95-00. This is a Jewish, co-ed day school founded in 1805. At one time, half of the Jewish children in Copenhagen attended this school. Today about 300 pupils are enrolled. If you want to visit this school, you should telephone ahead for an appointment.

Jewish Community Center, 6 Ny Kongensgade, 1472 K. Copenhagen. Tel: 33-12-88-68. Kosher meals are offered in the café, but check when the facility is open. Also located here are Bnei Akiva youth group, Hakoah Sports Club, and the Jewish Youth Club. Adults are active in Keren Kayemet (JNF), WIZO, and the Danish Zionist Federation. A museum and library display Judaica.

Resistance Museum, Esplanade in Churchill Park. Tel: 33-13-17-14. This building should head every tourist's must-see list. Its many exhibits tell the story of the Danish fight for freedom in 1940-45 and there are sections devoted to the

A tank in front of the Resistance Museum, Copenhagen, Denmark.
(Photo by Ben G. Frank)

rescue of Danish Jews. You will know you have arrived at your destination when you see a tank on the pavement in front of a brown wooden building with the words, "Frit Danmark" ("Free Denmark"). The entrance gives the appearance of a ship; you quickly remember how the Danes rescued the Jews in fishing boats. From May 6 to September 15, the museum is open Tuesday through Saturday, 10 A.M. to 4 P.M.; and on Sunday, 10 A.M. to 5 P.M. From September 16 to April 30, the museum is open Tuesday through Saturday, 11 A.M. to 3 P.M.; and on Sundays, 11 A.M. to 4 P.M. Closed on Mondays. Admission is free.

Exhibition cases 40-42 tell the story of the rescue operation of October 1943, when nearly all of Denmark's Jews were smuggled out on small Fishing schooners and ferried to Sweden. Many thank-you letters and plaques grace exhibition cases 83-85 (off to the side and down the steps). Ask the guard if you cannot find these cases.

You will see greetings from many synagogues and Jewish community centers, such as Beth Sholom Mens' Club of Pittsburgh, Adath Jeshurun Congregation in Minneapolis, and other congregations in Spring Valley, New York; Jersey City; and the Boro Park section in Brooklyn. National organizations also have dispatched their thanks, including a large impressive plaque from the Rabbinical Council of America, the largest Orthodox rabbinic group in the world. All voice the sentiment that Israel and Jews everywhere will never forget the rescue of Danish Jews from the Nazis to neutral Sweden. In the court-yard of the museum is a sculpture made by Knud Nellemose; it commemorates those who gave their lives to Danish resistance to the Nazis.

The Royal Danish Library (Bibliotheca Judaica Simon-seniana), 8 Christians Brygge. 1219 Copenhagen. This library houses one of the largest Jewish book collections in the world. About 80,000 volumes and manuscripts in Hebrew, Latin, Arabic, Aramaic, Ladino, Yiddish, Ethiopian, Persian, and many other languages occupy the shelves. Because it relates history, the library stands as a magnet for scholars from throughout the world. It holds the only illuminated copy of Maimonides' *Guide of the Perplexed,* penned in Barcelona in 1148.

Entrance to the Krystalgade Synagogue, Copenhagen. (Photo by Ben G. Frank)

KOSHER DINING IN COPENHAGEN

Kosher Dining in Copenhagen is not available, but there are grocery and product stores.

Sampson, 3 Rorhoimsgade, Copenhagen. Kosher groceries and provisions are available here.

Kosher Delikatesse (Butcher) 97 Lynbyveg. Copenhagen. Tel: 33-18-57-57. This establishment delivers kosher meals to hotels, airlines. Take-out is possible.

LODGING

The Hotel Villa Strand, Kystvej 12, DK, 3100 Hornbaek. Tel/FAX: (45) 49-70-00-88. This phone is only used during the season from April 1 until September 1. For the remainder of the year, call: (45) 43-96-94-00, FAX: (45) 43-96-91-37. This glatt-kosher hotel-pension, located just 45 minutes from Copenhagen, stands on the beautiful North Sea coast of Hornbaek. It features newly-furbished rooms and full board, including Jewish and Danish cuisine. A synagogue is located around the corner of the establishment. The hotel overlooks inviting sandy beaches.

SYNAGOGUES IN COPENHAGEN

Krystalgade Synagogue, 12 Krystalgade, is the main synagogue. Most community events occur in this Orthodox house of worship, including weddings and bar mitzvahs. Services are held Friday evenings in the summer at 8 and at 3:45 in the winter; Saturday mornings at 8. There is no mixed seating in the synagogue—women sit in an upstairs gallery. Erected in 1833, this beautifully designed building features inside walls painted white and decorated with gold. The prayer hall seats 650 persons, with standing room for about 100 people. The synagogue is near the main shopping area and the pedestrian street, Frederiksberggade, as well as close to major hotels, such as the SAS Royal.

Machsike Hadas, 12 Ole Suhrs Gade, 1354 K. Copenhagen. This synagogue maintains ties to Agudath Israel. It sponsors daily Orthodox services in addition to Sabbath services. In the summer, services also are held at 6 Granvaenget, Hornbaek, N. Seeland. About 20 families belong to this congregation.

Beth Chabad Denmark, Svend Trosts Vej 11, 1912Frb. Copenhagen. Tel: 3379-3326. Many activities are held here, including services, lessons, a "cheder" for children. Shabbat meals are offered as well as programs celebrating all the holidays. The group also sponsors an overnight summer and winter camp for children. Rabbi Yitzi and Rochel Loewenthal are in charge of the Chabad program here in Denmark.

ORGANIZATIONS

Association of Polish Jews, 74 Norre Farinagsgade. Tel: 14-30-92 or contact the Jewish Community Center.

Sweden

Sweden is peaceful. This country has not fought a war since 1814. Once for a brief moment, it wielded great power. Its large towns by and large were peopled by Hanseatic merchants who settled in a long and narrow country that today is bordered on the west by Norway, on the north by Norway and Finland, and on the east and south by the Baltic Sea.

Peaceful Sweden remains the envy of the Continent. You rarely see poverty or shabbiness.

Sweden encompasses an area of 179,896 square miles of forests and dark lakes. The 1990 population was put at 8,340,000, 94 percent of which is Evangelical Lutheran. Although religious observance is on the wane, the stern Lutheran ethic places high value on discipline, hard work, and achievement.

A BRIEF HISTORY

The story of Jewish settlement begins in 1774. A gem-carver, Aaron Isak, of Mecklenburg, Germany, became the first Jew granted the right to live in Sweden; he was invited by King Gustav III. A year later, his brother arrived. Aaron brought a minyan of 10 Jewish men and their families, so he could hold services. Eight years later, the Swedish Parliament passed a law, the so-called Jew Regulations of 1782, authorizing the settlement of Jews, but only in Stockholm, Gothenburg, and Norrköping.

The Jews who arrived at the end of the eighteenth century and first half of the nineteenth century came from Germany. In 1838, the king repealed restrictions that had been passed in 1782 and incorporated the Jews into the Swedish state. After several revisions, all limitations to full citizenship were removed by Parliament in 1870.

Jews were now entitled to hold political office and were emancipated. (The Law of Freedom of Religion in 1951 abolished the regulation of 1838 requiring that citizens affiliate with a religious organization).

In 1880, the Jewish population reached 3,000; in 1910, 6,112. In 1930, nearly 8,000 Jews resided in the country, with nearly half in Stockholm.

During World War II, Sweden sought and won complete neutrality as she had done in World War I. In 1940. the Swedes managed to stay out of the Soviet-Finnish War.

In the decade preceding the outbreak of World War II, Sweden's immigration policy was a restrictive one, according to *News & Views*, published by the World Jewish Congress. While there were Nazi sympathizers and while Sweden did maintain diplomatic relations with Germany, Jews were not persecuted. As the War went on, Swedish public opinion switched and Jews were admitted into the country. In fact, the Jews of Sweden were directly or indirectly involved in several important life-saving efforts during World War II, including the rescue of about 7,000 Danish Jews. A booklet put out by the Great Synagogue in Stockholm cites the name of Gilel Storch.

The pamphlet says he "is relatively unknown, although he was the driving force behind many projects, the most successful being the supplying of some 170,000 food packages to name given persons in Nazi death and work camps. Numerous testimonies prove the value of these packages, which were sent from Sweden directly or by way of Portugal." When the Nazis invaded Norway in 1940 and began to round up Jews, about 700 escaped to Sweden, which offered them asylum. Swedish Count Folke Bernadotte and Raoul Wallenberg later saved thousands of Jews from concentration camps.

A panel of historians studying Switzerland 's response to saving Jews in World War II, while it did not compare, said at the news conference, that Sweden, also neutral during World War II, had been significantly more helpful than Switzerland. Sweden, like Switzerland, had limited Jewish immigration between 1938 and 1942, but reversed its policy after officials learned of the mass killings of Jews." Every country in Europe is being asked to come to terms with its own action during World War II. Swedish neutrality carried a high moral price. The Swedish government allowed German forces to pass through the country on their way to occupied Norway. When it was clear that the Allies would win, Sweden began its refugee aid.

The largest and most important Jewish immigration to Sweden occurred immediately after World War II, when thousands of survivors were brought from the death camps. About 7,000 remained in Sweden, although the majority soon left for the United States, Canada, and Israel. After the upheavals in Communist Eastern Europe, 550 Jewish refugees arrived here in 1956 from Hungary. In the 1960s, 3,000 Jews emigrated from Poland. By 1970, Sweden had a Jewish population figure of 13,500; it is currently about 20,000, more than double the combined Jewish populations of Norway, Finland, and Denmark. Jews play a major role in the cultural life of Sweden, out of proportion to their numbers, especially in the fields of music, painting, and literary criticism.

Half of the Jews who inhabit Sweden today were victimized

by the Nazis or emigrated from Eastern Europe after the war. Today, about 12,000 Jews live in Stockholm, approximately 2,500 in Gothenburg, and 2,500 in Malmö; the remainder have settled throughout the country.

Swedish-Israel relations were somewhat tense because the former had offered long-term and hearty support for the PLO. The Swedes worked to have the Palestine Liberation Organization (PLO) chief, Yasir Arafat, enunciate so-called moderate positions toward Israel and renounce terror in December 1988.

JEWISH STOCKHOLM

Summer light stands for Stockholm—a city of islands, canals, and museums. Stockholm proclaims itself as the most beautiful and cosmopolitan of the Scandinavian capitals, replete with outstanding architecture and charm. Often called the "Venice of the North," the capital is the largest city of Sweden, with a metro population of 1,377,560. With water, water everywhere, you soon discover the city is built on 14 islands connected by about 50 bridges, under and around which ply more than 100,000 boats.

From downtown Stockholm with its modern business area to the Old Town (Gamla Stan) and its pedestrian streets; to the City Hall and its beautiful surrounding calm waves of water to boat rides in the canals alongside Renaissance buildings, you inhale this relaxing city. Visit the new Vasa Museum featuring the 1628 warship that was raised in 1961 from its watery grave after sinking, or the 75-acre Skansen Outdoor Museum of Swedish Life, a great tourist attraction of 150 reconstructed buildings spotlighting traditional handicrafts and domestic life.

This is Stockholm—clean, pure air and a wonderful traffic pattern. Much of Stockholm can be explored by foot. I immediately took a liking to the area around Nybroplan; the Number 47 bus goes there. Here is the Strand Hotel and its park areas; the Royal Dramatic Theater; the ferryboat to the Skansen Outdoor Museum; the Raoul Wallenberg Park;

Judaica House, which is the headquarters of the Jewish community; and the famous Great Synagogue.

Jewish Sites in Stockholm

The Jewish Museum, Halsingegatan 2. Stockholm. Tel: 8-318-404-56-08. Open every day, except Saturdays, from 12 noon to 4 P.M. Here you can discover the history of the Swedish Jews and their contributions to art, literature and culture of Sweden.

Judaica House, Nybrogatan 19. Tel: 662-6686 or 663-6566. This is the Jewish Community Center of Stockholm, the center of Jewish cultural and social activity. Located in the fashionable Ostermalm section of Stockholm, the center sponsors many programs, such as Israeli folk dancing and sports clubs. A kosher dining facility (dairy) functions in Judaica House, but check to see if it is open; a gymnasium and Jewish student club meeting rooms are part of the complex. Built in 1963, with a grant from the JDC (Joint Distribution Committee), the center also encompasses a meeting house for such groups as Bnei Akiva, Habonim, Maccabi, Keren Kayemet (Jewish National Home), WIZO (Women's International Zionist Organization), and other organizations. Most of the time, at least one shaliach (advisor and teacher from Israel) resides in Stockholm and maintains his or her office here. Offices, a mikveh, as well as a gift and book shop round out the facilities in the building. But above all, there are many cultural, social, and recreational activities. Please contact the center in advance to see if the cafeteria is open. Take the Number 47 bus to Nybroplan and you can walk a few short blocks to Nybrogatan 19. Two sightseeing guides have been recommended. They are David Fischer, Tel: 886-4521, and Birgit Blideman, Tel: 612-9494.

Next door to Judaica House is a **Jewish day school.** But one should inquire at the Jewish center for permission to visit. Kosher food may be available here when the day school is in session. Today, the school has advanced to include the ninth grade. "Our schools are bursting at the seams," declares Rabbi Morton H. Narrowe.

Raoul Wallenberg Park. During the six months between July 1944 and January 1945, tens of thousands of Hungarian Jews were saved from the Nazis by a 32-year-old non-Jewish Swede, Raoul Wallenberg. In desperation and fear of certain deportation, the Jews of Budapest appealed for help to neutral embassies. In response, the understaffed Swedish Embassy asked Stockholm to send extra personnel to help them cope with the large number of Jews in need. At the same time, arrangements were being made by the Swedish Foreign Department, the American War Refugee Board, and the World Jewish Congress to initiate a last-minute operation to save Hungarian Jews.

Wallenberg, who was unmarried and a skillful organizer and negotiator, volunteered for the job. He was able to save Jews by giving them the famous "schutzpass," a type of protective passport staling that they were under Swedish jurisdiction. After the Russian liberation of Budapest in January 1945, Wallenberg was picked up by Russian soldiers and taken to the Soviet Union, never to be heard from again. The Soviet government told Sweden in 1957 that Wallenberg had died in a Moscow prison in 1947, but witnesses claim to have seen him in prison as late as the 1980s. In 2000, he would have been 88 years old. In recent years, the Russians have acknowledged to the Swedes that Wallenberg had probably been killed in prison.

Synagogues in Stockholm

Rabbi Morton H. Narrowe, who for about 30 years was chief rabbi of Sweden, is now rabbi emeritus. He can be reached at the Great Synagogue. Born in Philadelphia, he is a graduate of the Jewish Theological Seminary of America. Rabbi Philip Spectre is now chief rabbi of Sweden and he, too, is a graduate of the Jewish Theological Seminary.

The Great Synagogue, Wahrendorffsgatan 3A, Stockholm. Tel: 8-679-2900. This brick building is one of the most beautiful synagogues in Europe and was designed by Fredrik Wilhelm Scholander. The seating capacity is 830 persons. Carol Herselle Krinsky, in her book *Synagogues of Europe: Architecture, History, Meaning,* claims this house of worship possesses "an Eastern identity." The community's **Administrative Building** is at Wahrendorffsgatan, 3 B, Stockholm.

In September 1870, Rabbi Ludwig Lewysohn dedicated

Rabbi Narrowe in the courtyard of the Great Synagogue in Stockholm. (Photo by Ben G. Frank)

The Holy Ark in the Great Synagogue in Stockholm. (Photo by Ben G. Frank)

The Great Synagogue. (Photo by Ben G. Frank)

the synagogue by kindling the gas-burning eternal light (Ner Tamid) over the Holy Ark (aron ha-kodesh). This date is confirmed by the Hebrew inscription over the main entrance to the synagogue. While the lamp is from that time, the cloth decorations around it are traditionally attributed to the time of King Gustav III, although no one is really certain of the truth of this claim. On the other hand, the eight-branched Hanukkah menorah is definitely a gift, according to the Hebrew text on which it stands, that was donated in 1792 after approval by King Gustav III. The legs of the menorah are in the shape of the royal G, which certainly stands for "Gustav." Those of the base upon which the menorah stands are formed in the shape of an S. The queen's name was Sofia Magdalena and the donor was Strelitz, so the meaning behind this letter is unclear.

The Raoul Wallenberg Room in the Great Synagogue is dedicated to Raoul Wallenberg, the Swedish diplomat who saved thousands of Hungarian Jews from the Nazis by issuing them diplomatic passports.

Most Jews here in the synagogue follow what probably is close to the Conservative movement of Judaism in the United States. Rabbi Narrowe describes the synagogue as Ashkenazic, Liberal, and Conservative—with an organ and mixed seating in one section.

Saturday morning services are at 9:15. Shabbat mornings are an exciting time to be in the synagogue, as the service is rewarding and the kiddush that follows gives travelers a chance to meet the Jews of Stockholm. Rabbi Narrowe gives the sermon in Swedish. The kiddush is held in the lecture hall, which features paintings of the past leadership of Swedish Jewry.

Winter brings darkness. Shabbat can begin as early as 2:30 on a Friday afternoon. A Monday and Thursday morning minyan is scheduled for 8, but check these times by calling the synagogue.

Tourists should note that few activities are scheduled in the summer, as most Swedes go on vacation, especially in July. The synagogue sponsors a popular Jewish summer camp that includes not only several hundred children, but senior citizens, too. Often, both a grandparent and grandchild will meet on the campgrounds.

The SAS Strand, Grand, and Diplomat hotels are near the synagogue. The Royal Viking Hotel, Vasagaten 1, near the central railroad station, is a little farther, but it is an excellent place to stop in the Swedish capital.

Two small Orthodox synagogues function in Stockholm: **Adas Yeshurun** and **Adath Israel**. Rabbi A. Katz is spiritual leader at both congregations, which in outlook are close to the Agudas Israel Orthodox group. About 200 families belong to the two congregations.

Adas Yeshurun is located in the school building next door to Judaica House, at Nybrogatan 19. The address is Riddargatan 5. Tel: 661-82-82. The synagogue is furnished with benches, Holy Ark, pulpit, and table that were in a small synagogue in Hamburg and miraculously survived *Kristallnacht5r*. These religious objects were sent to Stockholm's Orthodox Jews by the Orthodox Jewish community in Hamburg. "This synagogue and its furniture have great emotional value for all of Stockholm's Jewry. They express symbolically the faith that Judaism is eternal and that it lives throughout the world and in all ages," says a synagogue brochure. The other Orthodox house of worship, Adath Israel, is located at St. Paulsgatan 13. Tel 8-644-1995.

GOTHENBURG

Jewish Community Center, Ostra Larmgatan 12, 41107, Gothenburg. Tel: 17-72-45.

MALMÖ

Jewish Community Center, Karnregatan 11, 21156, Malmö. Tel: 11-84-60 or 11-88-60.

Synagogue, Foreningsgatan, Malmö.

Norway

Norwegian Jewry is unique. For example:
• One rabbi is in residence only about half of the year and lives in Israel the other half.
• An Arab runs the kosher provision store, which is stocked with kosher meat and food packages from Israel and Europe.
• The year 1992 was the 100th anniversary of Norwegian Jewry as a congregation, according to Norwegian Jewish leader Herman Kahan.

Kahan has written a book, part of which explains Judaism to this "caring," and "friendly" Norwegian society and another section on the history of this young Jewish community, a community that Kahan came to after the war, when he realized his sister was alive and living here. He fell in love with the people and country, which is attractive, clean, and very environmentally conscious. Although Norway can be expensive, it still offers some travel bargains.

There is a Jewish community here and it is alive. Except for the **kosher provisions store,** which is located at Waldemar Thranesgt 0171 (Tel: 22-60-91-66), you need only one address when you are visiting the city—Bergstien St. 13, 15, 17—which is the Community Center and synagogue (see below).

Nearly 1,000 Jews live in Norway, most in Oslo and its suburbs, with about 120 to 150 in Trondheim. A few Jews reside in Bergen. Actually, because less than 4 percent of its land is livable, most of Norway's 4 million-plus citizens inhabit Oslo, Trondheim, and Bergen.

Today, Norway welcomes tourists to its attractive, picturesque villages and spectacular scenery of fiords, cliffs, rugged uplands, and forests that once were the paths and sealanes of Viking warriors. They were those hearty warriors who sailed to North America between the ninth and eleventh centuries. Norway covers 125,057 square miles, with a 2,125-mile jagged coastline along the North, Norwegian, and Baltic seas. Norway lies back to back with Sweden along a peaceful 1,000-mile border. Actually, from 1814 until 1905, the country was held by Sweden. In the north, it shares a boundary with Finland and the former U.S.S.R.

Norway boasts the fifth largest merchant fleet in the world—more than 200 shipping companies. So one can see why the sea and the fishing industry remain paramount in Norway. The fiords, which are deep inlets of the sea extending back into the mountains sometimes for more than 100 twisting miles, complete the beautiful picture of this fine nation. Despite latitudes equal to Alaska, Norway's climate remains mild because of warm ocean breezes. A welfare state and the discovery of oil and gas have helped give the country a high standard of living.

A BRIEF HISTORY

For many years the history of Norwegian Jews was linked to Denmark's Jewish community since Norway was ruled by Denmark for 400 years until 1814, when Sweden took over. Norway may have been one of the last countries in Europe to admit Jews. The first Jews arrived here about 300 years ago, but 1851 seems to be the date they settled down. Immigration really got under way after 1881, with an influx of Jews from Eastern Europe. In 1890, 214 Jews lived in Norway, most of them in Oslo.

Norwegian Jews erected their first synagogue in 1920, when there were about 1,500 Jewish inhabitants.

Nazi Germany invaded Norway on April 9, 1940. Hitler needed this peace-loving land to secure the transports of iron ore from northern Sweden along the Norwegian coast in the winter when the Baltic Sea is iced. Norway could be exploited as a base to attack northern Great Britain. About 1,800 Jews inhabited the country, including several hundred Jewish refugees. Vidkun Quisling (who gave us the word *quisling*—traitor) was "minister president" of a puppet regime. He became dictator and turned Jews over to the Nazis. He was executed after the war.

In late 1942, 770 Jews were rounded up and shipped to Nazi death camps. Only 12 survived. Twenty additional Jews were murdered in Norway.

With the help of the Norwegian underground, some 930 Jews escaped to Sweden. This action was carried out with the aid of a group called the Norwegian Lifeboat Society.

After World War II, about 800 Norwegian Jews returned from Sweden. The Norwegian government, however, allowed several hundred Jews to enter from displaced persons (D.P.) camps, under the category of "war casualties." By the mid-1950s, about 1000 Jews resided in Norway, of whom 700 settled in Oslo, and 150 in Trondheim.

A democratic state, Norway fights anti-Semitism and is proud that the first secretary-general of the United Nations was Norwegian Trygve Lee, who helped gain passage of the 1947 U.N. Partition Plan Resolution creating the State of Israel. To fight a 50 percent mixed-marriage rate, many young Jews are sent to Stockholm, Copenhagen, London, and, of course, Israel to find a Jewish spouse. But the rate of mixed marriages here is believed to be lower than in Sweden and Denmark because many Norwegian Jews are newcomers from Eastern Europe and have not as yet assimilated fully.

Jews have been involved in the life of the country. Jo Benkow, born Josef Benkowitz, served as the speaker of the Norwegian Parliament from 1985 to 1993. He is said to have been the most influential Jewish politician ever in Norway. According to the *Jewish Bulletin*, February 11, 2000, Benkow was the head of the opposition Conservative Party in Norway from 1980 to 1984.

In the last few years, the Jewish Community of Detroit grew closer to Norway as one of Michigan's Jewish sons served as U.S. Ambassador to this Scandinavian country. Ambassador David and Doreen Hermelin served from 1998 to 2000 in Oslo. Memgers of the Jewish community describe Ambassador Hermelin, well-known for his philanthropy as a "total mensh," a wonderful human being.

Norwegian Jewry lauds its religious freedom, the absence of anti-Semitism, as well as government and public support for the Jewish community. The Jewish community here lives in a prosperous environment, so well off that the assimilation process may be accelerated.

The Oslo Synagogue. (Photo by Ben G. Frank)

JEWISH OSLO

Oslo, this bright, busy capital city of slightly less than a half-million, situated on 175 square miles and founded nine centuries ago in 1050, is a friendly city. From the new, modern Oslo Plaza Hotel to the comfortable, calm harbor area, the City Hall, the museums and restaurants, Oslo has many sites for the visitor. One of the most fascinating European tourist attractions is the open-air Vigeland Sculpture Park in Frogner Park. There, more than 200 bronze, granite, and wrought-iron statues of men, women, and children, reflecting the relationship between the sexes, draw tourists. Anyone visiting the Norwegian capital should pay a visit to Vigeland's present to the city of Oslo.

Informal Oslo proudly advertises that nearly everyone speaks English in this land of sailors and ships and merchant marines. The museums reflect the sea, especially the Kon-Tiki Museum on the Bygdoy Peninsula, which contains the raft of the anthropologist and adventurer, Thor Heyerdahl. Other museums include the Norwegian Folk Museum, also on the Bygdoy Peninsula. Oslo was also the site of the negotiations that led to Israel and the PLO signing "protocols" in Washington, D.C., in September 1993.

Jewish Sites in Oslo

Community Center and Synagogue, Bergstien St. 13, 15, 17. Three attached buildings—a senior citizen home, a synagogue, and a community center—make up the Jewish community complex on Bergstien Street. Friday evening and Sabbath morning services are scheduled.

The prayer times obviously depend on the season in these northern lands. For instance, in July, the Sabbath could begin at 8:20 P.M. and not end until 1:05 A.M. early Sunday morning. On Saturday mornings, after the services, a kiddush takes place. The telephone number of the office at the Community Center is 606-826. Leon Rothschild is gabai of the synagogue.

Herman Kahan is a leader of the community. His telephone number is 603-190; FAX: 461-394. Kai Feinberg, P.O. Box 740, Oslo, 0105. Tel: 22-30-29-29, is also a leader of the community.

The synagogue was founded in 1892 and the present structure built in 1920. After World War II, King Olav V, then Crown Prince, attended the reconstruction ceremony. The building had been miraculously spared by the Nazis in the war. In 1992, the 100th anniversary of the synagogue was celebrated.

The synagogue is located at Bergstien 15, 0172, Oslo. Tel: 22-69-65-70. It is difficult to find as it is in a residential community, situated on the east side of St. Hans Haugen Park. If you are walking, follow Ullevalsveien to Knud Knudsens Plass and follow the east side of the park to Bergstien Street.

The Jewish community is active. Zionist groups, B'nai B'rith, and WIZO meet at the Community Center, which is next door to the synagogue.

HJM—Help the Jews Home, Colletsgatge 43, 0456, Oslo. Tel: 69-23-70. Mrs. Jackie Feinberg, the group's secretary, can be reached at 14-11-13. An active Russian Jewry Committee has been on the scene in Oslo. Mrs. Feinberg reported that the group called "Help the Jews Home" was raising funds for Russian Jews. This group was established in 1990 by eight Christian, secular, and Jewish organizations.

Jewish War Victims Memorial, Stroensveten 105, in the Jewish cemetery, an enclave in the municipal cemetery. A large Magen David is engraved on the memorial's panels and it includes the names of 620 Norwegian Jewish men and women who perished in the Holocaust. From the center of the star rises a column in the shape of a truncated tree trunk, on which a memorial plaque is affixed. King Olav V and the Royal Family attended the unveiling ceremony.

The Jewish Memorial Park in the suburb of Hurum, on the Kjerrlgrav Hill, overlooking the Oslo Fjord. A planeload of Tunisian Jewish children crashed on this spot in 1949.

The Resistance Museum. Part of Oslo's Akershus Castle, the medieval stone fortress of the Viking king Harkon, this museum is close to the monument to heroes who lost their lives in World War II. Described as "informative," "interesting," and "stirring," Norway's Resistance Museum deals with Norwegian resistance against the German occupation, 1940-45. The building is known as the Double Battery and The Frame House. The basement consists of two stone vaults built in about 1650 to accommodate six cannons and an adjacent powder magazine. Later, a battery was positioned on top of the vaults, hence the name. The frame building above, erected in the mid-eighteenth century, was used mainly as a military storehouse right down to 1862, when the building was made available for use as a museum. The museum was opened to the public by the then Crown Prince, now King Harald, on May 8, 1970, 25 years to the day after the end of the war in Europe.

The Wergeland Monument. Each year on May 17, which is "Constitution Day" in Norway, Jews, especially Jewish youth, come together at the Wergeland Monument in the Var Frilser's Cemetery to honor Henrik Wergeland (1808-45), the national poet. They lay bouquets of red and white carnations at the foot of the statue of Henrik Wergeland. Wergeland was instrumental in having the ban against Jewish immigration lifted. Creating a welcome climate for Jews, he wrote a book entitled *Jodinden, The Jewess.* He did not live to see the ban against Jewish immigration lifted, as he died in 1845. Donated by Swedish Jews, the inscription reads: "To the indefatigable fighter for freedom and the rights of man and citizens." On the other side of the monument it says: "Grateful Jews outside the frontiers of Norway erected this monument to him."

Another monument to Wergeland stands in Studenterluden, a park on Karl Johansgate Street, which is the main pedestrian avenue, replete with shops and restaurants.

For further information on sightseeing in Oslo, contact the Oslo tourist office: Tel: 83-00-50.

Vegetarian Restaurant. Frisksport Vegeta Vertshus, 3-B, Munkedamsvei, Oslo.

TRONDHEIM

The northernmost **synagogue** in the world stands in

Trondheim, Norway. Originally a railroad station, this imposing structure is located at Arkitekt Christiesgate IB, near Nidaros Cathedral. The building—used by the Nazis as a warehouse in the war—was enlarged in 1955 by adding a Jewish community center that also includes a Hebrew school. More than 100 Jews live in the city. The sanctuary can seat 150 people, including a women's gallery. The telephone number of the synagogue is 47-52-20-30.

The Jewish War Victims Memorial in Trondheim is located in the Jewish cemetery. The monument consists of three granite slabs on which are inscribed the names of the 60 Trondheim Jews murdered by the Nazis.

Finland

Welcome to Finland, land of a thousand lakes, land of the "sauna." Five million people inhabit 130,119 square miles, in some places one person per square mile.

Bounded on the north by Norway, on the east by Russia, on the south by the Baltic Sea, and on the west by the Gulf of Bothnia and Sweden, Finland is as beautiful as a picture postcard, with 187,888 lakes—one lake for every 26 persons.

Much of the Finnish population lives in the south and that means they reside in and around the capital, Helsinki, a large industrial city, cultural center, and Baltic port.

This "white city of the North," with its numerous white buildings, rose in the 1550s and was built to be inhabited by humans. Helsinki grows on you. You cannot take in this city in one day. It must be observed and returned to in order to get the feel of it. Even with the end of the cold war, it still remains a bridge between the West and the vast expanse of Russia to its east. For those flying back from Russia or Baltic countries, Helsinki still positions itself as a welcome stopping-off spot.

Walk around Market Square and watch the people. Look out to the water buses in the south harbor. Stroll along Esplanade Park surrounded by shopping streets and hear the concerts at the bandstand. Buy some fruit in the market near the water.

The Jean Sibelius Memorial in Sibelius Park and Finlandia Hall are sights not to be missed.

The passenger ships of the Silja Line to Stockholm await you. A good way to arrive here from New York is on the daily Finnair jet flights.

A BRIEF HISTORY

In the Middle Ages, Finland was joined to Sweden. But in the eighteenth century, sections of southeastern Finland were ceded to the czar. Moreover, in the Peace Treaty of Hamina in 1809, Finland was formally ceded to the czar, but kept its status of an autonomous grand duchy that retained its previous law and institutions. In 1812, the country's capital was transferred from Turku to Helsinki (Helsingfors). While the Russian Revolution raged in 1917, Finland declared its independence on December 6. An ensuing civil war between Finnish Whites and Reds nearly devastated the country, with the Whites winning the conflict. Peace was signed in 1920.

Until Russia grabbed up Finland in 1809, Jewish settlement in Sweden was forbidden. When the Russians took over the country, a few Jews who served in the army were permitted to reside here. We call these ex-Jewish soldiers "cantonists." These "cantonists" were Jewish boys torn from their parents at a very young age and kept in the czar's military service for 25 years. But after that long quarter of a century of service, these veterans were permitted to settle anywhere in the czar's dominions, including Finland.

The edict of 1858 has been regarded by the Jews of Finland as a "Magna Carta," granting them precious rights and privileges, but still not complete emancipation. By 1880, about 1,000 Jews lived in Finland, but they had to stay in only a few cities, including Turku and Vyborg.

When independence was achieved in 1917, Jews were granted full civil rights. After the Russian Revolution, many

Russian Jews found a haven in Finland. By 1930, the Jewish population of Finland was about 1,700.

Zionism had a strong hold on Finland's Jewish population. In May 1939, Ze'ev Vladimir Jabotinsky, the leader of the Revisionist group in the Jewish State, visited Helsinki. Twenty years earlier, he had addressed the Jews of Finland. Only this time, with war beckoning, he desperately called on Jews to leave Sweden, Finland, Estonia, and Latvia and settle in the Jewish State. Jabotinsky called for a "clear nationalist feeling and a battle for liberation," according to Hannu Rautkallio. Nobody listened.

A few months later, the Russians attacked Finland in what became the Russo-Finnish Winter War, and Jewish lives were again lost as they rallied to the blue and white flag of Finland. The Finns fought the Soviets with "religious fervor." The Finns drew the admiration of the world as they mounted a desperate defense of their country. Many Jews served in the Finnish Army in that war of 1939-40 as well as during the Continuation War of 1941-44. The losses suffered by Finnish Jews were substantial; of the country's Jewish population, no less than one-fifth had served in the Finnish armed forces (more than 300 men, of whom 26 had been killed or reported missing—nearly 8 percent of the total number of Jews who served).

But even more unbelievable was the fact that Jewish soldiers fought in units that were alongside German soldiers in World War II. They actually did, and they did it on the Finnish-Russian border. In fact, during the war, the Finnish Jewish soldiers built a field synagogue by the River Suir, "no doubt, a very exceptional event in an Army fighting on the German's side during the war," writes Tapani Harviainen, a professor at the University of Helsinki.

Finnish Jews serving with Germans? How did it happen? The Finns say they were on the side of the Germans because in this case, the enemy of both nations was the then U.S.S.R. This unique situation actually began on August 23, 1939, with the signing of the infamous Molotov-Ribbintrop pact. Nine days later, on September 1, 1939, Hitler invaded Poland and Russia gobbled up the eastern part of Poland. The Soviets soon made harsh demands on Finland and the Russo-Finnish Winter War broke out on November 30, 1939, with the bombing of Helsinki. "It was naked, unprovoked, inexcusable aggression," wrote William L. Shirer. The war lasted 105 days and Finland, in 1940, ceded much territory to the U.S.S.R. But the fighting between Russia and Finland would start again a year later, in what became known as the "Continuation War."

The way the Finns tell it, Finland joined in the Continuation War in 1941 after it was attacked by Russia during the same time that the Germans launched their June 1941 invasion of the U.S.S.R. Thus, the Finns maintain, the Russians attacked first in 1941, and this was a "separate war." The Finns, continues the argument, were not "allied" to Germany, but merely a "co-belligerent." Therefore, "the Finnish campaign was a defensive struggle separate from the war of the great powers," says Eino Jutikkala.

However, in reality, one must also remember that as the Nazi Blitzkrieg swept across Russia in 1941, the Soviet Union seemed doomed and the Finns saw it as an opportunity to regain their land lost in the 1939-40 war. They did so briefly, but by 1943, the Russians hurled back the German invaders and broke through the Axis lines to assault Finland. Britain had declared war against Finland. The latter was obliged to make peace, once again ceding land and reparations to the U.S.S.R. At the same time, the Germans in their retreat through Finland ravaged Finnish land and killed many civilians.

The Finnish government withstood German pressure to harm Jews. By 1939, the Jewish population had grown to 2,000, and Finland gave temporary sanctuary to fleeing Jews and saved its Jewish residents. It gave shelter to a substantially larger number of westward-bound Jewish refugees than official statistics indicate, Rautkallio says. In 1944, 200 stateless refugees came to Sweden from Finland. Rautkallio states that Finland refused to hand over Finnish Jews to the Germans. The record shows that perhaps less than 20 non-Finnish Jews were surrendered to the Germans, the *Encyclopedia Judaica* puts the figure at 50 Jewish refugees from Austria and the Baltic countries, and Finnish Jewish publications and leaders today say 8. But it is clear that the Jews of Finland escaped being drawn into the Nazi net. As Raul Hilberg has affirmed, the process of the destruction of Jewry never extended as far as Finland. Finland was the only nation fighting on Germany's side against a common enemy that was never pressured to hand over the Jews, according to Rautkallio. He notes that the Germans were quite aware of the public outcry that would have been raised in Finland if there was so much as a hint of any coercive action against Jews. Persecution or anti-Semitism could hardly be discerned in Finland. Although quite late in the war, on Finland's Independence Day in 1944, Marshall Mannerheim attended a ceremony in the Helsinki synagogue.

Commenting on Rautkallio's book, Irving Abrahamson, in *Reform Judaism* magazine, said, "If, on the one hand, Rautkallio's book shows that the Finns took no part in the Final Solution, on the other it shows that the Nazis made no effort to impose the Final Solution on them."

In the end, Finland suffered many casualties. She lost 11 percent of her territory to the Russians. As Aini Rajanen points out, the Finns are "people who fought 42 wars with Russia and lost every one of them."

In World War II, there may have been up to 2,300 Jews in Finland, refugees and descendants of the cantonists; by 1949 there were 1,700 Jews in Finland.

Finland was the third nation, after the United States and the U.S.S.R., to recognize the State of Israel in 1948. Twenty-nine Finnish Jewish youths fought in Israel's War of Independence, proportionately the highest number in the Diaspora. More than 100 emigrated to Israel. Today, the Finns display strong support for Israel.

About 1,300 Jews live in Finland, 1,000 of them in and around Helsinki. Several hundred Jews reside in Turku, the oldest city in Finland, and 50 in Tampere. Those Finnish Jews, recognized as Jews according to halacha or through halachic conversions, are members of the community, which is Ashkenazic and mostly upper middle and middle class. The three Finnish Jewish communities of Helsinki, Tampere, and

Rafael Maimon of Helsinki, center, originally from Israel, with two of his employees in his restaurant in the Forum. Many Israelis gather in the restaurant section of the Forum, a huge shopping complex in downtown Helsinki. (Photo by **Ben G. Frank**)

Turku are united under the Central Council of Jewish Communities in Finland. Its executive board includes nine members, six from Helsinki and three from Turku. The Central Council represents the Jews of Finland, both nationally and internationally. This council is a member of the World Jewish Congress and the World Zionist Organization.

Some assert that at least half the Jewish population intermarries, and that rate is rising. "A marriage of two Finnish Jews has long been a rare exception," wrote Harviainen. Still, Jewish leaders note that many non-Jewish partners convert and the majority of the mixed couples prefer to send their children to the Jewish kindergarten and the Jewish school.

Jews voice their happiness with living in Finland. Why not? Finland's economy generally is good. There are no international problems, and no anti-Semitism hovers over the Jewish community. A very homogeneous society, Finland has no minority problems. Finns don't bother Jews, Jewish leaders told me. And while the people are reserved and not as gregarious as their neighbors, the Swedes, they love their country and their land and are trying to keep their national identity.

As for Finnish Jews, most of the older generations are independent business persons or shopkeepers, while the younger generation enters the professions.

Jews are active in all professions and walks of life. Max Jakobson was former Finnish ambassador to the United Nations and actually ran against Kurt Waldheim of Austria for the post of secretary-general of the United Nations. Jakobson lost when the Soviets vetoed his candidacy. Dr. Simon Parmet is a noted composer and conductor. Sam Vanni is a famous painter, a member of the Finnish Academy and the European Academy of Science, Art and Literature. In 1979, Ben Zyskowicz was the first Finnish Jew to be elected a member of Parliament.

Still active is a Finnish Jewish War Veterans League that was founded in 1979, with a membership in 1991 of 86 members, 70 of whom live in Finland, according to Gideon Bolotowsky.

JEWISH HELSINKI

Kosher Dining in Helsinki

Jewish Community Center. Malminkatu 26, next to the synagogue. Tel: (09) 586-0310. FAX: (09) 694-8916. E-mail: hjc@hjc.pp.fi. Kosher meals are available at the center if you phone in your order ahead of time. At the Community Center and in the synagogue one is likely to meet Russian Jews, many of whom wait here in Helsinki for their connecting flight to Israel.

Kosher butcher and delicatessen, Ritus, Uudenmaankatu 28. Tel: 644-951.

Jewish Sites in Helsinki

Synagogue and Jewish Community Center, Malminkatu 26. Tel: (09) 586-0310. FAX: (09) 694-8916. E-mail: hjc@hjc.pp.fi. All organizations meet here. The congregation is one of the few in Scandinavia holding daily services, which are scheduled Monday to Friday mornings at 7:45. Friday evening services are at 6:45 and Saturday morning services are at 9. The synagogue was built in 1906. Renovated and enlarged in 1926, this house of worship added a library to the building that same year. Unlike many synagogues in Europe, this synagogue is very visible. Services in the synagogue follow Orthodox Lithuanian ritual.

The Jewish Community Center, next to the synagogue, was dedicated in 1962. Facilities include a senior citizens home and an auditorium, lounges, meeting rooms, and a mikveh. Here the Helsinki Jewish community sponsors a day school. At one point, 80 percent of the Jewish children in Helsinki attended the school, founded in 1918. Enrollment has gone up because the Israelis send their offspring to the school.

Jewish organizations that meet at the Community Center include the 125-year-old Chevra Kadisha, the Chevra Bikur Cholim, WIZO Finland, which has several hundred members, as well as branches of the JNF and Keren Hayesod. Cultural

The synagogue in Helsinki. (Photo by Ben G. Frank)

activities are promoted by the Jewish Choral Society, the Club Judaica, and the Hebrew language club, the Chug lvrit.

Makkabi Sports Club, also located at the Community Center, is the oldest existing Maccabi sports club in Europe. Pictures of its famous athletes adorn the walls of its club room in the Jewish Center section of the complex.

The community publishes a bi-monthly magazine called *Ha' Kehila.*

Preserved in the synagogue is a wreath presented by Field Marshall Carl G. Mannerheim when he made a visit to synagogue services in 1944. The wreath memorialized the 23 Jewish soldiers who had died in the Russo-Finnish War. Mannerheim was president of Finland from 1944 to 1946. His statue stands tall in several places, including near the Parliament Building in Helsinki. His former home is a museum now.

The Mannerheim Museum, Kalliolinnantie 14, 00140, Helsinki. Tel: 635-443. The guides at this museum are excellent. To the Finns, Mannerheim is George Washington, Abraham Lincoln, and Winston Churchill all rolled into one. Jewish senior citizens maintain it was Mannerheim who saved the Jews.

TURKU

With a population of slightly more than 150,000, this seaport and one-time capital is one of Finland's oldest cities. Often called the "cradle of Finnish culture," for much of the country's early history occurred here, it is surrounded by great forests.

Synagogue and Community Center, Brahenkatu 17. Tel: 231-2557. This brick building, located on a corner site, also has a distinctive cupola that can be seen from a distance. The structure was built in 1912, with an adjoining community center erected in 1956. Several hundred Jews support the center. The community maintains a Burial Society, a Bikur Cholim society, and a Makkabi Sports Club. Also, Talmud Torah classes are held here.

Sugested Reading

Bertelsen, Aage. *October, 1943.* New York: Putnam, 1954.

Bradley, David. *Lion Among Roses: A Memoir of Finland.* New York: Holt, Rinehart & Winston, 1965.

Goldberger, Leo, ed. *The Rescue of the Danish Jews: Moral Courage under Stress.* New York: New York University Press, 1987.

Jutikkala, Eino, with Pirinen, Kauko. *A History of Finland.* Translated by Paul Sjoblom. Helsinki: Weilin and Goos, 1984.

Krinsky, Carol Herselle. *Synagogues of Europe: Architecture, History, Meaning.* Cambridge, Mass.: MIT Press, 1985.

Rajanen, Aini. *Of Finnish Ways.* Minneapolis: Dillon Press, 1981.

Rautkallio, Hannu. *Finland and the Holocaust: The Finnish Experience.* New York: Holocaust Publications, 1987.

Shirer, William L. *The Challenge of Scandinavia, Norway, Sweden, Denmark and Finland in Our Time.* Boston: Little, Brown, 1955.

Yahil, Leni. *The Rescue of Danish Jewry.* Philadelphia: Jewish Publication Society, 1969.

The Czech Republic
The Spotlight Shines on Prague

I stand on the banks of the Vltava River—in German, it is called the Moldau. Being in Prague, I naturally start humming Smetna's wonderful symphonic poem, "The Moldau," which salutes Bohemia's noble past and rich culture. Many Jews and non-Jews know that the yearning anthem of Zionism and later the National Anthem of the State of Israel, "Hatikvah," was adapted from the same Czech folk song on which Smetna based his famous E minor melody.

Cities often take on characteristics of their rivers or harbors as the case may be. Prague is such a city. It imitates the embracing calm and serene flow of the Moldau. The tourist wants to hug this Bohemian capital, Prague. Mention Prague and we feel good. Jews have a kind word for this Czech capital. It was, and can be again, a shining light of Jewish scholarship. It remains one of the few cities in Europe where Jewish sites have been preserved.

And yet for all our fondness, in our memory there is another side of the ledger that comes to mind:

In a speech to the British people in 1938, that arch-appeaser, Prime Minister Neville Chamberlain, said:

> "...how 'horrible, fantastic, incredible, it was that we should be digging ditches and trying on gas masks here because of a quarrel in a faraway country between people with whom we know nothing."

The "faraway" country was Czechoslovakia and the people

were the Czechs and Slovaks. Because the French and British sought to appease Hitler, the Munich agreement sacrificed Czechoslovakia to the Nazis. It would take fifty years for this wonderful country to begin to emerge from the consequences of Fascist and Communist totalitarianism.

In coming to Prague, you journey to the heart of Europe. Photograph Prague as you would a perfectly cut diamond, because Prague is the jewel of Central Europe. And as you travel through this city, remember history. History will tell you that Prague has always vied with Warsaw and Berlin for the title the "heart of Europe."

Prague is in the limelight now because Americans are flocking there for its beauty, charm, and vibrancy. Young people love it, just as they love Paris, only Prague is less expensive. Once, Paris, too, was the home of the American expatriates: Hemingway, Stein, Crowley, Fitzgerald, and Ford Maddox Ford. Today the spotlight shines on Prague, the "Left Bank of the New Century" the new Paris of American expatriates with writers, tourists, and students arriving here by the thousands to observe its Bohemian culture and patronize its cafes. They crowd Wenceslas Square—the downtown center of shopping and sight-seeing. And they rent apartments in the Old Town, if they can get them or if they can afford them.

A young Jewish man who lives in the new nation of Slovakia told me that while he is a Slovak citizen, whenever he sees the flag of the Czech Republic, he cries. He has good reason: "For 10 centuries, Prague (Praha) and the areas of Bohemia and Moravia ignited the torch of liberty in Central Europe. Sometimes it was the only light in a vast darkness." When it was independent, Czechoslovakia was one of the most progressive countries in the world. Timothy Garton Ash writes in his book, The Magic Lantern, "historically, Czechoslovakia was much the most democratic state in the region before the War." He believes culturally that "Prague is the Central European city."

But, like the former U.S.S.R., Czechoslovakia as a united state no longer exists. The year 1993 was a momentous one in the history of the former Czechoslovakia: the divorce between the Czech lands and Slovakia became official. When it was united (between 1918 and 1939, and 1945 and 1993),

Czechoslovakia was the size of New York state. Now the Czech Republic has 10.2 million people in 30,000 square miles with 1.2 million persons living in Prague.

The Czech Republic and Slovakia still stand at the major crossroads of Europe. "Not a single major European conflict has left the area untouched in its thousand year history," wrote Czech President Vaclav Havel in the October 17, 1993, New York Times. He added that "wars have started or ended in our territory, and the main threads of history have sometimes been wound together and unraveled here."

Bounded in the west by Germany, in the north by Poland, in the east by Slovakia, and in the south by Austria, the Czech Republic takes pride in its economic progress, with a budget surplus and a healthy export market to the West. By 1994, sixty percent of production came from privatized companies, and unemployment was low.

Now a member of NATO, Czech Republic is negotiating acceptance into the European Union.

For the traveler's purpose, Czech history starts when Slavic tribes pushed down from the north, perhaps as early as the first century A.D. Then came the Roman legionnaires, who were followed by waves of fierce Avars and Magyars and then Tartars and Turks-all of whom spilled rivers of blood through these lands.

A Slavic empire flourished until the tenth century. While the Slovaks chafed for a thousand years under Hungarian rule, the Czechs briefly enjoyed their own kingdom. Bohemia existed for several centuries. But then came the Hapsburgs who ruled for three hundred years, until 1918. Freedom lasted only twenty years until the flames of Hitlerism raged across this democratic nation. Following the war, Czechoslovakia was stifled by communism for forty years. In 1989, the Czech Communist world collapsed in the wake of the "Velvet Revolution," a peaceful mass revolt in which not one person died. The prognosis looks good. "The Czech Republic has a real chance of making the larger transition from planned to market economy, with relatively less economic pain than its neighbors: although I stress the word, 'relatively,'" writes Timothy Garton Ash.

A Brief History

Jews have lived in Czechoslovakia—always an important Jewish cultural center—for at least a thousand years. For much of the time, it was one of the richest and most advanced nations in Europe, with a high degree of religious freedom and. cultural development. Jews flocked there. As Jewish merchants moved eastward from the Rhineland in the West to the Fertile Crescent in the East, they plied the trade routes of Central Europe and probably arrived at the end of the tenth century in what we now call the Czech Republic.

Until the twelfth century, Jews lived under favorable conditions. With the Third and Fourth Lateran Councils (1179 and 1215), the Catholic Church cracked down on Jews and Jews lost many of the rights they had enjoyed. By the thirteenth century, sixteen Jewish communities existed in Bohemia and Moravia, all actively seeking religious freedom. It is no wonder that Jews by the thousands poured into these provinces. There they could live in peace and practice their religion. They became moneylenders, and because they also paid higher taxes than most people, they were somewhat protected by the king. But the king often turned against them and cancelled all debts to Jews. At other times, the Jews had the backing of the king and the nobles. During these periods, they were particularly creative: they established the first Hebrew printing house in Prague; they designed and published the Prague Haggadah. Prague took on cultural and economic importance, especially when Ferdinand I declared that Jews could not live in other towns. Jews owned land and they even farmed. They traded, practiced medicine, and served the court. They excelled in crafts. They contributed to Jewish learning and literature.

A momentous event occurred in Czech history in 1402. That year, the preacher Jan Hus reached the masses with the idea of Church reform. For his criticisms of Church practices, he was burned at the stake on July 6, 1415. The Hussite Reformation shook Europe a hundred years before Martin Luther emerged.

In 1522, 600 Jews resided in Prague. By 1541, the number had risen to 1,200.

A milestone in Czech history was the Battle of Mohacs on

August 29, 1526. In that conflict, Louis II of Hungary was defeated and killed, leaving the throne vacant for the ascension of Ferdinand I of Hapsburg as ruler of the Bohemian lands and Hungary. The Golden Age of Prague Jewry appeared on the horizon in that century and early in the next as Jews began to prosper economically. They gained privileges, economic freedom, and the right to live anywhere.

The Battle of White Mountain in 1620 saw the defeat of the Czechs at the hands of the Austrians. In one fell swoop, the Austrians overwhelmed the Czech people and their noblemen, executing 27 members of the Czech aristocracy and exiling 150,000 Protestants. Geoffrey Moorhouse in *Prague* writes: "The story of Prague since 1620 is essentially the story of alien domination. Unless the outsider can guess this fact, he or she will not understand this city, nor appreciate the wary, stoic temper of its people."

Even in Czechoslovakia as in other parts of Europe in the 18th century, Jews were viewed as an alien people. "But as, regrettably, they had come to be embedded physically within Christendom, it was necessary to ensure that formally, legally, morally and socially they needed in some way to be excluded from it," writes David Vital, in his book, *A People Apart: The Jews of Europe, 1789-1939.*

The Counter-Reformation, which was the response of the Catholic Church to the Protestant Reformation of the sixteenth and seventeenth centuries, "helped destroy religious freedom, national independence, and the educated classes of Czechoslovakia. In the Thirty Years' War, the Counter-Reformation was imposed on the Czechs, and they in effect lost their national independence." On the heels of the good life came oppressive laws, plagues, death, and pogroms. The Jewish quarter was burned to the ground and Maria Theresa (1740-80) banished the Jews from Bohemia and Moravia for three years. They were allowed to resettle, however, despite the anti-Semitism of this Holy Roman empress.

Joseph II of Austria (1780-90), who issued the *Toleranzpatent of 1782* ("patents of toleration"), improved the quality of life of the Jewish community. Yet he wanted the Jews to be totally assimilated and to be useful to the state as participants in a modern economic system. Jews took advantage of Joseph's reforms and expanded economic activities. They established factories and even worked in agriculture. Prague joined with Berlin and Vienna to become an important center of Jewish Enlightenment.

By 1848, the number of Jews in Prague reached the 10,000 mark, compared to Vienna, with only 4,000. Just as Jews began to achieve equal rights, the Jewish community of Prague dwindled as new Jewish centers arose in Berlin and Vienna. Yet by the 1900s half of the Jews of Bohemia resided in Prague. Those Jews were active in the politics and cultural life of the city, which once again became a major center of European Jewry.

After Czechoslovakia gained its independence in 1918, more and more Jews began to speak Czech. In Slovakia and Carpathian-Russia, they spoke Yiddish and Hungarian. Before 1918, the history of the Jews in Bohemia, Moravia, and Silesia was an integral part of the history of Austrian Jews, whereas the Jews of Slovakia and Carpathian-Russia shared their history with Hungarian and Transylvanian Jews.

Jews played an important role in the Czech economy during the years of independence, notably in textiles, food, and paper industries. Estimates vary, but at least thirty to forty percent of the total capital invested in Czech industry in the 1930s was initiated by Jews.

But the independence and the relatively good life would not last. An event took place in Bavaria in 1938 that began the countdown to World War II, although much of the world thought it was a reprieve. In Munich, the British and French appeased Hitler and sold out the Czech people, who then really had little choice but to cave in. But who cared? The world knew little of Czechoslovakia. Hitler gained the "rich rim of Czechoslovakia for nothing," writes John Lukacs, in *The Last European War.* "The ignorance of the Western democracies regarding Eastern Europe was and remains inexcusable."

At Munich on September 29, 1938, 20,000 Jews were literally handed over to Nazi Germany. Another 25,000 fled to the unoccupied part of the country, only to be caught in the Nazi trap within the next few years. The fate of the Jews would be in the hands of the Reich security main office in Berlin and that meant the hands of the notorious Adolf Eichmann, who would organize the deportation of Jews to death camps.

As for Slovakia in the east, it became Hitler's lackey after the Nazi dictator told them on March 13, 1939, to proclaim Slovak independence or to suffer occupation. On March 15, 1939, the Nazis seized and incorporated western Czech lands into the Reich as the "Protectorate of Bohemia and Moravia." Slovakia went on its way to fascism under clergyman Jozef Tiso. A government-in-exile was later set up under Dr. Eduard Benes. During World War II, a high percentage of Czech military units consisted of Jews. Almost fifty percent of Czech soldiers abroad were Jews.

When Czech independence ended in 1939, only the Czech Jews out of all the Jews of Europe could "look back warmly on the period between 1918 and 1939," says Charles Hoffman in his book *Gray Dawn: The Jews of Eastern Europe in the Post-Communist Era.* That indeed says a great deal for the people and nation of Czechoslovakia.

After the war and the Holocaust and the Communist coup of February 1948, the surviving Jews greeted the establishment of the State of Israel in May of that year. Between 1948 and 1950, 18,879 Jews left Czechoslovakia for Israel. More than 7,000 departed for other countries. In 1950, the Communist rulers barred Jewish emigration. Only about 18,000 Jews remained. Some 5,500 of them waited for a chance to settle in Israel. Few were allowed to go. And the Jews became fearful of this harsh Communist regime, which they suspected would inflict upon them suspicion and humiliation. The blow would come soon.

RUDOLF SLANSKY TRIAL

In 1951, Rudolf Slansky, the Secretary-General of the Czech Communist Party, and thirteen co-defendants were purged in a trial that was a signal that scapegoats were being sought for the crimes and shortcomings of the regime, which Slansky himself helped create. It was the morning alarm clock ringing and calling for an intensive anti-Semitic campaign. Peter Meyer calls it "the great anti-Semitic show trial."

The 1951-52 Prague show trials were watched with horror and revulsion throughout the free world. The purge even embraced a Nazi type of anti-Semitism. The Czechs actually followed the pattern of Soviet political trials. Staged by the Russians, these shows could easily have played at home to U.S.S.R. audiences.

Many of the accused were branded Zionists. Eleven of the 14 defendants were Jews. Eventually 11 were executed, 8 of them Jews. Paul Lendvai maintains that Slansky "was undoubtedly an innocent victim of the Soviet-sponsored purge since the specific charges against him were patently untrue."

So, after the trial, Czechoslovakia would be ruled as a closed society—except for the fresh air of the "Prague Spring" of 1968, and until communism was dissolved in 1989 and Prague once again basked in freedom.

Notable Czech Jews

Jewish contributions to Czech literature and culture were out of all proportion to the small minority of Jews in the country's population. Achieving international recognition were Franz Kafka, Max Brod, Franz Werfel, Oskar Baum, Ludwig Winder, Leo Purutz, and Egon Erwin Kisch.

Eduard Goldstuchker served as president of the Czech Writers' Union during the Prague Spring days of 1968 when the Czechs tried to release the severe grip of the Communist police state. Albert Einstein taught in Prague for a year in 1911. The composer, Gustav Mahler, a native of Bohemia, spent several years in Prague.

Most of these artists spoke German. Often they were middle class, secularized, and assimilated into the larger society.

Jewish Prague

Mother of cities, this elegant city is a chronicle in stone. It is a museum and an art gallery. As a tourist site, Prague is "in." And it is less expensive than Paris. Perhaps travelers flock here now because the Communist regime kept it isolated for four decades; it probably was the most closed of the large Eastern European capitals.

Above all, civilized Prague remains a delight, charmingly laid out on hills and slopes. Not damaged by the war, it remains "Europe's most ravishing city, a perfectly preserved confection of Gothic, Renaissance, baroque and rococo and decorated with an icing of art nouveau," writes one observer. People who visit the city are still charmed by the capital's beauty and location, and its architectural gems, cultural traditions, and extraordinary millennium-long history. Prague is a highly recommended tourist destination because many believe it is the soul of Europe. It truly rewards the Jewish visitor.

For centuries, this city has been proclaimed and acclaimed as "Golden Prague," where Jews have lived for at least a thousand years. Indeed, a thousand years ago, a Jewish Arab merchant, Ibrahim Ibn Jacob said this about Prague:

> The town is built of stone and limestone and it is the biggest town as regards trade. Russians and Slavs come here from the royal town with goods. And Muslims. Jews and Turks from the lands of the Turks also come here with goods and trade coins.

Destined to become an important trade route along a major commercial river, Prague attracted Jewish leaders in 995. Rewarded for the aid they rendered to Christians in their fight against the pagans, they set up their own residential area. They built a school in what is now the "Mala Strana," the Little Quarter or Lesser Town, as it is sometimes called.

These Jewish pioneers settled around the area of what is now Dusni Street. Their next move was to the area known as the Old Jewish Town that for the last hundred years or so has been called Josefov, after the Hapsburg Emperor, Joseph II.

Here is what Alois Jirasik said in an old Czech legend:

> Six gates marked the division. And beyond those gates, everything was different. Strange buildings which excluded an air of poverty and neglect. Architecturally, there was all manner of weird additions, balconies, protrusions, dark dilapidated courtyards. The streets were very different, too. They were short and narrow, meandering, seedy and unpaved. And Jews at every turn, people of different customs and manners.

But Prague is not a stagnant city-state. This old city is studded with new retail shops, computer companies, banks, and a visual explosion of restaurants and bars. Alongside these establishments move a well-educated and cohesive population. And Prague trades extensively with its neighbor and one-time bitter foe, Germany.

Today, in Prague, there are only about 1,200 "registered" Jews, out of approximately 3,000 Jews in the Czech Republic, although the latter figure could be much higher. The figures do not tell the complete story. Notice the word registered. There could be at least 10,000 Jews residing in the Czech Republic, many of them intermarried. Since being Jewish no longer carries political stigmas as it did under the Communist regime, the "unregistered" Jews may also participate in community activities. Still, due to a high degree of assimilation, which existed even in pre-war Czechoslovakia, many are simply not aware they are Jews and many of those that are aware do not identify with Judaism in any way.

So, cross the crooked medieval span of the Charles Bridge and look down onto the gentle Vltava River, which flows from the Bohemian hills and splits the capital Prague. Then enter into the Jewish Town.

You can stroll through Wenceslas Square, through the Old Town, past medieval architecture, past the big square in front of the city hall, down Pariska Street to the Jewish quarter, and then down the narrow cobblestone streets, through the old Jewish quarter. When you come to the banks of the Vltava River, set back your imagination ten centuries and visualize Jewish merchants traveling the trade routes and arriving at the very spot where you now stand. The Vltava still inspires romantic artists, writers, and historians.

Make sure you visit the Altneuschul. Then go on to the Klaus Synagogue, the Pinkas Synagogue, and the High Synagogue (also called the Town Hall Synagogue), which was built in the second half of the sixteenth century next door to the Jewish Town Hall. The latter is now the headquarters of the Prague Jewish community. Stand in the Maisel Synagogue reconstructed in 1885-1913. And be sure you take some time to wander through the Old Jewish Cemetery.

Inside the Altneuschul, "the Old-New Synagogue," in Prague. (Photo by Ed Robin)

From November to April, most of the synagogues and sites are open from 9 A.M. to 5 P.M., Sunday to Thursday. On Shabbat, the museums and offices are closed. On Friday, these institutions usually stay open until 1 P.M. In the summer, the hours are from 9 A.M. to 6 P.M. To obtain a guide, one can call the Jewish community at 2481-0099. The admission to the museum buildings is 80 kroners for all objects. For groups, admission is half price. The admission to the Altneuschul (Old-New Synagogue) is separate and amounts to 30 kroners and is also half-price for groups.

THE JEWISH TOWN

Prague may have existed as a settlement for six thousand years, but for the modern traveler, it is the Old Town that draws and inspires the tourist. A living museum of medieval architecture, it contains nearly two thousand historic buildings. Few are more popular with tourists than the synagogues, the Jewish Town Hall, and the cemetery of *Josefov,* the Old Jewish Town. Actually, these sites still remain central to Prague Jewry and will probably be so for as long as Jews live in this city by the Vltava River. More than 500,000 tourists, predominantly non-Jewish, visit the Jewish quarter or Jewish Town, as it is called, each year. During the peak tourist season, thousands daily stroll through the narrow streets.

Hear the words of Franz Kafka describe this ghetto, which he knew in his childhood:

> "Living within us are still those dark corners, mysterious corridors, blind windows, dirty backyards, noisy pubs, and closed inns. We walk down broad streets of the newly built towns. But our steps and looks are uncertain."

In 1896, a city-wide development project demolished the Jewish quarter, except for the Altneuschul, the Pinkas, Maisel, and the High (Hoch) synagogues. Many Jews moved out of the Old Quarter to new city areas. In 1870, more than half of Prague Jewry still lived in the Old Quarter. By 1900, less than one-fourth remained. Still, the Jewish ghetto has played an important role in Prague's history.

One million visitors come to the Old Town each year.

The **Jewish Museum.** The "exotic museum of an extinct race"—that is what the Nazis had in mind when they spoke of a Jewish museum. In Czechoslovakia, Jewish religious objects were saved because the Germans in their skewed insanity wanted to transform these museums into "museums of hate"—after all the Jews were annihilated by Nazi killer squads, of course.

Two notorious Nazis, Reinhard Heydrich and Adolf Eichmann, sadistically added items to the Czechoslovakia Jewish community's pre-war collection of Judaica by seizing Jewish books, manuscripts, and religious and art objects in Germany and other countries in Europe and bringing them to Prague for storage. This insane behavior saved an immeasurable wealth of Jewish cultural objects. At the end of the war, 8 buildings in the Jewish quarter and 50 warehouses throughout Prague were packed with Torah scrolls, ritual objects, musical instruments, paintings, furniture, and other stolen items. The Nazis seized these items from Czech and Slovak homes and from at least 168 synagogues that they destroyed in Bohemia, Moravia, and Slovakia.

Today, the Jewish Museum, founded in 1906, is housed in the surviving Prague synagogues that were not leveled by the Nazis. These former houses of worship possess a great collection of religious and secular Judaica, much of it from other European nations—a unique treasury of Jewish history. Actually, it may even be the richest Judaica collection in the world. One estimate is that there are more than 30,000 religious and artistic objects and a library of 100,000 volumes, most of which the Nazis had stolen from synagogues and from the homes of 92,000 Czech Jews who were deported to concentration camps, where 77,297 died.

The **Altaeuschul,** or **Old-New Synagogue (Staronova Synagoga),** corner of Cervena and Maislova streets, Prague. If you have time to visit only one site in Jewish Prague, this world-famous early Gothic synagogue should be it. Services are held every day at 8 A.M. Shabbat morning services are at 9 A.M. (The building is closed to sightseers on Shabbat). Erected around 1270, the "Altneuschul" stands in the ancient Jewish Town. Today, architects, artists, and scholars fix their sights on this and other buildings that were not touched by the Holocaust. The traveler should do likewise. Lest we forget, this is the oldest monument of Prague's ghetto and the oldest functioning synagogue in Europe. This synagogue of synagogues is among the most impressive of early European Gothic style. And during the summer tourist season up to 2,500 persons may visit the synagogue in a single day.

Located in this city of Gothic, neo-Renaissance architecture, the Altneuschul comes upon you very quickly. Its portrait looks better in photos. When you look closely you may see the marks of age. You realize it contains within its walls seven hundred years of Jewish history and the will to survive. Stories have been told and legends have been created. Thousands of people from all over the world have come to see this synagogue, one of the most important early Gothic brick buildings in Europe, and one of the world's oldest Jewish architectural monuments.

In the past, some sentimental visitors reported that the history of the Jews of Prague flashed on the walls before them. The blood of *pogroms* became visible to them on its whitewashed walls, they said. Jews were murdered in this building and the bloodstains, they were told, have never been whitewashed off the walls out of respect for the martyrs, according to Carol Herselle Krinsky in *Synagogues of Europe: Architecture, History, Meaning*. However, the stains have apparently faded away.

In 1254, Premysl Ottokar II granted certain Jews "privileges," which meant he would protect their houses, cemeteries, and organizations. Following up on this, Prague Jewry obtained permission to build a new synagogue and to hire masonry workers who were constructing nearby St. Agnes Church, which still stands.

Even the synagogue's name can be considered mythical. Interwoven into the history of how it obtained its name, the "Alneuschul"—the Old-New Synagogue—are numerous legends.

Construction of the synagogue was completed between 1270 and 1290. To differentiate it from another older synagogue, it was named "new." At the end of the sixteenth century, or at the beginning of the seventeenth century, another "new" synagogue was built and the former "new" synagogue came to be known in German as the "Alte Neu Schul," or "the Old-New

School," a name that was later written in one word, "Altneuschul." Thus we see that the Altneuschul's original name was the New or Great Synagogue (schul). The name, "Old-New" (*Altneu* in German), came into use only after other synagogues in the ghetto were erected in the late sixteenth century.

Another explanation is given by Jan Lukas, who recounts in *The Prague Ghetto* that "some experts maintain that the name 'Old New' developed precisely from the fact that the new part of the building was built on top of the old one which had been uncovered by the children at play."

Yet another source attributes the unique name to a vague expression that arose from the translation of the German word, *alt-neu*. The correct term, they say, is the Hebrew al-tnai, "on condition" or "temporarily"; that in fact, Jewish legend says the foundation stones for the construction of the Altneuschul were brought by angels from the destroyed Holy Temple in Jerusalem "on condition" (*al-tenai* in Hebrew) that the stones would be returned when the Temple was restored.

Still another legend maintains that the Jews were not permitted to change or to repair anything in the Altneuschul. When something had to be fixed or built onto the synagogue, the builder was always punished by misfortune or even death. For this and other reasons, the synagogue remained unchanged for many centuries.

At one time, according to yet another Altneuschul legend, the synagogue was protected against fire in the ghetto by angels who changed into doves.

A different folktale relates that the remains of the *golem*, the artificial creature made of clay and brought to life by the famous scholar, Rabbi Loew, are deposited in the synagogue— perhaps hidden away in the attic. Even today, it is said, no one dares to go up to the attic and the author was even told that during the Nazi occupation, two German soldiers climbed up to the attic to seek jewels and were never seen again. We shall discuss the rabbi and golem again when we visit the Old Jewish Cemetery.

Today, this oldest preserved synagogue in Europe still serves the needs of Prague's Jews. In the middle of the synagogue waves a historic banner of the Prague Jewish community. The right to have a banner of their own as a symbol of independence was first granted to the Jews of Prague by Charles IV in 1357. Attached to the western pillar of the main nave, the banner was altered to its present form in 1716 on the occasion of the birth of a son to Emperor Charles VI. The center of the banner bears the Star of David and contains a pointed Jewish hat that for centuries was the sign of Prague Jewry. The hat was also one of the traditional items of clothing of Prague's Jews. In certain periods Jews were not allowed to leave the ghetto without the mark of their religion.

There were times when conflict followed conflict. Historically, hatemongers—often incited by the Church itself—blamed the Jews for the Black Death in the fourteenth century, for example, and accused them of poisoning the wells "in order to destroy the whole of Christendom." The largest pogrom in the history of the Prague ghetto took place during Easter 1389. The killing was so onerous that this horrible event is still remembered in a special prayer that is read on Yom Kippur in today's Old-New Synagogue. Rabbi Avigdor Kara is the author of this elegy commemorating the pogrom that overwhelmed the Jews in 1389.

The synagogue's structure is in the shape of a reticulated nave. Its gateway is a portal with plant ornamentation. This original portal with a tympanum is decorated with stylized vine leaves. The hall-type double nave has a five-part rib vaulting supported by two octagonal pillars. The purpose of the fifth rib was to avoid giving a "cross" form to the vault, writes Rachel Wischnitzer in *The Architecture of the European Synagogue*. At the eastern wall stands the *aron ha-kodesh* (cabinet containing the scrolls of the Torah). The prized bronze chandeliers are from the sixteenth and seventeenth centuries.

"The synagogue is a grayish stone structure composed of a double-naved main room for men." The hall of worship is 49 x 29 feet. On three sides the main building is surrounded by low annexes that serve as a vestibule and a nave for the women. The latter section is connected with the synagogue's main room only by slit openings in the wall to enable the women to

hear a service. The floor of the main nave is somewhat lower.
Statue of Moses. Near the Altneuschul is a statue of Moses
by sculptor Frantisek Bilek. It is Moses on his knees in despair
after his descent from Mount Sinai. When he sees the results
of his anger: the fragments of the shattered tablets of the Law,
he despairs. He broke the tablets out of anger when he found
that his co-religionists had been worshipping idols.

Sculpted at the turn of the century by Bilek, the statue was
"meant to be the first of an unfinished series of numerous biblical characters and prophets to demonstrate the spiritual development of mankind." The original sculpture that was placed in
the small park next to the Altneuschul in 1935 was destroyed by
the Nazis. A copy was unveiled in the same spot in 1948.

Jubilee Synagogue, u.Jeruzalemska, 7, Prague. Located in the
Nove Mesto or New Town. This and the Old-New Synagogue
still serve the existing Jewish community. Services are held
Friday evenings and Saturday mornings. The organ is sometimes used and men and women can at times sit together. The
community calls it modern Orthodox. The Jewish community
decided to erect this synagogue "at the time of the Silver Jubilee
of Franz Joseph 1's ascension to the Austrian throne, which is
why it is called the Jubilee Synagogue in his honor."

The Jewish Town Hall, 18 u. Maislova, Prague. This impressive building is the heart of the Jewish community. This Jewish
Town Hall with its distinctive Hebrew clock, with Hebrew
numerals moving counterclockwise, serves as the community
center and boasts a kosher restaurant (see below). The present
rococo appearance of the Town Hall dates from 1763.

The kehila offices, rabbi's study, community archives, and
dining hall are all contained here in this early seventeenth century building located just up the street from the Old-New
Synagogue.

Karol Sidon is the new rabbi in Prague. He left
Czechoslovakia in 1983 and studied Judaism in Heidelberg,
Germany, and Israel. A writer and friend of Vaclav Havel, he
was one of the dissidents who had gathered around President
Havel. He became rabbi in Prague in 1992. A remarkable man,
born of a Jewish father and a Christian mother, he underwent

formal conversion. In 1992, he succeeded Rabbi Daniel Mayer, who had resigned.

Federation of Jewish Communities, 18 u. Maislova, P.O. Box 297, 11001, Prague. Tel: 0042-2-2481-0130, or 2481-1090. FAX: 0042-2-2481-0912.

Chabad of Prague, Bilkova u., 14, Prague. Always a warm welcome at this Chabad House. Tourists in Prague for Passover, for example, can attend the *Seder* Half the audience at this festive holiday celebration was from the U.S. The building is given high marks for its facilities, including a school and synagogue.

Reform Groups in Prague. There are two Reform movement groups in Prague. Both are members of the World Union for Progressive Judaism. The first is **Bet Praha.** In 2000, there was not as yet a Temple building. Address: P. O. Box 195, 11001, Prague Tel/FAX: 0042-2- 2482-26756. The other Reform group is known as **Bet Simcha,** Uruguayska 7, 12000, Prague. Tel/FAX: 0042-2-2481-2385.

Kosher Restaurants in Prague

Shalom Restaurant, located in The Jewish Community Town Hall, 18 u. Maislova, Prague. Offered here is cafeteria-style eating. Shabbat dinners. Open daily from 11:30 A.M. to 2 P.M. Closed Sunday.

King Solomon, Siroka 8, Prague 1. Tel: 4202-246-187-52. Open from 11 A.M. to 11 P.M. This restaurant offers a varied menu during the week and Shabbat lunch.

Golan Kosher Restaurant, Na Prikope 10, Prague 1. Tel: 4202-242-315-01. Open Sunday to Thursday, 11 A.M. to 11:30 P.M. Friday, from 11 A.M. to 4 P.M. and Saturdays, 6 P.M. to 11:30 P.M.

Jerusalem Kosher Restaurant and Shop (L'Mehedrin Dairy, café-style). Brehova 5, Prague 1, Near the Old-New Synagogue. Tel/FAX, 4303-2481-2001 Open from 8 to 11 P.M.

A **drug store,** at the corner of Maislova and Siroka streets, was set up recently by Charles Benibghi, who likes to help tourists find their way to Jewish sites.

Hotel Inter-Continental, Prague. Tel: 0042-2-2488-1111. FAX Reservation: 0042-2-2481-0071. This modern, luxury hotel is practically in the Old Jewish Town and is a fine stopping place for those who wish to visit the Jewish sites extensively.

Park Hotel, Prague. This is a more modest hotel than the Inter-Continental. On an outside wall of the hotel is a memorial to the Holocaust.

Precious Legacy Tours, Maiselova 16 (on the corner of Siroka) 100 00, Prague 1-Josefov. Tel: (4202) 232-1951; tel/FAX (4202) 232-0398; tel/FAX (4202) 472-1068. VIP Mobile phone, 0601-214-088; E-mail: legacy_tours@oasanet.cz; Web site: www.legacytours.cz. Luba Poleva, Ph.D., is owner, manager and chief guide of this Jewish travel agency and Judaica souvenir shop known as "Precious Legacy Tours." Among her guests have been Gregory Peck and Whoopie Goldberg. Luba Poleva is an official licensed tour guide for Prague, Vienna, Budapest and Cracow. Her agency offers Jewish tour services, tickets to all synagogues in the Jewish quarter, accommodations, private cars, Judaica art, souvenirs, books and Klezmer music. Also, meal vouchers for the Jewish Community Kosher Restaurant Shalom at the Town Hall and King Solomon Kosher Restaurant. Daily tours, (groups and individual) are conducted to the Jewish Quarter, and to Terezin. The agency is located next to the synagogue.

Mosaic Tours and Travel offers an opportunity to experience Jewish life in Prague in a service offered by Travel Judaica. Reservations in the U.S. for this tour, which includes a stay in a Prague hotel, and information about the tour to the Czech Republic are available from 1-800-Shalom-94. Mosaic Tours and Travel is located at 420 Lincoln Rd., Suite 448, Miami Beach, Florida 33139.

CEDOK

CEDOK Czechoslovak Travel—In Prague, one of the many Cedok branches is located at Bilkova 6, directly across from the Hotel Inter-Continental. In New York City, Cedok Czechoslovak Travel is located at 10 East 40th St., New York,

New York 10016. Tel: (212) 689-9720.

Charles Bridge

Of the fifteen bridges linking the two halves of Prague, the oldest and best loved is the Charles Bridge. After making Prague his capital in 1346, this Holy Roman Emperor and King of Bohemia, Charles IV (1346-78) built the bridge on the site of an old Slavic fort. Thirty stone saints line the bridge, the oldest stone bridge in Central Europe. Most of the stone saints were carved in the eighteenth and nineteenth centuries. Under Charles IV, a Czech national hero, Prague became an important medieval capital with the first university in Central Europe.

Another important figure in Czechoslovakian history and Jewish history in Bohemia and Moravia is that of Rudolf II (1552-1612), Holy Roman Emperor and King of Bohemia from the year 1576. In 1583, Rudolf transferred his court to Prague. This move improved the position of the Jews, and Jewish culture flourished. Rudolf was in constant touch with Marcus Mordecai Maisel, who served him as a banker and supplier of art objects for his art collection. He received Rabbi Judah Loew ben Bezalel (the *Maharal*—the Hebrew acronym for "most venerated teacher and rabbi") in an audience, it is said. Rudolf created the category of the *Hoflefreiter Jude* (1582): Jews who were attached to the court and enjoyed such privileges as exemption from taxes and from wearing the Jewish badge. From them the institution of 'Court Jew" developed.

But how King Randolph and Rabbi Judah Loew ben Bezalel met on the Charles Bridge comes from another legend. The Marahal, according to Elie Wiesel's account of the meeting in his book *The Golem*, was standing in the middle of the bridge waiting for King Rudolf. Onlookers argued that the rabbi might be run over because the king might not stop because "his horses run faster than the wind." "'Not this time,'" said the Maharal. People sneered. Soon, the horses came running as though they would trample the rabbi under their feet, "and then, suddenly they stopped." The king wanted to know why the Maharal risked his life. "I had to,'" said the Maharal. "'My people's lives are in jeopardy. Have you not signed a decree ordering them to

On the Charles Bridge, the crucifix surrounded by huge gilded Hebrew letters that
spell the traditional Hebrew sanctification, "Holy, holy, holy is the Lord of Hosts."
(Photo by Sam Urman)

go into exile?'" The king invited the Maharal to the castle and they became friends. The Maharal became a frequent visitor in the role of intercessor and defender.

Although Jews were persecuted in Prague, during his lifetime Emperor Charles IV protected the Jews. He was a statesman, writer, scholar, linguist, and builder.

At the end of the bridge named for him, you pass into the "Mala Strana," the Little Quarter-one of the three ancient areas of historical Prague.

On the Charles Bridge, the visitor will observe a great crucifix surrounded by huge gilded Hebrew letters that spell the traditional Hebrew sanctification, *Kadosh, Kadosh, Kadosh Adonai Tzvaot*, "Holy, Holy, Holy is the Lord of Hosts." According to various commentators, this piece, degrading to Jews, came about because in 1609 a Jew was accused of desecrating the crucifix. The Jewish community was forced to pay for putting up the Hebrew words in gold letters. The Nazis removed the gold.

Another explanation is that a Jew spit at the cross and for this he was to be put to death as punishment. When this man begged for his life, the king, seeking to have good relations with the Jews, said the Jewish community had to rectify the offense, and the Jewish man would have to put up a cross. A Jew is not allowed to put up a cross, but the man was forced to do so. By adding the words, *Kadosh, Kadosh, Kadosh,* the Jew felt exonerated from wrongdoing to his religion because the sanctification contains the words, *Adonai Tzvaot,* so that the man was in effect saying his god is *Adonai Tzvaot.*

High Synagogue, also known as the **Town Hall Synagogue, VysoKa (Radnicni) Synagoga,** u. Cervena, Prague. This synagogue is located across the street from the entrance to the "Old-New Synagogue," or the "Altneuschul." The High Synagogue, or "Hoch Synagogue," was built in 1565. The name High Synagogue probably comes from its unusual location on the first floor, which suggested its then exclusive and nonpublic character. Originally, it was accessible from a room on the first floor of the Jewish Town Hall. It was used as a prayer house by loaders of the Jewish community.

The High Synagogue and the Maisel Synagogue were financed and built by Mordechai Maisel (1528-1601), the so-called mayor of the Jewish Town Hall. The architect was Panacius Roder. In 1907, the High Synagogue's entrances on the eastern facade were removed and the existing entrance opposite the Altneuschul was constructed.

Like the other synagogues, the High Synagogue today is a museum. Exhibition cases and wall displays will mesmerize the visitor. Significantly, the High Synagogue contains several thousand synagogue curtains, draperies, Torah mantles, and binders that were seized by the Nazis from Czech Jews and from Jewish families throughout Europe.

The Prague Jewish community was especially known for its embroidery workshops. There is an exhibit showing the continuous development of synagogue textiles from the sixteenth to the twentieth centuries. An early baroque stone Holy Ark with combined columns on the sides, a symbol of the Torah crown, and an inscribed cartouche distinguish this synagogue.

When you leave the Old-New Synagogue or the High Synagogue, cross Maislova Street and walk down Stareho Hrbitova Street. On the left side of the street and to the left of the entrance to the Old Jewish Cemetery is the Klausen Synagogue.

Klausen Synagogue (Klausova Synagoga), u. Stareho Hrbitova, Prague. Located to the left of the cemetery entrance on u. Stareho Hrbitova, this synagogue, which stands as a museum, is especially noted for its permanent exhibition of Hebrew manuscripts and prints. The exhibits here contain examples of Jewish cultural and religious items.

Three small buildings that comprised the then-synagogue were destroyed by fire on June 21, 1689. That fire ravaged all of the 316 houses in the ghetto and most of the synagogues and public buildings.

The Klausen Synagogue was completed in 1694, thanks to Shlomo Kohen, a printer. The name "Klausen" may be derived from the Latin *claustrum.* Another source says the name Klausen comes from those small buildings, which were called "klauses." That is why some call this the Klaus Synagogue. The building was enlarged in 1883-84 and partly rebuilt in 1910, according to Carol Herselle Krinsky.

Interestingly, for lack of open space, the Klausen Synagogue was built on its location even though it faced the Old Jewish Cemetery. Shown in the synagogue is an exquisite baroque Torah Ark consisting of three sections. The vaulted ceiling of the synagogue is decorated with a rococo stucco from the eighteenth century.

By the way, the works of Kohen the printer are highly artistic. Well known are the Prague editions of the Pentateuch of 1518 and 1530 and the so-called "Prague Haggadah" of 1526. Kohen also printed selections from the writings of Rabbi Loew.

Chevra Kadisha Building, u. Stareho Hrbitova, Prague. The Chevra Kadisha building, to the right of the entrance to the Old Jewish Cemetery, once served as a mortuary. Today, it contains a heartbreaking display of poems, drawings, and letters from the children of the Terezin concentration camp. The majority of the Terezin children's material was created under the supervision of an established painter, Friedl Dicker-Brandejsova, to whom the children went to for lessons. Altogether 4,000 drawings survived, along with excerpts from illegal magazines published by the children in the camp. The present building, a Romanesque structure, was built in 1906.

Maisel Synagogue (Maislova Synagogue) u. Maislova, Prague. Originally built in 1592, this is now a neo-Gothic, triple-nave building designed by architect Alfred Grotte and remodeled between 1893 and 1905. It is named after Marcus Mordechai Maisel (1528-1601), who commissioned a number of buildings in the sixteenth-century Prague ghetto, including the High Synagogue (Town Hall) on Cervena Street. However, this synagogue was almost completely destroyed by the fire of 1689. Within two years (1691), it was rebuilt in baroque style.

This synagogue remains one of the most spectacular buildings in the Prague ghetto. A permanent exposition of silver and other synagogue objects from the collections of the Jewish Museum draws thousands of tourists. Here one observes synagogue crowns, shields, spice boxes, kiddush cups, and 8,000 silver pieces. The exhibit here is one of the largest collections of silver artifacts in the Czech Republic, with the oldest silver objects dating from the late sixteenth century. The largest part

The Chevra Kadisha building is located to the right of the entrance in the Old Jewish Cemetery in Prague. (Photo by Ben G. Frank)

of the collection consists of silver Torah ornaments. The visitor can view Sabbath lamps, pairs of silver candlesticks, and silver kiddush cups for benediction over wine. Most interesting, however, are silver spice boxes of various forms. They are used for the "Havdalah ceremony," which concludes the Sabbath.

Marcus Mordechai Maisel was a remarkable man. A Prague Financier, philanthropist, and head of the Jewish community, he was known as the "Maecenas of Science" and "the benefactor hero." A generous and fabulously rich merchant, his clients included the Imperial Court. He has been called the "First Jewish capitalist in Germany." Maisel helped Finance Rudolf II, who appointed him counselor during the Turkish wars. He had the streets of the ghetto paved. He bought a garden so that he could extend the area of the cemetery. He also built an infirmary and public baths. Above all, he organized the construction of the two synagogues—the High Synagogue and the Maisel Synagogue—upon which he lavished grand gifts and generous donations. Toward the end of his life in 1590, Maisel, who had so far been engaged in building public structures, bought a piece of land at the southern end of the ghetto on which to build a synagogue for his own use. In 1591, he obtained a special tax immunity privilege from Emperor Rudolf II to do so. A year later, during the holiday, Sirnchat Torah, the synagogue was dedicated. Architect Judah Tsoref Goldschmied de Herz designed the original building and Joseph Wald built it.

Historian David Gans, Maisel's contemporary, says in his chronicle that the building was unusually impressive. Supported by twenty pillars, its main, vast nave has been acclaimed by architects. Maisel and his wife donated a rich treasure of synagogal textiles, mantles, and curtains to the synagogue. This house of worship also served as the repository for a special banner that Maisel had made for himself on the basis of the privilege granted by Rudolf II in 1592 and kept in the Altneuschul.

During the Renaissance period, the Maisel Synagogue was the largest and most impressive house of worship in the Jewish Town.

Spanish Synagogue (Spanelska synagoga), u. Dusni, and Vezenska ulice, Prague. The building exhibits the distinctive

The Old Jewish Cemetery in Prague. (Photo by Sam Urman)

Moorish style that flourished in the 1880s. The exterior's design, which corresponds to the interior's Oriental decoration, gave the synagogue its name. Today, this synagogue, which is located opposite the presbytery of the Church of the Holy Spirit, is closed.

This Jewish house of worship is still called by some the "Old Schul," because it was built in the place of the original synagogue and was erected before the pogrom of 1389. The Portuguese rite had been followed there for many years. In 1868, the synagogue was demolished. The rebuilding was undertaken by Prague architect Vojtech Ignats Ullmann. The interior was designed by architect Joseph Nikias and is entirely Moorish.

The synagogue has a square, central ground plan and a large dome over the middle section. On three sides are balconies of metal construction that open into the main room. The interior was decorated between 1882 and 1893, according to a design by A. Baum and B. Munzberger. It includes a low stucco arabesque of stylized Islamic motifs that is richly gilded and polychromed in green, blue, and red. The same decorative elements are used in the carved decoration on the door around the organ, balcony railing, and wall lining with the ground floor. The windows were filled with painted glass in 1882-83.

During World War II, the Germans used the Spanish Synagogue as a warehouse. It was handed over to the State Jewish Museum after it had been partly restored.

In 1960, the first permanent exhibition of synagogal textiles was opened, and it ran until 1982.

The Old Jewish Cemetery, u. Stareho Hrbitova, Prague. Can you imagine a cemetery that some guidebooks call one of the ten most interesting sights in the world? U.S. President Bill Clinton visited the Old Jewish Cemetery on his visit to Prague in January 1994. And thousands of tourists come here each day.

Called a garden, it "evokes the spirit of the ghetto some feel and defies the passage of time." The Old Jewish Cemetery is one of Europe's oldest and best preserved Jewish burial grounds. About 500 years old, the cemetery contains between 12,000 and 20,000 gravestones. All are crowded into a very tight space and teeter at different angles. Slabs and tombstones date to the mid-fifteenth century. These tombstones are a chronicle of the Prague ghetto.

Actual burials took place here until 1787. The oldest-known tombstone—from 1439—is that of the Kabbalist and poet, Rabbi Avigdor Kara.

Because the tiny cemetery was not large enough to contain all the dead, it was necessary to gradually cover older graves with earth to provide a new burial layer. The result was that an uneven area appeared, and in some places it forms twelve burial layers. Parts of the tombstones from the older layers were raised to higher layers, which created the pile of tombstones that is typical of this cemetery.

All the tombstones carry Hebrew inscriptions giving the date of death and in some cases the name of the deceased and the date of burial. Poetic texts recall the merits of the individual and express the sadness of the relatives. On some stones you can see the biblical tribe, family name, and profession of the deceased. Hands outstretched in blessing represent a person from the priestly tribe of Aaron; a jug signifies the tribe of Levi; scissors are for tailors; a book identifies scribes; a violin is for musicians; and a tweezer marks a doctor.

The most significant tombstones are the large tombs confined by two oblique and two vertical stone slabs; most of these are in the central part of the cemetery opposite the main entrance.

The visitor really stands in awe here. Beneath the gravestones lie rabbis and scholars. Every human being is precious and significant. Yet we search for the tombs of the so-called mayor of the Prague Jewish Town, Mordechai Maisel, who died in 1661; the grave of Rabbi Loew; as well as the tomb of Hindel, the wife of Jacob Bashevi of Truenburg who died in 1628.

Rabbi Loew

One cannot really discuss the Old Jewish Cemetery and the Altneuschul or the Prague Town Hall without commenting on the legendary, and some say miraculous, Rabbi Judah Loew ben Bezalel. In the cemetery you will see the gravestone of Rabbi Judah Loew ben Bezalel, creator of the *golem*. His tomb, located in the rear of the cemetery, resembles a sarcophagus. This famous rabbi is supposed to have invented an artificial man we have come to regard as the golem, considered by Elie Wiesel to be "the most fascinating creature in Jewish lore and fantasy." As the story goes, Rabbi Loew is said to have constructed a clay figure that he brought to life in the Altneuschul with the help of God.

Owing to his profound knowledge, including the Kabbala, he thus entered popular lore as the miracle worker who could secretly give life and breath to the golem, which became a robot figure serving the rabbi as a reward for his good works. "Without the Maharal and the golem, the Jewish community of Prague might not have survived," Elie Wiesel maintains.

The golem, constructed to represent a human being, was to be the Rabbi's servant and defend the Jews from their persecutors, notably ritual-murder accusers. But it ran amok. Finally, legend has it, the rabbi was forced to destroy his creation by removing the magic name from underneath its tongue. He left the body of the golem in the attic and forbade any access to the attic in the Altneuschul. To this day, no one is to go up to the attic.

Rabbi Loew, who was also known as Der Hohe Rabbi Loew because of his great height, was a rabbi, Talmudist, moralist, mathematician, and philosopher. And he was a philosopher of great originality. His profound wisdom and wide-ranging scholarship influenced not only Jewish religious philosophy, but also ethics and pedagogy. He was the spiritual head of the Jewish community from the end of the sixteenth century until the early seventeenth century.

He was known as the Maharal. Maharal is the Hebrew acronym for "most venerated teacher and rabbi." Some people call him a wondrous magician who vanquished the angel of death. Known throughout the Jewish world as one of the greatest Talmudic scholars, he was acclaimed as the celebrated "Wonder Rebbe of Prague."

Born circa 1525, Rabbi Loew resided in Prague from 1573 to 1584, then from 1588 to 1592, and then again in 1597, until his death in 1609. When he died, he was serving as a rabbi and head of the yeshiva in Prague.

We think he was named after the Kabbalist Reb Yehuda

Loew, also of Prague. His tombstone states that he belonged to the royal line of David. We know he left Worms to study in Prague. He later married Pearl, the daughter of Rabbi Shmelke Reich, when he was thirty-two and she was twenty-eight. They had a daughter and one son.

He lived during the reign of Rudolf II, a time supposedly of the supernatural, which gave rise, obviously, to many of the legends surrounding him.

He is best known as the author of commentaries, essays on ethics, and mystically oriented writings. In his scholarly works he emphasized a logical progression from the simple biblical texts and post-biblical religious and legal writings called the Mishnah to the more difficult Talmud.

Rabbi Loew died at the age of ninety-seven, leaving behind a legacy of works covering every aspect of Jewish religious life and a legend that "consoles the hunted, the persecuted," according to Elie Wiesel.

Prague Town Hall. An impressive statue of Rabbi Loew adorns the entrance of the Prague Town Hall. It portrays a tall, severe figure with a high cylindrical hat and a long flowing beard fending off a naked woman who appears to be holding him. This statue was sculpted by Ladislav Saloun, a non-Jew who also designed Jan Hus's monument in the Old Town Square.

While working on the statue when the town hall was created in 1910, Saloun was inspired by a legend of Rabbi Loew's death: "Unable to approach the almost century-year-old scholar who was always absorbed in the study of holy books, death hid in a rose that was offered to the rabbi by his unsuspecting granddaughter. "

After you walk through the cemetery, you can visit the Pinkas Synagogue, where a further treasure awaits you.

Pinkas Synagogue (Pinkasova Synagoga), u. Siroka, Prague. At the other end of the cemetery in the heart of the old Jewish quarter is the Pinkas Synagogue. It was originally set up on the site of a Jewish house of prayer that existed before 1492. At that time, the house belonged to the Horowitz family. A descendant of the family, Zalman Munka Horovic, also known as Aaron Meshullam, financed the construction of the synagogue. Built in 1535, it was modeled after a late-Gothic, partly Renaissance synagogue built in 1479. One of the oldest and most valuable houses of worship in Prague, it was founded by Rabbi Pinkas and enlarged in 1535 by his grandson, Aron Meshule. The construction contains rib vaulting on Renaissance supports. The women's section was added in 1625 by Judah Tsoref Goldschmied de Herz.

Between 1954 and 1959, the interior of the Pinkas Synagogue was turned into the memorial for the 77,297 Bohemian and Moravian victims of the Holocaust, about 85 percent of the community. The names, and family names arranged according to communities, were inscribed on the walls of the main nave, balcony, and anteroom.

Today when you enter the Pinkas Synagogue, you see craftsmen painstakingly inscribing the names of the 77,297 murdered Czech Jews. The engraved names had been inscribed previously, but the Communists allowed the Jewish names to fade away. The memorial to the victims of the Nazi persecution under the Communists, it was closed to the public for more than twenty years. The names have to be inscribed again so they can live in memory.

Although the location of a synagogue near a cemetery is quite unusual, the Pinkas Synagogue was built close to the Old Jewish Cemetery because there was not enough space in the ghetto.

A memorial to Franz Kafka, the great Czech Jewish writer of universal fame, is located at his native house, No. 5, u. Radnice, Old Town of Prague. Kafka (1883-1924) attained worldwide respect and readership. He was born in the Old Town of Prague, in a house at that time located in Jachymova Street. This corner house next to the St. Nicholas Church was destroyed by a fire in 1897 and rebuilt in 1902. Only the portal of the old house was preserved. On July 3, 1966, a memorial tablet by academic sculptor Karel Hiadik was unveiled on the house standing at the corner of Kaprova, Maiselova, and Uradnice streets. A Kafka museum is located at this site of his birth.

Nearby is the Golz Kinsky Palace, a large, pink and white rococo structure that played an important role in Kafka's life. There, he attended school in the Palace and often visited his father's dry-goods store located on the ground floor. Kafka studied law at the German university and worked First in a law office and then for an insurance company. He wrote only in his spare time.

Because he was sensitive to noise, Kafka stayed and worked for some time in a small house on the Golden Lane in the area of the Prague Castle. The building was rented from its owner, Mrs. Michlova, by Kafka's youngest sister, Ottla. In the winter of 1916-17, Kafka wrote during the evenings and nights a number of shorter prose works and stories that he published in 1919.

In 2000, the area of the Old Town Square where the famous Jewish writer was born over a century ago, was scheduled to be renamed after Kafka, the author of such classics as *The Trial, The Castle* and *Metamorphosis*. It took a 37-year campaign for the naming to occur. Eduard Goldstuecker, 87, who led the drive, was a former Czech ambassador to Israel. In 1953, Goldstuecker began the campaign for the "best-known son Prague has today," he has said. He escaped death during the country's show trials of the 1950's. When released in Prague Spring, he fled to Britain. In 1992 he returned to Prague and began the campaign again.

Kafka did not live to bear the pain of the Holocaust. His works were suppressed by the Communists as "subjective and pessimistic." Now, of course, his writings are in great demand.

Kafka is buried in the New Olsany Cemetery alongside his parents. A stone marks their burial spot. A plaque also remembers his three sisters who died in the Holocaust. Located in Nad Vodovodem Street, this new Jewish cemetery includes prominent Jewish community leaders, such as the founder of the Jewish Museum, Dr. Salomon Hugo Lieben.

Hradcany Castle (Castle Hill) or Prague Castle—Look up to Prague Castle. Below the castle wall are hanging gardens and ancient roofs descending to the water's edge. Built by Bohemian kings, the castle was also the residence of Czech kings of old as well as of modern Czech leaders, such as Thomas Garrigue Masaryk and Eduard Benes. The Jews who came to Prague probably lived around the marketplaces in what is now Hradcany, a popular tourist attraction and a must-see on any visit to the Czech capital. It is a labyrinth of castles, churches, and museums perched on one of the seven hills on which Prague is built. Head for the sprawling edifice that dominates the city, the Hradcany or Prague Castle. Everyone looks to the castle for leadership as a symbol of strength.

After the Jews settled near the castle, they ran up against difficulties from the community and invaders torched the oldest Prague synagogue as well as the Jewish quarter that was located just below the castle. As a result, the Jews moved to the right bank of the Vltava River, which became the Jewish quarter we know today.

One occupant of the castle, Thomas Garrigue Masaryk (1850-1937), a profound writer and thinker, was certainly a friend to the Jews and to men of goodwill everywhere. Without Masaryk, "there would have been no Czechoslovakia," according to Josef Korbel in *Twentieth Century Czechoslovakia: The Meanings of Its History*.

By 1918, Masaryk and Czech leaders had convinced the French, the British, and U.S. President Woodrow Wilson that the Austro-Hungarian monarchy must be dismembered and that an independent Czech-Slovak state be set up. A declaration proclaiming the new nation of Czechoslovakia was signed in 1918 by Czech and Slovak émigré politicians in Pittsburgh, Pennsylvania.

Throughout his life, Masaryk fought anti-Semitism. Emil Ludwig writes that Masaryk had "a life-long sympathy for the Jews. As a Czech, he himself knew what it meant to be a member" of a downtrodden people. After World War I, anti-Semitism existed in most parts of Eastern Europe; it was much less of a problem in Czech lands.

During the Hilsner affair—a blood libel case occurring at the turn of the century—Masyrk wrote pamphlets declaring anti-Semitism an uncivilized and slanderous attitude. The Hilsner case involved trumped-up anti-Semitic charges against a young Czech Jew, Leopold Hilsner, who was arrested for the murder of a seamstress. Masaryk intervened; he did not have to do this. His pamphlets won the day and Hilsner's sentence was commuted to life imprisonment, and he was pardoned in 1916.

But Masaryk and Eduard Benes, who succeeded Masaryk, were not the only ones to occupy Prague Castle.

Even the hated Nazi invaders walked up the carpet-lined

stairways of the castle. Hitler proclaimed from the castle that Czechoslovakia no longer existed. And it was the home of hard-line Communist rulers who leaned hard on the people of this country for forty years. The popular playwright and intellectual, Vaclav Havel, a true dissident against the Communist regime and now Czech president, comes to work here every day, although he does not live here. In February 1990, in one of his First acts as president of Czechoslovakia, Havel re-established full diplomatic relations with Israel, ties that had been broken in 1967. Havel became the first head of state in modern Eastern Europe to visit Jerusalem in 1990. The next year, he hosted the then-Israeli President, Chaim Herzog, in Prague. He called Communist rule "20 years of timelessness."

WENCESLAS SQUARE

Most visitors will tell you that the first place they visit in Prague is Wenceslas Square, an 800-yard-long avenue of shops and restaurants. This is a great place for a leisurely stroll. Not only does stately Wenceslas Square cleave the heart of Prague, not only is it the "Main Street" of this wonderful metropolis, but it is also the symbol of Czech freedom and of a people's desire for liberty.

The square is named after Prince Wenceslas, later the "Good King" of the Christmas carol who lived more than a thousand years ago. His equestrian statue looks down on the square that bears his name. They say that today flowers are placed at its base in memory of those who died or committed suicide in Prague Spring. The statue was a symbol of good during the Velvet Revolution. Here in the middle of the square, President Vaclav Havel addressed the Czech and Slovak people. Here is where the hated Nazi troops entered in 1939. Here in Prague Spring 1968, Czech students hurled rocks at the Soviet armored tanks that crept into Wenceslas Square. And here in 1989, thousands gathered to celebrate the end of communism in what the world knows as the Velvet Revolution.

The 1968 Prague Spring was a symbol of hope and opportunity.

The people of Czechoslovakia wanted to ease the toughness of Communist rule. But on the night of August 20-21, 1968, troops of the Warsaw Pact invaded Czechoslovakia. Soviet airborne forces, including tank and artillery units, were landed in Prague and Bratislava. The invasion, said the Soviets, was a domestic affair. But the world did not buy it and was outraged. Telephone lines were cut and soldiers armed with machine guns took over Hradcany Castle. The invasion even then was a testimony to the failure of Marxism-Leninism.

But the Czechs fought back in their own way. They painted swastikas on the Russian tanks. They spat at the Russians. They turned street signs in the wrong direction to confuse the Soviets. They practiced passive resistance. Indeed, the tanks in 1968 were wholly inadequate weapons because in Czechoslovakia, they fired at "ideas with no hope of hitting the target."

The late Alexander Dubcek and other Prague Spring leaders were taken to Moscow, where behind closed doors in the Kremlin, Leonid Brezhnev forced Dubcek's government to surrender to undemocratic experiments. Among the Czechs was Frantisek Kriegel. A dedicated reformer, Kriegel, who had been called "that Galician Jew" by one of the Soviet leaders, was an abstainer to the Communist proposal to stop the reforms. The Russians kept him hidden and claimed that he was sick. The Czechs who were at the airport ready to depart for Prague said they would not leave until the Russians produced Kriegel. The Russians, who had every intention of keeping him, finally freed him and he took off with the delegation, according to Patrick Brogan in his book *The Captive Nations: Eastern Europe, 1945-90.*

But Prague still remained the "city of Kafka and Soviet tanks." Wenceslas Square had the submerged, slow motion quality of a nightmare. As Havel is said to have remarked, "The clocks had stopped." In the 1980s, however, Czechs kept alive the desire for freedom. At this time, 12,000 Jews remained in Czechoslovakia. Their average age was 60; it would stay that way for several decades, for there were only about 1,000 young people between the ages of 15 and 20. Some of these young Jewish persons would be among the those who brought about the Velvet

Revolution in 1989. In those 21 autumn days, without a drop of blood spilled, the people of Czechoslovakia broke the power of their Communist rulers. "It was a glorious, gentle revolution."

TEREZIN (THERESIENSTADT)

It is not easy to get to Terezin, forty minutes northwest of Prague. And yet they come day after day after day. On the bleak, rainy day I was there, I saw members of a teenage Canadian hockey team, a Danish college student, and an American university professor—all who spent one hour by bus to reach this city in Bohemia, this death station of the Nazis. Horrible things happened here in Terezin, especially to children.

To get there, you travel north from Prague. The fields at first are flat and neatly plowed. Farmland and sweeping highways spotlight a rich farm area that turns hilly as you approach the town of Terezin. The scenery actually gives little idea of the gruesome fortress town of Terezin, the star-shaped garrison town named for the Austria Empress Maria Theresa, who perhaps was a harbinger of the horrible inflictions hurled at the Jewish people there. In German, the town is called Theresienstadt. In the late 1700s, Terezin was a bulwark against the Prussians, who often would barrel their way down from the north. The name will probably send shudders down the spines of men and women of goodwill everywhere for hundreds of years to come, those who know the story of Terezin and the Holocaust.

About 277,000 Jews who had resided within the pre-Munich boundaries of Czechoslovakia lost their lives in the Holocaust. Approximately 25,000 escaped from Bohemia and Moravia before the war broke out, which left a Jewish population of about 90,000 in those two provinces. Only 10,000 of these Jews would survive.

In 1938, about 135,000 Jews resided in Slovakia, of whom 40,000 lived in the territory ceded to Hungary (Ruthenia and Sub-Carpathia). About 5,000 Jews emigrated voluntarily before the war, leaving about 90,000 Jews in Slovakia itself. According to Lucy S. Dawidowicz in *The War Against the Jews: 1933-1945*, a total of 110,000 Slovak Jews were murdered.

In 1941, the Nazis occupied this walled municipality; they emptied out its inhabitants and turned a citadel into a transit camp for Jews on their way to the death camps.

It was as if a whole town had been cleared to become a ghost town as well as a transport center to transfer Jews to the gas chambers in Poland and beyond. Today, it still maintains a drab look, especially in the fall or winter.

Officially, Terezin was a self-governing ghetto. But in reality, it was a concentration camp, probably without the gas chambers, although bodies of people who had died of typhus there were sent to the crematorium nearby, which the visitor can still see today. About 150,000 men, women, and children passed through this ghetto for Jewish prisoners between 1941 and 1945. At least 117,000 were tortured to death and murdered elsewhere. Of 15,000 children under the age of 15 who passed through the camp, fewer than 100 survived.

Nazis Reinhard Heydrich and Adolf Eichmann met on October 4, 1941. The Germans decided on the establishment of the Theresienstadt Ghetto on October 10, 1941, in a secret meeting at the Prague Castle chaired by Reich Protector Heydrich. The Nazis planned that from Terezin (in German, Theresienstadt), the Jews were to be deported to the East. Adolf Eichmann's plan was to evacuate the Jews from Terezin and transfer them to the concentration camps in Poland and beyond and then turn the whole area into a model German settlement. But Terezin took on an atmosphere that was worse than an "animal-like holding pen." At one point, nearly 60,000 persons lived in barracks designed to house 7,000 combat troops.

As a young child, the Czech author and one of the best-known Czech writers in the West, Ivan Klima, was packed off to Terezin. He writes about seeing the constant presence of death. "People died in the room where I lived. They died by the dozens," he wrote, adding, "the constant threat of the transports hung over the inhabitants."

Terezin also served as a "showplace," a facade for the International Red Cross monitors. The Nazis spruced up the camp to make the inspectors believe the Jews were being treated well. It was trickery par excellence—even in the midst

A sign above the entrance of the Small Fortress at Terezin declares Arbeit Macht Frei, "Work Makes You Free." That is the actual translation, but its real meaning was death. (Photo by Riva Frank)

of fake cultural activities, such as an orchestra concert given by the prisoners, transports from Terezin were continuously leaving for Auschwitz and Birkenau camps.

Several hundred Danish Jews were sent to Terezin because not all the Jews of Denmark escaped to Sweden. But the Danish government never gave up on their Jewish citizens and representatives from Denmark did visit the camp. And the government in Copenhagen sent food supplies to the Jewish Terezin. On April 14, 1945, the Danish prisoners left Terezin in Swedish Red Cross buses that were bound for freedom.

The Small Fortress at Terezin

A sign above the entrance of the Small Fortress declares: *Arbeit Macht Frei.* "Work Makes You Free," is the literal translation, but its real meaning was death. We know that now; the six million did not.

The first stop at Terezin might be the Small Fortress on the outskirts of town. This fort was built as part of the fortification system near the confluence of the Elbe and Ohre rivers. From the beginning, it was used as a prison. Jailed here, for example, were many nationalist leaders who wanted to overthrow Austrian rule. The 1914 assassins of Franz Ferdinand d'Este—archduke of Austria—were imprisoned here.

When Bohemia and Moravia were occupied by the Nazis in 1940, the Small Fortress became the prison of the Prague Gestapo. The first prisoners were brought there on June 14, 1940, and some 32,000 inmates, including 5,000 women, passed through the fortress during the war. The life of imprisoned Jews in this fortress was especially difficult, because it was a way station to Nazi trials, jails, prisons, and the concentration camps.

At the end of the war a typhoid epidemic killed many prisoners. On May 8, 1945, the first Soviet armored vehicles arrived in Terezin.

Between 1945 and 1948, the Small Fortress served as a detention camp for the Germans expelled from Czechoslovakia. During your visit, you will see the guards'

A cell block at the Small Fortress at Terezin. (Photo by Ben G. Frank)

office; the prison commander's office; the courtyards; the prison block cells, as well as 20 solitary confinement cells; the hospital block; the mortuary; places of execution; the SS barracks; and the national cemetery.

A documentary film is shown and there are special exhibits. It is also possible to purchase brochures, literature, and videotapes.

The Ghetto Museum at Terezin

After you visit the Small Fortress, turn right on the main road into the town of Terezin and you will come to the Ghetto Museum. On the front door are the Hebrew letters forming the word, *Yizkor*, "Remember." The museum was opened on October 17, 1991, fifty years after the beginning of the deportation of Jews from Czech lands.

Only after the 1989 Velvet Revolution could the building be handed over to serve as a memorial. Before the war, the museum building housed a school. During the ghetto period, it became, "L-417," and served as a home for boys 10 to 15 years old. Ironically, a "museum of Czechoslovakian police and revolutionary traditions of the Northern Bohemian region," was later set up in this former home of Jewish prisoners.

The exhibits are in good taste, well done, and include photographs, videotapes, and newspaper clippings of other materials in several languages. The exhibition is organized chronologically and begins with the Nazi take-over in Germany and ends with the liberation of Terezin.

In the Ghetto Museum, besides a tour of the permanent exhibition, there is an art gallery where you can see works of art created at the Terezin Ghetto. Guides are available.

Operating hours of the Small Fortress and Ghetto Museum, open throughout the year:

Winter: October 1 to March 31, 8 A.M. to 4:30 P.M.

Spring: April 1 to April 30, 8 A.M. to 5:30 P.M.

Summer: May 1 to September 30, 8 A.M. to 6:30 P.M.

The museum is closed December 24- 26 and January 1.

The Crematorium at Terezin

While the Communists controlled the country, local Terezin residents and guides often would not even tell you about the crematorium. While there were no gas chambers at Terezin, Jews and others were shot, tortured, or died from starvation or disease. The dead were disposed of in the crematorium, an old laundry building that usually is the third stop of a visit to Terezin. One can see the ovens.

A large Jewish cemetery is located near the crematorium. The site was visited by former Israeli President Chaim Herzog, who was on a state visit in 1991.

Between November 1 and February 28, the crematorium is accessible only with an official guide from the Ghetto Museum; otherwise, it is open every day, except Sunday, from 10 A.M. to 5 P.M.

Many travel agencies have tours to Terezin. The Federation of Jewish Communities, at 18 Maislova, Prague, Tel: 24-81-01-30, can advise you and is a good source for all of your questions.

The traveler can also go by bus from the Prague bus terminal to Terezin. Take the line to Litomerice and Usti Teplice.

Check the terminal bus timetable.

Suggested Reading

Ash, Timothy G. *The Magic Lantern: The Revolution of '89 Witnessed in Warsaw, Budapest, Berlin & Prague.* New York: Random House, 1990.

—. The Uses of Adversity: *Essays on the Fate of Central Europe.* New York: Random House, 1989.

Brogan, Patrick. *The Captive Nations: Eastern Europe, 1945-1990.* New York: Avon, 1990.

Dawidowicz, Lucy S. *The War Against the Jews: 1933-1945.* New York: Bantam, 1986.

Hoffman, Charles. *Gray Dawn: The Jews of Eastern Europe in the Post-Communist Era.* New York: HarperCollins, 1992.

Hoffman, Eva. *Exit into History: A Journey Through the New Eastern Europe.* New York: Viking, 1993.

Korbel, Josef. *Twentieth Century Czechoslovakia: The Meanings of Its History.* New York: Columbia University Press, 1977.

Krinsky, Carol Herselle. *Synagogues of Europe: Architecture, History, Meaning.* Cambridge, Mass.: MIT Press, 1985.

Kurlansky, Mark. *A Chosen Few: The Resurrection of European Jewry.* Reading, Mass.: Addison-Wesley, 1995.

Lendvai, Paul. *Anti-Semitism Without Jews: Communist Eastern Europe.* Garden City, N.Y: Doubleday, 1971.

Meyer, Peter, Bernard D. Weinryb, Eugene Duschinsky, and Nicolas Sylvain, eds. *The Jews in the Soviet Satellites.* Syracuse, New York: Syracuse University Press, 1953.

Moorhouse, Geoffrey, and the editors of Time-Life Books. *Prague. Amsterdam.* Time-Life Books, 1980.

Vital, David, *A People Apart, The Jews in Europe, 1789-1939.* Oxford, Oxford University Press, 1999.

Wechsberg, Joseph. *Prague: The Mystical City.* New York: Macmillan, 1971.

Weinberg, Gerhard L. *A World at Arms: A Global History of World War II.* New York: Cambridge University Press, 1994.

Weisel, Elie, ed. *The Golem: The Story of a Legend.* New York: Summit Books, 1983.

Wischnitzer, Rachel. *The Architecture of the European Synagogue.* Philadelphia: Jewish Publication Society of America, 1964.

Yahil, Leni. *The Holocaust: The Fate of European Jewry, 1932-1945.* Oxford: Oxford University Press, 1990.

Hungary
The Largest Jewish Community in Eastern Europe

This is Hungary: the sixteenth largest country in Europe, roughly the size of the state of Indiana. We now call this nation, the "Republic of Hungary." But from 1949 to 1989, it was known as the Hungarian People's Republic and it was Communist.

But that was more than a decade ago. Today Hungary is a proud member of NATO and is being considered for membership in the European Union. With its approximate 10 million persons—two-thirds of them living in metropolitan areas—its economy is considered on par with the Czech Republic, another shining light in Central Europe.

Looking at the map, however, one can see that the area lies in an exposed crossroad of Europe. It is easy to understand why this country has expanded and contracted over the centuries. Or as common wisdom suggests, it is not Hungary that causes the problem, it is its neighbors: Austria to the west, Slovenia, Croatia and Serbia to the south and southwest; Slovakia to the north; the Ukraine to the northeast; and Romania, including Transylvania, to the east. A number of those neighbors wanted and still desire to control the Danube, which runs right through Budapest.

Although not located in the Balkans, Hungary has historic ties to the area. As we shall see the Hungarian Kingdom at its height in the 15th century stretched from Croatia to Transylvania. Ottoman and Austrian conquests in the 16th century included most of Hungary.

Created in 1867, the Austro-Hungarian Empire lost World War I, which it and Germany initiated. In 1920, the Treaty of Trianon sliced nearly two thirds of the land off the Kingdom of Hungary and bisected out of the country 58.5 percent of its population. After being carved up, Hungary tried to regain lost lands and repeatedly failed. Encompassing 35,919 square miles, Hungary contains 10,186,000 people, including Gypsies, Jews, a few hundred Slovaks, Schwabians (German) and Romanians. About 75 percent of the country is Catholic, 22 percent Protestant.

The word "Hungarian" comes from the Turkik *on-ogur*, or ten arrows, which may refer to the region's early Magyar tribes.

The Hungarian people are known as Magyars and they make up most of the population. The language of 98.5 percent of the people is Hungarian, a language belonging to the Finno-Ugric linguistic group of the Ugric family. Among the Magyar languages of Europe, it is related to Finnish and Estonian. A most difficult language, the Magyar language is an orphan European tongue, belonging to neither Latin, nor German, nor Slavic languages.

Be that as it may, wherever there are large communities of Hungarians in the U.S., the language is preserved and spoken. Hungarians have a love affair with their language.

Where did this language and people originate?

In 896, the Magyars, a tough, pagan, Mongol tribe from Central Russia, swept into the area we know as Hungary. This pagan band fought across the steppes from the Ural Mountains to the Carpathians. Once settled in the Great Hungarian Plains, they abandoned their nomadic life and organized themselves into a state. They stubbornly held their land against invaders from all sides.

The Magyar clan chiefs had chosen a chieftain named Arpad to lead them in their migration. Under his leadership, the Magyars went on to ravage Central Europe until they were defeated by Otto I in 955. Arpad's grandson, Geza, accepted Christianity and his son Stephen I was crowned Hungary's first King, on Christmas Day, in the year 1000. December 2000 marked the 1000th anniversary of the crowning of King Stephan I.

The Danube basin offers invaders a hallway to Europe. In 1241, the Mongols, moving through the basin, invaded Hungary. After pillaging half the population, they withdrew. The native Arpad dynasty died out in 1301. From that date until 1918, Hungary was ruled almost continuously by foreign powers.

In 1456, the Hungarian army defeated the Turks at Nandorfehervar now located in the area around Belgrade. John Hunyadi was the commander of the Hungarians. It was here that the Hungarians stopped the advance of the Ottomans for about 70 years. In 1526, the Turks attacked once more and the Turks were victorious at the Battle of Mohacs. The Turks ruled for 150 years. But in 1686, the Turks were defeated at Buda. Actually the battle was over by noon time and Pope III Calixtus ordered that all the bells should be run at 12 o'clock noon in all Christian churches throughout Europe. Even today, in many places church bells are rung at noon.

Without fail, the Hungarian people placed their faith in the losers of every war since the 15th century, including World War II. And after that bloodbath, Joseph Stalin made sure the U.S.S.R. dominated Hungary.

All of this history tells us a great deal about the nation we shall be visiting.

In this country, Hungary, especially in the western marshes of what once was the great Pale of Jewish Settlement lived the majority of Hungarian Jews. We should say they may have existed in abject poverty, but they wrote into their history the highlights and tragedies of a wonderful Jewish community, today the second largest Jewish community on the continent, not counting Russia and the Ukraine. Hungary would become the only country in Eastern Europe in which Jews eventually achieved a modicum of security and social integration, according to historian Bernard Wasserstein. Commenting on his travels between the wars, travel writer Patrick Lehigh Fermor wrote that "in spite of endemic anti-Jewish feeling in Hungary, Jews had managed to play a considerable part in the country's life—it had been better for them there than in Russia or Rumania."

Nevertheless, here, alongside advancement was the always pervasive anti-Semitism, "endemic and occasionally violent." Pogroms were common. The pressure on the Jews of Hungary mounted and a large number of Hungarian Jews, like other

Eastern Europeans, migrated to the United States at the end of the nineteenth and beginning of the twentieth centuries.

It is the history of the Jewish community in Hungary that tells us not only about Hungarian Jews but also about Hungary itself. For imbeded in Hungarian history is the fact that Jews lived in the country long before the Magyars arrived in the area.

A Brief History

Jewish historical tradition mentions Jews in Hungary from the second half of the eleventh century. From that time, the pace of Jewish immgiration quickly picked up, with Jews arriving from Germany, Bohemia and Moravia. By the twelfth century, Jews had settled in Bratislava which was then ruled by Hungary.

We also know that Jews settled in Buda after the Mongol invasion in the 1250s; they had been granted that privilege by King Bela IV in 1251. This sovereign also gave Jews the "right" to maintain synagogues and he guaranteed them legal status. Jews assisted the King in managing the system and lent him money.

Jews, therefore, came to occupy important positions in the economic field, so much so that the nobles, feeling threatened, sought to curb Jewish advancement. Thus, the Golden Bull of 1222 included prohibitions directed at Jews.

In the reign of Anjou Louis the Great (1342-82) Jews were expected to convert to Christianity. When they refused, they were expelled—but as it usually turned out, not for long.

The Magyars were followed by the Ottoman Turks who conquered Buda and defeated the Hungarians in 1526 at the Battle of Mohacs. The Hungarian defeat paved the way for the country's occupation by the Turks. The Jews enjoyed religious tolerance. When the Turks stabilized relations, many Jews returned to Buda. We should never forget, Hungarian Jews say, that the Turks gave absolute religious freedom to the Jews. At least two synagogues existed in Buda at this time.

In the 1600s, Buda would become one of the most important communities of the Ottoman Empire before the Ottomans were chased out of all of Hungary.

The Austrians drove the Turks out of Hungary in 1686. The Turks had been defeated in Buda Castle and the victorious Christian army charged the Jews with cooperating with the Turks. Hundreds of Jews were killed in the ensuing slaughter. Others were sold into slavery. After Buda had been captured, the surviving Jews left Buda for Old Buda.

Although the Hapsburgs ruled autocratically, it was Emperor Joseph II, the son of Maria Teresa, who eased the lot of the Jews with his *Toleranzpatent* of 1782 ("patents of toleration"). By the mid 1850s, the Jews, often protected by owners of large estates and local administrators, made considerable advances in business and the professions. They enhanced their adoptive Magyar culture.

In the 1848 revolution, the Hapsburg ruler called on the Russians to help quell a rebellion. Because the revolution was in full swing, Jews were granted equal rights along with other religious denominations in Hungary. But it did not matter. The victorious Austrian government did not permit Jewish emancipation, until 1868, that is.

The Emperor Franz Joseph ruled for two decades before he changed the character of the relationship between the two countries. In the second half of the nineteenth century, Hungarian leaders realized that to build a liberal Hungarian nation under Magyar leadership they had to eliminate all religious discrimination, including that against the Jews. First, the Compromise of 1867 had created the Dual Monarchy. Under that act, the Hungarian Government would take control of its own domestic affairs while the Austrians managed foreign affairs, the military and financial matters.

The Emancipation Act of 1868 granted the Jews equality before the law. No longer were they excluded from owning property or holding public office. Some barriers still kept them out of politics and public life, but they certainly would play a large part in creating the Hungarian economy. The anti-Semitic mayor of *fin de siècle* Vienna, Karl Leuger, even referred to Budapest as "Judapest," suggesting that Jews dominated the city.

Because the Magyars ruled and dominated society, "considerable advantages were to be gained if one acknowledged one's Hungarianess, including the ability to speak Hungarian," writes Jorg Hoensch in his book, *A History of Modern Hungary, 1867-1986.* By 1889, 700,000 Jews who already had obtained equal rights considered themselves Hungarian.

A century later, the Jewish population numbered 932,000, representing 7.2 percent of the population. Jews made up 23 percent of Budapest's citizens, and 75 percent spoke Hungarian, their first language. Jews accounted for 54 percent of commercial business owners; they comprised 85 percent of financial institution directors and owners and 62 percent of commercial employers.

As a capitalist economy grew, so did the Jewish population in Budapest. In the half-century before World War I, Jews prospered and made significant achievements in science and in the arts. Pest itself became a center of Jewish life. The period 1867-1918 was indeed Hungarian Jewry's "Golden Age."

Large numbers of Jews entered the professions: Before World War 1, 45.3 percent of all lawyers were Jewish and 78.9 of all physicians. Jews also played prime roles in government. Between 1867 and 1918, 17 Jews were members of the Upper Chamber of the Imperial Diet, 103 Jewish deputies were in the Lower Chamber.

The Jewish economic role in Hungary was disproportionately large, represented by industrialists, bankers, and tradepersons. Jews were needed to fill a gap. Hungary was being industrialized and trade and banking flourished. The Jews helped build up Hungary's banking and industry. Jews started concerns in sugar refining, flower milling, textiles, and metallurgy, according to William 0. McCagg in *Jewish Nobles and Geniuses in Modern Hungary.* "Still, most of Hungary's Jews would spend their lives tediously eking out pennies to survive," adds McCagg.

More than anywhere else in Central and Eastern Europe, Hungarian Jews were not only fully assimilated, they were "the only middle class between a large landowning aristocracy and an impoverished gentry on the one hand, and millions of landless peasants on the other," writes Paul Lendvai in *Anti-Semitism Without Jews: Communist Eastern Europe.*

On June 28, 1914, a Bosnian Serb assassinated the heir to

the Austrian throne. Archduke Franz Ferdinand. The world shook; the course of history changed. Within days, Austria and Hungary presented Serbia with an ultimatum that made war inevitable. For Hungary, the war was a tragedy: about 2.5 million Hungarian soldiers became casualties. The end was near. The Hapsburg Empire collapsed.

Austria-Hungary signed an armistice with the Allies on November 3, 1918, and a few weeks later was declared a republic. The new state of Czechoslovakia also raised its flag.

In the truncated state, Hungarian Jews would suffer. All the problems of Hungary after the Great War, including an unstable economy, and the Communist dictatorship of Bela Kun, who was Jewish, were vented on the Jews. A quota system, *numerous clausus,* was introduced in Hungarian colleges and universities that limited Jews to five percent of the student body. Beyond the student population, many middle-class, assimilated Jews were targeted. Hungarian Jews would "become the victim of rampant anti-Semitism and terroristic outrages," writes Paul Lendvai. Hungarian Jews would face a worldwide depression, dictatorship, the Nazis, the Holocaust, and communism. But Communism collapsed in 1989 and a new Hungary arose. For over a decade now, Hungary has maintained a democratic government, with a parliament mostly containing center and right-wing parties.

Notable Hungarian Jews

Hungary owes much to its Jewish scientists, musicians, writers, artists, and journalists, who have been vital to the country's intellectual and cultural development. While the list of contributors is endless, let us name some of the luminaries.

In the area of science, there are Leo Szilard and Edward Teller, who helped father the atom and hydrogen bombs. Theodore von Karman, John von Neumann, Jeno Polya, a world-famous surgeon whose surgical methods are used to this day; Georg de Hevesy, and Jeno Wigner were major figures in the history of modern mathematics, chemistry, and physics—and all were sons of Jewish nobles. Dennis Gabor, 1971, Nobel Prize for Physics (Holography); George Olah, 1994 Nobel Prize for Chemistry and John C. Harsanyi, 1994 Prize for Economics.

The most surprising aspect of this galaxy of Hungarian "geniuses" is that many were related to each other and even attended the same schools.

The noted sociologists, Karl Mannheim and Oszkar Jaszi, and Sandor Ferenczi and Franz Alexander were at the forefront of psychology. Georg Lukacs was a well-known contributor to philosophical studies.

Theodor Herzl and Max Nordau were the early leaders of modern Zionism. Herzl, the founder of modern Zionism, was born May 2, 1860, in Budapest in a house that stood on the site now occupied by the Jewish Museum on Dohany Street. His bar mitzvah was in the Liberal Synagogue in Tabakgasse and he went to school in Pest. In 1878, after the death of his only sister, Pauline, who was one year older, the family moved to Vienna. As a journalist, he watched anti-Semitic outbursts in the streets of Paris during the sentencing of Capt. Alfred Dreyfus on trumped-up charges of espionage. Moved and shocked by this miscarriage of justice, Herzl wrote *The Jewish State*. And in 1897, he organized the first World Zionist Congress, which met in Basel, Switzerland. To Jews throughout the world, he is considered the father of Zionism and founder of the World Zionist Organization.

Arthur Koestler, a well-known author, was the son of an unsuccessful Jewish business person. He left Budapest in the early 1920s and lived in Vienna, Palestine, Berlin, Moscow, Paris, and London. More influenced by Weimar Germany and certain German thinkers, Koestler did not write in Hungarian or identify with Hungarian causes.

Bela Kun, part-lawyer and part-journalist, seized control of the Hungarian government; and on March 21, 1919, he established a Hungarian Soviet Republic. A number of intellectuals, including many Jews, marched under his banner. His dictatorship collapsed on August 1, 1919. After the failure of a Hungarian Army counteroffensive in a battle with Romania, Bela Kun fled first to Vienna and then to Soviet Russia. He was ultimately executed by Stalin.

Budapest

Budapest is not only considered by many to be the most beautiful city in Eastern Europe, but also a well-situated portal to Western Europe and the U.S. Climb the steps of Buda. Sit on a wall and gaze down at the bridges described by Patrick Lehigh Fermor as being "looped across the Danube in sparkling necklaces." After this gaze, it is well to look at this city's past. Buda and Pest and the densely populated Jewish Old-Buda were once three separate cities joined together to become Budapest in 1873, even at that time, one of the world's most beautiful urban centers. Budapest's growth was phenomenal and was surpassed in Europe only by Berlin. The growth rate was two-and-a-half times that of London in the first 90 years of the last century. In 1841, the population was 107,240. By 1939, it had risen to 1,115,877.

Today, two million persons live in this capital, which, Emil Lengyel says lies in the heart of Hungary but belongs to a different world—"a world of rich culture on the threshold of Asia." It is often called "the meeting place of Europe and the Balkans," with incidentally three English newspapers and an English radio station in a multicultural atmosphere.

Budapest still remains "Europe's most seductive capital," according to many of its visitors. The setting of Budapest is exceptionally beautiful and it costs no money to climb the hills on a Sunday afternoon and gaze out over the city spread out on the banks of the Danube. Anyone who has lived in a city alongside a river, such as Pittsburgh, Pennsylvania, knows the feeling when seeing the city below from on high. Actually, in Budapest, the Danube runs swifter than it does in Vienna. But it is not blue. As one Hungarian guide told me, the "blue" in Johann Strauss's "Blue Danube" was a figment of his wonderful imagination.

Although 850 miles from the Black Sea, Budapest enjoys the status of a harbor, thanks to the Danube; and without the Danube, Hungary could not have existed, writes Emil Lengyel. Budapest is the only large city that the majestic Danube flows through the middle of; in fact, the river evenly divides the city. It is, John Lukacs writes in *Budapest, Nineteen Hundred:*

Street scene in Budapest. (Photo by Scott Michaels)

A Historical Portrait of a City and Its Culture, "as if the Danube has been invented for the esthetic purposes of the city." And if you go to an observation post high up on the Buda side, you realize Lukacs is correct.

Buda was named after Buda, brother of Attila the Hun, according to *World Book Encyclopedia.* "Pest is derived from a Slavic word meaning oven, the name was given to the town probably on account of its great lime kilns," says *World Book.*

Most visitors are confused as to which side is Buda and which side is Pest. But it is really very simple. Buda rides the hills and slopes of the west bank, "garnished by gardens, crowned by castles, church spires and forts." Buda is characterized by medieval cobblestone streets and neo-Gothic buildings.

Pest, on the other hand, lies wide and flat, a tabular city, neat as a ledger, with wide massive streets, boulevards, and buildings. Crowded with shops and government buildings, Pest is the "busy corner" of Hungary.

But it does not really matter on which side of the city you stand. "Nature made Budapest one of the leading cities of the Danube," writes Emil Lengyel in *The Danube.* Budapest has become a city of museums and its architecture possesses a definite Austrian influence. One observes the embracing scene of the Buda Castle complex of buildings together with the Chain Bridge, both built in neoclassic style. Fitting in alongside the vistas are wonderful evenings at theater festivals, the opera, or ballet, and, of course, fashion and food-always part of this lovely East European metropolis.

Old and new blend well here. Visit the domed Royal Palace. It positions itself as an outstanding museum of art, sculpture, and history and it dominates Castle Hill. Today, the Royal Palace is a cultural center, including the National Szechenyi Library and the Hungarian National Gallery. And everywhere the views are magnificent.

Transportation here is good and remember, that while London was the first city to build an underground train system, Budapest boasts the oldest subway system on the European continent.

Indeed, we must mention **Imre Steinde Parliament Building** completed in 1902. This is the largest parliament building in the entire world. Its architecture combines Magyar medieval, French Renaissance, Westminsterian, and Gothic styles, with a neo-baroque ground plan and an interior filled with polychrome. Eighty-four pounds of 22-carat gold were used in its decoration, according to John Lukacs.

Throughout their history, each of the towns of Buda, Pest, and Obuda maintained active Jewish communities.

The **Buda-Pest Tunnel,** according to the *Encyclopaedia Judaica,* marks the area where a Jewish community was established by the end of the eleventh century. A cemetery was located near the Buda end of what is now the Pest-Buda Tunnel. We know that Jews moved here in 1250 after the Mongol invasion. In 1348 and 1360 the Jews were expelled from Buda, but they returned after a short interval.

From 1364, the Jewish quarter was located in Buda on the north and southwest side of what is today Tancsics Mihaly Street. This is where Jews lived until the Turks left Hungary in 1686. Here, they built two synagogues. The site of **Medieval Synagogue,** part of the historical section along Tancsics Mihaly Street, is located at Tancsics Mihaly 26. Open May to October, from 10 A.M. to 2 P.M., Tuesday to Friday and until 6 P.M. on weekends.

Whether they lived in the then-separate cities of Pest, Buda, or Old Buda, Jews built community institutions. Actually, Jews are first mentioned as being in Pest in 1406. Often these Jews welcomed merchants who between the thirteenth and fifteenth centuries brought various goods to Hungary from the Rhine district. At this time too, Polish and Lithuanian Jews participated in trade relations with Hungary and Bohemia-Moravia, according to *A History of the Jewish People,* edited by Haim H. Ben-Sasson. By 1504, Jews could own houses. In 1547 there were 75 Jewish residents in Buda and 25 newcomers. After the Austrian conquest in 1686, Jewish residence in the city was prohibited. As for Obuda, it possessed a Jewish community in the fifteenth century. An old synagogue here was demolished in 1817. An imposing new one, still in existence, was consecrated in 1820. By the mid-nineteenth century, nearly 1,500 Jewish families resided in Pest. In the 1848 revolution, a revolution that swept over much of Europe, many Jewish youths enlisted in Hungary's revolutionary cause.

The Pest Jews contributed much to the 1848 revolution, which turned into a war against Austrian oppression. But the fight for Hungarian freedom was quickly and firmly suppressed by Austria. Emancipation for Jews went out the window. After Austria granted joint rule with Hungary in 1867, the Jewish community of Hungary was emancipated in 1868. Hungarian Jewish families helped transform Budapest from a provincial bourgeois town into a large and cosmopolitan capital.

In 1869, there were 44,890 Jews living in Budapest; in 1890, 102,000; in 1920, 215,512; and by 1930, 204,371. In Hungary, as in other nations, Jews in ever-increasing numbers moved to larger towns and capital cities. After World War I, about 46 percent of all Hungarian Jews lived in Budapest, according to *A History of the Jewish People.*

JEWISH COMMUNITY

Much evidence exists that there is a revival of Jewish life in Hungary. In 2000, for instance, for the first time, there was not enough matzah baked in the Budapest community's baker in what used to be an Orthodox Jewish enclave in downtown Budapest before World War II. The kosher market in Hungary is expanding. The Jews in Central Europe face a shortage of Rabbinical supervisors to certify the kosher food products for which there is a growing demand.

The Hungarian Jewish community today stands as the largest Jewish community in Central and Eastern Europe. Estimates of its numbers vary. Usually the figure given is 80,000, although it probably is closer to 100,000. Some people say there are up to 150,000 Jews in Hungary if you include the many Jews who are not registered as Jews, as well as those who are considered "half-Jews" (those with one Jewish parent), according to Charles Hoffman in *Gray Dawn: The Jews of Eastern Europe in the Post-Communist Era.* Interestingly, many dedicated Jewish Communists were never told by their parents that they were Jewish.

Hungary and France are now the only European countries in which Jews represent as much as one percent of the population. Before World War I, Jews made up five or six percent of the population in some parts of Europe. In pre-World War II Poland and Hungary, the Jewish population was ten percent.

Today, about nine out of every ten Jews in Hungary live in Budapest. Unbelievable as it may be, anti-Semitism may be more pervasive in the provinces where there are no Jews than in cosmopolitan Budapest. Anti-Semitism is less evident now than it was in prior years, "despite the periodic charges and countercharges" in the political debate of the country. Many would like to blame the Communist fiasco on the Jews. It is true that in the beginning many totally assimilated Jews, Jews in name only—were in the top leadership of the Communist party, including Bela Kun, Matyas Rakosi, and Erno Gero. In the 1990s, one can find a latent anti-Semitism. Some Hungarians see Jews, including Christians of Jewish descent, as a non-Magyar minority. But others are quick to point out that this is not so, because many Jews are from families that have lived in Hungary for more than a century.

JEWISH SITES IN BUDAPEST

Your first visit of a Jewish site can be to what one might call a complex of Jewish institutions and monuments around the Jewish Community Center and headquarters of the Federation of Jewish Communities of Hungary, at 12 Sip utca, Budapest. This complex includes the beautiful Dohany Street Synagogue, the Jewish Museum, a Holocaust memorial in a nearby courtyard, and a memorial chapel known as the Heroes Synagogue at Wesselenyi utca, 5, 7, Budapest, which was dedicated to Hungarian Jewish soldiers who were killed in World War I. Services are held every day. During World War II, most of the ghetto area was behind the Dohany Street Synagogue.

MAZSIHSZ (Magyarorszagi Zsido Hitkozsegek Szovetsege,) Federation of Jewish Communities in Hungary) Sip utca, 12, 1075 Budapest. Tel: 342-1335 and 322-6478. This is the umbrella organization for the 28 Jewish communities in

Hungary. The congregations are organized around the synagogue. This is the group that makes representations on behalf of the Jewish community to the Hungarian government. Hungary for many years has had a liberal stream of Judaism called Neolog, which means "conservative." But some say that the type of Judaism that Hungarian Jews practiced in the nineteenth and twentieth centuries and known as neolog was similar to a form of Reform Judaism. Office hours are Monday through Thursday, 8 A.M. to 4 P.M.; on Friday, 8 A.M. to 2 P.M. The American Jewish Joint Distribution Committee and the World Jewish Congress also have their offices here. The Jewish Community building was built around 1860. Through its courtyard one can also reach the Dohany Street Synagogue. **BZSH (Budapesti Zsido Hitkozsegek Szovetsege) Federation of Budapest Jewish Communities,** is also located here at Sip Utca 12, 1075 Budapest.

JDC Office for Hungary, Sip ut., 12, Budapest. Tel: 269-6543. Here in Hungary, JDC sponsors programs of social services for Jewish seniors, including Holocaust survivors. For example, monthly cash assistance is provided by JDC through the Hungarian Jewish Social Support Foundation (HJSSF). As in other Eastern European countries, JDC finances a major portion of the Budapest Central Kitchen's budget which serves 1,500 seniors, including meals-on-wheels. Other activities of JDC include services to the aged, Jewish education, social and community development, religious activities. **Hungarian Jewish Social Support Foundation (Magyarorszagi Zsido Szocialis Segely Alapitvany)** Founded by JDC, it is also located at Sip ut. 12, Budapest. The purpose of this social welfare group is to use the funds contributed to it by the JDC for welfare programs in the community.

Balint Jewish Community Center, Revay ut.16, 1065 Budapest. Tel/FAX: 311-6669. A performance by a group of actors of the play, The Promised Land. A lecture on religion, tradition and culture by Rabbi Robert Frolich and Zsolt Kocsi in the Shalom Club. A piano concert, an excursion to the Jewish community of Szolnok. Hebrew language courses. These are but a few of the activities at the Balint Jewish Community Center supported by the American Jewish Joint

Distribution Committee. In this full-service, state-of-the-art building one can immediately see a wide range of Jewish oriented educational, cultural and social activities for all ages. Many Jewish groups meet here, such as Budapest's B'nai B'rith Lodge. Also located here is a dormitory for young Jews from other towns and cities who are studying at the Rabbinical Seminary or Pedagogium Jewish Teachers Training School. A Jewish monthly magazine is produced at this address. The Balint Center was established by JDC in partnership with the World Jewish Relief (WJR) of the United Kingdom, the Doron Foundation and the Federation of Hungarian Jews. Also giving funding to the building, which is probably the first full service Jewish community center to open in Eastern and Central Europe since the Holocaust, was the Balint family, a London family of Hungarian origin for whom the center is named.

Dohany Street Synagogue, 4-6 Dohany ut., Budapest, Remodeled it still remains one of the most beautiful synagogues in Europe, this great synagogue of Budapest, located at 4-6 Dohany ut., Budapest. The Hungarian government recently spent about $8 million in renovation and this house of worship right in the heart of the city, elicits highly complimentary comments from visitors throughout the world. The largest synagogue still in use in Europe, and second largest in the world behind Temple Emanuel in Manhattan, influences people in such a way that they say, "This is the most beautiful synagogue I've ever seen in my life. It makes me so sad to know that the people who worked so hard on it, can't enjoy it," wrote one visitor. The guest probably was referring to the 600,000 Jews killed in the Holocaust.

Designed by the German architect Ludwig Forster, this impressive Moorish style building features minaret-like towers that are 43 meters high, and crowned with bulbous cupolas. The Temple is 53 meters long and 26 meters wide.

When you walk into the synagogue you will notice the exquisite floor mosaics.

Established in 1859, it is probably the longest and largest synagogue in Europe and one of the largest in the world. Its length reaches 180 feet; it is 84 feet wide and 65 feet high; and

The entrance to the Dohany Street Synagogue, Budapest. (Photo by Ben G. Frank)

A view of the Dohany Street Synagogue, Budapest. (Photo by Ben G. Frank)

it seats a congregation of 3,000. The synagogue was designed by the architect Lajos Forster between 1854 and 1859. The interior was done by Frigyes Feszl. At one time it was known as Tabaktempel because the original street name was Tabak street. It seats about 3,400 persons and has an organ of 5,000 pipes. Franz Liszt and Camille Saint-Saens played their compositions on it. Once the Nazis surrounded the synagogue with a wooden fence to create the Budapest Ghetto.

Heroes Synagogue, Weselenyi utca 5-7, Budapest, where there are services every day. Friday night services are at 6 P.M. Saturday morning services are at 9 A.M. Daily services include a morning service at 7 A.M., Sunday service at 8 A.M., and evening service at 6:30 P.M. Call Jewish Center headquarters at Sip utca 12, to check on the service schedule, Tel: 342-1335.

In the courtyard of the garden of the Dohany Street Synagogue near the Heroes Synagogue is a memorial plaque to Channa Szenes (1921-44). This heroine grew up in Budapest and went to Palestine. She trained as a British commando and parachuted into Eastern Europe to locate downed Allied pilots and help the Jews. She remained with Tito's partisans in Yugoslavia. Szenes was captured shortly after she infiltrated Hungary to organize Jewish resistance in that country. After being tortured by the Hungarian fascists, she was executed on November 7, 1944 in a prison on the Buda side of the city. She was twenty-three years old. Szenes' remains were taken to Israel in 1950 and interned on Mt. Herzl. Before her death, she wrote the famous poem, "Blessed is the Match." In Israel and in the Zionist movement, her name became "a symbol of devotion and self-sacrifice."

According to Carol Herselle Krinsky in *Synagogues of Europe: Architecture, History, Meaning,* the Great Synagogue was constructed in a mode that was soon to become part of the architecture of monuments in Budapest. Besides gilded cupolas, the structure contains stone and terra-cotta trim and wrought and cast iron. The two octagonal banners are more than 41 meters high.

Krinsky says the Dohany Street Synagogue shows the "greater self confidence of Jews in the 1850's." During that period Jews were able to commission buildings with conspicuous street fronts in a supposedly Jewish style.

Martyrs Cemetery. Just outside the Dohany Street Synagogue and behind the Jewish Museum is a mass grave cemetery. On January 18, 1945, the Jewish ghetto was liberated thousands of Jewish bodies were buried here because they could not be taken elsewhere. The plaques do not mark individual graves; they are only markers put up by families and friends of the victims.

Weeping Willow Memorial Tree. This Holocaust Memorial, at the corner of Rumbach Sebestyen and Wesselenyi, Budapest, is a sculptured weeping willow tree. Cast in steel, its leaves are engraved on each side with the names of Holocaust victims as remembered by loved ones. Designed by the sculptor lmre Varga, it was first dedicated in 1988. On hand was the famous American movie star, artist, and author, Tony Curtis, whose parents came from Hungary. A plaque says the Memorial Tree was "dedicated to the 600,000 Hungarian Jews who perished in the Holocaust and to the many valiant heroes of all faiths who risked their lives to save untold members of Jewish men and women from certain death."

For further information on the Weeping Willow Memorial Tree Sculpture, in New York contact the Emanuel Foundation at 97-45 Queens Blvd., Rego Park, Queens, Tel: (718) 896-8300. In Budapest, contact the foundation at the Jewish Community Center, Sip utca 12. Hours are Monday through Friday, 9 A.M. to noon and 2 P.M. to 4 P.M. Tel: 121-5227. People who would like to make memorial gifts or have names listed on a leaf may contact the Emanuel Foundation.

Monument to the Swedish Diplomat Raoul Wallenberg. This monument is located on a grassy expanse on the Buda side on Szilagyi Erszebet Fasor, at the corner of Lupeny utca. Take metro train line 2 from Moszkva Terrace. Continue from there Bus 56 or Tram 56 to Szilagyi Erszebet Fasor.

During the war, the United States asked Sweden, who was neutral, to open a special section of its legation in Budapest to help rescue Hungarian Jewry. Raoul Wallenberg was then thirty-two years old and a distinguished Swedish diplomat who had studied architecture at the University of Michigan. Risking his life daily, he issued so-called "letters of protection" and

The Holocaust Memorial Tree, Budapest. (Photo by Ben G. Frank)

even Swedish passports. He hoped against hope that those who possessed these documents would be spared. Wallenberg saved between 50,000 and 100,000 Hungarian Jews from the Nazis by his dedication, determination, ingenuity, and skill, according to Harvey Rosenfeld in *Raoul Wallenberg, Angel of Rescue: Heroism and Torment in the Gulag*. He even got hold of advance copies of the daily lists of Jews to be deported so he could provide them with protection passports. Reportedly, he was shot at and even chased by cars and trucks. He continually used his daring and resourcefulness to save Jews.

But still terror reigned in Budapest. Wallenberg tried, but his protection could not reach everywhere. Bands of Arrow Cross Fascists drove Jews to the banks of the Danube, murdered them, and dumped their bodies into the river. About 130,000 Jews, mostly elderly and children, were first crammed into houses marked with yellow stars and located in the ghetto. The Gestapo under Adolf Eichmann may have directed the deportation, but it was the Hungarian fascists who beat and drove the Jews on the road to the death camps.

Many Jews starved along the way. Those who were too weak to walk were shot by Fascist guards. "The road to Vienna was lined with corpses," wrote Dr. Ilona Benoschofsky in *The History of Jews in Hungary*.

Wallenberg was arrested by the Soviets on January 17, 1945, imprisoned as a spy, and died, probably murdered by the KGB in Lubyanka Prison in Moscow in 1947. January 17, 2000, marked the fifty-fifth year of Raoul Wallenberg's disappearance. The Wallenberg committees throughout the world insist that his fate is unresolved and they continue the search. This "Swedish Angel of Rescue" will always be a hero to the Jewish people and men and women of goodwill everywhere.

Also active in Budapest during the terrible days of late 1944 was Charles Lutz of Switzerland, who helped Jews find shelter in safe homes or in neutral legations. "Wallenberg is the better known of the two because of the tragic conclusion of his mission, but Lutz was no less actively involved in the rescue operation," writes Leni Yahil in *The Holocaust: The Fate of European Jewry, 1932-1945*. In 1944, Lutz, a professional diplomat, not only represented his Swiss legation, but also other countries when he dealt with Jewish emigration from Hungary.

Memorial to Charles Lutz, Located in a small square next to 12 Dob ut., Budapest. At this site is the unique statue of figures sculptured by Tamas Szabo. Between 1942-1945, this Swiss diplomat saved 62,000 Jews from the death camps In December, 1944, most of the employees of foreign legations left the country, but Lutz stayed. It is said that in view of his influence and personal renown, the Germans ordered the fascist Arrow Cross Party that had been planning to blow up the ghetto, not to do so. In the 76 "protected houses" under the patronage of the Swiss Consulate, thousands were saved. Like Wallenberg, he had visited Palestine. Lutz was the consul at the Swiss consulate in Jaffa, Palestine between 1935 to 1941. He was always in touch with pioneering Zionist youth movements according to Leni Yahil. During that period, he secured the release of German prisoners, giving him leverage in his dealings with the Nazis during his later tenure in Hungary.

When standing near this Holocaust Memorial and in the cemetery area where thousands of Jewish victims were buried, it is fitting to recall the tragedy and nightmare of Hungarian Jewry at the end of World War II. If you walk through the Jewish area behind the Dohany Street. Synagogue, you undoubtedly will be in what was then the ghetto section where thousands of Jews were herded into and thousands more died a violent death at the hands of the Germans and the Arrow Cross. The Great Ghetto was the area surrounded by Dohany ut.-Nagyatadi Szabo Istvan ut., Kiraly ut., Rumbach Sebestyen ut., Madach Imre ut., Madach Imre ter, and Karoly Kiraly ut.

Old Pava Synagogue. The future home of the Holocaust Museum of Hungary, is to be at Pava ut., 39, IX district, Budapest. Tel: 36-1-215-8796. Today, this eclectic-style building is in rather poor condition, though it has a small, functioning prayer room. This museum will present the tragic murder of 600,000 Hungarian Jews by the Germans. It will also serve as a remembrance of the 30,000 gypsies who died in World War II. About 70,000 to 75,000 Jews survived and were saved by the Russian army which liberated the Jewish Ghetto in Budapest. This synagogue will be renovated.

Remember that Hungary fought alongside the Axis powers, although halfway through the conflict it tried to "disentangle" itself from Germany.

Memorial to Charles Lutz, Swiss diplomat who saved Jews in Hungary during World War II. (Photo by Ben G. Frank)

According to various Hungarian racial laws of 1938, 1939, and 1941, Jews were removed from professional and intellectual positions. Adm. Mikios Horthy was in power. Appointed originally only as a regent, he had transformed Hungary between the wars into a "Fascist dictatorship." His goal was to recapture lost lands.

In August 1941, 12,000 Jews were deported from Hungary and murdered because they were so-called "stateless Jews." Thus began the nightmare that was to last until Hungary was freed by Russian soldiers early in 1945.

Some Hungarians do not like to talk about their role in World War II. Or they answer lamely, "What could we do? We were surrounded by enemies." A Protestant cleric and historian, Jozsef Elias told *The New York Times* on April 18, 1994, "the fact is most Hungarians didn't reject Nazism, they accepted it."

When Hungary allied itself with Germany, Hungarian Jews received a reprieve from deportation. But many were pressed into labor battalions. Even in the beginning of the war, young Jewish men were sent to forced labor camps. In 1941, these boys were used as animals by Hungary's armed forces who were on the side of the Germans and who fought on the Soviet front. A lack of clothing during the Russian winter felled 50,000 out of the 70,000 Jewish youths.

Hungary participated in the German invasion of the Soviet Union in June 1941. Hungarian troops fought beside the Nazis in the Ukraine. The Hungarians suffered 200,000 casualties, including 130,000 dead, at the battle of Stalingrad in Russia during the winter of 1942-43. It is no wonder that Hungarian public opinion turned against the war.

The Nazis distrusted Horthy; they believed he might make a deal with the Allies.

Sunday, March 19—a date that will never be forgotten by Hungarian Jewry—dawned a beautiful day in the war-torn city of Budapest. Things would change very suddenly. If weather can reflect what happened that day on land itself, it was as if the sunny, bright-white day turned into a black night of plagues. The Nazi war machine moved its forces into its lackey Hungary and into the Hungarian capital. There was no resistance. Accompanying the German troops was the SS officer Adolf

Eichmann, who came to "solve Hungary's Jewish problem." Hungarian Jewry was doomed, according to Charles Hoffman in *Gray Dawn: The Jews of Eastern Europe in the Post-Communist Era*. In less than 24 hours Eichmann and his agents would arrest and deport to the concentration camps the top Jewish leaders of the city, including men, women and children.

Eichmann and his staff were determined to "resettle" the approximate 800,000 Jews as quickly as possible. Immediately, Regent Admiral Horthy appointed Dome Sztolyai as Prime Minister in what was billed as a "national government under a German protectorate." The *Encyclopedia Guide* says Horthy told Sztolyai that the Germans firmly demanded the solution of the Hungarian Jewish question. By April, Jews were required to wear the Yellow Star. In May, the ghetto was set up behind the Dohany Street Synagogue. Between May 15 and July 7, 1944, 437,000 Jews were rounded up in the countryside and sent to the concentration camp at Auschwitz and Birkenau. In July, there was an international outcry pointing out to Horthy that deportation meant sudden death. He had the deportations stopped on July 7, 1944, thereby saving the lives of the Jews in Budapest until the Arrow Cross fascist takeover on October 15, 1944.

From the end of July to October 12, Jews hid wherever they could to survive. Some were saved by Wallenberg, Lutz, and others. Wallenberg alone issued 13,000 passports. Interesting that before a person went into hiding he would tell everyone he was going to "Telech," which meant hiding. Also there were secret negotiations going on between various groups and the Germans, such as the Zionist Budapest Rescue Committee. According to *The Encyclopedia Guide*, "the personal message of Pope Pius XII and the firm communication from the American government also warned Horthy that he and all those who persecuted the Jews would be taken to account after the war." Papal Nuncio Angelo Rotta made frequent representations to cabinet ministers on behalf of the Jews. Rotta's demands were the first official protest against the deportation of the Jews lodged by representatives of the Pope. Thousands of Jews were saved because of special letters of accreditation supplied by the Holy See.

Horthy may have seen the handwriting on the wall; the allies had landed in Normandy. He had to know that the Russians would eventually succeed in breaking through and conquering Hungary. He tried to get an armistice with the Russians and he actually made a radio announcement that the war was over. But the Germans armed the Arrow Cross, who, along with Ferenc Szalasi, took over the country on October 15/16 and forced Regent Horthy to resign. For the next three months they hunted down Jews with the clear intention of rounding them up and sending them to their death in Germany.

In mid-November, Szalasi established a Great Ghetto in Budapest and Jews were moved into that area. About 25,000 Jews had found safety under the protection of the Swiss and Swedish embassies. While protected zones in the Great Ghetto were set up, we should remember that the ghetto was "protected" in name only. Arrow Cross troops, Hungarian soldiers and German troops appeared every day and looted, plundered, and murdered Jews without discrimination. "The Danube became a mass grave in those days since the hiding Jews caught by the Arrow Cross were escorted in great numbers to the bank, shot, and thrown into the river from the embankment," says the *Encyclopedia Guide*. On January 12, 1945, the Arrow Cross made plans to kill all the Jews on January 20, but the Russians had arrived two days earlier on January 18. Szalasi was captured by the American troops in 1945, was returned to Budapest and executed as a war criminal responsible for the death of about 100,000 Jews.

According to historian Jozef Elias, "whatever is said now about Horthy saving Jews is not true." Many people see Adm. Miklos Horthy as the man who presided over the deportation to Auschwitz alone of 438,000 Hungarian Jews, mostly from rural areas. Of this number, about 250,000 to 300,000 were exterminated. To others, he is seen as a leader who tried to resist German demands for the mass deportation of Budapest's middle-class Jews and who was finally pushed aside by Hitler in late 1944. After the German coup in Budapest in October 1944, Horthy was sent to Bavaria where the Americans wanted to arrest him for trial at Nuremberg. A Hungarian historian of the period, Francois Fejto, said Stalin intervened and exile in Portugal was arranged for Horthy. He died in 1957 in Portugal at the age of eighty-nine.

In 1930, 445,000 Jews resided in Hungary. After the infamous Munich Pact, Hungary added another several hundred thousand Jews to its population from Slovakia, Yugoslavia, and Transylvania for a total of about 650,000 Jews in Greater Hungary, according to Lucy S. Dawidowicz. She added in her book, *The War Against the Jews: 1933-1945*, that more than 450,000 Jews, 70 percent of the Jews of Greater Hungary, were deported or murdered under the occupation of the Nazis. Other researchers put that toll at approximately 600,000 Jews.

Dr. Ilona Benoschofsky, writing in *The History of Jewry in Hungary*, indicates that there were 700,000 Jews in Greater Hungary before the Holocaust. She says there were even 100,000 more who did not profess Judaism; still, the anti-Jewish laws applied to them.

Despite the rescue efforts of Charles Lutz and Raoul Wallenberg, by 1945, about three out of four Jews who lived in Hungary before World War II were dead. And Jews amounted to three-fourths of wartime Hungarian losses in life, according to Paul Lendvai. He added, "There is peculiar tragedy in the fate of Hungarian Jewry: it survived intact until the middle of 1944 and was then annihilated in less than eight weeks, when even the perpetrators knew that the war was lost." Almost 50 percent of Budapest's residents of Jewish origin died during the Holocaust period.

Approximately 85,000 Jews remained in Budapest by the end of World War II. According to Peter Meyer, the Russian soldiers who captured the capital in January 1945 acted beastly. Cashing in on their rigged election, the Communist party followed a negative policy and the Jews who were persecuted were often shoved into camps and treated as aliens. "Eastern Europe was not livable for Jews," wrote Meyer. Jews were allowed to emigrate to Israel until 1951. "After that time, Soviet hostility toward Israel greatly increased, restrictions on Jewish life grew more severe, and harsh measures were taken to prevent contacts between Israeli diplomats and local Jews," wrote author Charles Hoffman in *Gray Dawn: The Jews of Eastern Europe in the Post-Communist Era*.

Hungarian Jewry, until the late 1980s, was on the one hand

cut off from Jewry and on the other hand seemed more or less "content with their Goulash Communism and Goulash Judaism," wrote Hoffman.

Jewish Museum, Dohany ut., 2, Budapest. Tel: 342-0949. (Located to the left of the synagogue as you face this house of worship). It is not difficult to locate this museum in Budapest. Adjacent to the Dohany Street Synagogue and opened in 1932, the founders of the Jewish Museum wanted an institution that would, "awaken and maintain Jewish historical self respect because that is tied up with the Jewish-life ambition and is more important than the collection of treasures with absolute artistic values." During the war, the museum was a hiding place for Jews and many were saved.

Officially it opens on May 2 and can be visited from Monday through Thursday from 10 a.m. until 4 P.M. On Fridays and Sundays, the building is open from 10 A.M. until 2 P.M. On Saturdays and Jewish holidays, the museum is closed.

The Jewish Museum is open for visitors between the holidays of Passover and Succoth from 10 A.M. to 5 P.M. In winter, hours are from 10 A.M. to 3 P.M. The museum is closed in December.

Through original documents, manuscripts, and photographs, museum exhibits present the history of Hungarian Jews. Here are Judaic cups, rimonim, Torah crowns, candlesticks, spice boxes, and textiles along with an important collection of manuscripts. Especially meaningful are documents about Jewish participation in the Hungarian War of Independence (1848-49), as is the material introducing the Hungarian struggle for emancipation. Modern paintings, sculptures, and medals by twentieth-century Jewish artists are displayed.

As mentioned earlier, Theodor Herzl, the founder of modern Zionism, was born in 1860, in a house on this site. There is a memorial plaque marking the birthplace. The square on this site, just in front of the Jewish Museum, was recently named "Herzl Square."

Aided by the American Jewish Joint Distribution Committee, the rebuilding of the museum started in 1947. But little money was available for its upkeep during the Communist era, and for decades, only two permanent exhibits

A memorial plaque in the Jewish Museum marks the birth of Theodor Herzl, the founder of modern Zionism, who was born in 1860 in a house on the site of the Jewish Museum. (Photo by Ben G. Frank)

were on display: Highlights of Hungarian Jewish life during World War II and an anti-Fascist exhibit. Today, the museum presents the full Hungarian Jewish tragedy through documents, photographs, and newspaper articles.

Rabbinical Seminary, Jozsef Korut 27, Budapest. During the Iron Curtain period, it was the only rabbinical seminary in Eastern Europe. Founded in 1877, it is now old and dusty, a corner building not in very good physical shape. But its library and its history are fascinating. One can see the bullet holes in the books themselves—bullets fired during World War II. When the Russians were retaking Budapest at the end of that war, the Fascists used the roof as an army outpost against the Red Army. The building also served as a detention center during the war. The library contains 100,000 to 150,000 books. This author saw the dust on the books, dust that had accumulated during more than 40 years of Communist rule. But even in those dark days, there was hope for Jews.

Jews participated in the Hungarian Revolution in 1956 and in the events of 1989. "For 12 days in 1956, Budapest lived through one of the great dramas of the 20th century Europe," writes Patrick Brogan in his book, *The Captive Nations: Eastern Europe, 1945-1990*. It probably is hindsight, but now we know that the Revolution was in effect a rejection of Communism throughout the Eastern bloc. "Hungary cried, but no one heard," a former East European told this author. As Henry Kissinger wrote in his book. *Diplomacy*, America and its allies, "acted as if they were bystanders with no direct stake in the outcome." Soviet tanks crushed the revolt and 2,000 persons were executed, including Imre Nagy, who had formed an obviously liberal government. About 200,000 Hungarians escaped to the West, including about 20,000 Jews, according to Mark Kurlansky in his book, *A Chosen Few: The Resurrection of European Jewry*.

A little more than thirty years later, thousands of East Germans who would flee communism, also headed westward via Hungary. Again, one sees Hungary playing a large part in the final "knockdown" of communism as it allowed the East Germans entry onto their soil and opened the floodgates to them. The Berlin Wall soon came down and East European communism crumbled because everyone knew that in 1989 the Soviets, under Mikhail Gorbachev, would not send in their tanks.

The Library in the Rabbinical School—The library has more than 90,000 volumes which makes it the third largest Jewish library in the world. Founded in 1877, this facility contains the "Hebraica-Judaica," collection based on the collection of the famous rabbi of Padova: Delio Della Torre.

In the beginning of 2000, the Seminary was also given the title of "Jewish University."

Other Synagogues

Orthodox Center, Dob utca 35 and Kazinczy utca, 27, Budapest. This Orthodox complex contains a Talmud Torah, prayer centers, and offices. Services are held every day. The kosher restaurant, Hannah, which is supervised by the Orthodox rabbinate, is also situated in this center.

Main Orthodox Synagogue. The main synagogue entrance is Kazinczy utca, 27, Budapest. The synagogue certainly is well worth a visit, although it is closed in the winter. During that season, access to a smaller synagogue as well as access to the kosher restaurant can also be from Dob utca 35. The smaller synagogue conducts services every day.

Synagogue, Dessewffy utca, 23, Budapest. Services each day.

Synagogue, Nagyfuvaros ut, 8th district, Budapest. This is one of the older synagogues in Budapest, which survived the war. Congregation is mostly senior citizens. This district was known for the many merchants and craftsmen who lived in the area.

Lubavitch of Hungary-The Jewish Heritage Center, Wesselenyi ut, 4 1/1 1075 Budapest, VII district. Tel: (36-1) 258-0183; FAX: (36-1) 342-7876. E-mail: oberlander@zsido.com. The boys were studying Talmud. Each with his partner. This is the yeshiva of Lubavitch of Hungary which is very active in the community. Many activities are held here, such as lectures and promotions of Jewish tradition. Rabbi Baruch Oberlander is head of this Jewish Heritage and Education Center.

Rumbach Synagogue, 11-13 Rumbach Sebestyen ut, Budapest. Not far from the Dohany Street Synagogue is this beautiful synagogue designed by the famous Austrian architect, Otto Wagner. Sebestyen Rumbach (1764-1844) was the municipal health officer of Pest. Opened in 1872, the building is smaller than the Dohany Street Synagogue, but not "poorer looking." The women's gallery is separate and the bimah is in the middle of the structure. Oriental motifs are part of the atmosphere. During World War II, the synagogue was used as a detention barracks for refugees. The façade of the house of worship is accentuated by the octagonal pillars ending in two small towers.

Sim Shalom Community, c/o Edit Pragai, Mese ul, 12, 1121 Budapest. Tel: (36-1) 176-7095. In the year 2000 this group was still in the birth pang stage of development. Yet their group, probably the closest in Hungary to Reform Judaism, meets in various houses on Friday nights for an Oneg Shabbat. On Saturday mornings a service is held. Founded in the late 1980s, the group has met with representatives of the British Progressive Jewish movement and the Leo Baeck College in England. It is considered a member of the World Union for Progressive Judaism. Kati Kelemen is the rabbi of this group.

Schools

The former **Anna Frank High School for Boys and Girls,** is now called **Scheiber, Sandor General and Secondary School,** Laky Adolf ut, 38-40, Budapest. Tel: 211-4215. This institution is indeed one site that must be seen if one is to appreciate the great strides made by the Hungarian Jewish community to educate its children. A new, modern school, complete with computers, well-lit classrooms, a gym, a fitness room, and a multi-functional assembly hall, which obviously serves as an auditorium, gives meaning to the reality of the rebirth of East European Jewry. The main school auditorium hall also is used for religious services, dances, Channukah Ball, community lectures and conferences. Opened in 1998, it actually has been in existence for 81 years. Before its present name, Scheiber Sandor was known as the Anna Frank Secondary School. It was previously located in the Berkocsi ut, building of the Rabbinical Seminary. Today, about 400 students attend the school in classes which meet the needs of children between the ages of six and 18 years of age.

The goal of the school is to give the students the means to be Jewish.

Lauder Yavneh Jewish Community School, Budakeszi ut, 46 b, 1121 Budapest. Tel: 275-2240. Perched high in the hills of Buda section of the capital and in one of the city's nicest sections, is the modern, beautifully designed 21stst Century school. The attractive school is a contribution to the area's architecture. Its bright red paint on the outside give the various complex of buildings a rich, exciting look that depicts the values of the school and kindergarten which combines Jewish values with modern child-centered pedagogical approaches. Here one can see words translated into action: commitment and revival of Jewish life in Hungary. It is worth a drive to see this wonderful structure. But do call ahead if you want to visit this school or any Jewish school because of security.

American Endowment School, 44 Wesselenyi ut., Budapest. Also known as the **Reichman School,** named after the Reichman brothers now living in the United States. This Orthodox primary and partly secondary school was established in 1990 and is based on the principles of "Masoret Avot," (the traditions of the fathers").

The Lauder Foundation is located at 1 Vaci utca, 19/21, ste. 607, 1052 Budapest. Tel: 361-266-9168. FAX: 361-251-4257.

RESTAURANTS IN BUDAPEST

Hanna Kosher Restaurant, Dob utca. 35, Budapest. Tel: 342-1072.

Frolich Pastry Shop, Dob utca. 22. H-1072 Budapest. Tel: 267-2851.

Carmel Restaurant, Kazincy ut 29., Budapest, is not kosher, not even kosher style. But it does serve some traditional local Jewish dishes. Tel: 342-4585.

Gundel Restaurant, Allatkerti utca 2, Budapest. Tel: 321-3550. It is not kosher, but it is a first-class, expensive restaurant frequented by American tourists. Excellent food and entertainment, including Hungarian folk music via the violin.

The Scheiber Sandor school in Budapest. (Photo by Ben G. Frank)

HOTELS

Kings Hotel, Mehadrin Kosher, Nagydiofa ul., 25-27, 1074 Budapest. Tel/FAX: 352-7675. This 80-room hotel in the heart of the Jewish area is walking distance to synagogues, Jewish community offices. Strictly kosher: Mehadrin kosher. Meals are served in two restaurants under strict rabbinical supervision. A variety of Hungarian ethnic foods are offered, such as goose liver. Dining room is open on Shabbat. If you are not staying in the hotel make arrangements for meals on the Sabbath before the day of rest begins.

Hilton Budapest, Hess A., ter 1-3, H-1014, Budapest. Tel: 36-1-488-6600. FAX: 36-1-488-6644.E mail: hiltonhu@hungary.net. This hotel is located on the Castle Hill on the Buda side. View of the Danube, Margaret Island and the Pest side of the city. The hotel is a 10 minute-walk from the center of the city. Nearby is the Fisherman's Bastion, the Royal Palace, and museums.

Other five star hotels:

Mariott, Intercontinental, Kempinski, Meridien and the Four Seasons under construction in 2000.

City Panzio, Pilvax Koz, 1-3 H-1052, Budapest. Tel: 36-1-266-7660. FAX: 36-1317-6396. This is a three-star hotel right in the heart of the city, just off the Vaci shopping mall and in the center of the city.

Hungarian National Tourist Office, New York City. Tel: 212-355-0240.

Besides the first-class hotels on the Buda side of the city, such as the Hilton, there is a moderate business persons' hotel in the center of the city, known as the **Korona,** Kecskemeti utca, Budapest, 1053.

TRAVEL CENTERS AND TRAVEL GUIDES

Licensed tour guide Nandor Geray, H-1149, Bonyhadi ut. 106, Budapest. Tel: 36-1-383-3390. FAX: 36-1-251-3736. E-Mail: nandor@e73.kibernet.hu. Meet Nandor Geray, an excellent, knowledgeable licensed tour guide for Budapest and all of

The Kings Hotel is a strictly-kosher hotel in Budapest. (Photo by Ben G. Frank)

Hungary. He conducts Jewish heritage tours, general sight-seeing programs, trips to visit Jewish landmarks in Budapest or in the country-side. Mr. Geray is a Holocaust historian and can organize cultural programs and conduct small or large group tours. He speaks excellent English.

Jewish Cultural and Tourist Center of the Budapest Jewish Community and Aviv Travel, Sip ut., 12 1075 Budapest, Tel: 344-5409; FAX: 344-5131., E-mail: aviv@matavnet.hu. These two organization are the sponsor of the Jewish Summer Festival in Hungary held every year, usually the last week in August. For example in 2000, it was held August 27 to September 3. Highlights of the Summer Festival are the Jewish Book Fair, the International Cantor Concert, and other activities. Hungarian Jewish Culture is of course highlighted here with extravaganzas of music, film, dance, cabaret and Hungarian cooking, as well as klezmer with bands that come from Hungary, Holland, France, Austria and Turkey. Some of the daily activities include a sightseeing tour, called "Budapest Through Jewish Eyes," and the ongoing Israeli Gastronomy Festival with a daily change of menus. Aviv Travel was established in 1999 to meet the increasing demand for trips to Israel and the high standard tourist requirements of the Jewish Summer Festival. Aviv Travel conducts excellent tours and visits to the Dohany Street Synagogue and the Jewish Museum; a City Tour known as the Jewish Face of Budapest, a tour on the Danube River Aviv travel services include tourism in Hungary, city tours, car rental and bus trips, business and office services.

Laszlo Travel Budapest, Ltd., Travel Agency, Eotvos ut., 34, Tel/FAX: 36-1-3022-818. E-Mail: laszlotravel@g51.kibernet.hu. This travel agency conducts Jewish heritage tours, including visits to Szeged, synagogues, transfers, cultural programs, hotel and private apartment reservations. It can conduct general city tours in Budapest, full-day Danube-Bend programs, Lake Balaton tour, Horse Show in the Pustza, Hungarian Lowlands, or to the village of Holloko.

Szarvas, Hungary

The Ronald S. Lauder Foundation/JDC International

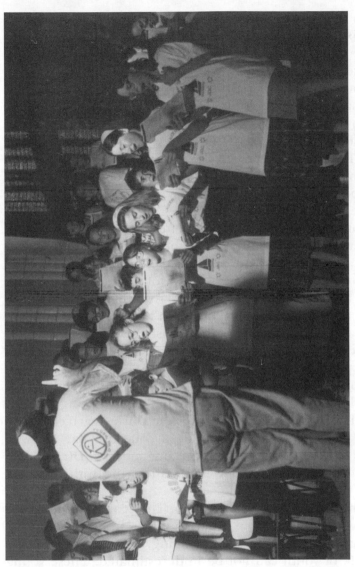

A scene from the Jewish Summer Camp at Szarvas, Hungary. (Photo courtesy of The American Jewish Joint Distribution Committee)

Summer Camp, Szarvas. Every summer 450 children from about six countries in East Europe come to this wonderful camp in this small town 90 miles southeast of Budapest. "Paradise in Szarvas," say the brochures, and they are right. "Welcome to the summer camp that changes lives," says the sign in the main hall of the camp which opened in 1990 and draws children from six to 18. And the sign is correct, too. For if the revival of Jewish life is to continue, the existence of this camp is a must. From here will come the leaders of the future Jewish communities of Eastern Europe. The camp of course includes sports, boating, hiking and summer camp recreational activities. The camp is a truly a mirror of East European Jewry. For many campers, the Szarvas experience is their first intensive contact with Jewish tradition and the two week camp session may be their only structured Jewish educational experience during the entire year. One counselor is quoted as saying, "Before they came to Szarvas, they knew that their father or their mother was Jewish. But they didn't care." Now they come to the camp, and they try to be Jewish, to learn about their Jewish identity." During each two-week camp session, counselors explain the basics of Jewish ritual. While the camp is not Orthodox, it is traditional and Shabbat and holidays are observed. Each child spends Friday mornings baking his own *challah*. The dining hall is strictly kosher. During each camp session, all 13-year old boys celebrate a collective Bar Mitzvah. Since its founding Szarvas has been operated by JDC, in close cooperation with the Lauder Foundation and with the assistance of the Jewish Agency.

Machol Hungaria- A Dance Camp. They come from all over Hungary. They come from other countries in Eastern Europe and they learn Israeli and folk dancing. The impact of dance in the life of youth can not be underestimated. These young people love it. To perform Israeli dancing is uplifting indeed and these Eastern and Central European young Jews enjoy every minute of it. The location is superb and provides a natural atmosphere for creative dancing, for getting to know Jewish students and for discussions on how to improve Jewish life in these newly revived Jewish communities.

Szentendre, Hungary

This is a small town just outside of Budapest. Great for restaurants, shopping and just a nice walk along the Danube. From here you can board cruises along the Danube.

Suggested Reading

Bierman, John. *Righteous Gentile: The Story of Raoul Wallenberg, Missing Hero of the Holocaust.* New York: Viking, 1981.

Balas, Egon, *Will to Freedom: A Perilous Journey Through Fascism and Communism,* Syracuse University Press, Syracuse, N.Y. 2000.

Brogan, Patrick. *The Captive Nations: Eastern Europe, 1945-1990.* New York: Avon, 1990.

Burant, Stephen R., ed. *Hungary: A Country Study.* Washington, D.C.: Library of Congress, 1990.

Dawidowicz, Lucy S. *The War Against the Jews: 1933-1945.* New York: Bantam, 1986.

Fermor, Patrick Leigh Fermor, *Between The Woods And the Water: On Foot to Constantinople from The Hook of Holland: The Middle Danube to the Iron Gates,* New York, Elisabeth Sifton Books, 1986.

Hoensch, Jorg. *A History of Modern Hungary, 1867-1986.* Text ed. New York: Longman, 1984.

Kissinger, Henry, *Diplomacy.* New York: Simon & Schuster, 1994.

Krinsky, Carol Herselle. *Synagogues of Europe: Architecture, History, Meaning.* Cambridge, Mass.: MIT Press, 1985.

Kurlansky, Mark. *A Chosen Few: The Resurrection of European Jewry.* Reading, Mass.: Addison-Wesley, 1995.

Lendvai, Paul. *Anti-Semitism Without Jews: Communist Eastern Europe.* Garden City, N.Y.: Doubleday, 1971.

Lengyel, Emil. *1,000 Years of Hungary.* New York: John Day, 1958.

——. *The Danube.* New York: Random House, 1939.

Lukacs, John. *Budapest, Nineteen Hundred: A Historical Portrait of a City and Its Culture.* New York: Grove/Atlantic, 1990.

McCagg, William O. *Jewish Nobles and Geniuses in Modern Hungary,* text ed. Boulder, Colo.: East European Quarterly, 1972.

MacLean, Rory. *Stalin's Nose: Travels Around the Bloc.* New York: Little, Brown, 1993.

Meyer, Peter, Bernard D. Weinryb, Eugene Duschinsky, and Nicolas Sylvain, eds. *The Jews in the Soviet Satellites.* Syracuse, N.Y: Syracuse University Press, 1953.

Rosenfeld, Harvey. *Raoul Wallenberg, Angel of Rescue: Heroism and Torment in the Gulag,* rev. ed. New York: Holmes & Meier, 1995.

Sugar, Peter F, et al, eds. *A History of Hungary.* Bloomington and Indianapolis: Indiana University Press, 1990.

Yahil, Leni, *The Holocaust: The Fate of European Jewry, 1932-1945.* New York. Oxford, Oxford University Press, 1990.

Young, James E. *The Texture of Memory: Holocaust Memorials and Meaning in Europe, Israel, and America.* New Haven: Yale University Press, 1993.

Slovakia
Jews Are Here to Stay

At Chanukkah in 1993, a significant event took place in the history of the Slovak Jewish community: a Chanukkah torch relay lighting ceremony—the first of its kind—was held in the city of Bratislava, the capital of the new nation of Slovakia. An escort of about twenty young Jewish runners accompanied the torch from the burial place of the great Orthodox scholar, Hatam Sofer, to the old Jewish section and the site of a former synagogue that stood in the path of the newly constructed bridge now spanning the Danube. The president of Slovakia, Michal Kovach, was on hand and Chief Rabbi Baruch Myers spoke.

Ceremonies in Eastern Europe are symbolic. This Hanukkah torch parade, similar to the carrying of the freedom torch by the Maccabees of old and run every year in Israel to the ancient town of Miron, signaled to the Slovak people that the Jews are in Slovakia to stay. This is crucial to the future of the Jews in Slovakia, for like in Russia and other countries in Eastern Europe, the Jewish community here sometimes appears to be uneasy. At the same time, there is no question that this Jewish community continues to revitalize itself.

Indeed, "anti-Semitism today [in Slovakia] is also a heritage of the war-time Slovak state, a vassal republic controlled by Hitler which expelled its Jewish citizens to German extermination camps and paid the Nazis set fees for each person deported," wrote Olga S. Hruby in *The New York Times,* November 11, 1991.

This is one Jewish community in Europe where American Jewish visitors, for instance, can make a difference in a people-to-people relationship. Slovak Jews need to know that there is also a bridge between the largest Jewish community from the Diaspora, the United States, and one of the smallest, Slovakia. If you really want to know how a small Jewish community exists in Eastern Europe, visit Slovakia.

Slovakia (Slovenska Republic)

Near the center of Europe, in the great Danubian valley, live the Slovaks. Today, most reside in a country called "Slovenska Republic," which covers 18,933 square miles and counts 5.3 million persons. Bordering the Czech Republic, Poland, Ukraine, Austria, and Hungary, it was once considered a "rural backwater" in the Austro-Hungarian Empire. But it is considered that no longer, because today it is strategically located between Ukraine and Hungary.

We know that Slovaks settled in Central Europe before A.D. 500. In the 800s, they were part of the Great Moravian Empire and around the year 900 they were conquered by the Magyars. Yet, throughout their long history, the Slovak people kept their own language, always "harboring nationalist feelings," longing for independence.

As Eva Hoffman writes in *Exit into History: A Journey Through the New Eastern Europe*, Slovakia's "brief moment of grandeur came in the 9th century when the Slovaks were united with the Moravians for the first time." The Great Moravian Empire was short lived and by the tenth century the Slovaks were conquered by Hungary, she adds. In fact, the Slovaks would endure Hungarian rule for most of their history. The Czechs at least enjoyed power and influence before bending to Austrian Hapsburg control.

Hungarians like to call the period between 1867 and World War I (1914) a particularly creative and productive era in Hungarian history; but for the Slovaks, it brought "relentless magyarization," including the increasing promulgation of

Hungarian as the official language. As a result, the Slovaks faced cultural extinction.

By 1918, powerful support existed among the Slovaks to unify with the Czechs, with the country to be called Czechoslovakia. So after World War I, much of the nation of Czechoslovakia was literally "cobbled together" from provinces of the defeated Austro-Hungarian Empire. Slovaks always felt the Czechs overpowered them intellectually and they resented Czech power. Constitutionally, there was no discrimination, according to author Josef Korbel. Czechs and Slovaks had common ties through ethnic identity. But over and over again the thousand-year history of separation had created two dissimilar societies and different cultural experiences. It soon became clear that the Czechs and Slovaks were "mismated," as Emil Lengyel puts it in *The Danube.*

Despite the assurances of the Czech patriot Thomas Garrigue Masaryk, who concluded what is called "the Pittsburgh Pact" in 1918 with Slovak Americans to win their support for a common state, Slovak self-rule never really occurred. During World War II Slovakia was a Nazi puppet state. The Slovaks "never had an opportunity to establish their own identity," it was said.

With the crumbling of the Communist states, the Czechs and Slovaks parted ways on January 1, 1993, a day the Slovaks waited a thousand years for. The Slovaks once again stand on their own two feet. But the terrain of independence is rocky, especially economically. In contrast to the Czech Republic where inflation and unemployment have been kept under control, Slovakia has suffered from economic and political gyrations. It must be recalled that it was the Slovaks who pushed for separation and the Czechs went along with it; many Czechs perhaps believed they were "carrying" the Slovak sections of the country and could do better on their own. The country is remote from Western Europe both geographically and culturally; and its relations with Hungary, a strong neighbor to the south, are tense. The economies of the Czechs, Poles, and Hungarians seem to be pulling ahead. It is hoped that Slovakia can catch up.

Vladimir Mercier and his party ran Slovakia from its independence in 1993 after the divorce from Czech Republic until September, 1998, when he was defeated by a coalition of four diverse parties. "His government was widely considered illiberal, discriminatory and corrupt, practicing crony politics," wrote Steven Erlanger in the *New York Times,* May 3, 2000. Many Slovaks thought that Merciar was "wrecking Slovakia's reputation abroad." And that may be just what was happening for it is not unreasonable to believe that many in Europe appeared to be blocking that country's entry into NATO and the European Union. Under Mercier, Slovakia seemed to be drifting away from the West. In 1997, NATO did not invite Slovakia to join that organization. Westerners have cited the instability of Slovakia's institutions, their lack of "rootedness" in political life and the shortcomings in the functioning of its democracy. But by 2000, with Mercier out of power, the European Union agreed to initiate accession talks with Slovakia. Thus, at century's end, the mood of the government led by Prime Minister Mikulas Dzurinda is definitely upbeat.

As time goes on, experts seem to agree that the Czech Republic got the better deal from the separation, certainly from an economic point of view. The economic news from Slovakia, while improving, is not promising. Some even say the Czechs all along wanted to go it alone. They probably were correct to do so.

Remember as you travel through this part of Eastern Europe that a dominant sentiment is suspicion: Where once there was one country—Czechoslovakia—there now are two separate states, including separate armies, separate borders and passport control, and separate trade policies. The Czechs and Slovaks are glad they divorced. Many Slovaks do not like the Hungarians. The Hungarians say the Slovaks are causing trouble by trying to divert the Danube River. Remember the Slovaks were under the thumb of Hungary for a thousand years. Noteworthy is the fact that 600,000 Hungarians live in southern Slovakia.

A Brief History

Who are the Jews of Slovakia? Once they were called "Highland Jews."

The history of Slovakia was often identified with Hungarian history—Slovakia was even called at various times Upper Hungary and Northern Hungary.

Slovak Jewish communities have flourished in the area since the thirteenth century.

By the fourteenth century, 800 Jews lived in Bratislava. Sometimes, they lived in an autonomous political unit headed by a communal leader. Generally, they were moneylenders engaged in commerce and finance.

After the Battle of Mohacs (1526), which began the rule of the Hapsburgs with Ferdinand I, Jews were expelled from the Slovak area towns and did not return until the beginning of the eighteenth century. From time to time, nobles granted them protection and some liberty.

The Austrian Emperor Joseph II (1780-90) granted Jews some limited civic rights, which made wider spheres of livelihood possible. This area in Northern Hungary became so popular for Jews that it was called "Magyar Israel." Many Moravian Jews arrived and created new areas of Jewish learning, especially in Bratislava itself. There, a yeshiva was established in 1700. The city became particularly prominent with the spread of the influence of Rabbi Moses Sofer, the Hatam Sofer, whose descendants for generations became rabbis of Bratislava and surrounding towns.

With the establishment of the dual monarchy of Austria and Hungary in 1867, the Hungarian Parliament passed an emancipation law the following year. The Jews of Slovakia became free men and women. The increased "magyarization" of the population, however, took its toll in the form of Jewish assimilation.

After the new nation of Czechoslovakia was established in 1918, Zionist activity emerged. For the first time, Jews had the right to declare themselves members of a Jewish nationality.

In the 1920s and 1930s, about 135,000 Jews, representing 4.5

percent of the Slovak population, lived in the Slovak region of Czechoslovakia. Political stability in the late 1920s brought prosperity for many Jews. Cultural and social life thrived around Zionist organizations and youth movements. The study of the Hebrew national culture and the increased focus on the Hebrew language led to close ties with the nascent Jewish community in Palestine. Jewish writers and journalists wrote in both German and Hungarian. However, in the late 1930s, as fascism spread over Europe, the position of the Jewish population deteriorated. The Munich Pact sellout resulted in the dismantlement of Czechoslovakia. Slovakia became a German satellite and agreed to set up a Nazi regime. Disaster lay ahead for the Jews. Jewish businesses became aryanized. Jews were fired from their jobs and were rounded up; they were shipped to the killing camps.

Thus began the Holocaust in Slovakia. By 1944, three-fourths of the Jewish community had been exterminated, and more than ninety percent of Jewish youth had been deported. Less zeal on the part of the Slovaks would have saved many Jewish lives. As early as 1941, Slovak leaders Tuka, Tiso, and Mach negotiated the question of deporting the Jews. Documents attest that in 1941, "Slovakia was the first state whose Jews the German Reich was prepared to take over." Adolf Eichmann gave Slovakia five hundred marks for each Jew as a guarantee that the Jews would not be returned.

The irony of it all: the first deportations from West Europe to the concentration camp Belzec took place on March 24, 1942. Two days later, the first Jews were deported to Auschwitz. They came first from Slovakia. On the following day, other Jews arrived from France. In her book, *The Holocaust: The Fate of European Jews, 1932-1945*, Leni Yahil writes that between March and November 1942, nearly 60,000 Jews were deported to Auschwitz and other concentration camps.

According to the book, *Tragedy of Slovak Jewry*, prepared by the Documentation Center of CUJCR, in Bratislava, and published in 1949, Slovak Jews "were exterminated so thoroughly and mercilessly during the years 1939-1945, that not one of the once happy and prosperous community has lived through the murderous storm without the irreplaceable loss of part or all of his family, without severe mental shock, or gravely impaired health."

Slovak Jewry lost about 110,000, including those deported in the spring of 1944 from territories that had been annexed by Hungary, according to Leni Yahil.

Bratislava

Welcome to Bratislava, the old city by the Danube—the capital of Europe's newest small nation, the Slovak Republic, and the country's largest city. Walk through Slovak National Uprising Square. Drive through this hilly metropolis, now trying quickly to shake off the forty-year Communist drabness, although it is succeeding somewhat. However, it will take time to undo the poor city planning of the Communists.

Even today—as in books—you cannot tell a city by its cover. There are some wonderful sites to see. Visit the gardens of Bratislava Castle. From there, you can see the splendid new bridge over the Danube. There is also the cathedral where 10 Hungarian kings and 8 Hungarian queens were crowned. Stop at the Baroque Old Town Hall courtyard and the Primatial Palace, which has its own art gallery and English tapestries based on Greek myths. And the Jewish community here is hospitable and will welcome the traveler.

With a population of 441,500 persons, Bratislava is crucial to Central Europe Jewish history. At the beginning of the nineteenth century, the noted Rabbi scholar Moses Sofer, the Hatam Sofer, made Bratislava the spiritual center of Hungarian Orthodox Judaism. The yeshiva in Bratislava once was the most important in Central Europe.

Throughout its history, the city was called, in Hungarian, "Pozsony"; in German, "Pressburg." The name Bratislava was coined by the Slovak archeologist P. G. Safarik in 1837. Some say the city was never a citadel of the Slovaks, for when it was separated from Hungary by the Versailles Treaty, its Slovak population was less than twenty percent. We must remember that Bratislava was the seat of the Hungarian Parliament for three centuries during the Turkish wars, and Hungarian kings were crowned in its cathedral. Actually, this old city on the Danube was the capital of Hungary from 1536 to 1683. It once stood as the second largest city in Czechoslovakia. Only thirty-five miles east of Vienna, it is now a center of rail and boat transport. Its factories churn out chemicals, textile machinery, and petroleum products. It is a working man's city, a factory town.

In the nineteenth and early-twentieth centuries, "a trip to Bratislava was considered a chic Sunday outing for Viennese noblemen."

Bratislava was the site in 1903 of the first Zionist convention in Hungary. Thirty-five years later, this metropolis, as capital of the German vassal state, lives in memory for the tragedy of the Jews' mass deportation to the death camps. That forced, deadly expulsion was set in motion and organized by one man, the late dictator Monsignor Jozef Tiso. Not only was he a puppet of the Nazis, but he headed Slovak fascism and even had his troops commit anti-Semitic atrocities.

After the war, Slovak history became Czech history. Under communism, Slovak Jew and Christian would suffer alike.

The postwar Jewish community was re-established on April 15, 1945, a few days after the country was liberated from the Germans.

By 1947, 7,000 Jews lived in Bratislava and a second synagogue opened. Jews had a difficult time reclaiming their property, however. Anti-Jewish riots erupted, and about 4,000 Jews emigrated to Israel just before the Communists took over. More left during "Prague Spring" in 1968, when Czechoslovakia launched fresh reforms, a new era of "socialism with a human face." This meant more civil rights, minority protection, and a possibility to emigrate.

Under the Communists, Jews could not easily or openly practice their religious or cultural customs. Jewish organizational property was turned over to government ownership and control. Any attempts to revitalize Jewish life were cut short and threats were made constantly. For example, in January 1952, the Communist newspaper, *Bratislava Pravda* warned that the country's "Jewish citizens are in the service of the American imperialists who are trying to undermine Slovak life."

The entrance to the Hatam Sofer Mausoleum in Bratislava, Slovakia. (Photo by Riva Frank)

Only several thousand Jews resided in Slovakia during the forty years of Communist rule. They lived under the threat of dismissal from employment, compulsory manual work, evacuation from their homes, and long prison terms.

Prague Spring 1968 brought relaxation of the strictures, but the reforms did not last long. With backing from the Russians, a new Communist political leadership in the country cracked down even harder. A year later, the Jewish population of Bratislava in 1969 was estimated at about 1,500.

Today, Bratislava Jewry is participating in Jewish life. In fact, the city was the scene of the Conference of European Rabbis in the spring of 2000 when the rabbis shifted their event from Vienna to this city to protest the Freedom Party's inclusion in the Austrian government.

As other Jewish communities are rebuilding their institutions, Slovakia's Jewry is moving forward to revitalize itself and to take care of its seniors who gave so much to keep this community alive. Because of the strong tradition of Jewish scholarship in this city, it is fitting that we visit first the burial place of Hatam Sofer.

JEWISH SITE IN BRATISLAVA

Hatam Sofer Mausoleum. The Hatam Sofer Mausoleum is a rarity among the sites of Slovakia. You would never know it is one of the most revered sights of Jewish Central Europe. It is located in what is called "Vajanskeho Nabrezie." It looks like a bus stop shelter. In a way it is, because people actually stand there while waiting for a bus. There are no Jewish monuments or memorials around it. But here rests perhaps the greatest Jewish scholar of the nineteenth century. He is Rabbi Moses Sofer, known as Hatam Sofer, rabbi, halachic authority, and leader of Orthodox Jewry. He was indeed the leader of premodern Orthodox Jewry "in its battle against the initial manifestation of the Reform Movement of Judaism," writes Jacob Katz in *From East to West: Jews in a Changing Europe 1750-1870.* His coffin, it is said, was made from the slabs of his lecture desk.

Twenty-three graves and 41 separate tombstones are in the

mausoleum today; once they were on the hillside of the cemetery behind the mausoleum. Visitors even leave notes just as
they do at the Western Wall in Jerusalem. The mausoleum
itself is part of the former Jewish cemetery that dates back to
the years 1670 to 1847.

A "man of letters," the Hatam Sofer was the rabbi of rabbis.
Rabbis came from all over Europe to Bratislava. He and his
yeshiva—the largest since the Babylonian yeshivot—influenced the development of Orthodox Jews in western and central Hungary. Torah study became widespread among large
sections of Orthodox Jewry. Yeshivot were established.

Hatam Sofer was born on September 24, 1762, in Frankfurt-
am-Main. A brilliant scholar, he was offered many positions.
But he accepted the offer of the Bratislava Jewish community
and on October 13, 1806, he became Chief Rabbi. In 1809,
when Bratislava was besieged by Napoleon's army, he fled and
organized a charitable activity.

He was a voluminous writer. His works comprise volumes of
responsa, sermons, commentaries, letters, poems, and a diary-
all bearing the imprint of his Orthodoxy. Hatam Sofer fought
for the usage of the Hebrew language and for the idea of a
return to Zion. He died on October 3, 1839. He educated
many hundreds of rabbis who became spiritual leaders all over
the world. He had devoted his life to religious judicial activity.

The mausoleum is visited by Jews from throughout the
world who come here to say their prayers and pay tribute to
Hatam Sofer. The key to the mausoleum may be obtained
from the Jewish Community Center. Arrangements for a visit
should be made in advance.

At the turn of the recent century, plans were underway to
begin a major reconstruction of the Hatam Sofer's gravesite.

KOSHER RESTAURANT AND HOTEL

Chez David Kosher Restaurant and Hotel, Zamocka 3, 81101,
Bratislava, Tel: 42-07-316-943 or 313-824. FAX: 42-7-312-642.
This attractive establishment is clean as well as reasonably

priced. The food is excellent. Among the many items on the menu are steak, cholent, and vegetable pâté. Rooms in the hotel are comfortable. This is a good place to meet the Jews of Bratislava, as well as Americans and Europeans working in the city and countryside.

SYNAGOGUES, COMMUNITY CENTER AND OTHER INSTITUTIONS

Synagogue, Heydukova St., 11-13, Bratislava. During the forty years of Communism, as an act of defiance, many brave Jews, upon entering this synagogue, would wave at the hidden cameras of the secret police. Before 1989, it was difficult to be Jewish, but not any longer. Many young people are coming forward and declaring that they are Jews, even admitting that they have one Jewish parent. This attractive synagogue schedules services on Monday and Thursday mornings, Friday nights, and Saturday mornings. The time of services depends on the season.

Today, nearly 3,000 Jews are registered in the Slovak Republic, of whom about 1,000 live in the capital city of Bratislava. Between 500 to 1,000 Jews reside in the city of Kosice. The rest are found in small communities scattered throughout the country. But the Jews are uneasy when they read that opinion polls indicated that more than half of the Slovak population fear Jewish influence. Czech Jewish leader Thomas Kraus told author Andrew Nagorski (in *Birth of Freedom*), "The Jewish community is nervous about the new state.... After independence, the standard of living will quickly drop and people will look for someone to blame." He predicted that in May 1992, "we would have a revival of anti-Semitism."

Here again, we see the phenomenon of "anti-Semitism without Jews."

Jewish Educational Center of Slovakia, Kozia 25, Bratislava. Eventually this center, administered by Chabad, will house a Jewish kindergarten, Hebrew school, holiday activities, as well as lectures. A Jewish summer day camp is also on the group's agenda. The directors of the Center are Rabbi Baruch Myers and Mrs. Chana Myers.

Community Center and Offices, Kozia St. 18, Bratislava. This building serves as the community activities center for the Jewish community, which now, according to Rabbi Baruch Myers, is composed of close to 1,000 Jews. For thirty years, the community was without a spiritual leader. Rabbi Myers, who became the first post-Communist rabbi in Bratislava, studied under the Lubavitch Rebbe in Brooklyn, New York. He told this author that not too many Jews are totally observant, but he had managed to set up the synagogue, a kosher kitchen, and study groups. An active Chabad movement holds meetings several times a week; there are activities for Jewish youth; a *shaliach* (adviser-educator) from Israel works with the community; bar mitzvahs are being celebrated. By 1990, a Jewish forum began holding meetings with several hundred in attendance.

Rabbi Myers was the subject of international headlines in 1993. Two teenage skinheads hurled the epithet "yuden raus"—"Jews, out"—at the rabbi. The Nazis had used that expression when rounding up Jews in the ghettos of Europe for deportation to the death camps. Myers was kicked and suffered minor injuries. He told this author he had been shaken up psychologically, but he indicated he would not be driven away. On December 6, 1996, Rabbi Baruch Meyers was again attacked again by skinheads. The attack took place at Rybne Square, where a Chanukah service was to take place the following day, and where a monument to the Holocaust victims is to be erected

The Headquarters of the Union of Jewish Communities in Slovakia. Kozia Street, 21, Bratislava. Although small in size, Bratislava Jewry sponsors a B'nai B'rith group with 55 members. Dr. Prof. Pavel Traubner of the Jewish community also told the author that 60 to 70 percent of the people in the Jewish community are 80 years old or more. And many in the Jewish community help older parents. Dr. Traubner said his dream "is a revival of Jewish life." He declared, "For now, we will help keep alive our survival. We will stay here."

Jewish Museum, Zhidovska ul., Bratislava. This museum is sponsored by the Slovak Ministry of Culture, Department of Jewish Culture.

Senior Citizen Residence, Svoradova ul. Bratislava. This attractive seniors' home was recently constructed.

Suggested Reading

Brogan, Patrick. *The Captive Nations: Eastern Europe 1945-1990.* New York: Avon, 1990.

Hoffman, Charles. *Gray Dawn: The Jews of Eastern Europe in the Post-Communist Era.* New York: HarperCollins, 1992.

Hoffman, Eva. *Exit into History: A Journey Through the New Eastern Europe.* New York: Viking, 1993.

Korbel, Josef. *Twentieth Century Czechoslovakia: The Meanings of Its History.* New York: Columbia University Press, 1977.

Lengyel, Emil. *The Danube.* New York: Random House, 1939.

MacLean Rory. *Stalin's Nose: Travels Around the Bloc.* Boston: Little, Brown, 1993.

Malino, Frances, and David Sorkin, eds. From East to West, *Jews in a Changing Europe, 1750-1870.* Cambridge, Mass.: Basil Blackwell, 1990.

Nagorski, Andrew. *Birth of Freedom.* New York: Simon & Schuster, 1993.

Tragedy of Slovak Jewry. Bratislava Documentation Center of CUJCR, 1949.

Yahil, Leni. *The Holocaust: The Fate of European Jews, 1932-1945.* New York: Oxford University Press, 1990.

Poland

Someplace Along the Polish Road, You Will Shed a Tear

"I realized I didn't know any Jews. So, I asked myself and I asked others: Where do Jews exist? I was told: Poland. And so I went to Poland."

—Alfred Doblin

Someplace along the line, dear reader, if you travel to Poland today, you will shed a tear.

This implies, of course, that not everyone will want to visit this rapidly advancing, modern country, a nation in no way displaying the poverty one sees in Russia, a nation quickly moving along the fast track of market reform and free enterprise. Yes, it is free at last from forty years of the drabness and darkness of communism imposed by the former U.S.S.R. You will find no Third-World country here. Actually, there are fine restaurants and extremely modern hotels, such as the Marriott in Warsaw. A high-speed train runs from Warsaw to Cracow. People are even friendly and extremely polite.

Logistics make Poland a launching pad to the former Soviet republics, as well as a distribution center to Scandinavian nations and others in the European Union. Its dynamic economy exhibits "dramatic recovery with sustained growth." Despite inflation, the country is moving fast, privatizing, and reforming. So welcome to Poland.

•In no other country since ancient Israel have Jews lived continuously for as many centuries in as large numbers and with as much autonomy as in Poland. Eighty percent of the Jews in the world during the Middle Ages lived in Poland. In the seventeenth century, three-quarters of the world's Jews resided in this land. In 1897, despite the effects of large-scale Jewish emigration, 14 out of every 100 Polish citizens were Jews. The tourist knows from history that in the 1920s, 1 out of every 5 Jews in the world still lived in Poland, about 10 percent of that country's total population. Nowhere else in the world did Jews form such a high percentage of the total population: 3,351,000 Jews made Poland the second largest Jewish community after the United States in 1939. Its capital, Warsaw, ranked as the second largest urban Jewish center with 350,000 people, or approximately 30 percent of the city's residents. By 1939, two-thirds of the world's Jews lived in Europe and three-quarters of them, half of all world Jewry, were concentrated in Eastern Europe. Remember, if you are a Jew residing in the United States or in the State of Israel, chances are your ancestors are from Poland, Czarist "Pale of Settlement," which included parts of partitioned Poland, or from Russia itself.

• Jews played a key role in laying the foundations of trade and industry in Poland. They created a vast network of religious, political, and social institutions. Artistic and cultural activity reigned: Yiddish literature, Kabbala, the mysticism that lasts to this very day, and Talmudic rationality. More than three-quarters of Polish Jews settled in cities and town, constituting 27 percent of Poland's urban population. About 40 percent were engaged in industry and handicrafts, more than 33 percent in trade and commerce, and about 6 percent in the professions. All came from this wonderful Jewish community.

• Poland was the spiritual and religious heart of the Jewish Diaspora, which for 1,000 years followed in the footsteps of matching the achievements of the Babylonian Exile or the Golden Age of Spain and produced one of the greatest world centers of Talmudic study.

• Poland's yeshivot and Talmudic libraries were the envy of world Jewry.

• Poland is a country with a long and serious history of anti-Semitism that often erupted and still does, but now is labeled "anti-Semitism without Jews." Indeed, Polish "skinheads" and other extremists use the term *Jew* as a label for any of their targets, Jewish or not.

• Poland's Jewish community in 1930 could boast 180 publications, including 20 daily newspapers, most of them in Yiddish but a few in Hebrew and Polish. By 1937, the number had grown to nearly 300. One newspaper, Haint (Today) employed 1,000 correspondents and was read by millions of Jews throughout the world. Contributors included David Ben-Gurion, the first prime minister of the State of Israel, and Sholem Asch, the noted Yiddish writer.

What hurts about visiting Poland? Three million Jews were murdered in the killing fields of this country. This is where the Germans erected their death camps, a half-dozen in Poland alone, including Auschwitz, a name that still sends shivers down the spines of people throughout the world. The Nazis made Poland the center for the extermination of all European Jews.

With all that pain, why go?

Some Jewish tourists visit Poland to seek their roots, to see the town their parents and grandparents called home, to physically observe and touch the "remnants," even a single surviving Warsaw Ghetto wall. Some place a pebble on a gravestone in the famous Jewish cemetery in Warsaw or stand in awe in front of the monument to the Warsaw Ghetto Uprising, which depicts the Jewish heroes and martyrs and marks the first armed, large-scale civilian resistance against the Nazis in occupied Europe.

Some recite psalms or a special prayer on the ground of the death camps or at the railroad platforms at Birkenau, where evil incarnate Dr. Joseph Mengele stood. Some journey here to make a statement that the Jewish people live, that "we are here." They walk with the young people who participate in the "March of the Living," where every two years, about 6,000 Jewish teenagers from 40 countries march from Auschwitz to Birkenau.

Jewish tourists do go and they do meet Jews. A minimum of 5,000-8,000 Jews reside here. There are probably thousands more who have not declared that they are Jews, although every day more and more do so. A Jewish community still exists in Poland, and in the opinion of many, it should be visited and helped despite the pain of the past.

Jews don't visit Poland dispassionately. Sholem Asch once said that the broad shallow river, the Vistula, the queen of Polish rivers, spoke to him in Yiddish. No matter what language you speak, the Vistula—"on whose bank the Jews dwelt for centuries"—will speak to you about the Jewish past in Poland, a past that must be remembered. Our roots are too deep in Polish soil to die. As long as Jews live there and Jews visit there, they will not wither away.

Location

"God wanted to place Poland at the heart of Europe. But, as with man, he missed. Our heart lies off-center on the wrong side of the Germany," says the author of *Stalin's Nose: Travels Around the Bloc*. Poland should "nestle" next to France, "not lie trapped, as it is, on the open plains between two hungry autocracies, Russia and Germany." Poland lies astride the invasion corridor from Berlin to Moscow; it is too important geographically for its status to be left to chance. This frequently partitioned nation was swallowed up first by Prussia, Russia, and Austria, and later by Germany and the Soviet Union. "In the course of its history, Poland has taken a large number of different forms. Almost every century has witnessed its territory modified and the political lines that bounded it changed." But Bernard D. Weinryb, author of *The Jews of Poland: A Social and Economic History of the Jewish Community in Poland from 1100 to 1800,* says Poland has always remained hemmed in. For much of the past 300 years Poland did not exist as an independent state. It possessed an "unusual talent" to lose its independence for such a long time. Only after World War I, did Poland win freedom. And then after World War II, its borders were shifted from east to west by 150 to 200 miles, meaning that a big swatch of Polish territory was absorbed by the former Soviet Union.

This large Central European nation, which covers an area of 120,725 square miles, is only about 60 miles from Berlin, and from east to west, it extends about 430 miles. With a population of about thirty-nine million, Poland is named for the *Polane,* a

Slavic tribe that lived more than a thousand years ago in the land we now call Poland. The name Polane comes from a Slavic word that means, "plain," or "field." Postwar Poland's population is more than 90 percent Catholic and more than 98 percent ethnically Polish.

A Brief History

And to think that it all began probably as far back as the tenth century, even though the first official documents attest to the Jews being in Poland in the twelfth century. After the Mongols overran Poland in 1240-41, many German Jews crossed the border into Poland, where they received a special invitation, also known as charters or privileges, from King Boleslav V the Pious, Duke of Kalisz, in 1264. These charters were called the "Kalisz Statutes," and they became the legal basis for the settlement of these German Jews. These privileges, too, were extended several times by King Casimir III.

To Jews, Casimir III, later known as Casimir the Great, looms large. In 1334, a year after he ascended the throne of Poland, King Casimir, who ruled from 1333 to 1370, issued a proclamation that substantially broadened those privileges originally granted to Jews. It is recorded in legend that Casimir had a Jewish mistress, Esther, and that their daughters were raised as Jews.

A crowning point, obviously affecting Jews, was the 1385 Polish Lithuanian Union. The Lithuanians wanted to rely on the Poles to stop the always present German threat. Pagan Lithuania sought a union with Christian Poland. They needed each other. In 1385, Jagiello, Grand Duke of Lithuania, "promised to convert his people to Christianity, to bind his armies to Poland's armies," writes Anne Applebaum, author of *Between East and West Across the Borderlands of Europe*. Jagiello became a Christian, married the Polish Princess Jawiga, and was named King of Poland. The Lithuanians converted to Christianity, too, and together, the Poles and Lithuanians defeated the Teutonic Guard Master at the Battle of Grunwald (Tannenberg) in 1410. This victory gave the Poles 200 years of growth and consolidation.

"The Jews are seen, accepted and defended as a group whose main business is money lending against pledges," according to the *Encyclopedia Judaica*. Jews are "protected moneylenders." The pledges were protected and ratified by King Casimir IV Jagiello in 1453, and later by other Polish kings.

Certainly not lacking in the case of Poland are the facts as well as legends concerning how Jews arrived in this nation. One legend connects the Jews with the 1492 Spanish expulsion. According to this tale, when Jews were dispatched from Spain by that country's king and queen, they wandered eastward. When they finally rested, they declared, "Poh Lin," which in Hebrew means, "Here, stay overnight." Also, Rabbi Moses ben Israel Isserles coined a pun on the Hebrew form of Poland and explained that it derived from two Hebrew words: "Poh Lin": "Here he shall rest." And again we have the same Rabbi Isserles who said: "It is preferable to live on dry bread and in peace in Poland, than in other dangerous lands."

A proverb began circulating that went something like this: "Poland, the heaven of the aristocracy, the paradise of the Jews, the hell of the peasants," according to Alfred Doblin.

THE FIRST JEWISH SETTLERS

Who were these Jews, these first Jewish settlers? While there were Sephardic Jews from Iberia and the Mediterranean basin, the bulk of the first settlers were Ashkenazim and they came from the west and southwest. In the Dark Ages in Western Europe, the Jews repeatedly had been accused of causing the Black Plague, of practicing witchcraft, and of committing ritual murder. So they fled from Bohemia to the "emerging kingdom of Poland." They were welcomed, and this was the beginning, some say, of Poland itself. Many of those merchants and their co-religionists were fleeing from the Crusades. Driven from Germany, they brought with them skills in various crafts and experience in trade. Other newcomers hailed from the Ukraine and from Khazar. Early Polish rulers encouraged them to establish shops and develop industry, wrote S. L. Schneiderman in *The River Remembers*. Jews were needed in the backward economy of Poland. They became innkeepers, artisans, and traders. They plied the overland route through Poland, which linked the Ottoman Empire with Central and Western Europe. No middle class existed between the landed gentry and the peasants. So the Jews brought with them their arts, crafts, trades, professions, and ability as merchants and financial agents. International trade and banking flourished.

Moreover, during the Middle Ages, Jews were not segregated. According to the privileges granted them between the thirteenth and fifteenth centuries, they could live anywhere. By the end of the fifteenth century, 10,000 Jews resided in Poland. Already it was believed by Jews in Germany that "Poland was the safest place for Jews."

Remember that after the 1492 expulsion from Spain, the only country in which Jews were permitted to engage freely in trade and crafts was Poland. By the end of the sixteenth century, therefore, Poland still was being hailed as "the new golden land of the Jews," writes Norman F. Cantor in *The Sacred Chain: The History of the Jews.*

In the sixteenth century, a Jewish parliamentary body, the Council of Four Lands (Vaad Arba Artzot), with headquarters in Lublin, was established and became an independent representative government of Polish and Lithuanian Jewry. It distributed the tax load among the various Jewish communities. Described as the highest institution of Jewish autonomy, it also concerned itself with matters of security and morals.

Between the end of the fifteenth century and the partitions of Poland in 1772, 1793, and 1795, Poland had expanded and reached its highest peak. Territorially it was the second largest state in Europe and ranked sixth in population. By the sixteenth century, Polish rule stretched from the Baltic Sea in the north to the Black Sea in the south and eastward to the gates of Moscow. Poland then was second only to France in size and population.

Polish nobility became the dominant political force, mainly because Polish farming was "primitive and feudal." The nobles realized that greater profits could be had if the lands produced more efficiently. So they turned to the Jews, according to Abba Eban in *Heritage: Civilization and the Jews.* Jews soon became active and valued partners to the nobility in many enterprises.

Jews who leased the land from the nobles were called *rendars*, and they enlisted other Jews to help them administer vast domains. Thus, the interests of Jews and Polish magnates coincided and complemented each other between the huge estates of the nobles and the private towns organized by the Jews. Jews "were made estate agents sent out to the outlying properties of the nobility to govern the serfs and produce revenue for the lords," writes Norman F. Cantor. He adds that Jews obtained the monopoly of the liquor trade in the countryside in the Ukraine. Polish peasants had to buy from Jewish tavern owners, often creating friction and hatred. It was part of the age-old Jewish problem—as tax collectors, managers of estates, or distributors of wine and liquor, you don't exactly make friends. An old Polish proverb, "What the peasant earns, the noble spends, and the Jews profit by," reflects the true sentiments of the masses.

The nobles opened up huge regions of the Ukraine wilderness and brought them under Polish rule. But this also brought difficulties: the Ukrainians were Eastern Orthodox, and they hated the Roman Catholic Poles, as well as their Jewish rendars.

THE CHMIELNICKI POGROM

To Ukrainians, he is a hero. To Jews, Ukrainian officer Bogdan Chmielnicki (1595-1657) is anathema. Chmielnicki hated Poles and Jews, and after an argument with a Polish nobleman, he fled across the Dnieper River to Zaporozh'ye, a Cossack stronghold. There, he roused the Cossacks to rebellion. And in 1648, he changed the history of the Ukraine and Poland because his revolt altered the balance of power in all of Eastern and Central Europe. The Cossacks now swore allegiance to the Russian Czar and thus, the Russians would go on to become a world power.

Poles and Jews suffered horrible deaths at the hands of the Cossacks. Jews were buried alive, sold as slaves and skinned alive. They suffered through several years of massacres.

Thousands were killed. Thousands were forced to convert to Christianity. Their homes were destroyed and their imposing wooden synagogues burned to the ground. From that moment on, Polish Jews began emigrating westward. The upheaval inaugurated Jewish poverty, especially in the villages of Eastern Europe.

By 1655, Poland began to decline for the Polish people and for the country's 1.5 million Jews. By the end of the eighteenth century, Poland disappeared from the map of Europe. Major changes occurred in the Jewish community in the seventeenth century. Jews tried to move out of money lending into other occupations, even agriculture and other branches of trade. But even during this decline, Poland stood strong as a reservoir of Jewish spirit and manpower that resisted assimilation and apostasy.

In the eighteenth century, Poland was partitioned out of existence; it became the "plaything of its neighbors and its political system was the laughing stock of Europe," says Robert I. Frost in his book, *After the Deluge: Poland and the Second Northern War, 1655-1660.*

Out of the wars and the Cossack uprisings grew the great messianic movements of Eastern European Judaism. And as the eighteenth century drew near, messianic claims of Shabbetai Zevi stirred the masses.

The Shabbetai Zevi messianic movement of the seventeenth century did not originate and develop in Poland, but it had an impact upon Polish Jewry. Zevi was born in 1626 in Smyrna, Izmir. Interested in Jewish mysticism, Kabbala, in 1648 he began to believe that he was destined to be the "savior of the Jews." Abba Eban says that "never before had one man united the Jewish people of all lands in a movement so inspired with enthusiasm and hope."

Zevi met and acquired a so-called "prophet," Nathan of Gaza. As the two wandered the Mediterranean area, the Turks, fearing an insurrection, arrested Shabbetai Zevi in 1666. Facing execution or conversion, he renounced Judaism and adopted Islam.

The impact of Jacob Frank was also great. Alfred Doblin says Frank was a Jewish sectarian. "He fantasized the Jews, got them to convert to Christianity." Incredibly successful, he was supported by the Polish king.

Polish-born Frank, who lived 1726-91, spent twenty-five years in Turkey before he came back to his homeland and founded the cult named after him. Like Shabbetai Zevi, whom he admired, he said people should seek the joy of life and communion with God through "ecstasy." Thousands of fanatical adherents followed him. He first became a Moslem and then a Christian. Several thousand of his followers converted to Christianity.

Jews felt they had been spiritually deserted by these false messiahs. But now a new movement came on the scene: *Chassidism.* Abba Eban defines Chassidism as "a special enchanting world, rich with stories, homilies, and endless wonders about the rabbinical court and dynasties that are the heart and center of the Chassidic vision."

Chassidism's founder was Israel ben Eliezer (1700-1760), who was of humble origin. We know him as the Ba'al Shem-Tov, literally, "the Master of the Good Name." After years of wandering and taking on various jobs, for example, as a beadle in a synagogue, teacher, herbal healer, and hermit—in 1735, he appeared as a pious miracle worker, according to Maurycy Horn in *Polish Jewry* History and Culture. His main power lay in the "force of his personality"; he offered hope to the Jews of Poland. Estimates state that half of Polish Jewry flocked to Chassidism. They believed he was a prophet; they found refuge in his wishful vision.

The 1648 *pogroms* and the closing of the Council of Four Lands in 1734 had sharply curtailed the once vibrant spirit of Polish Talmudic Judaism. The masses yearned for comfort; Chassidism filled the vacuum and became the greatest religious revival in the long history of the Jewish people.

In the nineteenth century, Poland became the seedbed for the intellectual movements that were to transform the Jewish world: Zionism, secularism, socialism, and neo-orthodoxy.

The Russians ruled Poland with an iron fist and again, after the 1863 Polish uprising, imprisoned thousands and exiled many of the Poles to Siberia. The czars, who had annexed large chunks of Polish territory, treated Poland as if it were nothing more than a "Province of Russia." They called it "Russification." These rulers of Russia kept the Jews as downtrodden as they could by confining them to a massive ghetto area of Russian Poland, called the "Pale of Settlement."

Before World War I, relations between Poles and Jews became strained. Jews were promised their own schools; that never happened. Jews were promised status as a minority with rights; that never happened. Jews were promised financial aid and support for schools; that never happened. All of these broken promises were symptomatic of Poland's difficulties, created bitterness, and even lead to deaths. Gerald Stillman reports in the publication *Jewish Currents,* April 1993, that between 1935 and 1939, some 500 Jews were killed and 5,000 injured in various pogroms throughout the country.

In 1936, Ze'ev Vladimir Jabotinsky, leader of the Zionist Revisionist Party and founder of Betar, its youth movement, pleaded with Jews to leave. They did not; many could not, and often those who wanted to were barred by highly restrictive immigration policies of Western nations, including the United States. Between the wars, as we shall see, Zionism, the national rebirth of the Jewish people, was one of the most important Jewish organizations in Poland. So, too, was the BUND, the acronym for the "General Jewish Workers Union in Lithuania, Poland, and Russia."

The BUND demanded cultural and national autonomy for national minorities, especially for the Jews. The BUND perceived the necessity of organizing Jewish workers into one national party. Generally, this group opposed political conservatives and Orthodox Jewish religion. The BUND saw that the only chance of solving the Jewish question in Poland was the building of a socialist society.

Despite the pogroms after the First World War, despite discrimination in Poland's universities, despite the increasingly hostile atmosphere, despite poverty and economic boycotts, a vast Jewish network of religious, educational, philanthropic, social, and cultural institutions flourished in Poland "without comparison elsewhere in Europe," according to Lucy S. Dawidowicz in *The War Against the Jews: 1933-1945.* Jews had political parties of all views and delegates and senators in the

Polish parliament. She adds that the rise of Nazi Germany, the death of Marshal Jozef Pilsudski in 1935, and Poland's accelerating Fascist course all brought near-disaster to the Jewish community. A torrent of anti-Semitic legislation, brutal pogroms, and an official government policy of "evacuating" the Jews from Poland overwhelmed them. By 1939, more Jews had left Poland than Germany, well over 400,000, and they went mainly to France, Belgium, and Palestine. To add insult to injury, the Polish government even studied the feasibility of settling Polish Jews on the island of Madagascar. In 1938, laws were enacted to revoke the citizenship of Polish Jews residing abroad.

The year 1938 will always be remembered as the year of Munich. On September 1, 1939, Hitler unleashed the German army and sent it into Poland. The long chapter on Polish Jewry was closed. A new disastrous chapter would begin. We know, of course, that after World War II, only about 200,000 Jews out of 3.5 million survived. Fifty years later, there would be only about 5,000 to 8,000 "registered" Jews in Poland. An even newer chapter would start.

Notable Polish Jews

Many Jews served as court physicians to Polish princes and magnates. Tobias Cohn (1652-1729) may have been the first physician to provide a detailed description of the disease known as *plica polonica,* a skin disease affecting the scalp.

A large number of Jewish moneylenders became involved in trade and helped establish villages on large tracts of land.

By far, some of the greatest Jewish scholars, luminaries of Talmudic scholarship, hailed from Poland. Among these rabbis were Yom Tov Lippmann Heller; Solomon Luria; Moses Isserles; Isaiah b. Abraham ha Levi Horowitz; Meir b. Gedaliah of Lublin; Mordechai b. Abraham Jaffe of Lublin; and the Chassidic masters, including Israel b. Eliezer Ba'al Shem Tov, the founder of Chassidism, to name a few.

Thirteen Jewish representatives sat in the first Polish Parliament in 1919. Noted among them was Professor Mojzesz Schorr, historian and Zionist, as well as being a member of the Polish Parliament.

Other important figures include Dr. Zygmunt Bychowski (1865-1934), prominent neurologist; Vladimir Medem (1879-1923), writer and leader of the BUND, which was founded in Vilna in 1897; Majer Balaben (1877-1942), historian, professor at Warsaw University, and once head of the Institute for Jewish Studies.

Polish Jewish musicians included Ignaz Friedman and Arthur Rubinstein, the singer Marya Freund, and harpsichordist Wanda Landowska.

Lazar Rundsztein was flyweight boxing champion of Poland in 1937.

Many of the leading Zionists and leaders of Israel came from Poland, the prime example being David Ben-Gurion, the first prime minister of Israel. Another noted Polish and later Zionist leader in Israel was Yitzhak Gruenbaum. A large part of the Israeli population had been born in Poland, and many were the organizers of the Jewish self-defense units in Palestine, known as the Haganah, which came out of Jewish defense movements in Poland, wrote Mark Kurlansky, author of *A Chosen Few: The Resurrection of European Jewry*. After the death of Theodor Herzl, the founder of modern Zionism, the leadership of the Zionism movement passed to Polish and Russian Jews, who carried on the idealistic work and vision. Poland once stood as one of the most important centers of the Zionist movement, with Polish Zionists playing an important role in World Zionist affairs. Various Zionist parties, like Hechalutz (a pioneering youth movement), were founded in Poland, as were groups such as the Revisionist Zionists. Unlike their German co-religionists, many of whom leaned toward assimilation, the Jews of Poland responded "wholeheartedly to the movement for a national revival." The first conference of the *Hoveve Zion*, "Lovers of Zion," movement was held in Katowice. Nahum Sokolow, who headed the Zionist movement in Poland, became a member of the World Zionist executive committee. A tremendous increase in membership in the Zionist movement occurred in Poland between the wars. According to the *Encyclopedia of Zionism and Israel*, "no other country with the exception of Palestine and, to a degree, Lithuania, experienced so encompassing a Zionist impact on

Jewish life." The encyclopedia also notes that the Polish government in the 1930s did not place obstacles before the Zionist movement "on the assumption that this would increase the stream of emigrants from Poland to Palestine." We will see that the Zionist youth groups in particular played a crucial role during World War II in the Jewish underground and the Warsaw Ghetto Uprising. In 1965, of the 17 cabinet members of Israel, eight were of Polish extraction; of the 120 Knesset members, about 30 percent had come to Israel from Poland.

Rosa Luxemburg (1870-1919) was swept up in the radical currents of the time. Born in the area of Russian Poland, she helped found the Spartacists, the forerunner of the German Communist Party. She was murdered by German rightwing soldiers in Berlin.

Julia Tuwim (1894-1953) wrote in Polish and is considered one of Poland's greatest modern poets.

Yiddish writers Solomon Rabinowitz, known as Sholem Aleichem (1859-1916); Shalom Abramovitsch, known as Mendele Mokher Soforim (1835-1917); and Isaac L. Peretz (1851-1915) immortalized the *shtetlekh* (Yiddish word for those Jewish rural communities of Russia and Poland). I.J. Singer (1893-1944) and Isaac Bashevis Singer (1904-91) were Yiddish novelists and short-story writers. The Singer brothers were born in Poland. I. J. Singer achieved fame for such novels as *Yoshe Kalb, The Brothers Ashkenazim, East of Eden,* and *The Family Carnovsky.* Isaac Bashevis Singer won the Nobel Prize for Literature in 1979. The books he is known for include *The Family Moskat, Gimpel the Fool, The Magician of Lublin,* and *The Manor.* Simon An-sky (1863-1920), folklorist and author of the famous play *The Dybbuk,* and Isaac Manger (1901-69) are also noted Jewish writers. To understand the life of Jews in Poland, the works of these authors make impressionable reading.

Sholem Asch (1880-1957), Polish-born, was the foremost Yiddish novelist of the early twentieth century. Also a dramatist, short-story writer, and journalist, Asch lived in Warsaw under the influence of Isaac Leib Peretz. Asch began writing in Yiddish in order to reach a worldwide Jewish audience. He lived and worked in several European countries as well as the United States and Israel. Some charged him with "becoming an apostate" and inciting further hatred of Jews, but he denied these accusations. He wrote *The Nazarene, The Apostle, Mary, Moses, Three Cities, The Mother,* and *East River.*

Polish Jewry Today

A Polish woman in her late forties recalls that as far back as thirty-five years ago the Polish Jewry community had only 5,000 members and was dying. "Thirty-five years later, I hear the same thing," she relates.

Never write off a Jewish community. The pundits said the same thing about the Jews of Vienna in the 1970s; that it was a dying community. Today, the Austrian Jewish community is a vibrant congregation. True, the history of Polish Jewry may be close to coming to an end, but it has not yet. Can organized communal life continue? Polish Jewry has received strong support from the American Jewish Joint Distribution Committee and from the Ronald S. Lauder Foundation. Other groups also have appeared on the scene.

In 1939, the Jewish population of the Soviet Union numbered 2.8 million. Nearly all Soviet Jews then and until this day lived in areas that once were part of Poland. Just before World War II, therefore, nearly 40 percent of the world's Jews lived in Poland itself or in former Polish territories. At least another 20 percent were descendants of Polish Jews who had emigrated to America.

For years, the population of the Polish Jewish community has been approximated at 5,000 persons. At the move into the 21st century, however, many Jewish leaders say the Jewish population is 5,000-8,000 and probably closer to 10,000 to 15,000.

Finally, what is effecting many Jewish communities in Poland is the fact that property restitution may soon come through, which will bring financial aid and independence to Jewish communities to help in the growth of schools, education facilities, and community institutions.

After Communism fell, the Poles began the process of returning to the market economy it once maintained. Along with Hungary and the Czech Republic, it has made progress economically.

A member of NATO, Poland is now negotiating entry into the European Union. It could take a few years. There are 38.5 million Poles living in an area almost as big as Germany and about the same size as New Mexico. The Poles talk of an emergence of a new, dynamic economy, Poland hopes to join the European Union by 2003, but it may take longer as it might with the Czech and Slovak republics.

Much information on Poland's Jewish Community can be gleaned from the community website: http:\\www.jewish.org.pl, or by e-mail: visitors@jewish.org.pl.

This is one community where Lubavitch is not active. Rabbi Haskell Besser, director of the Ronald S. Lauder Foundation, recounted that in a meeting with the late Lubavitch Rebbe, the Rebbe told Rabbi Besser that he should get involved "with the living in Poland," and not the dead. According to various sources, Lubavitch itself is not involved in activities in Poland.

Before the fall of communism, many Jewish parents masked or at least downplayed their Jewish identity because memories of the Holocaust were too painful and to be Jewish was not to their advantage. But now tens of thousands of full Jews, half-Jews, quarter-Jews, as well as non-Jewish spouses and in-laws are declaring their Judaism. In 1989, according to Rabbi Michael Schudrich, former director of the Lauder Foundation in Poland, and now the rabbi of the Warsaw and Lodz Jewish communities, thousands of young Poles began seeking their Jewish roots.

Now, Jews and other minorities feel comfortable in practicing Judaism. The restrictive policy of a Communist police state toward religion, toward Zionism, toward Israel, has been lifted.

Many of the young people tell of having one Jewish parent. During the Communist regime, these youths never thought of asking their mother if she was Jewish. As the story goes, that would have been like asking one's mother if she was a virgin when she got married. These people were one step past total assimilation. One young man knew so little, he did not even recognize he was Jewish when one day his mother blurted out, "By the way, my mother's mother was Jewish." According to Jewish law, that made the young man Jewish—Orthodox Judaism states that if your mother is Jewish, you are Jewish.

Because Rabbi Besser, the Lauder Foundation, the American Jewish Joint Distribution Committee, and other groups have been there tending to Jews who live in Warsaw, Cracow, Lodz, Lublin, Katowice, Wroclaw, Gdansk, and other cities, Polish Jewry can survive. "The Sabbath Candles Have Gone Out" is the title of the first chapter of Alexander Hertz's book, **The Jews in Polish Culture.** The lights may have been flickering, but they still can be seen.

"The eternal spark of the Jewish soul is never extinguished. We should not try to extinguish sparks that the Nazis and Communists failed to extinguish," declares Rabbi Schudrich.

Jewish Warsaw

If Warsaw is the heart of Poland and it is, then despite all, Warsaw is still the heart of Jewish Poland. But from 1939 to the year 2000, is like the difference between night and day. The Warsaw that Jews knew and loved is gone. And indeed, "the city, its people and its life will never be the same again." Once, one out of every three Warsavians was Jewish; today nobody even knows the exact figure—more than a thousand Jews, less than a thousand Jews.

The largest city of Poland, Warsaw lies on both banks of the Vistula River. The center of Warsaw and most residential areas are on the left bank.

In the years of the 900s, a small Slavic sect lived here. From the 1200s to the 1500s, Warsaw was the home of the dukes of Mazovia, a state that entered the Polish kingdom in the 1500s. In 1596, King Sigismund III moved the capital from Cracow to Warsaw. During the partitions, Prussia controlled Warsaw in the late 1700s; then the city became the capital of the Duchy of Warsaw from 1807 to 1813. In the next phase, the Russians controlled Poland until 1914 and after the German occupation in World War I in 1918, Warsaw became the capital of an independent Poland.

Today, Warsaw is bustling. In the Old Town square, which was reconstructed from utter ruin, we find the most elegant area in Warsaw and one of the most exciting in Poland. On an early Sunday morning, all is quiet except for the ringing of the church bells. This is what parts of Warsaw must have been like before World War II. Today Warsaw covers 170 square miles and has a population of about 1,700,000.

In 1781, 2,609 Jews lived in Warsaw, including several hundred in fashionable Praga, a suburb of the city on the east bank of the Vistula River.

In 1867, the Jewish Warsavian population reached 219,128.

Warsaw for the Jews symbolized study and cultural activities; Warsaw even had six full-time Yiddish theaters and a hundred Jewish troupes toured the country. Two major centers of Hebrew literary activity from 1880 to 1914 existed in Eastern Europe; Warsaw was one, Odessa in the Crimea, the other. Eventually, entire neighborhoods in the Warsaw suburbs were inhabited mainly by Jews, many of whom attended *shtibels*, Chassidic houses of prayer.

But between the world wars, the depression, the anti-Semitic policies of the Polish government, and the fall of Marshal Pilsudski, all "combined to keep the economic level of the Jewish community low," declared Lucy S. Dawidowicz. In his *Journey to Poland,* author Alfred Doblin was shocked by the poverty of the Jews. He described Jews in medieval garb with their own language, religion, and culture. He saw black-bearded Jews as vendors, elderly Jewish women, Jews in caftans and skull caps—they were not an "exotic tribe." They were lower middle-class workers, small businessmen, and laborers. By the 1930s, close to thirty percent of Polish Jews were receiving some form of financial assistance from Jewish communal funds.

There were renunciations of minority rights. There were *pogroms.* There were killings. There was anti-Semitism. There were numerous restrictive clauses. But there was not mass murder.

Warsaw remains a symbol of the tragedy of World War II. Without doubt, it had the distinction of being the "capital of the war," the first city to be bombed and the first to be turned into a battlefield.

Try to picture Stalingrad after that famous, devastating battle. Soviet officers who fought there maintain that Warsaw was the most destroyed city in Europe. Already ruined, Warsaw was burned to the ground during the German retreat. Early on, Hitler had decided to make Warsaw a "second Carthage," and in the 1944 Polish Uprising, the Germans bombarded the city, "literally to rubble," writes Eva Hoffman in *Exit into History: A Journey Through the New Eastern Europe.*

"Wartime in Poland lasted longer than for any other country, except Germany. In proportion to its size, Poland incurred far more damage and casualties than any other country on earth," according to Norman Davies in *Heart of Europe: A Short History of Poland.*

JEWISH SITES IN WARSAW

Because the Jewish community today is small, the tourist realizes that the major Jewish sites are pretty much within walking distance, so for our first visit we should head for Twarda Street and the NozykSynagogue.

Nozyk Synagogue, Twarda ul. 6, Warsaw. This synagogue is open to tourists at all times, but obviously they should not come to this house of prayer during services unless they desire to pray. There is no admission for those coming to pray, though contributions to the Jewish Community of Warsaw are always welcome, according to those who regularly pray there. The entrance to the synagogue building is up through a small staircase under a marquee from the side of the synagogue, facing the Yiddish Theater. A watchman sits in a small booth to the left of the entrance. He will buzz visitors in and he collects a nominal admission fee. A small bookshop is also located here.

During the Sabbath and holiday morning services, entrance to the synagogue is from the opposite end of the building, the location of the ornamental façade.

Since this is an Orthodox synagogue, there is separate seating for men and women. Women may sit in a partitioned-off area of the main sanctuary or they may go upstairs to the women's balcony.

If you are a male, you just may be the tenth Jewish man needed for a *minyan,* a prayer quorum. A daily, morning service is held, as of this writing.

The Nozyk Synagogue at 6 Twarda St., Warsaw. (Photo by Ben G. Frank)

This stately Orthodox synagogue was founded in 1900 and named after the founders, Zalman and Rywka, who died in the early part of the last century.

The *aron ha-kodesh (Holy Ark)* is located in the main hall and covered by the curtain (*parokhet*) with an inscription of the prayer, "Shema Yisrael." A member of the congregation led the prayers when I attended and his stand was on the right side facing the aron ha-kodesh.

How this synagogue, with alternating square piers and columns supporting the galleries, survived the Holocaust is a miracle. The Nazis used it as a stable. The dedication of the renovated synagogue, which is mainly Romanesque, took place on April 18, 1983, a day before the fortieth anniversary of the Warsaw Ghetto Uprising.

Jewish Visitors Information Center, Twarda ul 6, Warsaw. Tel: 620-3496. E-mail: visitors@jewish.org.pl. Sponsored by the Ronald S. Lauder Foundation, this office adjacent to the synagogue provides travelers with information about Polish Jewry, including maps, videos, publications and guidance, as well as Internet access by arrangement.

Union of Jewish Religious Communities in Poland, Twarda ul 6, 00-104, Warsaw. Tel: 620-4234. This organization coordinates activities for more than 15 synagogues in Poland and looks after Jewish cemeteries. It also attends to the religious needs of Polish Jewry.

Jewish Community of Warsaw, Twarda ul. 6, 00-104 Warsaw. Tel: 620-4234. Warsaw's Jewish community is located here. In 2000, its president was Helena Datner, the group's first female president.

TSKZ Jewish Social-Cultural Association of Poland, Plac Grzybowski 12/16, Warsaw (Yiddish Theater Building). This organization deals with cultural activities in Poland and is a lay organization, active in Jewish communities. There are **TSKZ** branches throughout the country and it is the largest Jewish organization in Poland. Together with the Union of Religious Communities, **TSKZ** was the officially recognized Jewish organization under Communism. Its bilingual Polish-Yiddish biweekly publication, *Slowo Zydowskie/Dos Yiddish Vort,* can be obtained in the Yiddish Theater lobby.

Shalom Foundation, Plac Grzybowski 12/16 ul, Warsaw. This group supports cultural programs and created the Polish Jewry photo album, "I Can Still See Their Faces."

The Ronald S. Lauder Foundation, Twarda 6 ul, 00-104, Warsaw. Tel: 620-3496. FAX: 652-2152. Website: http:\\www.lauder.pl. One might call this active group "the eyes and ears" of the Polish Jewish community. Here one finds a group of dedicated men and women. The Foundation supports schools, kindergartens and educational programs in 15 Central and Eastern European countries. In Poland, it supports Jewish day schools in Warsaw and Wroclaw; a kindergarten in Warsaw, a Sunday School program in Lodz, youth clubs, nightly adult education programs, and weekly Sabbath dinners in Warsaw, Lodz, Cracow, Wroclaw, Gdansk; holiday events, lecture series, a genealogy and archival research project, and an array of publications in Polish, geared to every age group. The director of the foundation is Jonah Bookstein.Tel: 652-2150.

Joint Distribution Committee, Twarda ul.6, Warsaw. Here, as in Eastern Europe, JDC aids the Jewish community in welfare and education activities. JDC supplies free medicine and serves hot kosher meals in canteens throughout the country. It also sponsors or advises the Jewish Sunday School and the Polish Union of Jewish Students.

Ronald S. Lauder Foundation, Youth Club, Twarda ul.6, Warsaw.

E.R. Kaminska's State Jewish Theater in Warsaw, Pl. Grzybowski, 16/18, Warsaw. Named after Esther Rachel Kaminska, this 400-seat theater was opened in 1970 at a cost of more than $1 million. Its founder and star performer, Ida Kaminska, fled Poland after the anti-Semitic outburst of 1968.

It has been said that Yiddish and the Hebrew language and culture, as well as the Yiddish theater, springs from Poland and it exists because the people and the community want to keep it alive and the government and the American Jewish Joint Distribution Committee support it. Productions are attended mainly by Poles.

In Warsaw, the first attempt to create a Jewish theater was recorded in 1837. In the 1890s, Yiddish productions were stimulated by Abraham Goldfaden, considered father of the Yiddish theater. Drama circles began to flourish in Warsaw and Cracow. The dramatists included such literary celebrities as Shalom Abramovitsch, known as Mendele Mokher Soforim, and Solomon Rabinowitz, whose pseudonym was Sholem Aleichem. The latter's plays still thrill the world, including *Tevye the Dairyman*, better known as *Fiddler on the Roof.*

We also recognize the Yiddish and Hebrew poet, Isaac Leib Peretz (1852-1915), and Ossip Dymov (1878-1942). Ossip Dymov, born in Bialystok, had been a publicist before he began writing for the theater. Only at the turn of the century did the Jewish theater start to actively develop.

In 1892, Esther Rachel Kaminska (1870-1925) made her appearance in Warsaw's Eldorado Theater. Kaminska, who would later found the theater in Obozna Street, won fame as an actress and performed in the first Jewish films. By her side, the great talent of her daughter, Ida Kaminska (1899-1978) grew.

The Jewish theater in Poland—chiefly in Warsaw and Vilna— gave premiers of plays, which were often dramatic adaptations by Sholem Aleichem. The audience also had the opportunity to acquaint themselves with Jacob Gordon's vast repertoire. The most creative period of the Jewish theater occurred in the 1920s and 1930s, when Yiddish theater companies were quite active in Poland, according to Lucjan Dobroszycki and Barbara Kirshenblatt-Gimblett in *Image Before My Eyes: A Photographic History of Jewish Life in Poland, 1864-1939.*

Even in the Warsaw Ghetto, the world's largest concentration camp, the Nazis permitted several theaters to operate. Between December 1940 and July 1942, five such theaters functioned. "The theatrical interlude in the Warsaw Ghetto was only one more element of the perfidious tactic of showing victims already doomed to death, a flicker of hope which would soon vanish on the way to the gas chambers," writes Zygmunt Hoffman in *Polish Jewry History and Culture.* After the war, Jewish theater commenced production.

It was not until 1955 that the State Theatre, named after Esther Rachel Kaminska, found a permanent home in Warsaw.

KOSHER FOOD IN WARSAW

Sad but true. At press time, apparently there are no longer strictly kosher restaurants in Warsaw. An opening of a kosher restaurant is now planned, however. There are non-kosher, kosher style or "Jewish style," restaurants, including **Café Eilat, Pod Samsonem, Menora** and **Warszawa-Jerozolima.** Visitors are advised to bring kosher food with them. However, **Warszawa-Jerozolima** says it can provide micro-waved kosher airline meals upon request. Unlike the U.S., Canada, or even some European countries, there are rarely any kosher products in the stores and even brand names familiar to kosher consumers in the West need not be kosher in Poland.

Restaurant Menora, Plac Grzybowski 2, Warsaw. Tel: 20-37-54. This establishment is open from 10 A.M. to 9 P.M. Once it was strictly kosher; it is no longer.

Warszawa-Jerozolima-Warsaw-Jerusalem, Restaurant, Smocza st. 27, Warsaw.This restaurant is located in the former area of the Warsaw Ghetto. Actually, the restaurant is in a basement. Included here are Israeli and Jewish music, traditional Polish Jewish cooking as well as Israeli Middle Eastern cuisine, such as falafel, tahina, humus and kebab. The Eastern European menu includes such delicacies as gefilte fish and chicken soup as well as stuffed chicken necks and tzimmes. Polish specialties are also served. Kosher airline food can be provided.

Café Eilat, Ujazdowskie al, 47, 00-536, Warsaw (opposite the Sheraton Hotel). A café near the U.S. Embassy where many young Polish intellectuals, Jewish and non-Jewish, gather. This establishment sponsors speakers, exhibits and programs on Jewish and Israeli themes, on Mondays and Thursdays, from 4 P.M. Located here, too, is the **Polish-Israel Friendship League.** Also, it is the mailing address of the Polish Council of Christians and Jews, according to Stanislaw Krajewski who is a leader in the Warsaw Jewish community. The Polish Council of Christians and Jews was established in 1991 to enhance mutual understanding between both Christians and Jews. Such an organization did not exist before 1989, the year Communism dissolved in Eastern Europe.

WARSAW GHETTO AREA

Those who know the tragedy that befell the Jewish people know this visit to the former Warsaw Ghetto area is not your usual simple walk-through, even though part of it is a nice, quiet area. It sports a beautiful green park and apartment buildings, children play, and shoppers hover about picking out bargains. Tourists bustle from place to place and melt into the busy scene. When the knowledgeable traveler visits the area of the former Warsaw Ghetto and its monument, he or she is reminded that between November 1940 and June/July 1943, "along this path of suffering and death," about 450,000 Jews were either driven away from the city to the gas chambers housed in the Nazi death camps, or were buried underneath these fine apartment houses.

The Jews, who accounted for thirty percent of the Warsaw population, were jammed into 2.4 percent of the city's area. We call that a *ghetto*,—in this case, a "concentration of Jews defined by racist criteria," points out Yisrael Gutman in *The Jews of Warsaw, 1939-1943: Ghetto, Underground, Revolt.* The section that you walk in—there are memorial stones in parts of it—was known as the Central Ghetto, including the streets of Wolynska, Szczeszluva, Ostrovska, Niska, Stawki, Nalewki, Gesia, Dzika (Zamenhofa), Mila, and Maranowska. We shall visit the "Memorial Route" soon.

Actually, as best as we can tell, the Holiday Inn hotel was the southern border of the Warsaw Ghetto. Near the Holiday Inn is 60-62 Zlota (Gold) Street and in the courtyard there is a remnant of the wall of the ghetto. Also at 55 Sienna Street is another wall remnant; a plaque was placed there by the United States Historical Memorial Museum.

"The sidewalks were filled with masses of people whose threadbare clothing reeked with the smell of rotting foodstuffs, and human sweat," writes Gutman. "Dead bodies rolled in the street." People dropped like poisoned flies. The ghetto was swarming with Jews brought from outlying villages. The smell of death was everywhere. Out of a half-million Jews, fewer than 50,000 remained by mid-1943.

The story of the Warsaw Ghetto actually begins with the victory of the Nazis over Poland. The Germans divided up Poland with the Russians, then later they established what they called the *Generalgouvernment*—an area of 39,000 square miles, composed of four districts: Cracow, Lublin, Warsaw, and Radom. This area became a dumping ground for Jews and Poles who had been expelled from Germany and parts of Poland. Now penniless and near starvation, these people were placed under German civil administration. Hans Frank served as Governor General. He was appointed on November 8, 1939, and set up his headquarters in Wawel Castle in Cracow.

With about 450,000 Jews jammed into the Warsaw Ghetto, the Nazis turned the area into a human stockyard. Isolated, they were forced into close, squalid conditions with dwindling food, fear, and intimidation. No hope for the future existed in their depressed minds.

Penned in on all sides, the sentence was death by starvation and disease. People became skeletons almost overnight. They were forbidden to teach or to learn. Escape from the ghetto was almost impossible. Marek Edelman, a survivor of the Warsaw Ghetto Uprising, said once that only one out of thousands was able to escape. You needed money to bribe the guards, including at times Polish police. Even before their scheduled final journey to the Treblinka concentration camp, many had died of disease and hunger. Others thought they could hide in the ghetto and somehow survive.

The Nazi goal was to isolate Jews, plunder their property, force them into slave labor, and actually starve them gradually to death, according to Israel Gutman in *Resistance: The Warsaw Ghetto Uprising.*

The Germans knew that by giving Jewish spoils to the Poles, the Nazis "gained ardent supporters. There is no doubt that Polish satisfaction with the fate of the Jews under the Nazis stemmed from economic considerations," wrote Joseph Kermisz in *The Warsaw Diary of Adam Czerniakow: Prelude to Doom.* But above all, was the dynamism shown by the Jews of Warsaw, "their tenacious resolve to hold onto life in spite of everything." With the intensification of German attempts to destroy the ghetto, resistance increased.

The Nazis concentrated Jews in cities at railway junctions and in the words of Martin Gilbert, author of *The Holocaust: A History of the Jews of Europe During the Second World War,* "into ghettos such as had not existed in Europe since the Middle Ages." The ghetto which was "shaped like a hammer head," covered 840 acres of slums and housed about 450,000, a figure that included Jews from the suburbs as well as towns, villages, and cities of Poland.

In the beginning of the Nazi occupation, Jews had no idea of the deaths that awaited them. The Germans used every possible ruse to deceive the Jews, even telling them in the extermination camps that the gas chambers were merely showers.

You could walk through the ghetto in forty minutes. Dan Kurzman, in *The Bravest Battle: The Twenty-Eight Days of the Warsaw Ghetto Uprising,* describes the ghetto as a "pressure cooker surrounded by a brick wall 10 feet high and 11 miles long." Glass splinters "embedded in plaster" were on top of the wall. The houses at that time were nineteenth-century, slope-roofed tenements, two to six stories high. The wall had twenty-two gates, reduced in the course of time to thirteen. At the final stage of the ghetto's existence, there were only four gates. At the gates stood the guards of three police forces, German, Polish, and Jewish. Every person, every wagon, and every vehicle that approached was thoroughly searched. Crowded in the narrow streets of the ghetto existed a population equal to that of a city in other parts of the world. Twenty-six thousand Jews lived in Pawia Street; 20,000 in Mila Street, and 20,000 in Gesia Street. They were for all intents and purposes at the mercy of the Nazis and the "representative of the regime," the Judenrat, which in effect was "the sole channel between hundreds of Jews and the authorities and the outside world at large," according to Yisrael Gutman. But they were handpicked by the Germans and some, like Adam Czerniakow of Warsaw, tried to mediate with the Germans, but to no avail. He later committed suicide. Others used their position to save themselves and their families. The Judenrat "was infiltrated by men who were controlled by the Germans and had been hired by express order of the authorities." A Jewish police force was established within the ghetto and "of all the frameworks and services for which the Judenrat assumed responsibility, the police force was the institution most remote from and alien to the traditions of Jewish communal life in the Diaspora."

Probably in 1940, the Germans decided to establish a ghetto to systematically segregate the Jews and by the fall of that year began to relocate them. On November 16, 1940, the Nazis sealed off the ghetto area. From that date until July 22, 1942, the isolated ghetto existed in its "normal format," according to Yisrael Gutman, but firom July 22, the Germans initiated the mass deportation of Jews and in the following seven weeks of deportation of Jews, "about 75 percent of the Jews were driven out of their homes and transported to the Treblinka death camp."

WARSAW GHETTO UPRISING

The Warsaw Ghetto Uprising was the largest single act of armed civilian resistance until the outbreak of the Polish Warsaw Uprising fifteen months later, as well as the most famous armed Jewish insurrection against the Nazis. The uprising came as a result of the German cold-blooded, organized, calculated, and deliberate act to destroy Jews.

A rabble army, without a decent weapon, held at bay the mightiest military power the world had ever known for 42 days and 42 nights; all of Poland in 1939 held the Germans off for less than a month.

Furthermore, Dan Kurzman maintains that the military encounter was one of "the most stirring, impossible and important battles in history." As for Jews, they had rebelled previously. But the uprising, "more than any other event, symbolically ended two thousand years of Jewish submission to discriminate oppression and finally genocide."

During the uprising, small episodes terrorized the Germans. Before the uprising, according to Yitzhak Zuckerman, whose code name was Antek, "all a German had to do was yell 'Raus,' and the Jews would come out. This time, no Jew came out. This time, the Germans came up to us and we killed them."

No longer did Jews feel they were going to their death, herded like cattle. Armed resistance gained mass support only when people understood that the Nazis planned to kill all Jews and that there was no way out of the ghetto, according to Israel Gutman. He asks why the Jews did not revolt sooner. They did not, he points out, because of extreme starvation and weakness. They were reduced to "utter impotence." They did not know death awaited them.

By January 1943, the Jews were expecting another action. Called "the second action" (*aktion*), it came by surprise on Monday, January 18, 1943, and lasted until January 22. Before that, Mordechai Anielewicz, who had been engaged in underground work, began to organize. He came back to the ghetto in October 1942. He was among the organizers of the Jewish Fighting Organization (Z.O.B.), whose definition was a "broad merger of political and ideological factions that bridged various and often antagonistic philosophies."

January 18, 1943 marked a turning point in the existence of the Jewish Fighting Organization. On that date, in the "second action," the Germans surrounded the ghetto. Until January 18, Jews were "passive prey." But then they fought back and those acts of resistance were very important. On January 18, with Anielewicz in command, a number of Jewish ghetto fighters attached themselves to the lines of the deportees being led to concentration camp-bound trains. Armed with pistols, and at a given signal, the freedom fighters opened fire; they shot a few German soldiers; they hurled some hand grenades and scattered the surprised Germans at the corner of Zamenhofa and Niska streets. The Jewish civilians ran and escaped.

After that day, the interval between January 22 and April 19, 1943, a space of 87 days, was used to train and prepare resistance. In April 1943, when the Germans once more moved to liquidate the Warsaw Ghetto, they again encountered armed resistance from the Jews.

The Nazis wanted the ghetto *judenrein* (free of Jews). And they wanted the job to be completed by April 20, Hitler's birthday. A year before, in April and May 1942, the ghetto contained about 350,000 Jews. The mass deportation or *aktion* of Warsaw Jews began on July 22, 1942, and continued until September 12, 1942. During those seven weeks, about 265,000 Jews were uprooted from Warsaw, transported to the Treblinka death camp, and murdered in the gas chambers.

The Germans entered the ghetto armed to the teeth on the morning of April 19, 1943; that night would be the first night of the Passover Seder. To this day, many Jewish families throughout the world pause during the Seder to recall the heroes of the Warsaw Ghetto. In that engagement thousands of German soldiers fought against a maximum of 1,200 Jewish fighters: "13 heavy machine guns against which the Jews had no equivalent armament; 69 hand-held machine guns, against which the Jews had none; a total of 135 submachine guns against which the Jews had two; several howitzers and other artillery pieces of which the Jews had none; a total of 1,358 rifles, as against only 17 rifles among the Jews," according to Martin Gilbert. The number of Jewish fighters varies. In *Admitting the Holocaust: Collected Essays,* Lawrence L. Langer says estimates of the Jewish Fighting Organization range from 250 to 800 out of 50,000 to 60,000 Jews who were still alive in the Warsaw Ghetto.

Author Ber Mark describes the Jews "as poorly equipped, inexperienced, minuscule and starving bands of ghetto warriors, with organized forces comprised of 600 members from the Jewish Fighting Organization," and about 400 from Farband and other groups. Thousands of these survivors participated spontaneously. The Jewish fighting units greeted the Germans "with a hail of grenades, bottles, bombs and rifle shots." The fighters trapped the invading Germans in a crossfire. The Jews fought from the rooftops and bunkers of the ruins. Their key element was surprise. They hid in cellars, bunkers, and sewers in the ghetto.

It is impossible to list all the names of the heroes of the Warsaw Ghetto Uprising. There was Yitzhak Zuckerman, Z.O.B. second in command, known as "Antek." He survived. There was Zivia Lubetkin, a Z.O.B. commander who, like others, escaped through the sewer system. She later became Zuckerman's wife. She and her husband and other ghetto fighters settled at Kibbutz Lohamei ha Gettaot in Israel. Marek Edelman, another commander, survived and still lives in Lodz, where he is a physician.

Of course, heading the list was Mordechai Anielewicz, the twenty-four-year-old commander who was born in Warsaw, attended Warsaw Hebrew High School, and was a member of Hashomer Hatzair, a pioneering socialist Zionist youth movement. At the beginning of the war, he escaped from the Nazis and helped organize Zionist activities in Russia-occupied Poland. According to Israel Gutman, writing in the *Encyclopedia of Zionism and Israel*, Mordechai Anielewicz was arrested by Soviet government troops as he tried to get to Palestine and was released after he volunteered to return to German-occupied Poland to help in the illegal activities of Hashomer Hatzair. He became head of Hashomer Hatzair in the ghetto and commander of the Z.O.B. and organized the remnants of the ghetto for the final battle in which he perished at MILA 18. He was "the handsome commander loved by all." In his last message sent to his deputy, Yitzhak Zuckerman, he wrote: "The dream of my life has been fulfilled. I have lived to see Jewish defense in all its greatness and glory."

Today, besides his reproduction in the statue of the Memorial to the Victims of the Warsaw Ghetto Uprising, another statue of Mordechai Anielewicz stands at Kibbutz Yad Mordechai, in Israel, in front of a bombed water tower damaged by Egyptian armed forces in the Israel War of Independence.

On May 16, 1943, Nazi commander Jurgen Stroop reported to his superiors that the Warsaw Ghetto "is no longer in existence." The action ended at 8:15 P.M. To celebrate, the Germans blew up the Great Synagogue.

But it would take months to end Jewish resistance. Jews defended building after building, bunker after bunker, street after street. They fought. Soon, however, starvation, exhaustion, and sickness took their toll. The skirmishes lasted in the ruins of the ghetto into July 1943. According to author Ber Mark, Polish sources cited evidence of armed groups of Jews fighting on "in the razed ghetto area in 1944!" Thousands of Jews were killed, thousands were burned in their hideouts, and 56,000 who had survived the fighting were shipped off to the death camps. But the legends of the Warsaw Ghetto will grow.

Memorial to the Victims of the Warsaw Ghetto Uprising, at the corner of Anielewicza and Zamenhofa streets, Warsaw. As a journalist and editor, I had seen pictures for forty-five years of that magnificent monument of the fighters of the Warsaw Ghetto and Jewish resistance. Its dedication in Hebrew, Yiddish, and Polish moves the viewer: "To the Jewish People— its Heroes and Martyrs."

In December 1970, Willy Brandt, world Socialist leader, former mayor of West Berlin, chancellor of West Germany, was in Warsaw for negotiations for the new treaty between Poland and the Federal Republic of Germany. He visited the Memorial and he fell to his knees before it. "This gesture...was not planned. Oppressed by the memories of Germany's recent history, I simply did what people do when words fail them," wrote Brandt, according to *The New York Review of Books*, July 14, 1994. Over the years, the world's leading figures have come to the site of the memorial for the heroes of the ghetto uprising, including presidents Jimmy Carter and Bill Clinton, as well as Pope John Paul II, who in 1978, then a Polish cardinal, became pope of the Roman Catholic Church. Solidarity also held demonstrations here.

The traveler should stand at the corner of Anielewicza and Zamenhofa. Now called Anielewicza, it is the former Gesia Street where the historic Jewish community was located. It has been renamed for the heroic commander of the Warsaw Ghetto Uprising, Mordechai Anielewicz. The streetcar, with the sign Anielewicza, today motors through the new section of the city. It covers concrete streets probably laid right on top of the ruins of the Jewish ghetto and the tram ends its route at the Jewish cemetery. Also at Anielewicza Street and Zamenhofa, a stone tells us the Dr. Ludwig Zamenhof, creator of Esperanto, the International language, lived on this street at no. 5.

"Of all the thousands of memorials created after the war to commemorate aspects of the Holocaust, Nathan Rapoport's Warsaw Ghetto Monument emerges as possibly the most widely known, celebrated and controversial," according to James E. Young in *The Texture of Memory: Holocaust Memorials and Meaning in Europe, Israel, and America*. A copy of the monument stands at the Yad Vashem Museum in Jerusalem, Israel.

Interestingly, the memorial's granite blocks were originally cut and stacked for the Germans to use them in a Nazi victory monument in Berlin.

The thirty-six-foot monument was unveiled on April 19, 1948, five years after the Warsaw Ghetto Uprising, before 12,000 survivors, military personnel, and government dignitaries.

As I stood before this wall of granite, it came alive for me and I agreed with Young's description of the seven persons on the front wall that represents the burning side of the underground bunker. "A muscular prophet figure on one knee picks up a rock, a young boy at the left, clutches a dagger, a young woman at the right cradles a Kalashnikov rifle, the leader Anielewicz clenches a homemade grenade. Even the mother engulfed by flames raises her right arm defensively as does the baby in her other arm." The ghetto is being swallowed by flames, but the men, women, and children in tattered clothes are led into battle by Anielewicz.

On the back of the wall, one sees twelve stooped and huddled figures, showing fear and despair—depicting the contrasting scene of Jews hopelessly on their way to the death camps. One sees only three Nazi helmets and two bayonets barely visible in the background. There is a rabbi holding a Torah scroll in one arm. He "looks up and reaches to heaven as if to beseech God." Two huge menorahs, symbolic of Judaism and the State of Israel, flank the main part of the monument.

As you walk in the area, you will note black memorial stones. The route is called **"A Memorial Route to the Struggle and Martyrdom of the Jews 1940-1943."** Some call it Memory Lane. People come by here every day, but April 19 is special. This is the day to commemorate the Warsaw Ghetto Uprising. People march along Zamenhofa and Dubois streets to Stawki Street and then to the Umschlagplatz Wall Memorial. The groups lay flowers, light candles, and say prayers. You, the traveler, can do the same.

The memorial route begins at the Monument to the Heroes of the Ghetto; runs down Zamenhofa Street past Samuel Zygielbojm Square and the mound and stone on the corner of Mila Street (dedicated to Mordechai Anielewicz and the Jewish Fighting Organization); then goes down Stawki Street, past the

S.S. Unit Command and the former school and Jewish transit hospital. It ends at the entrance to the Umschlagplatz.

Starting at the monument, we see the first monument built right after the war, in 1946, in the shape of a sewer top, to signify escape hatches—the only way out of the flaming ghetto. There are four memorial stones around the monument area. Nearby is the Tree of Shared Remembrance, an oak planted on April 19, 1988, to commemorate the murder of Polish Jews and Poles who perished saving Jewish lives.

To the left of the monument is a memorial stone dedicated to Emmanuel Ringelblum (1900-1944), historian and founder of the Underground Ghetto Archives.

At the corner of Lewartowski and Zamenhofa streets stand stones to Joseph Lewartowski and Michael Klepfisz. The former was a leader of the Communist party, and the latter was an activist in the BUND.

Then we leave Zamenhofa and come to Samuel Zygielbojm Square, where we observe a stone dedicated to Zygielbojm, the man from London who tried to alert the world to the murder of the Jews in Nazi-occupied Europe. But he felt he failed in his attempt to arouse the international community. In protest against the atmosphere of indifference to the tragedy of the Jewish people, he committed suicide on May 12, 1943.

The visitor should now head back to Zamenhofa Street toward Mila Street. There on the corner are two stones dedicated to Arie Wilner and Mordechai Anielewicz, both members of Hashomer Hatzair, the Zionist youth movement. Both died in the bunker, Mila 18.

MILA 18

Mila 18, on Mila Street, commemorates the site of the last bunker of the Warsaw Ghetto Uprising. Today a monument for all to see is mounted on top of what would have been Number 18.

Mila 18 was the central bunker of the Z.O.B., the Jewish Fighting Organization. At times, it housed about 350 persons,

Memorial to the heroes of Mila 18, the central bunker of the Jewish Fighting Organization in the Warsaw Ghetto Uprising.
(Photo by Ben G. Frank).

including 80 military personnel, according to Ber Mark. Zivia Lubetkin, a Dror activist who fought here. The Germans sought out this bunker. Probably tipped off as to its location, the German troops on May 8 surrounded the area, fired grenades, and injected gas into the bunker. The victims began choking, some committed suicide, others were killed by German gunfire. It is clear that almost all the fighters perished.

"Thus fell Mordechai Anielewicz, one of the finest and noblest warriors, who from the beginning put his life at the service of his people," according to Emmanuel Ringelblum, the noted Jewish writer who chronicled the events in the Warsaw Ghetto. After the war, those who came to Warsaw climbed onto the heaps of ruins. Nothing was recognizable. One could not tell where a certain street had been or where a house had stood. However, they discovered the spot, the hole, where the house on Mila 18 had stood. They took a great black stone, a mass of dull rock, stone, and dirt, and placed it there. In simple lettering in three languages, the following was etched on the stone: "Here on the 8th day of May, 1943, Mordechai Anielewicz, the commander of the Warsaw Ghetto Uprising, together with the staff of the Jewish Fighting Organization and dozens of fighters fell in the campaign against the Nazi enemy."

After visiting the bunker at Mila 18, we continue our walk down Dubois Street, which is a continuation of Zamenhofa. We come across memorial stones to Pawel Frenkiel, commander of the Jewish Military Union (ZZW), and Frumka Plotnicka, liaison-officer of the Jewish Fighting Organization. Still on Dubois Street, there are memorial stones to the leader of the Religious Zionist party, Rabbi Yitzhak Nissenbaum, and a stone dedicated to Janus Korczak (Henryk Goldszmidt), educator and writer who accompanied "his" children (orphans) on their last journey from the Urnschlagplatz to Treblinka.

We then turn left on Stawki Street and observe a memorial stone dedicated to Itzhak Katznelson, a poet-author who wrote "Poem of the Murdered Jewish Nation." He fought in the ghetto, but since he had a Honduran passport, he was sent to the Vittel concentration camp in France and later to Auschwitz, where he perished. The poem is one of the greatest literary expressions on the tragedy of the Holocaust.

Another stone cites the building at 5/7 Stawki Street, the headquarters of the S.S. And another stone at 6/8 Stawki cites a building in which the Jews were held before being transported to Treblinka. A stone to the left of the Urnschlagplatz Wall Monument cites the 450,000 Jews packed into the ghetto and murdered by the Nazis.

Umschlagplatz. Today it is a busy road. The cars speed by; watch how you cross the street. The wall in front of you—a fitting monument to the victims of the Holocaust—lists the first names of Jews who perished in the Holocaust and in the Warsaw Ghetto. In the early 1940s it was a large square at the northern edge of the ghetto, bordered by a railway siding, a "railhead for resettlement" to the German death camp. When the ghetto was established, food supplies were brought in to this railroad siding, which is located exactly at the foot of the ghetto. But from July 22, 1942, this loading dock became a one-way ticket to Treblinka. About 6,000 Jews were loaded into boxcars that first day the deportation began and then it was 10,000 every day after, until the ghetto was completely destroyed and no Jew could be found. In fact, whenever the Germans could not meet their daily 10,000 quota, they and their henchmen, the Ukrainians and the Latvians, even Jewish police, would guard and round up people right off the street. Chaos and hysteria ruled, thousands of men, women, and children were jammed into boxcars. Day after day, the "grisly caravans departed for the gas chambers with their loads of human flesh." Sometimes two trains would come at once. Everyone could carry only a single bundle; a three-kilogram bag. Very few escaped through the hospital, only to be picked up the next day.

As I stood on the Umschlagplatz and recalled one of the saddest events that occurred there. Janus Korczak (1878-1942), physician, children's writer, educator, and head of an orphanage, on August 5, 1942, accompanied his two hundred orphaned children to the Umschlagplatz and from there to the gas chambers at Treblinka even though he was not scheduled for deportation at that time. Korczak was a Jew who had been born Hersh Goldszmidt. However, he made Polish—not Yiddish—his mother tongue and he used his Polish name, Henryk. In other lands, he became known as Janus Korczak, which he used as a pen name. When the Germans came for his

The Umschlagplatz wall monument, dedicated to the hundreds of thousands of Jews who were deported by train from this railroad depot in Warsaw to the death camp. (Photo by Ben G. Frank)

two hundred children from the orphanage he headed, he brushed and polished the children and dressed them in their best clothes. He told them to take their schoolbooks so they could study when they weren't "working in the forest." Holding one child by the hand, he calmly signaled to the others, who were silently lined up behind him in neat rows, and they began marching toward the boxcars.

As we walk around the Umschlagplatz Wall Monument, we notice that the wall of the monument has white marble with a black band like a tallis (prayer shawl). The wall skirts a small rectangular area, one side of which is the outer wall of a school, the former Jewish hospital. The area inside the wall is symbolic. In the wall opposite the entrance from Stawki Street is a narrow opening that looks out onto a tree, a symbol of hope. Over the entrance is a black slab in the shape of a Jewish tombstone. Besides inscriptions dedicated to the Jews who were driven from the ghetto, there is a wall of four hundred first names in Hebrew, Yiddish, and Polish. Original paving stones have been preserved on the site of the former Umschlagplatz entrance, next to the former hospital and school building. On the other side wall of the school, next to the Wall Monument, is a white marble band with a verse inscribed from the book of Job (16:18): "O Earth, cover not my blood, and let my cry for justice find no rest."

Korczak Orphanage, 8 Jalikosowska St., Warsaw. This is a children's home and a statue of Janusz Korczak stands tall in front of this building. He is considered a hero of Poland. A moving statue of Janusz Korczak is located in the Jewish cemetery, which we shall visit next. Here, the statue shows Korczak holding a child in his arms and leading other children who are behind him.

Jewish Cemetery, ul. Okopowa 49/51, corner of Gesia Street, 01-043, Warsaw. Tel: 382-622. The "Pantheon of modern Polish Jewry, a forest of the dead." Open every day except Saturday, of course, from 10 A.M. to 3 P.M. This huge historic cemetery is not kept in the best of condition, but sincere efforts are made to keep it up. The cemetery's stone wall has gaping holes that were made by thieves who vandalized the marble tombstones and by plunderers who were still searching for gold teeth as in Auschwitz, according to S. L. Schneiderman. Here, despite the weeds, broken tombstones, and blurred engravings, lie the leaders, the writers, the doctors, and the men, women, and children of the last 150 years. You can inhale Polish Jewish history from the stories recounted on the tombstones.

Dr. Zamenhof, creator of the international language, Esperanto, is buried here, as is Esther Rachel Kaminska, world-renowned Yiddish actress. Also, Rabbi Osjasz Thon, leader of Polish Jewry and noted Zionist, lies here.

In a special pantheon lie I.L. Peretz (1851-1915), Yiddish writer; Jacob Dinesohn (1858-1919), Yiddish novelist; and S. An-sky (1863-1920), author, who wrote the famous play, *The Dybbuk*.

Here is the grave of the head of the Warsaw Ghetto Judenrat, the engineer, Adam Czerniakow (1880-1942), who committed suicide on July 23, 1942, rather than living and doing the bidding of the Germans who were on a path toward total annihilation of the Jews. Born in Warsaw, Czerniakow served as the head of the Warsaw Judenrat during the "Great Action." Realizing that the Jews were being taken for extermination, he wrote many of his thoughts in the now-published *The Warsaw Diary of Adam Czerniakow: Prelude to Doom*, an important source of information on the ghetto.

Jewish Historical Institute, Tlomackie 3/5 Warsaw, Tel: 827-9221. FAX: 827-8372. Often, in Europe, and very often in Poland, you end up talking about a synagogue that was. In the case of the destroyed Great Synagogue in Warsaw, part of it survives in what is now the Jewish Historical Institute. The Institute was once a wing of Warsaw's Great Synagogue at Plac Tlomacki. This classical prayer building contained a large dome and on top rested the Star of David. This was the synagogue of the middle class, the enlightened, and the emancipated. The assimilated came here, wrote Alfred Doblin. The Synagogue, which recessed from Tlomacka Street, could seat 1,100 persons. The buildings boasted a porticoed central section, domed receding wings, and projecting terminal elements. "It looked remarkably secular, usually an indication that the Jews wished to avoid imitating a church or looking exotic," says Carol Herselle Krinsky

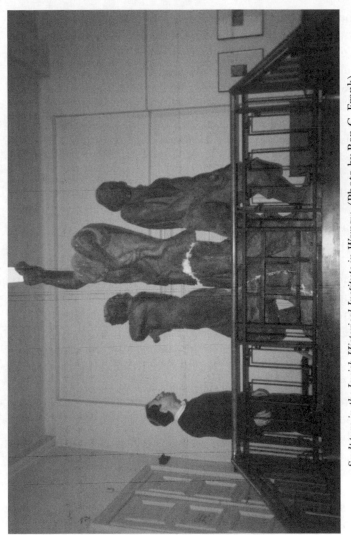

Sculpture in the Jewish Historical Institute in Warsaw. (Photo by Ben G. Frank)

in her book, *Synagogues of Europe.* It was erected in 1877, in German neo-Renaissance style. The Italian architect, Leonardo Marconi, drew the plans.

Heinrich Himmler, head of the Gestapo, ordered the synagogue destroyed at the so-called official end of the ghetto uprising. "A Wehrmacht sapper team under Stroop's supervision placed huge charges of dynamite under the building: the noise of the explosion shook all of Warsaw," wrote Ber Mark.

The Jewish Historical Institute contains one of the most outstanding collections of Judaica in the world, including manuscripts and the complete archives of Emmanuel Ringelblum, whose diary was found after the war hidden in sealed milk cans in the Warsaw Ghetto; it is one of the best records of the Warsaw Ghetto and is displayed for public viewing. Entitled *Notes from the Warsaw Ghetto,* it was not only Ringelblum's life work; it was also his death work. He did have an opportunity after the uprising in 1943 to be smuggled out of the country by the Polish underground, but he refused. He survived until March 1944, when he was discovered and shot by the Gestapo.

The Institute was once the magnificent library attached to the former Great Synagogue. Today, the library contains about 50,000 to 60,000 books and periodicals gathered from all over Poland after the war. Many important manuscripts are here as well as documents from the Warsaw, Lodz, and other ghettos during the war, as well as from theological seminaries. Paintings, sculptures, Judaica art objects, and other items, many from World War II, complete the vast holdings of this building, which survived the war and the restrictions of the Communist regime. Situated here, too, is a martyrs' museum devoted to the Warsaw Ghetto Uprising.

The **Jewish Historical Institute** was closed for a number of years due to renovations. It was scheduled to re-open by the summer of 2000. Ready for viewing were new exhibits of Jewish art, the Warsaw Ghetto and Holocuast and on Polish Jewish History.

There are plans to recreate a Museum of the History of Polish Jews. Suggested at one time for the location of such a building was the park in front of the monument to the Warsaw Ghetto Uprising located at Zamenhofa and Anielewicz streets.

These archives detail the history of Polish Jewry from the 16th century to the present. Divided into three periods: 1672 to the outbreak of World War II, the Institute holds records from synagogues in Cracow, Lublin, Radom and other cities. They included the important Ringelblum archives, which describe ghetto life throughout Poland. Also held here are survivor testimonials and accounts of those Jews who remained in Poland after the Second World War in order to rebuild Jewish life. The Institute receives support from the Polish government and from American-based organizations, such as the Ronald S. Lauder Foundation and the Society for Jewish Heritage in Poland.

The **Ronald S. Lauder Foundation Genealogy Project** at the **Jewish Historical Institute**. Tel: 827-9221. FAX: 827-1843. E-mail: laudergen@jewish.org.pl. Yale Reisner, who is on the staff of the Ronald S. Lauder Foundation, has been working on this project to assist those seeking "roots," relatives or survivors information about themselves or the fate of their families in Poland. This project at the **Jewish Historical Institute** provides genealogy and tracing consultations to visitors at no charge, although contributions to the preservation and cataloguing of Polish Jewish archives are welcome. The project helps people researching their ancestral towns, ascertaining the fates of Holocaust victims, tracing surviving relatives and documenting their own personal histories. Project staff speak English and several other languages.

Contributions can be sent to "The Javne Fund," 767 Fifth Avenue, suite 4600, New York, N.Y. 10153.

A twenty-minute walk from, let us say, the Marriott Hotel, brings you to the Jewish Historical Institute. Your landmark is a tall, white skyscraper structure with the word Sony on top. It stands on the very soil where the Great Synagogue once stood. Next door is the only surviving remnant, the Jewish Historical Institute.

The **Jewish Historical Institute** survived the war. East European Jewry, a reservoir of world Jewry, came to an abrupt end, and a chapter closed. After the war, the Zionist youth organization, Hashomer Hatzair, for instance, maintained that Jews should not live on the "cursed ground of Poland."

"We have to leave Poland, we have to get up and go," they said. "To most Polish Jews, it was unthinkable to renew their life on the Polish soil, soaked with the blood of millions of Jews," where Nazis found "thousands of collaborators among the local population eager to cooperate in the extermination of the Jews," states the *Encyclopedia Judaica*. Now began a mass migration of Jews from Poland and Eastern Europe, in 1945 to 1950.

The Polish attitude was disbelief that any Jew was alive. "You're still alive?" one Pole told a survivor, Harry Joskowitz, my wife's uncle. "You survived the war and you want your apartment, your houses back?" was the common attitude. The Poles indeed had expropriated businesses and real estate abandoned by the Jews.

This must be clearly stated. Many Poles experienced the annihilation of Polish Jewry as a colossal shock to their psyches. Many, however, found that "Hitler did the dirty work for us." Some did not think the work was so very dirty. The Poles considered Jews to be social outcasts and the Polish response to the Jewish plight fits in with the toothache theory of Yitzhak Zuckerman, "Antek."

Antek explains that Jews thought that once the world was aware of what was happening to them, someone would come to their rescue—certainly the Poles on the other side of the wall. "After the war, when I began reading memoirs of members of the Polish government in London, I was stunned by the extent of their alienation from and indifference to the Jewish issue, which was about as important to them as a toothache."

Jewish historians and leaders generally agree that the "Polish underground's supply of arms to the Jewish uprising leaders was scanty and inappropriate. They provided pistols when the Jews needed rifles and machine guns for the street fighting," writes Lawrence L. Langer in *Admitting the Holocaust: Collected Essays*.

And yet no matter how we view Polish anti-Semitism, we must remember the Poles did not start World War II. The Poles did not destroy Warsaw. The Poles did not order or build the death camps. The Poles did not serve as executioners; six million Poles, half of them Jews, died in the war. The Poles suffered great losses during the fighting and bombardments in

1939 and then in 1944. Approximately 2.5 million Poles were sent to Germany as forced laborers.

"Everywhere in the Nazi New Order, when faced with the plans to deport and murder local Jews, a proportion of the population attempted to aid and succor the Jews; a proportion assisted the Nazis and the majority remained inactive, somewhere in between," say the editors of *The Jews in Polish Culture.* There was no question about Polish complicity in a large segment of the population.

In discussing the Nazi policy towards Poles and Jews, a Polish underground hero who helped Jews and who tried to warn the world's leaders of the Holocaust, the late Jan Kozielewski, known as Karski during the war, told President Franklin Delano Roosevelt, "the Germans want to ruin the Polish state as a state, they want to rule over a Polish people deprived of its elites. With regard to the Jews, they want to devastate the biological substance of the Jewish nation." This underground leader went from world figure to world figure. Most of the people he appealed to did not believe him. Many did not want to believe the reports of the murder of Jews as early as the fall of 1942 or early 1943. Or, if they did believe, they did not want to do anything about it.

Elie Wiesel has written, "It is true that not all victims were Jews. But all Jews were victims." he said on the fiftieth anniversary of the liberation of Auschwitz: "The Jewish people-singled out for destruction during the Holocaust-have shouldered history's heaviest burden."

Although one-third of Jews managed to survive, says Lucy S. Dawidowicz, although the Jewish people and Judaism have outlived the Third Reich, the "Germans nevertheless succeeded in irrevocably destroying the life and culture of East European Jews." The thousand-year-old culture of Ashkenazic Jews that originated in the Rhine basin came to an end, she adds. But in *Tales of My People,* Sholem Asch maintains that "the terrible flame could destroy only the physical substance, not the spiritual essence of the Jew."

Estimates vary; however, at war's end only between 50,000 to 80,000 Polish Jews survived. An additional 180,000 were repatriated from the Soviet Union, which brought the total to somewhat over 200,000 survivors. A Jewish leader told me that every single Jew who survived had to have been saved by Poles. After the war, some Jews who remained in Poland saw communism as an answer to their problems. "For a Jew in Poland, at last, there was an answer to the Jewish question: No religion at all, for anyone," according to Mark Kurlansky. But in the 1968 anti-Semitic campaign, that belief would be meaningless.

Because this building also is a historical institute, we should recall the date of September 1, 1939, when "night" fell on Poland, the night the Nazi cancer continued its unchecked spread through the body politic of Europe. On paper, the September 1 invasion was labeled "Operation White"; we know it as *Blitzkrieg.*

Nearly two million German troops invaded Poland on that day. Poland was butchered; it never had a chance. The Jews of Poland were trapped. Martin Gilbert informs us that on the evening of September I, the Great Synagogue in Tlomackie St. was "full to overflowing. Large crowds also stood outside and prayed."

On September 17, 1939, Russia—who had betrayed Poland and free men and women everywhere by signing the infamous Molotov-Ribbentrop Pact of August 23, 1939, by which Hitler and Stalin agreed to divide Poland between the two of them—invaded Polish soil. Ten days later, Poland capitulated. The partition and occupation of Poland gave Hitler the opportunity to put his racial policies into effect.

After Stalin took over, in the late 1940s, only about 70,000-80,000 Jews remained in the country. By the mid-1950s, many Poles began to express discontent with government policies and resentment of Soviet domination and its Stalinist regime. In 1956, after worker unrest, %Wladyslaw Gomulka, who had been imprisoned in 1951, was freed from prison and again became head of the Communist party.

Stalin's crimes were made public. Yiddish papers blasted Soviet anti-Semitism. Approximately 2,500 repatriated Jews came back from Russia. The JDC and ORT were allowed to reopen. But many Jews moved out: 50,000 left in 1958 and 1959. At that time, approximately 30,000 Jews remained in Poland. As a result of the Six Day War and the anti-Israel stance of the former U.S.S.R., Poland, still a Communist satellite, broke relations with Israel in 1967.

Under the Communist regime, Polish media would now invent a new target for Polish hatred. The new enemy became the "Jewish conspiracy" and the State of Israel. The Polish government campaigned against Jews and intellectuals. It initiated and sponsored in 1968 a sweeping virulent anti-Semitic campaign, according to Eva Hoffman in *Exit into History: A Journey Through the New Eastern Europe.*

After the Six Day War, in 1967, Gomulka went along with Mieczyslaw Moczar, the interior minister. Student demonstrations were the pretext for the government's anti-Semitic campaign. Gomulka labeled the Jews "rootless cosmopolitans." He said the Jews were a "fifth column." Gomulka gave the Jews permission to go; large numbers did. Jews were dismissed from jobs. Organizations such as JDC and ORT were closed down. The Polish government in effect "liquidated" all organized Jewish life. Anti-Semitism "purged" Poland of nearly all its Jewish population. In 1968, it was "a matter of mental terror, of frightening Jews out of Poland," according to the late author Kazimierz Brandys in his book, *A Warsaw Diary: 1978-1981.* Mark Kurlansky states that Jews "could forfeit their homes and whatever property they might have and emigrate to Israel." He adds, "Only Jews were allowed to emigrate and Israel was the only acceptable destination."

"Not even in the heyday of Stalinism did the world see anything like the virulent, open and institutionalized racial discrimination practiced in the spring and summer of 1968 in 'People's Poland,'" Paul Lendvai says in his *Anti-Semitism Without Jews: Communist Eastern Europe.* While no one was killed, at least forty persons from Jewish and non-Jewish families were known suicides. One thing was certain, if you wanted to be Jewish, you left Poland in 1968; or if you stayed, you opted out of Jewish life.

The Lauder-Morasha School, Tel: 862-6330. This school is now located in an attractive building in the Wola District of Central Warsaw. Located here are an elementary and junior high school, with kindergarten through eighth grades. Subsequent grades to come, of course. At present, 166 students attend this school.

The Lauder Preschool, Twarda ul 6, Warsaw. Tel: 652-2162.

Note! Remember, a visit to the **Warsaw Jewish Cemetery** "alone is worth the airfare," writes Barry Lichtenberg in an article in the *Jewish Week,* September 3, 1999. "Thousands of beautifully designed and engraved tombstones huddle beneath towering oaks and fallen pines, emitting an ethereal glow."

PALACE OF CULTURE AND SCIENCE

The Palace of Culture is truly a bizarre sight.

In any book on Jewish travel and Jewish communities in Europe, certain national monuments and sites we visit invoke memory of past events. In Poland, moreover, international events-especially those between Russia and Poland—deeply affected Jews. Examples quickly come to mind: the 1939 Molotov-Ribbentrop Pact, the outbreak of World War II, and the 1989 collapse of communism. While not a monument, the Palace of Culture and Science building stands in the center of the city as a symbol. It was, after all, a Soviet gift to the Poles. Built in the early 1950s in the traditional Russian-Soviet architectural style, it was immediately labeled the "wedding cake." This massive structure contains 3,288 rooms, a Congress Hall for 3,000 people, three theaters, a swimming pool, and a museum. A view from the thirtieth floor gives the tourist a bird's-eye view of Warsaw. A Jewish leader told me he and his wife took courses there. It should have reminded them of the "looming specter of Russia."

Speaking of the Russians, some of the ire of the Poles and many other people today is the Molotov-Ribbentrop Pact, which many believe helped cause the outbreak of the war because of the secret protocol signed in Moscow by Nazi Ribbentrop and Communist Molotov on August 23, 1939. The two countries would carry out a joint attack on Poland and divvy up the area. Without the assurance of Soviet collusion, the German army could not have launched a unilateral attack on Poland. "Suddenly it became clear that if Hitler were to invade Poland, the Soviet Union would stand aside," writes

Martin Gilbert in his book *The Holocaust: A History of the Jews of Europe During the Second World War.* That was "ominous news" for the Jews of Poland. Hitler indeed invaded. Two years later on June 21, 1941, he stabbed the Soviets and unleashed a destructive war that would include the death of about twenty-five million Russians alone.

Survivors from Poland did fight. I heard about the Polish army unit, a certain group in Gen. Wladyslaw Anders' division, from my father-in-law, the late Rabbi Solomon Spitz. In 1941, the Soviets permitted a Polish army group to form under General Anders. Polish prisoners of war held by the Russians were allowed to join General Anders to fight with the allies. In March 1942, the new Polish unit crossed into British-controlled Iran. When the group arrived in Palestine, many Polish Jews left the unit and opted to stay in Palestine. Many, too, like my late father-in-law, joined the Jewish Brigade of the British Army in order to fight the Germans.

In 1944, the Soviet Army entered Poland and Stalin installed his Communist Poles as the new government in Lublin. On August 1, after the Red Army had reached the Vistula River, the Home Army of the London Poles launched an insurrection to liberate Warsaw before the Soviet troops arrived.

The Polish Uprising was an armed insurrection against the Germans, but, politically and more clearly, it was an uprising against the Russians. The Poles wanted to avoid a "Red Warsaw." The Soviet Army stood by and let the Germans slaughter the insurgents and utterly destroy the capital.

To this day, Poles also believe the Allies betrayed and sacrificed Poland at the February 1945 Yalta Conference held at that Crimean seaside resort. Here, the Western Allies accepted the new status quo in Poland and agreed to recognize the Stalin-backed Lublin government. Stalin would settle for nothing less than a Polish government controlled by Communists. He "scorned" his promises for a free election.

Summer-Winter Camp, Osrodek Wypocznikowy Srodborowianka, Literacka ul., 6, Srodborow, 05-400, Otwock, Poland. Forty-five minutes by car from Warsaw sits a very important institution for the Polish Jewish community.

While it was originally purchased by **JDC** and donated to **TSKZ,** the **Jewish Social-Cultural Association of Poland,** it is used as a winter and summer camp and summer vacation resort. In the past several years the camp has been used by the Ronald S. Lauder Foundation. Located in the midst of a lovely wooded area, the camp can also be reached by train. The **JDC,** which continues to use the camp for seminars, gives **TSKZ** monies for all its activities, including the running of Srodborow, as well as contributions to organize activities during summer vacations. But do call ahead if you plan to visit, as there are times when the camp is not being used. Contact **TSKZ** in Warsaw. See above.

TREBLINKA

"Before the War, on the Siedlec-Malkinia Railways, not far from the great axis running from Warsaw to Bialystok, there was a forgotten little station with the strange and beautiful name of Treblinka. It rose unexpectedly in a damp, sandy plain dotted with little pine woods and marshes," wrote Jean-François Steiner in his book, *Treblinka.* Here between 800,000 and 850,000 Jews were murdered by the Nazis, but here as in other camps, a revolt occurred on August 2, 1943; it was brutally suppressed and the camp destroyed.

This is one camp that has an unusual monument, to say the least. At least 17,000 huge stone slabs make up a symbolic cemetery. Engraved on the stones are the names of cities and villages from which the Jews were rounded up and brought here. The densely packed stones surround a huge 26-foot high obelisk-type stone sculpture shaped like a mausoleum and topped by a large menorah. It appears that the menorah is "carved into the cap" of the obelisk and is "jumbled" together. It protrudes in all directions. At the bottom of the obelisk, where there is a great crack, a stone plaque reads from top to bottom in Yiddish, Russian, English, French, German, and Polish, "Never Again."

Today, you can see that the railway, which once was abandoned, has been re-created symbolically with concrete sleepers to commemorate this railway that conveyed Jews to their deaths.

Martin Gilbert in his book, *The Holocaust: A History of the Jews of Europe During the Second World War,* says that in 1959, he ran his hand through the soil of Treblinka: "The earth beneath my feet was coarse and sharp; filled with the fragments of human bone."

At Treblinka, we again meet Janusz Korczak. In 1978, the hundredth anniversary of his birth, a stone was inscribed with his name and put with the thousands of others. It is the only stone dedicated to an individual, and Korczak is a Polish hero, too.

Treblinka itself is located in Sokolow Podlaski province near Warsaw. Jews in the Warsaw Ghetto between 1940 and 1943 who were deported to death camps probably died at Treblinka.

The Death Camps

* Auschwitz and Birkenau—Approximately an hour's drive from Cracow.

* Majdanek—Set up in the Lublin suburb of Majdan Tartarski.

* Sobibor—The camp was located in the small village of Sobibor on the Chem-Wlodawa Railway line, almost 5 miles south of Wloadawa.

* Belzec—A small town in the southeast of the Lublin district. Located on the Lublin-Zamosc-Rava-Russkaya-Lvov railway line—The death camp was located about a third of a mile from the Belzec railway station.

* Treblinka—Located 62 miles northeast of Warsaw.

* Chelmno—Situated on the Ner River, 37 miles from Lodz.

LUBLIN

My late father-in-law, Rabbi Solomon Spitz, was born here and went to the famous Lublin Yeshiva. In 1940 the Germans took thousands of holy books out of the hallowed yeshiva library, threw them down on the ground, loaded them into vehicles and burned them in the marketplace. The fire lasted twenty hours. And the Jews of Lublin watched this nightmare. They cried so that their voices rose above those of the Nazis: the Germans had to bring in their army band to drown out the agonizing shouts of protest.

Records, incidentally, say that the Germans confiscated 22,000 volumes and about 10,000 periodicals.

The city of Lublin, wrote a Chassid, "is the land of Israel." Yes, Lublin ranks as a special metropolis in the galaxy of Jewish life in Poland. In the 1920s, Doblin described Lublin as "not sleepy" like a small town in Germany, because the poverty suffered by the Jews kept them moving. Before the war, 97 percent of all the city's tailors were Jews; it is doubtful if there is a Jewish tailor there today. Lublin in 1939 contained a population of about 40,000 Jews. It was literally "a Jewish Oxford," famous for its yeshiva throughout Europe, famous for Talmudic and Kabbalist learning. Lublin, a center of Hebrew printing, was known for its fairs and market days. Annexed by Austria in 1795, and later incorporated into Russia-Poland in 1815, Lublin served as "the spiritual heart of Polish Jewry."

Jews arrived here in 1316. At first, they were denied rights, but King Casimir III permitted them to settle nearby in 1336. In 1602, 2,000 Jews made their home in Lublin. They were expelled in 1780. By 1806, 2,973 Jews resided here and by 1897 the figure jumped to 23,586.

Synagogue, 10 Lubartowska, Lublin. This synagogue is not used frequently. There are no daily services scheduled and rarely a minyan. Part of the building is used as a museum.

Yeshivat Hachmei Lublin, 85-83 Lubartowska St., Lublin, at the corner of Unicka Street. Today it is a medical college, but many Jews close their eyes and see before them youthful yeshiva students studying Torah, chanting afternoon prayers, or walking along the streets of this once great center of Judaism.

Today the medical college displays a modest plaque commemorating the yeshiva. Built with funds raised from all over the world, the yeshiva was opened in 1930. The building was designed by Agenor Senduchowski.

For centuries, the king of Poland appointed the rector of the yeshiva of Lubin. In 1935, 50,000 people, including high-ranking government officials, attended the ceremonies dedicating the new headquarters for the yeshiva. It consisted of 6 stories, 120 rooms, a huge auditorium, and even a scale model of the Temple of Jerusalem. In 1939, 500 students attended.

Lublin is renowned for its scholars and sages, one of them so great that he was referred to as the "Seer of Lublin." He was Rabbi Jacob Isaac ha-Hozeh. And living in Lublin were other great rabbis: Jacob b. Joseph Pollak, Jacob b. Samuel Bunim Koppelman, and Mordechai b. Abraham Jaffe.

At the densely wooded Grodzisk Hill, near the yeshiva, is the Old Cemetery. A great stone wall shields this sixteenth-century Jewish burial ground. The entrance to the cemetery is on Kalinowszcyna Street. Here rests another great Talmudic scholar, Rabbi Solomon Luria (1510-74), known by the acronym, Maharshal (Morenu ha-Rav Shelomo Luria).

Another great rabbi of Lublin buried in the cemetery is Meir b. Gedaliah (1558-1660), known as the Maharam of Lublin. The Maharam is an acronym for Moreinu-Ha-Rav Meir, "Our Teacher, the Rabbi Meir." This great halachic authority became head of the Yeshiva of Lublin at the age of twenty-four.

In Lublin, also, sat the Council of the Four Lands, which became an independent Jewish parliament and supreme court. It coordinated a system of autonomous Jewish institutions. The Council settled disputes between Jewish communities and appeals made by individuals against decisions rendered by other rabbis and courts. The Council existed from 1580 to 1764.

Majdanek

"If Auschwitz was hell on earth, then Majdanek was the morgue. Auschwitz could be smelled from afar, but Majdanek was in your living room," wrote Professor Eric Epstein in *Martyrdom and Resistance.*

The city of Lublin rises over Majdanek. The Nazis felt no need to conceal the camp from the local populace. In the summer of

1942, construction of the Majdanek concentration camp near Lublin, in the Majdan Tartarski quarter, was completed. It, too, was part of Operation Reinhard, named after S.S. General Reinhard Heydrich, who was assassinated by two Czech patriots on May 27, 1942, in the Czech town of Lidice. After his death, the Nazis began preparations for Operation Reinhard, the deportation of Jews to Treblinka, Belzec, and Sobibor. In Majdanek, more than eighty percent of the 350,000 murdered victims were Jews. It is pretty much preserved as it was. The visitor can see guard towers, barbed wire, barracks, and crematoria. Everything is still intact. In the back of one hall, there are empty canisters of Zykon B gas. There is a prisoners' clothing display, and prisoners' shoes are piled in the barracks.

Wiktor Tolkin's monument at Majdanek conveys impending danger because the top part of it is the "great weight of memory," which stands on a proportionately undersized base that creates a sense of top heaviness, even danger, for those standing beneath it. As you walk out from the base of the monument, you can see in the distance the dome covering a mausoleum of human ash and bones and to its right, a building with a tall chimney, which was the crematorium and gas chamber complex—the whole area symbolizes a valley of death.

KIELCE

The name of this town in southeast Poland will certainly live forever in Polish-Jewish history. Just one year after the Holocaust, the Jews of Poland woke up to a good, old-fashioned pogrom. "Jews were even taken off trains and murdered," said Yitzhak Zuckerman. He believed the event may have been instigated by the police or government, a well-organized plot. Forty-two Jews were murdered. The pogrom occurred on July 4, 1946. A monument was erected in the Kielce Jewish cemetery to perpetuate the memory of the pogrom's victims. The pogrom induced a major shock for the Jews—as if they needed one. The price of remaining in Poland, legally and illegally, increased greatly. That is why a mass emigration out of the country took place. Between 100,000 to 150,000 persons departed, including the Polish Jews who had been returning from Russia.

A synagogue is located at Rewolucji Pazdziernikowej but is now used as a center for archives. A monument to the memory of the pogrom's victims is located at 7 Planty Street.

CRACOW

And everyone crowds into the narrow little streets of the Jewish city and rushes for his place in the synagogue and Kazimierz is full of people and the old temples of Israel reflect the spell of the past.

—Majer Balaben, Polish Jewish historian

There in Eastern Europe, the Jewish people came into its own. It did not live like a guest in somebody else's house, who must constantly keep in mind the ways and customs of the host. There, Jews lived without reservation and without disguise, outside their homes no less than within them.

—Abraham Joshua Heschel

Friday night: *"Shabbos."* I use the Ashkenazic pronunciation because that is what was said on Friday nights by Polish Jews. They still say the *Shabbos* now. But now the younger ones pronounce it: *"Shabbat."* The square is empty. I fantasize it was as if you were watching a movie: a large, oblong square, bustling with people, full of people, men in their black gabardines and round hats, milling about the marketplace. Nearby are stone houses, colored blue, white, purple, and green. Then suddenly the film script changes. The same square, but there are no people. The buildings are there, but there are no Jews. You are ready to leave. But wait, faint at first are the sounds of the song, "Peace Be With You," *"Shalom Alecihem."*

You follow the sounds. You go in and there before you are almost fifty young people. This is the headquarters of the Ronald S. Lauder Foundation Youth Center on Kupa Street. Every Friday night, there is a Shabbat dinner where young people are invited to attend. Sometimes, American college students come to services and then to the program dinner.

Kiddush is recited. We sing Hebrew songs. We talk about Jews in nearby Ukraine. I realize a number of these young people are not Jewish, they are themselves from mixed marriages. Many will convert to Judaism. But these young adults, if they become Jews, are the future of Poland. For further information on youth groups in Poland, contact the Ronald S. Lauder Foundation in Warsaw, or in New York. In Cracow, contact Domick Dybek, Tel: 011-48-12-22-6855.

Jews once lived in the main square of the city. Today, there are very few signs of their one-time residence in the city center.

In 1335, King Casimir the Great founded this once rival city to Cracow on the southern side of town and called it Kazimierz. The Jews settled there soon after its establishment.

In 1495, King Jan Olbracht expelled the Jews from Cracow. The Jews moved to nearby Kazimierz, where they settled in a relatively small prescribed area northwest of the Christian quarter and were separated from the non-Jews by a wall. Cut off from the Poles, it would take the Jews four hundred years to get back to the environs of the Main Square in Cracow. Jews arrived in the fourteenth century.

But German and Bohemian Jews came to Cracow in the sixteenth and seventeenth centuries. Here they could live in peace. Those German Jews spoke Yiddish, similar to what the prosperous Cracovians spoke, which was mainly German. In the fifteenth century, Cracow Jews developed trade with Breslau, Danzig, Lvov, and Constantinople.

"Over the course of history," writes Henryk Halkowski, noted writer and historic guide of Cracow, "Jewish Kazimierz joined with Polish Cracow and together they became 'Ir-va-em be Israel,' (The Mother City of Israel)." Kazimierz was a predominantly Jewish quarter. By the end of the fifteenth century, Kazimierz consisted of a "quadrangle with a few streets enclosed on one side by the city walls and on the other by a wall with three gates leading to the non-Jewish city," says Bernard D. Weinryb.

By the 1570s, about two thousand people lived in Kazimierz, the Jewish section on the other side of town. Here in Kazimierz the famous Talmudic scholar and philosopher Rabbi Moses Isserles, known as Remuh, maintained his academy. Today his grave and synagogue remain places of pilgrimage. That six-teenth-century Cracow became the world famous center of Talmud education was due to Isserles, who is famous for his commentary to the treatise, *Shulhan Arukh*, the code of Jewish law. We shall learn more about him when we visit the only func-tioning synagogue in Cracow.

For more than four centuries, until emancipation in 1868, Jews of Kazimierz fought for rights to trade and work in Cracow. From the second half of the sixteenth century, a number of yeshivot were founded in Kazimierz, whose fame made Cracow a most important center of Judaism. By 1644, the community maintained seven synagogues, a main synagogue, the Old Synagogue, and Remuh Synagogue. Hebrew printing was intro-duced in Cracow in 1534. "This suburb was an independent town with its own municipal council until the partition of Poland in the eighteenth century," writes Rachel Wishnitzer in *The Architecture of the European Synagogue*. Until the beginning of World War II, Kazimierz remained the traditional residential quarter of Cracow's Jews. After the war, the section decayed.

A beautiful, ancient city, there is only one Cracow, the resi-dence of the leading Polish princes and a center of Polish cul-tural life. Cracow is one of the most magnificent cities in all of Poland. In the sixteenth century, this Renaissance city flourished. Until 1609, this was the old capital of Poland with straight and winding narrow streets, renovated monuments, and townhouses. History has been especially kind to this city on the Vistula. Alfred Doblin described it as the cleanest and most beautiful city he found in Poland in the early 1920s. It still is proud of its univer-sity and intellectual look. Who has not heard of Jagiellonian University; Wawel Hill, the seat of Polish kings, including Casimir; or the Cracow Marketplace? Cracow is virtually the only large Polish city that has preserved its old architecture.

The Vistulans or Wislanie lived here. Cracow dates from 465 when traveler Ibrahim ibn Yaqub from Cordova visited the town and mentioned it as a trade center.

Even after World War I, Cracow still retained its cultural center status. In 1921, 45,000 Jews lived here; in 1931, 56,800. By the outbreak of World War II, the city counted 260,000 inhabitants, between 60,000 and 70,000 of whom were Jews.

After World War II, 780,000 persons resided in this third largest city after Warsaw and Lodz. Huge steel works, Howa Huta, were built a few kilometers from the historical center. An ecological disaster, the Communists had attempted to break the traditionally intellectual and religious ties of the city.

In Cracow you can still see a street called St. Anne's Lane. Documents going back to 1304 called it Jews Lane. Jewish merchants held important positions in the city's economic life. At the end of the fifteenth century, a fire destroyed Cracow's Jews Lane and the Christian citizens succeeded in having the Jews expelled from the city. The Jews settled at neighboring Kazimierz, where they were assigned a self-contained area that later was to become the ghetto.

In the early twentieth century, the Zionists and the Socialists gained influence in Cracow and the city became a major stronghold of the Labor Zionists and the Revisionist Zionists.

Before World War II, 70,000 Jews lived in Cracow, about twenty-five percent of the population. When the Nazis entered, they were moved to the ghetto in the Podgorze section. In the ghetto, the "Eagle Pharmacy" was located at 18 Bohaterow Getta and was owned by the Pole, Tadeusz Pankiewicz, one of the leaders of the Resistance who succeeded in saving the lives of several Jews. In March 1943, the Nazis liquidated the ghetto and the last residents were sent to the concentration camps, among them the Yiddish poet and singer, Mordechai Gebirdg.

Sites in Cracow

Old Synagogue-Jewish Museum, 24 Szeroka, Cracow. It was built in the late fifteenth century on what was Broad Lane in the middle of the Jewish quarter, now called 24 Szeroka. At the far end of Szeroka Street, as you come out of the Remuh Synagogue, look to your right and at the end of the square stands the Alte Synagogue, today functioning as the Jewish Museum. Displayed here are some excellent exhibits, especially on the second floor—an exhibit of photos and drawings, the faces of Kazimierz Jews. The museum is open Wednesday and Thursday, 9 A.M. to 3:30 P.M.; Friday, 11 A.M. to 6 P.M.; and Saturday and Sunday, 9 A.M. to 3 P.M. However it is closed the first Saturday and Sunday of every month and when that occurs, the museum opens the following Monday and Tuesday. It has impressive collections of Jewish ceremonial art and works by Jewish painters. The original Gothic structure was destroyed by a fire; the Italian architect Matteo Gucci rebuilt it in Renaissance style in 1557-70. Some say the Old Synagogue housed the library of King Casimir the Great. Since 1958 the building has become a seat of the Judaic Museum, a branch of the Historical Museum of the City of Cracow.

In the room of the museum, on the second floor, such World War II photos with signs such as "Jews Are Forbidden to Enter the Park" are displayed. This room contains the history of the Jewish community of Cracow during 1939-45. The Old Synagogue is one of the most important synagogues of the medieval period in Poland. After the war the building was not used and was allowed to fall into disrepair. During the war, its massive bronze chandeliers were used to decorate the house of the Nazi governor general, Hans Frank. It is not known when the Old Synagogue, or Stara, was built in the former heart of this Jewish community, but it is believed to have been in the fourteenth or fifteenth centuries. Erected by Jewish refugees from Bohemia, it was patterned after the Altneuschul in Prague. The Old Synagogue of Kazimierz measures 17.70 by 12.40 meters, approximately 58 by 40 feet, is larger than the synagogues at Worms and Prague, and taller than the synagogue of Prague. Its two columns are slimmer than the piers of the latter synagogue, and its walls are thinner, too. "The parapet of bricks and stone, decorated with blind arcades, shows the influence of style of the medieval castles of the Cracow nobility," according to Earl Vinecour. It contains a double-naved, two-pillared edifice. The bimah [the Torah reader's platform] is not only slightly elevated between the two pillars, but is also enclosed in a canopied wrought-iron cage. From time to time, the Communists closed the building. During various insurrections against foreigners, patriotic speeches were given here urging Jews and Poles to unite in defense of their common homeland.

Popper Synagogue, 16 Szeroka St. Donated by the merchant Wolf Popper in 1620, it was rebuilt after World War II and is currently being used by the city of Cracow as a cultural center. Next door is the Ariel Café.

The High Synagogue, 38 Jozefa St., Cracow.

Kupa Synagogue, 8 Jonatan Warszauer. Erected during the building boom of the sixteenth and seventeenth centuries, restoration is now being undertaken.

Temple Synagogue, 24 Miodowa St., Cracow. It survived the war almost unscathed. It was built in 1860 to 1862, thanks to the efforts of the Association of Progressive Jews in Cracow. Magnificently restored, it is now open. There is a women's section in one of the balconies. It is only used when needed, such as on holidays.

Community Offices, also known as TSKZ Club, 2 Slawkowska St., Tel: 561-758, 562-349/22-98-41.

Ariel Jewish Artistic Café, 18 Szeroka St., Cracow. Tel: 21-38-70. There is folk and gypsy music and concerts of Hebrew, Yiddish, and Russian. Heard above the din of the coffee shop are tapes in Hebrew. You may find that many local Polish Jews and, from time to time, many Americans stop here for coffee, cake, and sandwiches, especially on the weekend.

Klezmer-Hois, ul. Szeroka 6, 31-053, Cracow. Tel/FAX: 411-12-45 or 411-16-22. Located here are a hotel, restaurant and café.

Alef, ul. Szeroka 17, 31-053, Cracow. Tel/FAX: 421-38-70. Located here are a hotel, restaurant, and café.

Hotel Eden, ul. Ciemna 15, 31-053, Cracow. Tel: 430-65-65. FAX: 430-67-67. In this hotel, you can obtain a kosher dairy breakfast, as well as El Al Israel Airlines kosher packets.

Vegetarian Restaurant Vega, ul. Szeroka 3, 31-053, Cracow. Tel: 431-01-29.

Hotel Ester, ul. Szeroka 20, 31-053, Cracow. Tel: 431-01-29. FAX: 429-12-33.

Ronald S. Lauder Foundation, Jewish Youth Group, 18 Kupa St., Cracow. On Friday nights, between 5:30 P.M. and 6 A.M., an oneg shabbat takes place. Young people, many of them students sit and say Kiddush. They sing Sabbath zemiros; they say the blessing over bread; they enjoy dinner and friendship. This is the fourth Jewish youth club and education center established by the Ronald S. Lauder Foundation since the Communist government fell in 1989. Rabbi Sacha Pecaric is in charge of this Foundation's headquarters here.

Synagogue, also known as the **Congregation of the Mosaic Faith,** located at Skawinska Street. It is now empty and not used.

Remuh Synagogue, 40 Szeroka St., Cracow. If you are in Cracow on a Friday evening or Saturday morning, you can pray at this mid-sixteenth-century synagogue, which was built by influential members of the Jewish community. Saturday service is at 9 A.M. Friday evening service's time depends on sunset. This is the famous, spacious, Remuh Synagogue, whose name goes back to Israel Isserles, father of Rabbi Moses ben Israel Isserles, who is buried with his family in the cemetery, adjacent to the synagogue. In 1553, Israel Isserles, as a wealthy merchant, obtained a permit from King Sigismund August, son of Sigismund I, to build a synagogue in Kazimierz. He did not erect a new building; he merely adapted a timber structure, which he owned, for synagogue use. A 1557 fire leveled the house of worship, so he rebuilt the structure in masonry. The Remuh Synagogue and Cemetery is now open Sundays to Fridays from 9 A.M. to 4 P.M.

Remuh Synagogue is named after the founder's son, the codifier Rabbi Moses ben Israel Isserles (ca. 1525-72). He was one of Judaism's great scholars. Remuh is the acronym of **R**abbi **M**oses **I**sserles, a great halachic authority. To this day, Isserles, born in Cracow, is venerated by Jews throughout the world. He is known as the "Maimonides of Polish Jewry," and the outstanding Ashkenazic codifier of religious law. Rabbi Joseph Karo codified the *Shulhan Arukh,* but that was intended for the Sephardim, according to writer, historian, and guide Henryk Halkowski. "Moses Isserles adapted [those laws] for the use of the Ashkenazim and in this form, as a collaboration of Joseph Karo and Moses Isserles, they became the oracle of Jewish life." He adds, "Even today the Orthodox regard the codex of Joseph Karo and Moses Isserles as defining the principles of their behavior."

Religious Jews undertake pilgrimages to Rabbi Moses Isserles' grave on the Lag B'Omer holiday, the anniversary of his death. He is buried in the Remuh Synagogue's cemetery.

The historic, mid-sixteenth century Remuh Synagogue in the Kazimierz section of Cracow, Poland.
(Photo by Ben G. Frank)

His tombstone was not damaged during the war.

The synagogue contains a nave with round-headed windows set high up in the walls, and a Roman barrel vaulted ceiling. "Tucked away" in a courtyard off the street, next to the ancient Remuh cemetery, it is a plain rectilinear building. The bimah is surrounded by a wrought-iron cage and the ark is similar to that of Old Synagogue. Before the Second World War, the synagogue was led by Rabbi Ozjasz Thon, who was also a member of Polish Parliament and a leading Zionist.

The Cemetery at Remuh Synagogue. Other graves besides that of Rabbi Moses Isserles, who is buried with his family, include Rabbi Joel Sirkes (1561-1640), head of the Cracow yeshiva and one of the greatest Talmudic scholars of Poland, and the famous Polish Kabbalist, Nathan Spira (1585-1633). Also buried here is Yom Tov Lippmann Heller (1579-1633), who also had been the rabbi of Vienna. The latter is most famous for his *Tosefot Yom Tov,* a commentary on the Mishnah. The Nazis razed all tombstones, but the cemetery, one of the best examples from the Renaissance, was restored in part by the American Jewish Joint Distribution Committee. A wall made out of tombstone fragments stands as a fitting symbol of the Holocaust.

Nissenbaum Restaurant, Szeroka St., 31-053, Cracow. Located next to the Remuh Synagogue, it was reported as non-kosher.

The Ajzyk Synagogue, at 16 Kupa, Cracow. Also known as **The Rabbi Isaac Synagogue** founded by Isaac Jakubowicz and his wife, Brindla Jakubowicz. He was a banker and elder of the Jewish community and obtained a permit to build a synagogue from King Wladislaw IV in 1638. The opening of the building, however, was delayed by litigation brought against the Jewish community by the priests of the Corpus Christi Church, who objected to passing a synagogue when they were bearing the sacraments, according to Wischnitzer. Still, despite the objection, building commenced and the 55 x 39-feet hall was constructed, and although the exterior has weathered, the portal facing Isaac Street is still beautiful. It is now possible to visit this synagogue from Sunday to Friday, from 9 A.M. to 7 P.M..

New Jewish Cemetery. Buried in their tombs in this cemetery are the famous leaders of Cracow Chassidim, the Epstein brothers and Raphael Landau. The cemetery was laid out in the nineteenth century and contains the graves of important Jews of the nineteenth and twentieth centuries, such as the painters Mauricy Gottleib and Arthur Markowicz; the Zionist leader and representative in the Polish Parliament, Rabbi Ozjasz Thon; the structural engineer Jozef Sare; the physicians Aaron Kirschner and Jonathan Warszauer; and many others. It is still used today for burial rites.

The Center for Jewish Culture in Kazimierz, Cracow, of the Judaica Foundation, Rabbi Meiselsa St., 17, Cracow. The Center for Jewish Culture in Kazimierz, Cracow, is one result of the revival of interest in Jewish history and culture in Poland that Joachim S. Russek, director of the Jagiellonian University Research Center on Jewish History and Culture in Poland, helped get underway in the mid-1980s. According to Professor Russek, also director of the Judaica Foundation, the goal of the center is to "help both physically preserve the Jewish heritage and to make it more accessible to all." This center provides cultural events; it runs a library; it prepares and distributes publications; it promotes research on Kazimierz; it supports restoration efforts. A recipient of a U.S. Congressional grant, the center possesses a wonderful lecture hall, a great coffee bar, and a fine place for American students to visit. Russek says the "Jewish landscape was an integral part of the Polish landscape, and he believes Poles have an obligation to take care of the entire history of Poland. Research students often come here.

The Center for Jewish Culture is housed in the former B'nai Emunah prayer house located at 17 Meiselsa, named after rabbi and Polish patriot, Dov Berush Meisels, who was in the Senate of independent Cracow and who rallied Jewish support in the 1863 rebellion against Russia. This former house of prayer was built in 1886 by a worship society, on a site where there had been a smelting facility of the Cracow goldsmith's guild until the seventeenth century. It was the work of the well-known Cracow architect and builder, Jacek Matusinski. The style of the building refers to the trends of the time, with Oriental elements. Inside, the most interesting elements were

The Center for Jewish Culture in Kazimierz is located at 17 Rabbi Meiselsa St., Cracow. (Photo courtesy of The Center for Jewish Culture)

The café at The Center for Jewish Culture in Kazimierz is a gathering place for students and visitors. (Photo courtesy of The Center for Jewish Culture.)

the *aron ha-kodesh,* the Holy Ark, as well as an iron column in the passageway separating the men's and the women's sections. A large memorial plaque for the founders and others who were connected with the prayer house was part of the synagogue. At the end of the nineteenth century the whole interior was covered with interesting polychromy. The building consists of a library, archives, and reading and study rooms. The center opened at the end of 1993 and operates under the auspices of the Judaica Foundation.

Schindler's List Tour. As I read the brochure citing the sites that would be seen on the tour of the places involved in the filming of *Schindler's List,* I could not help but recall that heart-tearing scene when the Gestapo is about to raid the Jewish Ghetto, which in the film version was right here on Szeroka Street in the Kazimierz section of Cracow. A proclamation is read which, paraphrased, said that King Casimir the Great invited the Jews to Cracow; they helped Poland prosper; they lived wonderful lives; they contributed to the community. But the Nazis made sure that that life would end. The Germans almost succeeded; they killed most of the Jews of Cracow. But as I walked along Szeroka Street, I realized Jews are still here; perhaps not in numbers, but something more spiritual. You may feel the same. And as you take the tour of *Schindler's List* sites, if you do, you will recall the film and what it portrayed; and the history of the Jewish people will become more realistic for you, the traveler. Viewers of the film *Schindler's List* certainly know some of the history and sights surrounding Cracow. **The Jordan Company and Jordan Book Store,** located right on Szeroka 2-Miodowa 41, conducts two-hour daily tours every day to the sights from the film. Participants can travel in a car or van. It is wise to make reservations beforehand, Tel: 011-48-12-21-71-66. The Cracow Ghetto was located across the Vistula in Podgorze. The ghetto took up the area bounded by the Vistula, Krzemionki and Lwowska streets, and Podgorski Square. A **Museum of the Ghetto** stands at Zgoda Square, now called PI Bohaterow Getta. From this spot, Jews were sent to the death camp. A drug store called "Pod Orlem" was here, and because it was on the edge of the ghetto, the pharmacy owners were able to save some Jews by taking them through a concealed passage, it is said. The Cracow Ghetto was "liquidated" in March 1943. A huge labor camp was set up and the tombstones of a Jewish cemetery were used in the construction of the camp buildings.

But before we see the site of the camp, the reader will note that Oscar Schindler's factory building still stands, only now it is used as an electronic parts firm. The Schindler plant is located at 4 Lipowa Street.

The camp itself, now destroyed, was situated on the site of the former Jewish cemetery in Jerozolimska Street and was known as **Plaszow.** It consisted of 34 barracks and 11 watchtowers. Inmates there included about 6,000 Jews who survived the deportations from the ghetto. At certain periods, the total number of inmates exceeded 20,000. We can still see the house where the Nazi commander and chief of the camp, Amon Goeth, resided. He was hung in 1946 for war crimes. Located on Jerozolimska Street, it still contains the balcony from which he shot innocent people during his so-called target practice. On the hill site of the Plaszow camp stands a gargantuan stone sculpture of sharply etched human figures with a huge horizontal gash across their bodies.

Guide. A highly recommended guide and historian, one whom visitors would be wise to engage if they so wish, is Henryk Halkowski, ul Dietla 34/8, 31-070, Cracow. Tel: 421-75-71. However it is best to call Mr. Halkowski on his mobile phone: 501-410-993. He is the author of *The Legends From The Jewish Town of Kazimierz* and *Jewish Cracow: History, Legends, People, Sites, Guide Book*. His E-mail address is: henryk@jewish.org.pl.

Jordan Company also has a wonderful Jewish bookshop at ul. Szeroka 2-Miodowa 41, Cracow. Tel: 21-71-66. It displays books and souvenirs on Jewish culture; it sells maps, postcards, audiocassettes, and guides.

Wawel Castle, Cracow. Built in the eleventh century, the town grew around Wawel Hill. In 1241, Tatars set fire to the city and burned Cracow to the ground. This was the seat of Polish kings for more than five hundred years and was of symbolic importance. Buried here is Jozef Pilsudski, who in the 1930s set

up a dictatorship in the country. Pilsudski (1867-1935), originally a Socialist, gained fame as a military leader and organizer
of armed opposition to Russia. As chief of state at the end of
War World I, he led the 1920 victory of the Poles over the
Soviet army outside Warsaw. Fed up with public life and cor-
ruption, he retired from public life in 1923. Three years later,
he returned to power after leading an armed coup. Sanacja
(purification) was the name bestowed upon the military
regime installed by Marshal Pilsudski. Most Jews felt that
Pilsudski, although he remained a dictator, spoke out against
violence toward the Jewish people. When he died, the con-
straints were lifted; a period of greater violence was ushered in.
Also buried here is King Kazimierz Wiliki. He founded Cracow
Academy, later renamed Jagiellonian University, "the second
in Central Europe after the one in Prague." Nicolus
Copernicus (1473-1543), who would later develop his helio-
centric theory, studied in Cracow in 1490-91.

OSWIECIM

On the marshes of the River Sola, a tributary of the Vistula,
lies the town of Oswiecim. Ironically, Jews settled there as early
as the thirteenth century, when the town served as the capital
of a Slavic duchy, all of which bore the same name.

More than a century later, in 1563, King Sigismund August
II confirmed the "privilege for Jews" to live in Oswiecim. He
denied them the right to own houses in the market square or
to build a synagogue. He also barred a further influx of Jewish
settlers. The Jews fought vigorously against such restrictions
and stressed their contribution to the development of the city.
The restrictions were finally lifted and in 1588 the Jews were
permitted to build a synagogue and to acquire ground for a
new cemetery. Thus in those days, Oswiecim became the spiritual center of the surrounding Jewish communities. In 1939,
about 6,000 Jews lived in Oswiecim.

After the liberation of Poland, Oswiecim developed
into an important industrial center with a population of
more than 30,000.

Synagogue, Plac Ksiedza Jana Skarbka 3, 32-600, Oswiecim. Tel: 33-844-7002. FAX: 33-844-7003. Web site: www.ajcf.org. At a distance of 1.9 miles from the actual site of the death camp here in Auschwitz, a small synagogue was dedicated in the fall of 2000. This house of worship serves as a place of prayer and reflection for Jewish visitors to the camp. There is no rabbi on the premises so formal services must be organized in advance. As noted, not one Jew lives in this town known as Oswiecim, the Polish name for Auschwitz. Funds for the building were raised by Fred Schwartz, a New York businessman. The synagogue was briefly revived after World War II by local Jews who survived the Holocaust, but was abandoned when most left Communist Poland for Israel. The Polish government returned the synagogue to the Jewish community in March 1998 under a restitution program for former Jewish religious properties. Although there was a theme of healing at the reopening rites, the atmosphere of good will was foiled somewhat after a large disco opened on private property about a mile closer to the camp. Protesters said that the opening of the club in the immediate vicinity of the largest Jewish graveyard in history was an affront.

AUSCHWITZ-BIRKENAU

This is Auschwitz-Birkenau, the "epicenter of the Holocaust."

"Please Behave Appropriately," says the sign on the entrance to Birkenau. "Respect the Memories of Those Who Suffered and Died Here."

I went to the Birkenau concentration camp before I went to Auschwitz. The two camps are located next to each other, separated only by a 21/2-mile "death march road."

Birkenau is named after "birch tree woods,"and was built after Auschwitz I, which was the first camp in the area. Auschwitz was originally intended as an intermittent camp for Polish political prisoners and then Russian POWs. As for Birkenau, it was built as an expansion to Auschwitz I, and was to serve as an extermination camp.

Memorial stones at the Birkenau death camp. (Photo by Riva Frank)

The author at one of the barracks at Birkenau. (Photo by Riva Frank)

A prison guard tower at Birkenau. (Photo by Ben G. Frank)

The author at the entrance to Auschwitz Concentration Camp. (Photo by Riva Frank)

The Germans razed the Polish village of Brezezinka, three kilometers from Auschwitz. Here they built this gigantic complex of barracks, gas chambers, crematoria, and burning pits—all fed by a rail spur diverted from the main line.

"Over the next four years, some 1.6 million people, 90 percent Jews, were murdered and burned at Birkenau, their ashes plowed into the soil, dumped into small ponds and scattered into the nearby Vistula River," writes James E. Young.

This huge, flat, grassy field is still the site of the barren, desolate shacks located here; the public, inhuman "latrines" are still here; the wreckage is still here. This last-built camp had the honor of housing the largest crematorium, which could burn 3,000 bodies a day.

This is as close as you are bound to get to reality. As Rabbi A. James Rudin, former national inter-religious affairs director of the American Jewish Committee, and others say that weather is playing havoc with the facility. Future generations may not be able to see the grisly horrors of Nazism firsthand. But the consensus seems to be not to rebuild the camp, otherwise it could become a "Holocaust theme park," complete with high-tech displays.

Here was the technology of genocide. It was the poison gas and the crematorium technology that combined to create mass murder. There were fifteen furnaces in every crematorium. It took only twenty minutes between the arrival of a trainload to be undressed and the arrival of the special detachment to strip the corpses of hair, gold fillings, and personal jewelry at the entrance of the crematorium, according to Norman Davies in *Heart of Europe: A Short History of Poland.*

There were four crematoria at Auschwitz: II, III, IV, and V.

The only way out of Birkenau was through the chimney, as one Nazi said. When you see the vast piles of hair, glasses, and suitcases on display in Auschwitz, you know the people who were there were turned to ashes.

I walked from the main gate at Birkenau along the railway track that brought the prisoners into the camp. The tourist should do the same. When the boxcars opened, an unbelievable stench enveloped the area, the floors had been covered with only lime and straw, and the journey could be several days and nights. When the prisoners stood at the platform, they were groggy, to say the least. Life had oozed from them in the hours spent in unsanitary boxcars. Like cattle, they had been shipped. They were weak. Night clouded their reality. The kapos shouted; the general selection was about to take place. New arrivals had no idea what was going on. They were confused, anxious, frightened.

I passed the spot where Dr. Josef Mengele is supposed to have stood selecting victims as they stumbled off the transports. They were directed to the left for the gas chambers, or to the right for slave labor..The "survivors" then passed by the remains of the pylon fencing. You can still see the fences. The Jews were stopped at the gas chambers. After undressing, hundreds of Jews were shoved into the gas chambers, furnished with showers and water pipes to give a realistic impression of a bathhouse. A Zykon-B pellet was dropped from above. They died instantly.

Today the gas chambers are steel wrecks; the retreating Nazis tried to blow up the camp, to cover up their crime. You can still see the barbed wire. Many Jews committed suicide by running right smack into the barbed wire.

I then went to Auschwitz or Camp I, the main camp, and there is the cynical sign at the main gate, *Arbeit Macht Frei,* translated by some, "Work Brings Freedom." The prisoners passed this sign each day on their way to work. On the small square by the kitchen, the camp orchestra would play marches to muster the thousands of prisoners so that they could be counted more efficient by the S.S.

After the war, the "blocks at Auschwitz I were converted into national pavilions, each with an exposition devoted to the national memory of a different country's citizens at Auschwitz," according to James E. Young.

In Block II, you see a model of the furnace, cans of Zykon-B gas, victims' hair.

In Block V, there are victims' glasses, prayer shawls, prostheses, canes, and crutches.

Block VII holds a swimming pool for the S.S.

Block X is where Jewish women were sterilized. There are descriptions of the sterilization process.

Each nation had its block. Block XXI tells the story of the Jews of Holland. You see a film of a train from Westerbork to Auschwitz and then back from Auschwitz to Westerbork to pick up more Jews.

What do we understand of the killers and victims through their remains? Young says that these remains "force us to recall the victims as the Germans have remembered them to us: in the collected debris of a destroyed civilization."

In Block XXVII, the Jewish prison blocks or exhibitions in Auschwitz I, you will hear on tape the chanting of "El Mole Rachamim," a Hebrew memorial prayer for the dead. I said a memorial prayer for the Joskowitz and Spitz families and as I did so, I remembered what Rabbi Besser told me. Holocaust survivors have very few relatives. How could they? For example, my wife's father lost all of his thirteen brothers and sisters and his parents somewhere in Poland, and my wife's mother lost six of her nine brothers and sisters and her parents somewhere in Poland. And to think that my wife's father did not have even one family picture or a single photo of any of his brothers and sisters to pass down to his children or grandchildren. That is what the Germans did to Jewish families—multiplied by six million dead—that is what you learn, recall, and feel at Auschwitz-Birkenau.

"The concentration camps are monuments to bestiality," writes Abba Eban in *Heritage: Civilization and the Jews.* He feels the camps are "kept as places of commemoration by governments and peoples who do not want to forget. Nothing like this violent bestial hatred had ever occurred in history," he continues. "If it had, the Jews would have known about it," he declares, adding, "had not they stood before in anguish, suffering and martyrdom."

This is the killing grounds, the killing fields, and the cemetery of the Jewish people. This was the "Auschwitz Moloch." The greatest mass murder ever committed in human history took place in this twenty-five-square-mile area. Neal Pease, writing in *Poland, A Country Study,* maintains that between 1939 and 1945, six million people, more than fifteen percent of Poland's population, perished in the war, including three million Jews murdered in the death camps of Poland.

One out of every two Poles was either killed, wounded, or enslaved during the war. The loss of more than 6 million Polish citizens, half of them Jews, from a total 1939 population of 35 million "represented a casualty rate of 18 percent compared with 0.2 percent in the U.S., 0.9 percent in Great Britain, 2.5 percent in Japan, 7.4 percent in Germany, 11.1 percent in Yugoslavia and 11.2 percent in the former U.S.S.R.," according to Norman Davies.

While estimates range as high as 4.5 million and as low as 1.1 million killed at Auschwitz, more human beings were murdered at Auschwitz than at any other place in history. Historians agree that between 1.1 million to 1.5 million were killed at Auschwitz, 90 percent of them were Jews. "When the Red Army arrived at Auschwitz," according to Rabbi A. James Rudin, "no one knew exactly how many people had been killed there and no one knows today." Auschwitz's first commandant, Rudolf Hoess, who was executed after the war for crimes against humanity, acknowledged he "personally arranged the gassing of two million persons between June-July, 1941 and the end of 1943." The Russians at one time said the death toll reached four million. And Poles still view Auschwitz as a place of national martyrdom. Most of the Jews killed at Auschwitz were not from Poland. Murdered here were Jews from Hungary, Greece, France, and other nations. Only ten to fifteen percent were Polish. Both Poles and Jews are extremely vulnerable when it comes to discussing the war. Both have experienced "national suffering."

Auschwitz was liberated by Russians who arrived at the camp at 3 P.M. January 27, 1945. One report says the camp was liberated by one Col. Grigori Davidowich Elishavetzki, a Jew. They found 648 corpses and 7,600 survivors: 1,200 survivors in the Auschwitz main camp, and 5,800 at Birkenau, including 4,000 women. There were also 650 survivors at Monowitz, the I. G. Farber Chemical Camp, according to Martin Gilbert in *Auschwitz and the Allies*. Most were deathly sick.

Tens of thousands of others had been forced to move out westwardly on death marches. Elie Wiesel, the writer and Nobel Laureate, as a teenager, was one of the 58,000 inmates marched out of the camp by the fleeing Nazis. Seven thousand skeletal and sick prisoners were left behind by the retreating Nazis to wait for the advancing Soviet army.

One of the Russians, Gen. Vasili Petrenko, then a colonel of the First Ukrainian Front, tells of finding the remains of four crematoria, one still intact, which the Germans did not have time to blow up when they fled. He said that he found the gas chambers where prisoners had been killed with Zykon-B gas and twenty-nine warehouses filled with the personal belongings of the camp's prisoners. Still horrified by those images today, Petrenko recounted his discovery of thousands of suitcases arranged in rows, and shoes and clothing methodically organized according to age and size. What shocked him the most, however, was seeing the eyeglasses, the masses of false teeth, and seven tons of women's hair packed in boxes. "It is unimaginable how many women had to be destroyed to produce seven tons of hair," he says. Many have argued that Aushcwitz, or at least the railroad tracks, should have been bombed; in 1944, they could have been.

The March of the Living. Every two years, 6,000 Jewish teenagers from 40 countries visit Jewish sights in Warsaw, Cracow, and Lublin, as well as the camps of Auschwitz, Majdanek, and Treblinka.

On *Yom Ha'Shoa* (Heroes and Martyrs Remembrance Day), these young people march six abreast from Auschwitz I to Birkenau, a route that some call the death march. After their visit in Poland, they go on to Israel.

Convent. In the mid-1980s, a painful controversy broke out when one of Auschwitz's original buildings, the warehouse where poison gas had been stored, was converted into a Carmelite Convent. Catholic nuns used the building to pray for those murdered at Auschwitz.

The change created an international furor that lasted almost ten years.According to Rabbi Rudin, who was "personally involved in the convent crisis," Jews felt the establishment of a convent at Auschwitz was an attempt to "Christianize" the Holocaust, to erase the particularity of Jewish suffering, and to deny that Jews were the principal target of Nazi genocide. Catholics were perplexed and often offended that anybody would object to a few nuns praying at the scene of mass murder. After all, Catholic priests died at Auschwitz.

In 1987, some European Jewish and Catholic leaders, including four cardinals, agreed the Carmelite nuns should move to a new convent to be constructed outside the camp. The nuns vacated the Auschwitz building, but only after Pope John Paul II intervened to resolve the controversy.

In 1999, hundreds of crosses that had been erected on the site by Polish Catholic extremists were removed. However, the large "papal cross" remains, demarcating where, in 1988, Pope John Paul II prayed for the 152 Polish Catholics killed at that location.

An **Inter-Religious Conference and Research Center** that attracts participants from throughout the world is near the convent, and is located at u.l. s.w. M. Kolbego 1, 32-600, Oswiecim. Tel: (0-381) 310-00. FAX: (0-381) 310-01.

Miedzryzec

This town has no Jewish community; no synagogue or Jewish Center. It does have a Jewish cemetery: three-quarters of the municipality of 16,000 were Jews who died in Auschwitz, Treblinka or other death camps. People visit towns such as this to remember and to preserve their heritage. The search for roots goes on.

Wroclaw

Now the second largest Jewish community in Poland after Warsaw, this town—with about 600 to 1000 Jews—is undergoing a Jewish revival. Once known as Breslau and located in Germany before World War II, Wroclaw was a center of the German Reform movement. After the war, the city became part of Poland.

Synagogue, 9 Wlodkowica St., Wroclaw. Tel: 364-01. The Ronald S. Lauder Foundation Youth Club is also located here.

TSKZ-Club, 28 Swidnicka St., Wroclaw.

The **Lauder-Etz Chaim Primary School,** Wlodkowica 8, Wroclaw. Tel: (07) 374-6117.

Katowice

Synagogue, 13 Mlynska St., Katowice.

Gdansk

The contact person in this city, according to the Ronald S. Lauder Foundation, is Jakub Szadaj, 8/7 Arctowskiego St., Tel. (home): (58) 47-98-02.

How to Get There. Lot Polish Airlines offers twenty weekly nonstop flights from New York City (JFK), Newark, and Chicago, to Warsaw.

Suggested Reading

Applebaum, Anne. *Between East and West Across the Borderlands of Europe.* New York: Pantheon, 1994.

Arad, Yitzhak, Belzec, Sobibar, Treblinka: *The Operation Reinhard Death Camps.* Bloomington: Indiana University Press, 1987.

Asch, Sholem. *Tales of My People.* New York: Putnam, 1948.

Brandys, Kazimierz. *A Warsaw Diary: 1978-1981.* New York: Random House, 1983.

Cantor, Norman F. *The Sacred Chain: The History of the Jews.* New York: HarperCollins, 1994.

Curtis, Glenn C, ed. *Poland, A Country Study.* Washington, D.C.: Federal Research Division, Library of Congress, 1994.

Davies, Norman. *Heart of Europe: A Short History of Poland.* Oxford: Oxford University Press, 1986.

Dawidowicz, Lucy S. *The War Against the Jews: 1933-1945.* New York: Bantam, 1986.

Doblin, Alfred. *Journey to Poland.* Translated by Joachim Neugroschel. New York: Paragon House, 1991.

Dubroszycki, Lucjan, and Barbara Kirshenblatt-Gimblett. *Image Before My Eyes: A Photographic History of Jewish Life in Poland, 1864-1939.* New York: Schocken Books, 1987.

Dubnow, S. M. *History of the Jews in Russia and Poland: From the Earliest Times Until the Present Day.* Philadelphia: Jewish Publication Society of America, 1918.

Eban, Abba. Heritage: *Civilization and the Jews.* New York: Summit Books, 1984.

Eliach, Yaffa, *There Once Was A World, A Nine-Hundred-Year-Chronicle of the Shtetl of Eishyshock,* Boston, New York, London, London; Little, Brown and Company, 1998.

Encyclopedia of Zionism and Israel. Edited by Raphael Patai. New York: Herzl Press/McGraw-Hill, 1971.

Engel, David. *In the Shadow of Auschwitz: The Polish Government in Exile and the Jews, 1939-1942.* Chapel Hill, N.C.: University of North Carolina Press, 1987.

Frost, Robert I. *After the Deluge: Poland and the Second Northern War, 1655-1660.* New York: Cambridge University Press, 1993.

Fuks, Marian, Zygmunt Hoffman, Maurycy Horn, and Jerzy Tomaszewski. *Polish Jewry History and Culture.* Warsaw: Interpress Publishers, 1982.

Gilbert, Martin. *The Holocaust: A History of the Jews of Europe During the Second World War.* New York: Henry Holt, 1987.

—. *Auschwitz and the Allies.* New York: Holt, Rinehart and Winston, 1981.

Gutman, Yisrael. *Resistance: The Warsaw Ghetto Uprising.* Boston: Houghton Mifflin, 1994.

Gutman, Yisrael. *The Jews of Warsaw, 1939-1943: Ghetto, Underground, Revolt.* Translated by Ina Friedman. Bloomington: Indiana University Press, 1989.

Halkowski, Henryk. "Cracow-City and Mother of Israel." from *Cracow: Dialogue of Traditions.* Cracow: Znak Publishers, 1991.

Hart, Kitty. *Return to Auschwitz, The Remarkable Story of a Girl Who Survived the Holocaust.* New York: Athenum, 1982.

Hertz, Aleksander. *The Jews in Polish Culture.* Translated by Richard Lourie. Evanston, Ill.: Northwestern University Press, 1988.

Hoffman, Eva. *Exit into History: A Journey Through the New Eastern Europe.* New York: Viking, 1993.

Korczak, Janusz. *Ghetto Diary.* New York: Holocaust Library, 1978.

Krinsky, Carol Herselle. *Synagogues of Europe: Architecture, History, Meaning.* Cambridge, Mass.: MIT Press, 1985.

Kurlansky, Mark. *A Chosen Few: The Resurrection of European Jewry.* Reading, Mass.: Addison-Wesley, 1995.

Kurzman, Dan. *The Bravest Battle: The Twenty-Eight Days of the Warsaw Ghetto Uprising.* New York: Da Capo Press, 1993.

Langer, Lawrence L. *Admitting the Holocaust: Collected Essays.* New York: Oxford University Press, 1995.

Lendvai, Paul. *Anti-Semitism Without Jews: Communist Eastern Europe.* Garden City, N.Y: Doubleday, 1971.

Levi, Primo. *Survival in Auschwitz.* New York: Macmillan, 1987.

MacLean, Rory. *Stalin's Nose: Travels Around the Bloc.* New York: Little, Brown, 1993.

Mark, Ber. *Uprising in the Warsaw Ghetto.* New York: Schocken Books, 1975.

Meyer, Peter, Bernard D. Weinryb, Eugene Duschinsky, and Nicolas Sylvain, eds. *The Jews in the Soviet Satellites.* Syracuse, N.Y: Syracuse University Press, 1953.

Nagorski, Andrew. *The Birth of Freedom.* New York: Simon & Schuster, 1993.

Polansky, Antony, Chimeri Abramsky, and Maciej Jachimezyk, eds. *The Jews in Poland.* Oxford: Basil Blackwell, 1986.

Read, Anthony. *The Deadly Embrace: Hitler, Stalin and the Nazi Soviet Pact, 1939-1941.* New York: Norton, 1989.

Ringelblum, Emmanuel. *Notes from the Warsaw Ghetto.* New York: McGraw-Hill, 1958.

Rosen, Moses, *Dangers, Tests and Miracles: The Remarkable Life Story of Chief Rabbi Rosen of Romania (as told to Joseph Finkelston).* London: Weidenfeld and Nicolson, 1990.

Rosenberg, Tina, *The Haunted Land, Faciang Europe's Ghosts After Communism.* New York, Random House, 1995.

Rottenberg, Dan, *Finding Our Fathers, A Guidebook to Jewish Genealogy.* New York, Random House.1977.

Schneiderman, S. L. *The River Remembers.* New York: Horizon Press, 1978.

Singer, Isaac Bashevis. *The Magician of Lublin.* New York: Fawectt, 1985.

Steiner, Jean-Francois. *Treblinka.* New York: Simon &: Schuster, 1968.

Suhl, Yuri. *They Fought Back: The Story of the Jewish Resistance in Nazi Europe.* New York: Schocken Books, 1975.

Swiebocka, Teresa, comp. *Auschwitz: A History in Photographs.* Bloomington: Indiana University Press, 1993.

Vinecour, Earl. *Polish Jews: The Final Chapter.* New York: McGraw-Hill, 1977.

The Warsaw Diary of Adam Czerniakow: Prelude to Doom. Edited by Raul Hilberg, Stanislaw Staron, and Joseph Kermisz. New York: Stein and Day, 1968.

Vital, David, *A People Apart: The Jews in Europe, 1789-1939.* Oxford, Oxford University Press, 1999.

The Warsaw Diary of Chain A. Kaplan. Edited by A. L. Katsh. New York: Macmillan, 1973.

Watt, Richard M. *Bitter Glory: Poland and Its Fate, 1918 to 1939.* New York: Simon & Schuster, 1979.

Weinryb, Bernard D. *The Jews of Poland: A Social and Economic History of the Jewish Community in Poland from 1100 to 1800.* Philadelphia: Jewish Publication Society of America, 1973.

Wiesel, Elie. *Night.* New York: Bantam, 1982.

Wischnitzer, Rachel. *The Architecture of the European Synagogue.* Philadelphia: Jewish Publication Society of America, 1964.

Wood, E. Thomas and Stanislaw M. Jankowski. Karski: *How One Man Tried to Stop the Holocaust.* New York: Wiley, 1994.

Young, James E. *The Texture of Memory: Holocaust Memorials and Meaning in Europe, Israel, and America.* New Haven: Yale University Press, 1993.

Zuckerman, Vilzhak ("Antek"). *A Surplus of Memory: Warsaw Ghetto Uprising: Memoirs of a Resistance Leader.* Translated and edited by Barbara and Benjamin Harshav. Berkeley: University of California Press, 1993.

Romania
Once a Large Jewish Community; Today a Small One

When the brawny arm-swinging, sword wielding, Roman legionnaires conquered Dacia, the land of the first Romanians, they chanted military songs rendered in Latin and composed in Rome. They certainly were not bellowing out the rousing Yiddish song, "Romania, Romania, Romania," as sung, let us say, by the great Israeli concert folk singer, Dudu Fisher, who melodically praises *mamaliga,* translated as "corn mush." We know it as polenta.

When you hear Dudu's song, you want to jump up and dance and dance and dance. For sure, Romanians know how to dance. Was not the Israeli dance, the *hora,* imported from this Balkan land?

All travel writers pick up sayings and descriptions that aptly describe a municipality or country. As a reporter in New Jersey, I read that when God looked down on Jersey City, he created the beautiful beach metropolis of Rio de Janeiro.

A similar story is told about Romania. Olivia Manning, in her novel *The Balkan Trilogy,* relates that God was so upset that he had been so generous with Romania and that he had given that country precious gifts such as "forests, rivers, mountains, minerals, oil and a fertile soil that yielded many crops," that to "strike a balance, he put here the worst people he could find." Of course, we scoff at this.

For hundreds of years, Romania has been "cursed by its geographic location" at the crossroads of Europe and Asia which has

made it "a transit point of intrigue and invasion by a succession of outside powers," according to Mark Sanborne in his book, *Romania.*" These invaders plundered, raped and murdered. Plucked right smack in the middle of invasion routes, barbaric hordes were followed by the Ottoman Turks, the Hungarians, the Austrians and finally the Germans.

Under its red, blue, and yellow flag, Romania encompasses 91,699 square miles and nearly 23 million citizens. Its current boundaries were set after World War II. Bordering it are the Black Sea in the southeast; the Republic of Moldova to the north and northeast; Ukraine to the east; Hungary and Yugoslavia to the west; and Bulgaria to the south.

Despite ugly urbanization, despite changes in its infrastructure, its somewhat run-down capital city of Bucharest, which counts 2,339,156 inhabitants, still displays a just-below-the-surface charm.

Tourist-wise, this is a beautiful country that proudly boasts breathtaking scenery, hiking trails and resorts.

Like many other territories in Europe, rivers and mountains define history and character, says author Robert D. Kaplan, author of *Balkan Ghosts: A Journey Through History.* Romania does not escape the impact of the Danube, which by itself touches seven countries on its 1,776 mile journey from the Black Forest in Germany to the Black Sea. The Danube flows past Budapest, past Belgrade and for 900 miles it forms Romania's southwest border with Yugoslavia and its southern border with Bulgaria. It then flows due north through Romania before turning east again and branching into a myriad of small waterways that flow into the Black Sea, notes Kaplan.

Romania, like other countries in East Central Europe, "was less productive, less literate and less healthy than West Central and Western Europe," wrote historian Joseph Rothschild in his book, *East Central Europe Between the Two World Wars.* As recently as the end of World War II, Romania was almost totally an agricultural country; that is, until the Stalinists got their hands on the economy and forced state-controlled industrialization down the throats of the people. Result: pollution, a pollution that today chokes Bucharest.

Once the food basket of Europe, Romania had been

prosperous, a land of plenty, wrote Olivia Manning in her novel, *Balkan Trilogy*. Golden beaches line her Black Sea coast. But to most Americans, Romania is "remote," and a "side show." As we have seen, Americans know very little about what goes on in this end of the world, known as the Balkans. But they are missing much.

Of all the countries in the world, Romania is "trapped between great historical forces," according to author Kaplan. He must have been referring to the Balkans, where much is in dispute, even in the 21st Century.

"No country has had a more muddled past than Romania," observed Manning.

Thousands of years ago, during the Bronze Age, 2200 to 12 B.C. Thraco-Getian tribes roamed the area known as Romania. Today's Romanians are in part descended from those Getai who lived north of the Danube River. Residing in the same area were the Dacians who established fortresses against the wild tribes of South Russia. Dacian civilization reached its zenith under Decebalus, who is still honored today in Romania. Decebalus fought the Romans in A.D. 105-106. Soon, however, Dacia was conquered and organized by Roman legions in A.D. 105. The Dacians, in turn, absorbed elements of Roman Culture including a Vulgar Latin that eventually evolved into today's Romanian language. Romanian is the only East European language that comes from Latin.

By the 200s, the Romans completely occupied the country. When they finally departed, anarchy walked in, according to R.W. Seton Watson in his History of the *Roumanians, From Roman Times to the Completion of Unity*. In would come major migrations from barbarian tribes, the Visigoths, Huns, Ostrogoths, Gepides and Lombards, Avars and Slavs. All swept over these lands in the next centuries, including "a race of Turkish nomads called Bulgars." In 676, the Bulgarian Empire, for instance, absorbed a large part of Dacia. Then in the Ninth Century came the Magyars who also swept over Eastern Europe, but settled in part in the area we now know as Hungary.

Between 1250 and 1350, the provinces of Moldavia and Walachia united to form what was the nation of Romania. By 1504, however, the principalities fell under Turkish rule.

In the 16th century, a Walachian prince, Michael the Brave, won a war of liberation against the Ottomans and the three states of Walachia, Moldavia and Transylvania were united.

For its part, Transylvania, known for its mythological vampires, was independent for about 170 years, but was returned to Hungary as part of the Hapsburg Empire. In 1848, Hungary revolted and proclaimed freedom of the press and religious rights. One of the first acts of the Hungarian DIET was to attach Transylvania to Hungary. "Romania had no voice in the decision, "says author Ronald D. Backman in *Romania: A Country Study.*

Walachia and Moldavia came under Russian protection soon afterward and remained under the Czars' influence until the Crimean War (1854-56). After that conflict, the Russian protectorate was effectively ended.

While they governed Romania, the Turks had imported a group of local supervisors known as the *Phanariot* who hailed from Greece. The Turks allowed them to run the Romanian provinces. These Greek satraps took their name from the *phanar,* the lighthouse district of Constantinople. Corrupt as they were, they also made a lasting impact on the life of Romania, for they brought culture, the French language and literature, as well as a good dose of nationalism.

After the Crimean War (1854-56,) the existence of Moldavia and Walachia was guaranteed. With the help of big power intervention, Walachia and Moldavia again were united under Prince Alexandru Ion Cuza in 1861 to form the nation of Romania. He simply announced to the world that the "Romanian nation is founded." But he was forced to give up power to Prince Karl of Germany, the second son of the reigning family of Hohenzollern-Sigmaringen, and cousin to King Wilhelm I. Prince Karl was chosen King in February 1866 and ruled Romania until 1914 as King Carol I. He may have been Romania's most beloved monarch, but Radu Ioanid, author of *The Holocaust in Romania: the Destruction of Jews and Gypsies Under the Antonescu Regime, 1940 - 1944* labels him an anti-Semite.

Romania was located in the heart of the Jewish world. However, we should remember that even at this stage in Romania's history, anti-Semitism had deep roots in Romania.

"The roots of anti-Semitism in Romania, as in most of Eastern Europe, stretch deeply in history," notes Ioanid.

The 1878 Congress of Berlin settled the issues resulting from the Russian-Turkish war. In the end, Romania was forced to accept Russia's annexation of southern Bessarabia from Moldavia, while in return it gained control over northern Dobruja, which included the Danube delta. Europe agreed to recognize Romania's formal and complete independence, in exchange for two main conditions: one, Romania must consent to the territorial deal with Russia, and two, that it guarantee equality of civil, political, and religious rights to all citizens, including Jews. This last condition was aimed at forcing Romania to repeal its laws discriminating against Jews.

Article 44 of the Treaty of Berlin stipulated that religion must not be used to exclude anyone from "the enjoyment of civil and political rights," according to historian Radu Ionid. It never happened. In fact, on January 17, 1879, Romania's Parliament made it impossible for Jews to become Romanians unless they converted. Now an individual petition and parliamentary vote were required for naturalization, a requirement that remained on the books until 1919. Between 1866 and 1904, only 2,000 Jews would be naturalized.

In 1912 and 1913, three Balkan wars were fought between Romania and Bulgaria and Serbia and Greece and the Ottomans. In 1912, the First Balkan War broke out. A coalition of Romanians, Bulgarians, Serbs and Greeks rebelled against Turkey and the Ottoman rule and was victorious.

But in the Second Balkan War, Bulgaria, unhappy about the land reward it had obtained in the First Balkan War, flexed its muscles and attacked its allies. Romania joined the Serbs and others against the Bulgarians, who lost. No one could know that this minor fighting in a far-away region was a prelude to a bloody world war, which, in effect, was the Third Balkan War.

Meanwhile, pre-war Romania still had a well-deserved reputation of being, along with Russia, the most "anti-Semitic country in Europe," wrote Ezra Mendelsohn in *The Jews of East Central Europe Between the World Wars*. Suffering from poverty and anti-Semitism, Jews had been emigrating. By World War I, about 90,000 Jews had left Romania.

World War I

On June 18, 1914, a Bosnian Serb assassinated Archduke Franz Ferdinand.

Romania's rival, Bulgaria, joined the Central Powers of Germany, Austria-Hungary, and Turkey. Romania, however, joining the fray in 1915, fought alongside Britain, France and Russia. But Romania's armed forces were described as too late and with too little preparation, according to author Edward Behr. Romania was attacked by the Bulgarians.

After the war, the Treaty of Saint Germain with Austria and Treaty of Trianon with Hungary aided Romania. Being on the winning side, Romania more than doubled its size and population. She obtained Transylvania, which had been ruled by the Hungarians. She received Dobruja from Bulgaria; part of Bessarabia from Russia, and northern Bukovina from part of the Austrian Empire, as well as part of Banat, which was given to the Old Kingdom of Romania.

For our purposes, this meant that more than a half million Jews were absorbed into Greater Romania. Romania thus became the third largest Jewish community in Europe, according to Aron Hirt-Manheimer, who wrote the introduction and commentaries in *Jagendorf's Foundry: Memoir of the Romanian Holocaust, 1941 - 1944.*

According to author Aron Hirt-Manheimer, the insistence of the Allies at the Versailles peace talks that Romania honor its obligation to grant Jews full citizenship and civil rights, often unleashed a violent xenophobic backlash, particularly among Romania's anti-Semitic university students and intellectuals who rallied the nation around the slogan: "Romania for the Romanians."

Finally, in 1923, Jews were granted full citizenship. The new Citizenship Law in 1924 "extended Romanian citizenship to all inhabitants of Bessarabia, Bukovina, Transylvania, Banat, Crisana Maramures, and Satu Mare, who had been born there of resident parents," explains historian Radu Ioanid.

Anti-Semitism in Romania got a big boost with the rise of Hitler and Nazi Germany.

Octavian Goga, a nationalist anti-Semite, came to power in

1937. He accused Jews of controlling Romania's financial assets. In actual fact, the Jewish population made up only 4 percent of the population, with more than 40 percent of Jews of working age engaged in industry and commerce and three percent in the professions and civil service.

Goga enacted profound anti-Semitic legislation that actually stripped about 200,000 Jews of their citizenship. Jewish businesses were seized. The regime lasted little more than a month but set the pattern for the next five years. Romanian Jewry would suffer greatly.

In February 1938, King Carol took complete control of the government and proclaimed himself "Royal Dictator." He tried to crush the Iron Guard fascists. A court sentenced its leader, Corneliu Zelea Codreanu, to 10 years hard labor for treason. Codreanu had built the Legion of the Archangel Michael into a powerful force in Romanian politics. But on the night of November 29/30, 1938, King Carol II ordered him to be killed. We shall see when we discuss General Ion Antonescu and the Iron Guard that it was Codreanu who formed the Legion of the Archangel Michael in 1927. This was an extreme right-wing movement, of which anti-Semitism was a major component.

Edward Behr, author of *Kiss The Hand You Cannot Bite: The Rise and Fall of the Ceausescus,* says that even though Romanian public opinion was "still overwhelmingly pro-British and pro-French, many Romanians now started to believe that given Romania's geographical position and the pro-German sentiments of neighboring Hungary and Bulgaria, self-interest dictated that they should work out an accommodation with Hitler's Germany." This regime, which already hailed anti-Semitism as an "official policy," would move straight into the arms of the Nazis.

Three Dismemberments

Just about at the same time that Romania was moving into the fascist camp, large parts of Romania were soon to be divided among Russia, Hungary and Bulgaria. The whole of Moldavia would be handed to the Soviets as the price of Russia's neutrality to that point in the War; that is, 1940. Southern Dobruja, would fall to Bulgaria. The Hungarians would march into and take over Transylvania.

In less than two months, Romania would lose forty thousand square miles of territory, and with it, six million citizens and five hundred million sterling pounds.

On June 26, 1940, the Soviet Union gave Romania 24 hours to return Bessarabia and cede it to Northern Bukovina. The Germans, who in 1939 signed a non-aggression pact with the Russians, advised King Carol to submit. He did. The Russians did not even wait; they marched right in. Romania pulled out almost without firing a shot. The humiliation and defeat was blamed on the Jews.

Two months later, in August 1940, with German and Soviet backing, Bulgaria took Southern Dobruja.

In the same month, Germany and Italy persuaded Romania to accept the retrocession of Northern Transylvania to Hungary. King Carol, who had looked to Britain and France for support, gave up the territory that it had gained from Treaty of Versailles after World War I, when Romania obtained its land gains of Bessarabia, Transylvania and Bukovina.

All these boundary changes were negative and fateful for Jews. The Hungarians, without mercy, would soon deport thousands of Jews from Transylvania to the gas chambers in Poland.

Meanwhile, with the fall of France and Britain's desperate plight in 1940, the corrupt Romanian King's position became untenable, according to various historians. As we have seen, bowing to the inevitable, Romania accepted Hitler's proposal regarding the loss of its territory. It was then that King Carol called on fascist General Ion Antonescu to form a new cabinet. In September, however, General Antonescu and the Iron Guard turned around and forced King Carol to abdicate, "blaming him for the loss of Bessarabia, Bukovina and Northern Transylvania," according to Radu Ioanid in his book on the Romanian Holocaust. Antonescu took over real power and the King's 19-year-old son, Michael, took his place in the Palace. But the latter was kept in a ceremonial role, since his father, King Carol, somewhat of a playboy to say the least, had ruled Romania from 1930 to 1940 along with his mistress of Jewish origin, Elena Magda Lupescu. After obtaining Antonescu's permission to flee to Spain, the deposed king and his lady friend stocked a nine-carriage train with a fleet of bulletproof automobiles, $2,500.000 worth of Madame Lupescu's jewelry, and a cache of gold.

Despite deep anti-Semitism, widespread popular violence did not break out in Romania until after Hitler invaded the USSR in June 1941. We should not forget that "Romania contributed more combat troops to the German war effort than all of the other Nazi allies combined," according to Mark Sanborne, author of the book *Romania.*

Romania's army was ill equipped, ill armed, ill trained and completely unprepared for war with the USSR, which had been invaded by Germany in June 1941. In the Romanian Army, the Romanian soldier could still be flogged. That army even conscripted civilian convicts. In the battles at Stalingrad, some Romanian units fought bravely considering that they had been left alone; their officers had fled the battlefield. Romania sustained heavy losses, especially at Stalingrad. When it was all over on the Russian front, Antonescu's troops looked like "ghosts in rags," according to Antony Beevor writing in his book, *Stalingrad.*

Total Romanian World War II losses came to 110,000 killed and 180,000 missing or captured. After Romania changed sides, about 120,000 would perish helping the Red Army liberate Czechoslovakia and Hungary.

In August 1944, Romania's King Michael overthrew the country's radical right wing premier and signed an armistice with the USSR. "Moscow forced Michael to appoint a Communist sympathizer to lead the government in 1945 and three years later Romania found itself under strict Communist control," writes author Bachman.

August 23 marks the anniversary of Romania liberation by the Soviet Army. Interestingly, to this day, it is celebrated as a national independence day.

The Red Army occupied Bucharest on August 31, 1944. And on September 12, 1944, Romania and Soviet Union signed an armistice. Romania was to pay reparations, repeal anti-Jewish laws, ban fascist groups and retrocede Bessarabia and

Northern Bukovina to the Soviet Union. Bessarabia would soon be called the Republic of Moldova and Northern Bukovina became part of today's Ukraine.

Actually, Romania's fate had been sealed when wartime leaders Churchill and Stalin met in Moscow on October 9, 1944. At the table, the two allied leaders drew up a list of Balkan and Central European countries. They listed the percentages and interests that each of them would obtain in the Eastern European sphere. Churchill agreed that there would be 90 percent Soviet preponderance in Romania. Romania would thus disappear into the Soviet camp. The Communists seized power, and the Iron Curtain descended with a huge bang. Moscow-trained Communist leaders took over. There is no question that the Communists were able to assume power because of the "decisive intervention of the Soviet Union," as Joseph Rothschild calls it in his book, *East Central Europe Between the Two World Wars*.

With the Soviet Army, and waiting in the wings, was Gheorghe Gheoghiu-Dej and Anna Pauker, Romanian communist leader, who organized the drive to turn Romania into a full-fledged Communist state, utterly subservient to Moscow. But as we shall see, Romania in the 1960s would pursue an independent line until Communism was overthrown in 1989.

Notable Jews

Rabbi Moses Rosen (1912-1994) Rabbi Moses Rosen was often called the "Red Rabbi," but he was not a Communist. To this very day, pictures of Rabbi Rosen adorn the walls of communal offices. A section of the Jewish Museum in Bucharest is devoted to Rosens's writings, public activities, and meetings with political and religious leaders around the world.

Rabbi Rosen was the spiritual leader of the Jewish community in Rumania during the Communist regime. Even today, years after his death, he is venerated by the community he loved and kept alive. He fought for adequate Jewish religious life in Romania. He took over from Rabbi Alexander Safran when the latter left the country, and was chairman of the

Federation of Jewish Communities of the Socialist Republic of Rumania from 1964.

He was born in Moinesti, Moldavia, where his father, Rabbi Abraham Aryeh, served as rabbi. Rabbi Rosen received a secular education along with traditional Jewish learning. He was imprisoned with some of the future leaders of the Romania's Communist Party. "Rosen was not a Communist, but he developed before and during the war into an ardent 'fellow traveler,' writes Charles Hoffman in *Gray Dawn: The Jews of Eastern Europe in the Post Communist Era,* adding, "he stoutly asserted that he would have made a pact with the devil in order to preserve Jewish life in Romania."

The Communists expected him to go along with their wishes. Rosen turned out less pliable than they expected. "The Communists," writes author Charles Hoffman, "were extremely ruthless in purging anyone who was thought to oppose them..."

From 1957, Rabbi Rosen was a member of the Great National Assembly (Parliament) of Romania; his original constituency being a quarter of Bucharest that at one time contained a large Jewish population.

"All of the things I accomplished—saving hundreds of thousands of Jews and bringing them to Israel—were possible only by working with Ceausescu. Could I do what I did by going against him?" Rabbi Rosen was reported to have remarked.

Romanian dictator Nicolae Ceausescu apparently disliked Rabbi Rosen because the rabbi fought the dictator's plans to demolish the Bucharest Great Synagogue, the Choral Temple and the Jewish Museum. "I still hold to the view that my efforts to obtain MFN (Most Favored Nation) status for Romania was in accordance with my patriotic duty. I carried out my duty both to my Jewish brethren and to the Romanian people," said Rabbi Rosen. The rabbi's "main achievement was the creation of legal conditions for adequate Jewish religious life in Rumania."

Rabbi Rosen was not the architect of the mass aliya. To stand against charges that he collaborated, he "overlooked the fact that the mass aliya was arranged mainly by the Israeli government, which had paid Ceausescu several thousand dollars a head or provided economic benefits to Romania in exchange for the immigrants," wrote Charles Hoffman in *Gray Dawn: The Jews of Eastern Europe in the Post-Communist Era*. It is a well-known fact that the Israelis paid $4,000 a person for an exit visa. Author Hoffman points out that the West Germans did the same thing to ransom tens of thousands of ethnic Germans living in Romania.

"Rabbi Rosen stands out as an exceptional figure among the tragic gallery of Jewish communal leaders who labored at the near-impossible task of maintaining Jewish life for forty years under the hostile and brutal watch of Communism," continues Hoffman in his book.

After 1947, the state controlled Jewish institutions. But Rabbi Rosen managed to keep the "Talmud Torahs" open with the support of the Minister of Cults. He always tested the limits, according to Hoffman.

With an independent policy in place after the Soviet Army pulled out in 1957, Romania, in the mid-1960s, allowed the Joint Distribution Committee (JDC) to return to its welfare and medical service work for the Jewish community. "In sum, Rosen's position in Romania and his ability to keep winning more concessions from the authorities came to be based on two external factors: his usefulness to the Romanian leadership as a 'good will ambassador' abroad, and his growing network of allies and contacts in the Jewish world and Israel, which in turn bolstered his status and influence within Romania," wrote Charles Hoffman."I continued to praise the Romanian Government for having granted us all our religious national and cultural rights. Whenever I obtained a concession, I had to pay the price by bringing it to the public's attention," said Rabbi Rosen.

Rabbi Rosen told author Charles Hoffman that when Ceausescu was deposed there were no Jews in high places in government, the dictator had long ago pushed them out.

Anna Pauker was the daughter of a Moldavian rabbi. She became a powerful figure in the Communist government, second only to Gheorghiu-Dej and was internationally known. "A good-looking Jewish woman in her early fifties, rather imposing and very bright, she became involved in the [Communist] movement as a student, and soon rose to a leading role in the party," according to Professor Egon Balas describing Pauker when she became foreign minister. Along the way to high position, she had been arrested in 1935 and served a prison term. She was almost executed in 1936.

After she was removed from power by Gheorghiu-Dej, Pauker simply became a non-person. The elimination of Anna Pauker and her group proved to be a godsend for Gheorghiu-Dej, according to author Behr.

It has been said that Pauker combined atheism and an unshakable faith in Stalin with considerable sympathy for Israel and for the Romanian Chief Rabbi, Moses Rosen. Her brother Solomon, a regular visitor to Bucharest, lived in Israel. But there are those who point out that Anna Pauker was ruthless, that she had her own husband, Marcel, and other right-wing persons, shot. Marcel indeed was executed in the Soviet Union as a traitor in 1938. Marcel and Anna had a son and daughter; she also had a daughter from a love affair with a French Communist leader, according to Professor Egon Balas in his book *Will To Freedom: A Perilous Journey Through Fascism and Communism.* She was sent to Moscow in 1941 as part of an exchange with the Soviets and returned with the Russian troops in 1944. After her expulsion from the party she was too well-known to be shot. She lived in retirement until 1960, "a bitter but dignified old woman."

Elena (Magda) Lupescu. She was a Jewish stenographer, but she once was considered the power behind the throne. Born in 1895, in Iasi, the provincial capital of Moldavia, Lupescu, it is said, snared King Carol II. It was the "Purim story in reverse." Even if she tried she could not have saved the Jews as Esther had done in the Bible, according to Robert D. Kaplan in his book *Balkan Ghosts: A Journey Through History (1930-1940).* Romanians felt humiliated because their king had deserted his real wife for a Jew. When King Ferdinand demanded his son break off the affair, Carol abdicated his right of succession and went into exile in Paris with Lupescu. Sources in Bucharest maintain that she really was born of a peasant family, but given over to a Jewish family, who raised her according to the Jewish religion. King Ferdinand died on July 19, 1927, and Carol's six-year-old son, Michael, was appointed king, but in reality a regency council ruled in his name. Carol came back in 1930 and he brought

Lupescu with him after dissatisfaction with the regency spread throughout the country. He had agreed to rule as a co-regent, but he broke his promises and pushed Parliament to proclaim him, King Carol II. He was known as a royal dictator rather than a democratic monarch. He formed links to the fascist Iron Guard. In 1938, however, he cracked down on the Guard and had 13 of its members killed, although "they were gunned down while escaping." He also suspended the Constitution and installed his own royal dictatorship.

Forced to abdicate in 1940, he fled into exile with Lupescu, his mistress, leaving his now 19-year-old son (1940-47) to take the throne. King Carol and Lupescu left Romania in the dead of the night in late 1940, in a nine car railway train fitted with the country's gold and art treasures. He had asked for asylum in Germany, but Hitler, because of Lupescu's Jewish origins, refused to have them. Crossing the Atlantic they settled first in Mexico, then in Brazil. There they remained throughout the war, eventually marrying in 1946. King Carol bestowed upon Lupescu the title of Royal Princess. After the King died in Brazil, she lived with Carol's former Prime Minister, Erners Urdarreanu. She died in 1977.

Brief Jewish History

For most American Jews if you mention the "Old Country," three nations come to mind, Russia, Poland and Romania.

As in other states in Europe, Jewish migration to Romania did not occur at once. We do know that Jewish merchants tagged along with Roman legions to the country that was called Dacia in the first few centuries of the Common Era.

Between the 11th and 14th centuries, those Jews expelled from Hungary entered Walachia, a Romanian principality founded at the end of the fifth century. A few served as physicians and diplomats for the sovereigns of Walachia. In the 16th century, Jews from Spain set up stakes in Romania. Others, searching for a safe-haven, moved up from the Balkan Peninsula. They found it in Romania.

When the Turks took over, they also placed restrictions on

the Jews who were considered a "non-Christian people with nebulous and often suspect external loyalties," according to historian Radu Ioanid, who adds that the Turks, however, actually let the Jews have a great deal of cultural autonomy as well as allowing them to pursue their livelihoods with a "minimum of official interference until the mid-nineteenth century."

When the Russians took over Bessarabia in 1812, more Jews moved into the area as well as into Moldavia which was founded in the middle of the 14th century.

What helped to bring Jewish settlers to Romania was that Walachia and Moldavia, stood on the trade route between Poland, Lithuania and the Ottoman Empire. But early in the history of Romania, commercial competition became a part of anti-Jewish hatred. In the first codes of law promulgated by the Greek Orthodox Church in Moldavia and Walachia, the Jews were seen as heretics and Christians were forbidden to have relations with them. Still by 1859, 118,000 Jews resided, in Moldavia and only 9,200 in Walachia.

The Russians peddled their anti-Semitism throughout the country. For much of the time and even until the mid 20th century, Jews were denied citizenship in Romania. Invading armies also caused difficulties for Jews. Author Sanborne says Jews came in large numbers after 1829. From 1859 to 1899, the number of Jews in Moldavia increased from about 118,000 to 200,000, while in Walachia, it grew from 9,000 to 68,000.

The winds of revolution of 1848 also spread to Romania. As in other nations, Jews fought in the 1848 Revolution alongside their fellow Romanian countrymen. S. Ettinger notes in *A History of the Jewish People*, that the Romanians were eager to win over "the few Jewish intellectuals to their cause." The major political parties, adds Jewish historian Ettinger, "outdid each other in their promises to the Jews."

But it never happened.

Anti-Jewish incitement became one of the important factors in the evolvement of the Romanian state, stresses Ettinger.

By 1859 there were about 130,000 Jews in Romania who were considered foreign subjects and who could not acquire land.

In 1866, the mob attacked Jews, destroyed the Choral Synagogue in Bucharest. The Assembly soon passed a law that only Christians could become citizens. The Government even declared that it never intended to give Jews civil rights.

The new national constitution denied Romanian Jews political emancipation, " a situation that would prevail until after World War I," declares historian Ioanid, adding "not until 1923 did Jews in Romania win legal equality."

At the Congress of Berlin in 1878, the European powers tried to persuade the Romanian Government to bestow equal rights on the Jews. Romanian leaders refused.

In the 19th century, Jewish leaders Adolphe Cremieux of France and Moses Montefiore of Great Britain visited the country and spoke to the authorities who pledged to stop the persecutions. But the promises were never kept. Indeed, after each foreign intervention, the Romanians raised the ante of hate. Over the next few years, even more pogroms occurred. While the physical attacks may have ceased, the "administrative persecution did not. Economic restrictions against the Jews were intensified," according to historian Ettinger.

By World War I, about 70,000 Jews had left Romania. The Jewish population was now 239,967.

The political unrest in the 1920s and 1930s brought the Iron Guard, a paramilitary organization with an extreme anti-Semitic program, to the fore. Indeed, King Carol II more and more was acting like a dictator and actually aided the Iron Guard. In 1933, the position of the now 750,000 Jews in Romania was different than say the Jews in France or Holland. According to the late, noted Jewish historian, Salo Baron, the Jews in Romania, more than any other group, felt a deep sense of insecurity. After Hitler came to power in German in 1933, even the main Romanian parties launched anti-Semitic *pogroms.* Jewish representation in parliament came to an end. In the mid-1930s, Jews were under attack everywhere. Jewish lawyers were disbarred. Iron Guard students prevented Jews from not only going to university classes, but as the literature indicates these fascist university students threw Jewish students out of classroom windows. The Germans aided in this anti-Semitic tirade with hate rhetoric and money to distribute it.

In 1937, 40 synagogues, two cemeteries, 19 schools, a library, a historical museum, two hospitals, nine clinics, two senior citizens homes and two orphanages were part of the Romanian Jewish infrastructure. In short, it was an active community.

Bucharest

"The Paris of the Balkans." "The Paris of the East." The "bread-basket" of the Balkans. Founded 500 years ago, Bucharest's tree-lined boulevards, *fin de siecle* architecture, its Arc de Triomphe, make it an attractive city. The History Museum and the Military Academy should be on every visitor's itinerary.

The **Palace of Parliament**, If ever there was an example of a dictator's grim reign and megalomania, this $10 billion Parliament building built by the late President Nicolae Ceausescu, is certainly it. It stands as the second largest public building in the world, (The Pentagon is the first, the Cyclops Pyramid of Egypt is third). Inside the hideously ornate Palace lived Nicolae and Elena Ceausescu when they were in Bucharest.

The palace is said to be 900 feet long, 600 feet wide; it contains 11 stories, with 1,500 rooms, 2,600 windows, 300 chandeliers and 4,200 gilded doorknobs and acres and acres of polished marble. The dictator built a Forbidden City of "fascist architecture to encircle a wedding cake structure larger than the Pentagon," wrote Robert D. Kaplan in his book *Balkan Ghosts: A Journey through History.*

While Romanians starved, this despot and his wife built this palace. About 17,000 men worked on the building, day and night. The best quality materials were used: marble from Romania itself, local wood such as walnut tree, sweet cherry tree, elm tree, and oak. Many men and women manufactured thousands of meters of carpets, silks, brocades, and gold and silver embroideries.

This palace is obviously a tourist attraction and guides told this author that visitors usually say, "this is a monstrosity, how could Ceausescu have done this to us." The other side says, "look at what we achieved; we are proud of what we have done."

Now 80 percent finished, it already has been used for concerts, forums, international meetings and conferences and the House of the Parliament. The Senate will soon move there.

Hopefully, it will continue to be used even more for educational purposes.

Former Communist Party Headquarters Building. Plata Revolutiei Nr., 1, or Calea Victoriei, Bucharest. A terrible canvas has been painted about President Nicolae Ceausescu and his family. Ceausescu and his wife forced Romanians to live in anguish and poverty. He relied on a huge security apparatus to spread fear and psychological terror around them, according to author Behr who adds, Romanians suffered "malnutrition, illegal botched abortions and the death of elderly people denied operations or treatment because of their age."

"Nowhere in Europe had the failure of Communism been more stunning, the economic, social and human disaster more desperate, the anguish of the people more heartbreaking," than Romania says Nestor Ratesh in his *"Romania: The Entangled Revolution."*

Author Charles Hoffman wrote that "even in the other satellite countries, the heavy hand of Communist rule had not been this oppressive, nor had the megalamaniachal drive of the rulers gone to such pathological lengths."

"One hell bent orgy of destruction," was the way author Robert D. Kaplan describes Ceausescu's last five years in power.

Personality cults are grotesque. Most Romanians agree that Elena Ceausescu was Nicolae's "evil genie." She frequently referred to her millions of subjects as "worms," to be controlled by hard labor and food rationing. From the very beginning, she consolidated power in her own right.

Ceausescu "played an active part in arranging Egyptian President Anwar Sadat's historic visit to Jerusalem in 1977. He served as host not only to Yasir Arafat, but to every Israeli prime minister in the last 20 years, it was reported. When President Nixon visited Romania he said Ceausescu was "the good Communist." The West in effect gave him the "ok" when French President Charles DeGualle visited Romania, which received most-favored-nation status in the 1970s and 1980s.

As Nicolae Ceausescu tightened the vice on his own people, "the West was willing to overlook his dismal domestic record because he was a thorn in the side of the Soviet enemy," writes Mark Sanborne.

Ceausescu produced sprawling steel and petrochemical plants. The only trouble was the country did not have the raw materials and energy, so they had to import the precious raw materials that cost dearly in terms of hard currency, according to Ronald D. Bachman, author of *Romania: A Country Study*. As for petrochemicals, while Romania is rich in natural resources, it has few raw materials for those industries.

But tyrants eventually always are toppled.

By the end of 1989, the Berlin Wall had come down, the Poles, Hungarians, Czechs had thrown off the Communist yoke. In Prague, students and parts of the crowd were beaten up, but no one was killed. Bloodshed had to occur somewhere in the former Communist Empire and it turned out to be Romania. The best estimates are that more than 1,000 persons, including the dictator and his wife, were killed in the revolution, if "revolution" is the right word as some Romanians cynically point out. Only a spark was needed; it came from a small city called Timisoara. There, Romanian state police wanted to transfer a young Hungarian priest who they said had been preaching against the regime. Both Hungarians and Romanians who lived in the city joined the protest against removing the minister. This demonstration set off a chain of events that led ten days later to Ceausescu's execution.

The events would occur thusly:

First, there was a civilian vigil outside the priest's home on December 15. When police were sent to remove the demonstrators holding candles in the square in Timisoara, the Romanian revolution burst open with a vengeance.

At one demonstration, the Romanian flag was unfurled at Party headquarters with the Communist coat of arms cut out, leaving a hole in the middle.

The Ceausescus' had given orders to shoot to kill. So on Sunday, December 17, 1989 troops fired on the people, but it only caused the demonstrations to grow. On Tuesday, December 19th a general strike was called, only this time the army let the citizens pass the barriers and fraternized with them. Ceausescu came back from a foreign trip and on December 20, he called for a rally in Palace Square in Bucharest. That, too, was his undoing as we shall see. He realized that the army had not put down the protestors, though civilians had been killed.

On December 21, Ceausescu spoke on the balcony of the Communist Party Headquarters. It was here that the crowd turned against him, relates Scott L. Malcomson in *Borderlands—Nation and Empire.* There were shouts of "Timisoara, Timisoara," and "Down with Ceausescu." Students demanded an end to the Ceausescu dictatorship. Pandemonium broke out. Not used to the managed crowds talking back to him, Ceausescu looked confused; his wife, Elena, also looking furious and offended. She even shouted to the crowd. Be quiet!" But they would not be silent, no matter how Ceausescu shouted. The crowd would not kowtow. From the back of the mass of people attending the rally came the boos, the catcalls and the chant of TI-MI-SOA-RA, according to author Edward Behr. Ceausescu and his wife were taken inside, where they spent the night.

The next morning, the pair tried again to speak to the audience from the balcony. When they were shouted down, when they saw that the insurgents had rushed into the building of the Communist Party Headquarters below and taken over, they realized that as the crowd surged forward, they would be lynched. The Ceausescus' fled on a helicopter that took them from Bucharest. The flight marked the climax of the Romanian revolution, according to author Nestor Ratesh. "The dictator has fled," said Ion Iliescu on television. He became Romania's president (1990-1996 and 2000-   ).

That night firing broke out, with armed cars firing on the crowds in the square. To this day, no one knows who started the shooting. Some call it an "operetta war."

Meanwhile the pilot abandoned the Ceausescus' on a highway. One of their two bodyguards commandeered two cars. The civilian drivers managed, by various ruses, to abandon the couple. One of the bodyguards then slipped away. The remaining guard then commandeered yet another car which was being washed by its owner. This man drove the Ceausescus' to an agricultural research station whose manger, by yet more ruses, succeeded in delivering the couple to the militia, who in turn handed them over to the army.

The Ceausescus' were given a very brief trial by a hastily

convened military tribunal. Several people whom they knew well and whom they treated during the trial with contempt were present. However, "even by the standards of the infamous Stalinist trials of the thirties, the proceedings were farcical. As we now know, the trial's purpose was not to bring the Ceausescus' to justice but to provide a legal pretext for executing them as soon as possible," opines Edward Behr. Even today some feel that the security police would only give up if they knew the Ceausescus' were gone. That may have been the reason their dead bodies were shown time after time on television for several months.

Found guilty of "crimes against the people, and genocide"— the prosecution maintained they killed 63,000 persons; they were sentenced to death by firing squad, on Christmas Day.

Their executioners placed them against the wall and fired some two hundred rounds into their bodies. The "conspiracy theories continue to echo in Romania today." Some say it was a plot hatched by "disaffected Communists."

Ion Iliescu, a former Central Committee secretary and deputy minister of the political executive committee who had fallen into disfavor with Ceausescu took charge and organized the new ruling party, National Salvation Front. Some say the NSF "stole the Revolution." Behr argues that the revolt was "not a carefully staged event." The plotters may have been waiting for such a moment as this.

More than a decade after the overthrew of Ceausescu, it is felt by observers of the Romanian scene that the people are generally disappointed; some say even bitter with life which they say is worse than 1989. According to *The New York Times* dispatch of December 19, 1999, a local poll pointed out that 61 percent said that life was better under Ceausescu. A visitor constantly hears the following refrain, "Then we had money, but there was nothing to buy. Now the shops are full, but we have no money."

JEWISH SITES IN BUCHAREST

"Jewish people will be here in Romania as long as the earth

will exist," a Jewish leader told me in an interview. But neither he nor any leader here could predict with accuracy how many Jews there would be and what kind of Jewish life they would lead? To understand the Romanian Jewish Community, one has to realize that 65 percent of the Jewish community is over the age of 65, or 9,000 persons; and that only 7 percent or 1,000 persons are between the ages of 0 to 35 years of age. With these kinds of demographics, how can there be a Jewish community in 25 years?

Where is everybody?

For the last 60 years, demographics played havoc with the Jewish community. Before World War II, Romanian Jewry contained about 800,000 persons. Nearly one half of that number were murdered by the Germans and their Axis ally, Romania. That left about 400,000 Jews, of which 350,000 went to Israel before 1948. The aliya was stopped by the Government in 1954, but allowed to begin again in 1958. In the late 1960s there were 14 regular synagogues in Bucharest. Of the 44,202, 3.6 percent of the total population registered, in the city in the 1956 census, according to the *Encyclopedia Judaica*.

In 1969, it was estimated that 50,000 Jews lived in Bucharest. By 1977, only about 40,000 remained. Today, there are about 14,000 Jews in Romania.

The Jewish community will not roll over and play dead. Yes, answer Jewish leaders emphatically, there will be a Jewish community in 25 years. Mixed marriages will exist and people will be accepted into the community on their sincerity. Romanian Jewry has not yet reached the percentage of mixed marriages in Bulgaria, which has reached 90 to 95 percent.

Today's Romanian Jews gather at the **Jewish Community Center** at Popasoare 18 in Bucharest. Here one can find a kosher restaurant, a cultural center, community resource center. The problem is to bring those Jews into Jewish leadership positions.

What hurts this community is the lack of young people. There are activities for young people, including choirs, Zionist youth movements and an active program by the Jewish Agency. If the economy does not disintegrate completely, Jews will survive. This is another Jewish community in Europe that certainly could use the help of young American Jews who could live in the country for a year and help the community. One such American Jewish young man, a JDC Jewish Service Corp Volunteer in Romania, Yosef Hirsh, helped establish an organization called OTER, Organization of Young Jews, which meets frequently to learn more about Jewish tradition and history. In Bulgaria, a JDC Jewish Service Corp Volunteer, Hadara Stanton travels to outlying Jewish communities where she works with the local Jewish leadership.

The Federation of Jewish Communities in Romania (FEDROM) is the national, community-based infrastructure representing Romanian Jewry.

A program for senior citizens sponsored by FEDROM and its Social and Medical Assistance Department is called the Dignity Program. The average age of one seventh of the Jewish population is above age 77. Assisted by FEDROM, their life expectancy is higher than that of Romanian seniors. And what is important to understand in Romania, is that over 85 percent of the senior Jewish Holocaust survivors served by FEDROM, are single.

FEDROM not only serves Jews in Bucharest, but 49 Jewish communities throughout the country, 11 affiliated communities and significantly 22 small towns that have only one Jewish person in each municipality. Most of the social and medical welfare assistance programs in Romania are financially sponsored by the American Jewish Joint Distribution Committee, although FEDROM also participates in the cost.

Choral Temple, Sfinta Vineri Str., 9-11, Bucharest, 70478. Tel: 312-25-38. For 40 years, this synagogue sheltered and kept the Jewish community alive. During the Communist era, this was the headquarters of the Jewish community. Judaism survived here, especially under the leadership of Rabbi Moses Rosen.

This is a synagogue that one can truly say has kept its appearance since it was opened in 1867. It actually was founded by German-Austrian members. According to Carol Herselle Krinsky, author of *Synagogues of Europe: Architecture, History, Meaning,* the architects patterned the Temple after the

Monument to the Holocaust in front of the Choral Temple, Bucharest. (Photo by Ben G. Frank)

large Vienna-Templegasse synagogue of 1855-58.

Before the Choral Synagogue was built, 29 synagogues existed in Budapest. Today, only this Choral Synagogue functions. I found author Charles Hoffman's description of the Choral Temple, to be quite accurate: "A large, handsome Moorish-style structure whose interior walls are painted in delicate hues of blue, beige, and gold."

Throughout its history, the synagogue was plagued by vandals. The Iron Guard severely damaged the building in the 1930s. After World War II, the synagogue was repaired by various Jewish organizations. Even today at the turn of the recent century, remodeling is still going on at the site. This is a good place to discuss the deep-rooted anti-Semitism that existed in Romania.

"The roots of anti-Semitism in Romania, as in most of Eastern Europe, stretch deeply in history," notes author Radu Ioanid.

In his 1930 pamphlet, *"The Jews in Roumania,"* Jewish historian, Salo Baron wrote: "Anti-Semitism is in general widespread and deeply rooted among the Christians in Roumania." "Rumanian anti-Semitism was particularly virulent," declares Bauer, who notes that a crude anti-Semitism "affected most of Romania's working class," a safety valve used to divert discontent from the nation's real difficulties and calamities, including a succession of cruel invaders and corrupt officials.

Official anti-Semitism was widely shared at all levels of Romanian society. Indeed, Romania was "the last European nation to grant Jews citizenship, and did so only under duress," according to Hirt-Manheimer. "Thus, the Jew was the traditional scapegoat. The Romanian learned to curse the Turk, the Russian and the Hungarian. But he beat the Jew," according to author Hirt-Manheimer.

Jewish Community Offices, Sfinta Vineri Str. Bucharest 70478. Alex Sivan is director general of the Federation of Jewish Communities in Romania. Tel: 312-25-38. Julian Sorin is secretary general.

A new building is under construction and will be used for administrative offices.

Monument to the Holocaust. Located in front of the Choral Temple, Sfinta Vineri Str., 9-11, Bucharest.

Temple Yoshua Tova, George Ianesco St., Bucharest.

Jewish Community and Cultural Center, Popasoare st., 18, Bucharest. Here one can find the kosher restaurant, the cultural center, and the community resource center.

Located on the first floor, is the kosher restaurant. Served here are meat dishes. Lunch is offered every day, Monday to Sunday, from 12 to 3 P.M. The room resembles a large dining hall, not a restaurant. On Friday nights an Oneg Shabbat is held at dinner. The restaurant is open on Saturday. Make reservations in advance.

On the second floor of this building is a large hall for meetings, concerts and performances.

A youth club meets on the third floor. Telephone: 321-3940.

In the basement of the building, a sports center/gym functions.

OTER, Organization of Young Jews in Romania, Popasoare, 18, Bucharest. Young people in their 20s and 30s, hold discussions, parties, sports activities, holiday celebrations, seminars. They attend the dance camp in Hungary. OTER publishes a newspaper. Topics include Jewish holidays, Jewish life cycle, famous Jews throughout history.

B'nai B'rith This organization meets in the library in the Choral Synagogue.

Social Assistance Department of the Federation of Jewish Communities, Dimytrie, Racovitza 8, Bucharest. Tel: (401) 314-86-84. FAX: (401) 322-4067. Nilu Aronovici is president. E:Mail: fcerdas@com.pcnet.ro. "You cannot forget so many Jews here." Jews in this country are given special food, parcels eight times a year at holidays, lunch meals on wheels, and clothes. Every Jew receives medical assistance.

Medical Center, Calea Calarasi, 57 B, Bucharest, Tel: 321-5160. This center is sponsored by the American Jewish Joint Distribution Committee.

Jewish Museum, Mamulary, 3, Bucharest. Once, there were eight active synagogues on Mamulary Street. Now there are none; only memories. And those memories live in the one synagogue, now the Jewish Museum. This was once called the "Tailors Synagogue." It is only five minutes from the Choral Synagogue and eight minutes from the Jewish Center. Nearby

A display of books in the Jewish Museum, Bucharest. (Photo by Ben G. Frank)

is the Great Synagogue. Ritual objects are housed in the Jewish Museum. Lazar Dubinowsky, the sculptor, designed a monument to the Holocaust, a black rug with footsteps showing an escape from Auschwitz, which obviously never occurred. The histories of Jewish communities of Bucharest, Timisoara, Iasi, Cluj, are featured as are Jews in the Romanian army, and the role of Rabbi Rosen in keeping alive the Jewish community.

Jewish Agency, Kogalniceau, 57, Bucharest, Tel: 312-52-94.

The Great Synagogue, Vasile Adamache 11, Bucharest. This was one of the most beautiful synagogues in Romania. Today, it houses a Holocaust Exhibition, which tells the story of the murder of Romanian Jews in World War II.

Statistics never completely tell the tale of the killing of the Jews in Europe during the war and Romania is no exception. But for the record, of the 380,000 Romanian Jews who died in the Holocaust, 260,000 were killed in Bessarabia, Bukovina and Transnistria. Between 120,000 to 150,000 Transylvanian Jews were also murdered. Most of these Jews were from Northern Transylvania which had passed to Hungarian rule in 1940. They were sent to their deaths in a sudden mass deportation in 1944.

Most Jews of Old Romania survived; a paradox in a country of such widespread anti-Semitism. Fifty seven percent of the Jewish population under Romanian rule during the war (including the Jews of Bessarabia and North Bukovina) survived the Holocaust.

Former president Emil Constantinescu publicly acknowledged Romania's responsibility in the Holocaust and the Ministry of Education has mandated the teaching of the Holocaust in the schools, says Holocaust historian Radu Ioanid.

"Romanian soldiers, police and Iron Guards initially murdered tens of thousands of Jews in vicious pogroms in Moldavia, Bukovina and Bessarabia, as well as in the Ukrainian cities they conquered with their German allies," according to Mark Sanborne in his book, *Romania.* The Romanians also allowed hundreds of thousands of others to perish from disease and starvation in a place called Transnistria (see below).

As Dr. Jean Ancel of Yad Vashaem has observed: The crimes were not committed by Romanian individual accomplices but by the entire state apparatus: the Romanian army, gendarmerie, police, civil authorities, prefectures, city councils and tribunals. Premeditated and uncoerced, the Romanian regime presided over the extermination of tens of thousands of Jewish civilians—old and young, women and men—in retaliation for illusory offenses. It was the recurring blood libel on a colossal scale. Instead of falsely accusing a single Jew of ritual murder, thousands of Jews were unjustly indicted for shedding the blood of Romanian soldiers."

Romanian troops and Einsatzgruppe D, "vied with each other," for the distinction of murdering Jews," according to Holocaust historian Yehuda Bauer.

Much of the killing of the Jews of Greater Romania occurred in Transnistria which comes from the Romanian, "trans-Nistru, the land across the Dniester River, according to author Aron Hirt-Manheim. Thousands of Jews from Bessarabia, Bukovina and from Dorohoi in Old Romania and other regions were shipped under conditions worse than cattle to Transnistria, a region between the Bug and the Dniester, two large rivers in the Ukraine. This area of Transnistria, twice the size of New Jersey, belonged to the Soviet Ukraine before Romania was given control of the region by Germany in August, 1941, just after the Germans and Romanians invaded the Ukraine.

Even though there were no gas chambers there, Jews perished by "terror, the threats, the nocturnal death marches, the sealed wagons, the starvation, the plagues, the humiliation, the public executions, the fires," wrote Elie Wiesel in the foreword of Rondu Ioanid's book, *The Holocaust in Romania: the Destruction of Jews and Gypsies Under the Antonescu Regime.* Jews would die from exposure, sickness and hunger after being housed in pigsties and village stables or slave camps on the shores of the Bug River.

In the Auschwitz gas chambers and in the shooting pits of Russia, death came quickly, notes historian Yehuda Bauer, but in Transnistria, death was slow.

But what contributed to the fact that 57 percent of the Jews under Romanian rule survived the Holocaust. The answers appear to be: Romanian self-interest, national pride, *real politik,* and the fearless stand of the Jewish leaders—all helped save Jews.

Holocaust historian Leni Yahil notes that despite Romanian persecution and killing of Jews since their arrival in the country from Russia in the 19th century, "the leaders of the Jewish community succeeded in maintaining relations with the heads of state and though they could not prevent drastic measures, they did succeed in limiting and mitigating them." She claims Jewish leaders and community members used "methods of self-protection such as bribery, intercession, evasion and mutual aid to save Jews."

Jewish leaders such as Rabbi Alexandre Safran and Dr. Wilhelm Filderman continually intervened with Romanian individuals and tried to save as many Jews as possible. In addition, "those who survived could not have done so without leaders such as Siegfried Jagendorf—the man who mastered the game of survival in the wilderness of exile," says Aron Hirt-Manheimer in his comments in the book, *Jagendorf's Foundry: Memoir of the Romanian Holocaust.*

Siegfried Jagendorf, for instance, convinced the Romanian officials in Moghilev to recruit a small task force to repair the city's nonfunctioning electrical system as well as a foundry. The handful of persons grew to 15,000 who survived the war.

Jewish leader Dr. Filderman had a lifeline to General Ion Antonescu, the Romanian dictator, as they were school classmates. When Antonescu and his government first consented to the 1942 German request that the Jews of the Old Kingdom and Southern Transylvania be deported to the death cams in Poland, Dr. Filderman "framed the Jewish question in terms of national honor," according to author Aron Hirt-Manheimer. Germany had no right to ask the Romanians to turn over its Jewish population. Jews were willing to pay a "king's ransom" to redeem the Jews of Romania. "It was this intermingling of factors combined with external pressures from the Swiss, Vatican, Americans and others, that induced Bucharest to begin formulating a more independent policy in dealing with its Jewish minority," says writer Aron Hirt-Manheimer.

Of course, the man who bears the responsibility of the murder of Jews in Romania was General Ion Antonescu—who gained power near the end of the King Carol rule in 1940. At the same time, he was also responsible for saving many Jews. "But this in no way absolves him from his huge war crime against the Romanian people, " wrote Rabbi Moses Rosen. His government was responsible for the murder of at least 200,000 Romanian Jews during the war, through pogroms carried out by his army and the deportations to Transnistria.

Despite continual German demands for the deportation of Romanian Jews, Gen. Antonescu in 1942 finally refused transporting Jews to their death. He even brought back some veterans, seniors and widows from Transnistria. The Jews in Bucharest did not have to wear the yellow star and henceforth, Romania never sent Jews north to the German camps. In 1943, Antonescu stopped the killing of about 50,000 surviving Romanian deportees in Transnistria by the retreating German troops because these terrible murders would give him a "bad reputation," according to author Hirt-Manheimer. He may also have read the writing on the wall in that by early 1943, especially, after the battle of Stalingrad, there were signs that the Axis powers would not be victorious.

Later, Ira Hirschmann who had gone on a secret mission to Turkey for President Franklin D. Roosevelt to negotiate with Eichmann's agents for the rescue of Jewish children would save about 100,000 Romanian Jews, including thousands of children, in exchange for four visas to Alexandre Cretziannu, Romanian minister to Turkey. The visas saved the Romanian diplomat's life.

Who was General Antonescu and how did he get to rule Romania? To understand his rise to power, we have to return to Romania between the wars. This country had "the distinction of having the largest fascist movement in the Balkans," according to Charles Bachman in his book *Romania: a country study*. This extreme nationalist, far-right, anti-Semitic, semi-legal fascist group was known as the Iron Guard and was founded in 1930 by Corneilu Zelea Codreanu who had backing from industrialists as well as from Mussolini and Hitler. Officially, called "Archangel Michael," its fanatical members were known as Legionnaires. They wore green shirts, boots and little bags of "sacred" Romanian soil hanging from their necks. These terrorists and assassins would constantly beat up Jews and leftists.

Codreanu himself a demogogue and a shrill anti-Semite, has been described as a "murderer, a Jew baiter and a thug."

King Carol, who in August 1940 decreed his own anti-Semitic racial laws, eventually cracked down on the extreme right-wing Iron Guard. The Iron Guard had gained 66 seats at the election of 1937. The King, jealous of Codreanu's power, dissolved that party. He also ordered Codreanu shot on the night of November 29/30, 1938.The King killed 13 Iron Guard senior leaders in prison and arrested thousands of others. The King brought General Antonescu into the government. But with the fall of France and Britain's desperate plight in the latter half of 1940, the King's position became untenable. The country was beginning to display a fascination with the Nazi political model and Romanian lands had been taken away and given to Russia, Hungary and Bulgaria and the people held the King responsible for this loss of land. In September 1940, King Carol was forced to abdicate in favor of his son Michael. Not long thereafter Romania became a satellite of Nazi Germany. The government's first act was to cancel Romanian citizenship for Jews. By this time, with the King gone, Antonescu had grabbed all the power. Since young King Michael's influence was obviously reduced, the General assumed the title of Conducator (leader). His strength lay in the fact that he represented the armed forces. At first, General Antonescu cooperated with the Iron Guard, but it was only a matter of time, until it, too, clashed with Antonescu. In November 1940, the fascist Legionnaires launched a reign of terror and killed and murdered advisors to the King in revenge for Codreanu's killing. The revolt was put down by the Army, but not before the Legionnaires in January 1941 carried out a "particularly ghastly massacre and mutilation of nearly 200 Jewish civilians in a slaughterhouse." Jews were beheaded and hung on iron hooks in the slaughterhouse. Author Robert St. John summed up his impression of the Romanians: "volatile, unpredictable, corrupt beyond imagination and cruel beyond forgiveness."

Romania, ally of Hitler, would go down to defeat in World War II. Near the end of the war, on August 23, 1944, King Michael arrested Antonescu and his ministers and declared a cease-fire. The next day, Romania, which had signed an armistice with the Allied powers, now declared war on Germany. The Russian army occupied Bucharest on August 31, 1944.

Antonescu and his henchmen as well as their families were executed by the Soviets. Romanian revisionists have attempted to rehabilitate Antonescu, saying he was only "moderately anti-Semitic." Holocaust historian Radu Ioanid notes "Romania's attempt to rehabilitate a World War II fascist leader comes as no surprise. Other countries in East Europe," he says, "attempt to rehabilitate war criminals." Yet the case of Romania is the "most egregious; nowhere else in Europe has a mass murderer, Adolf Hitler's faithful ally until the very end, a man who once declared war on the United States, been honored as a national hero, inspired the erection of public monuments and had streets named after him."

Jewish Theater, Teatrul Evreiese De State, T.E.S., Iuliu Barash Str., Bucharest.

Jewish Agency for Israel (Sochnut), Bv. Kogalniceau 57, Bucharest. Tel: 312-52-94.

Monument to the Struma ship, Cemetery, Cimitirul Guirgiului, Soslaua Giorgiului, Bucharest. This monument, while not exactly in the center of the city, is dedicated to the cargo ship Struma and the 769 men, women and children who only wanted to reach the Jewish homeland in the then British mandate of Palestine. All they desired was to escape fascism, survive the Nazis and make a new life. They had boarded the ship in the Romanian port of Constanta. The passengers had been promised a decent ship, but not only was it technically unfit for passengers—it did not even have a kitchen—Though not seaworthy it sailed on December 11, 1941, and reached Istanbul. The Turks refused to allow the passengers to depart from the ship. The British too, were extremely intransigent and refused to allow any of the passengers to move on to Palestine. To the British they were illegal immigrants. The Turks demanded that the British solve the problem and the latter again refused to become involved. "Finally

A poster at the Jewish Theater, Bucharest. (Photo by Ben G. Frank)

Monument to the Struma ship, Bucharest. (Photo by Ben G. Frank)

on the night of February 23, 1942, the Turks towed the Struma to a point outside their territorial waters and, despite the passengers' appeals for help and even attempts at resistance, cut the ship loose and sent it floating without food, water, or fuel," writes Holocaust historian Leni Yahil. An explosion occurred shortly afterwards and the Struma sank immediately. Leni Yahil said that Turkish rescue boats did not go out to pick up survivors until the next day. They found a single person in the choppy waters. The ship was sunk by a Russian submarine for unknown reasons.

Ronald S. Lauder Elementary School and Kindergarten is located behind the Jewish Theater, Iuliu Barash Str. 15, Bucharest. Founded in 1997, the school has four kindergarten classes and two elementary school grades. Languages taught here are Romanian, Hebrew and English.

Joint Distribution Committee, Sfinta Vineri Str., 9-11, Bucharest. 70478.Tel: 401-614-8684. Shortly after it was founded in 1914, the newly-founded American Jewish Joint Distribution Committee responded in 1915 with financial support because of the dire conditions of the Jewish community in Romania during in the First World War. Between 1919 and 1938, JDC allocated more than $55 million to help Romanian Jews face a difficult post-war economic conditions as well as rising anti-Semitism, once the Fascist Iron Guard took power. Even when the Jews were deported to Transnistria, JDC was permitted to provide limited assistance. While the majority of the Jews in Bucharest survived, they, too, had to be aided by JDC. The Communists forced the JDC to leave the country in 1949. When Nicolae Ceausescu drew closer to the West, he allowed JDC to return to Romania in 1967, giving it the distinction of being the only volunteer relief organization invited to operate in an Eastern European country. Since those days, JDC has provided food, shelter, clothing and medical attention to the elderly and impoverished. The group is in reality a safety net to needy Jewish seniors. Education is also a major area of concentration for JDC which is now focusing on restructuring the Talmud Torah system set up by the late Chief Rabbi Rosen.

All the relief and welfare contributions of the JDC are distributed by the local community.

Iasi (Jassy)

This was the Moldavian home during World War I of the Royal family. Queen Marie and other members of the Royal family fled here after the Germans captured Bucharest.

Because it is flat, Moldavia has suffered invasion after invasion, including six invasions by the Russians in the 18th and 19th centuries. "A hotbed of Romanian nationalism," notes author Robert Kaplan, in describing this land. In 1859, Alexandru Ian Cuza proclaimed the first state of modern Romania here.

This was also the home of Elena Magda Lupescu. In Iasi, the Moldavian capital, just before World War II broke out, about 100,000 people inhabited the city, 50,000 of them were Jews. The town had a tradition of anti-Semitism. Official and local propaganda in the early 1940s made Jews out to be "enemy aliens," "Bolshevik agents," and "parasites on the Romanian nation," cites Ioanid.

Professor A.C. Cuza (no relation to Alexandru Ian Cuza, the first prince of modern Romania, who declared independence in 1859) taught at the University of Iasi. One of Professor Cuza's disciples was Cornelieu Zelea Codreanu, the founder of the fascist Legion of the Archangel Michael. Codreanu began his career in Iasi in the 1920s.

The Romanians accused the Jews of hiding so-called Romanian deserters, who were really Soviet paratroopers when the latter moved into Bessarabia in 1940.

Another horrifying incident occurred during those days in 1941. The Romanians crammed about 4,300 Jews from the Iasi region into padlocked cattle cars, which traveled around an area in the countryside for almost a week. Nearly 3,000 of these occupants died of thirst and asphyxiation aboard those death trains.

On June 28/29 1941, thousands of Jews were killed in one of the most savage pogroms of World War II, the Iasi pogrom, perhaps the most infamous Holocaust event in Romania during

World War II. The pogrom was orchestrated by the Romanian army, police, and town citizens. The police summoned 6,000 Jews to come to their headquarters to change their identity cards. They were immediately set upon by soldiers and policemen and beaten to death in the most horrifying manner,"using the butts of their rifles to smash open the skulls of men, women and children," noted Rabbi Moses Rosen.

"Huge piles of bodies filled the large courtyard of the police station and a river of blood ran into the street, as everyone of the Jews was butchered.". In his book, Rosen adds, "This happened in the morning, the center of a European town, with the Christian population looking on."

To this day, it is difficult to say exactly how many Jews died in the pogroms at Iasi. Estimates range from 3,200 to about 13,000, according to Ioanid. He adds that the lower figure was that of revisionist Romanian historians. Some Communist officials had put the death toll at 10,000 and others at the 13,000 figure. Author Sanborne says 7,000 Jews were massacred on that single day in June 1941. One Nazi official commented disdainfully: "*pogroms* are a Slavic specialty."

The crimes committed by the Antonescu regime here at Iasi and in the transit camps in Transnistria were among the "most atrocious of the Holocaust," according to historian Ioanid.

Under the Ceausescu regime, the government diluted or denied the responsibility of Romanians in the slaughter of the Jews, placing all blame on the Germans.

Synagogue, Sinagogilor st. 1, Iasi.

Community Center, str. Elena Doamna, 15, Iasi. Tel: 032-11-44-14.

Kosher restaurant, str. Elena Doamna nr. 15, Iasi. Tel: 032-11-78-93

Arad

Community Center, str. Tribunul Dobra, 10, 2900, Arad. Tel: 057-28-13-10.

Senior Citizen Home and Kosher restaurant, are located in the same building, at Episcopiei nr 22, 2900 Arad. Tel: 057-28-07-31.

Cluj

Synagogue, Horea St., 21, Cluj
Community Center, str. Tipografiei 25, 3400 Cluj. Tel: 064-19-66-00.
Kosher restaurant, str., Paris nr 5-7, Cluj. Tel: 064-19-16-31.

Sighet

Synagogue, Basarabia st. 8, Sighet.
Community Center, str. Viseului 8, 4925, Sighet. Tel: 062-31-16-52.

Timisoara

Synagogue, Resita st. 55, Timisoara.
Community Center, str. Gh. Lazar, 5, 1900 Timisoara. Tel: 056-20-16-84.
Kosher restaurant, str., Marasesti nr 1 e, Timisoara. Tel: 056-20-16-84.

Suggested Reading

Bachman, Rondald D., *Romania: a country study.* Washington, D.C.: Federal Research Division, Library of Congress, 1989
Balas, Egon, *Will to Freedom: A Perilous Journey Through Fascism and Communism.*Syracuse: Syracuse University Press, 2000.
Baron, Salo, "The Jews in Roumania" (pamphlet). New York: American Jewish Congress, 1930.
Bauer, Yehuda, *A History of the Holocaust.* New York: Franklin Watts, 1982.
Behr, Edward, *Kiss The Hand You Cannot Bite:The Rise and Fall of the Ceausescus.* New York: Villard Books, 1991.
Ben-Sasson, H.H., *A History of the Jewish People.* Cambridge, MA: Harvard University Press, 1969.
Fermor, Patrick Leigh, *Between The Woods And the Water, On Foot to Constantinople from the Hook of Holland: The Middle Danube to the Iron Gates.* New York: Viking, 1986.

Hirschmann, Ira, *Caution to the Winds.* New York: David McKay Company, Inc., 1962.

Hoffman, Charles, *Gray Dawn: The Jews of Eastern Europe in the Post-Communist Era.* New York: Aaron Asher Books, HarperCollins Publishers, 1992.

Hoffman, Eva, *Exit Into History: A Journey Through The New Eastern Europe.* New York: Viking, 1993.

Ioanid, Radu, *The Holocaust in Romania: the Destruction of Jews and Gypsies Under the Antonescu Regime, 1940-1944.* Chicago: Ivan R. Dee (Published in association with the United States Holocaust Memorial Museum), 2000.

Jagendorf Siegfried, *Jagendorf's Foundry: Memoir of the Romanian Holocaust, 1941-1944* Introduction and Commentaries by Aron Hirt-Manheimer. New York: HarperCollins Publishers, 1991.

Kaplan, Robert D., *Balkan Ghosts: A Journey Through History.* New York: St. Martin's Press, 1993.

Krinsky, Carol Herselle, *Synagogues of Europe: Architecture, History, Meaning.* Cambridge, MA: MIT Press, 1985.

Lukacs, John, *The Last European War September 1939/December 1941.* Garden City, New York: Anchor Press/Doubleday, 1976.

Malcomson, Scott L. *Borderlands-Nation and Empire.* Boston and London: Faber and Faber, 1994.

Rothschild, Joseph, *East Central Europe between the Two World Wars.* Seattle and London: University of Washington Press, 1974.

Sanborne, Mark, *Romania.* New York: Facts On File, Inc., 1996.

Seton-Watson, R.W. *A History of The Roumanians: From Roman Times to the Completion of Unity.* Cambridge, MA: Cambridge University Press, 1934.

Treptow, Kurt W., editor, *A History of Romania.* Iasi: The Center for Romanian Studies, The Foundation for Romanian Culture and Studies, 1997

Vital, David, *The Future of the Jews.* Cambridge, MA, and London: Harvard University Press, 1990.

Yahil, Leni, *The Holocaust: The Fate of European Jewry, 1932-1945.* New York. And Oxford: Oxford University Press, 1990.

Bulgaria
Located in the Powder Keg
of Europe

Bulgaria, is one of the least known tourist destinations in Europe. That's a shame! This is a beautiful country with enough five-star hotels, first class restaurants, and good guides to show you the sites and try to make you feel at home.

Where else but in Sofia can you travel 15 minutes to nearby Vitosha Mountain and ski on some of the best slopes in the world? As tourists, you can not meet a more friendly and truly happy people than these eight million men, women and children of Bulgaria, who are going through difficult economic times, but still manage to wear that welcome sign on their sleeves.

History pervades the atmosphere. These Balkan lands are the sites of wars and conflicts, ethnic cleansing and mass murder. World War I started next-door in Serbia and need we be reminded of the recent war in Kosovo—a touchy subject in Bulgaria, despite the 1999 visit of President Bill Clinton to Sofia, where he thanked this nation for their help in that war. The importance of the Balkans in U.S. foreign policy was underscored by Clinton, when he noted that he was proud to be the first American president to visit Bulgaria.

The tourist quickly recognizes that capital city Sofia pales before the shining lights of Prague and Budapest. But by traveling to Bulgaria you will see a part of Europe that is certainly worthwhile to explore for its culture, history and Jewish community.

Bulgaria Saved Jews

While the dramatic rescue of Danish Jews is well-known and has been heralded around the world, not many know that Bulgaria, a close ally of Hitler in World War II, refused to allow the Germans to send its Jewish citizens to their death. "Not one Bulgarian Jew was sent to the death camps in Poland," according to historian Dr. Michael Bar-Zohar. Actually, Bulgarian Jewry became the only Jewish community under the Nazis "whose number increased during the Second World War," according to Bar-Zohar.

Not only did the 50,000 Jews survive, but after World War II, nearly the whole community picked itself up and emigrated to Israel. Remaining in Bulgaria were about 5,000 to 7,000 Jews.

This is not to say the Bulgarians did not commit crimes in World War II. They did. They rounded up 11,343 Jews from Thrace and Macedonia which the Bulgarians occupied on behalf of the Germans, and shipped them off to Auschwitz. "The deportation and the way it was carried out by Bulgarian officers, Bulgarian soldiers, and Bulgarian policemen, has left a dark, grim shadow over Bulgaria's past," according to Ben-Zohar.

In 1943, the Bulgarians may have robbed Jews; they may have expelled Jews to the countryside; their police may have picked up Jews and forced them to work as slave laborers, but they never carried out the orders to deport Jews from Old Bulgaria.

"The fact that not one Bulgarian Jew was transported to Auschwitz was not matched by any other country in Europe," notes Bar-Zohar.

Still, other satellites—Croatia, Slovakia, Vichy France—continued their anti-Jewish policies. "The stand taken by Bulgaria was, therefore, in that sense, extraordinary," wrote Holocaust historian Yehuda Bauer in his book *A History of the Holocaust*.

Why did the Bulgarians desist from massacring Jews? Some say that by 1943, the news of the fate of Polish Jews had reached Bulgarian politicians. By March-April 1943, the Germans had been defeated in Stalingrad. The tide was turning in the Allies' favor. An outcry arose from a number of Bulgarian legislators, the Church, even from King Boris III himself, who halted the deportation of the Jews from within the boundaries of Old Bulgaria.

The drama of Bulgarian Jews' deliverance is indeed worth telling and we shall discuss it when we visit the Holocaust exhibit in the main synagogue in Sofia.

The Country and Its History

President Bill Clinton said so himself: "This is a wonderful country! Come here and help," he messaged to Americans when he spoke in Sofia on November 22, 1999.

Anyone who comes to visit, study or work here should take a real close look at this country. Plains, plateaus, hills, mountains, gorges, deep river valleys are all part of the scene. Actually, mountains cover most of Bulgaria. This pleasant, lush-green country welcomes tourists to its picturesque villages and sandy beaches along the Black Sea.

Bulgaria is a country about the size of Tennessee, and is located in the heart of the Balkan Peninsula. Covering nearly 43,000 square miles, it borders on Macedonia and Serbia in the west; Romania and the Danube River in the north; the Black Sea on the east and Turkey and Greece on the south. Eighty-six percent of the population is Bulgarian; 10 percent ethnic Turks and the remaining four to five percent are mostly Gypsies, Armenians, Russians, Macedonians and Greeks, according to author Steven Otfinowski. Regarding religion, 85 percent of the population are Bulgarian Orthodox, 13 percent Moslem. As in most Balkan countries, most people have left the farm and headed to the cities. Today, seventy-one percent of the population lives in urban areas.

Today, Bulgaria has made a commitment to democracy and economic reform spearheaded by the government of Prime Minister Ivan Kostov, who has led the country to the doorstep of the European Union. There are many who believe that with belt-tightening reforms and privatization programs firmly in place, this former Soviet bloc country's economic renaissance looks set to last. Only time will tell.

The world's nations should pay attention to Bulgaria and its neighbors. This is a tinder box of the world that has blown up into violence, into wars, into internecine battles, and that ugly term, "ethnic cleansing" in a land once called Yugoslavia, a neighbor of Bulgaria. Bulgaria's location at the "nexus of the European and Asian continents brought strong cultural and political influences from both the east and west," according to author Glenn E. Curtis in his book, *Bulgaria, a country study.*"

Keep in mind, too, that this nation is located on the border of Asiatic Turkey. Just across from the Black Sea are the Russians whom the Bulgarians throughout history have embraced as brothers and liberators. The Russians actually freed Bulgaria from 500 years of Ottoman rule in 1877-1878. If any country in Europe epitomizes a Balkan past, it is Bulgaria, the last country to be freed from the Ottomans.. The Turks in large part turned the Bulgarians into vassals.

Much of Bulgaria's history is rooted in the past. About 3,000 years ago, a people known as the Thracians were probably the first to arrive in Bulgaria. Although the Thracians disappeared, their geographical name, Thrace, remains to this very day a geographic section of the Balkans, namely Greece. The Thracians were followed by the Romans, by the Huns under Attila who nearly destroyed the entire country; and by the Slavs who migrated to the area from southern Poland and Russia in the Sixth Century.

Less than a century later, a group of fierce warriors called Bulgars- thundered across the plains of Central Asia on horseback into what we now call Bulgaria. The Bulgars, who have always been vulnerable to invasions, were warriors who had migrated from a region between the Urals and the Volga to the steppes north of the Caspian Sea. They quickly moved across the Danube into the Balkans. In 681, with 285,000 persons, the Bulgars crossed the Danube under Khan Asparukh into a land they claimed as their own and began interbreeding with the Slavs.

"The word Bulgar comes from an Old Turkic word that means one of mixed nationality." The Bulgars intermingled with the Slavs and out of this "co-mingling of the two groups, a new people were born—Bulgarians," explains author Steven Otfinoski.

According to the *Encyclopedia Judaica,* "the faith of the early Bulgarian Christians was, however, a syncretistic mixture of Christian, Jewish, and pagan beliefs." Boris I converted to Christianity in 864—probably his most important act—and the King showed no mercy to those who would not follow him, says Jewish historian Vicki Tamir in her book, *Bulgaria and Her Jews: The History of a Dubious Symbosis.*

Twice in its history did Bulgaria reach the apex of power. First, Simeon I, known as Simon the Great, (893-927), came to power in 893 and gave himself the title of Czar—a Slavic version of "Caesar." He ushered in a golden age of art, literature, and trade. Simon conquered Albania, Macedonia, Serbia and some areas of the Byzantine Empire. He extended the boundaries of Bulgaria. After Simon died in 927, Bulgaria's power declined. In 1018 the country was swallowed up by the Byzantine Empire.

By 1186, however, Bulgarians broke free from Byzantium and established the Second Bulgarian Kingdom (1185-1393) under Ivan I, who again made the country a Balkan power.

Bulgarian power did not last long. By the end of the 13th Century, the Turks had taken over all of Bulgaria. In 1453, the Turks broke the back of Byzantium. Constantinople fell to the invaders and with them came five centuries of Turkish suppression. The Turks brought with them their government and their culture and their Moslem religion. By the end of the 16th century, two-thirds of the population of Sofia was Turkish.

This is not to say that Ottoman rule was all bad. As historian Vicki Tamir notes, when it was working efficiently, Ottoman rule "provided a more orderly system of government than the Bulgarian people had hitherto enjoyed." Still, from the 16th century to the 18th century, suffering Bulgarians unleashed a series of revolts. All were brutally put down by the Turks. To this day, Bulgarians talk of the "Turkish yoke."

By the late 19th century, Turkish oppression was heavy. The Turks cruelly put down an insurrection in 1876 and this aroused indignation in the west. In 1877 Russian forces attacked. By January 1878, the Russians stood before Constantinople. "The Ottoman era had come to an end," as historian Vicki Tamir notes. During that Russo-Turkish War

(1877-78) Russian troops had marched in and enlisted Bulgarian patriots to fight with them. At the Battle of Shipka Pass, the Russians and Bulgarians, including Bulgarian Jews, were hopelessly outnumbered by Turkish troops, but they bravely resisted. Some 13,000 Turks would die in the fighting as well as 5,500 Russians.

After five centuries of Turkish rule, Bulgaria was liberated.

The Treaty of San Stefano in 1878 established Bulgaria as an autonomous republic within the Ottoman Empire. The Turks had ceded about 60 percent of the Balkan Peninsula to Bulgaria. But the West would not stand for this treaty which would have allowed "the Russian Bear" to enter the Balkans.

The Treaty of San Stefano never went into operation. The Big Powers simply revised the Treaty of San Stefano when they met at the Congress of Berlin in 1878 and reduced the area of the country by more than half. Southern Bulgaria was turned into a Turkish autonomous province. Macedonia remained part of the Ottoman Empire and it and Thrace were put beyond Bulgarian control.

"Bulgaria emerged mutilated," notes historian Tamir. Bulgarians felt "a burning sense of injustice was meted out to it by the great powers," says R. J. Crampton, author of *A Concise History of Bulgaria.*

With the signing of the Treaty of Berlin, the Bulgarian state was born. In 1879, Alexander of Battenberg, a German prince, was appointed Bulgaria's ruler. He did not last long. He was forced to abdicate. In August 1887, Prince Ferdinand of Saxe Gotham took the throne which he kept for 31 years, first as the Prince of Bulgaria, 1887-1908, and then as King of the Bulgarians, 1908-1918. In 1908, he declared Bulgaria independent and the country became a kingdom.

THE BALKAN WARS

During the next 60 years, Bulgaria was to go to war four times, including two Balkan wars, to redress its grievances, only to fail each time.

In 1914, when World War I broke out, Bulgaria feigned neutrality. But within a year, it sided with Germany and the Austro-Hungarian Empire. Bulgaria wanted "to back the powers more likely to satisfy her territorial ambitions," notes historian Tamir. Germany took advantage of this and actually stripped the country of its goods and services. Left to starve, Bulgaria was totally defeated. The people blamed King Ferdinand's regime for the humiliation. On October 3, 1918, Ferdinand abdicated and left the country in favor of his 24-year-old son Boris III, who was to play a major role in deciding the fate of the Jews in his kingdom.

Bulgaria was devastated by the Great War. Jews fought heroically with their Bulgarian neighbors. As historian Tamir notes: "A disproportionately large amount of Jewish blood was spilled for the Bulgarian fatherland during the two Balkan wars and World War I." Under the Treaty of Neuilly, Bulgaria was forced to pay heavy doses of reparations to Serbia and its allies. Bulgaria lost Macedonia, which it had taken during the war. It lost southern Dobruja to Romania. It lost the border town of Tzaribrod to Yugoslavia and the Aegean coastline to Greece.

The world of the 1930s brought wave after wave of economic crises, the overthrow of legitimate governments, and in their wake, authoritarianism across Eastern Europe. Boris III promised a return to constitutional government; it never happened. He took complete control of the country.

Meanwhile, the Germans had also penetrated Bulgaria economically which was very impressed with German technology and military might.

WORLD WAR II

When Romania was dismembered in 1940, Bulgaria received something out of that deal with Hitler. The so-called Vienna Award restored southern Dobruja to Bulgaria. "Public jubilation in Sofia was such that Bulgarian gratitude to Berlin would henceforth know no bounds," wrote Vicki Tamir. Bulgaria tied her destiny to Germany. The age-old dream of a

Greater Bulgaria, as laid out by the San Stefano Treaty, had finally, with the help of Hitler, been fulfilled.

Therefore, on March 1, 1941, in Vienna, in the presence of the Italian and Nazi leaders, Bulgaria signed the Tripartite Pact and became an official ally of Germany, Italy and Japan. German troops entered the country on their way to attack Yugoslavia and Greece. Author Bar-Zohar notes that Bulgaria was ready to do almost anything to satisfy her German ally: "Of all Germany's vassals, Bulgaria held the honor of being the most willing to cooperate with the Reich on Jewish matters.". Because the Germans wanted to free its troops for the Russian front, Bulgaria got Thrace and Macedonia as an occupying power.

During World War II, the Bulgarians, even though an ally of the Germans, never declared war on the Russians. In fact, the Embassy of the USSR functioned and flew its flag, the hammer and sickle; while down the street, the Nazi swastika flew over the Embassy of Germany.

In August 1943, King Boris made a visit to Hitler. It was to be his last. Historians tell us he argued furiously with the Nazi leader. The latter demanded a Bulgarian commitment to send troops to the Eastern front. Boris III declined. On August 28, at the age of 49, the king of Bulgaria suddenly died. Mystery has surrounded his death ever since. Some believe he was poisoned.

The Soviet Union invaded Bulgaria on September 8, 1944. The Fatherland Front, a group of parties led by the Communists took power in the country. The typical Communist takeover occurred. So-called non-Communist ene-mies of the people were shot or sent to camps. Private property was seized. The Red-dominated Fatherland Front quickly gained control. A one-party system was imposed at the end of 1947. Communism would rule with an iron fist.

Georgi Dimitrov, the chief Communist leader, became head of the government and ruled the country from 1947 to 1949. By 1948, the Communists possessed total control of the nation. But severe shortages of goods and services would constantly wretch the nation.

Bulgaria of all the East European countries, was the most closely allied to the USSR. It also was the Warsaw Pact country "most dependent economically on Soviet aid," says Glen E.

Curtis, in *Bulgaria, a country study*. Todor Zhivkov and the Communist Party maintained a solid grip on the nation. He would rule from 1956 to 1989. He was forced to resign in the 1989 repudiation of Communism. He was arrested and later charged with abuse of power and misuse of government proper and money. Despite being sentenced to seven years imprisonment for misusing state funds, Todor Zhivkov wangled a hasty release and lived comfortably in an affluent Sofia suburb until he died in August 1998.

A somewhat tarnished reputation still hovers over Bulgaria. Pope John Paul II was wounded in an assassination attempt by a Turkish nationalist who claimed the plot had been hatched by Bulgarian and Soviet intelligence agents. Bulgaria was listed by U.S. State Department as a sponsor of terrorism and a supplier of arms to terrorists. Zhivkov also initiated a drastic policy of forced assimilation. In 1984 and 1985, Bulgarian authorities forced the Turks to adopt Bulgarian names. Some of the people who refused to change their names were killed by Bulgarian troops. Others were forced to leave the country. The Turks would not give in and 300,000 fled to Turkey.

Later, the first non-Communist Bulgarian prime minister, Philip Dimitrov, in a visit to Turkey, apologized to his former Turkish citizens. The Turks were invited back; about 200,000 returned.

On November 9, 1989, the Berlin Wall was torn down boulder by boulder. In November 1989, 5,000 persons marched on the National Assembly in Sofia, the largest unofficial demonstration in over four decades. A week later, dictator Todor Zhivkov resigned. The Communists changed their name to Bulgarian Socialist Party. In June 1990, free elections were held and the Socialists (i.e., former Communists) won a majority of seats. The new Socialists had no intention of dismantling the state they had spent the past 40 years building.

Totalitarianism may have been disbanded, but it would take time for democracy to take hold. A decade was to pass until the Bulgarians decided they really wanted democracy. "If Bulgaria is to be integrated into Europe, the government will have to continue to confirm to the democratic practices established in the post-totalitarian years," writes R.J. Crampton in *A Concise*

History of Bulgaria. The country is trying to rid itself of old gods. In 1999, Bulgaria finally tore down of some of the Communist statues. It even dismantled the mausoleum of Georgi Dimitrov, who for 45 years had been deified by the ruling Communists. Bulgaria has been given preliminary consideration for membership in the European Union. But it could take several years until she becomes a member.

Bulgaria probably will never return to the Communist system. But how it moves on the bumpy road toward a democratic system of government and a market economy depends in large part on its economic progress.

Notable Jews

Sarah who became **Queen Theodora**. In 1346, King Ivan Alexander divorced his wife and married a beautiful, intelligent Jewess from Turnovo, at that time the capital of Bulgaria. But Sarah converted and became Queen Theodora. Like Queen Esther, however, she did protect her people. Author Michael Bar-Zohar notes, "while Bulgaria often followed the written politics of her neighbors, including anti-Jewish legislation and the expulsion edicts toward the Jews adopted in 1355, they were never implemented. The story does not end there. In 1356 the Turks crossed Bulgaria, and unable to check Murad's military drive, Ivan Shishman concluded a peace treaty with the sultan and in 1375 gave him his sister Maria (or Mara) daughter of the Jewish woman, in marriage. Thus a Christian Jewish princess was converted to Islam, presumably to please a Muslim sovereign who had fallen in love with her, as her Christian father had fallen in love with her Jewish mother.

"It is one of the many ironies of history that the last Bulgarian king of an indigenous Bulgarian dynasty, was, according to Jewish law, a Jew." Together with the people's eloquently attested uneasiness with Orthodox Christianity, this attitude towards Judaism might in part account for the absence of Christian fervor and fidelity to the Cross when the Turks appeared on the scene, and conversion to Islam became the order of the day, declares historian Vicki Tamir.

Emil Shekerdjiski. He was a young Communist writer and organizer who led a partisan band against the Nazis. In World War II, he fought to the death rather than fall into the hands of the Germans. During the Communist era, the Library in the Jewish Center was named after him, according to Charles Hoffman in his book, *Gray Dawn: The Jews of Eastern Europe in the Post-Communist Era.*

A Brief History

Jews lived in Bulgaria even before Slavs and Bulgars settled the country. They probably arrived here during the time of the First Temple in 600 B.C.

After Emperor Trajan's victories over the Dacians in the second century, Jews in this area moved into northern Bulgaria, including Romania.

With the destruction of the Second Temple in A.D. 70, more Jews immigrated. Scholars have recorded a gravestone, discovered in Nikopol in the Second Century, which featured a drawing of a Menorah.

Even today, Bulgarian Jewish leaders are quick to point out the Bulgars came from the lands of the Khazars. The latter and the proto-Bulgarians resembled each other in looks and in customs. This is important in view of the Khazar conversion to Judaism in the Eighth Century. A strong Judaizing movement existed in that part of the Crimea during the time when the Bulgars crossed the Danube. Thus, a significant number of Bulgars already were Judaized before settling in the area.

Asparukh's army was neither ignorant of nor averse to Jewish religious practices, which were effectively established by 740. Ninth Century Bulgaria was ripe for conversion to another religion. "Had there been a concerted effort on the part of the rabbis to present Judaism as an institutionalized religion, a church of some authority, they could have transformed Bulgaria into another Khazar state, a Jewish kingdom on the Balkan Peninsula," states historian Tamir.

When King Boris I (852-89) converted to Christianity in 863, the Jews were not persecuted though they had been accused of proselytizing among the Bulgarians. His son Simeon (893-927) symbolizes a Golden Age for Bulgaria and its Jews. During this period, large numbers of Greek Jews emigrated to Bulgaria, including Nikopol, Vidin and Sofia. Even though members of the Eastern Church, the Bulgarian church never invoked the vicious hatred of Jews of the Greek and Russian Orthodox churches.

The Jewish religion was known to the population. The Bulgarians sent questions about Christianity to Pope Nicholas asking about regulations concerning such items as, when do the first fruits arrive; on which day does the Sabbath fall, Saturday or Sunday; how should animals be eaten and slaughtered?

By the 10th Century, Jewish settlements existed all along the Danube. A century later, Jewish traders and merchants came here from Italy and the area of what later would become Yugoslavia. The Bulgarian attitude toward Jews was favorable, according to the *Encyclopedia Judaica*. Many Jews fleeing the Crusades found safe haven here where Jewish life prospered during the Second Bulgarian Kingdom (1185-1394).

From the fourteenth through the sixteenth centuries, substantial numbers of Iberian, German, Hungarian and French Jews arrived in Bulgaria.

While the vast majority of the Jews in Bulgaria today are Sephardim, it was not always so. Actually, the Ashkenazim predate the Sephardim. By and large, until the Sephardim arrived in the 15th century, the Jews of Bulgaria and Greece as well as those in Serbia, were Romaniots. The Romaniots had their own special prayer book, which was eventually replaced by the Sephardic prayer book. Only a minority spoke Bulgarian.

The Ashkenazim may have established synagogues in Sofia, Plovdiv, Varna and Russe, but it would fall to the Sephardim to dominate Jewish life in Bulgaria. Over the years they even maintained ties with the Spanish Embassy. Today, if you can prove you are a descendant of Sephardic Jews, you can even emigrate to Spain.

Rabbi Joseph Caro, author of the *Shulkhan Arukh,* settled in

Nikopol in 1523 and set up a yeshiva there. He wrote a famous work, known as "House of Joseph."

By the 19th Century, the Ottoman Empire began to crumble and in 1878 Bulgaria shook off the "Ottoman yoke." "The Bulgarians, unlike the Romanians, accepted the Congress of Berlin's guarantee of equal rights to the Jewish community and Jews entered the new nation as full citizens, according to Steven Mark Mallinger in his booklet, *A Brief Introduction to the Jewish Community of Bulgaria.*

A cultural renaissance existed in pre-World War I years. Jewish histories were written. Sephardic rabbinic commentaries were issued. A Hebrew publishing house in Sofia produced books on mysticism. Newspapers and other publications, including Ladino tracts, were read by the community. Cultural events, specialized studies and a deep sense of learning were in the atmosphere. On the eve of the First World War, Jews numbered about 50,000, less than one percent of the Bulgarian population of about six million at the time.

Anti-Semitism increased during the 1930s, mainly because of Nazi influence imported from Germany and because of local marginal political groups.

Between 1939 and 1941, Bulgaria served as a gateway for thousands of European Jews fleeing Hitler.

But as the 1940s dawned, Jews found themselves in danger. When the war broke out, anti-Jewish legislation was introduced so that Bulgaria would conform to Nazi Germany's policies. Jews were restricted.

Bulgaria's rulers stripped its Jewish citizens of their civil rights and much of their personal and communal property. Most able-bodied men were sent to forced labor camps.

On December 24, 1940, "the Law for the Protection of the Nation," patterned after Nazi Nuremberg regulations, was passed and went into effect on January 23, 1941. But as we have noted, deportations of Bulgarian Jews within the boundaries of the nation proper were never carried out. Jews from Macedonia and Thrace, however, were sent to the gas chambers. *The Encyclopedia Judaica* states that 11,384 Jews were deported to their death.

According to Jewish community figures, 49,172 Jews lived in Bulgaria in the fall of 1944, three quarters of them residing in urban areas, including Sofia, with 27,700 and Plovdiv, with 5,800.

With war's end, what started as a trickle turned into a mass exodus to the Jewish homeland. Between 1949 and 1951, 44,267 Jews left for the State of Israel. This emigration hit the 90 percent mark of the Jewish population figure. Unlike Jews in other European countries leaving their former homes, Bulgarian Jews only moved to Israel. "No other Jewish community in the Diaspora has ever voluntarily uprooted itself *in toto*," points out Vicki Tamir in her book, *Bulgaria and her Jews: The History of a Dubious Symbiosis*. No other sizeable group adjusted as fast and as well to Israel as the Jews of Bulgaria, she added.

In 1945, the ax of Communist repression come down hard on Jewish life. Jewish contact with fellow international organizations was halted. All Jewish schools, hospitals, reading rooms and even some synagogue buildings were transferred to state government. Jewish schools were closed. Zionism was suppressed. The synagogues and rabbinate were left to fend for themselves. In the 1950s, Jewish clubs were used as Communist indoctrination units.

Certain Jewish holidays were banned, such as Passover and Rosh Hashanah. Even Purim was reinterpreted as a "rebellion of the oppressed Jews against the monarch and his clique." Jewish books were removed from the libraries; summer camps were closed. Jewish communal institutions were Jewish in name only. No recognized rabbis could administer religious instruction. Communist indoctrination would take place as Jews mingled with non-Jews, according to author Charles Hoffman. All young Jews were being educated by the Communist Party.

The Bulgarians followed the Soviet line so strongly that it was hard to discern which was tougher. The world was shocked in August 1955, when a Bulgarian air force plane shot down an El Al Israeli airplane that had crossed over into Bulgarian air space by error. Bulgaria severed diplomatic relations and trade with Israel following the 1967 Six-Day War. Often attacking Israel verbally, they unleashed anti-Israel invective in the halls of the United Nations.

But hateful propaganda could not dampen Jewish hearts.

They hoped for a return to Israel. It came in 1989. Communism fell. Arriving, too, were what everyone calls "the changes" of 1989, when Communism moved to a form of socialism and more freedom for the populace as well as the subsequent revival of Judaism.

The Jewish Community Today

"A small candle of Jewish life has survived here," notes Robert Djerassi, assistant to the country director for Bulgaria of the American Jewish Joint Distribution Committee.

"I was born in Bulgaria, the same year as the State of Israel, 1948," he likes to say. Now, for the first time in a half-century, the community has a future, he adds.

At the beginning of the current millennium, between 5,000 to 7,000 Jews called Bulgaria their home. Of these, between 3,000 and 4,000 live in Sofia, with 800 in Plovdiv, 220 in Varna, and 200 in Russe. According to statistics, Bulgarian Jewry should have long ago ceased to exist. The demographers say that with those small numbers, of which 90 to 95 percent are mixed marriages, they can not build a united community, let alone keep it alive. Not only that, but 50 percent of the community is above the age of 60 and 20 percent falls between the ages of 30 and 50 years old. Only 1,000 persons are between the ages of one and 18.

When discussing Eastern European Jewry, one must take into account that many Jews have kept secret the fact that they are Jewish. Djerassi opines that if you count so-called "hidden Jews," the number might reach 10,000 persons.

Despite the high rate of intermarriage and an aging population, Bulgarian Jews have not only kept Judaism alive but also have been engaged in putting forth a serious program of Jewish education. And they did this in the short time since the fall of Communism in 1989.

Problems abound: community leaders are trying to rectify the lack of Jewish education with adult classes, lecture series, and a new Jewish school. Today, prayer books, *mezuzot, dreidels* and sabbath candle holders are handed out freely to Jews.

A publishing house known as "Shalom Publishing" produces three to four books a year. They are translated into Bulgarian, including, for example, Dumont's *Jews, God and History*.

One should not always believe statistics. Jews sometimes have a strange way of surviving. There is an old Jewish proverb that warns against "sounding the death knell for any Jewish community."

East European Jewish communities may soon obtain some financial aid. During World War II, Jewish property and assets were confiscated by the Bulgarian Fascists. After the War, most of these assets and properties were "donated" to the Communist government, says Stephen Mark Mallinger, adding, "Bulgaria has been recently recognized for its progress in restoring private property to its Jewish citizens under Government Decree 225 of November 11, 1992. However, the communal properties, the schools, hospital, synagogues, lost in previous years, remain a sensitive issue." The community continues to work with both the government and legal authorities to settle the issue fairly. Hope exists that the Jewish community will obtain funds from restitution of the property taken over by the Communist government. These funds of course will help support efforts to build a strong community through education, seminars and projects, say Jewish community leaders.

The point is that in all these countries, the Jewish community of the future probably will not be Orthodox. In fact, religion may not play a huge role in the community. It may not be even be Judaism as we know it. But make no mistake about it, these Bulgarian Jews of the 21st Century are proud to be Jewish. And many will keep alive Jewish tradition, especially some of the young ones, many of whom even in their teens went through the ritual of circumcision. Jews here celebrate all the holidays and send their young children to Jewish day schools. They will belong to B'nai B'rith and other organizations and visit Israel. Like Jewish communities around the world, they, too, crowd the synagogues on high holidays. They will carry on Jewish life.

Sofia

What impresses one about Sofia is its past. Drive a short distance on the Tzarigradsco shose, (Tsars Boulevard) and you will be moving along the same road as many Jewish traders and merchants did when they traveled to Constantinople (now Istanbul). Drive on to Plovdiv, Bulgaria's second largest city, and then onto Edirne, and finally to Istanbul.

Stop off at the city center where the Parliament now stands and recall the year 1878: The Russians are about to capture Sofia from the Turks, who prepare to torch their city. Rabbi Almoz Nino pleaded with the Pasha to spare the capital. The Turkish commander did not set fire to the city and when some Turkish soldiers started a few fires themselves, a Jewish Fire Brigade rushed to the scene and put out the flames.

Indeed the Bulgarians called Constantinople "Tzarigrad, the City of the Emperors," though they really meant the earlier Roman-Greek-Orthodox Emperors and not the Turkish Sultans who replaced them in 1453.

Sofia gives you the impression of an unplanned town. This is not a high-rise building city; there are no real skyscrapers. About 1.4 million persons make Sofia the country's largest city. It sits in the foothills of the Vitosha Mountains in the western region of Bulgaria.

There are a number of good hotels, including the Kempinski, the Sheraton, and the Gloria Palace.

Founded nearly 2000 years ago by Roman Emperor Trojan, Sofia is the second oldest capital city in Europe, after Athens.

The Byzantines gave it the name Sofia in honor of Saint Sofia, whose cathedral was built centuries earlier in the heart of the city by the Romans. The Turks occupied the area in 1382. The Ottomans changed the skyline of the ancient city, building massive onion-domed mosques. In 1878, Sofia was named the capital of Bulgaria.

From a small town of 20,000, Sofia grew into a metropolis. "Today," says Steven Otfinoski, author of *Bulgaria*, "one in every nine Bulgarians lives in Sofia and 20 percent of Bulgarian industry is located here."

Home to 400 parks, the great National Museum and many other monuments attract and intrigue tourists.

JEWISH SITES IN SOFIA

Beit Am. The first stop the visitor should make is the five-story Beit Am, known as the Jewish Community Center and community headquarters at 50 Stambolijski Blvd., Sofia. This 1927 building is the address of the Jewish community of Bulgaria. You have a chance to hear not only Hebrew, but also the medieval Spanish dialect known as Ladino or "spanyol," spoken by the "seniors" or "pensioners."

Cultural events and holiday programs including the four-day "Esperanza Sephardic Cultural Festival," complete with concerts, performances, discussions, and fine cooking, all eminate from this building.

OJB "Shalom," (The umbrella organization of the Jewish Community) is located in the Beit Am, 50 Stambolijski Blvd., Sofia, Tel:00359-2-870-163, FAX: 981-11-39. E-mail: shalom@ibn.bg. Its president is usually regarded as the head of the community.

JDC-Joint Distribution Committee, 50 Stambolijski Blvd. Sofia. Tel: 00359-2- 981-43-32; or 00359-2-988-5001, FAX: 00359-2-981-45-27. E-mail: jdcbul@ibn.bg. It is certainly clear that without the aid of the American Jewish Joint Distribution Committee—and here we mean economical, financial, social and moral aid, as the Bulgarians themselves put it—the Jewish community might not have survived after the governmental changes of 1989. At least 80 percent of the social, welfare, educational costs of the Bulgarian Jewish community is borne by the American Jewish Joint Distribution Committee. For example, Jewish seniors receive health care and clothing. Here in Sofia, JDC even provides a dental clinic located in the local Jewish school.

Because of JDC and the Lauder Foundation assistance, as well as World Jewish Relief and other sponsors, Jewish life is being maintained and expanded.

Ronald S. Lauder Foundation, 50 Stambolijski Blvd., Sofia, Tel/FAX: 00359-2-980-3462. E-mail: lauder@mail.ibn.bg.

Bendichas Manos, 50 Stambolijski St., Sofia. *Bendichas Manos,*

First Lady Hillary Rodham Clinton was greeted by Robert Djerassi, assistant to the JDC Country Director for Bulgaria and a Bulgarian Jewish leader, at Beit Am, the Center of the Jewish Community in Sofia. Center is Emil Kalo, president of "Shalom."

The entrance to Beit Am *in Sofia.* (Photo by Ben G. Frank)

A few of the woman of the Bendichas Manos, the "Blessed Hands." This is a group of Bulgarian Jewish women who are keeping alive the Sephardic tradition through arts and crafts. Shown here are some of the colorful hand-made yarmulkes. (Photo by Ben G. Frank)

A few members of the young leadership of the Bulgarian Jewish Community at a café in Sofia. (Photo by Ben G. Frank)

which means "Blessed Hands,"is a wonderful art organization that occupies only one room. But its work keeps alive the Sephardic Jewish tradition through their arts and crafts. Their activities offer them a sense of belonging; a feeling for their roots, an opportunity to provide them with some additional money in these very difficult times in Bulgaria. More than 50 members aim at reviving the ethnic memory of Bulgarian Jewry through beautiful Sephardic art. They are eager to revive the tradition of their Sephardic heritage. They produce a large variety of articles: *yarmulkes, chalah* coverings, Passover and Rosh Hashana covers, Sabbath candlesticks, bookmarks. All the products are handmade and are available for purchase.

Center for Informal Jewish Education, also known as the Resource Center, 50 Stambolijski St., Sofia, Tel: 00359-2-986-2635. E-mail: jcenter@ibn.bg. By American standards, the room does not look like much. A few computers and a FAX machine attract immediate attention. Bookshelves line one wall. Without being sarcastic, the future Jewish community may come out of this one room, the meeting place of the youth of Bulgaria who gather for meetings and who supply others with Jewish education pamphlets and material. Yes, here is the future. The Resource Center publishes information on Jewish history, Zionism, Israel, and holiday celebrations. Also located in the **Informal Jewish Education Center** is the **B'nai B'rith Youth Organization, (BBYO),** 50 Stambolijski St., Sofia. About 50 members belong to this relatively new organization of young people between the ages of 13 and 18. Teenage programs are held on Saturday.

Kosher Restaurant, 50 Stambolijski, Sofia. The restaurant is open Monday through Friday, beginning at noon. It is closed on Shabbat (Saturday) and Sunday. It is kosher.

A **Café** is located in the Center for Informal Jewish Education (youth club) on the fifth floor of the building at 50 Stamboljiski Blvd., Sofia. The café is open every day from 5 P.M. to 10 P.M., except Thursdays. On Friday and Saturday nights, the hours are from 8 P.M. to 10 P.M.; on Sundays, from 10 A.M. to 2 P.M.

B'nai B'rith, 50 Stambolijski Blvd., Sofia. (Contact the "Shalom" office).

Pensioners Club, 50 Stambolijski Blvd., Sofia. Even on days when many were sick, even on bitterly cold days, they still come. They are there every day for the programs: lectures, arts and crafts, and the gym. They receive hot lunches, perhaps the only good meal they will eat the entire day. They are the "Pensioners" whose allotments have eroded with the bad times. Many of the pensioners live alone but come to Bet Am every day to sit together and chat over coffee or tea. They are lawyers, engineers, economists. All have relatives in Israel. Some long for the old days when they had good jobs. Mistakes were made under Communism, they admit, but errors were also made in the changeover to capitalism. Some prefer to call it "wild capitalism."

Jewish Agency (Sochnut), 50 Stambolijski St., Sofia, Tel: 00359-2-980-0893, FAX: 00359-2-980-0894. This organization helps put out educational material, sponsors courses on Israel, including the Hebrew language, and encourages *aliya.*

WIZO, 50 Stambolijski St., Sofia. (contact the "Shalom" office).

Maccabi, 50 Stambolijski St., Sofia.

The Jewish News newspaper, also known as **Evreiski Vesti,** is located at 50 Stambolijski, Sofia. This paper serves the organizations of **"Shalom."**

Ronald S. Lauder Foundation Jewish Day School (State School 134), 78 Pirotska st., Sofia. At this Jewish school, one can see a revival of Jewish life in Eastern Europe, even though this school offering Hebrew and Jewish subjects is located in a state school and only has a few grades for Jewish education. As new first grade classes enter and current classes advance, the number of grades dealing with Jewish subjects will obviously increase.

Hashomer Hatzair youth organization is not located in the Bet Am, but at 56 Stambolijski St., Sofia. Tel/FAX: 00359-2-899-759.

Synagogue, 16 Exarch Joseph St., Sofia, 1000. Tel: 359-2-831-273. This may very well be the largest Sephardic synagogue in Europe. It is also the last remaining Jewish house of worship in the capital city. Since the fall of Communism, it has undergone much reconstruction. The synagogue

The "Pensioners Group" meets at Beit Am in Sofia. (Photo by Ben G. Frank)

remained open during the Communist era. But probably out of fear, out of believing that prayer in a synagogue was a remnant of capitalism—did not Marx say religion was "the opiate of the people"?—young people never went there.

This synagogue uses Sephardic prayer ritual. Services are at 10 A.M. Saturday morning. Services are often held in the small prayer hall.

The synagogue displays a Sephardic style with the bimah in the center of the hall, Carol Herselle Krinsky, author of *Synagogues of Europe: Architecture, History, Meaning,* says that its architectural plans probably derived from Byzantine rather than indigenous European or Islamic sources. Still, it has a semblance of cupola architecture. Construction of the synagogue began in 1903 in the community which was organized like the French Consistory. Located in the center of the city and on its own block, the building is near the famous Alexander Nevsky Cathedral. Seating capacity is about 1,170 persons. Its dedication on September 23, 1909, was a gala affair. A holiday not only for Jews but for the whole Bulgarian Community was declared; King Ferdinand cut the ribbon. For 40 years, the synagogue enjoyed wonderful times, that is, until World War II. The emigration to Israel in 1948 also obviously reduced the number attending services.

Although the synagogue, now a landmark, was closed during the years 1943-44, when most of the Jews were deported to the countryside, the house of worship was not desecrated. Allied bombs hit the building several times during World War II. Later, the Communist Party's attempts to turn the synagogue into a concert hall would fail. If this was not enough, the large synagogue was damaged by an earthquake in 1977 and was repaired at government expense. After you visit the beautiful Sephardic-designed synagogue at Exarch Joseph St. 16, in Sofia, built in 1909, you might notice that the Synagogue, the Mosque, and the Church in the center of Sofia are equidistant from each other. This is called the Triangle of the Three Houses of Worship, which shows the timelessness and stability of Bulgaria's three religions.

The **Jewish Museum** is located on the second floor of the Synagogue. This museum is open from 9 A.M. to 1 P.M. on

Tuesdays and Wednesdays, and on Thursdays and Fridays from 1 P.M. to 5 P.M. Since there is a wonderful exhibition regarding the story of the Holocaust as it pertains to Bulgaria, one should stop at the Museum to relive and learn about the Holocaust in Bulgaria.

The Holocaust Memorial Exhibit in the Synagogue. Here again, as in Romania and Hungary, sources say that Bulgaria may have wanted to remain neutral, in World War II, but Germany and Italy would not permit it. Some historians say that the country "blundered" into the Nazi camp. What is clear is that Bulgaria became increasingly dependent on Germany. And what probably clinched the deal was that Germany held out the promise of regained territory. This set off old nationalistic dreams, so much so that the government clamored for an alliance with the Germans. Although she had signed a Treaty of Friendship with Yugoslavia, Bulgaria immediately deserted Yugoslavia and joined the Axis powers. Bogdan Filov, who was pro-German, served as prime minister and Peter Gabrovski became interior minister in a new government. Both brought fascism to the country. Alexander Belev, a fervent anti-Semite was soon to become the Commissar for Jewish Affairs. These supporters of the Nazis were also going to solve the "Jewish question."

As we have seen, on March 1, 1941, Bulgaria signed the Tripartite Pact with Germany, Italy and Japan. By joining the Axis powers, King Boris III would gain the territory he coveted, according to author Bar-Zohar. He also would have to pass anti-Semitic legislation, which he eventually did, even though as Bar-Zohar tells us, he was "far from being an anti-Semite."

Interestingly, Bulgaria did not send troops to fight alongside the Germans in Russia, although the Germans used Bulgaria as a military base.

In the beginning at least, the Bulgarians also did not want to be outperformed by their Nazi partners when it came to the treatment of Jews. They, too, passed a law similar to Germany's Nuremburg Laws and in January, 1941, the King signed it.

In August 1942, the Bulgarian parliament passed a bill depriving Jews in the occupied territories of Bulgarian citizenship. That piece of legislation would cost those Jews their lives.

Bulgarian and German officials signed an agreement to deport 20,000 Jews from Macedonia and Thrace. They knew there were only about 12,000 Jews from Macedonia and Thrace, but they decided secretly to add 8,000 Jews from Old Bulgaria to make up the difference, according to author Bar-Zohar. In the spring of 1943, nearly 12,000 Jews of Thrace and Macedonia, living in terrible conditions, were deported to their deaths.

But back in Old Bulgaria, Jews who already had been rounded up and prepared for death in March 1943 were somehow saved. When it became public knowledge that these Jews from Bulgaria proper, too, would be deported, there was an outcry in the press, from the Orthodox Church, and within the parliament. "All these protests had the whole-hearted support of the king," says R.J. Crampton in his book *A Concise History of Bulgaria*. Metropolitan Cyril also helped, and sent a telegram to King Boris, asking him to show mercy toward the Jews, according to Bar-Zohar. "Once again, the Church stood firm against the government's policy. There is no doubt that in the entire history of the Holocaust, the Bulgarian church stood high above any other Pravoslav, Protestant, or Catholic Church, in her bold and unyielding struggle to rescue the Jews," writes Bar-Zohar. Historian Vicki Tamir confirms that "the most courageous stand was that of the Church."

The Jews of Bulgaria were saved. A leading member of Parliament, Dimitry Peshev, had gathered up a delegation and had protested the impending deportation. Interestingly, nearly 60 years later, a bust of Peshev was unveiled in January 2000 in a gallery at the Council of Europe's headquarters in Strasbourg that honors politicians and intellectuals who have made special contributions to European civilization. Peshev had been deputy chairman of the Bulgarian National Assembly during World War II at the time when Nazi Germany started the deportation of Jews to concentration camps.

Although a member of the fascist establishment, Peshev "undramatically, modestly, but sincerely tried to save thousands of Jewish lives." His action will remain perhaps the greatest single exploit in Bulgarian resistance, notes historian Vicki Tamir.

Jews scheduled for deportation from Bulgaria were released on March 10, 1943. That is the day of their salvation. Author Bar-Zohar argues that King Boris III had intervened and stopped the deportation, recalling that the King felt he changed his position regarding Bulgan Jews, but did not have the power to save the Jews of Thrace and Macedonia.

"Peshev's eleventh-hour initiative, combined with the staunch struggle of the Church and the intellectual elites, had shaken the king and made him come to his senses. It had torn him from his meek obedience to the Germans. He could no longer afford the luxury of looking the other way," wrote Bar-Zohar.

But the Germans and their Bulgarian lackeys did not stop there. They would try again in May 1943. May 24, 1943, was an important day in the struggle to save Bulgarian Jewry. The Communists, too, got on the bandwagon. Later, Todor Zhivkov, the Communist leader, was to claim that he was there. Bar-Zohar says that Communist leader Zhivkov "was very sympathetic to the Jewish cause." He had written the first Communist flyer against the persecution of the Jews. But according to records, Zhivkov was nowhere to be found during that day of protest.

The dramatic protest occurred on May 24, 1943, when many Sofia Jews attempted to march to the royal palace to protest, but they were stopped by the police. Stephen Mark Mallinger, author of *A Brief Introduction to the Jewish Community of Bulgaria,* says that on that day, Rabbi Daniel Tsion delivered an impassioned plea to the crowd urging them to action. The protestors were joined by official and unofficial protests from pro-Jewish public leaders.

Once again, the King again ruled out the plan to deport Jews from Old Bulgaria, even though he agreed to the plan to expel the Jews from Sofia to the countryside. Bar-Zohar notes that the decision to deport the Jews only to the interior of the country was officially approved by the government in a meeting on May 24, 1943.

King Boris turned the forced labor into a scheme to protect the Jews from a much worse fate. The Jews and the road construction became King Boris' biggest bluff during the war.

"All Jewish males were drafted for compulsory, unpaid hard labor," notes Vicki Tamir. Jews were to be scattered throughout the country.

Not only did the church plead with the king not to deport Jews in May, but diplomats, writers, religious leaders, and labor groups, including the Communists, added their protests.

In May1943 the Jews of Sofia were resettled in the provinces in what could have been a first step toward deportation to the death camps. But the Bulgarian Jews would survive the war. By 1944, Bulgaria wanted to extricate itself from the war. This nation also wanted to appear more reasonable in the eyes of the allies. By August 24, 1944, the Commissariat for Jewish Affairs had been abolished and all anti-Jewish legislation was officially abrogated on August 29. The Decrees of Abolition were published on September 7, 1944, an important day in Bulgarian history as that is the day the Soviet Union declared war on Bulgaria and launched the Red Army across the border. A few days later, a coalition government of the Fatherland Front took over and organized Jewish life was re-established. In September 1944, 34 Jewish communities were in existence.

"Only years later did the truth about these days come to light," says Bar-Zohar. The events of May—the protests, the letters, and the delegations—were a dramatic expression of the support many brave Bulgarians extended to the Jews. But they didn't change the fascist government's plans. Even before May 24, King Boris had decided not to send one single Jew out of Bulgarian territory, maintains author Bar-Zohar.

After King Boris died, a new government came into power.

Also, in May 1944, secret talks were held in Turkey between the Bulgarian minister and Ira Hirschmann, representative of the U.S. War Refugee Board. All anti-Jewish measures were annulled. In August, Sofia demanded the evacuation of German troops. On September 7, 1944, Bulgaria declared war on Germany. World War II ended in Europe nine months later.

Holocaust Memorial Plaque. A memorial plaque was placed on the back of the Parliament building and in front of the Academy of Art in 1993. It cites the saving of the Jews of Bulgaria. It also takes note of the 11,363 Jews killed in Thrace and Macedonia.

Senior Citizens Home. High up in the hills of the city is a new white building that will serve as a home for seniors. Funding came from the World Jewish Relief, the Claims Conference as well as a per capita commitment from the municipality. The local "Shalom" organization is raising funds from various sources to support the home.

Summer Camp at Kovacevski, Opened in 1996, this facility hosts a winter camp and seminars year round. But it is in the summer that much progress is made on educating Bulgarian Jewish children.

Plovdiv

About 500 Jews live in this well-organized Jewish community where at least 10 organizations and clubs meet in a center that holds many activities and organizes events. The synagogue in Plovdiv is the only functioning synagogue in Bulgaria, other than the beautiful house of worship in Sofia. On March 10, 1943 as we have seen, the Jews in Plovdiv also were saved from deportation. In the center of the city stands a monument commemorating the Bulgarians who stood by the Jews as the latter faced deportation to Nazi concentration camps.

Holocaust Monument, Tzar Kaloyan Square, Plovdiv. Situated almost halfway between the community center and the synagogue is "the monument of gratitude." The words inscribed in Bulgarian, Hebrew, and English, declare, "With gratitude to all who contributed to our salvation on March 10, 1943—from the grateful Jews in Plovdiv." Every March 10, the entire Jewish community gathers at the monument to commemorate the day of remembrance. The community hopes that soon "Tzar Kaloyan Square" will be renamed "Spasenie na Plovdivskite evrei Sqr" ("The Saving of the Jews of Plovdiv Square").

"Shalom" Jewish Community Headquarters, 20 Hristo G, Danov st., 4000, Plovdiv.Tel: 359-32-268-023. Tel/FAX: 359-32-632-622. This is the headquarters of the Jewish community.

Synagogue "Zion," 13 Tzar Kaloyan str. Plovdiv. Considering the attachment of the community to Israel, it figures that the name of the Synagogue is "Zion." There is an entrance to the synagogue on Tzareva Livada st. It is only a five-minute walk from the synagogue to the community center.

A BRIEF HISTORY

The ancestors of today's Jews in Plovdiv were part of the Sixteenth Century immigration from Spain. These were the exiled Jews who were welcomed by the Sultan of Turkey Bayazid II to help his stagnant economy. Jews had lived in the area but in small numbers.

When the Spanish Jews arrived after their expulsion from Spain, they immediately built synagogues, schools, and libraries. Historians such as Joseph Benaroiah, vice chairman of the Regional Organization of Jews, "Shalom," in Plovdiv, note today that until they learned Bulgarian, Jews spoke Ladino, which he describes as a mixture of Hebrew and Spanish.

As time went on, both Bulgarian and Ladino were spoken. Today, in fact, we still have in Plovdiv a rich treasure of Ladino songs, proverbs, and even cuisine.

In 1878, at the time of the liberation of Bulgaria from the Turks, there were 1,164 Jews out of a total town population of about 30,000. The Jews had backed the struggle of the Bulgarian people from their Turkish oppressors.

Between the liberation of Bulgaria and the Second World War, the Jews in Plovdiv immersed themselves into the economic and cultural life of the Jewish community. Many Jews served in the Bulgarian Army.

Bulgarian Jewry is well known, as we have seen, for its strong backing of Zionism, even in its infant stages at the end of the 19th century. The first Zionist Association in the country was established in Plovdiv. The first translation of Herzl's book, *The Jewish State,* was published in Bulgaria. As historian Benaroiah notes, "Zionism was viewed by Bulgarians and Jews as a natural and logical movement connected with the 2,000 year aspiration of the Jews to regenerate their own state."

In any discussion of the history of the Jews of Plovdiv, mention of the saving of Bulgarian Jews must be made. Even

An American Jewish Joint Distribution Committee board delegation visiting the synagogue in Plovdiv, Bulgaria.

before March 1943, Jewish men between the ages of 18 and 55 were called up for forced labor in work gangs. But on March 10, 1943, when the first group of Jews were waiting with their luggage in the local Jewish school, ready to be dispatched to concentration camps in Poland, the order to stop the deportation came. On that day, the local Bishop of Plovdiv, Cyril, obtained permission from authorities for the Jews to return to their homes. Later in Israel in 1962, Bishop Cyril said, "We would not have had the courage to ask for abrogation of the anti-Jewish laws if we were not supported by the whole Bulgarian people. We just expressed its will." Every March 10, the Jews of Plovdiv bring flowers to the graves of the patriarchs Stephan and Cyril in the Monastery of Bachkovo.

In 1948, 5,000 out of 6,000 Jews in Plovdiv left for Israel. With the Communist takeover, the Jewish "municipality" was closed down, as was the Jewish school. The synagogue did not have a rabbi. There was very little Jewish life.

After the fall of Communism in 1989, Jewish life revived, and the "Shalom" organization was restored. The synagogue was saved and work began on its restoration.

A Sunday school exists and Hebrew is one of the languages offered in a high school. Jewish holidays are celebrated in the community center. "The Jews in Plovdiv are loyal citizens of their country and town," wrote Community historian Benaroiah. "Jews in Plovdiv have never lived in a ghetto and they do not today. Anti-Semitism has never been a government policy and it is not today," added Benaroiah.

Always sympathetic to the struggles of the Bulgarian people, Jews, though small in numbers, have become part of the economic and cultural life of Bulgaria.

Suggested Reading List

Bar-Zohar, Michael *Beyond Hitler's Grasp: The Heroic Rescue of Bulgaria's Jews.* Holabook, MA: Adams Media Corporation, 1998.

Bauer, Yehuda, *A History of the Holocaust.* New York, Franklin Watts, 1982.

Crampton, R.J. *A Concise History of Bulgaria.* Cambridge, MA: Cambridge University Press, 1997.

Curtis, Glen E. *Bulgaria, a country study.* Washington, D.C.: Federal Research Division, Library of Congress, 1993.

Fermor, Patrick Leigh, *Between the Woods And the Water, On Foot to Constantinople from the Hook of Holland: The Middle Danube to the Iron Gates.* New York: Viking, 1986.

Hoffman, Charles, *Gray Dawn: The Jews of Eastern Europe in the Post-Communist Era.* New York: Aaron Asher Books, HarperCollins Publishers, 1992.

Hoffman, Eva, *Exit Into History: A Journey Through The New Eastern Europe.* New York: Viking, 1993.

Kaplan, Robert, *Balkan Ghosts: A Journey Through History.* New York: St. Martin's Press, 1993.

Krinsky, Carol Herselle, *Synagogues of Europe: Architecture, History, Meaning.* Cambridge, MA: MIT Press, 1985.

Malcomson, Scott L. *Borderlands-Nation and Empire.* Boston-London: Faber and Faber, 1994.

Mallinger, Stephen Mark, *A Brief Introduction to the Jewish Community of Bulgaria, Sofia, Bulgaria.* RIVA Books, 1996.

Otfinoski, Steven, *Bulgaria.* New York: Facts On File, Inc., 1999.

Rosen, Moses, *Dangers, Tests and Miracles: The Remarkable Life Story of Chief Rabbi Rosen of Romania (as told to Joseph Finkelstone).* London: Weidenfeld and Nicolson, 1990.

Tamir, Vicki, *Bulgaria and Her Jews: The History f a Dubious Symbosis.* New York: Sepher-Hermon Press, Inc., 1979.

Yahil, Leni, *The Holocaust: The Fate of European Jewry, 1932-1945.* New York and Oxford: Oxford University Press, 1990.

Index